The Keyboard Music of
J.S. Bach

Second Edition

D0781037

David Schulenberg

Routledge
Taylor & Francis Group
New York   London

Routledge is an imprint of the
Taylor & Francis Group, an informa business

VISUAL & PERFORMING ARTS

Routledge
Taylor & Francis Group
270 Madison Avenue
New York, NY 10016

Routledge
Taylor & Francis Group
2 Park Square
Milton Park, Abingdon
Oxon OX14 4RN

© 2006 by Taylor & Francis Group, LLC
Routledge is an imprint of Taylor & Francis Group, an Informa business

Printed in the United States of America on acid-free paper
10 9 8 7 6 5 4 3 2 1

International Standard Book Number-10: 0-415-97400-3 (Softcover) 0-415-97399-6 (Hardcover)
International Standard Book Number-13: 978-0-415-97400-4 (Softcover) 978-0-415-97399-1 (Hardcover)

Library of Congress Cataloging-in-Publication Data

Schulenberg, David.
    The keyboard music of J.S. Bach / by David Schulenberg. -- 2nd rev. ed.
      p. cm.
    Includes bibliographical references and index.
    ISBN 0-415-97399-6 (hb) -- ISBN 0-415-97400-3 (pb)
    1. Bach, Johann Sebastian, 1685-1750. Keyboard music. 2. Keyboard instrument
music -- Analysis, appreciation. I. Title.

MT145.B14S415 2006
786.092--dc22
                                               2006003775

Visit the Taylor & Francis Web site at
http://www.taylorandfrancis.com

and the Routledge Web site at
http://www.routledge-ny.com

Contents

Preface

This is a guide to Bach's keyboard music for the student, teacher, listener, or scholar seeking information, analysis, and performance ideas for individual works. It can serve as a reference book, but it can also be read from cover to cover or chapter by chapter—preferably with score, instrument, or recording at hand.

The first edition, published in 1992, received gratifyingly positive reviews. The chief incentive for the present edition has been the appearance since then of an enormous amount of relevant new material. Hence this is in large part a new book, incorporating information from new biographical writings, new critical editions, and new general and critical studies published during the last fifteen years. The chapter on performance practice has been expanded, and references to editions and scholarly literature are thoroughly updated. In response to comments about the first edition, I have added additional references to works that may have served Bach as models or as spurs to invention. I also have reframed the introductory sections of many chapters to define more clearly the place of Bach's works within the context of European music, and more specifically within Bach's compositional development. A few pieces have been shifted from one part of the book to another as their chronology or even authorship has been clarified, and several peripheral compositions discussed in the first edition have been deleted.

In carrying out these changes I have tried to maintain the focus of the first edition, which was to provide a musically literate reader with useful information about the background, origins, and musical text of individual works, much of which is buried in scholarly literature that is all but inaccessible except to specialists. I have also aimed at balancing scholarly matters with interpretive discussions and suggestions about performance practice, and I have included suggested completions—now containing a few corrections—for several fragmentary works. In discussing individual works, I have resisted the tendency, particularly prevalent in writings about Bach, to express subjective observations about the music in the form of assertions about the composer's intentions or compositional procedures. I also have avoided criticism of a fashionably subjective nature, preferring to couch my interpretive views in the form of analytic comments. Music analysis may be no less subjective than the type of writing that describes a listener's personal responses by attaching adjectives to themes or asserting their extra-musical significance. But good analysis, although it may be offered in technical or abstract terms, describes the dynamic processes of a work, including its expressive or kinetic high and low points. Especially in Bach's music, these processes are intimately related to the articulation of a work into sections and the particular harmonic, motivic, and contrapuntal devices used in each. Identifying the formal plan of a work or important features of its harmony or counterpoint is directly relevant to where one hears its main breathing points or its most dramatic gestures.

The nature of this book limits the depth to which I have been able to delve into individual works. But where it seemed important to do so I have presented extended discussions of individual issues: the compositional history of movements in the *Well-Tempered Clavier* and *Art of Fugue,* the tonal design of the Chromatic Fantasia, the interpretation of dotted rhythms in the B-minor overture, to name a few. I have announced few new discoveries or approaches; often a well-advertised innovation turns out to be a restatement of an old idea. But at many points I have offered what I believe are my own interpretations of the music or its sources, and I have tried to contribute to continuing debates over such questions as the interpretation of Bach's notation of rhythms and ornaments, the authenticity and dating of certain works attributed to Bach, and the nature of and reasons behind his revisions in particular compositions.

Chapter 1 discusses such basic matters as the precise extent of the repertory under discussion and the use of editions and sources. Chapters 2 and 3 present overviews of performance practice and Bach's stylistic development, respectively. The remainder of the book consists mainly of commentaries on the individual works, grouped into chapters according to genre and, very approximately, chronology. Each chapter (after the first three) opens with a general introduction to the group of works covered, followed by discussions of individual compositions.

Some individual commentaries open with lists of sources and editions; these are intended to be representative, not comprehensive. Dates or copyists' names are included in the listings of sources only where these are firmly established in the existing literature. For certain pieces whose texts are defective in recent editions, I offer lists of emendations at the ends of the individual commentaries. These lists are not meant to serve as detailed accounts of variant readings, nor is space available to explain the philological or analytical reasoning underlying each suggestion. In general, the readings listed are those of the sources, as opposed to those in available editions; readings in brackets or followed by question marks are my own conjectures.

An enormous amount has been written about Bach and his music. To keep the number of references and the size of the bibliography within reasonable limits, I have cited only those writings and editions that have been particularly helpful, or that readers might find valuable. Where citations are lacking, information about musical texts and sources usually comes from one of several standard sources: a critical edition (usually one of those named for a given work), the Schmieder thematic catalog (BWV), or the newly revised catalog of the Berlin Bach manuscripts (Kast 2003).

In writing the first volume I was helped by numerous friends and colleagues, among whom I must mention Peter Kirwin, David Kopp, Michael Marissen, Robert Marshall, Robert Mealy, Joshua Rifkin, Russell Stinson, Peter Watchorn, Christoph Wolff, and Peter Wollny. A stimulus toward preparing this second edition was the Japanese translation completed in 2000 by Nozomi Sato and Sachiko Kimura, whose exacting work led to many changes and corrections in the present edition. Andrew Talle was generous enough to share with me material relating to the copyist formerly known as Anonymous 5, and Frieder Rempp and Ulrich Bartels kindly provided a list of contents for volume V/12 of the *Neue Bach-Ausgabe* prior to publication. Gregory Butler and Joshua Rifkin also were generous in providing material from forthcoming publications. A number of reviewers, both named and anonymous, also provided perceptive criticisms. I gratefully acknowledge the constant spur provided by the challenging writings of Peter Williams, by whom any author and particularly any Bach scholar is constantly reminded that questions are more useful than answers. The late Howard Schott offered sound and helpful advice and encouragement, as well as a model of scholarly generosity and modesty to which any writer might aspire.

My most profound thanks go to my wife Mary Oleskiewicz, scholar, teacher, and virtuoso traversa player, without whom this book would not have been written.

A Note on Musical Examples, Measure Numbers, and Pitch Names

Unless otherwise indicated, measure numbers and readings for each work are those of the most recent scholarly edition cited. In citations of measure numbers, lower case letters (e.g., 5a, 27b) indicate the first and second halves of measures, respectively. Upper case letters (5A, 27B) refer to first and second endings. Measure numbers for parallel passages are often given in the form "mm. 63–5 || 56–8," where the sign || means "are parallel to" or "are closely based upon."

The examples have been checked, where possible, against original sources. They are, however, for illustration only and do not present critically edited texts.

The notation has been altered in the interest of legibility, economy of space, or clarification of the point illustrated.

Pitches are named using the Helmholtz system, which is descended from the German keyboard tablature occasionally used by Bach. Middle C is c′; the notes below and above it are b and d′, respectively. The pitches an octave lower are B–c–d; an octave higher, b′–c′′–d′′. Notes below C (two octaves below c′) are designated by double letters (AA, BB).

1
Bach's Keyboard Music
An Introduction

Bach's keyboard works form one of the oldest and most important repertories of instrumental compositions that have remained in use since their conception. Although most of his vocal music was largely forgotten soon after his death, his keyboard works continued to be highly valued and assiduously studied, at first by a relatively small circle of pupils and admirers, then in ever-widening circles that now encompass virtually everyone who has ever performed or listened to Western art music.

Nevertheless, the performance and interpretation of Bach's music for more than two and half centuries have hardly constituted a uniform or unbroken tradition. Every generation has had its own image of Bach's music and of Bach himself. The image presented in this book has been shaped by modern Bach scholarship and colored by modern Bach performance. Since 1950, Bach studies have been one of the richest and most active spheres of musicological activity, producing a new edition of his collected works as well as discoveries that have overturned previously held convictions about their dating, their manner of performance, and their relationships to eighteenth-century music and culture in general. Performers, drawing on this scholarship and on the work of instrument builders, on research into historical performing practice, and on practical experience, have revealed new aspects of the works and revised the ways in which their sound and their expressive content are understood.

The first three chapters of this book provide introductory matter that will be especially useful to those who are not professional Bach specialists. The remaining chapters furnish a commentary on Bach's keyboard works. The commentary includes essential historical background on each work as well as discussions of relevant editions, literature, and the music itself. The works treated in each

1

chapter are roughly contemporary with one another and belong to the same or closely related genres; for example, chapters 4–7 deal with early works (suites, fugues, toccatas, etc.), chapters 10–12 with the *Well-Tempered Clavier* and compositions leading up to it, chapters 13–15 with the later suites and partitas. The reader is invited to skip forward to discussions of whichever pieces are of the greatest interest.

The Repertory

The boundaries of the subject covered in this book have been the subject of considerable debate. Here, "keyboard music" means those compositions for a single keyboard instrument that lack a full-fledged pedal part and do not fall into any of the genres that imply the use of the organ, such as the *pedaliter* chorale prelude. Roughly two hundred of Bach's pieces meet this definition, falling into three general categories: (1) suites, partitas, and similar works; (2) preludes and fugues, including pieces under such titles as fantasia, toccata, and sinfonia; and (3) a miscellaneous group containing variation sets, sonatas, a concerto, and transcriptions of works originally composed for other instruments.

Although Bach's intentions regarding the instrumentation of his ensemble works were usually very precise—far more precise than was once thought—he rarely designated an exact medium for the music discussed here. These works have long been regarded as being for the *Clavier*, but the meaning of that term has changed with time. During Bach's lifetime it was probably a generic term for any musical keyboard, although by the later eighteenth century some German writers used it with the specific meaning of "clavichord," and in nineteenth-century Germany it became synonymous with "piano." Today, although pianists everywhere play this music, the works are most often regarded as having been meant for the harpsichord. But eighteenth-century documentation for this view is surprisingly sparse, and Robert Marshall (1986) argued that, although some of this repertory really was conceived for the harpsichord, much of it was not. He therefore proposed a division between works for harpsichord—essentially, group 1 in the list above—and generic "clavier" works comprising most of the remaining pieces. He argued further that many of the "clavier" works were meant for organ without pedals.

The first part of Marshall's hypothesis had the substantial merit of corresponding with Bach's intentions insofar as they can be discovered from explicit indications of medium in the most authoritative sources. But a composer's expressed intentions are not the only way in which to understand a composition, nor the only possible basis for an interpretation. That many of the "clavier" works were, in practice if not in principle, composed for some type of harpsichord is argued in chapter 2 and in the discussions of individual pieces. Nevertheless, the term "keyboard music" is adopted here as the best English expression that can be applied to the repertory without making questionable assumptions about the intended medium.

Keyboard music, so understood, forms one of the four main divisions of Bach's output, the others being organ works, works for instrumental ensemble, and vocal music. The distinction now made between organists and harpsichordists, and thus between organ music and "keyboard" music, might have surprised Bach and his contemporaries, who appear to have been equally at home on both types of instruments.[1] Nevertheless, the distinction between organ and "keyboard" music is a real one, based on differences in style and genre that are usually quite clear. Moreover, the keyboard works have a somewhat exceptional place in Bach's *œuvre*, for they were the one part of it that was not written in direct fulfillment of any of Bach's official duties.

If we discount his school years and a brief early stint as a "lackey" (*Lacquey*) at Weimar, Bach began his professional career as an organist, serving in the cities of Arnstadt (1703–7) and Mühlhausen (1708) and at the ducal court of Weimar (1708–14). He was then promoted to *Concertmeister* at Weimar, subsequently serving as *Capellmeister* to the Prince of Cöthen (1717–23). From there he went to Leipzig, where he remained *Director musices* (director of church music) and *Cantor* of the St. Thomas School for the rest of his life. Except at the St. Thomas School, where his position as *Cantor* was that of a teacher, in each of these posts Bach was expected to produce music of a particular type. Thus, most of his organ works date from the Weimar years and earlier, although many were revised at Leipzig. At Weimar and Leipzig he also wrote church cantatas on a regular basis, at least for a portion of his tenure in each city.[2] The music for instrumental ensemble was long thought to have been written mainly at Cöthen, but some of these works must date from Weimar, others from Leipzig.

Keyboard pieces, however, flowed from Bach's hands in substantial numbers throughout his career. This must reflect a continual association with stringed keyboard instruments, especially the harpsichord. Bach was officially employed as a keyboard player—that is, an organist—only at Arnstadt, Mühlhausen, and from 1708 to 1714 at Weimar. But titles could be misleading. Although designated a mere lackey while serving at Weimar in 1703, Bach went from there to Arnstadt, where he was described as having been the Weimar court organist.[3] When he returned to Weimar in 1708, now officially as court organist, he must have participated in rehearsals and performances as a harpsichordist.[4] This he certainly did at Cöthen and Leipzig, in instrumental works like the Brandenburg Concerti, in secular cantatas composed for the Leipzig Collegium Musicum, and occasionally in sacred works as well. The only contemporary report of a specific performance in a church mentions Bach playing harpsichord—that is, directing the ensemble while improvising a basso continuo realization—in the *Trauerode* (BWV 198) of 1727.[5]

Yet there is little if any evidence for Bach's having performed solo "clavier" pieces in public or as part of his official duties anywhere. It is reasonable to suppose that Bach would have played solo keyboard music during private palace performances for princely patrons, or on special occasions such as the aborted contest with Marchand in 1717.[6] But only the organ had a tradition of use in public recitals during Bach's day, and Bach's public appearances as a "clavier" soloist might have been confined to the occasional keyboard concerto. The music considered in this book would have been used primarily for private practice and study, even if certain pieces (such as the Chromatic Fantasia and Fugue) might have been played occasionally in public.

Sources

In order to consider the history and text of Bach's keyboard works in any detail, it is necessary to pay some attention to their sources, that is, the manuscripts and early printed editions in which they are preserved. Source studies have been a prime area of Bach research. The sources are not only documents for the music; they open a window onto the working habits and even the personalities of those who produced them, starting with Bach himself. Apart from helping to establish the reading of a disputed passage, or in following Bach's thought as he corrected details of counterpoint or reorganized whole sets of pieces, study of the sources has led to insights into how Bach's music spread beyond his own circle: who played what, how widely individual pieces were disseminated, and how those outside Bach's circle understood (and misunderstood) what he had written.

Only a fraction of Bach's keyboard pieces were published during his lifetime. Most, even the few that appeared in print, circulated mainly in manuscript copies. Bach's own manuscripts (autographs) survive for some works, but autographs are lacking for most, including almost all of the earlier pieces. Some early works are preserved in but a single manuscript copy, and this is one reason for the disputes that have arisen over Bach's authorship of certain pieces. Even where autographs do survive, these are generally fair copies or revision scores, not first drafts, making it difficult to establish when the pieces were originally composed.[7] Still, it is fascinating to reconstruct the process of correction and revision that can be seen in some of the autographs. Even in pieces for which no autograph survives, it is often possible to trace the course of Bach's revisions by comparing the readings of copies made from different versions of his score.

Since 1950, Bach scholarship has gone to extraordinary lengths to identify the handwriting, paper, and other aspects of the sources. Scholars have traced watermarks in the paper to specific paper mills, providing dates for the manufacture of the material, and they have codified the gradual changes over time in the handwriting of individual copyists, including Bach himself. Through such research has come steady improvement in our understanding of when pieces were written, how they were revised, and which copies are closest to Bach in time and place and therefore most authoritative. Because of the sheer number of Bach's keyboard pieces and of the sources containing them, the "clavier" works have been the most difficult of the four main groups of Bach's works for scholars to investigate from the point of view of sources. Many questions pertaining to dating, compositional history, and even Bach's authorship remain open and perhaps unanswerable.

The manuscripts range from single sheets of paper inscribed with a few lines of music to massive compilations of separate manuscripts that have been bound together. Manuscripts may be in Bach's hand (autographs) or in the hand of someone else (copies). Many extant manuscripts of Bach's works are in hands known to be those of his pupils, who probably paid for the right to make copies (a common practice); some pupils seem to have served Bach as apprentices, making copies not for themselves but for sale or archival use by Bach (see Beißwenger 2002, 13–4).

Today the greatest concentration of Bach manuscripts is in Berlin, but there are major collections in other European cities (Leipzig, Dresden, Göttingen, Vienna, Brussels), and important sources can also be found in London, New Haven, Washington, and Tokyo.[8] Among the copyists are pupils and associates of Bach who were important musical figures in their own right. Other copyists have yet to be identified by name although the distinctive features of their handwriting have been recognized. Scholars continue to make progress in matching the handwriting of such personages as Anonymous 5 and Anonymous 300 with that of actual figures named in court or university records.[9] The most important manuscripts are autographs and contemporary copies made by members of Bach's immediate circle. But for certain works the only surviving manuscripts were made by peripheral figures, sometimes of the later eighteenth and early nineteenth centuries. Such manuscripts were not necessarily copied from autographs; in many cases they were derived from lost manuscripts of doubtful accuracy, and editors must puzzle out what Bach's original readings might have been. A few copyists were responsible for assembling large manuscript collections, and as these are cited frequently they are described at the end of this chapter.

The printed sources that interest us are primarily those published (or prepared for publication) by Bach himself, beginning in 1726 with the Partitas and ending with the posthumously issued *Art of Fugue*. With a few minor exceptions, no further publications of Bach's keyboard music came out until the early nineteenth century, when editions of previously unpublished works began to appear in profusion. Music printing and publishing in the first half of the eighteenth century were different enterprises from those of today or even the later eighteenth century; how this bears on our understanding of the music will become clear in chapters 15–18.

Catalogs and Editions

Since 1950 the thematic catalog by Wolfgang Schmieder (BWV) has been the basic reference source, listing Bach's works as well as providing dates, bibliographic entries, and much other useful information. Despite the ongoing production of an even more massive compilation of data—the *Bach-Compendium* (BC)—Schmieder's BWV numbers remain the standard way of referring to both authentic and inauthentic works that have been attributed to Bach. The BWV numbers are not chronological; compositions are listed by medium, beginning with vocal works, then music for organ, music for "clavier," and finally works for other instruments and for instrumental ensemble.[10] Within each group are subdivisions for various genres. Ordering within the subdivisions follows no obvious principle, although at times it reflects the arrangement of pieces in the old Bachgesamtausgabe (BG).

That edition, produced between 1850 and 1900 by the German Bach Society (*Bach-Gesellschaft*), was one of the first and most successful scholarly editions of any composer's complete works. It remained the basis for most subsequent editions of Bach's keyboard music until the late twentieth century, and it remains indispensable for Bach scholars. But the New Bach Edition (*Neue Bach-Ausgabe*, or NBA), begun in the 1950s and by 2006 largely complete, presents the findings of more recent Bach research, and its texts are usually superior to those of the BG. This is especially true for the keyboard works, although publishers continue to put out reprints based on the BG and other nineteenth-century editions. Some of these reprints are now showing up on the Internet, either free or for sale. But it is impossible to recommend either reprints or online Bach editions, most of which are unaltered reproductions of old, unreliable printed editions.

The NBA is enormously expensive and available only in major research libraries, although the keyboard volumes are being reissued in versions for practical use. The original volumes of music are accompanied by separate volumes containing editorial reports—lists of sources and readings, accounts of how works originated, and discussions of editorial problems. As useful as these *kritische Berichten* are to serious scholars, they are impenetrable to readers who lack German or the patience to master their arcane organization and content. Even the score volumes can be difficult to interpret, especially when, as in the case of the *Well-Tempered Clavier* or the French Suites, they present multiple versions of each work. As one would expect in an editorial project produced over a period of more than half a century, older volumes do not reflect current knowledge or scholarly views, and there are inconsistencies between volumes in organization and even accuracy. Despite the huge accumulation of data represented by the NBA, many critical mysteries in the history of Bach's keyboard music—when individual pieces were first drafted and how they reached their familiar forms—remain unsolved.

Thus the NBA is hardly the last word on Bach's keyboard music, and the chapters that follow cite alternative editions for many individual works. Like the NBA, these other editions are of the type often described as Urtext editions, from the German word meaning "original text." The term is a misnomer, since in most cases what is printed is not Bach's original but rather a product of extensive revisions and reworkings—usually his own, but in some cases possibly involving other hands. Some self-declared "Urtext" editions even add fingerings and suggestions for dynamics, articulation, or ornamentation. Even if carried out according to the latest theories on "authentic" performance, such markings presuppose decisions that may insinuate themselves unbidden into one's interpretation of the music. For example, fingerings in modern editions are usually based on the late nineteenth-century pianistic principle of maintaining as smooth a legato as possible. The hand contortions that are sometimes needed to insure legato can lead to questionable decisions about tempo or registration. Even the harpsichordist who owns a perfect new instrument and follows the latest word on historically informed performance practice may be subtly influenced by a faulty text or an editor's fingerings.

Some Major Manuscript Sources for Bach's Early Works

The *Andreas Bach Book* (ABB) and the *Möller Manuscript* (MM) are the earliest of the major Bach sources.[11] Compiled by Bach's older brother and teacher Johann Christoph Bach of Ohrdruf, both are known by the names of later owners. Schulze (1984a, 52–6) identified the principal copyist, and Hill (1987) showed that MM is probably the earlier of the two manuscripts, copied while Bach was at Arnstadt (1703–7); ABB corresponds more or less with the beginning of the Weimar period (from 1708). Hill also produced an edition (1991) of selected compositions from the two manuscripts, including works by both Bach and others. Both manuscripts contain a repertory of "free" pieces for both organ and harpsichord—suites, preludes and fugues, sonatas, and transcriptions of French and German orchestral music. The contents include many of Bach's most important early works, several in his own hand. Most of the texts are accurate, but many of the non-autograph copies include French ornament signs that may not derive from the composer. Although these signs are included in modern editions, some are inconsistent with the French keyboard tradition or with Bach's practice as documented in later works.

P 801, P 802, and *P 803* are a complex of manuscripts related to Johann Gottfried Walther, the Weimar organist and composer who was a friend and relative of Bach. P 801 and P 802 include copies not only by Walther but by his pupil Johann Tobias Krebs, who also studied with Bach. So did Krebs's son Johann Ludwig, whose hand appears in P 803. P 802 contains chiefly chorale settings, but P 801 and P 803 include important copies of Bach keyboard works as well as harpsichord works by Dieupart and other French composers, and transcriptions of orchestral music. Most of Walther's copies apparently can be dated to the period around 1714–7. Bach's works appear mostly in early versions that presumably date from Weimar, in generally accurate copies, although occasionally one suspects that Walther or another copyist added ornaments and other performance markings.[12]

P 804, unrelated to the previous group, comprises fifty-seven separate fascicles, each originally an independent manuscript. Known in the nineteenth century as the "Kellner miscellany," it belonged to Johann Peter Kellner, an organist, composer, and acquaintance if not an actual pupil of Bach, whose works he began copying around 1725. Stinson (1989a) is a comprehensive study of this and several other Kellner manuscripts. Kellner's Bach copies include the sole sources for some pieces, and the *earliest* surviving sources for others. Not all of the Bach works were copied from scores obtained from Bach himself, and Kellner's addition of ornaments and other changes has raised questions about his dependability. An especially serious issue concerns the reliability of his attributions, particularly where Kellner merely provided a title for a copy in another hand. Some pieces were even left anonymous but have been generally accepted as Bach's.[13] The traditional attributions are accepted here, but it remains curious that Kellner should have copied or collected pieces that Bach's pupils apparently ignored during the same period.

The *Mempell-Preller* collection consists of separate manuscripts in several libraries; these manuscripts originally belonged to Johann Nicolaus Mempell, cantor from 1740 at Apolda near Weimar, and to Johann Gottlieb Preller, apparently his pupil and later cantor at Dortmund. The two most important manuscripts are LEm mss. 7 and 8; the most complete discussion of the collection remains that of Schulze (1984a, 67–87). It is uncertain how either copyist obtained the works by Bach, although Preller might have been in contact with former pupils or associates of Bach at Weimar during the 1740s.[14] Preller's copies tend to contain many fingerings and ornament signs, only some of which are found in other sources. His copies have therefore been taken as documents of performance practice; some of Preller's texts are published as appendices in volumes of the NBA. But these texts are unlikely to derive directly from Bach's performance or teaching; rather they provide evidence for the manner in which one provincial organist was playing Bach's music around the middle of the eighteenth century. Together with the other copies described above, they suggest that teachers were actively supplementing Bach's texts in manuscript long before nineteenth-century editors such as Czerny did so in print. Nevertheless, the Mempell-Preller collection remains important as the sole source for several of Bach's earliest compositions.

2
Some Performance Issues

It is no longer unusual to hear Bach's keyboard music performed on the harp-sichord; indeed, new recordings on the piano have become something of a rarity, and study of historical performance practice has become a required part of the curriculum in many institutions. Yet many players and teachers remain untouched (or unimpressed) by so-called historically informed performance, and much of what passes for "authentic" playing on "original" instruments is not what it purports to be. Performance practice is too large a topic to be discussed adequately in any one book, let alone a single chapter, but certain issues recur so often in Bach's keyboard music that it is worth mentioning them briefly before considering individual compositions.

The most fundamental issues for anyone concerned with historical perfor-mance practice are philosophical ones. These issues were once framed in terms of historical authenticity, understood as performing music as it was originally played, or as the composer intended. But no reputable performer or scholar today claims that using an old instrument or a supposed copy thereof, or even play-ing it according to the latest ideas about historical performing practice, assures authenticity. Few suppose that it is possible to discover and reproduce Bach's intentions concerning the performance of a particular work, especially when it is unclear that he had a specific intention even about something as fundamental as the medium of the "clavier" works. Hence the debate over authenticity has turned to more sophisticated questions. *Should* a performance reflect the composer's intentions, or at least the conventions and conditions of performance that the composer might have originally anticipated? If the answer is yes, is this because the performer bears a moral duty to the composer, or is it because a historically informed performance is potentially richer than one based solely on present-day assumptions and intuitions? Is it because a well-crafted composition possesses some sort of integration that is reduced when it is not performed on the instrument and in the manner for which it was envisioned?

Even if a performance cannot be authentic in the naive sense of recreating an actual historical one, it can attempt to follow documented performance conventions, or to operate within historically documented ranges for individual parameters such as tempo or dynamic level. Authenticity in this sense is relatively uncontroversial, especially when applied to such mundane things as the realization of ornament signs or the interpretation of rhythmic notation. Temperatures rise when historical "accuracy" is used as a criterion of value—a historically informed performance being considered *better* than one that is not—or when the use of historical practices affects not only the sounds but the expressive character of the music.

That expression is central to the issue became clear from a notorious debate over the dotting of the French overture. The differences between the participants came down to the fact that what seemed majestic to one sounded jerky and awkward to another.[1] One might suppose that it would be best to play such pieces in a way that conveyed "majesty" to present-day listeners, even if this meant ignoring eighteenth-century conventions. But Bach's majesty is not the same as Beethoven's, Verdi's, or Copland's, and musical compositions, or at least those of a master composer like Bach, do not express simple affects like majesty. They are complex, integrated works in which sonority, rhythm, ornamentation, and other aspects of performance practice are as much a part of the musical fabric as the written notes, all operating together to produce what some listeners will experience as expressing a particular emotion, others as something potentially quite different.

In the absence of relevant documents, we cannot know what Bach meant to express in his music or how Bach's contemporaries felt when they heard it. Precise answers are unlikely to be forthcoming even to more concrete questions, such as how Bach tuned his harpsichords and clavichords. Nor would we necessarily want to replicate those practices, even if we did know what they were. But research into historical instruments and practices has consistently led to new ideas about how music can be performed today, opening up previously unimagined possibilities of interpretation. And the fact that some things are unknowable does not invalidate all research into historical performance practice. One needs, however, to frame questions of a type that can be answered: not "What does the French overture express?" or "How did Bach play this overture?" but "What was the range of tempos used in early eighteenth-century overtures?" and "In what ways did Bach's contemporaries interpret dotted rhythmic notation?"

Even questions of this sort lack simple answers. Anyone confronting an unfamiliar ornament sign, or, worse, the *absence* of expected information in a score (such as a tempo mark), naturally craves a definite, readily internalized solution. Some modern authors oblige, giving rules claimed to come from old treatises, perhaps even quoting relevant passages. Yet the evidence cited may not apply to the music in question; for instance, does a book published at Berlin in 1753 tell us anything about the performance of music composed at Weimar in 1714? Did the word *cantabile* in a score or title mean the same thing to Walther or J. S. Bach that it does today? Useful answers are likely to be framed in terms of probabilities and possibilities, not absolute black and white dogmas.

Bach's music presents a special problem for the student of historical performance practice: it is often the first "early" music that a beginner encounters, yet it is one of the most complex, difficult repertoires ever created. Pupils often begin their study of Bach with the Inventions, but these are not easy pieces, and many students confront them in a stylistic vacuum, before knowing the music of Bach's contemporaries. Pupils gain insights into Bach's music by hearing good performances of works by Bach's forerunners and contemporaries—composers such as Corelli, Couperin, and Telemann, who provided models for Bach's works. Bach's own pupils had access to such music—indeed, they evidently studied it before graduating to his own works (see appendix B)—and they were, of course, surrounded by authentic performances of eighteenth-century music. Teachers today can hardly provide the latter. But they owe it to their students to gain some familiarity with recent, stylish performances of the music from which Bach himself learned.

Instruments

Although copies of harpsichords and other early instruments are now widespread, how these instruments sound and play depends on the manner in which they have been designed, built, and maintained. Actual surviving instruments from Bach's day are rare and largely confined to museums. Most are no longer in playing condition, and many that can be played have been altered in ways that have destroyed or obscured information about their original state. An unplayable wreck may be of greater value to a qualified scholar than an instrument that has been heavily restored.

The most basic fact to emerge from the surviving evidence is that keyboard instruments of Bach's day were far less standardized than those of today. Each of the main categories (organ, harpsichord, clavichord, fortepiano) comprised many varieties, differing in range, action, number of keyboards, and other fundamental characteristics. Harpsichords, for example, included distinct Italian, French, and German types, the latter sharing elements of the first two (see Koster 1999, 59). There were also smaller varieties of harpsichord such as the spinet, and hybrids such as the lute-harpsichord (*Lautenwerk*). Some German makers were interested in experimental harpsichords that might possess three manuals or unusual stops.

Although it can be hazardous to generalize about early instruments, the stringed keyboard instruments available to Bach, including early fortepianos, seem to have differed from the modern piano in having relatively light but efficient actions. This, together with the well-defined attack and release on each note, would have given the practiced player precise control over articulation and ornaments. In addition, individual tones on the older stringed keyboard instruments may take a bit longer to achieve full resonance, but they fade more quickly, and this has implications for tempo, among other things. Most harpsichords seem richer in upper overtones, as compared to the modern piano, making attacks clearer and inner voices audible even through a complex contrapuntal texture.

In Bach's day, keyboard players rarely specialized exclusively on one type or another, and there is little evidence of systematic differences in articulation, ornamentation, fingering, and other aspects of technique and style as applied to the various keyboard instruments. Butt (1990, 140) concludes that the same principles governed articulation in all the instrumental media used by Bach. This made it possible for the latter to transfer pieces such as the solo concertos from violin to either organ or harpsichord, with little change in the notes played. Even if certain of Bach's keyboard pieces constitute "demonstration counterpoint" meant for an abstract "clavier," they presuppose the qualities of an eighteenth-century instrument, not a present-day one.[2]

Although we possess a list of the instruments that Bach owned at his death, it fails to indicate much beyond the relative size and value of each.[3] Earlier documents, including one relating to Bach's acquisition of a harpsichord for the Prince of Cöthen in 1719 (see Germann 1985), also provide less information than one would like. Hence, precisely what types of instruments Bach owned or employed for his solo keyboard music remains a matter of conjecture, and efforts to connect particular compositions with particular instruments are speculative. In view of his reported interest in instrument building and in innovative combinations of sounds,[4] one may assume that Bach took an interest in unusual instruments. But there is little evidence that he ever composed pieces specifically for the latter, save for a few organ pieces and several works possibly intended for the lute-harpsichord.[5]

The sources for Bach's keyboard music rarely give an explicit indication of instrument, more often using an ambiguous term such as *Clavier* or *manualiter*. Although Bach must have realized that certain pieces would suit one instrument better than another, he accepted the custom of composing in a manner that made keyboard works readily transferable from one instrument to another. Thus the occasional dynamic markings in his keyboard music can be disregarded when playing on a one-manual harpsichord, without grave loss to the musical effect. Even the simple pedal parts found in some of the early pieces, as well as a few sustained bass tones in later compositions that seem to call for organ pedals, do not imply use of any particular type of instrument.[6]

Reflecting these uncertainties, recent years have seen deepening skepticism about certain orthodoxies concerning historical performance. During the

1970s, historically informed performances of Bach's keyboard music tended to be confined to harpsichords based on one or two eighteenth-century French models; now one can again hear Bach's keyboard music played on all manner of harpsichords, as well as clavichord, organ, and even fortepiano. Given the current fashion for broad interpretive freedom, players may need to be reminded that assumptions about what is idiomatic for particular instruments cannot be taken for granted. The harpsichord is not necessarily best suited for "austere" pieces or those that look like *motus perpetui*, nor need the clavichord be confined to pieces calling for "a light touch and understatement" (Levin 2000). The presence of arpeggiated figuration in early works containing simple pedal parts, such as the praeludium BWV 921, does not necessarily exclude the organ.[7] Apart from being unhistorical, such assumptions limit the player's imagination as to what an instrument can actually do. It is true that the harpsichord cannot produce the same dynamic variety as the piano, but early fortepianos and most clavichords do not have wide dynamic ranges either. On the other hand, modern harpsichordists, aided by uncompromising instrument builders and restorers, have shown how the various types of articulation, ornamentation, and other performing devices used historically on the instrument can compensate for the "missing" resources of the modern piano.

The Clavichord

Because most if not all of the music considered in this book was intended primarily for private study or "pastime," many pupils, amateurs, and even professional musicians would have played Bach's music on the clavichord and on the spinet and other small varieties of harpsichord, regardless of whether such instruments best serve the music.[8] The clavichord permits sensitive control of dynamics, and larger examples of the instrument, when well made and properly played, have a surprisingly wide dynamic range although they remain quiet by comparison with other types of instruments. Forkel declared the clavichord Bach's favorite instrument (1802 , 17/NBR, 436), but his claim has been disputed on the basis that Forkel was confusing his own preferences (or those of his informants) with Bach's. Still, at his death Bach owned "3 *Clavire* nebst *Pedal* [*sic*]"; the phrase has been variously interpreted but most likely referred to a set of three clavichords, two of them fitted with manual keyboards and one with a pedalboard, set up as a single instrument for practicing organ music.[9]

    One objection to the clavichord, especially in Bach's more austere contrapuntal works, such as the *Art of Fugue*, is its weak sustaining power. But this objection largely evaporates when the music is played at a reasonable speed; the difficulty of Bach's music is no excuse for drearily slow tempos. A more serious objection is that during Bach's lifetime the great majority of clavichords were probably small "fretted" (*gebunden*) examples on which two, sometimes three adjacent pitches were struck at different points on the same string. On such an instrument the notes D♯ and E, for example, cannot be played or held simultaneously. A trill or a slur involving both notes must be distinctly broken to prevent a thumping or pinging sound that occurs if one attempts to play one of these notes before the finger holding down the other has been completely raised. Although even small fretted clavichords can be well made, possessing a beautiful if tiny tone, they were a concession to the limited budgets and space of poor students and amateurs. Most are no more adequate for serious music making or practice than the cheap upright pianos on which so many twentieth-century students had to practice, or the electronic keyboards that have replaced them.

Although we know of large unfretted clavichords from as early as 1693, it is unlikely that these ever became widespread. On a fretted clavichord, not only are some passages unplayable as written, but the player's choices of ornamentation and articulation are restricted. This in turn limits one's ability to play as expressively as one would like in such pieces as the preludes in C-sharp minor and F minor in part 1 of the *Well-Tempered Clavier* (WTC). Still, it is possible that Bach conceived some of his simpler pedagogic pieces specifically for the use of pupils at a clavichord. Speerstra (2004) has argued that many more pieces were intended for the clavichord, but this relies heavily on evidence dating from after Bach's death, including the report of his pupil Agricola that Bach played his suites and sonatas for unaccompanied violin on the instrument (see chap. 16). But Bach's music never requires *Bebung* or *Tragen der Töne*, varieties of vibrato and portato, respectively, that were valued by later generations as unique capabilities of the clavichord.

Nevertheless, it is true, as C. P. E. Bach wrote (1753–62, i.introduction.11), that the clavichord is the most demanding keyboard instrument, the one "on which a keyboard player can most conveniently be judged." A practiced clavichordist can not only control dynamics sensitively but can voice chords and bring out individual notes or voices in a contrapuntal texture—the same techniques that good pianists use to project details of Bach's counterpoint. The best players must have mastered such skills and applied them to Bach's music during his lifetime. But to play Bach's contrapuntal keyboard music on the clavichord can be a maddening exercise, especially in the more remote tonalities (difficult because of the short accidental keys). When a repertory of music explicitly for the clavichord emerged during the second half of the eighteenth century, it was characterized by thin monodic textures consisting primarily of melody and a simple accompaniment, very different from and much easier to play than Bach's.

Harpsichords

Harpsichords are larger, more complicated mechanically, and therefore more expensive than clavichords. German makers seem to have been more diversified or experimental in their output, building instruments that show greater variations in size, compass, and registrational possibilities than the harpsichords of their French and Italian contemporaries (see Koster 1999). At his death, Bach owned instruments of distinctly different values, implying distinct designs and sounds as well. Whether he was unusual among professional musicians in owning several harpsichords, as has been claimed, is uncertain.[10] Bach's suites, like the French pieces on which they were modeled, were certainly meant for harpsichords of one sort or another. Couperin assumed that a beginner would start on a lightly quilled harpsichord, and French composers explicitly demanded the harpsichord in many titles, as did Bach in the first, second, and fourth parts of the *Clavierübung*. By extension, pieces whose style or texture resembles that of Bach's suites, such as the F-major prelude in WTC2, might be assigned to the harpsichord. Even the *Art of Fugue* contains similar writing.

Some of Bach's keyboard works contain passages in sustained style for which the organ or the modern piano may seem more suitable than the harpsichord. Yet, even in a quasi-vocal piece like the E-major fugue of WTC2, the clear articulations of the harpsichord will facilitate phrasing and the crisp delineation of individual motives. In addition, the harpsichord's capacity for minute variations in the breaking of chords, which can range from a near-simultaneous striking of all notes to a distinct arpeggiation, provides a means for shading each verticality. To what degree these devices were part of the historical technique of harpsichord playing is uncertain, since treatises rarely discuss such details of actual playing. Modern harpsichordists have cultivated a technique described by Quantz and Forkel that allows precise control of articulation and arpeggiation. Yet modern players may be more concerned than were their eighteenth-century predecessors with projecting the structure and expressive character of pieces to large public audiences. This in turn may have led to the cultivation of habits and techniques that Bach would have considered mannered or exaggerated. Yet it is hard to believe that the sensitive articulation and timing of most present-day harpsichordists, which seem so idiomatic to the physical instrument, are entirely a modern invention, especially as these techniques have exact parallels in practices documented for eighteenth-century winds and bowed strings.

All this merely proves that the harpsichord is a *suitable* medium for the keyboard pieces—not necessarily the optimal or the intended one. Few of the compositions that were already regarded in the second half of the eighteenth century as "clavier" pieces can be considered the exclusive domain of harpsichordists.[11] Clavichord and fortepiano remain possibilities, and Marshall (1986) made a case for the organ in certain works. No doubt Bach was well aware of the capabilities of all these instruments and could use each of them to bring out aspects of any piece. But this is merely to say that a good performer makes the most of a performance situation. It remains necessary to consider the question of best medium carefully for every work, in conjunction with the piece's date and sources, its genre, and its internal musical characteristics.

Organ and Fortepiano

Much of Bach's clavier music is theoretically playable on the organ, but what does a *manualiter* piece gain from being played on such an instrument? The organ would seem useful in works containing long sustained notes, especially pedal points. But it is clear from the music for unaccompanied violin that Bach often notated sustained tones that he did not expect to be physically held. One could "realize" these violin compositions exactly as notated by playing them on the organ—or on modern contraptions, including the violins with specially modified bridges and bows that were invented for this purpose during the twentieth century. But to do so actually eliminates features that Bach wrote into the music, which presupposes the special timing and phrasing required for playing three- and four-note violin chords in eighteenth-century style. By the same token, releasing and restriking otherwise unsustainable pedal notes becomes part of the interpretation of the A-minor fugue of WTC1 when played on the clavichord or harpsichord. A large organ can produce more sound than either instrument, and will probably make a greater impression on shallow listeners whose musical sensibilities have been formed by the high decibels of amplified music or modern orchestras. But one might ask in every piece whether organ performance adds anything more than momentary visceral excitement.

The argument for the fortepiano is weak from the historical point of view, since such instruments were rare and quite expensive during Bach's day. We have evidence of Bach's playing and selling such instruments during his later years, implying that he might have had such an instrument in his house for a while. But the fortepianos that Bach would have known were small, soft, and better suited for accompanying quiet chamber music than for playing solos in public.

The Modern Piano

In principle the modern piano can do almost everything the harpsichord and clavichord can do. Yet ornaments that can be played crisply and with little effort on the harpsichord seem heavier and require stronger fingers on the piano. Chords—especially the swiftly broken chords used so frequently in harpsichord playing—practically voice themselves on the harpsichord or organ, yet pianists must carefully weigh each note. The greatest problems for pianists playing Bach arise not from the instrument per se, but from habits carried over from other repertories—for example, the *horror vacui* inculcated in many players at an early age through the insistence on legato pedaling in nineteenth- and twentieth-century music. Such pedaling, and the concomitant disregard of slurs in eighteenth-century music—which imply some degree of non-legato after the slur and on unslurred notes—discourage the pianist from using the finely honed silences that are one of the modern harpsichordist's most valuable resources.

Some pianists argue that use of the damper pedal is essential to the true nature of the instrument. But legato pedaling—like the continuous vibrato of modern string playing—is an innovation of the mid- or late nineteenth century. Its appropriateness in Mozart, Beethoven, and even Chopin is open to question, let alone in Bach. An articulate, unpedaled approach to the modern piano need not be dry or percussive, but it does require placing a certain amount of weight on each note and paying the same attention to each attack *and* each release as a good organist or harpsichordist does.

To do so makes musical sense; the purpose is not simply to imitate the older instruments. Pianists certainly ought to use dynamic accents on appoggiaturas and suspensions, and there is no reason not to increase and decrease volume to reflect the rise and fall of melodic lines. Such attention to "light and shade," as Quantz and others referred to it, was normal in eighteenth-century performance in other media. Still, too much reliance on the unique resources of the piano to shape or "bring out" certain aspects of the music—inner voices, for example—risks producing a mannered effect. Harpsichordists shape lines through careful attention to articulation and judicious use of ornaments, arpeggiation, and rhythmic nuance. Pianists have more means at their disposal, but in attempting to rectify the apparent limitations of Bach's instruments they might be wary of gilding the lily.

Temperament and Registration

Keyboard temperament has been a much-studied problem, particularly in relation to the author of the *Well-Tempered Clavier*. In Bach's day temperament was a favorite subject of debate for both theorists and practitioners, including organ builders and players. Because it raises certain computational issues, temperament has always been of special interest to mathematicians and, more recently, computer scientists. As in the eighteenth century, some feel a compulsion to publish theories of tuning illustrated with elaborate charts and tables that are of little relevance to either aurally perceptible distinctions or historically documented practices.

Temperament is a necessary first step in tuning any keyboard instrument that is to be used for playing in more than one key. Three pure or "just" major thirds do not make a pure octave, nor do twelve perfect fifths lead back to the note on which they began (that is to say that for singers and for players of non-keyboard instruments, B♯ is not the same note as C). By Bach's day, theorists and instrument makers had devised various systems for altering, or tempering, pure thirds and fifths, to make possible the participation of keyboard instruments in the increasingly broad range of keys and modulations used in eighteenth-century music. Since even some of Bach's earliest keyboard music employs distant keys and enharmonic equivalents, he is likely throughout his life to have been familiar with sophisticated tuning systems, including more or less equal temperament—precisely equal temperament being unattainable except through an electronic synthesizer.

Equal temperament is only one of various types of so-called well-tempered (*wohltemperierte*) tuning systems that Bach would have known. There survive no unambiguous accounts as to how Bach tuned his instruments, and it is entirely possible that he used different systems at different times and for different types of music. By selective citation of individual pieces or other documents, one can adduce internal "evidence" that Bach used one sort of tuning or another.[12] But in the absence of sufficient documentation for Bach's preferences, such claims invariably turn out to be little more than an expression of personal preference. Assertions such as Lindley's (1990, 180) that "the tuning theorist whom Bach most respected was J. G. Neidhart" cannot be verified, nor can doodles on an autograph title page be unambiguously interpreted as a code for a particular temperament.[13]

Nevertheless, Bach's concern with "pure" temperament is documented by his rejection of the system adopted by the organ builder Gottfried Silbermann.[14] Any system that produces very sharp "Pythagorean" thirds or other out-of-tune intervals—as in temperaments described by Werckmeister and Kirnberger—distracts the ear away from Bach's music to the peculiarities of the intonation. Some *wohltemperierte* systems are more subtle than others in their distribution of the impurity that arises unavoidably in any circular temperament. But the more sophisticated unequal systems are harder to tune and less likely to be noticed by any but the sharpest ears. Neidhart, known today as an advocate of "well-tempered" tuning, argued as early as 1706 for the superiority of equal temperament and continued to do so despite his defeat in a celebrated tuning competition with Nicolaus Bach of Jena—an event of which Sebastian must have been well apprised. Accounts of organs inspected and passed by Sebastian Bach mention their having been tuned "according to Neidhart,"[15] which may have meant equal temperament, the system with which Neidhart's name seems to have been most commonly associated. Werckmeister, whose earlier unequal temperaments are often cited, advocated equal temperament in a work published in 1707.[16] Bach did not necessarily read the works of either theorist, but he must have been aware of the principal arguments on both sides of the controversy.

Later theorists argued that unequal temperament invests different keys with distinct characters.[17] Proponents of unequal temperament still praise the shadings that such systems can give to certain keys, and which in some instances produce a pleasing variation as one passes between distantly related tonalities. But the argument from character is based on the naive idea that the expression or affect associated with each key must have some physical basis in the acoustic structure of the scale itself. In fact, "key characteristics" are more psychological and cultural in nature. They may originate in the associations of certain instruments with particular keys—Baroque trumpets with C and D major—or in the physical sensation of playing particular scales or chords on a keyboard instrument. Bach's transposition of several pieces by half step, as in the B-Minor *Ouverture* BWV 831, makes it doubtful that he linked the choice of key with a work's expressive character. This would seem to favor the case for equal temperament; so too does the fact that at Leipzig and elsewhere church organs were pitched differently from other instruments, making the organ a transposing instrument.

On the other hand, it would have been possible to tune an organ in an unequal temperament whose central (most pure) key was B♭, not C. Writers such as Quantz and Telemann advocated tuning systems in which major thirds are purer than in equal temperament (see Oleskiewicz 2000, 204–8). Although not intended for keyboard instruments, the temperaments described by such musicians were evidently used in chamber music, and one wonders how, for instance, the fortepianos were tuned for King Frederick's private palace concerts at Potsdam, where Bach played in 1747.[18]

What is certain is that tuning systems that made possible the use of all keys were receiving praise during Bach's lifetime. A few years after his father's death, Carl Philipp Emanuel Bach wrote of a "new type" (*neue Art*) of temperament, using language similar to that with which he described a "new fingering" (*neue Finger-Setzung*) associated with his father.[19] The implication is that Emanuel Bach associated this "new" type of temperament with his father; that this was equal temperament is evident from a tuning treatise by the instrument maker Barthold Fritz (1757), which indicates that Emanuel Bach approved of equal temperament. Hence, we can be reasonably certain that by 1753 Sebastian's music was being played on clavichords tuned in equal temperament. But neither the instrument nor the tuning necessarily coincided with the composer's intentions or practices. Bach might have tuned his own instruments according to pragmatic recipes dependent on ear and personal taste. The resulting temperaments could well have contained subtle shadings of certain keys, as in the more refined temperaments described by Neidhart, and there seems no harm in using one of these.

Registration

Registration is the art of selecting a combination of strings or pipes for a piece, or a passage within a piece. Like the modern pianist's concern with "color" or "sound," registration can become an obsession overriding more important concerns. But the considerable ingenuity and expense devoted to building colorful instruments, especially in Germany, during the late Baroque suggests that some of Bach's contemporaries shared this obsession. His cantatas and other orchestral works reveal his own interest in instrumental color, and he must have exercised some ingenuity in choosing organ registrations. Nevertheless, registration in Bach's day would have been influenced by conventions that limited the range of choices available in certain genres.[20]

The choices available on harpsichords are more restricted than on all but the smallest organs, and in any case novelties in this sphere wear off quickly. For this reason, and because they tend to distract attention from more substantial musical qualities, harpsichordists today tend to avoid the colorful registrations that were fashionable during the mid-twentieth century, especially on hybrid instruments not based on historical antecedents. Hence, it is worth remembering that German makers of Bach's time did construct instruments with unusual stops, such as "lute" and sixteen-foot ranks, and that in pieces such as the Goldberg Variations Bach would certainly have expected the player to take full advantage of the capabilities of any given instrument.[21] Moreover, in two pieces that do call for two manuals, the Italian Concerto and the B-Minor *Ouverture*, the changes of manual are occasionally quite tricky, suggesting that Bach was willing to tolerate technical awkwardness for the sake of variety in sound.[22]

Nevertheless, it proves difficult to introduce changes of manual or registration in the course of other pieces without doing violence to their architecture. For example, in the Chromatic Fantasy (BWV 903/1) one might wish to introduce a hush at the beginning of the *Recitativ* section by shifting to a quieter manual or registration. Yet there is no obvious point at which to return to a fuller registration before the end of the movement; wherever one does so, the sudden return to a higher dynamic level produces a discontinuity. Similar problems occur in quasi-ritornello-form movements, such as the preludes of the English Suites. Bodky (1960) devoted an entire study to prescribing manual shifts in such movements, intended to make explicit the imitation of the solo/tutti contrasts of a concerto. Yet the design of such a movement emerges from its built-in motivic and textural contrasts, regardless of the registration or dynamic level used for each passage.

In Bach's contrapuntal textures, lines often cross between the hands, which in such cases should presumably play on the same manual. All voices do not always "breathe" simultaneously between phrases; the soprano may rest while the alto line continues, making it impossible to jump between manuals at that point. In concerto-like pieces the contrast between "tutti" and "solo" may be clear at the beginning but grow ambiguous later, making arbitrary the assignment of a given passage or line to the loud or the soft manual. Adding an extra rank of strings or pipes for a closing section may provide a momentary dramatic effect but can upset a piece's symmetrical formal design, creating a vulgar effect. In short, to insist on an austere approach to registration is not to rely on the historically unfounded "aesthetic convention" that "a composition should embody only one affect."[23] Rather it is a way of being faithful to the music, and if a clever registration creates practical or architectural difficulties as one works one's way through a piece, one's ingenuity might be better exercised in other domains.

Articulation

Present-day harpsichordists and organists (like players of other historical instruments) are particularly concerned with nuances of articulation and rhythm at the local level. The two are intimately connected; eighteenth-century treatises on wind and string playing illustrate in great detail how specific patterns of legato and non-legato notes were related to particular meters and rhythmic patterns. Keyboard treatises provide less detail, but they make it clear that eighteenth-century keyboard articulation tended more toward non-legato than did nineteenth- and twentieth-century playing.[24] Thus, modern harpsichordists follow the suggestions of writers such as the flutist Quantz, who offered specific articulation patterns for numerous motivic figures, the precise pattern of detached and partially detached notes depending upon the rhythm and the melodic intervals of the line.[25]

Specialists in early music often refer to the resulting articulate style of performance as being more akin to speech than to song in the nineteenth-century sense. Indeed this style of performance may have had some connection to rhetoric, the art of formal speech, which formed the basis of instruction and theory in the arts prior to the nineteenth century. Although its significance for Baroque music is often overstated or poorly defined (see Williams 1983b), the use of rhetorical devices or "figures" in speech and poetry is analogous to the use of certain devices in music, leading to the theory of musical rhetoric. Renaissance and Baroque writers took great delight in attaching Greek and Latin names to all sorts of verbal devices, most of them having no obvious musical parallel. But devices such as *repetitio* (repetition) and *chiasmus* (presenting ideas in the order ABBA) represent patterns common to music and speech, and music theorists described many purely musical devices as well.

Figures of the latter sort, which Marpurg (1756) called *figures de composition*, are close to what we would call motives. In early eighteenth-century music, these often take the form of elaborations or embellishments of single notes or chords: a broken triad, or a written-out turn of four notes. Many Baroque melodic lines, including Bach's, are comprised of such figures, and what at first glance looks like a homogeneous series of eighths or sixteenths is revealed upon analysis to comprise "a series of motifs, patterns, cells, *figurae*" (Williams 1979, 477). One way for a player to make his or her performance of such a line "rhetorical" is by articulating individual motives, sometimes even individual notes, in ways that we know were practiced during the late seventeenth and eighteenth centuries.

Single Notes

One can deduce from string and wind treatises that it was normal to articulate unslurred notes separately, that is, with small silences before and after each note. Stronger notes might be preceded by stronger articulations, that is, slightly longer silences, creating agogic accents on notes that fall on beats, especially downbeats. By placing articulations before accented beats, the player clearly defines the metrical structure of each measure. This does not mean that every beat receives equal emphasis; rather, beats within each measure are distinguished by subtle distinctions in the duration of both the actual sounding notes and the "silences of articulation" that precede them. Notes off the beat, or on weak beats, are detached, whereas notes on accented beats may receive a dynamic accent while also being held for a slightly longer duration than would otherwise be the case. In short, accented notes can take more time than unaccented ones—and not only in French music, where the common practice of *notes inégales* meant that in pairs of notes written as quarters, eighths, or sixteenths (depending on the meter), the first of each pair occupied a greater portion of the beat than the second.

In light of such practices, it is misleading to characterize lines in eighteenth-century keyboard music simply as legato or non-legato. A uniform non-legato is as out of place in most eighteenth-century music as is a uniform legato. For the unslurred notes of a melody, players employed a variety of articulations ranging from true staccato to tenuto tones that are nevertheless distinctly separated from one another.

Slurs

Slurs in Bach's music never mark whole phrases, nor were they introduced arbitrarily or for the convenience of the player. Rather they fall on particular types of recurring figures, such as an appoggiatura and its resolution, and they more often begin on accented than unaccented beats, rarely extending for more than four notes. Some figures can be slurred in more than one way, and Bach sometimes wrote signs ambiguously or indicated different slurs for the same passage (see Butt 1990, 122–30 and 136–39). But the notes under a slur usually arpeggiate a single harmony (sometimes with a passing tone or two), or they may embellish a single tone by circling around it or prefixing an appoggiatura. A slur is therefore an indication that the notes are an embellishment of an underlying chord or melodic tone.[26] Some writers directed keyboard players to hold down all the notes of a slur,[27] thereby running the slurred notes together into a single *Gestalt*. In much the same way, a Baroque violinist incorporates a slurred figure into a single gesture played with a single bow stroke, constituting a single rhythmic impulse.

The practice of holding down slurred tones is effective on the harpsichord and even the organ for audibly projecting a short slur to an audience. The momentary dissonances arising when the slur encompasses adjacent tones are not intrusive and rather contribute to the warmth or fullness of the sonority. The slur also has rhythmic and dynamic implications: because slurs usually begin on beats, especially accented beats, the first note of a slur may be slightly lengthened and will seem louder than the others, even on a non-dynamic instrument. The final note of a slur is not only likely to be detached, but it may seem softer than the others and may also come rhythmically a bit late.

Nowadays it is commonly assumed that one can freely add slurs in eighteenth-century music. Adding slurs may even seem a technical necessity on bowed strings and woodwinds, and it may be justified if slurs occur in parallel passages elsewhere in a piece, or on the same motivic figure in another composition. Yet if the notes in question do not belong to a single harmony, or do not constitute an integral figure embellishing a single tone, they were probably not slurred in the eighteenth century. In particular, figures that cross the barline or that extend from a weak to a strong beat need not be slurred to retain their integrity; only in special circumstances did Bach and his contemporaries write the type of slur between upbeat and downbeat that is so common in Viennese Classical music.[28] By the same token, slurring into a beat is not the only way to join upbeat to downbeat in a single gesture; detached upbeats seem to be the rule in Bach's music.

Many of Bach's melodies incorporate figures comprised of two or three slurred notes alongside an unslurred one. Such motives are defined by a specific *combination* of slurred and unslurred notes (e.g., groupings of sixteenths in patterns of 1 + 3 or 3 + 1). In such a combination the little articulations or silences preceding and following the slur do not break up the gesture but become a part of it. On the violin, the *Gestalt* of such a figure comprises two quite different strokes of the bow, on the keyboard an alternation of downward weight (slur) and upward release (single note).

Broken Chords

A technique not usually associated with articulation and rhythm but in fact intimately related to it, at least on the harpsichord, is the breaking of chords. Modern harpsichordists often take it for granted that all chords should be broken to some degree, if only to prevent the impression of a harsh or clunky accent on every chord. On bowed strings, chords of more than two notes must be broken, even though this is not indicated notationally. Following clues in eighteenth-century treatises and notation, Baroque violinists today place the lowest note of such a chord on the downbeat, holding out only the highest one. Rameau (1722, iv.3.5), probably assuming use of the harpsichord, tells keyboard continuo players to break all chords swiftly, the first note in the right hand being struck together with its underlying bass note. Players in Germany presumably followed the same practices.

Just as a violinist controls the speed of a broken chord for expressive purposes, the ability to break chords at varying rates is a crucial element in the modern harpsichordist's vocabulary. By varying the precise speed of the arpeggiation, it is possible to give the effect of either a harsh or a gentle attack, and to accentuate the top or the bottom note, respectively. Moreover, because a slow arpeggiation takes time, breaking a chord that falls on a strong beat accords with the lengthening of metrically strong parts of the measure. These routine types of chord breaking are not indicated notationally; in the rare cases where Bach actually dictates arpeggiation, the sign may have implied a slower, more measured breaking than usual, as is implied by the "realizations" of arpeggio signs shown in French tables of ornaments.

Fingering

It was once thought that the instructions for playing scales in old treatises, like the fingering numerals in some musical manuscripts, furnished important clues to historical keyboard performance, especially articulation. Indeed they do, but more by way of suggestion than prescription. For instance, so-called paired scale fingerings (3–4–3–4), such as Bach prescribed in the Applicatio BWV 994, do not necessarily imply corresponding pairs of slurred notes (as Williams points out, 1980–4, 3:220). One can produce a smooth legato or almost any other type of articulation while using such a fingering; the trick is to turn one's hand in the direction of the scale, lifting the thumb up from the keyboard, as the virginal player is doing in the oft-reproduced frontispiece from *Parthenia*.[29]

The Applicatio is one of just two pieces with fingerings known to come from Bach himself. Emanuel Bach later credited his father with a "new" style of fingering, including increased use of the thumb in scales and other passages. But Emanuel Bach still recommended older fingering patterns in many contexts, and his contemporaries often played scales and arpeggios without the thumb-under technique that later came to seem indispensable in keyboard playing. As in other aspects of his art, Sebastian must have integrated older practices alongside new ones; he could not have conceived his peculiar style of keyboard music had he been bound to the more modern approaches to technique and fingering that were probably emerging in the playing of his own sons and pupils.

The technique implied by early fingerings differs considerably from that used by most modern players, harpsichordists as well as pianists. Fingerings in modern editions—even the exemplary ones by Jones—follow present-day pianistic conventions, which are based above all on the principle of constant legato. But, as we have seen, in eighteenth-century playing notes were not usually sustained for their full written values, and this has all sorts of consequences for fingering and other aspects of technique. For instance, when playing a line that jumps between registers, one is not bound to connect the notes; instead notes preceding leaps can be detached and the hand shifted to where the new note must be played. In polyphonic passages, or in sustained melodies that might imply legato to a modern pianist (or organist), finger substitution and awkward finger crossings are rarely necessary. Rather, one can use the same finger to play successive melodic notes, so long as they are not too quick. Hence the hand is tensed or stretched less frequently than in "modern" playing, although it may spend more time in the air, shifting position, just as a Baroque violinist's bow may actually be off the string more often than it is on it. This is not to say that the keys are struck from above, except perhaps in lively dances; placing the fingers gently on each key before playing will avoid audible thumps, which are particularly obvious on the clavichord.

Even rapid scales and arpeggios can be played without thumb-under fingerings, and what looks like a routine legato passage to a current-day pianist would have seemed more textured to Bach and his pupils. For instance, Bach might have written the opening of the C-minor fantasia BWV 906/1 under the assumption that it would be played with a fingering that grouped its initial downward arpeggio into two distinct sets of triplets: c'''–g''–eb'', c''–g'–eb' (each fingered 5–3–2). In the C-major fugue of WTC1, when the bass enters with the subject (m. 5), the left hand must play the eighths c–d while holding down tenor c'. The latter is played by the thumb, forcing the repeated use of the fifth finger on c–d, and perhaps on the following e as well. Bach evidently expected the player to play those notes non-legato; far from being an unintended consequence of the polyphonic texture, the articulate character of the subject in this entry is a positive feature that can be integrated into one's conception of the piece as a whole.

Ornaments and Embellishment

Even more than articulation, ornaments are fundamental to historical Bach performance. The performance of appoggiaturas, trills, and other standard ornaments is one of the first topics encountered in many historical treatises, implying that learning to sing or play ornaments clearly and expressively was a basic part of the education of a young musician. Through the seventeenth century, German treatises tended to repeat accounts of ornamentation that derived from early-Baroque Italian sources, such as Caccini's *Nuove musiche* of 1601. But Bach's early years coincided with a surge in publication of keyboard pieces in both France and Germany, some of them equipped with ornament tables documenting new symbols and probably, to some degree, new approaches to ornamentation. The manuscripts MM and ABB also include ornament tables, copied by Johann Christoph Bach (directly or indirectly) from French sources. In the 1720 *Clavier-Büchlein* for Wilhelm Friedemann, Sebastian adopted the custom of equipping a volume of keyboard music with a table of ornaments.

Today such tables are understood as explanations for how to play ornaments. But written-out "realizations" can suggest only a possible range of notes and rhythms indicated by each ornament sign. Bach and his contemporaries—at least those at musically sophisticated courts and cities such as Weimar and Leipzig—enjoyed the advantage of regularly hearing music performed with ornaments, both written and unwritten. For them, ornament tables and treatises would have served not as instructions in how to play ornaments, but rather as guides to understanding which signs a particular composer used to designate ornaments that were already well understood.

Today Bach is known as one who wrote out ornaments and embellishments that other composers left to be improvised, a practice noted by Scheibe in his famous attack on Bach's style. But as Birnbaum noted in his reply (BD 2:304 [item 409]/NBR, 346), the same was true of the French composers whose works Bach imitated. What Birnbaum had in mind were the French signs for small, formulaic ornaments, not the more elaborate types of embellishment that cannot be reduced to recurring formulas. Neither Scheibe nor Birnbaum, writing in the 1730s, is likely to have known that in Bach's earlier works, and in early versions of familiar works, the composer's notation of ornament signs was relatively spotty. Ornament signs in some works, including many early compositions preserved in ABB and MM, may have been added by others. Even in the WTC, which although not printed was revised several times and copied by numerous pupils, ornament signs appear sparingly. Bach must have expected players to supplement the written signs, as Bach himself apparently did in revised versions of the French Suites.

But where Bach did indicate ornaments, signs are sometimes drawn hastily or unclearly and therefore are subject to varying interpretations.[30] Even his pupils and the engravers of his printed works, who presumably worked under his direction, sometimes confused different ornament signs, as variants in the French Suites and ambiguous signs in the Partitas and the Goldberg Variations suggest. Over the course of his long career, Bach's notation of ornaments changed, and no doubt his way of playing them; there can be no one way of realizing the ornament signs in his music. His practice may never have been precisely that documented by Emanuel Bach, whose *Essay* (1753–62) includes a detailed discussion of ornaments. But Bach must in general have followed consensuses documented by his German contemporaries.

Thus Georg Muffat stated as early as 1698 that trills began on the upper note, at least in music for instrumental ensemble. Fischer indicated the same in a keyboard ornament table (1696), as did most subsequent authors. Exceptions have been noted in treatises from as late as 1730 (see Neumann 1978, 302–3), but these are clearly just that, exceptions to what had become the usual practice. The underlying principle is that the upper note of these trills is usually dissonant, functioning as an appoggiatura; this was in keeping with the increasing cultivation of dissonant appoggiaturas as both written and unwritten ornaments in late-Baroque music, used to heighten the expression of a melodic line. That the first, upper note of a trill was normally placed on the beat, not before it, is implicit in instructions for the performance of appoggiaturas, although the latter present a more complex case. C. P. E. Bach (1753–62) gave the rule that the appoggiatura is always played on the beat and normally takes half the value of the main note to which it is attached. But Emanuel's precepts do not necessarily apply to his father's music, and this rule seems not to have been stated verbally by any earlier writer, although it is enshrined in the ornament tables of d'Anglebert and Sebastian Bach himself, at least as interpreted literally.

Early in his career, Bach might have followed the less systematic approach to appoggiaturas (*accents*) implied by seventeenth-century sources. These suggest that appoggiaturas—more properly, various types of passing-note ornament— might be placed before, after, or even straddling beats, lasting various amounts of time. Emanuel Bach still made a distinction, not indicated notationally, between long (or "invariable") and short ("variable") appoggiaturas; both fall on the beat, but only long appoggiaturas follow the rule stated above. Sebastian usually wrote long appoggiaturas as regular notes; hence those which he no-tated as small notes, or through the sign for an *accent,* were probably meant to be played short. During his lifetime, short appoggiaturas, especially of the type known as the *tierce coulée* (which fills a descending third at the end of a phrase), were sometimes played before the beat, at least in French music.[31] But C. P. E. Bach's vehement rejection of this manner of performance cannot be dismissed, especially as one of his examples is practically a quotation from the aria of the Goldberg Variations.[32]

It is sometimes thought that the rules of counterpoint can settle questions about the interpretation of ornament signs, such as where to place appoggiaturas. Yet "forbidden" parallels crop up occasionally in Sebastian's music. Those arising from ornaments are positively objectionable only when they become blatantly obvious, as may occur with the long appoggiatura, or when individual notes of an ornament are played too mechanically or in time.[33]

Modern "classical" training inculcates literalistic interpretations of notation, and therefore it may not be helpful to give pupils written-out realizations of orna-ments. One sometimes hears ornaments executed as if they are not ornaments, that is, as if each sixteenth note with which they are notated in a "realization" must be clearly articulated. Some pianists make the opposite mistake of playing trills like pretty colorations of individual notes, suffused by the damper pedal with a pleasant haze. But trills and other ornaments, despite the name, are not mere decoration. They impart harmonic tension to the music through their incorporation of accented dissonances, thus becoming expressive inflections of the melodic line; a long trill can begin slowly and speed up without ever becom-ing a mere reflexive buzz.

Embellishment

Improvised embellishment is even more remote than ornaments from the experience of most classically trained musicians today, although it is the basis of jazz and was common in European concert music well into the nineteenth century. Embellishment is more complex and irregular than the formulaic ornaments that can be represented in shorthand by simple signs. Bach's music frequently incorporates written-out melodic embellishment that was meant to imitate improvisation, especially in slow movements, where it takes the form of flurries of small note values. Bach's embellishments include conventional slide and scale figures, classified by theorists through such terms as *esclamazione* and *passaggio*, as well as appoggiaturas and turning figures of various sorts, often in configurations that put dissonances or chromatic notes on accented beats. Other embellishments take the form of broken chords, usually with dissonant passing tones inserted. Hence it is useful to analyze Bach's more ornate melodies by identifying the harmonies that they arpeggiate and the non-chord tones with which the harmonic tones are embellished. The challenge for the player is to bring out the expressive implications of the dissonances, by giving them extra time or a slight dynamic impulse, without losing track of the underlying beat.

Baroque treatises give extensive instruction in how to improvise melodic embellishment, but this was an art best practiced in certain adagios whose intentionally simple style invited glossing by the player. Common in the sonatas of Corelli and in Italian opera, such movements are rare, if they occur at all, in Bach's music. Although experienced players may find opportunities for free embellishment in Bach's music, the danger is that one's own embellishments will sound banal or will clash stylistically against what Bach actually wrote.

Rhythm and Tempo

Ornaments and embellishments, whether or not notated, derive much of their expressive significance from the tension that their irregular notes create against a regular beat. We are accustomed to setting the beat (or the metronome) to whatever note value we like, but for Bach and his contemporaries the time signature dictated on which note the beat falls. Thus the beat is on the eighth in a passepied notated in 3/8, on the quarter in most adagios (in common time), on the half-note in overtures and fugues notated *alla breve*. Tempo was determined largely by convention, recognizable from such clues as a dance title or a dance rhythm embedded within a movement. The rhythmic patterns that characterized each dance were surely meant to be heard clearly; some of these patterns, especially the shifting hemiolas of the courante, can be difficult to grasp in Bach's own settings and are best studied first in the simpler examples by composers such as Dieupart.

Florid embellishment may cause some deceleration of the beat; one might, for instance, play the sarabandes of the second and third English suites more slowly than others, in light of their many *agréments*. Yet the beats themselves are best not subdivided, even if that may seem necessary when learning the music. Even in heavily embellished adagios and sarabandes it is crucial that one still count halves or quarters, not eighths or sixteenths; subdividing causes the written-out embellishment to lose the character of passionate improvisation that it was meant to imitate. This will also happen if the tempo is too slow, making the music unduly solemn and dull.

To be sure, relaxation of the tempo at cadences can be heard in most good performances of eighteenth-century music. The freedom that eighteenth-century music permits within the beat also allows time to be taken at phrase endings (which often occur just after, not on, a downbeat). But a ritard that would be appropriate in a Romantic work may be out of place in a Baroque one, even at the end of a movement. Bach usually maintains a piece's prevalent rhythmic pattern right up to the last barline, and even in the final measure of a piece one can often maintain the beat while slowing only a little; if one takes too big a ritard, the written-out arpeggiations so common in final bars (especially in dance movements) may seem superfluous or dragged out. As in all notational matters, Bach was generally quite precise in indicating the value of final notes, which may range from a whole note to an eighth (followed by rests).

This is not to argue for the metronomic playing that arises from a literal reading of Baroque notation. Freedom within the beat is suggested not only by the principles of articulation noted earlier, but by written-out embellishments whose small note values often fail to add up properly. Six thirty-seconds followed by four sixty-fourths, all written on one beam (as in the ornamented version of the sarabande from the Third English Suite, m. 9), probably signify not contrasting rates of speed but a single accelerating gesture that starts slower and ends quicker than a literal reading of the notation would indicate. Ornaments, leaps in melodic lines, and broken chords may all invite one to take additional time on or immediately after the notes in question.

In certain types of pieces, Bach's contemporaries understood conventional alterations of the notated rhythms. The most famous of these alterations today are *notes inégales*, in which the first of a pair of sixteenths, eighths, or quarters is played longer than the second; which note values are affected depends on the time signature and the genre of the piece (in Bach's allemandes, for example, sixteenths would have been played unequally). No contemporary German writer adequately described the practice, but Bach must have had opportunities to hear French musicians who employed it, and he can hardly have been unaware of this or other widely recognized rhythmic conventions. Over-dotting, another convention, is sometimes confused with inequality, but the two apply to different types of pieces and involve differing notation and performing practice. Inequality can be used in almost any French dance, and was probably heard in many other types of music as well, not all of them French in origin.

Over-dotting is especially famous today from its use in overtures. But imprecise notation of dotted rhythms occurs in many types of music, resulting in the so-called "variable" dot. In Bach's overtures, notes following a dot can, as a general rule, be shortened to the value of a sixteenth; the preceding longer note will be lengthened in compensation. To be more precise, the dot is replaced by a rest of variable length, and an overture will lack energy and precision unless there is space before each of the shortened notes. In other words, overture-style over-dotting involves not only rhythmic modification but a distinctive manner of articulation (and of bowing on string instruments).

These rhythmic conventions, as well as what has been said about articulation, ornamentation, and embellishment, make sense only when the tempo of a piece is within appropriate limits. Many controversies that arose in the twentieth century over issues of Bach performance, such as the debate about overture dotting, can now be seen as the result of misapprehensions about tempo. To understand the tempos Bach probably had in mind for various types of pieces, it helps to examine simpler examples by Bach's contemporaries, whose tempos can be established from verbal accounts and even choreographies. Quantz arrived at a system of tempos and rhythmic notation which, although not directly applicable to Bach's music, gives an idea of how a younger contemporary of Bach expected sicilianos, allegros, and adagios, and other standard types of piece to be interpreted.[34]

Perhaps inspired by Quantz, or by the somewhat comparable system of Bach's pupil Kirnberger, some modern writers have sought mechanical solutions to the problem of tempo, supposing that Bach was a secret adherent to the proportional or mensural rhythmic theory of the Renaissance. Walther and other contemporaries repeated old definitions of time signatures, but neither Walther nor Kirnberger suggests that late-Baroque tempo was determined by precise proportions.[35] Naturally there are cases in which an arithmetically simple tempo proportion (such as 1:2 or 2:3) can be effective in, say, a prelude and the following fugue. But even minute differences in tempo can have important consequences for the character of a piece, and a tempo that is effective on a particular instrument in a particular room may need to be modified under other circumstances. Any tempo system born of rationalistic zeal may in practice need to be so heavily modified that it is no longer truly a system.

It is appropriate to conclude this chapter with the fermata, which had several uses for Bach. In an aria or a work for instrumental soloist, a fermata might indicate a cadenza; in a chorale it signified the end of a line, that is, a phrase ending or breathing point. Both usages occur in Bach's solo keyboard music, where, however, fermatas are largely confined to the ends of movements. Because Bach appears to have been inconsistent in his notation of final fermatas, they are usually assumed to be decorative, of no relevance to performance. Franklin (1992) explains the absence of a fermata at the ends of certain movements (especially in the WTC and the Goldberg Variations) as an indication that each movement forms part of a group with the next one, and that the two are in some proportional tempo relationship. Is it possible, however, that Bach was simply too busy to be wholly systematic and rational in his notation?

3

Bach's Style and Its Development
in the Keyboard Works

Bach's music was the product of a mingling of ideas and influences from current and earlier German, French, and Italian traditions, which he integrated into a personal style that developed over a period of half a century. It was once customary to regard this style as a conservative one; now it is clear that the style incorporates many "progressive" traits (as argued in Marshall 1976a). Still, musicians of Bach's generation were conservative in the sense that they usually composed within established genres. Genre governed not only medium and function but also determined the form, length, texture, and other aspects of a work. Hence, for Bach, as for any Baroque composer, it can be misleading to speak of a single style; he cultivated various styles, each appropriate to the genre within which he was working at a given time.

Like most composers, Bach took the works of esteemed older contemporaries as his models, learning from them the types of rhythm, melody, and texture appropriate to the genres in which he worked. Although the music of Vivaldi, Telemann, and other contemporaries can seem simple when compared to Bach's, this should not obscure the fact that, throughout his life, Bach was eager to learn and adopt whatever was of value in the current music of Italy, France, and Germany. Bach was never isolated musically, even though portions of his career were spent in relatively provincial locations. Hence his development as a composer and his choices of style in various genres reflect those of European (and especially German) music generally.

Nevertheless, Bach's mature keyboard works reveal certain personal tendencies. It was characteristic of Bach that, although in principle following the conventions of each genre (such as the use of binary-form movements with dance titles to form a suite), he transformed the genres in which he worked by expanding traditional formal structures and admitting technical and stylistic features borrowed from other genres. For example, the dances of the English Suites, although adhering to the traditional rhythms and general character of their French models, incorporate invertible imitative counterpoint—a traditional device, but not traditionally associated with the suite. Suites were associated with the French style, but five of the six English Suites open with a large prelude in the manner of a concerto—that is, Italian orchestral style. Some of the music whose influence might be detected in these suites was, at the time of composition, old if not outmoded—dances and fugal movements by Froberger and even Frescobaldi, for instance. Other apparent influences, such as Vivaldi's concertos, were very new, at least to German musicians. Indeed, the synthesis of old and new is a fundamental element of the style.

For this reason, it is not easy to characterize compositions by Bach in simple terms. Not all dotted pieces are "French," nor is every "impetuous" piece Italian, and we cannot be sure we understand all the connotations that national styles or their mixture had for Bach and his contemporaries. It is possible, for example, that Bach's early "French" overtures reflect opera sinfonias heard at Hamburg, not the music of francophile German courts. Mattheson (1739, 234) described overtures as possessing nobility (*Edelmuth*), but for him the overture has no specifically royal or French connotation. This poses a problem for the fashionable practice of reading political or sociological metaphors into Bach's music on the basis of superficial elements of style.

This is not to deny that Bach's music has been used in the service of various ideologies. Forkel saw in Bach's fugues an expression of "the unified spirit of a people," perhaps a liberal idea in 1802, but by the 1930s it could be transformed into the rightist fantasy that "Bach's fugues and [King] Frederick's battle plans are spiritually united."[1] In the aftermath of World War II, the historian Hans-Georg Gadamer regarded Bach's achievement as "the creation of a world of order which requires no Romantic inspiration or sentimental humanization"[2]—a modernist reaction to German nationalism and its excesses. Gadamer reflects a view that can be traced to Bach's own time, when his adherence to contrapuntal textures was not only recognized as a fundamental trait of his music but was viewed as a conservative feature—an impersonal focus on musical technique at a time when a proto-Romantic sensibility favored more immediately accessible emotionality in music.

Today such politically charged terms as "conservative" and "progressive" are of little use in analyzing Bach's style. The view of Bach as an old-fashioned contrapuntist goes back to a cliché of eighteenth-century writing on music, which distinguished a strict (*gebunden*) contrapuntal style, derived from Renaissance polyphony in four or more parts, from free or *galant* composition in which melody and bass are the only consistently maintained voices.[3] Bach paid more attention to counterpoint than did most of his contemporaries. But this did not necessarily ally him with any particular earlier composers since, except when he was employing the *stile antico* (the Baroque version of sixteenth-century polyphony), Bach's counterpoint is fundamentally different from that of his predecessors.

The motivic material of Bach's contrapuntal works usually incorporates figures from current style. Froberger had already used fugal imitation in his gigues, and later seventeenth-century composers such as Buxtehude considerably extended the motivic and expressive vocabulary of fugue. Bach's fugues continue in that direction, incorporating violinistic figuration, declamatory motives reminiscent of recitative, and virtually every other type of writing available in music of the early eighteenth century. In addition, the individual parts move with unparalleled melodic freedom and rhythmic independence; this contrasts with the texture of many seventeenth-century works, especially those in more than three voices, where the parts tend to move in stepwise intervals, often outlining diatonic triads. With earlier composers the bass is often static, and chromaticism is reserved for pieces in which a special expressive effect is desired. With Bach, however, any part may move through dissonant melodic intervals (chromatic half steps, tritones, diminished sevenths). Even in relatively lighthearted pieces, there may be more chromaticism and more frequent passing dissonances than would previously have been expected except in music meant to be unusually expressive, learned, or speculative.

Bach's detractors could recognize the learning in his music but not the expression. Its complexity led some contemporaries to regard his music as turgid and incomprehensible—that is, more concerned with its own technique than with conveying a clear "affect" or expressive character. There was some truth in this, for Bach usually avoided the direct, easily understood representation of the so-called affects that was prized by more simple-minded critics. Yet even his most complex, dissonant voice-leading is normally controlled by the principles of tonal harmony, which today is usually explained in terms of chord symbols standing for harmonic functions. Bach himself might have explained his more complex passages as being governed by or derived from simpler progressions through a principle of "composition by variation" (see Schulenberg 1995).

As essential as it is in Bach's keyboard music, counterpoint is hardly the only important element. His stylistic development can be traced equally well in terms of his adoption of various contemporary French and Italian genres, rhythms, and melodic formulas, or his use of ritornello-based designs and (a neglected topic) sonata forms. Unfortunately, problems in dating individual works make it difficult to trace Bach's development accurately. Scholars have persistently proposed chronologies for Bach's compositions, yet these efforts have been based on a small number of landmarks—a few datable autograph manuscripts, and certain manuscript copies that can be assigned to reasonably well-defined periods. Particularly for early works, scholars have had to base their guesses on internal evidence, relying on the assumption that the appearance of particular stylistic features in a given work can place it within a certain time period.

But a feature recognized by a modern author, such as ritornello form, may not have been one recognized by the composer; its presence in a given work is a matter of subjective analysis. Attaching a date to such a feature is at best an educated guess, based on suppositions as to when and where Bach might have first heard or picked up the feature from music by another composer. As in art history, connoisseurship based on isolated stylistic details is heavily influenced by current scholarly fashion and prejudice. Making the venture even more dubious is the fact that developments within any given genre follow a logic unique to that genre. Fugues, for example, do not always show developments parallel to those found in preludes or dance movements; the seemingly archaic *Art of Fugue* is a late work.

Most of Bach's best-known works date from relatively late in his life; for this reason, Bach's music is still often discussed as if it showed little stylistic development at all. One hears of "Bach fugues" or "Bach chorales," as if these show a style that did not change to any appreciable extent in the course of his lifetime. Bach himself contributed to the impression through his manner of revising older works. For example, the G-minor organ fugue BWV 535/2 originated early in Bach's career, but his thorough reworking of the melodic lines brings its style close to that of much later pieces, at least insofar as the melodic surface is concerned.[4] It is possible that many other works were significantly revised, but the low survival rate of sources from the early period makes it difficult to reconstruct Bach's early development.

The Early Keyboard Works

A quick survey of the keyboard works can nonetheless give some idea of the development of Bach's style (or styles). No surviving music can be securely placed earlier than Bach's Arnstadt period. The latter (1703–7) presumably saw the creation of most of the early suites, fugues, and other compositions discussed in chapters 4–6 and perhaps the toccatas as well (considered in chap. 7). Many chorale settings that also probably date from this period lack pedal parts and thus could be considered "clavier" pieces, but only a few of these—especially individual movements from the chorale *partite* (variations)—seem suited to the harpsichord or clavichord. The rest, like the big *pedaliter* preludes and fugues, must be regarded as primarily organ pieces.[5] These reflect two seventeenth-century traditions: both the exuberant *stylus fantasticus* of Buxtehude and other northerners, and the more restrained style of Pachelbel and other central German composers. These traditions ultimately drew on the early-Baroque music of Frescobaldi and Froberger, echoes of which can be heard in Bach's keyboard works.

The suites are the least complex of the early works, though not necessarily the earliest. They are comparable to suites by Bach's older German contemporaries, such as Pachelbel, Reinken, and Böhm, who were in turn indebted to Froberger and to the French *clavecinistes* of the seventeenth century. But two of Bach's early suites open with overtures in orchestral style, showing that Bach was already concerned with adapting up-to-date orchestral styles and genres to the keyboard.[6] The early suites also reveal Bach's mastery of French *brisé* notation, of the various dance rhythms, and of the distinction between the idioms of organ and harpsichord (or perhaps clavichord)—something that is not always apparent in the keyboard pieces of other German composers, such as Kuhnau.[7]

Yet the early sonatas, toccatas, preludes and fugues, and like works are close to the German organ tradition; indeed, some might have been intended primarily for organ. Like the ensemble sonatas of the seventeenth century, of which they are the keyboard counterparts, they often consist of loosely connected sections too brief to be considered self-contained movements. Reflecting the *stylus fantasticus*, some sections may introduce striking "rhetorical" motives, virtuoso figuration, or dramatic shifts of register, tempo, or key. Each such work, however, usually includes a lengthy fugal section that could have stood on its own and perhaps did so at an early stage in the work's history; in at least one instance (the toccata BWV 914) the fugue is transmitted separately, although this does not necessarily reflect its original state. Conversely, some fugues surviving as separate pieces might have been envisioned as sections of larger compositions. A fugue is by definition unified or integrated motivically, in the sense that it is based on a single main subject. But even in fugue the improvisatory, additive impulse underlying Bach's early works (and seventeenth-century style generally) is evident in the tendency to end with a free postlude that is unrelated to the main body of the movement.

Some of these early fugues might have been composed as part of Bach's self-instruction in composition, which was described many years after his death in a letter by his son Carl Philipp Emanuel.[8] That this self-instruction included study of music by others is confirmed by a number of Bach's early fugues that borrow subjects from older composers. Among the latter, however, are the relatively recent Italians Albinoni and Legrenzi, not Frescobaldi or the French and German composers mentioned by Emanuel (apart from Reinken). Modeling of a different sort can be assumed in the famous Capriccio BWV 992, which appears to have been inspired by the Biblical Sonatas of Kuhnau, published in 1700; several of the latter pieces were copied in ABB. Both the programmatic rubrics of the Bach work and some of the motivic material recall the sonatas of the earlier composer, to whose position Bach eventually succeeded at Leipzig.

A close relationship with earlier pieces can also be assumed in the early Praeludium et Partita BWV 833 (preserved in MM). This is an example of the variation-suite, in which the courante, and often additional movements as well, is a variation of the first dance movement, the allemande.[9] Reinken and Buxtehude, among others, wrote such suites, probably drawing on earlier models by Frescobaldi and Froberger; one suite given anonymously in MM employs variation technique in all four movements.[10] Bach later made keyboard arrangements of portions of two of Reinken's variation-suites (see chapter 6); an allemande and courante by "Richter," included in the *Clavier-Büchlein vor Wilhelm Friedemann Bach*, form a variation pair, suggesting that Bach found pedagogical value in this sort of piece when it came time to teach his own children. The underlying principles are explained in a treatise by Friedrich Erhardt Niedt (1989), portions of which appear in a manuscript copy that belonged to one of Bach's Leipzig pupils.

Weimar

Bach had worked at Weimar briefly in 1703, when he was described as a "lackey" but was probably already serving as court organist. He joined the court on a more permanent basis in 1708 as organist and chamber musician, after spending about a year (summer 1707–summer 1708) as organist at Mühlhausen. One of the few precisely datable works from this period is Bach's cantata for the installation of the Mühlhausen city council in 1708 (BWV 71); this shows solid compositional technique, imaginative instrumental and vocal scoring, some striking harmony, but also a somewhat short-winded, episodic approach to composition at the larger level. One can infer that at this point Bach had not yet fully assimilated the lessons in large-scale design, learned from contemporary Italian music, that would inform his Weimar vocal works. In Bach's earliest keyboard works the form is likewise episodic, extended by the addition of sections with little regard for a large-scale rounded or symmetrical design; many fugues, for example, make no lasting modulations away from the tonic, or place their most remote tonal excursions near the end.

The adoption of more cogent, integrated formal designs was one of the principal accomplishments of Bach's Weimar years. This was also the period in which Bach can be said to have come into his own as a composer; there are many distinctive earlier pieces, but it is not always possible for us to recognize their style as that of the mature Bach. That Bach from the beginning had been straining to expand the vocabulary of the traditional genres can be seen in such audacious early experiments as an extended chromatic passage in the G-Minor *Ouverture* BWV 822 or the overextended fugue (called a capriccio) in E, BWV 993.[11] But alongside capable voice leading and mastery of the keyboard idiom, there are occasional clumsy passages, and longer movements often ramble. Moreover, the effort to combine sophisticated counterpoint with imitations of orchestral and even vocal style sometimes comes into conflict with the requirement of writing notes playable by a single performer at the keyboard.

Bach gradually overcame these difficulties; the crucial developments seem to have taken place between the end of the Arnstadt years and the middle of the Weimar period, that is, from about 1707 to around 1713.[12] The beginning of the development might have been sparked by the ambition to create lengthy but motivically unified fugues and other movements, such as occur in the seven *manualiter* toccatas (discussed in chap. 7). Further steps in this direction occur in a number of large preludes and fugues that probably belong to the Weimar years. Discussed in chapter 9, these are roughly comparable with the great preludes and fugues for organ, which also seem mostly to have been composed at Weimar.

A critical development in the keyboard works of this period was Bach's assimilation of the Venetian concerto style. The process probably had begun by the time (around 1713) when Bach carried out the concerto transcriptions discussed in chapter 8. Forkel would attach great importance to the transcriptions and to Vivaldi's influence on Bach, perhaps reflecting a Bach family tradition (see Forkel 1802, 24/NBR, 441–2). What the concerto meant to Bach and what it has meant to later historians are different things; recent scholarship has focused on disciplined motivic work and especially ritornello form. But these can also be found in arias and other Italian music of the same period (see Schulenberg n.d.). What particularly attracted Bach and his contemporaries to the concerto may have been the imaginative use of the orchestra as well as the effective use of repetition and other types of regular patterning that had been avoided in the *stylus fantasticus*. Dramatic surprises might still occur in the new style, but these are now integrated into rational formal designs, and the striking effects no longer seem to be used for their own sake. Bach's fugues now tend to follow long-range modulatory schemes instead of additive designs, and improvisatory postludes disappear; episodes are clearly distinguished from expository passages, often resembling the solo sections of a concerto in their reduction of the texture to two voices.[13]

The fruits of Bach's Italian studies can be seen not only in the quasi-ritornello forms of certain preludes and fugues, and in the soloistic figuration of many episodes, but also in a distinctive type of embellished adagio. This too is prefigured in what are probably somewhat earlier works (e.g., the Reinken arrangements BWV 965–6), but it achieves its mature form around 1714, in several of the Weimar cantatas and one or two movements from the concerto transcriptions. Italian style is also present in movements from the English Suites, which were once dated to Cöthen but are now thought to have been composed, at least in part, at Weimar (see chap. 13). Five of the six suites adopt the Venetian concerto style for their preludes. But they employ French style in the ensuing dances, and these reflect Bach's knowledge of recent French music, including works by Grigny and Dieupart that Bach copied at Weimar.[14] Imitations of Froberger or Kuhnau are now rare or absent, the dance movements instead showing the melodic and rhythmic formulas of current French music. The latter, however, are often worked out in imitative counterpoint, as in the gigues of Froberger, Reinken, and other Germans.

Cöthen and Leipzig

The English Suites might be the earliest group of keyboard pieces that Bach himself assembled into a collection, on the model of published collections by French and German contemporaries; the toccatas, concertos, and other groups of pieces do not occur as complete sets in any early source. Although the English Suites may have been completed when Bach left Weimar in 1717, his revision and organization of his keyboard pieces into sets seems to have begun in earnest at Cöthen in connection with the pedagogic needs of his growing family. For example, the *Clavier-Büchlein* (Little Keyboard Book) of Wilhelm Friedemann Bach and the first of the two books for Anna Magdalena Bach were begun at Cöthen.[15] These sources contain the earliest copies of the Inventions and Sinfonias, some of the French Suites, and movements from the first part of the *Well-Tempered Clavier* (WTC1), also compiled at Cöthen. At least some of this music, as well as various other small preludes and fugues never incorporated into the famous sets, was probably composed prior to being entered into the famous Cöthen manuscripts; certain movements in WTC1 and even a few in WTC2 (assembled much later) are archaic in style. Nevertheless, these works are generally distinct in style from those mentioned previously and, if composed at Weimar, must date from the later part of Bach's tenure there.

The French Suites, probably begun at Cöthen, were completed only at Leipzig. They represent a considerable development of style beyond the English Suites—a development continued in the Partitas, which constituted Bach's first keyboard publication, appearing in installments from 1726 to 1731. The six partitas collectively formed the first part of the *Clavierübung*, which was followed in 1735 by a second volume containing an Italian concerto and French *ouverture*. Both the concerto and the dances of the suites and partitas largely abandoned the invertible counterpoint that figures so prominently in the English Suites. Indeed, elements of what is now called *galant* style had been becoming increasingly apparent in all of Bach's work, even in fugal movements. The most obvious of these elements are "sigh" figures and singing melodies accompanied in parallel thirds or sixths, which, although they occur in works from Weimar and earlier, are now met more frequently.

Today the word *galant* implies the pre-Classical style of the mid-eighteenth century, as in the music of Bach's sons. The style was already fully established in Germany by 1731, as signaled by the premiere of Hasse's opera *Cleofide* that year in Dresden (which Bach attended). To contemporaries the word implied fashionability and an absence of counterpoint, and even Bach's most *galant* efforts would have struck listeners as more contrapuntal, more challenging harmonically, than the works of other composers. But although the *Clavierübung* shows a deliberate lightening of touch, a direct appeal to popular taste, the music retains a strong contrapuntal component. Following a pattern that Bach had set from his earliest days, the music is also more challenging technically than that published by his contemporaries, including Handel, Rameau, and Domenico Scarlatti—although the hand crossings in works of the latter two bring their music close to Bach's in difficulty, at least at a superficial level.

Contrary to modern suppositions, *galant* music is not necessarily inexpressive. Eighteenth-century writers assumed music in the newer homophonic genres to be the only genuinely expressive type, older contrapuntal genres being considered to be of mainly theoretical or pedagogical value. Today we recognize the expressive qualities of Bach's fugues, as we also recognize the contrapuntal element in the apparently homophonic music of, say, Mozart. But in view of the bland, formulaic efforts made by other eighteenth-century composers in the contrapuntal genres, it is understandable that Bach's younger contemporaries would have assumed his music to be equally inexpressive. For them the most attractive feature of the *galant* style was its ability to express easily understood emotions in what was judged to be a natural manner. Bach obviously did not share the disfavor in which some writers, such as Scheibe, held the old polyphonic forms. But there can be no mistaking the adoption in his later keyboard works of the expressive language of *galant* music, especially as represented by new types of melodic ornament, such as the long appoggiatura.

Besides growing increasingly *galant*, the three sets of suites—the English, the French, and the Partitas—reflect other ongoing developments in eighteenth-century style. For example, the individual binary-form dance movements grow longer, in some cases becoming indistinguishable in proportions and style from sonata movements of the period.[16] The same tendency is evident when the preludes of parts 1 and 2 of the *Well-Tempered Clavier* are compared. Paradoxically, during his last decade or two Bach intensified his interest in strict canon and in *stile-antico* fugue. The *stile antico* is evident in several fugues of WTC2 (completed around 1742), the six-part ricercar from the *Musical Offering* (1747), and throughout the *Art of Fugue* (published posthumously in 1751). Canon plays an important role in the last two publications and also in the Goldberg Variations (1741). Yet these four collections temper "research" into archaic polyphonic forms with elements of *galant* style; they also incorporate a considerable amount of pure keyboard virtuosity. Hence, even in works that seem to have been intended as models of contrapuntal rigor, Bach retained his stylistic eclecticism and the conception of the keyboard player as a brilliant soloist. And the purposes of the music, insofar as we can judge, remained those of earlier works: models of composition and improvisation as well as instruments of expression.

4
The Early Suites

Bach's earliest keyboard pieces are often charming, sometimes earnestly rhetorical, and occasionally quite inventive. But they have remained little known to all but specialists, and they are quite different from the later pieces that are more commonly studied. None of the early suites, sonatas, preludes, fugues, and other works were ever gathered into an ordered collection like the WTC or the *Clavierübung*. Some of the pieces allude to stylistic traditions that are unfamiliar even to many harpsichordists. One seeks in vain in most of them for unmistakable hints of Bach's later style, although one does sense a certain audacity, as in the chromatic modulations of the G-Minor *Ouverture*. Nevertheless, these pieces share favorite motivic ideas, characteristic cadential formulas, and other small touches with Bach's early work in other genres, making it clear that we are dealing with a distinct musical personality, if not the familiar Bach of Cöthen or Leipzig. One surprising side of this personality is a modestly elegiac character that contrasts with the exuberance of the composer's early organ music; one hears this especially in the allemandes and courantes, which tend toward minor keys even when the tonic is major.

These pieces must already have been fairly obscure by the time Bach reached Leipzig; they tend to survive only in early or peripheral sources or in manuscripts written by collectors like Kellner who seem to have sought out unusual or early pieces. Bach himself might not have kept copies of all of these pieces, and with few exceptions he seems not to have revised them or made them available to his pupils after his departure from Weimar. It is possible to attach only rough dates and a relative chronology to the pieces discussed here and in the next two chapters. But it is safe to say that most if not all were drafted before Bach arrived in Weimar. If Bach ever used any of them in his teaching, they were later replaced by other pieces; whether Bach wrote them for that purpose, for his own performance, or as exercises in composition is impossible to say since we know nothing of the circumstances under which they were written.

We begin with the suites, not because they are necessarily the earliest but because they are the least complicated of the early pieces. Simplicity is no firm guide to chronology, but the five relatively simple works considered first in this chapter are probably among Bach's earliest surviving compositions. Although the term "suite" is used here for all seven works, they bear various titles in the sources: *Suite, Partita, Ouverture*. That the first two titles were essentially synonymous is clear from the fact that one work (BWV 832) appears as both a *Suite* and a *Partie* in different manuscripts. Each of the two *ouvertures* BWV 820 and 822 could have been described more precisely as "overture with suite," the last word referring to the movements that follow the overture proper. The diverse titles for what is essentially the same type of work reflect the fact that the idea of an ordered set of short keyboard pieces was relatively new in the years just after 1700. The terminology remained unstable throughout Bach's lifetime, as his own varying titles show (*Suite, Prélude avec la suite, Partita*). The word *ouverture*, however, clearly connoted a piece in orchestral style, if not an actual transcription, and of Bach's *ouvertures* only the Fourth Partita includes the allemande-courante pair that most often opens a keyboard suite. The French word *ouverture* is used here for a suite in orchestral style, the English word "overture" for the opening movement of such a work.

We know from the successive versions of some of Bach's later suites that movements could be added to or subtracted from such works. Thus, his suites are not closed cycles but open sets of pieces in the same key, arranged in a certain order; the latter was determined chiefly by convention, not personal choice. That musicians around 1700 were beginning to think of groups of dances as having a definite form is suggested by the "better order" (*meilleur ordre*) in which Froberger's keyboard dances were arranged in posthumous printings (beginning with an Amsterdam edition of 1698). But only where the movements show thematic or harmonic parallels, as in the variation-suite, is there a concrete cyclic element. Other suites remain loose anthologies of pieces that share a common key and (perhaps) similar proportions and character. Especially in his early years, Bach, in composing keyboard pieces, may have set out to write not suites but individual movements that could be grouped together at a later date; this might explain the presence of only two movements in the *Partie* BWV 832 as found in its earliest source.

The manuscript collections ABB and MM provide clues to where the young Bach got his ideas about how to write keyboard suites. Most of the copies in those manuscripts, however, are probably several years later than the works described below. Williams (2001, 18) emphasizes that an imaginative musician could pick up useful ideas from mediocre as well as good composers, obscure as well as famous. Potential sources included not only imaginative works by

French and German musicians such as Lully and Buxtehude, but also the stodgy suites and sonatas of a Johann Kuhnau, and the feeble partitas and fugues of a Johann Krieger.

It is appropriate to open this survey of Bach's keyboard music with the two *ouvertures*. The F-major work (BWV 820) is smaller in scale and simpler in texture and technique than the one in G minor (BWV 822). Either piece might be a transcription; in fact the G-minor work was designated as one in NBA V/10, although there is no documentary evidence for this.[1] ABB and MM, the two manuscript collections compiled by Bach's older brother, contain transcriptions of orchestral music by Lully and others. Similar transcriptions had previously been published among the *Pièces de clavecin* (Paris, 1689) of d'Anglebert, whose music is not represented in ABB or MM but whose influence is felt in many works in both manuscripts.[2] But no orchestral model for either of Bach's early *ouvertures* has been found, and there is no reason Bach could not have written such pieces as original keyboard works, perhaps after having heard opera overtures of this type at Hamburg. Handel, who arrived in Hamburg in 1703, wrote comparable pieces, including two early keyboard suites that he probably later adapted as orchestral works.[3]

Ouverture in F, BWV 820

> *Sole independent source*: ABB (no. 13). *Editions*: BG 36; NBA V/10; Dadelsen (1975); Hill (1991).

This *ouverture*, or suite in orchestral style, is typical of the genre in being heavily weighted toward the overture, which is followed by four relatively brief dances: entrée, minuet (alternating with trio), bourrée, and gigue. The opening gestures of the overture and of the entrée have similar contours, as do those of the minuet and trio, but this is not enough to make the work a variation-suite (there is no common harmonic ground).

BWV 820 occurs early in ABB, within a group of pieces in French genres, including an *ouverture* by Telemann and Böhm's Suite in D in overture style. At least some of these pieces, including the *partie* by "J. E. Pestel" that immediately precedes BWV 820, might be transcriptions—perhaps even transcriptions by Bach.[4] That BWV 820 might be a transcription as well is suggested by the thin, predominantly two-part texture, even in the overture. Such a texture could have been the result of copying only the outer parts of a work for four- or five-part ensemble. Sometimes an inner voice enters and then drops out for no good reason; in such cases the voice might have been a somewhat arbitrary late addition, as in mm. 14–5 of the minuet. Yet these are insufficient grounds for concluding that the piece is not original—or for filling out the harmony with additional inner voices (as suggested in NBA V/10, KB, 63). As in countless other eighteenth-century keyboard pieces, the harmony is usually sufficient as it stands and will sound full enough on a reasonably resonant instrument.

Even if BWV 820 is indeed a transcription, its model might have been the work of a francophile German composer, not a Frenchman. That the composer was Bach himself, and that the work is original, becomes more plausible the more closely one studies it. Both subject and countersubject in the fugal portion of the first movement employ short repeated motives of a type common in German keyboard fugues, including Bach's early efforts. Also reminiscent of other early works attributed to Bach are the weak harmonic implications of the fugue subject, which merely oscillates between III⁶ and I⁶ even when combined with the countersubject (mm. 18–21). Bach evidently had not yet learned the importance of composing fugue subjects that imply strong harmonic progressions. In addition, the closing phrase of the fugue, with its four measures of tonic prolongation and chopped-off final chord, is entirely within the German organ tradition. In organ music the cutting short of the last chord (which surely requires no rallentando) might have been meant to exploit the natural reverberation of the final sonority throughout the church; here one must settle for the after-ring of the strings of the harpsichord.

The ornament signs, which are found only in the first part of the overture, are not necessarily original. If realized in what was the normal manner by 1700—that is, starting on the upper note, as shown in the tables in ABB and MM—the ornaments may imply a more thoughtful character than the "fleeting, scurrying quality" that has been found here (Williams 1989, 187). The fugue has been criticized for the disproportionate lengths of its sections (NBA V/10, KB, 60), yet it is one of Bach's more satisfactory early fugues, if only because it is one of the least ambitious. Like most fugues composed before 1700, it lacks lasting modulations, and despite brief excursions to the related keys of C, B♭, and G minor, it quickly returns to the tonic after each of them. Nor is contrapuntal work a major concern; although there are four entries in the initial exposition, the fugue is essentially in three voices, often reduced to two. Its strength lies not in its counterpoint but in the intensive motivic development of the ideas in the subject and countersubject. The reprise at m. 89 of a passage from the initial exposition serves as a sort of recapitulation. Although only accidentally anticipating sonata-allegro form, this reprise follows a skillful retransition in which the two hands both have running sixteenths—a type of texture common in the episodes of Bach's early fugues, here serving as the climax of the entire movement.

An *entrée* is a dance in the style of the first (dotted) half of an overture; the first movement of the Pestel suite in ABB is labeled *Entre* (*sic*) despite the inclusion of a fugal section in triple time. Although it bears the traditional pompous character, the entrée in BWV 820 includes an expressive turn toward the minor in the closing phrase, beginning in m. 25.[5] And although the movement shares the general features of an overture, the eighth notes in the manuscript are not dotted except in m. 26, suggesting that one should not play them dotted elsewhere. But it remains possible that some sort of rhythmic inequality was applied to eighths throughout the movement, even to the point of having an effect identical to dotting. Although no ornaments are indicated, a trill would be idiomatic on each of the dotted quarters preceding sixteenths (as in m. 1, right hand, and the imitation in m. 2, left hand).

The three-measure phrasing of the minuet can be traced to French examples; d'Anglebert's *Pièces de clavecin* contains such a minuet right after an entrée, as in the present suite (d'Anglebert's entrée is an arrangement of one in Lully's *Triomphe de l'amour*). The trio is a different sort of movement, a genuine trio that one can imagine scored for two oboes and bassoon, moving in four-measure phrases. It may require a somewhat slower tempo than the minuet if its rather intricate counterpoint is to be heard clearly, or if one is to clearly articulate the sudden modulation from D minor to C minor in m. 14.

Bourrée and gigue are both straightforward little dances, although the bourrée contains an expressive touch characteristic of Bach's early style: a slurred "sigh" motive that droops downward through a fifth instead of a half step (m. 7). The gigue is almost a *moto perpetuo*, similar to but more restrained than the one in Handel's early D-minor suite HWV 437.

As in most of Bach's early keyboard works, the text is not without problems. Some arise because the youthful composer (or the copyist) left certain points vague. The repeats in the minuet and trio produce discontinuities in the bass line when played as written; presumably one was expected to improvise appropriate alterations. The trio and the last two dances are simple rondeaux in da capo form, a design that Bach continued to use until the first French Suite (see chap. 14). Possibly one was meant to repeat the entire portion of the movement that follows the double bar, yielding the form AABABA. Bach would spell out such things more clearly in later works.

The ornament signs in the overture are stylistically appropriate, even if not Bach's. Since ornaments are absolutely essential in a piece of this type, these might as well be played. Christoph Bach probably played the "little notes" (*petites notes*) before the beat, a documented option for the *ports de voix* on the downbeats of mm. 8 and 9 and useful for avoiding a clash between the leaping appoggiatura f′ on the downbeat of m. 2 and the chord in the left hand.

Emendations (see preface): *Overture*, 4, r.h., 1st chord, add sign for downward arpeggio; l.h., 3d note, orn.: trill. *Entrée*, 18–19, no ♯ on c′, f″; 24, no accidentals (flat is later addition in manuscript). *Minuet*, 8, r.h., last note, a″? 9, l.h. rhythm quarter, half?

Ouverture in G Minor BWV 822

> *Sole source*: LEm ms. 8 (unidentified copyist, dated 1743). *Edition*: NBA V/10.

Bach's other early *ouverture* was unknown to the editors of the BG; in the NBA it is labeled "a probable arrangement of a foreign composition." Its style is more confident than that of BWV 820, and it incorporates more Italian features alongside French ones. Several movements, including the opening dotted passage, contain as convincing an imitation of orchestral style as in any of Handel's early suites. Yet, like BWV 820, the suite bears the hallmarks of the young Bach and seems no more—perhaps somewhat less—likely to be a transcription. The fugue is highly economical in its use of motivic material and contains a remarkable modulating excursion. The following movements include an aria with written-out Italianate embellishment and two minuets consisting entirely of invertible counterpoint; neither type of movement is likely to have originated in an orchestral work. An awkward passage near the end of the overture (mm. 142–3) has been cited in support of an orchestral origin (NBA V/10, KB, 84) but is perhaps just a clumsy bit of four-part writing such as occurs in some other early works of Bach.[6] Several passages in the last movement (a gigue) involve repeated notes that might be thought unsuited to the keyboard, but only at a tempo that is probably faster than appropriate for this variety of gigue. Because the chromatic modulations in the first movement seem to point squarely to Bach, it has even been suggested that he interpolated this passage into an existing piece (NBA V/10, KB, 80), but this is in order to save the hypothesis that Bach did not write the rest of the music.

Small parallels between this work and the *Ouverture* in F, insignificant in themselves but suggestive when taken together, support a common authorship. As in BWV 820, the opening dotted section of the overture closes on a dominant pedal, and the fugal section is highly sequential; several passages use the same sixteenth-note motive as BWV 820.[7] There is another reprise near the end of the fugue (mm. 104ff.), although this now precedes rather than follows a passage in which the outer parts both move in sixteenths (mm. 118ff.). The gigue is again in da capo form, although belonging to a different rhythmic type.

On the other hand, the dotted portion of the overture abandons the simple imitative counterpoint of BWV 820 for a more brilliant orchestral texture characterized by flying *tirate* (quick upward scales). The fugue, longer and even more insistent in its repetitions of the principal motive, makes substantial modulations, with decisive cadences to III (m. 38), V of v (m. 55), and VI (m. 90)—the sort of clearly articulated tonal design that would be taken for granted in later works. Preceding the cadence to VI is the extraordinary chromatic passage, which works its way downward through the circle of fifths from D minor to G♭ major (mm. 56–76) and then back up to E♭. The modulations are a bit mechanical, as if Bach had just discovered the circle of fifths and was eager to use it—and some sort of well-tempered tuning—in an exploration of remote keys. A portion of the chromatic passage recurs later with altered accidentals (mm. 94–102 || 68–74), resulting in a completely different modulation: to G minor instead of G♭. The change is ingenious, but because the modulations occur so quickly the passage has a slightly madcap quality. Nevertheless, it reveals a fascination with exotic keys, and the most remote tonalities occur in the center rather than near the end, resulting in a more symmetrical design than in some of Bach's other early fugues.

The aria is at least as inventive as the overture and may be the high point of the suite. The designation *aria* is common in suites and ensemble sonatas by Pachelbel and other seventeenth-century composers, often attached to brief dance- or song-like movements in binary form that serve as the basis of variations. But the inspiration for this example lies in the embellished adagios of Italian sonatas or concertos for violin or oboe, a type that Bach would favor at Weimar. Although sharing its binary form with many such movements, it is unusual in having a second "half" slightly shorter than the first—either a sign of the composer's not quite having achieved a mature sense of proportion, or a legacy of Bar form (as in a chorale) with its short *Abgesang*. Although brief, the movement is fairly sophisticated; for example, the right hand in m. 11 (Example. 4.1) contains a so-called polyphonic melody pointing toward the mature Bach, especially if emended as shown. The movement also contains rhetorical writing characteristic of Bach and other German composers in the first decade of the new

Example 4.1 *Ouverture* in G Minor BWV 822, aria, mm. 10b–14.

century: the leap of a ninth up to the repeated a♭˝ in m. 11, and the threefold statement of a descending motive in mm. 14–15, each statement articulated by rests. The music-rhetorical figure involved in both passages—the insistent iteration of a note or a simple motive—is common in earlier German keyboard music and can be traced to Frescobaldi.[8] Bach uses it within a tonal scheme whose crux is the fermata on the unexpected chord on the downbeat of m. 13; the rhetoric dramatizes the modulation from the subdominant back to G minor.

The *gavotte en rondeau*—that is, a gavotte in simple rondo form—might have been modeled after d'Anglebert's piece of the same title. But Bach develops a smaller number of motives with greater insistence than is usual with his French predecessor. The repeating sigh figure introduced in m. 2b plays a role as well in the following movement, which lacks a title in the source. The NBA calls it a bourrée, perhaps on the model of the *bourrée anglaise* in the partita for unaccompanied flute BWV 1013; but it is closer to a rigaudon. The young composer's harmonic invention, evident in the overture and the aria, re-emerges in the repeated pauses on diminished chords (mm. 2, 6, 13, 20) and a Neapolitan harmony in the closing phrase (m. 17). This interest in dissonance and chromaticism is rare in French dances; and although the written-out *petite reprise* in the last four measures is a familiar device in the French *pièce de clavecin*, it also occurs in music by Corelli and other Italians.[9]

The little suite of minuets constitutes a second rondeau movement. Although the manuscript omits the final *da capo* indication, minuet 1 presumably should be repeated after the last one. The resulting form anticipates the minuet of the First Brandenburg Concerto with its three trios. In such cases it is unclear whether repeats should be taken in the restatements of the first minuet, as Zaslaw (1989, 501–4) argues was done in Viennese Classical symphonies. The numbered endings in Couperin's rondeaus indicate that the rondeau theme was repeated only the first time.

The First Brandenburg Concerto, probably composed no more than ten years later, would also echo the invertible two-part counterpoint of the first two minuets. These recall the canonic minuets of later eighteenth-century composers, including Haydn and C. P. E. Bach; the idea could have been suggested by canonic dances in the French harpsichord repertory. As in some examples of the latter, the two-part writing and the crossing of voices in minuet 2 imply performance on different manuals. Minuet 3 retains the essentially two-part texture, and its bass and treble both repeat motivic material from the first two minuets. But this movement is a weak effort, with banal if not faulty melodic writing and voice-leading.[10]

The suite ends with a French gigue characterized by dotted rhythms; imitation recurs, but not systematically. Like the gigue of BWV 820, this is in da capo form, but the symmetry of this movement is not an asset. It lacks the subtle rhythmic irregularities that give interest to d'Anglebert's gigues of the same type, and the second half falls into Italian-inspired sequences too routine to be interesting despite the stylistic contrast that they introduce (mm. 8b–11a, 14–8).

Although the source is neatly copied, it contains many apparent errors. In a work that survives in a single source by an unidentified copyist, one should consider imaginative emendations.

> *Overture*, 136, r.h., source has two voices only, middle voice should read c′–d′–c′? 144, chord, bass c, not d? *Aria*, 11, treble, notes 9–11, c–d–eb? 13, r.h., in place of the tie suggested in NBA V/10, one might play the notes c″–f♯″–a″ as a swiftly broken upward arpeggio (restriking c″ and rushing the two 16ths); 16, r.h., note 5, f♯′? g′? *Bourrée*, 19, treble as in m. 1? tenor bb, d′ (quarters)? (see also note 9). *Minuet 3*, 15, r.h., note 2, for a′ (quarter) read b′–a′ (eighths) (cf. m. 7)?

Praeludium et Partita del Tuono Terzo, BWV 833

Sole source: MM (no. 44; Johann Christoph Bach). *Editions*: NBA V/10; Dadelsen (1975); Hill (1991).

Like BWV 822, this suite was unknown to the BG, and when it appeared some commentators were reluctant to accept it into the Bach canon. But the identification of the copyist as Bach's older brother has dispelled any serious doubt. Although the word *partita* often means "variation," as in the works of Frescobaldi, the bilingual title page of Krieger's *Musicalische Partien* gives *partita* as an Italian equivalent for a series of dances.[11] An anonymous, roughly contemporary *Partie* follows a plan close to that of BWV 833: prelude, allemande-courante variation pair, sarabande with double, and final movement.[12] Hence Bach was not alone among German composers of the post-Kuhnau generation in writing pieces of this type.

BWV 833 is a relatively ambitious example, although it avoids the orchestral pretentions of the two *ouvertures*.[13] Hill (1985, 252) sees it as having a roughly symmetrical design, the two outer movements (praeludium and air) framing the dances. Indeed the allemande and courante share a common harmonic ground, making them a variation pair like the sarabande and its double. But the latter are relatively short, and like most Baroque suites this one is weighted toward the opening. The dances are more energetic than the outer movements; even the allemande is characterized by repeated notes and leaping motives, perhaps inspired by similar writing in Krieger's allemandes; the double of the sarabande is an allegro reminiscent of seventeenth-century violin writing.

The prelude is marked andante, in a work of this date perhaps a conscious Italianism to be taken literally ("going," "walking"), as a warning against a slow tempo. The imitations, though simple, are handled skillfully, but the most distant modulations occur late, an expressive move toward C minor taking place just four measures from the end.

The courante, although notated in 3/4 (MM gives the time signature as "3"), is really in what we would call 6/4. As in many courantes, the barlines signify beats rather than measures;[14] two measures here correspond to one in the allemande. The two movements share some motivic material, but their main common point is the harmonic ground, which turns to the minor mode in the closing phrase of the first half (as in the entrée of BWV 820). The courante inserts two measures (29–30) into the ground plan, but because several other measures of the model are compressed, it is no longer than the allemande, comprising twenty measures of 6/4.[15]

The sarabande, with cadences on the third beat of every fourth measure, is of a type more common in the seventeenth than the eighteenth century. There is hardly any sign of the accented second beat usually taken to be typical of the dance, and although only the double is marked allegro, the sarabande proper may not have been meant to go slowly; the allegro marking of the double may reflect only the replacement of eighths by sixteenths as the prevailing note values. Still, these cannot go too quickly if the intricate figuration is to sound clear and graceful.

The most original movement of the suite is the final air, an imitation of an Italian-style aria with ritornellos; the latter employ figured bass notation, hence resembling those of a continuo aria. Yet the melodic style is simpler, more like a simple German lied, than would be typical of a genuine Italian aria of this date. Despite the Italian tempo mark and texture, the title is French, and, unlike the aria of BWV 822, the movement lacks Italianate embellishment. Indeed it is more a rondeau than a da capo form; *Dal Segno* at the end signifies only a repetition of the opening ritornello.[16]

Still, the rhetorical pauses in the opening ritornello are reminiscent of similar gestures in Handel's early cantatas, and one wonders what models served for this movement—arias heard at the Hamburg opera?[17] It certainly precedes Bach's earliest actual arias of this type. As a translation of a vocal idiom to the keyboard, it resembles the *Lamento* of BWV 992 and points forward to the recitative section of the Chromatic Fantasia. Quasi-vocal writing is evident in the pauses in the opening theme, which is broken up into small "speaking" motives, and in the motives themselves, short descending gestures whose contour and sequential treatment recur in other early works. The latter include the Sonata in D (BWV 963) and the opening movement of the cantata *Aus der Tiefen* (BWV 131). The air shares some of their elegiac character and, like the double of the sarabande—also marked allegro—is best not rushed.

By Bach's later standards the movement goes too far in imitating the vocal idiom, for the figured bass notation leaves unclear what sort of realization the composer had in mind. Since the bass has the melody in the ritornellos, a discreet right-hand accompaniment is appropriate, without elaborate counterpoint. Two added parts will suffice, amplified at cadences as in the suggested realization (Example 4.2).[18] Should this accompaniment be played on the quieter upper manual, if available? And should the harmonic filling-in continue after the end of the ritornello, in the "solo" passages? Open fifths between treble and bass suggest that some filling-in is necessary. But entries of the upper part occasionally overlap the ends of the ritornellos (e.g., in m. 20), making it impractical to divide accompaniment and melody (or ritornello and "solo") between manuals.

Emendations: *Prelude*, 14, add d′ on downbeat to allow soprano to enter with first note of the subject (compare m. 19)? 27, Hill (1991) shows extraneous c″, d″, and fermata. *Allemande*, 2, l.h., beat 1, Hill (1991) shows extraneous B♭ (16th); 4, l.h., add natural on B, implied by the parallel harmonic structure of the courante (m. 8). *Courante*, 1, arpeggio

Example 4.2 Praeludium et Partita in F, BWV 833, air, mm. 1–21, with suggested inner voices (parentheses indicate later additions in MM)

sign possibly directs downward not upward direction; trills on ascending notes are better played as mordents or left out in mm. 5 (on b♭´), 33 (on a´), 35, and 36 (but mordent signs in example 4.2 are best realized as trills, if played at all). *Sarabande*, 7, l.h., last note g not a.

Partie in A, BWV 832

Chief sources: MM (no. 38, Johann Christoph Bach; titled *Suite*, allemande and air only); Gb, Sammlung Scholz (without title); B Br II 4093 (formerly Fétis 2960; title: *Partie*). *Editions*: BG 42; NBA V/10; Dadelsen (1975); Hill (1991).

Bach's authorship of this little suite was once rejected on stylistic grounds, and as recently as 1984 it was listed in a thematic catalog of the works of Telemann.[19] But the sources listed above independently attribute it to Bach.[20] MM, while giving only the first two movements, also adds a few ornaments and a few obvious mistakes, but its attribution to Bach can hardly be doubted.[21]

Whatever the original title—a point on which the sources disagree—all five movements are plausible products of the young Bach, despite their stylistic heterogeneity. The key of A major was uncommon in keyboard music around 1700. But BWV 832 modulates to much rarer tonalities, and the allemande contains some long scale figures that imply a composer who thought seriously about keyboard fingering, as C. P. E. Bach later claimed of his father. The one odd movement is the *Aire pour les Trompettes*. The title could be a borrowing from the *Air de Trompette* in a group of pieces arranged from the opera *Alcide* by Marais and Jean-Louis de Lully; Eichberg (NBA V/10, KB, 71) notes a fleeting motivic resemblance. But the French piece is a real trumpet tune;[22] like the one by Purcell called the Cebell (Z. T678), it is in duple time and its melody is playable on the natural (valveless) instrument. That is hardly the case here. Indeed, the music has little in common with Baroque trumpet writing, and the title might be an allusion to harpsichord registration.[23] The latter would suggest playing the melody on a separate solo manual, but that is impractical. In any case, trumpets are not the only brass instruments alluded to; m. 21 contains the octaves of the post horn, also cited in the Capriccio BWV 992 (see chap. 6).[24]

Despite small motivic parallelisms (noted by Hill 1985, 253) and the use of similar cadential formulas in different movements, this is not a variation-suite. But the plans of the first two movements do have some points in common; both are in the usual binary form, and both reach somewhat exotic keys midway through the second half: C♯ minor in the allemande, F♯ minor in the air. The sarabande also contains some notable harmonic progressions, passing from a chord of the mediant (C♯ minor) to that of the Neapolitan (B♭) in the space of just six measures (9–14); the Neapolitan is part of an expressive excursis in the minor mode.

The simple two-part writing in both bourrée and gigue might have contributed to the assignment of the suite to Telemann, but it is also characteristic of Bach's later bourrées, and we have already seen it in BWV 820. The easy arpeggiations of the left hand in the gigue are less typical of Bach's later music, but they are not a mere Alberti bass. They constitute the lower voice in a two-part texture that is inverted after the double bar.

> Emendations: *Aire*, 12, soprano, note 8, d″ not c♯″; 15, l.h., note 1, delete g (blot in MM; produces parallel octaves); 16, soprano, note 2, cautionary ♯ in Hill (1991) is editorial (♮ is possible); 22 and 24, l.h., upward stems on a and e (quarters) are editorial.

Suite in B♭, BWV 821

Sole source: SPK P 804/24. *Editions*: BG 42, NBA V/12.

The Suite in B♭ is one of many works published in the BG as Bach's but banished to a supplementary volume of the NBA containing works of uncertain authorship. On a stylistic basis this little suite is no less plausibly Bach's than the others considered in this chapter. But it has the misfortune of being preserved only in a copy of uncertain provenance that found its way into the Kellner miscellany (P 804). Several of the "Neumeister" chorales attributed to Bach show parallels with the last movement, and other details also suggest Bach: the first half of the allemande swerves toward the Neapolitan (m. 8) in a manner reminiscent of the untitled dance in BWV 822, and there are melodic formulas common in Bach's early pieces.[25]

The overall form—three dance movements framed by a prelude and an *echo*—resembles that of BWV 833. The prelude is again imitative but livelier, and limited to three voices except at the end, hence resembling a trio sonata. A few hard-to-play passages, especially some parallel sixths in running sixteenths (mm. 10, 13), are justified by the logic of the voice leading and hardly speak against Bach's authorship.[26]

In texture the allemande resembles the prelude and comes close to quoting it (compare m. 16 with m. 11 of the prelude). This is only one of several connections between movements. As in BWV 832, the allemande and courante, although not forming a variation pair, are related by their unusual harmonic designs. The first half of each ends in a minor key, that of the allemande in the relative minor (vi), of the courante in the mediant (iii). The right-hand solo over a pedal point at the opening of the courante forms a continuation of the passage for right hand alone at the end of the allemande. It also recalls courantes in two of Handel's suites (HWV 430, 439); could this be an echo of something Bach heard in Hamburg? The harmonically inspired character of the melodic material—chord-derived figuration for the right hand with simple *brisé* accompaniment in the left—is the sort encouraged by Niedt's composition treatise. Similar ideas occur in the courante of the variation-suite BWV 833, whose final cadence (m. 38) corresponds precisely with that of the little written-out *petite reprise* (m. 27).

The sarabande is altogether different from that of BWV 832 or 833. Rhythmically and melodically it is more in the French mold (e.g., in the cadential formula in mm. 15–6), but the imitative opening is unusual. Two unexpected arrivals on G-minor triads (mm. 4, 7) give this opening a delicate pathos shared with other early Bach works. The cadence to F *minor* in m. 16 could be another expressive touch, but the flats there may be a mistaken extension of those in the preceding measure; it would be more in keeping with the French gesture imitated here to return to F major for the cadence itself.[27]

The concluding *echo* opens with a motive similar to that of the sarabande. Echo movements in suites are a rarity, but they had been common in German and Dutch organ music since the early Baroque. The device, best known to harpsichordists from the echo movement in the B-Minor *Ouverture* BWV 831, also occurs in the last *partita* (variation) on *O Gott du frommer Gott!* (BWV 767), which contains a passage very similar to mm. 41ff. here. Echoes also occur in one of the "Neumeister" chorales (*Ich hab' mein' Sach'* BWV 1113).

The "Neumeister" chorales also furnish a parallel for the coda of the echo movement, which is notated as a treble line with figured bass together with the rubrics *adagio* and *forte Tutti*. Predictably, this has elicited the suggestion that the movement was arranged from a lost orchestral work (see NBA V/10, KB, 48). But, as Stinson (1989a, 123) notes, the closing passage bears a remarkable resemblance to the conclusion of *Alle Menschen müssen sterben* BWV 1117, in the same key and bearing the same adagio marking.[28] Realizing the figured bass in this passage is less problematic than in BWV 833 and 992; a simple chordal texture with full harmonies in both hands is clearly intended and easily improvised.

Apart from the coda, the echo movement is in the form of a rondeau. In the source, the repetition of the initial section after m. 18 is indicated by a dal segno—implying that a further dal segno (not marked) should be taken before the coda. That, however, might be more repetition than the rather slender musical content can bear. Forte and piano measures alternate regularly up to m. 34; by then the novelty of the echo effect has worn off. Yet the movement was planned with some care. The first *couplet* (mm. 9–18) moves to G minor and D minor, the keys reached at the double bars of the allemande and courante, respectively. The second *couplet* (mm. 27–39) moves toward "flatter" tonalities, Eb and then F minor, on the way passing through a few compelling chromatic progressions; this is the high point of the entire suite. The coda, unrelated to the rest of the movement, brings the suite to a grand ending, like the codas of some of the early fugues.

Emendations: *Allemande*, 17, r.h., last three notes: f″–d″–eb″? *Sarabande*, 15, treble, note 4, a♮″ not ab″? 16, treble, note 1, a♮″ not ab″, and alto, note 3, a♮´ not a♭´? *Echo*: the only figures in P 804 are 7 (m. 45, on g) and 7/5 (m. 48, on g).

Suite in F Minor BWV 823

Sole source: P 804/45 (Kellner). *Editions*: BG 36 (appendix); NBA V/10; Dadelsen (1975).

This work also has been thought inauthentic, and the BG designated it "Fragment of a Suite." Kellner's copy ends with the customary *Fine*, indicating that he thought it was complete, but his lapses as a copyist in other works have led scholars to question his attribution.

Indeed, it is not obvious that "the style of all three movements confirms the ascription to J. S. Bach" (Eichberg, in NBA, V/10, KB, 65). If Bach's, the suite must be somewhat later than those previously discussed; Dadelsen suggested (1975, 133) that it stems "from the middle of Bach's Weimar period, before 1715." It might be a bit earlier, for the English Suites could be no later than that, and they seem more mature. In BWV 823 there are still a few gaucheries: the low rumbling accompaniment through much of the sarabande, and implicit parallel octaves in a recurring passage of the gigue (mm. 24–31, 44–51). The sequence of movements is unconventional: prelude, sarabande, gigue, and although Kellner might have omitted some movements, the internal forms of the first two movements are also exceptional. The prelude is a "rondeau with three couplets," as Eichberg puts it, and the sarabande is in da capo form, which we have seen in other early dances by Bach but not sarabandes. The prelude is, additionally, a sort of chaconne, its *couplets* forming a series of variations upon a bass; the A section of the sarabande is likewise constructed over a descending tetrachord in the bass.

Is the style that of Bach? The key is unusual but not unknown at this date, and if anything speaks in his favor, as do the unusual forms of the first two movements. The embellished melodic lines of the prelude and especially the sarabande include formulas present in many authentic works, and the top voice of the sarabande can be played on a separate manual, as in the sarabandes of three of the French Suites (which may not be much later). The third couplet of the prelude comprises sequences of running figuration in both hands, a texture found in many of Bach's early keyboard works. In short, until a conflicting attribution is found, Bach does seem the most likely composer.

Dirksen (2003) seeks a way out of the apparent dilemmas of the piece by suggesting that it is an original Bach composition for lute from the 1740s. This would not be excluded by the dating of Kellner's unique manuscript,[29] but the slightly sketchy character of all three movements remains compatible with a keyboard setting. The gigue is of a type that Bach also included in the Fifth Cello Suite BWV 1011 and the Second French Suite BWV 813, neither of which is likely to date from after 1723.

Emendations: *Prelude*, 1, 5, etc.: ornament: *Schleifer* (slide), not appoggiatura; 9: ornament: inverted turn with natural. *Sarabande*: title includes the words *en rondeau*; 2, 10, 12, 18, 22: appoggiaturas are written as 8ths, not 16ths; 3, 5, 19, small values (16ths, 32ds) are slurred; 6, l.h., c´ is half-note without dot.

Suite in E Minor for Lute BWV 996

Sources: P 801 (Walther); privately held copy by Heinrich Nicolaus Gerber; B Br II 4093 (= Fétis 2960; in part by J. J. H. Westphal). *Editions* BG 45; NBA V/10.

If Bach did write BWV 823 for the lute, it would not have been the only such piece that was played on keyboard instruments. Seven of Bach's works are usually designated solo lute compositions, but they survive more in keyboard than in lute sources, and most require modifications to be playable on known varieties of eighteenth-century lute. Although their texture is thinner than usual for Bach's keyboard music, the composer may have had keyboard instruments in mind for these pieces, at least as an alternative medium. All three copies of BWV 996 are at least partly in the hands of organists, and the Brussels manuscript gives it in a keyboard version transposed to A minor.[30] Walther's copy carries an indication that the suite is for the lute-harpsichord, but the handwriting is unidentified and the entry is probably a later conjecture.

Although its practicality on the lute has been questioned, BWV 996 has been recorded on the instrument, essentially as written.[31] Certainly Bach meant it to be an idiomatic lute work, writing it in a lower and smaller range (restricted to three octaves) than usual in his keyboard music. Many passages contain figuration more suited, at least in principle, to the lute than to keyboard instruments, and the inner voices and even the bass are often broken up in a way that would not be necessary in keyboard music. On the keyboard one might sustain certain notes longer than written, even add a few chord tones or alter the register of an occasional bass note. But further adaptation is likely to do violence to Bach's harmony and voice leading, which, as in the unaccompanied violin and cello music, is entirely self-sufficient.

The E-Minor Suite is clearly the earliest of the designated lute pieces, but its relatively mature style implies that it is somewhat later than the suites considered above. The prelude, as in English Suite no. 6, is actually a self-contained prelude and fugue, but the fugue is relatively short and the initial section resembles that in a toccata or similar early work. The initial flourish on the tonic chord—a standard device in preludes and improvisations[32]—bears the indication *passaggio*. Term and gesture both recur at the beginning of the Prelude and Fugue in G Minor BWV 535a for organ. Despite its brevity, the fugue achieves considerable intensity as the texture builds to four real parts in mm. 46–54 and again in the closing measures.

Bach's assimilation of the French style in the first two dances is flawless apart from a prosaic sequence in the allemande (beginning in the middle of m. 13). The sarabande is as compelling as any in Bach's later suites, revealing his characteristic mixture of French and Italian styles. The latter is evident in the melodic embellishment, of far greater sophistication than in the ornamented slow movements of the earlier suites. As in BWV 820, the last two dances, a bourrée and a gigue, are further from French models. Indeed the gigue is hardly a gigue at all but rather a freely contrapuntal movement in binary form.

5

The Early Fugues

Bach's name is inseparably associated with fugue. Yet it is impossible to say when or how Bach came to recognize his special talent for fugal writing. C. P. E. Bach's testimony that his father studied fugue on his own suggests that this took place during his years at Arnstadt (1703–7).[1] Although such reports may have intentionally downplayed Bach's dependence on teachers (as Williams 2004, 14 and *infra*, suggests), by the age of eighteen—barely out of childhood—Bach was indeed on his own. For a brilliant young musician this would have been a time of rapid development and self-instruction. Bach is unlikely to have disregarded what he might have received from his older brother or other teachers. But any genius is, in a profound sense, self-taught, and Bach would also have been storing away, in memory if not yet on paper (given the expense of the latter), all manner of ideas derived from music by other composers that he had sung, played, and heard. At the same time, by working out these ideas in increasingly complex and sophisticated compositions, he would have been teaching himself the art of writing fugues. By the time he reached Weimar in 1708, Bach must have mastered various types of fugal writing—not only in those keyboard pieces actually called fugues, of which only a few survive from that date, but in the fugal sections of larger keyboard pieces and vocal works.

Fugue is essentially a texture, not a form or genre. Any composition might employ *fuga*, that is, imitation, but before Bach's time few pieces were designated fugues as such. We have already seen a few fugues as parts of the suites considered in chapter 4, and there will be more in the sonatas, fantasias, toccatas, and other works discussed in chapters 6 and 7. It is possible that Bach wrote some of the self-contained pieces considered in the present chapter in emulation of much older ricercars, fantasias, and other fugal works by Sweelinck, Frescobaldi, or Froberger. Some works of this type were composed and studied as models of specific contrapuntal techniques, falling into sections that may demonstrate inversion, stretto, combinations of multiple subjects, and so forth. Several of Bach's early fugues (BWV 896, 949) suggest similar "research" as they work out the contrapuntal possibilities of their subjects. But only a few allude to the *stile antico*, the imitation of sixteenth-century vocal polyphony that continued to be cultivated well into the eighteenth century. The idiomatic keyboard style found in most of Bach's early fugues would have allowed them to serve as sections of larger works: *praeludia*, toccatas, and sonatas. Such pieces are typical of Bach's immediate predecessors, including the north Germans Reinken and Buxtehude and the central German school of Pachelbel.[2]

Thus the Fugue in B♭ on a theme by Reinken (BWV 954) might have been destined for a complete transcription of one of Reinken's chamber sonatas, like BWV 965. Several early fugues conclude with free *pedaliter* codas such as occur at the ends of Bach's, Buxtehude's, and other composers' *praeludia*, where the coda balances a free section at the beginning of the piece. In the absence of a separate prelude or prelude-like section, players might sometimes have improvised one, and in several instances Bach brought together preludes and fugues composed separately. Copyists sometimes took the matter into their own hands, without the composer's authorization, as may have been the case with the B-Minor Fugue BWV 951, which in some sources is preceded by a prelude in the same key (BWV 923).

BWV 954 is one of several early fugues in which Bach followed the old tradition of borrowing subjects and other material from existing pieces, including works by the Italians Corelli and Albinoni.[3] These were not necessarily study pieces, for, with the exception of BWV 946, they are relatively mature in style. Each is a new composition, not a transcription, sharing only the subject and sometimes a few additional motivic ideas with its model, from which it departs in fundamental matters of style and form. These fugues might have served as personal homage to the composers of the original subjects; probably too Bach was eager to show what he could do with subjects whose potential had hardly been exhausted by the works in which he found them. These fugues must also reflect a tradition of virtuoso improvisation on existing subjects. Several are large display pieces, among the most impressive of Bach's early works.

The presence of simple pedal parts in the closing passages of several works raises the question of medium, as do occasional sonorities in the bodies of works that cannot be played by two hands alone. In the closing sections of two works (BWV 949 and 950), the pedal is limited chiefly to holding a few pedal points that can be dropped without significant loss. Elsewhere, as in BWV 955, the apparent need for pedals to play a few notes might be traced to the composer's not yet having mastered the art of keeping his distinctive style of counterpoint within the confines of what can be played by two hands. Yet, even if some of these pieces were intended for organ (or pedal clavichord), the absence of contrapuntally independent pedal parts distinguishes them from "organ fugues" as such. The subjects are not limited to motives playable on the pedals, and the bass is as lively as the other voices, except in the codas. The absence of an independent pedal part means that the formal design cannot be articulated by climactic pedal statements of the subject (e.g., at the end), as is often the case in organ fugues. All these features make the present "clavier" fugues a distinct category of composition.

A second question arising in some of these pieces is that of attribution. Like Bach's early suites, these fugues are preserved in manuscripts of greatly varying dependability. Discoveries over the last two decades have clarified the authorship and even the genre of one piece formerly included among them.[4] At the same time, more pieces have emerged that bear attributions to Bach, and a few of these have even been published in the NBA.[5] This chapter considers only works certainly or very likely by Bach; some others are mentioned in appendix A. That the present pieces survived at all may be due only to accident or because later collectors regarded them as curiosities. Bach cannot have used them in his teaching except during the earliest period. Still, BWV 951 and possibly several others exist in more than one version, implying that Bach found at least these pieces worth saving and revising either for teaching or for his own performing.

Chronology and Style

The chronology of these pieces is quite uncertain. No autographs survive, and most surviving manuscript copies were made long after the music was composed, forcing scholars to date the works on the basis of their style, an imprecise enterprise at best. The loss of early sources also leaves us with no idea of what struggles—one assumes there were some—the young composer underwent to bring these pieces to their present forms. Although the counterpoint of these works is often strong and imaginative, it does not always measure up to Bach's later standards. Passages in four parts are rare—in four-part fugues the first voice often drops out at the entry of the fourth—and clumsy parallelisms, harsh passing dissonances, and excessively wide spacings between parts sometimes arise. Presumably this is due not so much to weak contrapuntal technique per se as to inexperience in the difficult art of writing meaningful counterpoint playable on a keyboard instrument.

What attracted Bach to fugue in the first place may have been not contrapuntal artifice but the particular sorts of drama attainable only in fugue: the gradual accumulation of sonority during the initial exposition, and the climaxes achieved through strategically placed entries of the subject (as in a final bass entry). Bach's interest in fugue as drama might explain his avoidance in the early works of both the *stile antico* and the somewhat mechanical permutational schemes used in some of Reinken's works. Even those fugues that focus on contrapuntal work avoid the abstract subjects of the old ricercar, preferring dance-like or rhetorical themes. Such subjects could lead to problems, however, for the pauses and repeated motives embedded in some of the more "rhetorical" subjects are not particularly suited to complex counterpoint.[6] Idiomatic keyboard writing in the subject of a fugue could also cause difficulties; the wide leaps in the subject of the closing fugue of BWV 992 make for a lively theme, and are perfectly playable by themselves, but they produce awkward spacings and voice-crossings when combined with other parts. Subjects (or countersubjects, as in the G-Minor Toccata) containing octave leaps are more easily maintained in *pedaliter* works—there is a notable example in Buxtehude's E-minor organ praeludium (BuxWV 142)—and Bach must have gradually learned what sorts of subjects are appropriate to a given type of fugue.

As Bach's keyboard counterpoint matured, his sense of form also developed. The Capriccio BWV 993, one of several early fugues that stress idiomatic keyboard writing, has an improvisatory structure: expositions combine the subject with continually changing counter-material, and each episode likewise introduces new material. BWV 946, although concerned more with strict counterpoint than with keyboard display, is also improvisatory in the sense that the order of subject entries follows no obvious plan. Later fugues generally have more cogent structures that reflect some acquaintance with the rounded modulatory schemes and ritornello design of the Venetian concerto. The two versions of the Fugue in B Minor after Albinoni show Bach's progress very clearly. The earlier (BWV 951a) is a patchwork, whereas the later (BWV 951) is conceived more as a large formal unity, even containing hints of the recapitulatory structure found in most quick concerto movements and in many of Bach's later fugues.

The term "recapitulation" is used here not in the sense familiar from the study of Classical sonata form, but to refer to any transposed restatement of episodic material.[7] Recapitulation in this sense is largely irrelevant to Bach's earliest fugues, which contain few extended episodes. But as his fugues began to incorporate long episodes, often in a soloistic style reminiscent of a concerto, recapitulation became an essential device. It made possible a sense of order lacking in those rambling early fugues (e.g., BWV 993) that give the impression of having been improvisatorially extended. Such works obey an earlier, more literally baroque, aesthetic that placed a high value on variety and the absence of pattern. This aesthetic, though congenial to a composer still under the sway of the seventeenth-century *stylus fantasticus*, was at odds with the incipient classicism that can be perceived in, for example, the sonatas by Albinoni that supplied several of Bach's subjects. By the time of the final version of BWV 951, Bach had apparently accepted the need for more predictable formal patterns.

BWV 951 in its final form might date from Bach's last years at Weimar (1714–7). But most of these fugues must predate the works discussed in chapters 7 and 8. Except for BWV 951, the early fugues cannot be counted among Bach's great works. But they show that Bach posed difficult compositional challenges for himself and on the whole met those challenges successfully.

Prelude and Fugue in A, BWV 896

Chief sources: MM (No. 34; Johann Christoph Bach); P 804/3 (Mey; fugue only). *Editions*: BG 36 (fugue only); *BJ* 9 (1912) (Wolffheim; prelude only); Hill (1991, both movements); NBA V/9.2 (both movements).

Although this piece is furnished with a short prelude in the copy by Bach's older brother, the prelude is lacking in the later copy from which the BG edition was made, and the two movements did not appear together in print until Hill's 1991 edition.[8] Neither movement calls for pedals; suggestions of *brisé* or *luthé* style in the prelude, together with the dance-like character of the fugue (in a gigue-like 6/8), make both suitable for the harpsichord. The title *Praeludium ex A#* in MM seems to refer only to the prelude; it might have been meant to apply to both movements together, but the frequent omission of work titles in MM (as in other manuscripts) makes it unlikely that the two movements were conceived as a unified praeludium.[9] Still, the fugue is one of Bach's strongest early efforts in a strictly contrapuntal idiom, and this might account for its having been furnished with a prelude.

Hill (1987, 435–6) notes parallels between the prelude and "a type of keyboard aria" cultivated by earlier German composers; similar rhythmic textures occur in the eighth of Buxtehude's *partite* on La Capricciosa (BuxWV 250) and in variation 6 of Bach's Aria variata BWV 989. The continuous dotting of the upper part has nothing to do with the French overture; it might be a sort of written-out inequality but is best explained as a staggering of vertical sonorities, a product of the broken (*brisé*) style. The homogeneous rhythm makes for a sort of species counterpoint in three voices, but the texture is treated freely, with an implied voice crossing at the start of m. 7. The piece consists of just two phrases of six measures each, both concluding with wistful cadences on the weak part of the measure. The second cadence is repeated in a written-out *petite reprise* (mm. 11–2 are a varied repetition of 9–10).

The fugue has a vivacious gigue-like subject, which is developed in a systematic exploration of strettos and inversions. The initial exposition—in four real parts—leads to paired stretto entries by the lower and upper voices, respectively (mm. 24bff.). A second exposition, opening with an entry in the dominant, begins precisely at the midpoint (m. 34) and includes the entry in the most remote key, a stretto entrance on B (tenor, m. 35). This modulation, although ephemeral, is sensibly placed just after the center of the piece. In this sort of fugue, however, greater interest attaches to contrapuntal work than to modulation. The crowning events occur in the final exposition with the combination of *rectus* and *inversus* versions of the subject in stretto (mm. 48ff.) and in a pair of simultaneous entries (m. 56). This is, in simple form, the same design that Bach would use in many later fugues that demonstrate the artifices of counterpoint—for example, the fugue in B♭ minor in WTC2.

The inspiration for this type of fugue might have come from Reinken's fugal gigues, which offered a model for strict contrapuntal writing outside the *stile antico*.[10] But unlike Reinken's gigues, BWV 896 offsets rigorous expository passages with episodes. The latter, although short and restrained, are just sufficiently distinct in style to set the expository sections in relief. The episodes suggest another possible model, the dance movements in Kuhnau's Biblical Sonatas, which the fugue seems to quote at several points.[11]

> The edition of the fugue in the BG was based on a late, inferior source, but the copy in MM is not faultless either. Hill (1991) is inaccurate; emendations for NBA follow: *Prelude*, 1–2, bass, tie obscures imitation of sop.; 7–9, bass, editorial rests not justified; 11, alto, note 2, f♯′? (to avoid parallel fifths). *Fugue*, 3, sop., note 6, d♯″ (present in P 804); 36, bass, last note, d♯? 47, alto, note 4, d′ not d♯′.

Fugue in A, BWV 949

> *Chief sources*: ABB (No. 19; Johann Christoph Bach; also a second copy in an unidentified hand); P 804/37 (Mey). *Editions*: BG 36; Dadelsen and Rönnau (1970); Hill (1991); NBA V/9.2.

BWV 949 is another fugue in A, preserved like BWV 896 in copies by Johann Christoph Bach and from the Kellner circle. The use of A major in both fugues may be only a coincidence, but as BWV 949 is another contrapuntally organized fugue it is possible that Bach associated rigorous counterpoint with the use of what was at the time a fairly adventurous key on the far "sharp" side of C.[12]

Hill (1987, 447) considers BWV 896 "probably a considerably earlier composition than BWV 949." But the pieces have much in common. As in BWV 896, the subject of BWV 949 moves by step after an initial "repercussive" motive, and the few episodes are brief and restrained. The present subject is more square, without strong dance implications, but the writing gradually grows more exuberant, with hints of violin style in the episodic passages. Figuration emerges triumphant over contrapuntal work in a short *pedaliter* coda. Elsewhere as well BWV 949 is the more adventurous of the two pieces. Only BWV 949 modulates to F♯ minor, even introducing the subject—in inversion—in that key (m. 35). In addition, two *rectus* entries of the subject are altered chromatically to permit modulations to the relative minor (mm. 22, 61). There is no tonal design underlying the piece as a whole; instead the design turns on the introduction of the inversion a little before the midpoint (m. 35). But this does coincide with the least ephemeral of the modulations to F♯ minor, the only one marked by a strong cadence in that key (m. 41). Unfortunately the significance of this moment is later upstaged when a significant-sounding flourish (m. 60) leads to merely a second arrival on F♯ minor.

The fugue must be one of the earliest of Bach's to have a regular countersubject—two countersubjects, actually. More importantly, there is little motivic material anywhere that is not directly related to the subject or the first countersubject. Unfortunately, this single-mindedness is not to the piece's advantage, nor is the obsession with the relative minor. The fugue repeats itself several times; the second of the two altered entries in the relative minor is almost a reprise of the first one, but because it is not part of a larger recapitulation the parallelism seems accidental.

Hence this fugue is less successful than BWV 896. Another potential problem, the occasional rough passing dissonances of both works, arises from the melodic logic of the individual lines and is barely noticeable at a sufficiently lively tempo. More problematical here is that the subject is essentially an ascending pentachord, and rather too many expository passages consist of little more than parallel or contrary movement within the triad outlined by the subject. Such polyphony is easy to write and occurs frequently not only in Bach's early works but throughout the earlier Baroque. It leads to a proliferation of sequential progressions over stepwise bass lines and to more frequent doublings of the third of the triad than would occur in Bach's later music (see, e.g., mm. 64, 65, 66, and 67). The almost obsessive working-out of simple motives in both parallel and contrary motion, and in inversion, no doubt provided the composer with valuable lessons and was a precursor of later counterpoint using more distinctive material. But the tolerance for octaves and fifths on successive strong beats is a sign that Bach—like most composers around 1700—still had his eyes firmly on the musical surface, paying less attention to voice leading at deeper levels or to the larger design than he would be doing just a few years later.[13]

The coda calls for four pedal notes, and this together with the break in the texture at the diminished chord in m. 80 sharply articulates the coda from the rest of the piece. Nevertheless, the *pedaliter* close is a natural extension of the main body of the fugue, thanks to the use of related motivic material. The passage is easily enough adapted for instruments lacking pedals.

> All editions of BWV 949 contain some questionable readings. The voice crossing in m. 28 is editorial. In m. 36, sop. b´ on the third beat is the product of an alteration in ABB; the original a´ is more compelling. Further emendations (for NBA): 19 and 67, sop., note 3, g♮´ (also tenor, note 2, in m. 67)?

Capriccio in E, BWV 993

Chief sources: P 804/7 (Kellner); P 1087 (Preller); B Br 4093 (Fétis 2960; in F); P 409 (in F). *Editions*: BG 36; NBA V/10.

Bach wrote two very different early works entitled *Capriccio*: the present one and BWV 992 (see chapter 6). Both are connected in some way to one of his brothers; otherwise they have little in common. Kellner's copy of BWV 993 bears the subtitle *in honorem Johann Christoph Bachii*, to which several later copies add *Ohrdruf*, presumably to identify the dedicatee rather than the place of composition. Although the piece is found in neither MM nor ABB, this cannot be because BWV 993 is later than the works in those manuscripts. Perhaps Sebastian gave his older brother a special dedication copy too precious to have been kept in the larger collections. Christoph lived until 1721; whatever the reason for Sebastian's writing a piece in his honor, there is no possibility that *honorem* meant *memoriam*.

The word *capriccio* also raises questions. It is attached to several diverse compositions in MM and ABB and may have meant nothing more than a free, otherwise unclassifiable piece. BWV 993 is a fugue, but an exceptionally long one containing lengthy episodes that sound inspired by violin style; in this it resembles the first of two ambitious but rather clumsy capricci in ABB (nos. 10 and 44) attributed to "Polaroli."[14] Bach's piece is more accomplished, touching on an unusual variety of tonalities and figuration and extending longer than any other single movement in Bach's early keyboard works—120 long measures, not counting the brief *pedaliter* coda. It is tempting to suppose that the work was intended as a summing up of everything that Bach had learned through his first twenty years or so, with a grateful bow to his older brother. But although the Capriccio makes somewhat greater demands on the player than the works previously considered here, and explores the remote keys of D♯ minor and G♯ minor, it avoids the relatively sophisticated counterpoint displayed in works like BWV 896 or 949. One therefore wonders in what way such a piece was understood to honor Bach's older brother and teacher; could it have had something to do with the key, unusual for its time? In its rambling episodic structure it resembles two long fugues attributed to W. H. Pachelbel. Bach's older brother was a student of Johann Pachelbel, and perhaps such pieces were characteristic of fugal improvisation in the Pachelbel school; perhaps, too, Christoph had given the subject to Sebastian.

Veracini, in his unpublished treatise *Il trionfo della pratica musicale*, gave a definition for *capriccio concertato* that might apply to this type of fugue (see J. W. Hill 1979, 269). But although the design of BWV 993 somewhat resembles that of a concerto movement, an equally compelling analogy might be made to the rondeau. There is only one regular exposition, at the beginning, after which the entries of the subject alternate with lengthy sequential episodes, which form the real substance of the work. Some employ violinistic arpeggiation reminiscent of Italian sonatas or concertos, but most of the material is closer in inspiration to north Germany than to Italy.

The rondo-like structure does not preclude use of the same design elements employed in Bach's other early fugues. The most remote key, D♯ minor, is reached at about the middle of the piece (m. 61), and there is some sense of accumulating tension in two of the last three episodes, thanks to the massive chords accompanying the figuration in the right hand (mm. 81b–89a, 92–97). The last two statements of the subject are accompanied in three sustained voices, sounding quite grand after the rather nervous passagework in two and three parts. Yet, despite the variety of figuration and the sure command of counterpoint, modulation, and keyboard idiom, the piece is too long to hold interest consistently. The structure remains episodic, and the flurry of thirty-seconds in the coda is almost as irrelevant to the rest of the work as the solemn closing passage of BWV 946. The pedal notes cannot be omitted and must be taken with the left hand if there are no pedals; as in some works by Pachelbel, it is possible for the left hand to play the pedal notes an octave higher, which makes them easier to manage. A few pedal markings in the body of the piece appear to be copyist's additions and can be disregarded.[15]

Fugue in B♭ BWV 955

Earlier version (BWV 955a): *Sources*: P 595/9 (Ringk); P 247/2 (in G).
Edition: BG 42, appendix (in B♭).
Later version: *Sources*: P 804/17 (title by Kellner); P 425/2 (Kellner circle).
Editions: BG 42; Dadelsen and Rönnau (1970); NBA V/12.

Bach's authorship of this work has been disputed, yet its sources, style, and quality justify its inclusion here. Although Heller (1995) argued strongly for its attribution to Bach, it will appear in a volume of the NBA reserved for doubtful "clavier" works. Questions are raised by the relatively unauthoritative sources and somewhat anonymous style, but less well documented works have been accepted into the Bach canon. Reluctance to accept this work may be due to an old alternate attribution that, as Heller showed, can probably be dismissed.

It remains conceivable that the work acquired its attribution only because a pupil or collector found a copy of it among Bach's papers, perhaps with a few corrections or alterations in his hand. The accomplished contrapuntal technique and clear formal organization are compromised only at a few spots where the composer evidently could not avoid calling for pedals in an otherwise *manualiter* fugue. It is true that BWV 955 shows few stylistic fingerprints of Bach, especially in the opening exposition, whose generic subject and countersubject, reminiscent of choral writing, are practically ready-made for invertible counterpoint and sequential development. The latter half of the subject introduces a lively *figura corta* motive, but only with the first episode (mm. 24–6) does the style become distinctly instrumental. The new episodic motive, resembling an inverted mordent, is not memorable in itself. But it is the basis of most of the subsequent episodes, undergoing a somewhat different development in each one. In each episode the repetitions of the motive, articulated by "rhetorical" rests, relate it to the "sigh" figures found regularly in Bach's early works; so too does the half step present in the motive when it appears in G minor in the final episode (mm. 69–70a).

What appears to be an earlier version of the fugue, also probably in B-flat originally, does not differ greatly. The melodic material was embellished with motives and passing dissonances characteristic of Bach, and the bass was taken up an octave in mm. 45–7 to eliminate an unduly wide spacing.[16] Pedals remain necessary, however, at a few points where tenor and bass are momentarily separated by wide intervals (mm. 48, 78–9).

BWV 955 was once regarded as Bach's reworking of a composition by Johann Christoph Erselius, who in 1731 became organist at Freiberg Cathedral in Saxony; he owes his small share of immortality to whoever added the words *di Erselio* to the title *Fuga* atop the copy in P 247.[17] Agricola praised him in 1768 as "one of Germany's strongest [*bravsten*] players" (Adlung 1768, 1:229). But Erselius, born probably in 1703 (Heller 1995, 131), belonged to the generation after Bach and is unlikely to have furnished the latter with a model for this or any other composition. Moreover, the G-major version bearing Erselius's name contains a few errors implying that the copyist himself made the transposition, perhaps to permit the use of pedal for the entries in mm. 27 and 48. These would otherwise pass above middle C, the highest note on many Baroque pedalboards.

> The text of the later version seems dependable, save for ornaments and appoggiaturas that give the piece a mannered quality and might have been added by a copyist.

Fugue in B♭ on a Theme by Reinken, BWV 954

> *Sole source*: P 804/14. *Editions*: BG 42; Dadelsen and Rönnau (1970); NBA V/11.

BWV 954 is preserved in a single copy by an unidentified copyist who failed to name the composer. Yet its style, together with the existence of two other fugues by Bach on Reinken's themes (in the sonatas BWV 965 and 966), strongly implies Bach's authorship.[18] Keller (1949) described these as "large keyboard fugues in concerto style [*grosse konzertarte Klavierfugen*]," and although the analogy to concerto style is far from exact, all three fugues transfer the thematic material of Reinken's seventeenth-century consort fugues to a new type of piece influenced by current Italian instrumental style. Moreover, Bach abandoned the rigid permutational structures of Reinken's originals for more flexible designs that include at least one long episode in each case.

The theme of BWV 954 is from the second of the ensemble sonatas in Reinken's *Hortus musicus* of 1687.[19] Of the three fugues, the present one seems the earliest (a conclusion previously reached by Siegele 1975, 19). Its tonal design is relatively simple, there are occasional unmotivated breaks in the sixteenth-note pulsation, and like the fugue of BWV 966 it does not go beyond the three-part texture of Reinken's original. On the other hand, BWV 954 makes the greatest number of changes in Reinken's subject, which, as in the two other fugues, is virtually the only material taken from the model. BWV 954 is, moreover, perhaps the most immediately gratifying of all the early fugues to play and the most successful in reconciling the impulses of the keyboard virtuoso and the contrapuntist.

The subject, originally for violin, is rendered more brilliant by Bach's elimination of most of the repeated notes found in the original, except for those in the opening motive (Example 5.1). As emended by Bach, the subject provides the motivic material for most of the subsequent passagework; only one extended episode contains figuration not directly derived from the subject (mm. 71b–80). The fluency of the figuration, especially in the bass, marks an advance over earlier fugues; instead of the stolid bass lines in halves or quarters typical of earlier fugues (and Reinken's original), the bass here almost always moves in small note values. This reflects Bach's adoption of the motoric pulse of the Italian sonata and concerto style and the abandonment of the declamatory or rhetorical manner of his earlier works. Only in a few spots, for example the brief series of "sighs" and chromatic harmony in m. 41, does Bach seem unable to resist a momentary return to the rhetoric of his earlier style, which makes sense in this context only if the tempo is somewhat slower than the opening bars may suggest. Although there are still some poorly hidden consecutives (e.g., in m. 11), the overall form of BWV 954 has a firm tonal basis, organized symmetrically with an entry of the subject in the subdominant at the center (m. 47) and statements in minor keys (g and c, respectively) on either side of it (mm. 37, 54). The style is brilliant throughout, but the most striking figuration—scales descending through three octaves (c‴ to B♭)—serves to dramatize the return of the subject in the tonic, after the last episode (mm. 71b–80).[20]

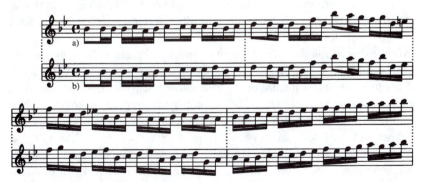

Example 5.1 Fugue subjects from (a) Reinken, *Hortus musicus*, Sonata 2 (basso continuo omitted), and (b) Fugue in B♭ on a Theme by Reinken BWV 954.

Perhaps the surest sign of Bach's mastery of the new style is his ability to bring the fugue to a convincing conclusion without a thematically irrelevant coda. Instead, a short extension of the final entrance of the subject (bass, m. 90) leads naturally and unpretentiously to the final cadence, without any break in the rhythmic texture.

Fugue in C on a Theme by Albinoni, BWV 946

Chief sources: LEm Go.S.11 (F. W. Rust); LEm ms. 1 (J. A. G. Wechmar); GB Ob Ms. M. Deneke Mendelssohn c.55 (Gleichauf). *Modern editions*: BG 36; Dadelsen and Rönnau (1970); NBA V/9.2.

The little Fugue in C is one of three Bach fugues on themes from Albinoni's Opus 1, a set of trio sonatas published in 1694.[21] As Talbot (1995, 153) shows, a few ideas beside the subject come from its model, implying that Bach knew the entire movement and not just the theme. But his style here is distinctly less developed than in the two other "Albinoni" fugues, BWV 950 and 951. Unlike them, BWV 946 was not immediately recognized as deriving from another work, since Bach transposed the subject, which no source identifies as Albinoni's.[22]

The model for BWV 946 was one of Albinoni's simpler fugues, the closing presto of the trio sonata op. 1, no. 12 in B♭. Although the syncopations in the subject might have formed the basis for strettos and expressive dissonances, their treatment by Albinoni is more playful than learned. The subject would have been suitable for a serious work in the manner of a seventeenth-century ricercar, but Bach's fugue, like Albinoni's, has little contrapuntal artifice, and its four parts sound together only rarely. The confinement of the subject to entries on the tonic and dominant and the lack of substantial episodes suggest an early date; Talbot (1995, 156) finds "facile note-spinning and pointless harmonic meandering," among other weaknesses. Such criticisms, although justifiable by the standards of Bach's mature works, deny the composer, still perhaps in his teens, due credit for tackling a rhythmically difficult subject in a variety of two-, three-, and four-part textures. Where Albinoni consistently maintains three diatonic voices, using recapitulation and repetition to fill out his design (as Talbot notes), Bach substitutes the constant change and occasional chromaticism of the *stylus fantasticus*. The most intense of the brief chromatic passages—mm. 44b–45a, in four parts and quoting the B-A-C-H motive in retrograde—provides a mild climax just before the *pedaliter* coda. The latter, although thematically unrelated, echoes the voice leading of the chromatic passage (sop. c″–b♭′–a′, bass F♯–G). The pedal notes are essential, and although the passage can easily be adapted to be playable on manuals alone, on harpsichord or clavichord it lacks the intended gravity unless filled out with arpeggiations or other embellishment.

The NBA includes alternate readings from Gleichauf's copy, but it is unclear whether the latter represents a distinct version; both traditions contain apparent errors. Emendations: 6, sop., notes 2–3 (tied), f′ not a′. 14, sop. g″ (dotted quarter) is apparently in the sources, but it creates impossible dissonances, and only a″ as suggested in BG makes sense; 28, flat on e′ (alto) misplaced, belongs on sop. note 3 (b′)? 45, sop., note 4, g♮′ (as in BG), not g♯′?

Fugue in A on a Theme by Albinoni, BWV 950

Chief sources: P 804/51 (Kellner, in G); P 595/3 (Ringk); P 288. *Editions*: BG 36; Dadelsen and Rönnau (1970); NBA V/9.2.

BWV 950 is a more mature example of the type of fugue essayed in the Capriccio BWV 993, in which entries of the subject alternate with extended episodes that continually introduce new material; the fugue ends with a free *pedaliter* coda. Here the episodes are almost always in two parts and more clearly imitate Italian violin writing—appropriately enough, considering the source of the subject.[23] The counterpoint is more fluent than in the works considered above, and even the extraordinary passing dissonances of m. 28 or 31 sound like natural products of the two moving lines. Unlike BWV 946, which contains only fleeting echoes of Albinoni's original (apart from the subject), here the soprano continues to follow the first violin line for another measure after the entry of the second voice. Bach, unlike Albinoni, does not use this line as a regular countersubject, but he does make two further quotations from the model; both citations provide motivic ideas that recur in several episodes.[24] Albinoni restricts the entries of the subject to the tonic and dominant; Bach includes entries in C♯ and F♯ minor in an exposition at the center of the fugue (mm. 48b–59a).

The coda gives way to Germanic toccata-style figuration; harpsichordists can let go of the two pedal notes (after initially striking them). The fugue as a whole perhaps runs on a bit too long, like BWV 993. But one should not overlook Bach's attempt to use stretto for dramatic effect in mm. 75–7, where a descending series of partial entries heralds the last full statement but one (bass, m. 78). The effort to dramatize an important moment toward the end of the fugue is less successful than in BWV 954, but it involves the same type of quasi-orchestral writing, at a similarly climactic moment.

The transposed version in G given by Kellner is probably his own, as various other alterations suggest. Particularly suspicious are the trivialization of Bach's athletic bass line in mm. 16–7 (given as the main text in the BG and editions based upon it) and a variant in the bass of m. 70 that results in parallel fifths.[25] Yet the G-major version provides necessary accidentals at several points, as well as a more cogent rhythm in m. 8 and more convincing ornaments.[26]

The text presents many puzzles; the BG's eclectic readings are more convincing than those of the NBA, which contains parallel fifths, unlikely accidentals and ornament signs, and other probable errors. Emendations: 8, sop., notes 6–7 (d′–c♯′′), dotted 8th–16th; alto, notes 5–6 (b′–a′), 8th–16th; 13, 17, 29, 31, etc., trill not mordent; 21, 23, 32, d♯′′ throughout (disregard editorial natural signs); 25, r.h., note 5, e♯′; 57, alto, last note, a′; 70, r.h., 1st beat, a (8th), a′–a (16ths), and 2d beat, both g′s natural, as in BG; 84–5, sop., a more regular pattern would be note 7 d′′ not f♯′′, note 11 d ′′ not e ′′, etc.; 87, alto, note 2, b not d′? 89, beat 3, BG maintains motion in 16ths by inserting a second b′ (16th) tied to the following chord; 94, tempo mark *allegro* is editorial interpretation of "allo" and "Mo" (*moderato?*) in the sources; 97, l.h., e not d♮; 98, BG adds c♯′ (quarter) on downbeat; 99, l.h., add A (half note) on downbeat. The NBA's mordent signs are transcribed literally from P 804, but most fall at cadences where a trill is demanded.

Fugue in B Minor on a Theme by Albinoni, BWV 951

Earlier version (BWV 951a): *Chief sources*: LEm Rudorff 16 (Mey); LEm Poelitz 9 (Johann Christoph Bach, with longer ending); Durham Cathedral Library, E 24. *Editions*: BG 36 (appendix); Dadelsen and Rönnau (1970); NBA V/9.2.
Later version: *Chief sources*: P 801 (Walther, 1714–7); LEm ms. 8 (Preller); P 648 (with BWV 923); Gb (Scholz, with BWV 923). *Editions*: BG 36, Dadelsen and Rönnau (1970); NBA V/9.2.

The third "Albinoni" fugue might have been first drafted at about the same time as BWV 950.[27] BWV 951a, the earlier version, is archaic in its use of old-fashioned cadence formulas, "obstinate" figures (at mm. 51, 54–5, 78), and occasionally awkward counterpoint and jerky rhythms. But the existence of a distinct revised version suggests that Bach recognized that in this work he had accomplished something special.[28] The relatively widespread dissemination of BWV 951 (and 951a) cannot have been due to superficially attractive features, which are lacking. Most of the copies are late, implying that the work achieved its greatest renown after Bach's lifetime, as did the toccatas and other relatively mature works from his earlier years. Still, the existence of copies by both Walther and Bach's brother Johann Christoph implies that the fugue was valued at an early date for its tortuous but always expressive and inventive working-out of Albinoni's chromatic subject. Indeed, it is arguably Bach's greatest *manualiter* fugue prior to the WTC.

Especially in its revised form, BWV 951 is important for several reasons.

The revisions changed an old-fashioned fugue into one that is distinctly closer to the fugues in concerto style considered in chapter 9. Remarkably, a group of later manuscripts from Berlin and Vienna contains both BWV 951 and 951a, indicating that musicians there were aware of and took an interest in Bach's revisions.[29] Another group of copies attaches the prelude BWV 923, useful today as a companion piece even if the pairing does not stem from Bach (see chap. 10). A different prelude is attached to one copy of the early version, showing that players used the early as well as the later version in performance; this music was not merely for study.[30] Walther and Preller, whose copies of the revised version represent a Weimar tradition particularly close to Bach, designated BWV 951 as a harpsichord piece, making it one of the earliest *manualiter* works to bear a reasonably dependable indication of this type.[31]

This is also one of Bach's earliest surviving pieces in B minor, a key in which he would write some of his most profound later music. Only two other early works (not counting chorale settings) are in this key; one, the organ fugue on a subject by Corelli BWV 579, furnishes an obvious parallel to BWV 951.[32] The two borrowed subjects open with the same downward leap, and the trio sonatas from which they were taken are roughly contemporary.[33] Yet the differences between Bach's two fugues outweigh the similarities.

The "Corelli" Fugue is, like its model, a double fugue, or rather a "simple" fugue in which the opening statement of the subject is already accompanied by the countersubject (which is never presented in an exposition of its own). The "Albinoni" fugue has a countersubject of the usual type, which Bach treats quite freely. The expository passages in BWV 579 are rich in the chains of suspensions made famous by Corelli. These recur in Bach works from the same period, including the "Reinken" Fugue in Bb (BWV 954)—but not BWV 951. In addition, the "Corelli" Fugue alternates between expositions and episodes in a manner reminiscent of ritornello form, although the episodes do not sound like the solos of a contemporary concerto. Both BWV 951 and the Albinoni fugue on which it is based are graver, more austere works; there is episodic passagework in both early and late versions of BWV 951, but in neither version does the figuration represent more than a brief respite from contrapuntal rigor. Despite the key of B minor, there is little chromaticism in Bach's "Corelli" Fugue. But BWV 951 shares with its model a saturated chromatic harmonic texture; the subject contains a descent in eighth notes through the chromatic hexachord, and the fugue accordingly tends toward a heavy harmonic rhythm in which every eighth bears a change in harmony.

As in BWV 950, Bach quotes directly from Albinoni's original at two points beyond the subject itself. One quotation consists of a prominent alternation between tonic and dominant chords that would otherwise be inexplicable (Example 5.2). Bach does not merely quote; the idea is used, as in the original, to begin a new section after a cadence to the dominant. Also borrowed is an ascending

Example 5.2 (a) Albinoni, Trio Sonata in B Minor op. 1, no. 8, second movement, mm. 29–30; (b) Bach, Fugue in B Minor BWV 951a, mm. 59–60.

chromatic hexachord—the inversion of the motive used in the subject—heard in the closing phrases of both pieces (Example 5.3). These two borrowings were somewhat obscured in the revised version (BWV 951).[34] The latter turned the bass of the tonic/dominant alternation into sixteenth-note arpeggiation, a reference to the countersubject; Albinoni had instead reintroduced the subject at this point. At the close, instead of merely repeating the chromatic motive in the upper voice (as in Example. 5.3b), the last five measures of the revised version work it into a sort of three-part stretto.

The form of the work remains close in conception to that of BWV 993 and 950, alternating between expositions and episodes; the latter draw more consistently on the subject and countersubject for their motivic material in the revised version, but both BWV 951a and 951 return to the tonic after each significant tonal excursion. If the early version manages to produce some sense of accumulating tension toward the end, this is a product of the unbroken sixteenth-note motion in mm. 70–80, containing both the final episode and the penultimate entry of the subject. But the chief appeal of BWV 951a lies in the rhetoric of its details, not in any large-scale drama.

Why Bach should have returned to BWV 951a is not immediately apparent, for the early version, despite the inventive counterpoint, contains no particularly striking contrapuntal developments, harmonic progressions, or modulations. Hill (2002, 176) not unjustly describes the episodes as "aimless" (*ziellos*). Perhaps Bach was moved to do more with a memorable subject whose possibilities he had not exhausted. The revision brought the work into line with some of the structural principles that govern the later Weimar fugues. Inconsequential motivic ideas that had been introduced and quickly abandoned, like the triplets of m. 45 or the "obstinate" passage introduced at m. 50, were eliminated. Plain successions of consonances were embellished by passing motion, a device also

Example 5.3 (a) Albinoni, Trio Sonata in B Minor op. 1, no. 8, second movement, mm. 33–6; (b) Bach, Fugue in B Minor BWV 951a, mm. 84–7.

used to avoid the barely hidden parallel fifths in mm. 20–2.[35] Some old-fashioned, irregular passagework was replaced by more consistently patterned figuration, as in mm. 34–7. Yet, despite lengthening many passages and inserting several entirely new ones, Bach did not fundamentally alter the character or design of the work. The inserted passages fall within the last third of the piece, starting in m. 68. The new section modulates to G (m. 86), a key absent from the BWV 951a and a welcome relief from the predominantly minor tonalities. Bach also added a new entry of the subject in the tonic (m. 78), reinforcing the rondeau-like character of the design.

Nevertheless, the new modulation to G, or III of IV, complements an earlier move to A—that is, III of V (m. 50b). Hence the revised version has a symmetry lacking in the more improvisatory older plan. Bach makes the symmetry explicit by also inserting a brief recapitulation. Only three measures are involved, but the restatement of a striking Neapolitan harmony from earlier in the piece is sufficient to tie the two ends of the piece together.[36]

The NBA's text for BWV 951a contains suspicious G♮s where one would expect sharps (mm. 23, 75) as well as unlikely parallel octaves in the final cadence (shorter version).

Canzona in D Minor BWV 588

Chief sources: MM (no. 27, Johann Christoph Bach, last 16 measures only); P 204 (Schwenke, 1781); lost copy by Kittel (basis for BG); LEm ms. 7 (Preller, ?spurious ornamented version). *Editions* BG 38, NBA IV/7.

BWV 588 is generally known as an organ piece, but although requiring pedals for a few notes it is essentially *manualiter* and is Bach's only known example of the genre, which goes back to the sixteenth century.[37] Title, subject, and texture place it more precisely in a seventeenth-century tradition of contrapuntal keyboard pieces modeled after Frescobaldi's ricercars and canzoni. Indeed, the subject resembles that of the *Canzon dopo la Pistola* (Canzona after the Epistle) in Frescobaldi's organ mass for the Blessed Virgin, part of the *Fiori musicali* (Rome, 1635), of which Bach owned a copy that he signed and dated 1714. BWV 588 was probably composed before that date, yet it cannot be as early as the tentative little fantasias BWV 563 and 570 with which it is sometimes grouped. Its concern with chromatic counterpoint in a somewhat archaic style aligns it with the fantasia BWV 917, with which it must be roughly contemporary. Over the next decade or two Bach would write comparable pieces in other media; Williams (2003, 193) mentions the organ fugue BWV 538 and Cantata no. 25. But the closest thing to it in his output for "clavier" is the first section of the incomplete *Fuga a 3 soggetti* in the *Art of Fugue*.

The work, like many seventeenth-century keyboard canzoni, consists in essence of two four-part fugues, the first in duple time, the second in triple time, with appropriately altered versions of the same subject and chromatic countersubject. Williams (2003, 194) calls the second part "less inventive" than the first, referring perhaps to the excessive reliance on sequences; even the new form of the subject contains two of them. Although the subject appears only on tonic and dominant, tonal planning is apparent in the placing of the most remote tonality, E minor, after the middle of the second section. Fingerings in Preller's copy assume *manualiter* performance, the left hand taking the bass even at the three points where BWV 588 exceeds the convenient reach of the hands. This was not necessarily Bach's solution, for Preller's over-ornamented version (given in the appendix of NBA IV/7) is unlikely to stem from the composer.

6
Miscellaneous Early Works

The fantasias, sonatas, and other remaining pieces from Bach's early years probably belonged to a larger collection of efforts that have mostly failed to survive. These works vary greatly in length and style, and although they now look like a mixed bag of miscellaneous pieces, some of them represent genres that must have seemed well established at the time they were written. For instance, several little fantasias belong to a tradition of short, modestly contrapuntal four-voice preludes cultivated in the circle around Pachelbel. Bach's transcriptions of ensemble compositions may derive from arrangements that were usually improvised and rarely written down. Yet the diverse titles for these pieces could also reflect generic ambiguities arising from the youthful composer's experimentation. BWV 922 has the general shape of a praeludium, that is, a prelude and fugue, yet the ostensibly imitative section lacks a fugue subject of the traditional type and seems more concerned with modulating into remote tonalities through what is essentially a long series of broken chords. The one-movement sonata BWV 967 is generically akin to the short instrumental movements (often called sonatas) that open contemporary vocal works, including Bach's early cantatas, yet it is longer and more complex in form and texture than most.

Besides these pieces in so-called free genres, the young Bach also wrote many settings of fixed melodies: chorale compositions of all sorts, as well as at least one set of variations on a secular melody. Although variations on both sacred and secular "arias" were enthusiastically cultivated by Pachelbel and other German predecessors, Bach produced relatively few examples. Throughout his career he would compose individual settings that employ a given technique (such as canon) or use a single ostinato-like motive, but a long series of such settings based on a single melody evidently did not appeal to him. We tend to think of chorale settings as organ works, but many of Bach's, including most of the Neumeister chorales, do not demand pedals.[1] Certain types of chorale settings were clearly meant for clavichord or harpsichord, such as an anonymous piece in allemande style based on the tune "Auf meinen lieben Gott," copied by Johann Christoph Bach in ABB.[2] Comparable writing occurs within Bach's four reliably attributed sets of early chorale variations, of which all but BWV 768 may have been meant primarily for domestic performance on stringed keyboard instruments.[3]

The medium of the free pieces is similarly ambiguous. The little fantasias BWV 563 and 570 are essentially *manualiter*, yet they have traditionally been regarded as organ works because of their sustained style and the presence of a few pedal points or other notes not easily played on manuals alone. On the other hand, the sonata BWV 963 has been considered a "clavier" work since its publication as such in the nineteenth-century BG. Whether the distinction has any historical basis is impossible to say without knowing the original functions of these pieces—if they had any set functions. If meant for both church and domestic use, this would be one reason for their ambiguity of medium. Precise dates are equally elusive, although all could have been at least drafted before Bach came to Weimar in 1708. The seven *manualiter* toccatas belong to this group as well, but because they form a distinct set of pieces in a relatively mature style, they are treated separately in chapter 7.

Praeludium in C Minor BWV 921 (with Fantasia in C Minor BWV 1121)

Sources: ABB (No. 32; mainly Johann Christoph Bach, last three measures autograph, followed by BWV 1121, both anonymous); P 222 (Johann Christoph Schmidt, 1713); LEm ms. 7 (Mempell). *Editions*: BG 36; Hill (1991); NBA V/9.2.

Although representative of "unruly virtuoso and improvisatory elements in Bach's early works" (Wolff 2001),[4] BWV 921 is a far cry from the wilder and emptier products of Buttstett, whose superficially comparable writing might have provided stimulation (inspiration would be the wrong word). The much younger Bach is more expert in his voice leading and more purposeful in his modulations and his exploration of diverse meters and types of figuration. Although designated a *praeludium* in ABB, BWV 921 has little to do with Bach's other preludes, apart from its dependence on arpeggios and chordal figuration.[5] There are five brief sections in four different meters; the central section is the longest, consisting in part of variations over a very simple ground bass. This section is also the quietest, framed by more fully scored passages. The *arpeggiando* chords of the opening return briefly (mm. 76–7) just before the last, climactic section, which is marked *prestissimo* (young Bach liked superlatives). The latter calls for a simple pedal part, which is also implied by the wide chord in m. 6.[6]

How the *arpeggiando* marking in m. 1 was understood is uncertain (see chap. 9). The successive time signatures raise the possibility of proportional tempos, the quarter note of the 4/8 section being equal to the dotted quarter of 6/8. If so, do both equal the half note of the common-time sections, and the dotted half note of the 24/16 coda? The last measure bears the French time signature "2," implying a doubling of tempo and thus a terrifying, abrupt conclusion. This would be in keeping with the demonic character of the piece, whose repeating ideas constituted the type of passage that was sometimes termed a *perfidia* (see Hofmann 1998).

Bach himself notated the last three measures in his brother's copy (the tempo indication and the "Pedale" marking are thus in his hand; facsimile in NBA V/9.2, vii). As in the coda of BWV 993, which likewise divides a climactic line of melodic figuration between the two hands, the pedal notes can be taken by the left hand. But this makes it difficult to achieve the incisive articulation obtained when the notes of the upper line are divided between the two hands (what Rameau later called a *batterie*). Perhaps this is why the pedal notes are missing from the copy in P 222 by Schmidt (not the Dresden composer of the same name). Today we tend to think of the *arpeggiando* chords, but not the pedal notes, as being idiomatic for a stringed keyboard instrument; Bach may not yet have been thinking along those lines.

In ABB the next piece is a fantasia in C minor, also in Bach's hand but, like BWV 921, anonymous, and, moreover, in tablature; it is found nowhere else. Bach's authorship of both is now generally accepted, and in recent years the fantasia has been upgraded to BWV 1121 from its former listing as Anh. 205. But it is indicative of continuing uncertainty that the NBA gives the *pedaliter* BWV 921 in a volume of "clavier" pieces and the fantasia, which is entirely *manualiter*, with doubtful works in its organ series (they appear together in Hill 1991). Although Bach failed to sign his name to either piece, he copied no other works but his own into MM and ABB; Schmidt named him as composer of BWV 921. The different forms of notation for the two pieces weigh against their forming a pair, as does their stylistic disparity. Akin to BWV 563 and 570, the fantasia is strictly contrapuntal and metrically stable, whereas the praeludium is free and in perpetually changing time. But of course this makes the fantasia an effective foil to the praeludium, and it may be anachronistic to suppose that the youthful Bach (or his older brother) had a definite intention as to whether two such pieces formed a pair, that is, a single "work." In addition to the Bach fingerprint at the end of the fantasia,[7] dramatic moments in both pieces are marked by augmented-sixth chords in root position, bass and treble forming a diminished third.

Despite its Italian tempo mark, the fantasia uses French cadence formulas, and there is an echo of the closing part of an *ouverture* when the meter shifts from 6/4 to common time shortly before the end. Williams (2003, 575) finds the placement of cadences "rather arbitrary"; after a long section in the tonic they come rather rapidly in the scheme c–g–Bb–F–c–Bb–c. But the emphasis on Bb was not odd in a style where major and minor tonalities a step apart are closely related (a vestige of modality). There is a parallel in BWV 921, which twice arrives on Bb (mm. 34 and 56). The counterpoint looks strict on the page, since it is transcribed from tablature. But voices and motives come and go freely despite the occasional imitation; this is genuine keyboard music, working reminiscences of both orchestral and motet-style polyphony into an improvisatory texture. Its composer, not yet concerned with motivic unity or "architectural" design, possessed a sure mastery of voice leading and was not afraid of expressive leaps and dissonant chromaticism (as in mm. 44–6).

The sources indicate the diminished thirds unambiguously (BWV 921, m. 5, c#/eb″; BWV 1121, m. 42, f#/ab″). But in BWV 1121 the doubled f# in m. 16 is surely an error for f#/a, and in m. 34 a quarter rest is probably intended on the downbeat, in the fifth voice that enters momentarily on f; the notation here seems confused and perhaps the second c′ in the tenor should be a (do these apparent mistakes cast Bach's execution of the tablature in doubt?). The final chord is major, not minor as in Hill (1991).

Praeludium in A Minor BWV 922

Chief sources: B Br II. 4093 (Fétis 2960); LEm ms. 8 (Preller, with added ornaments and fingerings); P 803 (J. T. Krebs; title: *Fantasia*). Editions: BG 36; Dadelsen and Rönnau (1970); NBA V/9.2.

BWV 922 is more recognizable than BWV 921 as Bach's, though it cannot be much later; some of its figuration resembles that of the C-minor work.[8] It is remarkable not only for its dogged repetitions of a few motivic formulas, which recall those of BWV 921, but for the remote keys reached in the middle section. It includes an impressive coda whose recitative-like style also occurs in the transition sections of the toccatas; an expressive Neapolitan harmony is prolonged in a manner reminiscent of a passage in the E-minor Praeludium BWV 533a, which must be nearly contemporary.[9]

The work exists in two slightly different versions, with different titles. The Brussels manuscript, which also preserves the *manualiter* toccatas, seems more correct in designating the work a *praeludium*, that is, a "prelude and fugue." Krebs, who was responsible for the copy in P 803, designates it a *Fantasia*, but he also wrote *Fuga* at the beginning of the middle section (mm. 34ff.), suggesting that his initial heading applies only to the opening.[10] Krebs, who studied with Bach at Weimar, also gives a few ornaments and embellishments (mostly appoggiaturas) not found in the other sources. It is possible that Bach added these at Weimar, at the same time changing the title, but the piece has little in common with either earlier or later works that Bach designated *fantasia*.

As in most such pieces, none of the harmonically inspired figuration of the initial section comes back exactly. But there are echoes in the closing section, which contains somewhat similar chordal figuration (mm. 87–92) as well as momentarily dwelling on the Neapolitan (compare m. 29). The subject of what Krebs called the fugue is little more than a broken chord, used as the basis for a *perfidia*-like modulating extravaganza; the motive occurs twice in almost every one of the section's fifty-three measures. This would grow tedious were it not for the adventurous modulations, which reach F♯ minor in the first half, even hinting at G♯ minor. The second half (mm. 58–87) turns toward the "flat" keys D minor and G minor; it modulates somewhat less remotely than the first but achieves intensification through two deceptive cadences that land squarely on dissonances (mm. 66 and 68). In addition, massed chords as in BWV 993 increase the general level of sound near the end (mm. 83–6). Despite its impressive architecture, the section needs to be performed with delicate timing and subtle distinctions in the articulation and breaking of the chords on the strong beats; otherwise it will sound mechanical.

> The parallel fifths in NBA (m. 37) are not in P 803 or LEm ms. 8, which have sop. d′′ (not b′) on the downbeat. NBA's ornamented readings, shown in small type, are from the copy by Krebs (not Kellner as stated on p. 27fn.). Walther's copies contain similar emendations, and, as Krebs also studied with Walther, these do not necessarily stem from Bach, nor do the numerous ornaments (omitted in BG) in the "fugue." Certainly not Bach's are the even more excessive ornaments and senseless fingerings in Preller's copy, reproduced as an appendix in NBA. In m. 78, Krebs put appoggiaturas on both the second and third beats, the latter probably a mistake.

Fantasia duobus subiectis in G Minor BWV 917

Sources: MM (no. 52; Johann Christoph Bach); LEm ms. 7 (Preller, with fingerings and ornaments); LEm ms. 1 (Wechmar); LEb Go.S.11 (F. W. Rust). *Editions*: BG 36; Dadelsen and Rönnau (1970); Hill (1991); NBA V/9.2.

The Latin title of BWV 917 calls attention to its almost academic concern with invertible counterpoint, which prevails except in the brief opening flourish and an even briefer one at the end.[11] Apart from those flourishes, the piece follows the older tradition of the contrapuntal fantasia, not the later improvisatory one. Nevertheless, the motion in quarters or in *figure corte* that characterized pieces like BWV 563 or 1121 is replaced here by movement in steady eighths.[12] This, together with the transparent texture (mainly in three parts), helps the piece remain light and flowing even as it sets forth systematically all six permutations of its three subjects, giving the effect not of a counterpoint exercise but of a Corellian piece of chamber music.

The title mentions only two "subjects," but, as Hill (1987, 423) explains, the word *subjectum* must refer to what we would call a countersubject, as in the organ fugue BWV 574. The latter is entitled *Thema legranzianum...cum subjecto* (Theme by Legrenzi...with a subject) in Johann Christoph Bach's copy.[13] The implication is that BWV 917 also uses a borrowed or traditional "theme"—perhaps the descending chromatic tetrachord first heard in the alto, although the suspension motive in the bass is equally conventional (compare the countersubject of BWV 955). Against these two slower ideas Bach sets a running figure. Despite its brevity the piece is more polished than one would expect of student work, and it could be a few years later than the other pieces considered above. Similarly skillful rhythmic differentiation of the thematic ideas recurs in the fantasia in A minor (BWV 904/1), a mature composition also combining an ostinato-like descending theme with a running figure.

> The Wechmar and Rust copies, although late, lack the unlikely ornaments of J. C. Bach and Preller, given in NBA. BG 36 sensibly adjusts mm. 14 and 16 and mm. 22 and 23, respectively, to show parallel readings: 14, alto, notes 6–8, f´–c´–eb´; 22, bass, last 2 notes, G–Bb.

Prelude and Fugue in A Minor BWV 895

> *Chief sources*: P 804/9; US NHy LM 4982 (Johann Christoph Bach of Gehren [1673–1727]). *Editions*: BG 36; Dehnhard (1973); NBA V/9.2.

Comprised of two discreet movements, instead of one through-composed series of sections, BWV 895 superficially resembles several preludes and fugues that Bach composed around the time of the *Well-Tempered Clavier*, probably near the end of his Weimar period. Yet it is significantly more archaic in style than those pieces (discussed in chap. 10), and its sources are unrelated.[14] Instead, BWV 895 could be the only surviving pedagogic prelude and fugue from Bach's early years at Weimar. The Yale manuscript preserves it as part of a "systematic collection" of small preludes and fugues used by Pachelbel and his pupils (Belotti 2000, 15), suggesting that this is Bach's contribution to a tradition that was being continued by his brother Johann Christoph and other Pachelbel students. Its dimensions suggest that Bach could have used it as a teaching piece, although some of his early organ *praeludia* (e.g., BWV 533) are not much bigger.

Copied perhaps as early as 1710 or so by the Gehren cantor Johann Christoph Bach (a distant cousin of Sebastian, born in Erfurt), the Yale manuscript preserves it immediately ahead of instructions on how to tune and string harpsichords and clavichords.[15] Although there is no reason to think that these instructions were copied from an exemplar in Sebastian's possession, they do, together with the repertory of the manuscript as a whole, reveal a concern with the same musical issues that led to Bach's *Well-Tempered Clavier*. They also suggest that despite some organ-like writing, the repertory in the manuscript was played on stringed keyboard instruments, as the *brisé* textures of the present work imply.

BWV 895 is more sophisticated than others in the manuscript, and it is distinguished from early Bach works like BWV 921 and 922 in its concision and the absence of extroverted virtuosity. But the prelude, reminiscent of the *passaggio* that opens the lute suite in E minor BWV 996, remains a free improvisation, lacking the more organized type of design found in later preludes (as in BWV 899–902). The fugue subject was perhaps a good one for a pedagogic piece, since it is short and distinctive, but it is too simple and rhythmically too dull (unbroken eighths) to inspire challenging harmony and counterpoint. On the other hand, the *brisé* texture of some passages is not a weakness but rather a successful effort to incorporate idiomatic keyboard textures into fugue. The fugue lacks episodes and closes with a free coda; the sole subject entry not on the tonic or dominant is a late entrance on the subdominant (tenor, m. 24). These are all signs of an early date, perhaps even as early as the "1707/08" suggested by Zehnder (1995, 331).

The NBA's text, based on the Yale manuscript, is superior to previous editions that followed Kellner. But many ornament signs are unlikely, e.g., the mordent and trill in the second half of m. 15. Other emendations: *Praeludium*, 6, beat 3, alto, 16th rest followed by [dotted] 8th; 12, beat 2, add a second stem on a´ (quarter). *Fugue*, 20, beat 3, c´–b–a belong in the alto; ten. read a (quarter, tied). 31, beat 3, add alto e´ (quarter).

Sonata in D, BWV 963

Sole source: P 804/10 (Mempell). *Editions*: BG 36; NBA V/10; Dadelsen (1975).

Neither BWV 963 nor the much shorter BWV 967 (discussed below) has much in common with the type of keyboard sonata that became ubiquitous in the later eighteenth century. But the title is not necessarily original; it is given (like the attribution) only on a separate title page in Kellner's hand. Bach must have known Kuhnau's sonatas, but these lack substantial fugues. As applied to BWV 963, "sonata" is virtually synonymous with "toccata," save for the absence of an improvisatory opening section; otherwise the plan resembles that of the D-Major Toccata BWV 912. The second of the three main sections is in a contrasting minor key, and modulating transitions connect the larger sections. The last two of these are fugues of contrasting types; the second, in B minor, is in motet style, whereas the last is a lively if not comic piece in gigue rhythm.

The opening section is reminiscent of the seventeenth-century instrumental movements that furnished models for Kuhnau's keyboard sonatas. But this first section employs the same little descending motives as other early Bach keyboard works, and the short phrases divided between the hands recall antiphonal exchanges in the opening chorus of the early cantata BWV 131.[16] Like BWV 967, the movement falls into a rondeau-like or ritornello-based form. But instead of the virtuosity of Italian style one finds, as in BWV 1121, hints of French style (e.g., the falling thirds in the metrically weak phrase endings in mm. 4, 30, etc.). An early move to B minor anticipates the key of the middle section (m. 28); the prominence given this and related keys (rather than the dominant) reinforces the elegiac character also expressed by the numerous descending figures.

The transition from the gentle opening movement to the first fugue begins with a sudden F#-major chord and a pair of animated flourishes. The change of texture on a remote harmony is a rhetorical effect, imitating the surprising chords (often third-related) found at important junctures in vocal works from Monteverdi onward.[17] The effect is strengthened by the pedal notes called for only at this point.

The first fugue (movement 3 in the NBA) combines a diatonic subject with a chromatic countersubject, a favorite device for which the fantasia BWV 917 might have provided some practice; but this is a more earnest piece. The following adagio is a short example of a type of transition passage built from arpeggiated chords, used in works by Reinken and Böhm and also in Bach's toccatas. The close-spaced tempo markings at the end of this passage (presto, adagio, allegro) have antecedents in seventeenth-century toccatas and violin sonatas, where they probably indicate nuances, not radical tempo changes. The allegro measure uses the same motive as the presto one, written in half the note values, implying quicker notes but not literally twice as fast.

The title of the closing fugue (movement 5), *Thema all' Imitatio Gallina Cuccu*, must have been intended to mean something like "Fugue in imitation of the chicken and the cuckoo."[18] Birdsong occurs in keyboard fugue subjects at least as early as 1624, when Frescobaldi published a *Capriccio sopra il Cucco* ("Caprice on the cuckoo"), and similar pieces were written throughout the seventeenth century.[19] This fugue combines two traditional motives—in the subject and second countersubject, respectively—but it is hardly necessary to interpret these allegorically (as suggested by Osthoff 1991). Despite its charm, the fugue is one of the more disappointing in Bach's early works. The initial repercussive motive—an arresting idea—represents the hen (*gallina*). But the theme as a whole, like many striking themes in German keyboard music of the period, fails to imply a compelling harmonic progression, instead tracing a progression from I to ii and back to I again. Hence each statement of the subject oscillates between two weakly related harmonies, and as every measure of the subject (save the first) outlines a complete triad, there is no getting around its implied harmonies. When the other voices enter they are forced to jump between alternate notes of the triad—which is good for the cuckoo, but bad for maintaining contrapuntal or harmonic interest. There are also some inept phrase elisions, the subject at times entering in a way that suggests that something has been left out (e.g., at mm. 47, 54, 72).

> The sole source is carelessly written. BG's conjectural insertion of m. 10 in the first section makes sense and is retained in NBA, but the editorial pedal point on A in the first bridge (mvt. 2, mm. 5–7) is unnecessary. Harpsichordists can leave out the other pedal notes (mm. 1, 3–4, 14) or transpose them up an octave (mm. 2, 8–13). Emendations: *Movement 1:* 16, add ♯ on g´? 51, omit d♯´? 53, omit g´? 79, alto, g´ not a´? 82, add ♮ on c´´? 85, last two chords, a´/c♯´´, b´/d´´? 99, omit b´. *First bridge (mvt. 2):* 5–7, omit editorial A. *First fugue (mvt. 3):* 11, bass, omit last note (NBA: g; BG: g♯), probably a misunderstanding of tied b in ms.; 13–14, tie d´´–d´´ in ms.; 32, alto, notes 5–6, c♯´–d´ (conjecture from BG). *Second bridge (mvt. 4):* 4, r.h., adjust rhythm to follow m. 3 (a´ on downbeat, etc.)? 5, ten., 3d beat, f♯´ (dotted quarter, in place of rests)? 9, 1st chord, alto, g´ not a´? 4th chord, f♯´ not g´? *Second fugue (mvt. 5):* 43, ten., note 3, a not b?

Sonata in A Minor BWV 967

Sources: MM (No. 33); P 804/27 (Kellner); Stuttgart, Württemburgische Landesbibliothek, Cod. II, 288 (Lorenz Sichart). *Editions:* BG 45/1; Dadelsen (1975); Hill (1991); NBA V/9.2.

Though possibly a fragment, this one-movement piece could have been considered a complete sonata at a time when the word was often used to refer to a single instrumental movement at the beginning of a larger work (as in Cantata 182). The sketchy notation of several passages written in two voices (with figured bass) led to the suggestion that this is an arrangement of a lost chamber work (BG, repeated in NG and NG2). But the fully written-out passages are idiomatically conceived for keyboard and show no signs of being arrangements, and it is hard to imagine what the putative original of around 1700 would have looked like.

The first two phrases of BWV 967 today suggest a fully scored ritornello followed by a solo episode in two parts with figured bass. But the "ritornello" ends with a chromatic progression to V, like the opening phrase of a seventeenth-century German consort sonata. It is possible that the next phrase, far from representing a thinly scored solo passage, was actually meant to be realized with full chords as well, answering mm. 1–5. This would explain why phrase 2 starts with a full chord on the downbeat of m. 6; the first real contrasting phrase would then begin after the tonic cadence on the downbeat of m. 14. Even then, soloistic material is at first confined to the bass, whose running sixteenths combine with eighth-note "sigh" motives in the upper two voices, taken from the "ritornello." Hence, if there is a concerto model for this sonata, it is a Roman concerto grosso, not a Venetian solo concerto, and it is misleading to see it as representing an early stage in Bach's development of so-called ritornello form.

Although the style is early, this is not the work of a beginner, and had it been fully notated its sophistication would be more evident. The running figuration gradually attains greater prominence, reaching the top of Bach's keyboard near the end, in a climactic passage accompanied by fully notated chords (m. 61). There is a brief flurry of thirty-seconds at the very end, but this is not a separate coda, just a cadenza-like elaboration of the final phrase. The sonata's pathos derives not from the sigh motive as such but from the harmonic context in which the latter most often occurs: an oscillation between two 6/3-chords separated by half steps. First heard in the "ritornello" (m. 3), the idea is echoed in the second phrase (m. 7) and is one of the young Bach's most characteristic types of expressive rhetoric, recalling especially passages in the early Cantatas 4 and 71.

If the figured bass notation is indeed shorthand for full chords, then its realization should be as in the "orchestral" closing passage of BWV 821, not the "chamber" aria of BWV 833 (for both, see chap. 4). Presumably one need not be concerned about playing parallel fifths and octaves any more than Bach was about writing them in m. 2 (or in the similar opening passage of the G-major toccata). There are in fact only a few figures, but the need to fill in the harmony seems clear; mm. 6ff. are notated in just two parts, but when the passage is repeated with the two lines exchanged between the hands (mm. 46ff.), the right hand has three-part chords.

> All editions are inaccurate, heavily emended, or both, reflecting the nature of the sources. Emendations for NBA: 2, sop., note 3, c''; 9, bass, note 1, figure 6#?; 36 and 37, beats 3–4, sop, mss. read f''–b''–b''–d'', which makes sense if the chord is 6/4/2; 52, omit trill (in sources), or substitute mordent? 76–7, omit tie?

Capriccio sopra la lontananza de il fratro dilettissimo BWV 992

Chief sources: MM (No. 35; Johann Christoph Bach); P 595 (Ringk; final fugue only); B Br II 4093 (Fétis 2960). *Editions*: BG 36; NBA V/10; Dadelsen (1975).

Bach's most famous early work, BWV 992 was evidently modeled on Kuhnau's Biblical Sonatas (published Leipzig, 1700), with which it shares the use of programmatic rubrics for each section. Until recently the work was assumed to have memorialized the departure of Bach's brother Johann Jacob to join the retinue of King Charles XII of Sweden. In the brief family history compiled by Sebastian in 1735, Jacob's departure is set in the year 1704, but Sebastian mistakenly gave 1704 as the year of his own arrival in Arnstadt, so he might have been wrong about Jacob's departure as well.[20] Wolff (1992, 148–49) pointed out that the word *fratro* need not be understood literally and could refer to any close friend. Hence the separation (*lontananza*) referred to in the title could have involved almost anybody, and there is no reason to assume the piece is of autobiographical significance.[21] On the other hand, a lost manuscript of the D-minor toccata referred to Johann Christoph Bach as *delect[issimus] frater* (see chap. 7), so it is conceivable that the present work might reflect Sebastian's *own* absence from one family household or another.

The title *Capriccio* does not indicate caprice in the modern sense, but the work's emotional extremes have led one commentator (Vendrix 1989, 201) to comment on the its combination of "Traurigkeit und Humor." At the center is the famous *Lamento*, which is drenched in conventional symbols of grief and, although over-wrought by modern standards, need not be understood ironically (as suggested in the first edition of this book). Still, the plan of the work, which moves to the minor dominant for the Lament, dispatches the latter with the almost inordinately cheerful aria and fugue that follow. These last two movements both use post horn motives; is this because the "brother" has departed by post coach, or because he has sent mail? In any case, the emotional as well as the tonal trajectory leads from darkness to light, which would be a favorite theme in Bach's cantatas.

The opening movement represents, according to its subtitle, the efforts of unnamed friends to talk our *fratro* out of making his journey.[22] The affect is not unlike that of the *sinfonia* that opens Cantata 106 (the so-called *Actus tragicus*), particularly in the falling motive repeated many times in the latter part of the movement. The latter is thus an example of what is termed here an "obstinate" figure (mm. 14–5). Could this represent our hero's repeated insistences that he must leave, or is it simply abstract expressive rhetoric? Bach might have remembered a somewhat similar passage in the Albinoni trio sonata, also in B♭, that furnished the subject for BWV 946.[23]

The following section represents "various misfortunes [*casua*] that might occur to him in foreign countries"; this was prophetic if the work indeed concerns Jacob Bach, who wound up a prisoner in Istanbul after the defeat of Charles XII by the Turks. This is set as a fugue in motet style, like the corresponding section of BWV 963; with its numerous downward leaps and dissonances it is more an expression of grief than of physical danger. Entries occur more mechanically than in most of Bach's keyboard fugues, at intervals of one and one-and-a-half measures, but stiffness is avoided by the unusual modulating scheme, which begins and ends in different keys (G minor and F minor, respectively). The downward journey through the circle of fifths is accomplished by putting the fugal answers in the subdominant, as in the opening exposition of the organ fugue in C, BWV 531.

Example 6.1 *Capriccio sopra la lontananza*, BWV 992, third movement: a possible realization for mm. 13–5.

The "friends' general lament" is in F minor, a rare key in the early eighteenth century and not one expected within a work in B♭ major. The tempo is *adagissimo*; the rare superlative (an indication of Bach's seriousness) also occurs in the long arpeggiando bridge of the D-Minor Toccata in some sources. The lament is an ostinato movement, built upon a four-measure chromatic bass line of a type used since the early seventeenth century for operatic laments. Three statements for bass alone (the first, the seventh, and the twelfth and last) serve somewhat like ritornellos, although bass as well as treble undergoes variation. The vocal model is made explicit by the figured bass notation of mm. 1–4, before the upper part enters, and again in mm. 25–8; harmonic filling-in seems necessary not only here but elsewhere as well. The reference in the title to *general* lamentation implies heavy, full-voiced realization, as in BWV 821 and 963, each hand striking as many chord tones as possible. Measures 13–5 call for rhythmic filler as well, that is, some sort of contrapuntal motion to avoid a hiatus on each downbeat, although this could be provided by ornamenting the melody (Example 6.1). One wonders where Bach might have previously heard such music—perhaps at Hamburg, or in recently imported Italian cantatas at Weimar in 1703 or even Eisenach.

"Since they see that it cannot be otherwise," the friends bid their adieus in a short bridge movement. Baroque conventions of musical representation offered nothing directly applicable to this programmatic situation, and the music, like much of Kuhnau's in such cases, merely suggests an appropriate affect. But the transition to brighter keys is skillful, including a modulation from A♭ major to D minor in the space of four measures. Still, the return of B♭ major at the beginning of the next movement seems abrupt, in part because the *Aria di Postiglione* is a jolly little binary form,[24] utterly different from what has preceded. The departure itself is not represented, unless this is the meaning of the post horn motive, also seen in the *Aire pour les Trompettes* of BWV 832.[25] Although short, the movement is not simple; the phrasing is asymmetrical (5 + 7 mm.), and the counterpoint of m. 1 is inverted after the double bar, as in the little gigue of BWV 832.

The closing fugue combines two significant motives, like that of BWV 963. The subject contains a trumpet signal, and the octave leap of the post horn (apparently the *posta* referred to in the title of the movement) is heard in the countersubject.[26] Although entertaining, the incorporation of such motives into a fugue again creates awkward challenges for the player, and they do not encourage sophisticated counterpoint. Williams (1986c, 277–8) suggests that "some empty moments" might have been inadvertent products of Bach's composing the piece in tablature rather than score. But the thin textures of some passages, with wide gaps between the voices (e.g., mm. 38–43), reflect the unusual character of the motives, and they might sound full enough on the right type of harpsichord. The climax occurs in a series of sequences in which the post horn motive becomes the basis for flying figuration in both hands, at the end turning into something violinistic (mm. 42–8). Not coincidentally, this passage leads to the most remote tonality (D minor), but as the latter lasts until just six measures before the end, the return to B♭ is not entirely convincing. There is not even a final entry of the subject in the tonic, just a partial stretto (mm. 55–6). The latter contains the same harmonic formula (over a pedal point) that is elaborated in the closing passages of the echo movement of BWV 821 and the "Neumeister" chorale prelude BWV 1117.

Sonata in A Minor after Reinken BWV 965

Sources: P 803 (Walther); P 804/20 (Kellner); PL LZu Spitta Ms. 1752/3.
Editions: BG 42; Dadelsen (1975); NBA V/11.

Reinken's *Hortus musicus* (Musical Garden), published at Hamburg in 1687, was a set of thirty pieces for four-part chamber ensemble (two violins, viola da gamba, and harpsichord). The pieces are divided into six groups, each consisting of a "sonata" followed by four dance movements (allemande, courante, sarabande, gigue) in the same key; each "sonata" comprises an adagio, a fugue, and a free postlude. The fugues are permutational in design, that of the first sonata systematically presenting all possible combinations of subject and countersubject in such a manner that each voice states each theme four times in the tonic and four times on the dominant.[27] The gigues also are fugal. In each of the first two sonatas, the postlude consists of a brief adagio for the full ensemble followed by a solo for the first violin; the solo is then repeated by the gamba, although this repetition is omitted in Bach's arrangements. The dances are often linked by thematic resemblances, and in three cases the allemande and courante form a strict variation pair like those of BWV 833 and Reinken's own keyboard suites.

The importance of Bach's transcriptions was recognized by Keller (1949), who drew particular attention to the fugues. Although employing Reinken's thematic material, the fugues (including BWV 954, discussed in chap. 5) are essentially new compositions. Opinions on their dates have ranged from "before 1705" to circa 1720; the issue is made difficult by the uncertain dating of Walther's copy, the sole early source.[28] It is plausible that Bach might have drafted the three Reinken fugues at roughly the same time, perhaps even as early as 1705 or so. But we know from the B-minor Albinoni fugue BWV 951 that Bach could revise an early piece to produce something that retains many of the formal characteristics of the original, yet whose heightened harmonic tension and mastery of counterpoint must reflect profound stylistic development over a significant period of time. The Reinken settings may have had a comparable history, BWV 965 having undergone the most thorough (and latest?) revision.[29] Although Bach's awareness of Reinken and the *Hortus musicus* can presumably be traced to Bach's student years, the fugal movements—including the gigue of BWV 965—show more sophisticated compositional technique than early fugues such as BWV 896 and 949 or those on Albinoni subjects (with the exception of the revised BWV 951). His avoidance of the permutational schemes of Reinken's fugues also implies a certain distance in both time and place from Bach's first exposure to these works. In addition, the written-out embellishment in the prelude sections is closer to the adagios of the Weimar cantatas and concertos than to the air in the *Ouverture* BWV 822. Some awkward writing—the left hand must span a tenth in the gigue of BWV 965—implies that these pieces preceded the great preludes and fugues discussed in chapter 9, but they may not have come long before them.

It is impossible to say what led Bach to arrange the pieces, which were already somewhat old-fashioned even before he arrived at Weimar in 1708. Perhaps Bach's arrangements stem from an effort to preserve and at the same time to refashion works that he had admired in his youth. Yet the melodies and harmony are often conventional, and the writing for the strings is not always idiomatic; many passages betray the origin of the material in keyboard style (Example 6.2).[30] Even if the arrangements were an act of personal homage to a respected older musician, their existence does not necessarily indicate Reinken's particular influence on Bach. Conscious rejection of Reinken's style might even be seen in Bach's substitution of his own fugal technique for Reinken's rigid schema, as well as in the modern Italian violin style that can be heard in the figuration of the fugues and the written-out embellishment of the preludes. Whereas Bach's "Albinoni" fugues subject their Italian themes to the *varietas* favored in the *stylus fantasticus*, Bach smoothes out Reinken's fugue subjects and develops them in a more up-to-date style.

Bach apparently arranged only the first of Reinken's five-movement sets in its entirety. BWV 965, the resulting work, is called a sonata, although Reinken ap-

Example 6.2 Reinken: Courante no. 1 from *Hortus musicus*, mm. 21–2.

plied that word only to the opening movement. Except in the fugal sections, Bach's method of adaptation was the same process of variation by which Reinken had composed the courante of this set as a triple-time elaboration of the allemande. Although embellishing the outer voices, Bach generally preserves the salient voice-leading of all three original parts.[31] The middle line is often dropped an octave or incorporated into an idiomatic left-hand accompaniment that serves as a realization of Reinken's figured bass. The result is usually idiomatic keyboard writing, yet the arrangement is not an unqualified success.

In the opening adagio Bach adds a layer of Italianate embellishment to Reinken's relatively simple violin and gamba lines. No doubt this is how anyone would have treated the piece circa 1710. But by then Reinken's work was more than twenty years old, and Bach could be accused of embellishing it excessively and in a stylistically inappropriate manner. At one point Bach's embellishments fill the eloquent silences of Reinken's original (m. 12, second and fourth beats). Moreover, certain embellishments (e.g., in mm. 8–9) lose their ornamental quality, becoming motives that are exchanged in imitation between different voices. This rationalizes what otherwise might be an arbitrary improvisation, but the embellishments lose some of the fire and spontaneity normally associated with this type of writing.

The dances too are overworked in spots, as if Bach was trying too hard to add counterpoint or embellish the bass wherever the opportunity arose. To be sure, Reinken's originals lack the sophisticated rhythm of a French *pièce de clavecin*, and the old-fashioned bass lines are often stodgy, moving slowly, by whole steps, even in climactic passages. In the allemande of BWV 966 Bach left one such bass line untouched (mm. 15–7). But in BWV 965 a similar passage is reworked to resemble those episodes in Bach's early fugues in which each hand has running sixteenths (Example 6.3).

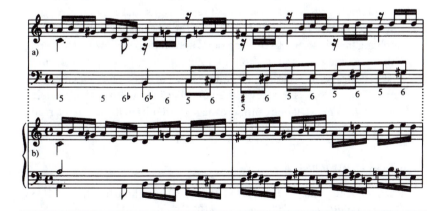

Example 6.3 (a) Reinken, Allemande no. 1 from *Hortus musicus*, and (b) Sonata in A Minor after Reinken BWV 965, allemande, mm. 24–5.

The fugue is one of the most ambitious of Bach's early *manualiter* efforts. As in the two other "Reinken" fugues, Bach omits the continuo line that originally accompanied the initial entry of the subject. His countersubject is a very free variation of Reinken's, but it is not maintained in the rigorous permutational manner of the original. The next three entries of the subject take place in the same measures as in the original, although not in the same voices. The bass entry in m. 13 corresponds to the second entry for the first violin, at the beginning of Reinken's second exposition. But from that point onward Bach's music is completely new. A fifth entry (m. 20) brings the opening exposition to a close, and thereafter each entry of the subject leads to a soloistic episode, more or less in concerto style but invariably based on material from the subject. The successive episodic passages grow in length, and the most substantial, in mm. 57–70, is the most up-to-date in style, at one point suggesting a parallel with Bach's Double Concerto BWV 1043.[32]

In the gigue, although Bach kept little of the original apart from its subject, he retained its basic design: the two halves of the movement are exactly equal in length, the second half using the inversion of the subject. Also as in the original, each half contains the same number of entries of the subject, which appears twice in each part. Unfortunately, the addition of a fourth voice led to a texture that is unusually dense for a gigue, and Bach, like Reinken, avoids entries on any degree except I and V. The counterpoint, moreover, often consists of parallel thirds or simple contrary motion; again, Reinken's subject is no help here, but the writing is not as imaginative as in the fugue in the opening movement.

> NBA is more accurate than earlier editions but might have followed the latter in emending *fugue*, 38, sop., note 10, a, not f♯ (to avoid a cross-relation), and *gigue*, 55, 3d beat, where alto and bass should probably have G♮s, not G♯s. In *allemande* and *courante*, all three editions insert first and second endings as well as conjectural repeat signs. But PL LZu gives the last three notes of *courante*, 22 (m. 22B in the editions) as 16ths, not 8ths, implying that these notes serve as a rapid upbeat to the following measure. Other possible emendations from PL LZu: *courante*, 12, sop., note 4, omit sharp; *gigue*, 50, sop., note 2, f♯″, not f♮″. Further suggested emendations: *Gigue*, 8, sop., 1st note c″ (tied over barline), not b′? 41, alto, note 8, b, not g? In m. 54, if one cannot manage the tenths in the left hand, read ten., a (quarter) for b–c′ (8ths).

Sonata in C, BWV 966

Chief sources: P 803 (Walther); LEm ms. 8 (J. A. Lohrber?); P 804/33 (Kellner). *Editions*: BG 42; Dadelsen (1975); NBA V/11.

BWV 966 is an adaptation of the "sonata" and allemande from the third set of pieces in Reinken's *Hortus musicus*. Bach evidently did not transcribe the three remaining dances, but this does not make BWV 966 a fragment, since in the original print the pieces are not grouped explicitly into suites.[33] The method of adaptation here is exactly as in BWV 965, but the style is simpler, particularly in the fugue, which is in three voices, as opposed to four. Of the three "Reinken" fugues, this comes closest to what is now termed concerto form in its rounded tonal design and the regular alternation between expositions and episodes. Moreover, as in BWV 955, a distinct thematic idea recurs in four of the five "solo" episodes. The episode motive, first heard in m. 16, is nearly identical to a figure that serves the same function in the "Dorian" toccata BWV 538/1.

The assimilation of Venetian concerto style is by no means complete. As in BWV 954, the subject and thus the fugue as a whole are pervaded by the running sixteenths employed in many concerto movements. But the pulsation in sixteenths is momentarily interrupted at a few seemingly random points (e.g., mm. 8, 50, and 64). The counterpoint is not perfect; mm. 7–8 contain empty octaves on the even-numbered beats, and there are parallel octaves in m. 9. The last measure of the fugue is filled out with an archaic formula that seems misplaced here (compare the close of BWV 949). Nevertheless Bach was on the way to incorporating Venetian concerto style into his own.

Aria Variata in A Minor BWV 989

Chief sources: ABB (no. 36; Johann Christoph Bach; title: *Aria. Variata. all Man. Italiana*); P 801 (Johann Tobias Krebs: . . . *all'manual-Italiana*); P 804/21 (Kellner: . . . *all Imitatione Ittalian* [*sic*]); B Br II.4093 (Fétis 2960). *Editions* BG 36; NBA V/10; Dadelsen (1975).

The Aria variata is, apart from the chorale partitas, the only assuredly authentic variation work of the early years (see appendix A for the doubtful BWV 990). Although it shares some things with the chorale variations, especially the full harmonization of the theme at the outset, it is more different from those works than alike, avoiding traditional types of cantus-firmus setting, for example. Puzzles about its title, instrumental medium, and text should not distract from its unusual and attractive features, especially the expressive harmony, which is intensified in the variations: the E–A progression in m. 7 becomes E–B♭ in most variations, and in the last one B major leads directly to G minor after m. 6, a striking effect that is echoed by the E–B♭ progression just two bars from the end.[34] Nine of the ten variations are limited to essentially two voices, and although each tends toward intensive development of just a few motives, there is more variety of figuration than in many similar compositions of the period. On the whole the writing is fluent and assured, closer to a work such as the Capriccio BWV 993 than to Bach's earliest fugues or other compositions. Archaic features include the insistent *figure corte* in variation 1 and the angular counterpoint of variation 9, as well as the "obstinate" repetitions in the harmonically significant m. 7 (variations 2 and 3).

The word *aria* in the title has the same meaning as in keyboard works by Pachelbel and other seventeenth-century composers, also used by Bach much later in the aria of the Goldberg Variations: a short binary form that serves as the basis of variations, mostly composed of lively figuration. Both title and content show parallels with an Aria with variations in the same key, usually attributed to Johann Christoph Bach (1642–1703)[35]: both works use full-voiced settings at beginning and end, triplet variations in the body of the work, and a penultimate variation consisting of sixteenths for both hands. The theme is probably the composer's; the adventurous harmony and unusual melodic leaps of BWV 989 are unlikely to have occurred in a popular tune. But this is not certain, and the work raises other puzzles as well. The title given in the BG, *Aria variata alla maniera italiana*, means "song varied in the Italian style." But this reading occurs only in a late, derivative source, and although the violinistic nature of some variations (2, 8) suggests Corelli, the more old-fashioned features are distinctly German.[36] Variants in the title have been taken as evidence that the piece was written for an "Italian manual" (NBA V/10, KB, 49), presumably signifying some special instrument, a possibility made plausible by a few odd passages.

The work exists in two distinct versions, Krebs, Kellner, and the important Brussels manuscript giving what may be an adaptation to avoid low AA; Krebs and Kellner, moreover, diverge in the theme.[37] All versions contain wide stretches in the lower staff, suggesting the need for pedals or a special type of keyboard. The odd bass formulas in the closing measures of variation 1 (as given in ABB) also suggest an unusual sort of keyboard, but the wide intervals between tenor and bass in the theme and last variation would remain unplayable on an instrument equipped with an ordinary short octave, whether or not it supplied the low AA. Since the latter note appears in a few other works probably composed at Weimar (BWV 806a, 903a), Bach may have had access there to an instrument that extended down to what was then in Germany an unusually low note. This piece might have been written expressly for that instrument, which, if equipped with pedals for AA and other low notes, would have facilitated performance; perhaps the theme was even meant for performance on two manuals and pedal, which would make it easier to play the numerous ornaments that ABB gives for the melody.[38]

A series of variations can be shaped by the relative levels of energy or intensity in successive settings, and the violinistic triplets of variation 2 mark an early high point of this type. But disagreements between the sources leave some doubt as to whether Bach had clear intentions for the order of variations.[39] Only

ABB includes what seems to be the climactic ninth variation, where both voices contain the running sixteenths that characterize the more virtuosic of Bach's early *manualiter* fugues. Similar figuration marks the final variation in two works from Pachelbel's *Hexachordum Apollonis*, a collection of "arias" with variations that would have provided models for BWV 989. Krebs and Kellner lack this variation, not necessarily because it was a later addition, but perhaps because it cannot be played as brilliantly as the notation in steady sixteenths would have suggested after 1715 or so.

Other textual variants suggest that, as in BWV 820 and 967, Bach's score left some details undecided.[40] Some of the ornaments in ABB may not be Bach's; the short diagonal lines in mm. 5–6 of the theme might be interpreted as *séparés*, a measured breaking of the two-note chords (Example 6.4).[41] ABB lacks the tempo marks given in the modern editions; if those in the other sources are Bach's, this is a further sign that the latter manuscripts give a revised version. Presumably one would have changed the registration for each variation insofar as the instrument permitted.

Example 6.4 Aria variata BWV 989, aria, m. 5.

7
The *Manualiter* Toccatas

The seven *manualiter* toccatas mark the culmination of Bach's early work for keyboard instruments without pedals. They also form the earliest group of "clavier" pieces now known by a collective title, but unlike the English Suites, WTC, and various other collections they do not appear to have been organized into a set by Bach himself. Their tonalities do not fall into any obvious pattern, although the predominance of minor over major keys—only two of the latter—is an old-fashioned trait shared with the English Suites. Although they were distributed more widely than the pieces considered in previous chapters, the toccatas tended to be copied on an individual basis, and not by Bach's Leipzig pupils, implying that Bach did not use them for teaching. Probably their older style had made them unfashionable by the time Bach left Weimar, but they were again attractive after his death as *manualiter* parallels to his great organ *praeludia*. This may explain why, apart from copies deriving from Bach's Weimar pupils and associates, most sources are later.

Individual works from the group are preserved in dozens of eighteenth-century manuscripts, but only one source contains more than three of them,[1] and the number of copies preserving individual pieces varies widely. This suggests that although certain toccatas were fairly well known during Bach's lifetime, others remained obscure. Two toccatas may have existed in separate manuscript copies by Heinrich Nicolaus Gerber, one of Bach's pupils from the early Leipzig years.[2] But Forkel (1802, 57; NBR, 469) mentioned them only in passing among Bach's "youthful efforts" (*Jugendübungen*), perhaps reflecting a tradition in the Bach circle that the toccatas were outmoded, or early experiments.

During the early Baroque, Frescobaldi, Froberger, and others used the word *toccata* for relatively extensive pieces that often combined an improvisatory introduction with one or more contrapuntal passages. But the genre was never strictly defined, and later toccatas, in both Italy and Germany, are often short, preludial pieces, like those of Pachelbel (which could have been used to introduce separate fugues or other compositions). Bach's toccatas are closer to a small group of north-German toccatas, especially one by Reinken (preserved in ABB), that resemble the early-Baroque type in being composed of distinct contrasting sections. Like the sonatas and other pieces considered in chapter 6, these toccatas bear a family resemblance to the *praeludium* and other quasi-improvisational genres cultivated by German organists during the seventeenth and early eighteenth centuries. But whereas the *praeludium* was evolving toward a well-defined two-movement form—what we call the "prelude and fugue"—for Bach the word *toccata* evidently continued to refer to a more diverse, heterogeneous succession of sections, some of which constitute self-sufficient movements, others serving as bridges or transitions.

Bach's toccatas are strong works, each with a distinctive design. All close with fugues, and all but one opens with an improvisatory prelude. Three include movements not in the tonic; in the Toccata in D the modulatory bridges connecting the more self-contained sections are particularly dramatic. In these bridge passages, and to a lesser degree in those of the other toccatas, one senses a kinship with recitative: melodic lines are fragmented by rests and chromatic motion, and declamatory motives alternate with sudden bursts of figuration and tremolos.[3]

The toccatas are more mature compositions than those discussed in chapters 4–6, but there are no firm guidelines for dating them. The early version of the D-Major Toccata is preserved in MM and could be dated around 1707; the toccatas in F♯ minor, C minor, and G appear in ABB and are therefore probably a bit later. These three works give an impression of greater fluency, but, like the superficial hints of concerto style in the G-Major Toccata, this is hardly sufficient to place them in a precise timeframe, especially in view of the presence of features familiar from seventeenth-century organ compositions. The most one can say for sure is that the seven works were completed before the end of Bach's Weimar period and might have been all drafted before his arrival there.

At least two works, those in D (BWV 912) and D minor (BWV 913), survive in distinct early versions, raising the possibility that Bach only revised these pieces during his Weimar years, as he presumably did BWV 535, 951, and other early compositions. The revision of the two toccatas did not affect the large structure of either work. But it included the insertion of brief passages as well as additional melodic embellishment, altered figuration, and refinements of voice leading. It has been supposed that the written-out embellishment in the slow sections was intended to make the music more idiomatic to the harpsichord (as opposed to the organ), and the unadorned four-part writing of the adagio in the early version of BWV 913 indeed sounds lame on a stringed keyboard instrument when played literally. But it is unlikely that Bach expected such notation to be interpreted as is, and the written-out embellishments might have been for the benefit of pupils (as suggested by Stauffer 1980, 170–1). Students today would find it instructive to practice the simpler early version when first learning the piece, for the embellishments of the later version obscure the outlines of the voice leading, and they encourage a slower tempo than is necessary.[4]

The other toccatas also show traces of revision, but whether by Bach is uncertain. Manuscripts by Walther, Preller, and Johann Christoph Bach, among others, give extra ornaments and other details, in particular for the slow movement of the Toccata in G. But some of these ornaments are stylistically dubious, and none can be unequivocally traced to Bach. More puzzling is the fugue of the E-Minor Toccata, which not only exists in a distinct, somewhat shorter version but also shares extensive portions with a work in the same key preserved anonymously in an Italian manuscript. These have been taken as signs of revision and borrowing by Bach, yet the most recent editor of the work argues that the alternate versions of the movement are later reworkings by other hands.

Another recurring question is that of instrumental medium. The opening sections of most of the toccatas contain monophonic solos in the bass as well as the treble that would be more forceful if played with the mixtures and powerful sixteen- and four-foot manual stops of an organ. Much figuration elsewhere is equally reminiscent of organ music. Although the harpsichord is appropriate for the arpeggiando bridge passages in the works in D minor, F♯ minor, and E minor, and for the lute-like opening of the latter, such writing hardly rules out use of the organ, which Bach would use at Leipzig as a substitute for the lute (or harpsichord) obbligato in the Saint John Passion. Yet, although Marshall (1986) and others have argued that they are organ works, the *manualiter* toccatas do not pose the practical problems for harpsichord performance presented by some earlier pieces. They lack the wide spacings and sustained pedal-points that would make organ performance clearly preferable, and Gerber's copy of the G-Major Toccata called expressly for *clavecin*. The likelihood that Bach and other players often practiced organ music on clavichords and harpsichords would have encouraged flexibility in the assignment of pieces to one medium or the other. But the period that saw the composition and polishing of the toccatas may also have been the one in which Bach learned to differentiate between the capabilities of the various keyboard instruments, knowledge later emphasized by Forkel. In short, the toccatas are probably best viewed as harpsichord pieces, but ones that imitate organ style.

The toccatas present difficult problems for editors. The edition in NBA V/9.1 is more reliable and draws on a far more complete understanding of the sources than anything previous. But many of its alternative readings (on *ossia* staves, in footnotes, and in an *Anhang*) are likely to be additions by other musicians or to derive from copyists' misreadings of a heavily revised autograph.[5]

Toccata in F♯ Minor BWV 910

Chief sources: ABB (no. 20; Johann Christoph Bach); P 801 (Walther). *Additional sources*: B Br II 4093 (Fétis 2960); P 804/47; P 228 (title annotation by C. P. E. Bach); P 287/9 (J. F. Hering); P 597/4 (S. Hering); B Br Fétis 7327 C Mus. 7 (J. L. Krebs); LEm ms. 8 (Preller); P 419 (Kittel); AmB 546 (Anon. 401, owned by Kirnberger); LEm Poel. 26 (Penzel, final fugue only).

The toccatas in F♯ minor, C minor, and G fall close to one another in ABB, where they rank among the most important of the pieces that Bach evidently gave to his older brother.[6] Because the chronology of the toccatas is not established, and Bach himself is not known to have ordered them in any way, it is most convenient to follow the BWV ordering, which although arbitrary does start with the work most commonly encountered in the sources. This is also the work that comes first in the Brussels manuscript, the only source to give all seven toccatas.[7] As shown by the above listing of sources (by no means complete), the work was widely distributed, preserved in manuscripts by many of the most important Bach copyists, but not his Leipzig pupils. Any of the *manualiter* toccatas would have given keyboard players who lacked advanced pedal technique the opportunity to play a virtuoso work reminiscent of the Weimar masterworks for organ. BWV 910, through its exotic key and the presence of two fugues—one on a chromatic subject (the descending hexachord)—would have been especially attractive to serious musicians.

Schmieder, perhaps in view of the impressive proportions, the challenging key, and the capable handling of chromaticism, at first (1950) proposed a relatively late date for this work and for the Toccata in C Minor. But the suggestion of a Cöthen origin for both pieces seems impossible, and not only in light of the inclusion of BWV 910 in ABB and P 801. The piece relies on the same archaic formal principles as do Bach's earlier multisectional works, now carried out at greater length. And therein lies a problem for all the toccatas, especially the three longest ones—those in D minor, C minor, and F♯ minor. All three tend toward excess, as in the arpeggiando passage connecting the two fugues of BWV 910, where the same figure is used twenty-one times to set forth a not especially compelling series of harmonies (see Example. 7.1). Individually, the two fugues are not especially long, and both show signs of tonal planning, as in the move to the relative major shortly after the center of the second fugue. Yet the second fugue goes to no other major keys, and there is but one further modulation to a major key (also to A) in the first fugue. Hence, the work as a whole has the same monochrome quality as the "Albinoni" Fugue BWV 951 and other early minor-key works. Also like the "Albinoni" fugue, the toccatas generally require slower tempos than do later works using similar notation. Even in the presto of BWV 910, the dense counterpoint and chromaticism force the sixteenths to go more slowly than in Bach's later works.

In this light, it is unclear whether the piece is helped or hindered by the similarity between the chromatic subject of the final fugue and that of the adagio that follows the opening prelude. The adagio is one of several slow imitative passages in the toccatas comparable to the motet-like first fugue in the Sonata BWV 963 or the Capriccio BWV 992. The present adagio is the most chromatic and the most heavily embellished of these three passages. Many of the ornaments and embellishments might be later additions, as in the corresponding movement in the D-Minor Toccata. Although they intensify an already expressive movement, they should not weigh down the tempo or obscure the underlying rhythm, which seems to be that of a sarabande.

The tempo marking of the first fugue—*presto e staccato*—is probably best interpreted as "lively and separated," the last word referring to the eighth notes of the subject. Both *presto* and *staccato* are common in the Italian concerto repertory, where *presto* is hardly distinguishable from later *allegro* as an all-purpose designation for a quick movement. *Staccato* implies articulate but not necessarily abrupt playing, like the similar term *spiccato* (used in the first movement of the oboe concerto by Alessandro Marcello that Bach transcribed as BWV 974). The combination of the two terms implies a more vehement manner of performance than would otherwise be the case—faster and more emphatically articulated. But exaggerated accentuation of each eighth would grow tiresome, and too rapid a tempo would turn the fugue into a blur—not that players will want to do that, given the difficulty of this section.

The fugue derives its energy not from the tempo but from the character of its subject, which is shorter and simpler than in many other early Bach fugues. The counterpoint too is fluent but simple, often consisting of essentially little more than parallel thirds or sixths that accompany the first part of the subject, a descending staccato scale in eighth notes. The episodes—at mm. 57, 67, and 80b—use an old-fashioned motive in sixteenths, which is combined contrapuntally with fragments of the scale motive in the third episode. The combination effects an intensification, heightened by its coinciding with a sequence that momentarily shifts the meter from common time to 3/4 (mm. 83–6). A few measures later the opening motive of the subject enters in a brief canon in the outer voices, marking the fugue's most remote modulation (D♯ minor, m. 91). But despite these efforts to produce a sense of accumulating tension, the fugue perhaps runs on for too long without letting up. The problem, if it is one, is not solved by increasing the tempo; it might even be alleviated by adopting a tempo slow enough to permit expressive rhythmic nuance.

After the fugue, the arpeggiando bridge follows somewhat awkwardly, even though the opening harmony (D♯⁷) is prepared by the cadence on F♯ major. One might favor the contrast afforded by shifting to a quieter manual, yet the full texture at the end of the section points against this, as does the flourish inserted just before it in three sources, presumably to ease the transition.[8] The

Example 7.1 Toccata in F♯ Minor BWV 910: bass line underlying mm. 108–31.

passage grows long, but there is no point in trying to hurry through its measured modulations, which lack clear direction until the bass begins a stepwise ascent halfway through (Example. 7.1).

The closing fugue is the climax of the work, not because it is more brilliant than the first fugue but because it is more expressive. In addition, it employs four instead of three voices, at least from m. 155 onward. Despite the notation in 6/8, its rhythm is that of the chaconne, which in French examples did not necessarily have a ground bass but did normally open on the second beat of a triple measure. Bach might have derived the idea of a fugue in chaconne rhythm from Keiser, whose Hamburg opera overtures include similar sections.[9] The present fugue has not only the rhythm but the refined grandeur and pathos of the greatest French chaconnes; the subject begins on the second eighth of the measure and makes its chromatic steps on the second note of each group of three eighths.

This rhythm calls to mind related works from Bach's Weimar period: the first chorus from the cantata *Weinen, Klagen, Sorgen, Zagen* BWV 12, later used in the B-Minor Mass, and the great organ Passacaglia BWV 582, which concludes in a fugue. The ground bass in BWV 12 is practically identical to the subject of the present fugue, whose second countersubject also appears in the cantata.[10] Cantata no. 12 was first performed April 22, 1714, and perhaps the toccata is from that time as well. Its chromatic density has been taken as a sign of a relatively late date (e.g., by Marshall 1986, 228); whether or not this is true, the rich detail of its chromatic voice leading makes the final fugue one of the most impressive single movements in the toccatas.

Toccata in C Minor, BWV 911

Chief sources: ABB (no. 25; Johann Christoph Bach); LEm ms. 8 (Preller); B Br II 4093 (Fétis 2960).

Both its BWV number and its position in many editions imply that the Toccata in C Minor is a companion to the one in F♯ minor. But there is little reason to consider them related in any special way, and the C-Minor Toccata, if not actually earlier, is less mature in style, its counterpoint simpler (confined to two parts for long stretches) and the range of its modulations more restricted. It also follows a different plan: after a prelude and another motet-like adagio comes a single very long fugue. The toccata shows some of the best aspects of Bach's early style—emphatic musical rhetoric, economical and intensive use of thematic material, inventive keyboard scoring. Yet the first two of these traits work against the success of the piece, for the fugue develops too limited a range of ideas for too long, even if its plan is original and its dimensions impressive.

One problem for the fugue is the somewhat ponderous character of its rhetoric. The opening figure in the subject is immediately repeated after a short rest, a familiar rhetorical gesture. But the figure that is repeated is itself somewhat repetitious, containing two downward arpeggiations of the C-minor triad, and in the course of the fugue it can grow tiresome. Another favorite rhetorical device occurs in several "obstinate" repetitions, as at mm. 138–40, which echo the opening of the Capriccio BWV 992. Although the passage is touchingly sweet in the midst of so much C minor—it connects the only two entries of the subject in major keys—it lacks a strong organic connection to the surrounding material. Elsewhere, the absence of significant contrast in key, texture, or motive leaves the fugue rather colorless, despite some imaginative figuration. For example, m. 69 introduces a countersubject that begins in the soprano and then migrates into the tenor, in the process crossing the subject and spanning more than three octaves (c′′′ to G). Related effects occur in mm. 115b–117a, where the countersubject is divided between soprano and bass, and in mm. 162b–164a, where the two opening gestures of the subject itself are similarly divided between two voices (and registers).

Like the Capriccio in E (BWV 993), which it resembles in many respects, the fugue makes gestures toward concerto style in its soloistic episodes and almost constant pulsation in small note values (sixteenths). But the sixteenths cannot flow as quickly as in more up-to-date Italianate pieces (e.g., the fugue of BWV 944), and a restrained tempo is necessary to accommodate the *figura corta* (sixteenth plus two thirty-seconds) first heard at m. 82b. The latter is introduced in an improvisatory passage placed about a third of the way into the movement, after a cadence in the tonic (m. 80b). This is an odd place for a cadenza, and one wonders if the piece did not originally end around here, perhaps after a short coda in place of the present cadence to the dominant (m. 85b). When the piece starts up again, it is now a double fugue (in the sense that a new countersubject is introduced together with the subject). Only beyond this point do expositions alternate with long sequential episodes (mm. 109–15a, 127–33a, 147–52a, 157b–62a). These episodes make increasing use of *figure corte*, hence intensifying the motion. But the conclusion, unlike that of BWV 910, is by way of a formulaic coda: a deceptive cadence to $IV^{6/4}$ (also heard in BWV 915), followed by *presto* sextuplets that recall the *presto* septuplets of BWV 967.[11]

Toccata in D, BWV 912

Early version (BWV 912a): *Sources*: MM (no. 28; Johann Christoph Bach); P 804/50. *Editions*: Hill (1991); NBA V/9.1.
Later version: *Chief sources*: B Br II 4093 (Fétis 2960); LEm ms. 8 (without the final fugue).

Perhaps the most successful of the toccatas is the one in D, not on the strength of any single section but because of its uniquely effective overall design, which has at the center a fugue in the relatively remote key of F♯ minor. The general plan is similar to that of the Sonata in D (BWV 963), but the toccata, apart from being on a larger scale, adds a free allegro after the opening section. Similarities between the toccata and the organ praeludium in the same key (BWV 532) have also been noted (e.g., by Williams 2003, 41). Not only do both works open with comparable figuration, but they share an unusual emphasis on the mediant (F♯ minor) and on remote "sharp" keys in general.[12]

From the outset, the toccata shows such exuberance that one may not notice the logic with which the initial upward scale is extended to two octaves (m. 6), then inverted (m. 9). Both the scales and the arresting tremolo figure (m. 8) return in later bridge passages, so these are more than mere formulas.[13] Even the ascending arpeggio at the very end of the toccata can be heard as echoing the broken-chord figure in the second half of each of mm. 1–5. This connection is particularly audible if one retains the ties that were originally present in the opening measures; their absence in the later version might be due simply to copyists' misunderstanding of notation that was somehow abbreviated or unclear.[14] Another echo of this figure occurs at the beginning of the second bridge (m. 111b).[15]

The allegro is, like the corresponding section in the G-Minor Toccata, a rondo-like movement that might have been inspired by the allegros of Italian solo concertos, inasmuch as some of the episodes use arpeggiated passagework. But both the main theme and the "solo" figuration are treated in imitation (or rather are exchanged between treble and bass), and the style closely resembles that of other early Bach keyboard works, especially the Sonata BWV 967. The allegro provides the first hints of the toccata's special preoccupation with "sharp" minor keys, modulating several times to F♯ minor but never remaining there for long.

The decisive move occurs in the first of two adagio transitions, when descending scales twice interrupt the recitative-like writing (mm. 75–6). The first fugue, which follows, is unexpectedly quiet and understated for a movement in F♯ minor, and apart from its considerable chromaticism it has little in common with the fugues in the same key in BWV 910. Like the "Corelli" fugue for organ BWV 579, it announces subject and first countersubject jointly at the beginning.

Actually there are two countersubjects, which are combined with the subject in five of the six possible permutations. The subject enters only six times in all, but the fugue is neatly articulated into three expositions. These alternate with two short episodes (at mm. 89 and 100, respectively), giving the fugue a pleasant symmetry.

The indication *con discrezione* occurs at m. 111 only in the later version, where, together with the added fermata, it assures the player that this is indeed the beginning of a new, transitional section. Froberger, Kuhnau, and other German writers use the word *discrezione* and its cognates to call for rhythmically free performance (see Schott 1998, 102–4). It is thus equivalent to *adagio* as used in many Italian works. Here the word could be interpreted as signifying a gradual slowing down, the fermatas signifying only a momentary dwelling on the notes that bear them, so that only by m. 114 are we clearly back in the improvisatory adagio mode. The dissolution of the fugue into this echo of the introduction, which is then interrupted by several bursts of scalar figuration, makes this bridge section the more dramatic one. Especially remarkable is the circuitous path back to D major, which is reached only after a long feint toward E minor, including a short cadenza on its submediant (C, in mm. 118–9). By dwelling on this and other indirectly related harmonies, the passage prolongs the excursion through dark minor keys and withholds the return to D major, creating a sense of suspense, even mystery; Bach would further exploit this device in the Chromatic Fantasia. The cadenzas are already present in the early version and must have been part of Bach's original, inspired conception of the passage.

The toccata closes with what is in principle a fugue, though it is governed more by harmony than by counterpoint. The subject is little more than an oscillation between two thirds that suggest tonic and dominant, respectively (d′/f♯′ and c♯′/e′). The harmonic basis of the counterpoint is reminiscent of the "fugue" in the Praeludium BWV 922. So too is the demonic affect arising from the perpetual motion in triplet sixteenths, although the figuration has parallels elsewhere (e.g., Buxtehude's C-Major Fugue BuxWV 174, no. 26 in ABB). The surface motion in thirds is the same that has been heard in the tremolos of mm. 78 and 114, which therefore are not mere novelties.[16]

Unusual for this period is the sudden shift from a major key to its parallel minor, which happens three times in the course of the final fugue: in E (m. 201), C♯ (m. 220), and finally the tonic (m. 261). The toccata's obsession with remote "sharp" keys resurfaces in the last third of this section, which opens with a statement of the subject in the bass—unaccompanied—in C♯ minor (v of iii) at m. 220. Shortly afterward the fugue reaches the most remote key of the entire toccata, G♯ minor (m. 227), then dissolves into harmonically inspired figuration. In the revised version, this passage culminates in a flurry of thirty-seconds, which in a later work would doubtless have led straight into the final cadence. Instead the toccata ends by reverting briefly to adagio style for an old-fashioned cadence in full harmony. Although perhaps disappointing by later standards, this permits one last reference to the beginning of the piece. BWV 915 accomplishes the same thing through a literal restatement; here it involves the subtler motivic echo mentioned earlier, as well as a harmonic one: the secondary dominant on G♯ in the penultimate bar recalls m. 8. The result is not only the most dramatic but the most organically unified of the toccatas.

The early version (BWV 912a) possesses all the salient features of the later one, the most important differences being the simpler figuration in the second adagio and at the end of the last fugue. Only the later version has the tremolos written out in the adagios, but both versions have them in the opening section, and MM indicates them in the first adagio through the abbreviations *trem* (m. 68) and *tr* (mm. 69 and 70). The parallel fifths in mm. 30 and 55 are avoided in the sources of the early version, at least on paper, by voice crossing (e.g., tenor leaps b–f♯´ in m. 30).[17]

Toccata in D Minor BWV 913

> Early version: *Sole source*: print (Leipzig: Hoffmeister und Kühnel, 1801).
> *Edition*: NBA V/9.1
> Later version: *Chief sources*: P 281 (Weimar copyist); LEm ms. 8 (Preller).

The D-Minor Toccata may be the most popular of the seven, thanks to its relatively transparent textures, which make it easier to play than the others. It is also arguably the most polished, if not the most ambitious or the most impressive, and this might be why it reportedly bore a dedication to Bach's "most dear brother" Christoph in a lost manuscript.[18] Thus, like the Capriccio BWV 993, which was ostensibly "in honor" of the Ohrdruf Bach, BWV 913 might have been presented to him in a special fair-copy autograph, explaining its absence from MM and ABB. The quasi-pedaliter texture of mm. 8–15, which can be played *manualiter* but invites the use of pedals if available, also recalls BWV 993 and 989, special pieces seemingly connected with Bach's older brother (Bach returned to this type of writing at the end of the Chromatic Fantasia BWV 903/1). The work appears in several sources as *Toccata prima*, but the numbering does not necessarily stem from Bach, and none of the other toccatas is reliably labeled *Toccata seconda*. BWV 913 was, however, the first of the toccatas to reach print, in 1801, albeit in the early version BWV 913a. The publisher Kühnel at one point owned MM and may have possessed other Bach manuscripts as well (Schulze 1984a, 39–41).

The design is similar to that of the Toccata in F♯ Minor, even to the point of including a long sequence of apreggiando figuration in the second adagio. But the present work avoids the chromaticism of the F♯-minor toccata, and its fugues are characterized by smooth sequences, many of them incorporating

Corelliesque chains of suspensions. Hence the style is closer to the new Italian sonata and concerto, although this does not necessarily have any bearing on the date. The introduction alludes to the *pedaliter* prelude and fugue, with its bass solos and the pedal points of mm. 8–11. It also includes a measure of figuration virtually identical to one in the Aria variata, but the toccata avoids the wide spacings found between bass and tenor in that work.[19]

Only a short rest separates the introduction from a passage in four-part motet style (m. 15b), corresponding with the adagio found at this point in several other toccatas. There is no imitative subject as such, but the passage is held together by its steady descending sequences, suspensions, and "sigh" figures, all favorite expressive devices in Bach's early works. A difficulty here is to project the meter: the suspensions are more expressive if the dissonances are heard as clearly falling on the strong beats, an effect helped by dwelling on the latter.

The following fugal section is labeled in the manuscripts with the word *Thema*, possibly just an equivalent for *Fuga* but perhaps referring specifically to the subject and maybe even implying that the latter was borrowed from another piece. The subject, whether considered to extend for two measures or just one, is little more than a concatenation of common formulas, recalling in this regard the fugue BWV 955. Essentially the same motivic ideas form the basis of the second fugal section, making the work a "variation" toccata. But neither imitative section is a fugue in the usual sense. The first begins like Bach's later inventions with the subject imitated in the tonic. The final section opens with a version of the same subject combined with a countersubject; the two ideas are immediately repeated in inverted counterpoint. This procedure, too, is employed in some of the inventions. As the latter were apparently written in connection with Bach's instruction of his son Wilhelm Friedemann, they might have reflected his tinkering with subjects during his own studies.

Both imitative sections have the rondo-like structure of some other early fugues. One might complain of the somewhat facile sequences, but these occur in other early works as well, such as the organ fugue in G minor BWV 578, and they are part of a successful emulation of Italian violin style. The first fugue reverts to a more rhetorical German style in its coda, which opens with "obstinate" repetitions of a motive reminiscent of seventeenth-century organ music (mm. 111ff.). The final fugue also flirts with the idea of a free close, falling into arpeggiated figuration unrelated to the theme as it approaches the end (m. 271). But the subject returns, and the fugue ends with one of the most successful (and exciting) closing phrases in any of Bach's earlier *manualiter* works, based on an ascending sequence that Bach might have taken from the first allemande of Reinken's *Hortus musicus* (Example 7.2).[20] The toccata concludes with an echo; the last two measures lack a dynamic indication, but the piano marking implied here could be found in comparable ending phrases in Corelli's opp. 5 and 6.

Example 7.2 Toccata in D Minor BWV 913, mm. 291–3; (a) early version (BWV 913a); (b) later version.

As in BWV 912, the early version differs above all in the less embellished form of the first adagio. The later version makes numerous small alterations in the two fugues, the first of which has an extra two-measure phrase (mm. 50–1). Both versions have been printed with a one-flat key signature, but the latter is absent from most of the manuscript sources and quite properly has been removed in NBA V/9.1.

Some details in the early version could be products of anachronistic editing in its only source, an early nineteenth-century print: meaningless discrepancies within sequences at mm. 19 and 206, the low D in the last measure, naturals on f´´ in mm. 11–2 and on B in m. 46, flats on b´ and B in the second beat of m. 99, and b♮´ (not flat) in m. 137.

Toccata in E Minor BWV 914

Chief sources: copy by H. N. Gerber (see Wiemer 1987); B Br II 4093 (Fétis 2960); P 213 (Johann Christian Westphal, completion of a partial copy by L. A. C. Hopff = Anon. 305).

The understated opening of BWV 914 lacks the *passaggi* present in the other toccatas, but next to BWV 912 it is the most satisfying of the seven works, if not the most ambitious or virtuosic. The biggest movement is the concluding fugue, which is preceded by a short introduction, a fugal allegro, and a rhapsodic adagio; many copies give the fugue alone, in a somewhat shorter form usually seen as an early version.

The low tessitura and light texture of the introduction lead one to wonder whether it was originally for lute, although the initial four-note motive is equally idiomatic for solo pedals. The following section resembles the motet-like adagios of several other toccatas, but it is labeled *Un poco allegro* (a warning against too

Example 7.3 Toccata in E Minor BWV 914: bass line underlying mm. 42–62.

slow a tempo?) and lacks the florid embellishment of some corresponding move-ments.[21] It is a fine double fugue, despite ending a bit abruptly just after the final entry (in the bass). One subject opens with an expressive rising half step; both subjects contain suspensions, which are developed in the brief episodes.

In Gerber's copy the adagio bears the additional title *Praeludium*, which led Wiemer (1987, 31) to suggest that this, together with the closing fugue, once formed an independent piece. This section differs in style from the adagios oc-cupying analogous positions in the other toccatas, for nearly every harmony is composed out through extended figures that amount almost to small cadenzas. Although seemingly a free improvisation, the greater part of the adagio is built over a simple linear bass line (Example. 7.3), a device recurring in later pieces like the prelude in E minor from WTC1. Eventually the writing coalesces into more regular figuration, still harmonic in inspiration but using a propulsive figure found also in BWV 922.[22]

The brilliant closing fugue in three parts became one of the more mysteri-ous pieces in the Bach canon with the discovery of an anonymous fugue that is nearly identical to the present one for a substantial number of measures.[23] Bach's borrowings in other Italian-inspired fugues (BWV 579, 950–1, etc.) are limited mainly to the subjects. Here Bach's opening and closing expositions are parallel to the analogous sections of the anonymous fugue, which also seems to be the source for two central expository passages (Example 7.4).

The Naples manuscript that preserves the anonymous fugue bears a "blanket" attribution to Benedetto Marcello, but, as Selfridge-Field (1990, 327) observes, the subject of the fugue is "not characteristic of Marcello's keyboard music." The fugue subject in BWV 914 leaves a "clear north-German impression" on the most recent editor (NBA V/9.1, 98), but this is less clear in the Naples version. There the opening figure employs violinistic barriolage, repeating b´ on each offbeat, in place of a Germanic zigzag pattern. Since the Naples manuscript also preserves pieces by Durante and Platti—both active in Germany after the time of Bach's toccatas—the possibility of a borrowing from Bach, rather than the reverse, can-not be ruled out. A motivically irrelevant cadence formula (mm. 39b–40a) in the style of Hasse sounds like a later intrusion, perhaps by a Neapolitan composer

Example 7.4 (a) Fugue in E Minor from Naples, Biblioteca del Conservatorio, Ms. 5327, fols. 46v–49r, mm. 1–4 and 47–9; (b) Toccata in E Minor BWV 914: mm. 71–4 and 125–7.

such as Durante, as does a lengthy episode involving repeated hand crossings. On the other hand, that Bach might have borrowed very substantially from an existing fugue is not out of the question. Within the Pachelbel tradition there are apparent instances of fugues by one composer being reworked by another, whether in a few details or at larger levels (see, e.g., Belotti 2001, 12–4). One can imagine Bach reworking a flashy virtuoso piece encountered within the same Italian repertory as the two "Polaroli" fugues in ABB. The latter works show that music by southern virtuosos was indeed circulating in Germany during Bach's early years.

The simplistic hand crossings of the Italian fugue might have dismayed members of the Pachelbel school, but can one be sure that passages of this type did not occur in Italian keyboard music "before the second half of the 1720s" (NBA V/9.1, KB, 98)? Virtuosos would not have published trade secrets early in their careers, yet they must have known of such things long before they appeared in print, as in Domenico Scarlatti's *Essercizi* of 1739 or Durante's 1747 sonatas. If he indeed encountered it in the anonymous fugue, Bach kept this particular trick to himself for decades before finding a way to work it into music he was not ashamed to publish as his own (in the First Partita, his Opus 1).

If Bach did borrow directly and liberally from the anonymous piece, he nevertheless made characteristic alterations. Bach's version of the subject is more refined but flows a little less easily because of the implied passing dissonances (escape tones). Everywhere, in fact, Bach's fugue has somewhat more complex readings, as in the interpolation of rests to avoid some barely audible parallel octaves (Example 7.4a, mm. 48–9). Still, in the passages common to the two fugues, the voices accompanying the subject remain somewhat perfunctory. Bach's episodes are distinctly richer in harmonic implications than are the expository passages, even though the first episode (mm. 90b–94) retains a motive taken directly from Italian violin style (and from m. 2 of the subject). It is at this point that Bach's fugue diverges from the one in Naples; the latter's long central episode is dominated by a banal sequence involving repeated hand crossing, a technique that Bach would never incorporate into a fugue except in the fragmentary BWV 906/2.

As in many such cases, it is possible that both extant pieces derive from a lost original. Traces of the latter have been seen in a shorter version of Bach's fugue that ends five measures earlier, just after the final entry of the subject in the bass—the same type of ending seen in the toccata's first fugue. The view that this version is a later abbreviation (NBA 9.1, KB, 97) may not be sufficient to account for numerous other variants. All stylistically plausible, these point to an earlier state of the piece closer to the Naples fugue in some details.[24] Although the problem must remain unresolved, in its familiar version the fugue, and the toccata as a whole, is one of Bach's most successful early essays in the Italianate style also seen in BWV 913.

Toccata in G Minor BWV 915

Sources: P 1082 (Preller); B Br II 4093 (Fétis 2960).

Despite its lively allegro and two expressively embellished adagios, the G-Minor Toccata has always been less popular than the others, perhaps because of its long fugue, which is extremely awkward to play. Only two manuscript copies survive, both relatively late and inaccurate;[25] Preller even left out a measure of the subject at the opening of the fugue, an error perpetuated in some nineteenth-century editions. Bach's obituary listed only six, not seven, "clavier" toccatas (BD 3:86 [item 666]/NBR, 304); if Bach's own score of this work had been lost, this would explain its being overlooked by copyists and eulogists. Parallels have been drawn to works by Reinken, especially in the lengthy fugue on a gigue-like subject. But, like the apparent quotation near the end of BWV 913, the similarities are more in the nature of common formulas than the distinct modeling seen in the fugue and sonatas derived from Reinken's *Hortus musicus*.

This work centers on two main sections, an allegro in B♭ and a closing fugue. But the most striking aspect of its plan is the recurrence of the opening flourish at the very end, giving the toccata the most literal example of formal closure in Bach's works of this type.[26] The actual amount of material that returns is very little, yet the gesture is striking as it includes a deceptive cadence to a full-voiced $IV^{6/4}$ chord (m. 5). This cadence has further echoes near the ends of the two adagios (mm. 16, 75); like the motivic connections that were observed in BWV 912, these reinforce the unity of the toccata.

As in BWV 910, the first adagio resembles a sarabande. But it is shorter, and most of it is the free elaboration of a sequence comprised of $V^{6/4/2}–I^6$ progressions in D minor (mm. 8–9), C minor (10–11), G minor (12), and F (13–14). The allegro, like that of the Toccata in D, must have been inspired by Italian style, coming somewhat closer to what we recognize as concerto-ritornello form thanks to the clearer imitation of solo/tutti contrasts. These are accomplished through variations in texture and a couple of piano/forte alternations. Yet the underlying texture is, as in BWV 912, invertible two-part counterpoint; here the more important of the two subjects is the one stated at initially in the bass. The idea of working out one or two simple subjects is not so different from that seen in the "fugues" of BWV 913, although the predominance of *figure corte* and the absence of suspensions make the present movement more Germanic. Since it is in B♭, a third away from the tonic, its function within the plan of the work resembles that of the central fugue in BWV 912. But the relative major is less remote tonally than the mediant, and the transition passages on either side of it are less dramatic; the allegro ends by returning to G minor via a single deceptive cadence (mm. 67–8).

The fugue, alone of those in the toccatas, makes a show of using the type of strict counterpoint seen previously in BWV 896 and 949. It is in four parts, with a regular countersubject, and both subject and countersubject are used in inversion (first at m. 99).[27] The subject contains an ascending sequence, and this, when combined with the driving triplets of the countersubject, generates considerable excitement in the first exposition.[28] But the subject also contains an old-fashioned rhetorical "iteration"—it closes with a three-fold statement of a simple turning motive—and this repetitiveness may be one reason the remainder of the fugue fails to sustain the initial excitement. The gigue rhythm, although maintained steadily for 111 measures, is not in itself dull; Bach would write many equally long works in homogeneous rhythmic textures. But, as in the gigue of BWV 965, the inversion of the subject and the permutations of the two subjects, even the occasional episodes, do not provide sufficient variety. Nor is the inversion of the subject set out in its own distinctly articulated exposition or systematically combined with the upright version, as Bach might have done in a later work.[29]

Hence, as in the fugue of the C-Minor Toccata, the overall impression is somewhat diffuse, despite clear evidence of tonal planning: a move toward the subdominant that begins near the midpoint of the fugue (m. 129) includes two entries in a major key (E♭). The same section includes a momentary softening of the texture into parallel thirds in the first of two brief episodes (mm. 150–3); this provides relief from the prevailing counterpoint (compare mm. 139–41 in the C-minor work). After moving as far to the subdominant side as F minor (iv of iv, m. 164b), the fugue re-establishes the tonic with a bass entry (m. 176), in a passage that recovers some of the urgency of the opening exposition.[30]

NBA V/9.1 shows Preller's later embellishments for the first adagio on *ossia* staves (mm. 7, 17) , but even the main text here and in the second adagio includes ornaments possibly added by someone other than Bach. Footnotes in the same edition show less ornate readings from the Brussels manuscript, and these are probably closer to Bach's original even if the copyist did not always give them correctly (e.g., ties omitted in mm. 14 and 72, g′ for b♭′ on the third beat of m. 14).

Toccata in G, BWV 916

Chief sources ABB (no. 27; mostly Johann Christoph Bach); P 281 (Weimar copyist).

The bright G-major tonality, unclouded by excursions to remote minor keys, and its clear three-movement form distinguish BWV 916 from the other toccatas. In the lost Gerber copy reported in BG 36 it was called *Concerto seu Toccata pour le Clavecin* (Concerto or Toccata for Harpsichord). As in the Toccata, Adagio, and Fugue for organ BWV 564, the plan does bear a general resemblance to that of an Italian concerto, and Wollny (2002, 246) dates the two chief sources to around 1713, Bach's supposed year of concertos (see chap. 8). But even if Bach was consciously borrowing an Italian form, he filled it with detail from the German keyboard tradition and, as in the other toccatas, reserved the weightiest movement (the fugue) for last. Use of the harpsichord, as indicated by Gerber, seems entirely appropriate, although as in the other toccatas there is nothing that would entirely rule out the organ.[31]

Like BWV 912, the piece starts out with a scale, here worked into a full-length allegro movement. The opening phrase serves somewhat like a ritornello, alternating with "solo" episodes and articulating landmarks in a cogent tonal design. Similar things have been pointed out (Hill, 1995) in works by older Italian contemporaries, especially Torelli. Yet the short-winded phrases and the opening flourish on the tonic triad belong to the German toccata or *praeludium*. Moreover, despite the massive chords in its third and fourth measures, the "ritornello" is too short to provide closure at the end of the movement, which therefore concludes with a free codetta in German organ style.

The adagio has much in common with corresponding passages in the other toccatas, adopting their freely imitative style as well as Italianate melodic embellishment. But the latter is concentrated in the first few measures, after which the movement settles into motet style. The subject, first recognizable with the alto entry (upbeat to m. 61), emerges through a sort of de-embellishment of the previous soprano phrase (m. 60), itself a variation of the opening measure. One wonders whether the movement originally used a simpler form of the theme throughout; conversely, the embellished melodic style of the opening phrases might have continued beyond m. 65, as indeed it does in Preller's copy (LEm, ms. 7). Perhaps Bach envisioned Italianate embellishment extending to every entry of the subject throughout the movement, as in the adagio of the First Brandenburg Concerto, which could date from almost the same time. But even Preller's copy eventually settles into plainer style, and the gradual shift from embellished adagio to walking andante seems essential to the plan of the movement. It is difficult to find a single suitable tempo; some flexibility is doubtless appropriate, although the adagio should not go so slowly as to render the written-out embellishements lifeless. Simple ornaments can be applied throughout the movement; ABB suggests some possibilities, although as usual some of Johann Christoph Bach's ornament signs are doubtful.[32]

The fugue is in three parts. Although its subject includes the skipping rhythm of a French *canarie* (gigue), its running sixteenths bring it close to the type of gigue found in the suite BWV 996. The impressive design is built around expositions in minor keys at mm. 114 (E minor) and 142 (A minor), that is, one-third and two-thirds of the way through, respectively. Yet, as in the other toccatas, the counterpoint is occasionally awkward to play, and there may be insufficient variety. Unlike BWV 954 and other pieces, in which repeated scale figures are reserved for crucial or climactic moments, this fugue is saturated with them, thanks to their presence within the subject. These scales echo the opening of the toccata, but, having found that the opening of the subject makes a fine stretto, Bach introduces similar strettos in three of the four main episodes (mm. 96, 112, and 149). The last exposition opens (m. 154) with two more, incomplete, stretto entries, and the final phrase opens with yet another stretto (m. 173b).

Example 7.5 Toccata in G, BWV 916, mm. 173b–177.

The piece concludes with scales cascading down to G, followed by a long silence (Example 7.5). Such an ending is not unknown in German organ music, although in the present context it also suggests Italian wit or *bizzarria*. Composers and copyists are unlikely to have filled out the final measure with rests unless the notation meant what it says. Hence one should resist the temptation to lengthen the final note or to end with an unnecessary allargando.[33]

8
The Concerto Transcriptions

During his Weimar years Bach made keyboard versions of some twenty concertos by various composers. The originals were mostly by Italian (more precisely, Venetian) composers, including Vivaldi and Benedetto Marcello. But they also included at least one work by Telemann and three by the talented young Prince Johann Ernst of Sachsen-Weimar.[1] The composers of three works are unknown. Five arrangements are for organ, with pedal; sixteen or seventeen are *manualiter* and are generally assumed to be for harpsichord. Two concertos exist in both *manualiter* and *pedaliter* versions.

Many of these arrangements are significant keyboard pieces in their own right and for that reason alone would merit careful consideration here.[2] They also have been considered important documents for Bach's musical development. Although this is open to qualification—we have already seen numerous Italian influences in earlier works—the works that Bach transcribed contain features of the mature Venetian Baroque style that are barely suggested in his earlier keyboard works. Bach appears to have taken up similar features in his own works during the following years.

Forkel thought that it had been by transcribing the concertos of Vivaldi that Bach had learned to conceive music outside a specific instrumental idiom; arranging the works for keyboard "taught him to think musically."[3] The source of Forkel's view is unknown, and he proved to be misinformed on some matters.[4] His agenda here is to further his early-Romantic view of Bach as a composer for whom music was something pure or abstract, higher than the mere virtuosity or digital exercise that he (wrongly) characterizes as typical of Bach's early works. But it is possible that Forkel is echoing ideas conveyed to him by Friedemann or Emanuel Bach. And although today we tend to admire Italian Baroque composers for their spontaneity and occasional *bizzarria*, Forkel's emphasis on the classical virtues of "order, connection, and relation" in Vivaldi's compositions may have reflected Sebastian's own view (as stated in his later years) of a style that had swept Europe in the early decades of the century through its vitality, expressive power, and sheer novelty.

Views on the dating of Bach's transcriptions have varied widely (see Heller 2002). Recent writers have followed Schulze's suggestion (1984a, 146ff.) that they date from the period beginning in mid-1713, after Prince Johann Ernst returned from university studies in Utrecht, presumably bearing newly printed editions of Venetian concertos. A letter written in April 1713 by Bach's student Philipp David Kräuter mentions his anticipation of hearing both French and Italian music at Weimar, which would be useful for learning how to compose "concertos and overtures" (see Schulze 1984a, 157). Yet the transcriptions vary in their degree of musical finishing, and at least several underwent significant revision, suggesting that Bach worked on them over an extended period. Surely, if Weimar became an early center for concerto performance in Germany, it was not merely because of the teenaged prince's journey to Holland. At the time, many German musicians and patrons were buying prints and manuscript copies of new Italian music; Weimar exchanged music with other German courts (Schulze 1984a, 165–7), and Bach's arrangements presumably drew on the resulting fund of music.

Despite his title as organist, Bach would have been involved in the performance of secular music, including concertos, from his initial appointment in 1708; in his letter of resignation to the Mühlhausen authorities he had referred to himself as a member of both the ducal *Hoffcapell* and the *Cammermusic* (BD 1:20, item 1). Hence the transcriptions could have served not only for Bach's private study (as Forkel implied) but as virtuoso solo pieces. Bach is unlikely to have had a need to study works by the teenaged prince. But by 1717 concertos were being played as organ solos during recitals at Amsterdam, and the practice might have been fairly widespread.[5] Other German composers, including the Weimar city organist Walther, also transcribed Italian concertos.[6]

A few of Bach's *manualiter* concertos are little more than unembellished keyboard reductions, and these might have been made for study purposes. Concertos were normally disseminated in parts, not scores. As the number of real voices in such works was rarely greater than four, and in many passages was reduced to two or three, a student would have found it convenient to score the outer parts onto just two staves. In the process, melodic lines could have been embellished or altered for more convenient performance at the keyboard. But Bach could surely have improvised an idiomatic keyboard version from just the original outer parts. The apparently unfinished form of some of the arrangements could be due to their having been left in a more or less preliminary state, whereas the more elaborate transcriptions might have been the products of revisions carried out later, perhaps for the benefit of pupils.

The sources for the *manualiter* concertos are relatively late and few in number, and the absence of concordances and even attributions for several raises questions of authorship.[7] The traditional numbering (1–16) comes from BG 42, which Schmieder followed; NBA V/11 adds BWV 592a at the end. For the first eleven concertos, this is the order of the most important source, a manuscript copy by Bach's Eisenach cousin Johann Bernhard Bach.[8] With the exception of BWV 982, and possibly also BWV 977, the arrangements copied by Bernhard Bach were of Italian works. It is conceivable that the sequence was determined by Sebastian himself; the volume opens with a splendid D-major work of Vivaldi, arrangements of weaker pieces falling toward the end. A few movements in the transcriptions toward the back of the book (e.g., the second adagio of BWV 981) remain incompletely adapted for keyboard performance, as is also the case with several of the transcriptions not included in P 280. Otherwise it is difficult to discern any pattern in the ordering of the works.

Forkel mentions in particular that Bach studied Vivaldi's treatment of "ideas," presumably meaning thematic material and figuration. In adapting Vivaldi's violinistic "ideas" to the keyboard, Bach would have discovered new ways of writing for keyboard instruments—discoveries that proved useful when he later arranged his own violin concertos for organ and harpsichord. But Bach would have gained valuable lessons in musical form as well. At the largest level, he would have gained a deepened appreciation for the possibilities inherent in what we call ritornello form, and he would have learned how to give large movements a rational, symmetrical architecture articulating a reasoned tonal structure—in contrast to the somewhat arbitrary, rondo-like patterns of his own earlier works. Equally important would have been the recognition that simple repetition and regular periodic phrasing, far from being marks of banality—as they seemed in the older German *stylus fantasticus*—were essential elements in the new style, whose rational architecture depended upon the recurrence of themes and other structural units, both literally and in sequence. Crucial to articulating this type of formal architecture were new varieties of sequential and cadential formulas; even more important was the principle of recapitulation, which is demonstrated at the large level in many of the works transcribed. Several movements follow early versions of sonata form, that is, expanded binary rather than ritornello designs, with recapitulations in the modern sense. Recapitulation also occurs in the sense employed previously in the discussions of fugue, that is, a transposed restatement of a passage from an episode (a ritornello, like a fugal subject, is constantly "recapitulated").

Bach's method of transcription ranged from verbatim reduction to wholesale rewriting, including the embellishment of treble, bass, and even inner voices, as in the Reinken arrangements. Bach's arrangements are generally more elaborate than the plainer and possibly earlier ones of Walther, whose choice of models (perhaps dictated by what was available to him) was also much weaker.[9] Although some unidiomatic passages remain, Bach usually rescored passages that were not suitable to a keyboard instrument, and he enriched the texture with additional counterpoint and imitation. Several transcriptions are transposed, usually to bring the highest notes of the violin parts down into the four-octave range used in most of Bach's keyboard works of the period (C–c′′′). In the two cases where Bach left both *pedaliter* and *manualiter* versions of the same concerto (discussed by Leisinger 2003), the *manualiter* version occasionally required more ingenuity, since the left hand was no longer free to play both the bass and a high inner part. Bach's usual solution in such cases was to embellish the bass rather than preserve the not very complicated counterpoint of the originals.

These were not the only passages in which Bach tended to add embellishment to the bass rather than an upper part. In quick movements the solo violin part could receive little new elaboration. The simpler bass lines were more readily embellished, yielding two relatively equal voices and avoiding the chordal filler that would otherwise have had to substitute for the continuo realization of the original. In slow movements, tradition dictated an embellished melodic line, but Bach was sparing in his elaboration. Although he did add embellishments in several slow movements, he left others largely as he found them, in several instances because they were already embellished; the embellishments in the slow movements of BWV 972, 973, and 978 are Vivaldi's own.

The transcriptions have not been well served by editors, the only modern critical editions being those of BGA 42 (Naumann, 1894) and NBA V/11 (Heller, 1997).[10] Performance questions are raised by the repeated notes and chords that are a common feature of Italian orchestral style; in BWV 974, 975, 978, and 982 Bach makes no effort to disguise them or adapt them to the keyboard idiom. Four or six repeated chords in a slow movement pose an interpretive challenge on any keyboard instrument, and rapidly repeated sixteenth-note chords in an allegro can present a technical challenge, depending on the tempo and the nature of the keyboard action.[11]

Repeated notes in Bach's instrumental music sometimes bear slurs, indicating the technique known as "bow vibrato" or "slurred tremolo"—that is, a pulsation of the note without re-articulating it, a sort of measured shimmer.[12] Although it is possible that string players would have used this technique in several slow movements that contain repeated chords, the latter do not bear slurs in either the originals or the transcriptions. On the contrary, in both original and transcription the slow movement of BWV 978 calls explicitly for staccato chords. Hence, it seems that one is to play such chords cleanly, with crisp articulation, bearing in mind that the incomplete damping of an authentically set-up eighteenth-century harpsichord will leave a clear after-ring following each chord. Over-interpretation, for example in the form of imaginatively varied arpeggiation for each repeated chord, would impede the forward motion and fail to convey the intended orchestral effect.

The traditional division of Bach's *manualiter* and *pedaliter* transcriptions between harpsichord and organ, questioned by Marshall (1986), has much in its favor. Walther's arrangements, including three without pedal, are explicitly for the organ. But the copy of BWV 974 by Christoph Graupner (1715–60), son of the Darmstadt composer of the same name (Talle 2003, 147–55), has a title specifying "Clavessin." A few sustained notes would sound more clearly on the organ,[13] and occasional stretches of a tenth, as well as other awkward moments, suggest that Bach assumed the presence of pedals, although they might just mean that he did not quite finish adapting the music for two hands at one keyboard.[14] Some passages are distinctly more effective on the harpsichord,[15] and several transcriptions exceed the four-octave range of Bach's organ music.[16] Still, Bach seems to have intentionally avoided high d‴ in two cases, raising the possibility that the transcriptions were made for varying instruments and purposes.[17] The suggestion that Bach made the transcriptions for performance on a small instrument, played for the prince during the latter's final illness (Sackmann 2003, 136), is of course unprovable. But unless they were used in palace concerts, the transcriptions could have been envisioned for playing primarily on small harpsichords and even clavichords.

Such instruments would have lacked the second manual which might seem an obvious necessity here, as in Bach's later Italian Concerto. But this view is predicated on modern assumptions about the primacy of the tutti/solo opposition in concertos and its reflection in the use of contrasting loud and soft keyboards. The distinction in sound between ritornello and episode, now taken for granted as a principle of both scoring and structure in the concerto, would have been less marked in performances of Bach's day, which used only a few ripieno players. Solo episodes are entirely lacking in some movements, and even where they are present in the originals, the transcriptions do not contain corresponding dynamic markings; the *pianos* in BWV 976 mark echoes within the ritornello, played in Vivaldi's original by the tutti. Similar echoes occur in the compositions transcribed as BWV 975 and 978, but the arrangements of these works lack dynamic indications.[18] Although appropriate changes of manual can be managed in some of the pieces—and the slow movements of BWV 973 and 982 can be played with melody and accompaniment on separate keyboards—Bach's elaboration of the bass or treble line often leaves no convenient place for changing keyboards between "tutti" and "solo." In such instances, both must be played on one manual, and the contrast in sound between tutti ritornello and solo episode is instead written into the notes themselves.[19]

Problematical in this light are the criss-crossing scales at the end of BWV 973, which are virtually unplayable on a single keyboard. Yet dividing them between manuals raises the questions of where one should begin divided performance, and what registration can be used on each manual to prevent one voice from overshadowing the other. Presumably both lines should be equally loud, yet on most harpsichords divided manuals require light or unequal registration. A dazzling virtuoso climax was clearly intended here, and the scales are barely playable

Example 8.1 Concerto no. 2 in G, BWV 973, third movement, mm. 55b–60.

on a single keyboard, either by redistributing the notes between the hands or through the use of old-fashioned fingering (without thumbs), one hand being held well above the other (Example 8.1).[20]

Concertos after Vivaldi

Only six of the *manualiter* concertos are known to be based on works by Vivaldi (see Table 8.1). But he remains the composer most frequently represented, and Bach also arranged four other works by Vivaldi, three in *pedaliter* settings

Table 8.1 Concertos after Vivaldi

Transcription			Original				Sources (of Transcription)
No.	BWV	Key	R.	Op./No.	M.	Key	
1	972	D	230	3/9	414	D	P 280, P 804/55 (3d mvt. incomplete), B Bc XY 25448 (J. A. Kuhnau, BWV 972a)
2	973	G	299	7/8	449	G	P 280, P 804/54 (without 3d mvt.), Poel. 29
4	975	g	316a	4/6*	(423)	?g	P 280
5	976	C	265	3/12	417	E	P 280, P 804/15 (lacks 2d mvt.)
7	978	F	310	3/3	408	G	P 280
9	980	G	381	4/1*	514	B♭	P 280

*Alternate version
R = number in Ryom (1986)
M = volume number in *Le opere di Antonio Vivaldi*, ed. G. F. Malipiero et al. (Rome, 1947–72)
P 280 and P 804 are in SBB; Poel. 29 is in LEm

for organ and one in the concerto for four harpsichords (BWV 1065). Of these ten works after Vivaldi, six are based on originals published in Vivaldi's opus 3 (Amsterdam, 1711). The remaining four also appeared in print (in either op. 4 or op. 7), but Bach knew three of them in distinct pre-publication versions that he must have obtained in manuscript copies.

Vivaldi's *opera* 4 and 7 were printed as sets of five part-books each. Their contents are now identified as "solo" concertos, that is, works for *violino principale* plus four-part string ensemble (and continuo). Opus 3, on the other hand, was issued in eight part-books—four violins, two violas, and two bass parts. In neither type of work were any of the parts explicitly meant to be doubled; all these works are chamber music, playable by one instrument per part, and the scoring in opus 3 varies between that of a "solo" concerto and what is now usually called a concerto grosso. The resulting variety of texture was surely one of the great attractions of this set for Bach and his contemporaries, but it is not something that can be readily conveyed in a solo keyboard transcription. Perhaps for this reason the concertos from opus 3 selected for *manualiter* transcription are of the "solo" type, in which only one violin has a soloistic part. Still, players should bear the original scoring in mind; a passage scored for the four violin parts, like the opening tutti of the last movement of BWV 972, was conceived for four players, not a large modern string section.

Concerto no. 1 in D, BWV 972

The full D-major chords and forthright dotted rhythms of the opening passage make this a suitable work to start off the series, whether or not Bach actually intended it for that purpose. Yet the first allegro confounds modern expectations of what a Vivaldi concerto movement should be like. It is barely recognizable as a ritornello form; the opening tutti is hardly a ritornello at all (the opening three-and-a-half measures never come back), and apart from a short excursion to the relative minor the entire movement remains in the tonic. Still, the movement demonstrates how much Vivaldi could accomplish in a series of short phrases confined to a few harmonies. The music seems simple, yet it maintains considerable tension through its varied figuration and the judicious use of dominant prolongations. Although Bach did not follow this model in his own concertos, one phrase is echoed in the prelude of the Fourth English Suite, which comes as close as any of Bach's original keyboard works to concerto style.[21]

Although the bass is frequently varied or rewritten, Bach hardly altered the top line at all. The only significant embellishment is the substitution of figuration in thirty-seconds for sixteenths in the central solo of the last movement (mm. 58ff.). In the slow movement the written-out embellishment is taken verbatim from the original, even though the figuration is much more repetitive than what Bach used in his own decorated adagios.

A variant version of the concerto has been designated BWV 972a. Here the left hand has a few passages whose less embellished forms are consistent with Bach's early versions of other works.[22] Other readings, however, look more like mistakes involving either wrong or omitted notes in inner voices.[23] Therefore it is hard to say to what degree the score published in NBA V/11 corresponds to an actual earlier draft of Bach's.

Concerto no. 2 in G, BWV 973

Of the four Vivaldi works that Bach transcribed from sources other than opus 3, only this one follows the same version as the later print. Particularly striking here is Bach's embellishment of the slow movement, which is a model of its type and should be carefully considered by anyone who envisages adding embellishments to other movements. Bach wisely avoids filling in the rests in Vivaldi's violin line (mm. 2, 9, 11, etc.); these rests articulate a beautifully asymmetrical phrase structure. The diminished-seventh chord in m. 14, where treble and bass for the first time rest together on a long note, is marked by only a mordent; a more elaborate embellishment at this point might have ruined the eloquent effect of the pause on a dissonant harmony. Similar restraint marks the closing phrase of the movement (from m. 19); flourishes occur on the beats preceding cadential formulas, not on the cadences themselves—that would be anticlimactic—and the final chord is again elaborated by a bare mordent.

Bach also added inner voices to the original two-part texture, which was scored for solo violin accompanied by unison violins and violas (without basso continuo). In the transcription, melody and accompaniment can be played on separate manuals, as in the slow movement of the Italian Concerto. That the same is possible here can hardly be an accident, and it facilitates several passages where melody and accompaniment cross (mm. 16–17, 19).

The other movements remain closer to the original, and the embellishments in the first movement are mostly Vivaldi's own. These include the variation of the ritornello motive at the first entrance of the soloist (mm. 22–3), the variation of the entire solo theme in its second appearance (mm. 46–53), and the soloist's variation of the second phrase of the ritornello just before the end (m. 117–24). But in both allegros Bach added a second scale moving in contrary motion to the rushing scale figures of the closing phrases. Hence, the criss-crossing scales at the end of the last movement (shown in Example 8.1) are a heightened version of what happens at the end of the first. Bach also eliminated several dramatic rests in the last movement, where a series of striking staccato chords is homogenized through the addition of running sixteenths (Example 8.2). He did otherwise in the closing passages of BWV 976 and 978, retaining Vivaldi's dramatic interruption of the prevailing motion, and would imitate this idea at the end of the Fourth Brandenburg Concerto (mvt. 3, m. 229).

Example 8.2 (a) Vivaldi: Concerto in G, R. 299, and (b) Concerto No. 2 in G, BWV 973, third movement, mm. 43–44a.

Concerto no. 4 in G Minor BWV 975

The first two movements of this arrangement correspond closely with the version in Vivaldi's opus 4 (Amsterdam, ca. 1716). But the last movement is completely different, and the slow movement also shows important variants.

One has to agree with Vivaldi that the later version is better. And although Bach's transcription is fully worked out, it fails to reflect the subtle scoring of the opening ritornello. The first phrase (mm. 1–8) was repeated piano by the tutti, after which the soloist had a forte passage accompanied by the ripieno (mm. 17–23a).[24] It would be not impossible to play the piano phrase (mm. 9–16) on a softer manual. But there are no dynamic markings in the transcription, and it would be difficult to make all the leaps between manuals necessary to reflect the rapid alternations between forte and piano in the original at mm. 73bff.

In the slow movement, Bach again embellished the melody, and he inserted a chromatic element into the bass as well. Although not adding any inner voices, he provided an effective realization of the basso continuo by transforming the lower voice into a sort of Alberti bass (Example 8.3). Slurs in mm. 7–8 suggest that the chord tones in the left hand should be held out, but one wonders why the slurs are not present from the beginning. The first ritornello, in A minor (mm. 9–10), enters awkwardly after a half-cadence to an A-major chord; this passage is absent from the published version of the concerto, and the remaining ritornellos were rewritten.

The final movement is in binary form. The print substituted a through-composed movement, as also in the work transcribed as BWV 980. Although some composers continued to use binary form for the quick movements of their concertos, Vivaldi apparently came to regard such a form as inappropriate in a

Example 8.3 (a) Vivaldi: Concerto in G Minor R. 316a, and (b) Concerto no. 4 in G Minor BWV 975, second movement, mm. 1–3a.

genre that was becoming increasingly defined by the contrast between solo and tutti. Here (but not in BWV 980) Bach elaborated the binary form by providing written-out repetitions in which the bass is varied.[25]

Concerto no. 5 in C, BWV 976

This was originally the work that closed Vivaldi's opus 3. It is one of the longest and most brilliant concertos of the set, and the dotted rhythms in the closing phrase brought the collection to a ringing finish. Bach left them intact and did not fill in the rests with figuration as he did in BWV 973. Elsewhere, however, the arrangement is inconsistent in the degree to which it elaborates the original. The largo is not much more than a literal reduction, but treble and bass are considerably varied in the last movement, and the figuration in the upper part in mm. 64–79 is a realization of an arpeggiando passage originally notated as three-part chords. The fugal opening of the largo, in four real parts, is rare in an Italian concerto but perhaps an aspect of the original that caught Bach's attention; Vivaldi might have borrowed the subject from Marcello, who uses the same idea in the same key to open Concerto III in his 1708 set (from which Bach transcribed the preceding work).

Kellner's copy (in P 804) omits the largo as well as part of the final solo episode of the last movement (mm. 106–10). Scholars have suspected that here Kellner made arbitrary or erroneous deletions, as he did elsewhere. Yet the fact that Kellner also has an extra measure in the preceding passage, essentially repeating m. 104, makes one wonder whether his readings derive from an otherwise unattested early draft—perhaps one based on a pre-publication version of Vivaldi's original.

Concerto no. 7 in F, BWV 978

The third of the works transcribed from Vivaldi's opus 3 is an "easy" Baroque concerto that many violinists encounter early in their training, probably unaware of the impact that its clear, concise architecture and inventive scoring had on Bach. A curiosity of the outer movements is that both re-establish the tonic through sequential statements of the ritornello theme in A minor, C, and (in the first movement) F.[26] This makes for a slightly abrupt return to the tonic, but Bach evidently was not troubled by it.

Bach's substantive alterations are in the bass line, including the imitation of the violin figure at the opening of the first movement (the original lacks the imitation). The second movement, which Bach transcribes quite literally, is marked *Largo*, which in Vivaldi's opus 3 is associated with special scoring of some sort. Here the term, which literally means "broad," cannot signify a particularly slow tempo and seems instead to have something to do with the three tutti chords played in every other measure, alternating with the soloist's arpeggiation. Bach retains Vivaldi's staccato sign on the chords, implying accented attacks, but there is an arpeggio sign as well, which must be executed quickly.

Concerto no. 9 in G, BWV 980

In Bernhard Bach's copy of BWV 980, a later hand correctly identified it as a version of the work that opens Vivaldi's opus 4.[27] But the first movement of the published concerto differs after m. 28 from the version transcribed here, and the second and third movements are entirely distinct. In the version of the concerto transcribed by Bach, the overwhelming weight, as in BWV 975, falls on the first movement. This is no fault, but the motivic material is dull, and in the published version Vivaldi added variety to the figuration, rewriting the last two solo passages (here, mm. 63–8 and 71–6). Vivaldi's scoring brings the somewhat barren thematic material of the manuscript version to life, but the movement does not transfer well to the keyboard. The ritornello involves close imitations at the unison between the two violin parts; Bach adapts this to the *manualiter* idiom, transposing the second violin part an octave lower, but the result is a pale reflection of the original (Example 8.4). Bach would incorporate a more inspired imitation of the Vivaldi model in the canonic opening of the Sixth Brandenburg Concerto.

The last movement is a sonata form like that at the end of BWV 975. The opening themes of the two movements are practically the same, apart from the difference in mode,[28] and Bach's arrangement embellishes the bass as in the varied reprises of BWV 975.

Example 8.4 (a) Vivaldi: Concerto in B flat, R. 381, and (b) Concerto no. 9 in G, BWV 980, first movement, mm. 1–2.

Concerto no. 6 in C, BWV 977

Sources: P 280 (Johann Bernhard Bach); P 804/56 (Mey).

The original of BWV 977 has not been found among Vivaldi's known works. Yet the copy by Mey bears the title *CONCERTO in C.♮. di Vivaldi. accomadato. sul Clavicembalo. di Giov. Seb. Bach.*[29] Although Mey's title may be faulty, the work is strongly Italianate in style—more so than the two other transcriptions of unidentified works (BWV 983 and 986), which might have been German imitations of the Venetian style. As BWV 976 is the sole surviving document for the alternate version of Vivaldi's op. 4, no. 1, it is possible that the present transcription also preserves an otherwise unknown work by Vivaldi. National style is, however, hard to judge three centuries later; Schering's guesses (1902–3, 242) about BWV 979 (German) and 987 (Italian) proved wrong, although his suggestions of an Italian origin for BWV 977 and a German origin for BWV 983 and 986 remain plausible.

The original key of BWV 977 is likely to have been D, since the Fs in the opening ritornello could not have been played on violins.[30] The plan is as much that of a sinfonia (or overture) as a concerto. The first movement is a compact ritornello form, but the adagio is short—only nine measures, ending in a half cadence. Nevertheless, the first seven measures are worked out imitatively in four parts, as in Vivaldi's op. 3, no. 12. Like BWV 975 and 980, the work ends with a short dance in binary form, here labeled explicitly a *giga*.

Example 8.5 Concerto no. 6 in C, BWV 977, third movement, mm. 30–2.

Possibly a second solo violin or a solo cello joined the principal violin in the solo sections of the first movement (e.g., mm. 27–32). But the accompaniment of the melody in parallel tenths and sixths in those passages could just as easily have belonged to the ripieni or been added by Bach. No clear tutti/solo contrasts are implied in the last two movements, but a movement without solo passages would not be unusual in an early concerto; similar scoring occurs in the last movement of BWV 975 and apparently also in BWV 981.

Whatever its origin, this is one of the more attractive and idiomatic of the transcriptions. The outer movements contain effective keyboard writing, as in a series of descending sevenths in the left hand (mvt. 1, m. 16) that look bizarre on paper but seem perfectly natural in performance.[31] The adagio is less effective, for its dense four-part writing is a little studied, like the opening of the C-Major Sonata after Reinken.

The gigue makes a little excursion to the minor at the end of each half. This might have been inspired by Corelli's C-major violin sonata (op. 5, no. 3, last movement), which is practically quoted in mm. 32b–33. Unfortunately, the preceding phrase is faulty in both sources, and the passage requires a little re-composing to make sense (Example 8.5). Even then it is unsatisfactory; perhaps Bach's score contained corrections at this point, and one might delete the whole phrase, skipping from m. 30a to 32b.[32]

Concertos after "Marcello" and Torelli

Benedetto Marcello was the better known and more prolific of two Venetian nobles who were brothers and composers. Bach is thought to have transcribed one work by each (see Table 8.2). But although Benedetto was thirteen years younger than Alessandro—and evidently not always on good terms with him—the two concertos transcribed by Bach are similar in many respects. Both are serious, well-crafted pieces; in addition to similarities in their motivic material, the quick movements of the two concertos reveal symmetrical architectures involving extensive use of recapitulation. The usefulness of this procedure for composing lengthy, rationally organized movements would have impressed Bach. Particularly

Table 8.2 Concertos after "Marcello": Sources

Transcription			Original			Sources (of Transcription)
No.	BWV	Key	Composer	Op./No.	Key	
3	974	d	Alessandro (?)	—	c (d)	P 280, P 804/4, DS ms. 66 (C. Graupner, jr.)
10	981	c	Benedetto	1/2	e	P 280, DSB P 801 (Walther), B Br XY 25448 (J. A. Scheibe), LEm ms. 8

notable are the final movements, sonata-allegros resembling the last movements of BWV 975, 977, and 980, but longer and more serious than those dance-like pieces. Bach and Walther probably did not consider the two concertos to be by different composers (if indeed they are); the manuscripts omit the first name, and Alessandro is not mentioned in the brief entry in Walther (1732; the omission was noted by Hanks 1972, 214).

Concerto no. 3 in D Minor BWV 974

This is an arrangement of the oboe concerto ascribed to Alessandro Marcello in an anthology entitled *Concerti a cinque* (Concertos in Five Parts, i.e., "solo" concertos), containing works by various composers and published at Amsterdam around 1716. The concerto became known in the twentieth century under the name of Benedetto Marcello, in a somewhat embellished C-minor version preserved in a German manuscript.[33] Selfridge-Field (1990, 365) describes the attribution to Alessandro as "reasonably secure," leaving open the possibility that Benedetto may after all have been the composer.

Bach's setting apparently depended on a version transmitted in manuscript, since the first movement lacks six measures that elsewhere begin a recapitulation in the tonic (following m. 44a). Hence the movement is in a concise sonata form; indeed, like some other early Venetian concertos it is so concise, and so restrained in style, that it has more the character of a sonata than a later concerto movement. In the middle of the movement, however, Bach rewrote a passage to serve as both a climax and a demonstration of how to achieve a crescendo on the harpsichord (Example 8.6).

Nothing so dramatic happens in the last two movements, although Bach considerably embellished the adagio. The Darmstadt copy by Christoph Graupner, Jr. gives a few readings closer to the original concerto and therefore presumably earlier; notable among these is the avoidance of d‴ in the third movement.[34]

Concerto no. 10 in C Minor BWV 981

The concerto by Benedetto Marcello was second of a set of twelve *concerti a cinque* published at Venice in 1708. The original solo part (*violino principale*) of

Example 8.6 (a) Alessandro Marcello, oboe concerto, and (b) J. S. Bach, Concerto no. 3 in D Minor BWV 974, first movement, mm. 34b–35.

the printed edition is lost, and Bach's transcription is thus the sole source for the otherwise missing part, although in this work soloistic writing was apparently confined to the first two movements. The contrapuntal character of the original, and indeed of the entire set, may explain Bach's interest in the work; this concerto must have been particularly impressive, accounting for the preservation of Bach's arrangement in four copies even though the last two movements are barely adapted for the keyboard. The unidiomatic character of the transcription has led to the suggestion that BWV 981 was intended for an instrument with pedals (Leisinger 2003, 83), but perhaps it is simply unfinished; there is, however, evidence for some revision.[35] However unsatisfactory the arrangement, it could serve as the basis for a reliable reconstruction of the lost original solo part.[36]

Originally in E minor, the concerto is in the four-movement form today associated with the *sonata da chiesa*. The first movement, an adagio, opens with dotted rhythms that might, as in several concertos by Corelli, refer to the French overture (despite the time signature of 3/4). This was evidently set aside for solo figuration in the second half (from m. 20). Bach is likely to have taken this figuration unchanged from the original, as it contains repeated notes more apt for the violin than for the keyboard, and in the original key it would not have descended lower than a♭.

The ritornello of the first allegro evidently started with imitative statements of the opening motive by each of the three violin parts; the viola and bass remain silent until m. 8b. The movement comes close to sonata form, material that originally leads to a cadence in the dominant (mm. 21b–29a) being restated at the end in the tonic (mm. 37b–45a). The final movement comes even closer to sonata form, longer and with more extensive recapitulation than the corresponding movement of the work attributed to Alessandro. The entire second half (from the double bar onward) consists of previously heard material transposed upward or downward by a fifth; only the phrase in mm. 16–22 is never restated.

Such schematic recapitulations can become tiresome in a solo keyboard performance, and there is little opportunity for adding embellishments on the repeats. Moreover, despite having reworked the first two movements, Bach left the tutti passages of the third (slow) movement as verbatim reductions that seem to call not only for embellishment but for the elimination of some awkward spacings. A number of ornaments in NBA V/11 (given in parentheses in BG 42) come from Walther's copy in P 801; as in similar cases they are likely to represent the copyist's additions. The same can be said of two fragments that J. T. Krebs added in P 801 at the end of the first movement. Although they have been interpreted as sketches for a transition between movements 1 and 2, these appear to be embellished readings for two parallel passages within the first movement (mm. 16–8 and 36–8), confirming the impression from other sources that Bach's Weimar pupils were in the habit of adding their own decorations to his works.[37]

Concerto no. 8 in B Minor BWV 979

Arrangement of: Torelli (?), Violin Concerto in D minor. *Source:* P 280 (Johann Bernhard Bach).

Torelli was the most important member of the first generation of concerto composers, and if the work transcribed here is really his, it might be the earliest of the pieces arranged by Bach.[38] Zehnder (1991) argued for a stronger influence by Torelli on Bach than was previously recognized, but the only tangible evidence for the hypothesis appears to be that furnished by the present arrangement. Like many seventeenth-century ensemble sonatas, the original work comprises numerous sections of varying character, some of them mere transitions. But it focuses on two large allegro movements (nos. 4 and 8 in Table 8.3), each con-

Table 8.3 Sections In BWV 979

No.	No. In NBA	Tempo Marking		Length (Measures)
		BWV 979	Lund ms.	
1	1	none	none	4
2	—	Allegro	Allegro	43
3	2	Adagio	Adagio	6
4	3	Allegro	Allegro	67
5	—	Adagio	Adagio	5
6	4	Andante	Adagio pianissimo	28
7	5	Adagio	Adagio	11
8	6	Allegro	Vivace	87

structed in highly regular fashion around three statements of a ritornello—full-fledged themes, not the "short ritornellos" (*kurz-Ritornellen*) that have been seen, not entirely convincingly, as Torelli's legacy to Bach (see Hill 1995).

Bach expended considerable care on the keyboard adaptation, which was clearly intended to make a dazzling effect. In the first, preludial, allegro (no. 2), Bach added sixteenths in the bass (they are already present in the solo part); he also used sixteenths to fill in dramatic rests in m. 27 (beats 2–3), but not in mm. 36–9. In two adagios (nos. 3 and 6), five-part chords for the strings (with divided violas) were elaborated into precisely notated arpeggiation.[39] String figuration, especially that involving repeated notes, was replaced by idiomatic keyboard writing throughout most of the two main allegros, but not in the climactic retransition passage of the first of these movements (no. 4, mm. 38b–41). Here repeated chords in sixteenths intensify the return to the opening material and tonality. Bach's alterations elsewhere in no. 4 included a recasting of the ritornello theme, whose opening phrase (mm. 1–3a) originally consisted mainly of eighths; Bach elaborates this into a stream of running sixteenths. The passage was originally assigned to the soloist, unaccompanied, a striking gesture that is not represented in the arrangement but would have been remembered by anyone who knew the original.

Played by a virtuoso string band, the original concerto would make a strong impression. In the keyboard version, the reliance on running figuration in two parts, together with the limited variety of arpeggiated figures, might grow wearying, especially as Torelli tends to repeat fairly ordinary sequences. But surely this arrangement was an effective concert piece for harpsichord, regardless of whatever purposes some of the other, less brilliant or less finished, transcriptions might have served.

Concertos on German Models

Of the seven remaining works, five are known to be arrangements of German compositions (see Table 8.4). The appearance of Telemann among the composers

Table 8.4 Concertos on German Models: Sources

Transcription			Original			Sources (Of Transcription)
No.	*BWV*	*Key*	*Composer*	*Op./No.*	*Key*	
14	985	g	Telemann	—/—	g	P 804/28 (Mey)
11	982	B♭	J. Ernst	1/1	B♭	P 280
16	987	d	J. Ernst	1/4	d	P 804/34 (Mey)
13	984	C	J. Ernst	—/—	?C	P 804/52 (Ringk), Poel. 29, LEm ms. 8
—	592a	G	J. Ernst	—/—	G	Poel. 29
12	983	g	?	?	?	P 804/35 (Mey), Poel. 29
15	986	G	?	?	?	P 804/46 (Mey)

of the originals should elicit no surprise, for by 1713 he had established himself as the leading German composer of his generation, having held positions at the courts at Erfurt and Eisenach, among others. He had connections as well with the court of Weimar, dedicating his first publication—six violin sonatas (1715)—to Prince Johann Ernst, whose own opus 1, a set of six concertos, appeared posthumously in 1718, edited by Telemann. Telemann was also godfather to Sebastian's son Carl Philipp Emanuel, born at Weimar in 1714, and Bach must have had considerable admiration for the slightly older composer, whose early works show imaginative adaptations of current French as well as Italian style.

Telemann's early concertos are more compact and more economical in their use of motivic material than the better-known works of Vivaldi; phrases tend to be shorter and virtuosity is more restrained. Similar qualities also characterize the other works considered below. Although these lack the spaciousness and verve of Vivaldi's concertos, at its best the style produces music of considerable eloquence.

The young Prince of Weimar modeled his own concertos more closely on Telemann's than on Italian imports, to judge from the available examples. But Johann Ernst is likely to have known at least the Italian concertos transcribed by Bach and by Walther, who dedicated his *Praecepta* to the prince on the latter's twelfth birthday in 1708. Walther's elementary textbook contains little directly relevant to concertos, or indeed to any of the newer French and Italian genres. But presumably the prince received oral instruction about the concerto from Walther as well as from Telemann and Bach.[40] Johann Ernst's inexperience reveals itself in the brevity and inconclusiveness of several movements, but the unusual plans of certain movements and perhaps even of whole concertos (see BWV 982 below) reveal originality. Indeed, the music is superior to some of the minor works that Walther transcribed, and there are attractive details of melody and scoring. Like a much more accomplished princely amateur, King Frederick II of Prussia, Johann Ernst seems to have had an especial affinity for expressive slow movements.[41] His early death, preceded by a long illness, may have made him something of a romantic figure to his contemporaries. But there is no evidence to support Schering's suggestion that Bach's arrangements of the prince's works were intended as private, posthumous homage.[42]

Concerto no. 14 in G Minor BWV 985

Easily underestimated because of its brevity and restraint, Telemann's concerto is a very fine work, and it received careful attention from Bach. Bach followed an early form of the concerto; a later version has an extended solo passage after m. 44 of the last movement.[43] As in the Marcello and Torelli concertos, the quick movements of Telemann's work have a logical, clearly articulated design that must have appealed to Bach. Another reason for Bach's interest would have been the spare rhetoric of the adagio, whose high point is a series of chromatic modulations that pass quickly, via deceptive arrivals and surprising dissonances, from G minor through B♭ minor to the tonic C minor (mm. 9–14). The imitative ritornello of the last movement recalls that of the first allegro in BWV 981; an even closer parallel can be found in a trio sonata by Albinoni, published in the same set from which Bach borrowed three fugue subjects.[44] Bach may have borrowed from the present concerto as well; the closing flourish of the first movement reappears at the end of the sonata in the same key for viola da gamba (BWV 1029).[45]

Bach's substantive changes are confined to restrained embellishment of the bass and occasional alteration of figures not idiomatic to the keyboard (e.g., mvt. 3, mm. 15–16a). The adagio is an almost exact copy of the original, which is scored for soloist and continuo only.[46] As a result, it may seem a little bare. But even the empty tritone between bass and treble in m. 9 (second beat) might be left as is, without ornamentation or harmonic filler. This is the sort of well-placed harmonic surprise that Telemann often places at a strategic location in a movement; in a keyboard setting it can be more effective without additions.

Concerto no. 11 in B♭, BWV 982

This first concerto from Johann Ernst's opus 1 is something of a hodgepodge, perhaps assembled posthumously from heterogeneous fragments. The first movement is a very competent ritornello form reminiscent of Telemann, but the last movement suffers from a too-late return to the tonic just seven measures from the end. The second and third movements, originally for solo violin and continuo alone, form an adagio-allegro pair in the foreign key of G minor, and the second movement seems to open in the middle of a phrase.[47] Bach may have edited the prince's composition or worked from memory, for (as in BWV 984 and 592a) the transcription lacks several measures of the original; a few others are added. In any case he probably worked from a pre-publication version, as a manuscript copy of the original concerto (in ROu) lacks the ripieno parts in mm. 41–57 of the last movement, leaving a duet for two solo violins—a scoring apparently imitated in Bach's arrangement (the viola part is ignored).

In the adagio, the opening and closing passages (marked *piano*) were originally scored for continuo alone. Bach's version is therefore a written-out realization; it is fairly elaborate, in four real parts. The solo line is marked forte, perhaps indicating that it is to be played on a separate manual.

Concerto no. 16 in D Minor BWV 987

Like BWV 979, this work consists of relatively short, linked movements. It begins with an expressive grave (*Adagio e staccato* in the original) that opens with a chromatic "speaking" passage—a very different, perhaps more Germanic, call to attention, although a model for the present alternation of slow and quick sections could be found in Italian works (e.g., Corelli's op. 5, no. 1). Johann Ernst marked the quick sections *piano e presto*, but the word *piano* is probably just a way of indicating a solo passage, and Bach leaves no opportunity for changing manuals. The longest movement is the central allegro, whose opening ritornello suggested the *Follia* to Schering (1903–4, 569); the staccato triadic theme might actually be imitating that of the third movement of Vivaldi's "Grosso Mogul" Concerto R. 208a.[48] The last movement, a short vivace, has some points in common with the prelude of Bach's Third English Suite.[49]

Concerto no. 13 in C, BWV 984

The model for this transcription is lost, but Johann Ernst's authorship is established by titles in LEm ms. 8 and in the two sources of the organ version BWV 595. The latter comprises only the first movement, in a somewhat longer version that one would assume to be later than that of BWV 984 were it not for some redundancies and awkward modulations.[50] The present version still suffers from rather sudden modulations (G to E minor, m. 18; A minor to C, m. 54). Apparently the prince, or his teacher Walther, had a good understanding in the abstract of how to structure a concerto movement, but tended to think in terms of long, stable tonal blocks connected by too-swift transitions—missing the point that the drama of a good concerto lies in skillfully negotiated modulations, not facile diatonic sequences. The somewhat more varied figuration of the *manualiter* version suggests that it is the later one, perhaps representing Bach's own abbreviation of the original.

The second movement, in F minor, ends with a sort of Phrygian cadence on the dominant, which at first seems a mistake inasmuch as C major is the tonic of the following movement. But the latter begins with a harmonic progression back to F (I–IV), producing a musical pun that is effective in connecting the two movements. In both arrangements the first movement is the most Vivaldian of the prince's concerto movements transcribed by Bach (as Sackmann 2003 has also noticed). The *manualiter* transcription is worked out with considerable panache, as in the cascading arpeggios of movement 3, mm. 57–62. All three movements being dominated by prosaic sequences, Bach's task here was much like Handel's in pieces like the G-major Chaconne BWV 442, where the simplicity of the material called for virtuoso variations that are elegant and imaginative, but not wearingly complex.

Concerto in G, BWV 592a

BWV 592a is a *manualiter* alternate to the organ arrangement of the same concerto (BWV 592). Relegated to an appendix in BG 42, it appears in the main text of NBA V/11. The two transcriptions stem from an unpublished work of

Johann Ernst, and although the *manualiter* version might have been based on the *pedaliter* one, if so it is a thorough reworking and not merely a simplified arrangement. The lateness of the source and the fact that the copyist remains unidentified raise questions about Bach's involvement in BWV 592a. Although the manuscript contains three other transcriptions generally accepted as Bach's, at least one of these is also slightly suspect (BWV 983, anonymous in the only other copy). Still, the arrangement is a good one, and it departs from the model at the same point as does Bach's organ transcription.

The original concerto evidently enjoyed some popularity, and the *manualiter* arrangement is worth rescuing from obscurity. The somewhat greater embellishment of the upper line in the *manualiter* version again suggests that it is the later of the two keyboard versions. Both discreetly revise one phrase (first movement, mm. 60–5), which becomes a measure longer than in the original. But many imaginative touches, such as the switch to triplets for the solo passages of the first movement, are the prince's own, and his distinctive scoring of the last movement forced clever rewriting in both transcriptions (Example 8.7). This movement seems artless, but it is so good-natured and so imaginatively transcribed that it ought to be heard more often, if only as an encore piece.

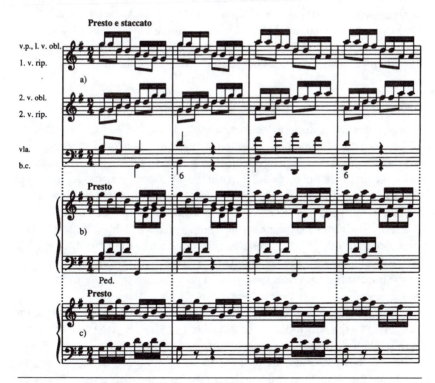

Example 8.7 (a) Johann Ernst von Sachsen-Weimar, Concerto in G, (b) J. S. Bach, Concerto in G, BWV 592, and (c) Concerto in G, BWV 592a, third movement, mm. 1–4.

Concerto no. 12 in G minor, BWV 983

BWV 983 is an unusual work, its fiery first movement answered first by an expressive adagio, then by an echo movement that resembles a siciliano or pastorale (and therefore should not be taken too quickly). The counterpoint in the ritornellos of the first two movements must have pleased Bach, although the imitations in the episodes of the outer movements (mvt. 1, mm. 57–61; mvt. 3, mm. 14–6) could be his own additions, as also the alto's ornamented imitation of the bass in the second movement (m. 37). Heller (NBA V/11, KB, 115) rightly points to the redundant modulating scheme of the first movement, which together with the last movement suffers from a few prosaic sequences; none of the movements moves very far from the tonic and the relative major.

The opening theme of the first movement somewhat resembles that of a weaker concerto by Luigi Mancia, transcribed by Walther, and there are other near-quotations from Venetian works. Yet the work is not unimaginative, and the adagio is expressive; the counterpoint here and the echoes in the concluding presto suggest a German composer.[51] The attribution of the arrangement is a bit weak, but the style, especially the scrupulous voice leading in the four-part ritornellos of the first two movements, contains nothing foreign to the other arrangements. The staccato markings in the slow movement, presumably taken over from the original, would have implied vigorous bow strokes but not necessarily very short notes. On the keyboard they suggest not too slow a tempo, and they might also be indications not to add further embellishment.

Concerto no. 15 in G, BWV 986

This is a charming work, more compact than BWV 983 and thus more likely to be based on a German original if not an early Venetian one. The "speaking" repeated notes in the adagio recall those in the grave of BWV 985, whose model is by Johann Ernst. But this work is free of the occasional weak modulations and sequences noted in the prince's other concertos, and it might be by a master composer such as Telemann, as Schering suggested (1902–3, 242). Perhaps this concerto even furnished the model for the longer work by Johann Ernst that Bach arranged as BWV 592/592a, which also introduces triplets in the initial episode of the first movement. The figuration of a brilliant (tutti?) sequence in mm. 33ff. of the present first movement also bears a resemblance, in Bach's arrangement, to the opening of the last movement of BWV 592a.

Other notable features include the imitation of the ritornello theme at the dominant by the bass in the first movement (m. 5); never repeated, the imitation might have been Bach's embellishment of a simpler original texture. Also "Bachian" but probably part of the original composition is the progression involving the Neapolitan in the middle of the same movement (mm. 26–7); the progression recurs in intensified form as the climax of the brief adagio (m. 9). The finale, although the shortest of all the binary final movements in these concertos, is nevertheless a complete sonata form, analogous in meter, key, design, and general character to the concluding movement of Bach's Third Brandenburg Concerto. Its opening on the second quarter of a measure of 12/8 allows the final chord to fall on a downbeat, reflecting a concern for correct musical prosody (cf. Mattheson 1739, 147).

9

The Virtuoso Fugues

Five large virtuoso keyboard fugues, each paired with a prelude or fantasia, stand apart from Bach's early, generally shorter or more archaic works, and the later compositions that he gathered into the WTC and other collections. Among them is the Chromatic Fantasia and Fugue BWV 903, probably Bach's best-known keyboard piece outside the great collections. With one exception (BWV 906), these pieces probably originated toward the end of Bach's Weimar period (1714–7). Arguments have been made for placing BWV 903 at Cöthen (Stauffer 1989) or BWV 894 in the Leipzig period (Stinson 1989b) on the basis of notational evidence or patterns of manuscript transmission. But large display pieces like the Chromatic Fantasia might at first have been withheld from circulation, serving as Bach's private repertory for performance on special occasions. Eventually, however, these pieces—above all the Chromatic Fantasia and Fugue—circulated relatively widely and, unlike Bach's earlier keyboard works, remained in use long after they had been composed. There is evidence that Bach revised them later, at Cöthen or Leipzig, in one or two cases perhaps bringing together separately composed preludes and fugues. The later datings proposed for some of these pieces might apply to the revised versions.

Unlike the works considered in previous chapters, these consist of long, self-contained, formally closed movements, without the improvisatory opening, closing, or transitional passages that Bach used to construct large pieces out of relatively small parts (as in the toccatas). This was possible, to some degree, because these works adopt certain formal elements of the concerto—ritornello form in the first movements of BWV 894 and 904, extensive "solo" episodes in the fugues of BWV 903 and 944, clearly articulated and directed modulating schemes. They also employ types of motives and phrasing characteristic of Italian orchestral compositions of around 1710, emulating the motivic economy or consistency and the relatively predictable nature of such works. The latter comes about through the use of repetition at various levels: sequence at the micro-level, transposed repetition (referred to here as recapitulation) at the large level.

Hence the present works are distinct from both the rambling, episodic fugues of the toccatas, and from the preludes and fugues of the WTC, which are generally more concise and avoid flashy virtuosity. To some degree the present works are the *manualiter* equivalents of the great preludes and fugues for organ, which also date mostly from Weimar. Although some of the latter were revised and widely circulated, they too were never gathered into a named collection. Indeed the present *manualiter* pieces are also playable on the organ, but only BWV 904 is arguably closer to organ than to harpsichord style. Moreover, at least one movement in each of these works is explicitly assigned to the harpsichord in one or more sources. Hence, with the possible exception of BWV 904, it is safe to refer to these as virtuoso *harpsichord* pieces.

Doing so raises the question of what purpose these pieces served. Since public harpsichord recitals were unknown, one imagines Bach playing these pieces in informal private concerts or in palace performances at Weimar, Cöthen, and elsewhere. But the two contemporary accounts of Bach's clavier performances—the aborted contest with Marchand and the Potsdam performance that led to the *Musical Offering*—describe improvisations, not prepared compositions. A witness who heard him during his Leipzig years reported that, before improvising, Bach was in the habit of playing a written piece, to "set his powers of imagination in motion."[1] If this was already Bach's practice during the Weimar years, one wonders what compositions Bach might have brought with him to an event like the 1717 contest with Marchand.[2] Perhaps the Chromatic Fantasia or the A-minor fugue BWV 894/2 represents the sort of music that Bach played on such an occasion. In any case, these pieces include formulaic passagework and sequences that could have been incorporated into improvisations, and they may even be idealized examples of two types of improvisation that Bach must have been prepared to carry off: the free fantasia, with its open form and wide-ranging modulations, and the virtuoso fugue worked out in relatively simple counterpoint, with episodes made up of arpeggiated passagework. Such pieces might have been what C. P. E. Bach had in mind when he wrote to Forkel that his father, although usually composing away from the keyboard, in certain compositions "took the material from improvisations on the clavier"(BD 3:289 [item 803]/NBR, 399).

Fantasia and Fugue in A Minor BWV 904

Chief sources: P 320 (J. N. Gebhardi?); P 804/25 (Kellner; fantasia only); P 288/11 (Kellner; fugue only); Mus. ms. 30112 (fugue only); P 617 (Johann Gottlob Freudenberg; fugue only). *Editions*: BG 36; Dadelsen and Rönnau (1970); NBA V/9.2.

BWV 904 is the most old-fashioned of the three large fantasias and fugues that Bach is known to have written for harpsichord.[3] The word *fantasia* means something different in each; here it may reflect the grave character and moderately contrapuntal texture that BWV 904/1 shares with a few organ works of the same title (BWV 562, 563, 570).[4] The two movements are preserved separately in the earliest sources, and Stinson (1989b, 455–9) argues that the organist Kittel, one of Bach's last pupils, could have been "the architect of the pairing."[5] As Stinson (1989b, 460n.) notes, the opening thematic material of both movements includes the progression e″–f″–e″. Although fleeting, the motivic parallel helps make the pairing plausible, even if it is not original.

Both movements avoid outright virtuoso display, but the counterpoint is sometimes awkward to play, the parts dividing oddly between the hands and the voices crossing in ways rarely encountered in Bach's keyboard works.[6] This could be interpreted as arising from an organist's lingering tendency to compose counterpoint that occasionally presupposes the availability of pedals. But it also reflects the uncompromising character of the music, in which every dissonance and each convoluted chromatic interval is full of meaning. One would like to linger over the details (and moderate tempos certainly ease the player's task), yet not at the expense of losing sight of the grand design of both movements.

Kellner, who copied the two movements separately, designated the fantasia *pro Cembalo*, the fugue *manualiter*. But even if the latter indication referred to the organ, as Marshall (1986) argued, there is nothing in the music pointing specifically to that instrument. On the other hand, the fact that the movements are preserved separately in most early copies supports the idea that they originated separately. Stinson (1989a, 107), arguing for a "post-1725 origin" for the fantasia, points to its "extraordinarily symmetrical design," which closely resembles ritornello form. Equally symmetrical schemes do, however, occur in what are probably Weimar works.[7] In any case the fantasia, although formally a textbook example of ritornello design, lacks concerto-like material except perhaps in the arpeggiated figuration of the last episode. The "ritornello" is a twelve-measure phrase constructed over a descending chaconne-like bass and repeated at regular intervals in E minor, D minor, and in the tonic at the end. Its stark initial statement, in five and six voices, is a splendid opening gesture for a concert; the texture is reduced to four voices for the D-minor statement. There are three episodes, all using a suspension motive related to one in the "ritornello" (compare treble in mm. 3–4, alto in 12–3).

The fugue is in three sections and has two subjects; the central section introduces the second subject (m. 37), and the last section (m. 61) combines the two.[8] The design is an old one, predating Bach, who used it throughout his career; the "Legrenzi" Fugue for organ BWV 574 is a probably somewhat earlier example. Such fugues are particularly effective when there is a strong contrast between the two subjects, as is the case here. The first subject is characterized by rhetorical pauses and repeated gestures, the second by its chromaticism and by its more restrained motion—longer note-values, fewer leaps.[9] Each outer section closes with a statement of the first subject in the soprano; the final statement (beginning at m. 74b) is extended slightly and combined with the second subject.

The sources show notable inconsistencies, especially with regard to ac-cidentals. As in other highly chromatic pieces (e.g., the A-minor prelude of WTC2), Bach may have changed his mind about several notes, such as alto g′ (g♯′?) in fugue, m. 23 (beat 2), and b′ in the final (soprano) entry in fugue, m. 74. The NBA's b♭′ in the latter passage, although found in the principal sources, seems a mistake, and the final chord (m. 80) should surely be major.

Fugue in A Minor BWV 944

Chief sources: ABB (no. 56; mainly Johann Christoph Bach; with fantasia); LEm ms. 8 (Preller); P 618 (J. W. Häßler). *Editions*: BG 3; Dadelsen and Rönnau (1970); NBA V/9.2.

The fugue BWV 944 is even more of a display piece than BWV 904, closer to Italian concerto style although not necessarily later in date. Indeed, its presence in ABB suggests that it is earlier, although it is probably one of the last entries in that manuscript. There it is preceded by a short fantasia, but most other sources give only the fugue, and it is possible, as Hill (1987, 360) suggested, that "Bach himself suppressed the fantasia." Suppressed, or simply abandoned—for the fan-tasia consists of only ten measures of not very striking chords, marked *arpeggio*. As such it is little more than a framework for improvisation or a preliminary sketch, like the series of five-part chords that represents the earliest form of the prelude in C♯ from WTC2. Where Bach's finished works use similar shorthand, the arpeggiation of the first few chords is usually written out to suggest how the remainder should be realized. No such suggestion occurs here, and the vary-ing number of voices in the chords makes it impossible to use exactly the same arpeggio pattern for each.[10]

The arpeggiando fantasia is obviously suited to the harpsichord, and the title in Johann Christoph Bach's copy (*Fantasia in A♭ pour le Clavessin*) can be as-sumed to extend to the fugue as well, as signified by the marking *Fuga seq[uitur]*. The running figuration and three-part texture of the fugue are eminently suited to the harpsichord; a few sustained bass notes might be restruck if they cease to sound. The subject is often said to be a version of that of the organ fugue in A minor BWV 543/2, and there is a family resemblance. Otherwise, however, the pieces are distinct.[11] BWV 944 is the more integrated work, drawing virtually all its motivic material from the subject and containing a great deal more recapitulation. The first and only exposition in a major key (C) falls near the exact center (mm. 93–108) and closes with a passage previously used at the end of the first exposition (mm. 27–32). The last third (from m. 122) is mostly patched together from recapitulated material. Monotony, always a danger in the absence of strong contrasts, is avoided by the ever-inventive writing, in particular a sequence that contains some remarkable chromatic juxtapositions (e.g., V– I in A minor followed immediately by V⁷ of B♭ in mm. 62–3). A dominant pedal point from the end of the second section (mm. 117ff.) returns to lead directly into the coda (mm. 177ff.). Hence, the coda is not a motivically unrelated improvisation, as in the early works, but a natural extension of the main body of the piece—a further distinction from the organ fugue BWV 543/2.

The present fugue's great length and its perpetual motion in sixteenths make it tempting to play it as quickly as possible, as a demonstration of digital dexterity. No doubt it was written partly for just this purpose, and it makes a brilliant display piece. But as in other "motoric" pieces, a tempo that reduces the constant sixteenths to a mechanical blur may be less exciting than a slower speed that permits rhythmic nuance.

Prelude and Fugue in A Minor BWV 894

Chief sources: Earliest readings: P 804/29 (Kellner, dated 1725); P 1084 (Mempell). Slightly revised readings: P 801 (J. T. Krebs). Intermediate (?) readings: US NHy LM 4717b; LEm ms. Rudorff 9 (Johann Bernhard Bach). Late readings: SBB AmB 549 (Anon. 401 = Kühn?). *Editions*: BG 36; Dadelsen and Rönnau (1970); NBA V/9.2.

The other big A-minor work, BWV 894, comes even closer than BWV 944 to the mature Venetian concerto. Johann Bernhard Bach, who was responsible for the most important manuscript copy of the concerto transcriptions, also made one of the earliest copies of the present work, under the title *Praeludium pro Clavicembalo*. Eppstein (1970) argued that BWV 894 was itself drawn from an actual keyboard concerto, but the sources do not support this, and the internal evidence is inconclusive. Still, the material of BWV 894 recurs in the outer movements of the Triple Concerto BWV 1044, which is scored for flute, violin, harpsichord, and ripieno strings (the same instrumentation as in the Fifth Brandenburg Concerto, with the addition of a second *violino di ripieno*). The extensive differences between BWV 894 and BWV 1044 imply that both works go back to an earlier, lost model; they also raise some doubt as to whether Bach was really responsible for BWV 1044.[12]

There can, however, be no questioning Bach's authorship of BWV 894. The prelude follows a design remarkably close to that of the opening allegro of the harpsichord concerto in D minor BWV 1052. The latter dates from the 1730s but is probably descended from a much earlier work, now lost, that can be assigned to Weimar (see Breig 1976, 32–3). The formal crux in both movements is a cadenza (or a series of cadenzas) placed just after the midpoint, after a cadence to the subdominant.[13] Moreover, the final ritornello in each movement is prepared by a climactic flurry of passagework. Yet, despite the clear ritornello structure, a predictable suggestion to divide the "tutti" and "solo" passages of the prelude between manuals (Bodky 1960, 334) is not practical. Particularly at the center of the movement (mm. 53b–63a), where short cadenzas alternate in rapid succession with fragments of the ritornello, it is awkward for the player and ineffective musically to shift to a softer manual for the brilliant soloistic phrases.

The fugue is reminiscent of BWV 944; both are allegros or prestos in perpetual motion, and both subjects are based on the same underlying progression.[14] The two fugues also have comparable formal schemes. The fugue in BWV 894 employs relatively little exact recapitulation, but like BWV 944 it makes only a single strong move to a major key, cadencing to C a little more than halfway through.[15] There is also a substantial coda, again based on material from the subject.

Despite its attractive features, the present fugue is in some ways less successful than BWV 944. The slower harmonic rhythm of BWV 944—which often has but a single harmony per measure—counters the effect of the incessant rushing figuration and permits it to achieve considerable breadth. In BWV 894 the harmony changes on almost every dotted eighth, which can prove wearying. Sequences are omnipresent in both pieces, but BWV 894 lacks the chromatic progressions that raise certain sequences in BWV 944 out of the ordinary. Most seriously, the fugue of BWV 894 is too much like its prelude for the two movements to form an effective pair. Measures 2–3 of the subject are a virtual quotation of m. 3 in the prelude, and further parallelisms also occur.[16] One wishes that there were an intervening slow movement—as there is in the concerto version, which inserts an adagio drawn from the organ sonata BWV 527.

The work, especially the praeludium, may have passed through several stages of revision, but these were limited to small refinements and the expansion of one passage (the concluding "solo" of the praeludium) by two measures. NBA V/9.2 presents "early" and "late" versions for both movements, although the early version of the fugue is represented only by a few readings on "ossia" staves, not a separate score. On the other hand, *ossia* staves are used to show a few intermediate readings from P 801 in the early version of the praeludium (in m. 41, G should be corrected to A). NBA V/9.2, KB, 95–101, describes two further intermediate versions, but these rarely present their own readings, following instead the earlier or later version, but not according to a consistent pattern. Hence, as in BWV 903, all surviving versions of the work may derive from a lost autograph whose successive revisions were never notated with sufficient clarity to prevent copyists from sometimes overlooking or misreading Bach's corrections.

Chromatic Fantasia and Fugue in D Minor BWV 903

Early version (BWV 903a): *Sources*: DS Mus. ms. 69 (Christoph Graupner, Jr.); "Rust" copy (lost; signed "J. L. A. Rust, Bernburg 1757"). *Edition*: Leisinger (1999); NBA V/9.2, Anhang I.
Intermediate (?) version: *Source*: P 803 (two copies: J. T. Krebs, Samuel Gottlieb Heder). *Edition*: NBA V/9.2, Anhang II.
Later version: *Chief sources*: P 651 (Agricola); P 275/5 (Müthel; fantasia only); P 289 (J. F. Hering); AmB 548 (Anonymous 414 and Anonymous 401; with fingerings added); P 551 + P 535 (Gebhardt; fantasia and fugue separately, with arpeggios of fantasia written out on a loose sheet); P 212 (Forkel; indirect basis of his 1802 edition); print, ed. Griepenkerl (1819). *Editions*: BG 36; Dadelsen and Rönnau (1970); Leisinger (1999); NBA V/9.2.

Few of Bach's solo keyboard works have been as admired as the Chromatic Fantasia and Fugue. Already for Forkel it was "unique, and never had its like" (1802, 56/NBR, 468). The work's mystique derives from its apparent opposition to everything that Bach stands for; it seems romantic, not baroque, improvisatory rather than strictly architectural. This view is not entirely without justification. Comparable chromatic passages occur in other instrumental pieces by Bach, but only in the G-minor organ fantasia BWV 542/1 in such concentration and with so little regard for the usual niceties of modulation. The free fantasia would become a favorite genre for younger composers, notably C. P. E. and W. F. Bach; a fantasia by C. P. E. Bach from the 1740s constitutes a link between BWV 903 and later works, opening like the Chromatic Fantasia with measured figuration before proceeding to recitative-like writing.[17] Yet whatever influence BWV 903 might have had on later fantasias was probably less than that of actual improvisations which Sebastian's sons would have heard in their youth.

NBA V/9.2 lists over forty manuscript sources, many of them late, showing that BWV 903 was widely played and remained influential well after Bach's death. Not surprisingly, it was among the first of Bach's keyboard pieces to be edited (or rather revised) to suit later musical fashions. Griepenkerl's 1819 edition included ornaments and embellishments together with numerous indications for dynamics and articulation, all claimed to stem from Friedemann Bach.[18] Then, in the mid-nineteenth century, Hans von Bülow issued his notoriously romanticized piano edition. In 1890 even Naumann accepted slurs and dynamics of doubtful authenticity, contrary to the BG's usual procedures. Schenker's 1910 edition was, despite its "elucidatory" analytic commentary (translated in Schenker 1984), merely an annotated version of the BG text.[19] Not until 1970 was there an edition based on a reasonably accurate evaluation of the sources, and editors still have not settled important questions such as the precise status of what seem to be intermediate versions.[20] The edition by Leisinger (1999) is the most reliable;

the NBA includes *ossia* readings that could represent late revisions by Bach but might equally well be spurious.

Again there are indications that the two movements were originally separate. Some sources give only one movement, and the fantasia—but not the fugue—seems to have been originally notated without the one-flat key signature. Important variants occur in both movements, particularly in the first half of the fantasia, whose earliest version (BWV 903a) descends to low AA. This note appears at the end of a descending arpeggio (m. 23) and might have been intended for the special instrument apparently used in the Aria variata BWV 989, a probable Weimar work. The instrumental recitative in the fantasia seems to have been inspired by a Vivaldi work (see below), and this too would support a Weimar origin for the fantasia. Parallels in the figuration of the Fifth Brandenburg Concerto have been cited in support of a Cöthen dating (Stauffer 1989). But although the familiar version of the concerto is dated 1721, it may well have been composed by the time Bach reached Cöthen. Like BWV 903, it exists in an early version distinguished especially by a shorter form of an improvisatory passage, that is, the harpsichord "cadenza" near the end of the first movement. Perhaps Bach revised the two works for court performances at Cöthen and Berlin, respectively.

The title appears in various ways. Usually it is clear that the adjective "chromatic" applies to the fantasia; P 803, for example, specifies *Fantasie chromatique pour le clavecin*. The fugue has a chromatic subject, but a separate title like the *Fuga cromatica* of P 535 appears to be late, perhaps reflecting an awareness of the *Recercar cromatico* of Frescobaldi; Marpurg had drawn attention to the latter by citing the subjects of the two pieces side by side in his *Abhandlung von der Fuge* (1753–4, 1:83).

It is especially important in the fantasia that the player understand which notes are chord tones and which ones are anticipations, passing tones, suspensions, and the like. Harmonic analysis in the ordinary sense is less useful for this

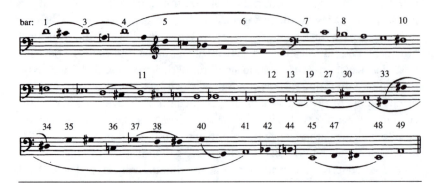

Example 9.1 Chromatic Fantasia BWV 903/1: bass line sketch for mm. 1–49 (open note-heads = tones of primary importance; filled note-heads = tones of secondary importance; slurs and ties connect notes belonging to the same harmony).

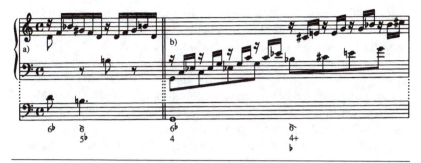

Example 9.2 Chromatic Fantasia BWV 903/1: (a) m. 7a, and (b) m. 12, with figured bass sketch.

purpose than understanding the voice leading that underlies the embellished surface. As Schenker recognized, such understanding can emerge through a form of analysis documented from Bach's time: extracting the essential bass line and outlining the basic voice leading in the form of figures, as in Example 9.1. This reveals, among other things, that the baffling chromatic progressions at several points in the opening section are all elaborations of essentially the same progression: what look like augmented-sixth chords in mm. 7, 9, and 11, as well as the C-minor harmony in m. 12, all arise through similar chromatic voice leading (Example 9.2).

The fantasia falls into two distinct sections, which we may refer to as prelude and recitative, respectively, although each borrows to some degree from the style of the other. Tonally the first half moves in a relatively straightforward way to the dominant (m. 49); the second half returns to the tonic, but only after some remarkably remote modulations. The first half is essentially an arpeggiando prelude, though the figuration ranges from regular sequences using broken-chord motives to free cadenzas. The early version gives mm. 3–20 in a somewhat longer but less striking form that nevertheless follows essentially the same scheme as the later versions.[21] Up to m. 33 the harmony is rather conventional, save for the chromatic progressions mentioned above. But the C-minor harmony at m. 12 constitutes a momentary dislocation into a remote "flat" realm, anticipating the more extensive tonal dislocations that occur later. These begin in earnest at m. 33, where Bach reverts to the indeterminate arpeggio notation used in the fantasia of BWV 944. In addition, what has been a steady descent in the bass from d′ to A (see Example 9.1) now gives way to irregular voice leading, whose diminished fourths and other odd intervals resist reduction to a simpler line.[22] The passage alludes to "flat" (G minor, m. 33), then "sharp" (E minor, m. 34), and again to "flat" tonalities (B♭ minor, m. 38).[23] The only lasting modulation is the one at m. 45 to A minor, the minor dominant, although by this point the rapid key changes are likely to have wiped out one's tonal bearings.

Hence one is prepared for the violent tonal lurch that launches the following section. The title *recitative* for this section is evidently original; presumably it applies to the entire remainder of the fantasia. The imitation of recitative is less literal but at the same time more idiomatic to the keyboard than later examples in works by Bach's sons.[24] Sebastian might have drawn on earlier examples of instrumental recitative instead of imitating the vocal idiom directly; Kuhnau's Biblical Sonatas had already contained one or two fairly explicit examples. But a more immediate model was the slow movement of Vivaldi's "Grosso Mogul" concerto, which Bach arranged for organ as BWV 594.[25] Vivaldi's violin line is highly embellished, in a distinctly non-vocal manner, but it is accompanied by basso continuo alone, notated as in simple ("secco") recitative. Bach, in his organ transcription, realizes the figured bass and rewrites the bass notes and chords as quarters separated by rests, making explicit the "short" accompaniment that was probably the normal way of realizing Vivaldi's original notation (see Tagliavini 1986, 248 and 250).

The recitative in the Chromatic Fantasia employs the same explicit short notation, and its chromaticism is more extreme than Vivaldi's, the cadenza-like passages more brilliant. But even the pedal point at the end of the fantasia has some precedent in the Vivaldi work, which ends with an ascending progression over a dominant pedal (Example 9.3). In the corresponding passage in the fantasia (mm. 75–9), the treble descends chromatically through a full octave over a tonic pedal; the underlying gesture is essentially that of a plagal cadence, marvelously prolonged.[26]

Despite its chromaticism, the harmony at the end of the recitative is reasonably straightforward. Not so the beginning, which seems to cast all normal harmonic logic aside with a sudden move from A to D♭ (m. 50).[27] From there until m. 63, where the music re-enters the realm of D minor (via V of iv), the keys tonicized bear no obvious relation to the tonic. Distant and even arbitrary modulations were part of the language of recitative, but one still expects them to make sense, and in fact the modulations make more sense than the notation might suggest. The dominant chord tonicizing D♭ in m. 50 is enharmonically equivalent to the

Example 9.3 Vivaldi, Concerto *il grosso Mogul* in D, R. 208, second movement, mm. 20b–23.

Example 9.4 Chromatic Fantasia BWV 903/1, mm. 50–68: harmonic outline (lowest staff shows bass of mm. 50–8 in enharmonically equivalent notation).

one tonicizing C♯ minor in m. 61 (as indicated by the asterisks in Example 9.4). Moreover, the intervening passage is essentially a sequence over a descending bass line.[28] Hence the opening section of the recitative is essentially a digression in C♯ minor—that is, iii of V. The latter, to be sure, represents a very distant relationship to the tonic D minor. It is easier to understand the fantasia as modulating at its very center to one of the most remote keys imaginable, just as Emanuel Bach half a century later placed the central sections of two free fantasias a tritone and a half step from the tonic, respectively.[29]

Did Bach have any specific expressive intent here? The way in which the work stands apart from Bach's other compositions has made it irresistible for some commentators to weave romantic fantasies around it. Schleuning (1969) linked it to the seventeenth-century *tombeaux* of Froberger and Louis Couperin, with which it has almost nothing in common stylistically. Wiemer (1988, 165–6) supposed that it might have been a lament for Bach's first wife, Maria Barbara. But she died in 1720, raising difficulties for Wiemer's proposal if the fantasia indeed dates from Bach's Weimar years. In any case, despite its generalized chromaticism, the work lacks specific symbols for lamentation, such as the chaconne bass employed in BWV 992. But could the mere presence of remote modulations have had particular connotations? Bach and his contemporaries sometimes used chromatic progressions to represent transformations, whether between joy and sorrow, life and death, or love and hate. In Bach's cantatas, remote key-successions occasionally reflect profound theological ideas, although not nearly as often as is sometimes supposed.[30] It would be arbitrary to attach any particular meaning to the transformations in this work. We have no documentation of how Bach's contemporaries heard such compositions, but later writers took it for granted that music could move metaphorically between "light" and "shade."[31] By the end of the century we find an account of musical modulation as something like passing "into another world"(*wie in eine andre Welt*); this occurs in Wilhelm Heinse's 1794 novel *Hildegard von Hohenthal*, a work related in spirit to the proto-Romantic descendents of the Chromatic Fantasia.[32]

The fugue, despite its chromatic subject and virtuoso episodes, is inevitably something of a letdown. Several exceptional features reflect its pairing with so extraordinary a fantasia: the protean character of the subject, which appears in various forms, and the octave doublings of the bass in the final phrase, otherwise unknown in Bach's keyboard works. The free treatment of the subject has drawn attention from commentators, beginning with Marpurg (1753–4, 1:83), who showed that in the answer (mm. 9ff.) the original half-step a′–b♭′ (m. 1) is replaced by the third d′–f′.[33] The passing tone e′ in m. 9 is an embellishment, but the point was lost on Bülow, who arbitrarily "corrected" the answer in his edition, eliminating the surprising dissonance (d′/c′′) formed when the second voice enters. In fact, one can hear the d′ of the alto (m. 9) as a continuation of the same pitch sounded by the soprano on the preceding downbeat.

If the fugue indeed deserves its epithet "chromatic," it is not because of its subject; Bach wrote other fugues on equally chromatic subjects. Rather, like the fantasia, the fugue moves to tonalities not normally encountered in D minor, here B minor and E minor. Yet the fugue suffers from the absence of major keys. The subject may have been unsuited for use in the major, but the excursions to unexpectedly "sharp" minor keys do not compensate for the overwhelmingly minor coloration. Still, the fugue was planned with a clear sense of tonal design, and the modulations to the remote keys of B and E minor are at the center (mm. 83–97). As in BWV 944, most of the last third of the piece is patched together from recapitulated material; this is no failing, although one might criticize the somewhat pedestrian sequences first announced in mm. 118–25 and restated not much farther along (at m. 147).

Fantasia and Fugue in C Minor BWV 906

Chief sources: Autograph of the fantasia in the possession of the Bethlehem Bach Choir, housed at Lehigh University (facsimile: Marshall 1976b); Dl Mus. 2405-T-52, Aut. 3 (autograph of the fantasia, with fragment of the fugue; facsimile in Schulze 1984b). *Editions*: BG 36 (fugue in appendix); Dadelsen and Rönnau (1970); NBA V/9.2.

The C-Minor Fantasia and Fugue is much later than the other pieces considered in this chapter, but because it was never incorporated into a larger set it is most conveniently treated here. The fantasia is indistinguishable in form from "the allegro of a sonata," as Forkel (1802, 56/NBR, 468) put it, and is close in style to the more extended sonata-form preludes in WTC2. The fugue survives only as a fragment of what was probably to have been a much longer movement.

What is probably the earliest source, the Bethlehem (Pennsylvania) autograph of the fantasia, is a fair copy, and the original draft could have been written earlier; the Dresden autograph was probably written around 1738 or later.[34] Marshall's (1976b) proposal that the fantasia might have been conceived for use in the C-minor Partita, or that both movements together might have been considered for inclusion in WTC2, has not been widely accepted. But the virtuoso character of the present work, both of whose movements involve hand crossing, is not entirely foreign to WTC2; hand crossings occur in the prelude in B♭, which is also a sonata-form movement of ambitious proportions.

Commonly described as binary form, the type of sonata movement represented by the fantasia is actually in three main sections, the double bar marking the end of the first, a short retransition (mm. 28b–33) preceding the final section. The title "fantasia" may seem inappropriate for such a movement, but there is a fantasia by Friedemann Bach in the same form (F. 14 in C), and the title evidently was considered appropriate for a sonata movement containing fairly unusual figuration. It is conceivable that Sebastian wrote the present work expressly for his eldest son, who was a noted virtuoso and might have been the original owner of the Dresden autograph. Hand crossing seems to have been a popular entertainment in the Bach household during the 1720s and 1730s; it occurs in the First Partita (published 1726) and in Emanuel Bach's first published work, the Minuet W. 111 of 1731. The technique naturally calls to mind the sonatas of Domenico Scarlatti, but Rameau is another possible influence.[35] Hand crossings also occur in the anonymous fugue that Bach perhaps reworked as the last movement of the E-Minor Toccata BWV 914. Hence, by the time of the C-minor fantasia, hand crossings are unlikely to have been a novelty to Bach. They are incorporated into the symmetrical architecture of the piece, crossings by the left hand over the right in the first section being balanced by crossings of the right over the left in the second.

By the late 1730s, Bach's sons—at least Emanuel—were composing full-fledged keyboard sonatas in *galant* style.[36] This fantasia's affinity to such pieces is evident not only in its clearly articulated sonata form but in the triplets, the periodic phrasing, and the leisurely underlying quarter-note pulse. But Sebastian's hand is recognizable in the contrapuntal texture—limited to two or three essential parts, but these engaging in frequent imitation—and in the somewhat quirky chromaticism, especially in the final phrase.

Although an attractive and extremely effective work in performance, the fantasia has a slightly manic character due to the packing of so many virtuoso gestures into a simple, compact structure. The first section ("exposition") consists of two equal periods—$2 \times (4 + 4)$ measures—and the third ("recapitulation") is a simple period ($3\frac{1}{2} + 4\frac{1}{2}$ measures). No matter how deliberate the tempo, extraordinary gestures like the dissonant chromatic sequence in the closing phrase (mm. 37b–38) fly by quickly. But by the time this piece was written, the old sense of chromatic lines as deeply expressive—each interval fraught with harmonic tension—was perhaps eroding under the influence of equal temperament and a general lightening of style. This impression is strongest in the climactic chromatic lines that move first in parallel, then in contrary motion (m. 33) just before the return. Although not quite ornamental—each chromatic step retains a vestige of harmonic significance—the long chromatic lines in small note values might even receive slurs, like the similar figure in the augmentation canon of the *Art of Fugue* (m. 29).

It is curious that, except perhaps at the cadences, the only substantial interruption in the flow of the triplets occurs early, in m. 8.[37] There the repeated sixteenths in the left hand should probably be interpreted literally (without "assimilation" to the prevailing triplets); the passage is made more effective by prolonging the initial (upper) note of the trill. This will emphasize the expressive cross-relation (f♯/f′), which was to become a favorite mannerism in the *empfindsam* style of Emanuel Bach (Example 9.5). Assimilation is more plausible in mm. 21–3, where the thirty-seconds might be altered to triplets.[38] It may be, however, that the thirty-seconds in this passage represent the notes of a mordent, quickly played, which Bach wrote out in order to avoid any ambiguity about the necessary accidentals.[39]

The fugue, had Bach finished it, would have been remarkable not only because of its hand crossings (the only substantial ones in a Bach fugue) but because of the elaborate chromaticism and permutational counterpoint of the opening section. In fact, Bach may have completed the work in some form, for the entry in the Dresden autograph seems to start as a fair copy. But certain details underwent changes, probably as Bach was copying. Thus, in mm. 34–5, Bach altered one of the two new themes introduced at that point, showing that here he was revising, perhaps even composing, as he wrote.[40] The hand crossings begin in m. 38,

Example 9.5 Fantasia in C Minor BWV 906/1: (a) m. 8; (b) m. 21.

and Bach broke off work on the manuscript after reaching the downbeat of m. 48. Perhaps Bach had doubts about the propriety of introducing hand crossing into a fugue, or perhaps the stylistic disparity between the opening section and that on which he was now working had grown too great. Forkel already noted the change of character that occurs at m. 25, questioning Bach's authorship of the remainder of the fragment (Forkel 1802, 56/NBR, 468). Indeed, mm. 25–33 could almost be by Friedemann Bach. These measures constitute a sort of free coda at the end of the initial section. But neither this coda nor the exposition of the new subject, which follows, has any significant motivic connection to the opening section. Nor can the subject be combined contrapuntally with the new themes introduced at m. 34.

Schreyer (1910–3, 2: 34–6), although doubting Bach's authorship of the fugue, was apparently the first to suggest that the movement was to have been a da capo form, like a number of large virtuoso fugues for other instruments.[41] But there is no fermata (signifying a *Fine*) at the end of the first section, and it is unclear whether one would place it at the middle of m. 33 or on the downbeat of m. 34. Nor do mm. 32b–33a constitute a conventional final cadence, despite forming a V–I progression. Having introduced new material at m. 34, Bach (at this stage in his career) would surely have developed it at length in episodes alternating with entries of the principal subject; indeed, the latter enters just as the fragment breaks off (m. 46). Hence, to repeat mm. 3–33—whether after the downbeat of m. 48 (at the end of the extant fragment),[42] or at the conclusion of a longer reconstruction—is at best a provisional solution. One such completion, by Edward T. Cone (1974), emphasizes contrapuntal development of the chromatic subject; Example 9.6 shows another approach.[43]

Example 9.6 Fugue in C Minor BWV 906/2, mm. 48ff. (suggested completion).

Example 9.6 (Continued)

Example 9.6 (Continued)

Dal Segno
(bar 5)

Example 9.6 (Continued)

The Arpeggio Notation in BWV 903

The incompletely notated *arpeggio* passages in the Chromatic Fantasia are the most extensive in any of Bach's frequently performed keyboard works. The written-out breaking of the first chord (m. 27a) suggests that each subsequent half-note chord should simply be broken once upward and once downward. But the number of notes in the chords varies, making it impossible to maintain precisely the same pattern for each chord. And one wonders what to do in places such as the second half of m. 33, where one voice has passing motion in quarter notes.

Notation of this sort is quite common in eighteenth-century keyboard music, but few sources provide detailed explanations of how to interpret it, perhaps because the manner of playing seemed self-evident at the time. Unfortunately, verbal explanations are ambiguous on such matters as the number of times each chord is to be rolled.[44] Nor do they entirely accord with written-out "realizations," which suggest that some players took such passages to be invitations for virtual free improvisation or composition.[45]

For the Chromatic Fantasia we have written-out realizations, including one inserted into the manuscript P 551, as well as verbal instructions in the preface to Griepenkerl's 1819 edition of the work; Leisinger (1999) reproduces both. Although late, each has a tenuous claim of belonging to the Bach tradition; the copyist of P 551 might have had some connection with Kittel,[46] and Griepenkerl was a pupil of Forkel, who had studied with W. F. Bach. Both take a simple approach, differing on the question of how to deal with passing tones: whereas P 551 incorporates the passing tones into the descending part of the arpeggio (see Example 9.7a), Griepenkerl arpeggiates the chord twice, the second time with the passing tone. Griepenkerl's practice makes the changing notes more audible, but it seems contrary to the rhythmic notation, which shows the passing tones only as quarter notes off the beat.[47] A compromise—admittedly without any historical source—would be to play upward arpeggios (only) for both the chord on the beat and the same chord incorporating the passing tone.

Another question is what to do when successive chords fall in different registers. P 551 supports the common-sense idea that one can omit the notes of the left hand from the descending part of the arpeggio, when the left hand must move to another register for the following chord (Example 9.7a). One may further speculate that chords notated as whole notes (such as the one that opens BWV 944) can be broken twice (Example 9.7b), and that it is permissible to end a phrase with an upward arpeggio (e.g., in m. 42).[48]

Example 9.7 (a) Chromatic Fantasia in D Minor BWV 903/1, m. 33, with realization of arpeggios from P 551; (b) Fantasia in A Minor BWV 944/1, last two measures.

10

The *Clavier-Büchlein vor Wilhelm Friedemann Bach* and Related Works

Bach came to Cöthen late in 1717 and remained there until spring 1723. At Cöthen he had no duties as a church musician, and thus it is assumed that he concentrated on the production of secular music for the court, as well as pedagogical works for his pupils, including members of his own growing family. It was during this period that some of his best-known instrumental works, the Brandenburg Concertos and the works unaccompanied violin, were revised and put into definitive form, if not actually composed. Cöthen autographs survive not only for those works but also the first part of the *Well-Tempered Clavier* (WTC1) and the Inventions and Sinfonias. In addition, the Cöthen years saw the commencement of little keyboard books (*Clavierbüchlein*) for Wilhelm Friedemann and Anna Magdalena Bach.

The autographs of WTC1 and of the Inventions and Sinfonias are fair copies that were probably meant to serve as the basis for further copies by Bach's pupils. The idea that they also served as a sort of teaching portfolio, taken to job interviews (as envisioned in Wolff 2000, 225–6), presupposes that the authorities were concerned with Bach's ability to provide technical training in keyboard playing and composition, as opposed to singing and Latin. In any case they differed from the little keyboard books in that the latter served as family albums for domestic music teaching and recreation, not as templates for further copies. Anna Magdalena's book—the first of two manuscripts known by her name—is the earliest source for the French Suites and is discussed in chapter 14. Friedemann's book (hereafter, CB) contains a variety of pedagogic pieces, including early versions of the Inventions and Sinfonias as well as some of the preludes of WTC1.[1]

Friedemann's book was begun (according to the title page) on January 22, 1720, two months after Friedemann's ninth birthday. The pages were only gradually filled with music; the majority of the entries are thought to have been made from 1721 to early 1723. Some of the pieces entered by Sebastian into the volume appear to be first drafts; others are fair or revision copies. Still others are in Friedemann's hand, including copies of several works by composers other than Sebastian Bach. The book probably drew on a stock of pieces that Bach had already assembled for teaching. These pieces cannot all have been composed specifically for Friedemann, but the pedagogical needs of his children would have encouraged Bach to keep an eye open for easy pieces by other composers even as he created new teaching material.

It cannot have been common for ten-year-old children to receive books that would be filled with sophisticated keyboard music. A child such as Friedemann, born into a family of professional musicians, was predestined for a life in music and would at some point have begun acquiring a personal collection of music by copying out pieces for study. But the music in CB is extraordinary; so too is the planning evident in the book's design, which no doubt reflected Sebastian's considerable experience by this date as a teacher. The father must already have had clear ideas about how and what to teach, and the son must already have shown the brilliance for which he was later famed. Friedemann is often said not to have fulfilled his early promise, but during a long career he would produce some extraordinary music, much of it reflecting the lessons in counterpoint and keyboard technique that are memorialized in CB.

The relatively orderly way in which teaching pieces by Sebastian Bach were entered into CB implies that sequences of such works already existed in some form; Hofmann (2001) argues the case for eight preludes that were later incorporated into WTC1. Bach must have composed a considerable number of teaching pieces by the time he left Weimar, where he had put together what is probably the earliest of the major keyboard collections, the *Orgelbüchlein* (Little Organ Book)—a set of chorale preludes. The title of Friedemann's book (Little "Clavier" Book) complements that of the organ volume, whose title was added to the manuscript only at Cöthen.[2] The majority of the pieces in CB were incorporated into WTC1 or the fair copy of the Inventions and Sinfonias. But some remained outside the great collections, as did a number of preludes, fugues, and other compositions not found in CB that might have belonged to Bach's larger repertory of teaching pieces. This chapter considers pieces from the latter group alongside the better-known ones in CB. A number of the pieces excluded from CB (such as the fugue BWV 952) look like prototypes for pieces included there or in other collections. These pieces suggest that Bach's pedagogic compositions evolved from relatively conventional, half-improvised preludes, fugues, and binary forms into more rigorous and challenging works like the Inventions and Sinfonias. Some of the left-over pieces were eventually incorporated (not necessarily by Bach) into further collections, including the "Six Little Preludes" and perhaps even the organ Pastorale BWV 590.[3]

The instrument for which these "clavier" pieces were intended is, as usual, uncertain. It has been assumed that the clavichord is the "most likely candidate" for the "avowedly preparatory compositions" (Marshall 1986, 234) with which Bach evidently commenced his sons' musical instruction. But Couperin (1717), writing for Parisian amateurs, assumed that beginners would be taught on a lightly quilled harpsichord. A family of professional musicians in Germany might not have been so well off, but Bach was not poor and his pupils would surely have had opportunities to play on harpsichords at least occasionally. Within CB, one can play up to the prelude in C♯ minor (no. 22) before encountering the note collisions that limited the practicality of fretted clavichords for music outside a restricted range of tonalities.[4] Such instruments remained common into the latter part of the century, but if these were indeed the chief instruments on which his pupils practiced, Bach made no concessions to the practical difficulties that they created. An allemande by J. C. (?) Richter, which falls just a few pages after the prelude in C♯ minor, is designated explicitly for *clavecin* (harpsichord), which is doubtless the instrument on which Bach's pupils would have wanted to play these pieces, given a choice.

The word *clavier* did at some point come to imply specifically the clavichord, but probably only after the time of CB.[5] The word *clavecin* attached to the Richter work cannot have been intended to distinguish it from others in the volume, for two other suites (CB 47–8, by Telemann and Stölzel, respectively) are in a brilliant style equally suited to the harpsichord, yet their titles do not mention any instrument. Bach added a movement (the trio BWV 929) to the Stölzel suite, and this piece, like the preludes, fugues, and the rest, is playable on the clavichord. Yet the arpeggiated chords of some pieces (BWV 846a/1 = CB 14, BWV 848/1 = CB 21), the lively violinistic figuration of others (BWV 779 = CB 35, BWV 796 = CB 53), and the contrapuntal textures of the inventions and sinfonias are more idiomatic to the harpsichord than the clavichord, whose greatest strength (as Friedemann and Emanuel would recognize in their mature compositions) is in textures that combine an expressive, lyrical melody with a relatively simple accompaniment.

Friedemann's book contains five main divisions:

1. tables illustrating clefs, the names of the notes, and an *Explication* of ornament signs and their meanings
2. a group of simple pieces, starting with a demonstration of keyboard fingering and including several preludes and two chorales (CB 1–13)
3. eleven preludes, later included in WTC1 (CB 14–24)

4. the fifteen two-part Inventions, here termed *Praeambula* (CB 32–46)
5. the fifteen Sinfonias, today often called three-part inventions but here designated *Fantasias* (CB 49–[63])

Similar elements occur in other pedagogic sources of the period, and Bach's models would have included manuscript collections belonging to the Pachelbel tradition in which his teacher and older brother had studied (see Belotti 2001). The scheme of Bach's manuscript suggests that it was conceived as a graded course in keyboard instruction, although the compositions were not simply copied from beginning to end. Blank pages were left at various points to be filled in later—but not always according to the plan sketched above. The suite by Richter (CB 25) was one of several items copied by Friedemann in the gap between the third and fourth groups of pieces. Several pieces falling within the second group are also in Friedemann's hand and may be early compositional essays of his own. Sebastian added a three-part fugue (BWV 953 = CB 31) just before group 4. The placement of this last work is no more readily explained than the fragmentary state of several other pieces, such as the chorale prelude *Jesu meine Freude* (BWV 753 = CB 5), which Sebastian broke off after reaching the end of a page in group 2.

Only four pieces in CB bear attributions, and only one attribution is to Bach; this is for the trio BWV 929 (= CB 48/5), distinguishing Bach's contribution from the rest of the suite by Stölzel. There is little reason to doubt Bach's authorship of the pieces that he entered into the book, especially when these show his revisions and corrections, as in the Inventions and Sinfonias. In several other cases—as also in a few little preludes preserved only in Kellner's copies—the style appears to be that of Sebastian Bach, and his authorship has rarely been questioned. Yet the pieces in question are too short and simple for their attribution to be determined confidently on the basis of style alone. The absence of independent concordances with attributions makes it conceivable that some of these compositions are by others, perhaps Friedemann or other Bach pupils.[6]

Tables of Notes and Ornaments

The opening material—illustrations of clefs, notes, and letter names for pitches—was traditional in instructional books. More modern was the ornament table, especially associated with publications of keyboard music in the French style. Such tables cannot have been meant to explain how to play ornaments, for musicians would have learned this through oral tradition. Rather, for experienced players the tables would have indicated which sign a particular composer used for each ornament. For beginners, ornament tables would have served the same function as tables of clefs or notes, teaching the pupil the names and the manner of notating things with which he or she was already well acquainted through aural experience.

Ornament tables are necessarily schematic. Even Bach's table employs rhythmically ungrammatical notation for a few things that could not, in any case, be precisely notated. Hence, attempts to puzzle out the performance of his ornaments through a literal interpretation of such a table are destined for failure. The table in CB is a rationalized, simplified version of ornament tables published by d'Anglebert and Dieupart. Bach had included d'Anglebert's table in his manuscript copy of Grigny's First Organ Book,[7] but Bach's own table is shorter, omitting signs not encountered in his scores. Williams suggests (2004, 165) that the sources on which Bach drew would have seemed old-fashioned in 1720, and Bach's practices in later years might have differed; certainly he did not consistently use all of the signs shown here.

In any case, Bach's table, like his notation of ornaments in actual compositions, is a personal synthesis of several traditions. The ornament that Bach calls by the French word *accent* is equivalent to the appoggiatura called a *port de voix* by d'Anglebert and other contemporary French musicians, played on the beat if the tables can be believed. Yet the term derived from the Italian *accento*, often used for unaccented passing tones in the older, early-Baroque Italian tradition. Following d'Anglebert, Bach signifies the appoggiatura by attaching what looks like a comma or a hook to the front of the notehead to which it applies (Example 10.1). But unlike d'Anglebert, Sebastian places the sign on the line or space representing the actual ornamental tone, not on that of the main note. Moreover, the sign is often accompanied by a slur; since the slur and the comma look alike, notes graced by such an *accent* often seem to be preceded by a pair of slurs or hooks.[8] An appoggiatura indicated in this manner is probably identical to one notated as a small eighth note (or other value). But in neither case can one assume that the length of the appoggiatura was governed by the rules later given by C. P. E. Bach; these apply only to the long type of appoggiatura that he described as "variable."[9] Most appoggiaturas in French harpsichord music are better played as the short or "invariable" type, and the same is true in Bach's works in French style; long appoggiaturas lack the spontaneity and gracefulness of the shorter type, and without the capability to swell gracefully on the dissonant note a keyboard instrument can make a long appoggiatura seem pedantic.[10]

Example 10.1 (a) D'Anglebert, *Cheute ou port de voix en montant*, from *Pièces de clavecin*; (b) CB: *accent steigend*.

Example 10.2 (a) D'Anglebert: [cadence] *sans tremblement*; (b) CB: *cadence*; (c) D'Anglebert: *double cadence* [avec tremblement]; (d) CB: *Doppelt-cadence*.

Another distinction between Bach's practice and that of his French contemporaries lies in his treatment of the turn and its relatives. For d'Anglebert, a simple turn standing alone ("sans tremblement") was evidently a *Cadence* (Example 10.2a)[11]; a *Double cadence* seems to be the pair of turns that precedes the trill in example 10.2c (the second turn is the rising one indicated by the arc at the beginning of the turn sign). Bach probably used the word *Cadence* in the same sense as d'Anglebert (Example 10.2b). But Bach, somewhat illogically, applied the expression *Doppelt-cadence* to a trill preceded by a single turn—that is, to the ornament that comprises only the second half of d'Anglebert's cadential formula (Example 10.2d). The result is a long trill that begins with a turn played on the beat. C. P. E. Bach later referred to this ornament as the "trill from below" or the "trill from above," depending on the direction from which the prefix begins.[12] This ornament is distinct from the *tremblement appuyé*, a trill with an elongated first (upper) note, the latter being signified by a straight, not curved, preliminary extension of the symbol. The *tremblement appuyé* is absent from the ornament table in CB—one of several signs that occur in Bach's music but not in the table, either because Bach did not use it at the time, or because he did not think it important enough to show a ten-year-old pupil.

More significant than the labeling of the ornaments is their relationship to the musical text. Are they a part of it or are they inessential additions, "ornaments" in a literal sense? Although ornamentation was a mandatory element of performance practice (e.g., in cadential trills), Bach probably thought of ornament *signs* as unnecessary—until he began to prepare works for study by his pupils. His early works rarely use the signs illustrated in CB, and early copies of the Inventions and other works show substantial differences in ornamentation. This implies that Bach did not initially regard the signs as fixed parts of the text. But later versions of the French Suites and other works are almost as replete with ornament signs as those of the French *clavecinistes*; were these signs meant as suggestions, reminders, or prescriptions for proper ornamentation? Conceivably, things originally offered as suggestions gradually became prescriptions. One wonders too whether in the process of writing out the ornament table and other pedagogic material, Bach codified and regularized his notation and terminology. A precocious ten-year-old might have noticed and demanded explanations for any inconsistencies in Bach's ways of playing or notating individual ornaments.

Preludes and Related Pieces

The word *prelude* could connote either a little teaching piece (as a prelude to more advanced studies?) or an improvisation (as a prelude to a written-out fugue or suite); the verb *preludieren* actually meant "to improvise." Both meanings could be attached to many of the pieces designated preludes in CB. The short pieces in group 2 probably were not Friedemann's first exercises at the keyboard. That function might have been served by simple minuets and other dances learned by rote (as Couperin suggests). This would explain the relatively sophisticated nature of even the first short pieces in CB, which demand as much care and thought in performance as the best French *pièces de clavecin*.

Applicatio BWV 994 (CB 1)

The Applicatio might be viewed as a continuation of the introductory matter preceding it. The term is perhaps not a title but a label: "Fingering," demonstrated in a little piece of eight measures in which virtually every note bears a fingering numeral.[13] The piece resembles a *Prelude oder Applicatio* that opens a somewhat earlier German keyboard book (see NBA V/5, KB, 74). The first measure is almost identical in the two pieces, as is the archaic fingering used for scale passages. But in these Sebastian makes 1, 3, and 5 the "good" (accented) fingers of the right as well as the left hand; this might have seemed a more modern approach than that taken in the other work. Still, the use of "paired" fingerings (3–4–3–4 and 1–2–1–2) seems to contradict what is often thought to have been Emanuel's claim that his father invented modern thumb-under fingering (C. P. E. Bach 1753–62, i.1.7). In fact Emanuel merely indicated that his father had expanded the use of the thumb, especially in "difficult" tonalities; Emanuel still gives paired fingerings as alternatives in the simpler keys. Paired fingerings remain useful in Bach's music for the occasional scale passage that must be played by the outer fingers of the hand while holding down an inner voice with the thumb (e.g., in the A-minor fugue of WTC1, m. 42). A player who practices these fingerings will find that many other types of passages are facilitated as well. Not only Emanuel Bach but his brother Friedemann seem to have continued using such fingerings, at least in keys involving few accidentals (see Faulkne r 1984, 22).

Efforts to connect such fingerings with particular schemes of rhythm or articulation are rarely convincing, since, with practice, one can learn to play most passages in Bach as smoothly as one wishes, using either "modern" or paired fingering.[14] Neither the Applicatio nor the other fully fingered piece (the prelude BWV 930) is sufficiently long or complex to provide fingerings for more than a handful of common figures, and these contain few surprises. Bach's fingerings do imply articulate (nonlegato) performance in certain contexts, as in the use of the same finger for successive changing notes (in m. 4). Several passages in BWV 930 likewise imply that strong articulations were tolerated, even encouraged, before strong beats and ornaments.[15] In addition, the Applicatio implies that Bach expected pupils to train the weaker fourth and fifth fingers for playing ornaments, and to cultivate somewhat unusual stretches between the outer fingers of either hand. A few of the stretches demanded here may seem rather wide for a boy of ten. But perhaps the young Friedemann already had the unusually long fingers visible in the reputed portrait by Friedrich Georg Weitsch (see Boyd 1999, 49),[16] or was taught on an instrument with unusually narrow keys. Even if the keys were no narrower than on a modern piano, a light action and a shallow key-dip would have made chords like that in m. 4 comparatively easy to play.

Despite its brevity the piece shows Bach's imprint. Unlike the anonymous prelude from which it may derive, it falls into a symmetrical binary form. The second half opens with an inversion of the opening motive, which is treated in quasi-imitation in both sections.

Chorale Preludes

What we call chorale preludes comprise various types of pieces that would have served differing purposes during Bach's lifetime. Although such compositions are now associated with the organ, the playing of chorale settings was by no means confined to church or liturgical use. The two examples in CB (*Wer nur den lieben Gott lässt walten* BWV 691 [CB 3] and *Jesu, meine Freude* BWV 753 [CB 5]) are at least equally suited to the harpsichord or clavichord. Both are *manualiter* examples of what Breig (1990a, 260–1) has termed the "monodic" organ chorale, in which a decorated chorale melody is accompanied by lower voices that can be played on a different (softer) manual. The same is true of *Jesus, meine Zuversicht* BWV 728 in the first *Clavier-Büchlein* for Anna Magdalena Bach, which is somewhat more subtle and counter-intuitive in some of its decoration of the chorale melody. BWV 753 is a fragment; Example 10.3 suggests a continuation.

German keyboard players must have routinely improvised pieces of the present type, which also occur among the works of Böhm, Buxtehude, and oth-

Example 10.3 *Jesu, meine Freude* BWV 753, mm. 9ff. (suggested completion).

ers. Such pieces are related to the allemande, which could be based on a chorale melody (ABB contains an anonymous example; see Schneider 2002, 127–9), and to the custom of creating dance movements as variations, as in Froberger's suite *auf die Mayerin* or the variation set attributed to Bach as BWV 990 (see appendix A). The style of the decoration derives partly from the Italian adagio but also from French organ and harpsichord music. Some of the more tortuous figures, as well as the occasional chromatic voice-leading in the lower parts, recall the slow movements of Bach's concertos and sonatas, which drew on the same store of improvisational formulas.

Chorale settings of this sort might have played a regular part in Bach's teaching regimen. There is a second copy of BWV 691 in Anna Magdalena's 1725 *Clavier-Büchlein*, and the work is also known in a spurious version (BWV 691a) in which ritornellos are added at the beginning, end, and between phrases.[17] BWV 691a might be the work of a Bach pupil; another such arrangement, BWV Anh. 73, is attributed in one source (LEm R 25) to C. P. E. Bach.[18] The existence of such arrangements suggests that short chorale preludes could serve as the basis for more extended exercises in composition or improvisation. The same process, carried out on a larger scale, produced the chorale fantasia *Vor deinen Thron tret' ich* BWV 668 as well as the Triple Concerto BWV 1044.[19]

Little Preludes

The little preludes in group 2 were apparently drawn from a larger repertory of such pieces. A few more were copied in the gap between groups 3 and 4, and other sources contain additional preludes. The surviving repertory is shown in Table 10.1, which lists the pieces roughly in order of increasing complexity; this does not, of course, necessarily correspond with the order of composition.[20] The titles vary in the sources; CB uses *Praeambulum* and *Praeludium* for different pieces, but the two terms seem to be equivalent.

Although Bach was responsible for the ordering of the pieces in groups 3, 4, and 5—that is, the preludes of WTC1 and the Inventions and Sinfonias—he is unlikely to have put all of the little preludes into any particular order. Unlike the pieces in the three other groups, those forming group 2 in CB do not constitute an integral set. Later manuscripts and printed editions put selections from the repertory into various arrangements. The so-called "Twelve Little Preludes" draws on pieces in CB as well as Kellner's manuscript P 804, even though one of the "Twelve" (BWV 999) is actually for the lute, and another (BWV 929) is not a prelude but Bach's insertion for a suite by Stölzel.[21] The "Six Little Preludes" has a slightly better claim to being an original Bach collection, appearing as a group in some late eighteenth-century copies. On that basis they appear together in NBA V/9.2, although one must look elsewhere (e.g., Dehnhard 1973) for a dependable modern edition of all the preludes in a single volume.

Table 10.1 Little Preludes and Related Pieces

BWV	Key	Chief Sources	Copyist	BG	NBA	Remark
939	C	P 804/53	anonymous	36:119	V/12	no. 2 of the "12"
940	d	P 804/53	member of Kellner	36:123	V/12	no. 6 of the "12"
941	e	P 804/53	circle,	36:123	V/12	no. 7 of the "12"
942	a	P 804/53	1726–7	36:127	V/12	no. 12 of the "12"
927	F	CB 8	WFB, 1722–3/1725–6	36:124	V/5	no. 8 of the "12"
		P 804/53	Kellner circle, 1726–7			
924	C	CB 2	JSB, 1720	36:118	V/5	no. 1 of the "12"
924a	C	CB 26	WFB, ca. 1726	36:221	V/5	"Variant" of BWV 924
926	d	CB 4	JSB, 1720–1	36:122	V/5	no. 5 of the "12"
928	F	CB 10	JSB, 1720–1	36:124	V/5	no. 9 of the "12"
930	g	CB 9	JSB, 1720–1	36:126	V/5	no. 11 of the "12"
925	D	CB 27	WFB, ca. 1726	36:121	V/5	no. 4 of the "12"
932	e	CB 28	WFB, ca. 1726	36:238	V/5	fragment
931	a	CB 29	WFB, ca. 1726	36:237	V/5	not by JSB?
943	C	P 804/2	Mey, by 1727	36:134	V/12	
933	C	various	various	36:128	V/9.2	no. 1 of the "6"
934	c	various	various	36:128	V/9.2	no. 2 of the "6"
935	d	various	various	36:130	V/9.2	no. 3 of the "6"
936	D	various	various	36:131	V/9.2	no. 4 of the "6"
937	E	various	various	36:132	V/9.2	no. 5 of the "6"
938	e	various	various	36:138	V/9.2	no. 6 of the "6"
999	c	P 804/19	Kellner, after 1727	36:119	V/10	no. 3 of the "12"

The four preludes BWV 939–42 have been banished to NBA V/12, a volume of doubtfully attributed works, because of their anonymity in their one source, P 804, where they are preserved alongside BWV 927 (also anonymous). But these could be the sort of improvisatory, lightly contrapuntal pieces that served as prototypes for the Inventions. Less austere than the latter, all but BWV 942 include at least a few passages in three or four voices. Yet the imitative structure never involves more than two parts; where chords do occur, they involve simple polyphony reminiscent of basso continuo realizations, such as one finds in the easier keyboard preludes and fugues of Bach's contemporaries. If Bach tossed off such pieces for favored pupils, it would explain why he continued to use the title *praeambulum* (implying improvisation) for the early versions of the Inventions, which, however, had developed into something more rigorous and original in conception.

The two shortest of these preludes, BWV 939 in C and BWV 940 in D minor, open as variations on conventional formulas, that of BWV 939 recalling the first prelude of WTC2. In all four preludes the opening motive is imitated in the bass, and the form hinges on a modulation to the dominant, articulated by something resembling an elided cadence at the exact center. Hence even these simple exercises offered pupils a demonstration of imitative texture within a tonal design.

Example 10.4 Prelude in A Minor BWV 942, mm. 8–10 (with suggested emendation for m. 9, left hand).

The slightly longer BWV 941 and 942 more obviously resemble the Inventions, already composed when the copies in P 804 were made. BWV 941 in E minor is the most likable of the set, with its jaunty arpeggio subject and simple quasi-stretto after the medial cadence to the relative major (m. 11). But BWV 942 in A minor comes closest to the Inventions, not only in its restriction to two voices but in its more tortuous melodic lines and more sophisticated, dissonant counterpoint. The initial imitation introduces types of passing dissonances (sevenths and augmented fifths approached by leap) that are rare outside Bach's music, especially in ostensibly simple pieces for beginners. The sole source for BWV 942 contains an error in m. 9; Example 10.4 suggests an emendation.[22]

One other very brief prelude appears in both CB and Kellner's collection. BWV 927 in F (CB 8) does not modulate; indeed the score contains no accidentals at all, a real rarity for Bach! But right at the center (the middle of m. 8), a weak cadence to the tonic coincides with a momentary change of texture. Friedemann's copy of this piece is the only fragment in the entire volume that he later completed, adding the last seven measures some time after he had copied the beginning of the piece.[23] Sebastian might have left this piece in a somewhat sketchy form, for the surviving sources show differing types of notational shorthand (as well as some corrections) in m. 14 (Example 10.5).

The first prelude in CB, BWV 924 in C, would have provided instruction in both keyboard playing and composition or improvisation, for it resembles illustrations in Niedt's *Musicalische Handleitung* of how to "vary" a bass line. We tend to view such pieces as demonstrating how melodic ideas can be generated from the arpeggiation of block chords. But to musicians whose understanding of harmony derived from figured bass, the "chords" would have constituted a simple four-part contrapuntal texture. The counterpoint is not simplistic; an

Example 10.5 Prelude in F, BWV 927, m. 14 (right hand): (a) reading of CB; (b) reading of P 804/53; (c) suggested interpretation.

initial series of 4–3 suspensions in mm. 1–3a gives way to less regular sequences of 6/5- and 9-chords by m. 4. Voice crossings reminiscent of Corelli's trio sonatas are already implicit in m. 1, where alto c′′ resolves to tenor b′ on the fourth beat. Hence it is not quite accurate to refer to this type of piece as one that "measure for measure uses the same compositional scheme [*Zerlegungsschema*] to break a series of chords" (Hofmann 2001, 159). Besides, after just eight measures the style changes entirely, with the cadenza-like elaboration of the dominant that begins at m. 9. Hence even this little piece illustrates Bach's apparent unwillingness (which Hofmann points out) to write entire compositions based on the same repeated elaboration of simple voice leading.

Friedemann later copied a similar prelude, BWV 924a, sometimes described as a "variant" of BWV 924. It is more than that, since the harmonic schemes of the two pieces diverge after m. 1. The general plans, however, are similar, and a pedal point on the dominant—with a bass in leaping octaves as in BWV 939—is the eventual goal in both pieces. Since BWV 924a is in Friedemann's hand, one wonders whether he, rather than Sebastian, was the composer. But Friedemann's score shows no compositional revisions, and it may well be a copy of an alternate realization by Sebastian of the scheme used in BWV 924.

The second prelude in CB, BWV 926 in D minor, is an expanded version of the same general design.[24] The score, in Sebastian's hand, is apparently a first draft showing several layers of corrections at one point. Measure 43 (six measures from the end) originally contained a dramatic cessation of surface motion, as in several of the Vivaldi concertos. In its final form, however it extends the sixteenth-note motion of the preceding measures through m. 43 (Example 10.6).[25]

The Prelude in G Minor BWV 930 is, like the Applicatio, a binary form with most of the fingerings marked. It is, however, a larger piece, and the second "half" falls into two subdivisions. Only a few fingerings appear for the last four measures of the bass, leaving it unclear how Bach dealt with the leap from dominant to

Example 10.6 Prelude in D Minor BWV 926, mm. 42–4, showing successive versions of the bass.

Example 10.7 (a) Prelude in G Minor BWV 930, mm. 39–42; b) C. P. E. Bach, *Probestück* in C, W. 63/1/3, mm. 16–18A.

tonic in the final cadence (Example 10.7.). Probably the fifth finger played both notes, producing a strong articulation of the final tonic note; this is how Emanuel Bach fingers such progressions in his *Probestücke* of 1753.

The Prelude in D, BWV 925 is more heavily scored, its texture (in three to five parts) recalling some of the preludes of the English Suites. Despite its brevity and the absence of any substantial modulations, it closes with a rather pretentious four-measure tonic pedal. A fermata on the downbeat of mm. 15, where the coda begins, suggests that the piece might have originally ended here.

Two further preludes, BWV 928 in F and BWV 932 in E minor, are on a larger scale than those discussed so far. The Prelude in F could almost be the opening section of a large-scale movement in concerto style, like the prelude of the English Suite in the same key (BWV 809). Both preludes also continue to show an affinity to the Inventions, opening with imitation of the soprano by the bass (and by an inner voice in BWV 932). BWV 928 subsequently reverses the order of entries, soprano imitating bass when the subject is restated in the dominant (m. 5b). BWV 928 also has a strongly marked return that heads a miniature recapitulation section (mm. 20–4 || 1–5).

With its three voices—more rigorously maintained than in BWV 939–41— BWV 932 is close to some of the Sinfonias (e.g., BWV 790 in D minor, whose principal subject opens with the same motive). Unfortunately, Friedemann copied only the first page of BWV 932, which remains a fragment. Since the fragment is a fair copy, it almost certainly stems from a score by Sebastian; despite a few corrections it contains no signs of having been Friedemann's own work (as suggested in the NG2 work-list). The breadth of the fragment suggests that this was a relatively extended work, comparable in scope to BWV 928. It reaches the dominant only after eight long measures, and the blank page that follows would have allowed space for at least one further modulation (to G or A minor) before returning to the tonic. Perhaps it was even longer, and Friedemann broke off the copy when he realized he lacked space for it, thereby depriving us of a very attractive work. Example 10.8 gives a hypothetical completion based on the assumption that only one page is missing.

Example 10.8 Prelude in E Minor BWV 932, mm. 11ff. (suggested completion).

The little Prelude in A Minor BWV 931 is less likely to be entirely by Sebastian. It does not closely resemble any of Sebastian's preludes, nor is there any imitation or substantial motivic work of any kind. This may be a clue to the piece's identity. The bass line is more coherent than the upper voices, opening with a formula employed in the last movements of the chamber sonatas BWV 1021 and 1038. These sonatas share a common bass line and seem to have been employed in the teaching of "composition as variation" (Schulenberg 1982). Perhaps BWV 931 was the product of a similar exercise set out by Sebastian and realized by Friedemann Bach.[26]

Against this hypothesis must be weighed the fact that the copy of BWV 931, in Friedemann's hand, employs several French ornament signs not included in the table at the beginning of CB. Among them is the comma or hook after the note to indicate either a mordent (*pincé*), as in m. 1, or a turn at the end of a trill (*tremblement et pincé*), as in m. 2. Friedemann also places strokes through the stems of several chords, presumably to indicate arpeggiation, perhaps with an ornamental *acciaccatura* or *coulé* (passing note) in the two-note chords. He also seems to misplace the signs for *accents* or *ports de voix*, setting them even with or above the main note. The departures from his father's practice raise the possibility that Friedemann was copying from some foreign source.

The manuscript P 804 contains an additional *praeludium* in C (BWV 943) copied by Mey, apparently an associate of Kellner. BWV 943 is an elegant little imitative fantasia in three parts, comparable to the Sinfonias. But as in BWV 941 the middle voice is distinctly unequal to the outer ones, only the latter participating fully in the contrapuntal work. The part writing contains a few rough moments; the harsh passing 9/4-chord (B/e''/c''') in m. 51 could be alleviated by moving the upper voices up a step, although this would exceed the piece's four-octave range. The chord as written emerges from the logical melodic leading of each part, and as in BWV 941 the angularity is rather a point in favor of Bach's authorship. Moreover, the piece has the rational design we expect in Bach's mature works, reaching a cadence in the dominant at almost the exact center (mm. 28), introducing the subject in inversion immediately afterward. The motivic material and the general character could have been suggested by the prelude in G from Fischer's *Ariadne musica*, on which Bach drew in the WTC. The prelude might be paired—purely for the convenience of the modern player, as there are no documentary grounds for doing so—with the little Fugue in C, BWV 953.[27]

The "Six Little Preludes" BWV 933–8 are not found in CB or any other early source, but they do occur in several independent copies stemming from later associates of Bach or his sons.[28] Whether the set was assembled by Bach or someone else,[29] it presumably drew on the same repertory of miscellaneous pieces mentioned earlier. Unlike the Twelve Little Preludes, these form a coherent collection based on ascending keys (C–c–d–D–E–e). All six preludes are in binary form, with central double bars.

These pieces are more substantial and less improvisatory, on the whole more sophisticated and refined in style, than most of the other "little preludes," suggesting a relatively late date. But there are significant variations in style, perhaps reflecting different dates of composition. Unusual for the set is the dissonant counterpoint near the end of no. 2 (BWV 934, mm. 38–9), the product of successive dissonant chords incompletely spelled out by the two-part texture. This movement might be the earliest of the group, its first eight measures following a harmonic scheme parallel to that of the courante in the French Suite in the same key (BWV 813).[30] Otherwise the two movements are so similar that one wonders whether both were originally composed as teaching pieces, one afterwards being incorporated into the suite, the other left out because it was not quite suitable in style or length for inclusion in the suite. Similar considerations arise in connection with no. 5 in E (BWV 937), which recalls the allemandes of BWV 817 and 819, and nos. 3 and 6 (BWV 935 and 938), whose two-part imitative counterpoint invokes the Inventions, especially the one in E (BWV 777), also in binary form.

On the other hand, nos. 1 and 4 (BWV 933 and 936) might be relatively late, related to an effort (evident in the preludes of WTC2) to create stylistically up-to-date teaching pieces during the 1730s or 1740s. "Late" signs in no. 1 include *galant* parallel thirds and "sigh" motives; no. 4 extends upward to e′′′, a note rarely used by Bach. Number 4 is also the one prelude from the group to use trio-sonata texture, which, together with its opening subject, recalls variation 2 of the Goldberg Variations. One passage (mm. 29–32), however, practically quotes the gavotte of the Sixth English Suite (BWV 811), a much earlier work. The high tessitura of BWV 936 has raised suspicions that the last ten measures or so might originally have been an octave lower; Hofmann (1992, 62) suggests instead that the present text could be the product of an anonymous reviser.[31] But the small inconsistencies that Hofmann finds here and elsewhere could be the types of problems that Bach would have eliminated had he actually assembled these pieces into an "official" set such as the WTC.

There remains the lute prelude BWV 999. Like most of Bach's lute music it is equally playable on keyboard; Kellner, who made the sole copy, was an organist not otherwise known to have been interested in lute music.[32] More problematical is the fact that the piece, which opens in C minor, ends in G.[33] Kellner writes the final chord—on G, with "Picardy" third—as a quarter note, implying that the piece is not over at that point and that a subsequent section in C minor could follow. Bach wrote another prelude (BWV 872a/1) whose initial arpeggiando section likewise ends on the dominant, a fugato following.[34] If a similar continuation was envisioned for BWV 999, either Bach never wrote it, or Kellner failed to copy it.

Suites, Dances, and Other Pieces

Two stylistically tentative allemandes (BWV 836–7) entered early in CB may be Friedemann's compositions. BWV 836 contains hints of his later quirky brilliance in the sudden chromaticism of mm. 8ff., now amusing but probably meant in earnest. The tripartite form of the piece is probably an illusion, the third section being intended to replace the second, which ended in the wrong key.[35] BWV 837 is a fragment, but both are given in fair copies, implying that they were completed before being copied here. If Friedemann's, their stylistic models were furnished not by Sebastian Bach but by composers like Telemann and the two other German composers represented in CB. The inclusion of their music shows that Bach welcomed his sons' study of fashionable *galant* keyboard music; further evidence for this can be found in the 1725 *Clavier-Büchlein* for Anna Magdalena Bach (see appendix B).

Telemann's three-movement suite (CB 47) lacks an attribution and was accordingly listed as BWV 824. Bach might have seemed a likely composer, as the gigue's imitative subject resembles that of the Fourth French Suite (BWV 815). Moreover, a recurring passage on a dominant pedal point (e.g., mm. 21–8) calls to mind the pastorale in part 2 of Bach's Christmas Oratorio (BWV 248). But the attribution in another source to Telemann makes better stylistic sense.

The *Partia* (CB 48) by Stölzel is a duller work, save for the *Menuet Trio* (BWV 929) that Bach added at the end. Perhaps it is an arrangement of an orchestral suite; Bach might have picked it up in 1721 on a visit to Gera, where Stölzel had been *Capellmeister* before moving on to Gotha.[36] Its inclusion shows that Bach found value even in minor compositions. Its overture would have served as an easy example in keyboard form of an important orchestral genre; Bach would write his own more sophisticated example in the D-major Partita a few years later. The correct part writing, rational forms, and logical if schematic development of motives in sequences and over pedal points would have taught pupils how to write correctly, in a socially acceptable style. There are in fact glimmers of originality, as in the sudden move to the subdominant in the Air Italien (mm. 3–4, echoing a passage in the overture, m. 54). Sebastian probably did not check his son's copying, for Friedemann seems to have telescoped two similar measures of the bourrée into one (Example 10.9).

Example 10.9 Stölzel, *Partia* in G Minor, bourrée, mm. 9ff., with suggested emendation.

The allemande and courante by Richter (CB 25) form a variation pair, like that in Bach's Praeludium et Partita BWV 833 but in *galant* style. Friedemann failed to complete his copy of either movement, but the parallelisms between the two halves of each binary movement make them easy to reconstruct. The composer was probably Johann Christoph Richter (1700–85), who would become court organist at Dresden in 1727; the 1725 *Clavier-Büchlein* for Anna Magdalena Bach includes further music by younger Dresden composers, perhaps acquired by Sebastian during visits to the regional Saxon courts.

Minuets BWV 841–3

The three minuets (CB 11–3) were copied at the end of group 2 by father and son jointly. One of the simpler dances, both musically and choreographically, the minuet had become a traditional type of teaching piece, useful for introducing pupils to the French style even though minuets are rarely as subtle or complex as other types of French harpsichord pieces. Although rhythmically straightforward, the two G-major minuets have the type of contrapuntally saturated texture characteristic of Bach, and his revisions in the second minuet are typical of those he applied in other compositions; these considerations caste doubt on the supposition that these were collaborations between father and son.[37] Plath, noting the low tessitura of BWV 843, suggested that it was transposed downward from C in order to form a "cycle" with the other two (NBA V/5, KB, 82). This is unprovable, but in their present state the pieces form a little suite of three movements increasing in musical and technical sophistication.

The first minuet—the simplest in style and entirely in Friedemann's hand—recurs in Anna Magdalena's first *Clavier-Büchlein* of 1722, where it might have been intended to complete the French Suite in the same key (BWV 816). The third is the most interesting musically, no longer a true minuet thanks to the energetic *figure corte* (eighth–sixteenth–sixteenth) introduced in m. 1 and soon dominating the texture. The motive occurs as well in the second minuet, although its occurrences there in mm. 2, 6, and 14 are products of Sebastian's embellishment of Friedemann's copy. The insertion of these figures might have served as an instructive example of compositional procedure or improvisation, but they inject a nervous quality that is not necessarily an improvement to the broken-chord figuration that they decorate (cf. the revisions to the C-major Invention).

Fugue in C, BWV 953; Fugue in C, BWV 952

Bach wrote three similar fugues in C, all short and in three voices, their material consisting largely of running passagework. BWV 953 occurs in CB (no. 31) in a probable composing draft; the very similar BWV 952 is known only from a few eighteenth-century copies, in which it circulated with other "leftover" pieces such as the B-minor "Albinoni" fugue.[38] Evidently, neither fugue was substantial enough to be incorporated into the first part of the WTC. Yet, when Bach assembled WTC2 he included a third fugue in C whose original form (BWV 870a/2) was similar in style and dimensions to BWV 952 and 953.

The uncertain provenance of its sources has raised questions about Bach's authorship of BWV 952. But it is remarkably similar to BWV 953 in structure; both, for example, reach a cadence in E minor in m. 23. Both also come to rest on a pedal point (a) around m. 14, just before the midpoint. But in BWV 953 the pedal note takes the form of eighths separated by rests, and, through an ingenious harmonic misdirection (m. 16b), the note a is reinterpreted as iv rather than the more obvious i. This is one of several hints that BWV 953 might be the latest of the three pieces, although its counterpoint is initially very simple, accompanying the subject with chords in a way that one imagines was typical of improvised fugues (seen also in BWV 902/2). But the subject of BWV 953 is violinistic, whereas that of BWV 952 (and BWV 870a/2) is based on an old-fashioned zigzag motive. And the counterpoint of BWV 953, after the initial exposition, is less conventional than that of the two other fugues, involving the hands in the type of counter-intuitive involutions found in the Sinfonias (as in the passage over the "punctuated" pedal point, mm. 14–6).

Fughetta (Fugue) in C Minor BWV 961

Chief sources: P 542; P 823; LEu N. I. 10338 (formerly M. pr. Ms. 20[i]). *Editions*: BG 36; Dehnhard (1973); NBA V/9.2.

Three two-part pieces in C minor are, like BWV 952, orphans whose legitimacy has been questioned. The simplest of these, the Prelude BWV 919, was accepted (with reservations) as Bach's in the first edition of this book. But it is hard to maintain his authorship in the light of the work's conflicting attribution and compositional weaknesses (see appendix A). The little Fughetta BWV 961 (called *Fuge* or *Fuga* in some later sources) is more surely Bach's, though preserved only in manuscripts of uncertain provenance. Its subject, consisting solely of eighths in 12/8 meter, implies a gigue, but sixteenths take over in the second half; hence the initial section must be taken at a leisurely pace. The piece is a true two-part fugue, if a loosely constructed one, lacking any full statements of the subject in the second of its three sections (mm. 11–7). This somewhat improvisatory scheme allies the piece with other works that probably preceded the more rigorous Inventions; the pedestrian character of the counterpoint and figuration would account for its evident abandonment by Bach.

NBA V/9.2 gives a faulty text deriving from P 823 and the Leipzig manuscript, which if older are not necessarily more accurate than P 542. The latter, used by Beethoven's patron Prince Karl Lichnowsky during studies at Göttingen, probably stems from Forkel and was, together with the late copy in P 804/1, the basis of the musically more satisfactory editions in BG 36 and Dehnhard (1973).

Fantaisie sur un Rondeau BWV 918

Chief sources: LEu N. I. 10338 (formerly M. pr. Ms. 20ⁱ); P 319. *Edition*: BG 36; Dadelsen and Rönnau (1970).

The most interesting of the three C-minor pieces mentioned above is the "Fantasia upon a Rondo" BWV 918. Its source situation is more precarious than for BWV 961, as it survives complete only in the undependable Leipzig manuscript that also includes the latter. Yet BWV 918 is one of the more imaginative of Bach's smaller works. Although it could never be a crowd-pleaser, it demonstrates how a popular *galant* genre could be turned into an austere fantasia comparable in its rigorous counterpoint to the canons of the *Art of Fugue*. In two equal parts throughout, it can be played as a duet on two matched keyboards.

The title and key call to mind the *rondeaux* movement of the C-minor Partita. Perhaps Bach drafted BWV 918 as a possible movement for the partita, even an opening one (as in BWV 823). But apart from the two-part texture the pieces have little in common. The title as given in the Leipzig manuscript implies that Bach based the piece on the theme of a French *pièce de clavecin* in rondo form, but there is no assurance that the title is Bach's. The rhythm at the opening, which consists of an upbeat of five eighth-notes in 3/4 meter, is indeed very French.[39] But otherwise the quirky little theme seems more characteristic of Bach than anyone else. The piece remains a sort of rondeau, the main theme returning three times in the tonic: at mm. 28, 80, and at the end (m. 120). Between these refrains come polyphonic *couplets* in which motivic ideas more or less closely related to the theme are worked out in two-part imitative counterpoint. The distinction between theme and *couplet* becomes blurred when fragments of the theme are developed in inverted counterpoint during the *couplets* (as at m. 36), and later when the second restatement of the theme is expanded through the canonic treatment of its first two phrases.[40]

Preludes and Fugues (Fughettas) in C, D Minor, E Minor, F, and G, BWV 870a and 899–902

Principal sources: P 1089 (Vogler, 1727–31); P 804 (Kellner, BWV 902/1a + 902/2 in fascicle 5, the rest in fascicle 38); SBB Mus. ms. 10490 (Michel, later readings)
Editions: BG 36 (BWV 902/1a in appendix); Dadelsen and Rönnau (1970;

BWV 901 and 902/1 only); Dehnhard (1973; lacks BWV 901); NBA V/6.2.

Compared to the individual preludes and fugues considered above, these five prelude-and-fugue pairs are longer and, in most cases, probably earlier works that preceded the composition of WTC1. Although the brevity of some movements suggests that Bach wrote them for teaching, this cannot be assumed. Ultimately Bach did include one of the preludes and three of the fugues in WTC2, but only after substantially revising them. The five pairs are preserved together in a relatively early manuscript copy by Vogler, Bach's Weimar pupil, and independently in a later one by Michel, C. P. E. Bach's copyist. Hence these pieces are more likely than the "Six Little Preludes" to have been gathered together by Bach himself, but that remains uncertain, as does the date when he might have done so. The sources differ on the exact labeling of each movement; Vogler, the copyist closest to Bach, uses *Prelude, Praeludium, Fuga,* and *Fugetta* (*sic*), the diminutive form perhaps referring not to length (these are not particularly short pieces) but to the character of these fugues, which are less rigorous and, in their frequent sequences, more predictable than most of those included in the WTC. A connection with a type of prelude and fugue traditional in the Pachelbel circle is suggested by the thematic concordance noted below for BWV 902. The preludes are all serious pieces, more rigorous in their adherence to a few motives and more formal in their designs than the improvisatory type of prelude seen in BWV 895 (see chap. 6) or in "verset" sets by earlier composers. Yet they are also remote from the arpeggiando type common in CB and WTC1.

The five works constitute a series in ascending keys, beginning in C and concluding in G; the discontinuous BWV numbering reflects the fact that they were not recognized as a set prior to Hofmann (1988b; see also Brokaw 1985, 24–5). Dürr published them together for the first time in NBA V/6.2, alongside WTC2.[41] Only the pieces not incorporated into WTC2 are discussed in this chapter; see chapter 12 on the preludes and fugues in C, G, and A♭ (the latter incorporates the fugue in F, BWV 901/2, transposed up a minor third).

The Prelude and Fughetta in D Minor BWV 899 is most notable for the fugue subject, which is composed of the simplest imaginable four-note motive (d′–e′–f′–e′ in even dotted quarters). This subject behaves like a harmonically neutral cantus firmus, against which lively counterpoint is woven, as in a seventeenth-century hexachord fantasia. The counterpoint has the same lively style as in BWV 870a/2, generally up-to-date but including the zigzag motives of older organ music. The major event of the fugue is a demonstration of invertible two-part counterpoint at the twelfth, a point that is brought home by the wide separation of the outer voices in mm. 33–40. The prelude is in four imitative parts, with expressive chromatic counterpoint and a clearly articulated tripartite design (thematic statements in mm. 1, 7, and 17). Even more than in the C-major

prelude (BWV 870a/1), the bass tends to sit on pedal points rather than participating fully in the polyphony; this makes performance on a stringed keyboard
instrument less than entirely effective, as does the cantus firmus–like writing
in the fugue. Together with the somewhat ad hoc character of the imitations
(those in mm. 2, 8, and 18 are at the sixth and only approximate), this might
have ruled out inclusion of the piece in the more rigorous later sets. Unusual
too is the I–V–V tonal design of the prelude, echoed in the order of entries in
the first exposition of the fugue.[42]

The Prelude and Fugue in E Minor BWV 900 is the most impressive of the
group. The prelude has the same type of tortuous, dissonant part writing as the
allemande of the English Suite in the same key. It differs in introducing the inversion of the subject and countersubject right at the start, in the first imitative
entry (m. 2), and in the somewhat surprising outbreak of scale figuration in
thirty-seconds at the end of each of the three sections—all this within a concise
eighteen-measure framework. A similar sort of acceleration occurs in the fugue,
the longest of the group, whose subject, moving primarily in eighths, is of the
old-fashioned rhetorical type, punctuated by silences. The latter are filled in
by the countersubject's figuration in sixteenths. These are among the points of
style recalling the "Chromatic" fugue BWV 903/2, with which this fugue shares
what seem to be characteristics of Bach's Weimar virtuoso works: the sequential
phraseology of the subject; long episodes in two voices, often setting figuration
in sixteenths against "walking" eighths; and a flashy final cadence that immediately follows a statement of the subject in the soprano (embellished from m.
98 onward). The long stretches of the fugue given over to episodic passagework
in two parts, by comparison with the somewhat similar BWV 870a/2, might be
why Bach eventually admitted the latter into WTC2 but not BWV 900.

The Prelude and Fughetta in F, BWV 901, although not as imposing as BWV
900, is the most refined of the group, and this might be why Bach adapted the
fugue for WTC2, albeit only after transposing it to A♭ and doubling its length.
As in BWV 899 and 900, the prelude is a simple three-phrase form, but its voice
leading is less rigorous and its thematic material treated more freely (only the
initial four-note arpeggio recurs regularly). The fugue, the only one of the group
in four parts, recalls the type of late-Baroque vocal polyphony echoed in BWV
955 (see chap. 5). The subject opens with a motive found in many Baroque choral
fugues;[43] the countersubject uses an equally conventional though very different
idea, a descending chromatic hexachord. The four voices sound together only in
the last phrase, and if Bach originally wrote the piece in three parts this might
explain why Vogler, who copied an early version of the piece, left out the tenor
in the first half of m. 23; perhaps the autograph contained revisions and was
hard to read in this passage.

BWV 902/1 in G is by far the longest of the preludes, even without its repeats.
The first measure is practically identical to that of a prelude in the same key attributed to Pachelbel.[44] It is of a type with the E-major prelude of WTC2, in binary

form with two repeated halves of equal length. The initial pedal point of both pieces was a traditional opening for a prelude, but later passages in the G-major prelude, especially the triplet filigree and the expressive move to the minor at the end of each half, sound like passages in the partitas, which probably date from the 1720s.[45] A true sonata form, the movement includes a medial cadence to E minor (mm. 36) in the middle of the second half, as well as a distinct retransition and a real recapitulation section (from m. 41). There exists a busily ornamented copy by Preller (given in NBA V/6.2, p. 334) which, even more than in other cases, disfigures the serenely lyrical original and cannot derive from Bach.

Only Kellner copied an alternate prelude in G, known as BWV 902/1a, which is shorter and simpler than BWV 902/1. Kellner's prelude is akin in some ways to the prelude in D minor BWV 875a, which Bach later expanded for use in WTC2. It is easy to see the shorter G-major prelude as the earlier one, yet it could just as well be later. Its running sixteenths over a bass of repeated eighths are a borrowing from *galant*-influenced orchestral writing (compare the opening chorus of the Magnificat BWV 243, composed in 1723). Its freewheeling character resembles that of the Praeambulum to the Fifth Partita (1730, in the same key), for which it might have been a short preliminary sketch.

A prelude need not be similar in length to its fugue to form an effective pair, as Bach had realized by the time of WTC1, where several fugues are dwarfed by their preludes. The longer G-major prelude BWV 902/1 is nicely contrasted by its fugue, which, however, more closely matches the character of the shorter prelude BWV 902/1a; the latter is almost exactly the same length. Both the fugue and the shorter prelude also end with strokes of wit: the fugue with a sudden burst of figuration, the prelude with a sudden *interruption* of the prevailing figuration (as in the Vivaldi concerto in the same key arranged as BWV 973). The enormous disparity in length and style between the fughetta and the better-known prelude BWV 902/1 might account for Bach's having used a third prelude for the revised version of the fugue in WTC2. The latter prelude remains in binary form, and it opens, like BWV 902/1, over a tonic pedal point.

It is curious that Bach abandoned another movement in the same key with a somewhat similar character—the opening Cantabile of BWV 1019a—when he put together the six sonatas for harpsichord and violin. The cantabile movement remained in use as an aria for soprano and strings (most likely its original form) in Cantatas 120a and 120. In each case Bach's sense of stylistic propriety evidently led him to eliminate a splendid keyboard piece from a collection to which it did not belong.

Prelude in B Minor BWV 923

Chief sources: P 401 (Kayser, fragment); P 648 (later 18th cent., with BWV 923); Gb (Scholz, with BWV 923). *Editions*: BG 42; Dadelsen and Rönnau (1970); NBA V/9.2.

BWV 923 was probably not a teaching piece, but it is included here as a miscellaneous work more mature in style than those considered in chapter 6. It poses several puzzles: was it meant to stand alone? is it complete? is it even by Bach? Recent editors have paired BWV 923 with the "Albinoni" fugue BWV 951, to which it is attached in a number of eighteenth-century manuscripts. Yet the prelude appears alone in its earliest source, the fragmentary copy by Kayser, where it is a late addition at the end of the latter's manuscript of WTC1 (see chap. 11).[46]

In fact the prelude is closest not to anything in the WTC, and certainly not to the Chromatic Fantasia (BWV 903/1), with which it shares its general style as well as at least two distinctive harmonic progressions.[47] If the progressions here are less compelling than in BWV 903, it may be because BWV 923 was never finished. After a striking opening, it dissolves into a long series of chords, presumably shorthand for arpeggios that Bach would have spelled out had he ever revised the piece. In addition, the modulation back to the tonic in the last six measures is too sudden and too late to be completely successful. Yet the prelude remains worth playing for the remarkable improvisatory fantasia that constitutes its first half, and as the only possible companion piece for BWV 951. Particularly thrilling is the implied crescendo and acceleration as the chromatic sequence in mm. 15b–17a builds from two to four voices, culminating in a cadenza on an unexpected G^6 chord.

The later version BWV 923a is a spurious adaptation (see appendix A). An alternate attribution to Wilhelm Hieronymus Pachelbel (1686–1764), oldest son of Johann, raises questions about the authorship of BWV 923 itself. But Kayser and Scholz, who both had access to reliable Bach manuscripts, independently attribute the prelude to him.[48] Nothing in the available works of the younger Pachelbel approaches BWV 923 in the ingenuity of its harmony or figuration.[49]

Air with Variations in C Minor BWV 991

Source: P 224 (autograph). *Edition*: NBA V/4.

Bach's composing score in the 1722 *Clavier-Büchlein* for Anna Magdalena is the sole source for this apparently unfinished piece. The fragment consists of an ornate sixteen-measure melody in binary form, for which Bach wrote the bass for the first nine-and-a-half measures only. He also wrote out the upper line for one variation and for the first eleven-and-a-half measures of another. The whole piece was subsequently crossed out (not necessarily by Bach). The text, as edited in NBA V/4, contains apparent errors (mm. 3, 8A), and the simple gavotte-like melody given as the first variation is more what one would expect as the original theme, perhaps one borrowed from another composer. The four blank staves that follow in the manuscript imply that Bach intended to compose at least one more variation. But what he did write is not very promising, and his failure to complete the piece does not seem to have deprived us of anything very significant.[50]

The Inventions and Sinfonias

Group 2 of CB was apparently meant to be preliminary to group 3, the eleven preludes later incorporated into WTC1. The next group of pieces, the Inventions, represents a further advance in complexity and technical difficulty, leading to the final group, the Sinfonias. The order of the pieces in the book does not necessarily reflect the order in which the pieces were composed. But the Inventions and Sinfonias were all entered into CB at about the same time, many in what appear to be Bach's composing drafts. Within each group there are similarities of style, dimensions, and overall conception that support the idea that all originated during a brief period of concentrated work. These pieces seem later than the isolated preludes and fugues discussed previously; they are more rigorous, rarely introducing free motivic material after the initial passage, and they are free of even the occasional awkward detail in voice leading or structure. These pieces also reflect Bach's acceptance of *galant* "sigh" figures and expressive "singing" melodies into his keyboard polyphony. This is not to say that the pieces are easy to play or contrapuntally obvious; the Sinfonias are more difficult than many pieces in the WTC, and the counterpoint is often dissonant and counter-intuitive. But the combination of learned and popular elements has helped these pieces win their place in the canon of pedagogic works still taught to keyboard players.

Antecedents of the Inventions include *bicinia* from the sixteenth century and later, as in the organ book of Nivers (1665) and among Pachelbel's Magnificat fugues. The four duetti in Bach's *Clavierübung* belong to this tradition as well, as shown by their publication alongside liturgical organ pieces. It is less easy to fit the Inventions into it, as they are shorter and more clearly intended for study at stringed keyboard instruments. Previous little pedagogical pieces in strict three-part counterpoint like the Sinfonias are even harder to find, since four-part writing had been the norm. Bach's original title *praeludium* for the Inventions suggests that they arose from earlier introductory or improvisatory pieces. But the rigorous two- and three-part counterpoint of the Inventions and Sinfonias suggests a significant change in conception from the relatively free style of a piece like BWV 900/1.

CB must have originally included all fifteen Inventions and all fifteen Sinfonias, under the titles *Praeambulum* and *Fantasia* respectively. The last two leaves of music are missing and with them presumably the last *fantasia* and half of another. Except for a few inventions copied by Friedemann, all are in Sebastian's hand (see Table 10.2 below). The systematic order of the keys of the pieces suggests that Bach planned both sets ahead of time. But within a year or two of their entry into CB, Sebastian had recopied all thirty pieces, changing their order and slightly revising them.

Tonality, still a new and far from fully codified subject, was a concern of German music theorists at the time. Franklin (1989b, 255) notes the near-identity between Bach's fifteen tonalities and sixteen "primary keys" described by both Niedt and Mattheson (who did not agree on exactly which ones they are). Whether Bach read the arguments of the theorists is unknown, but he must have been aware of Mattheson's polemic exchange on a related topic with Pachelbel's old pupil Buttstett during these very years (1714–7). Mattheson's *Exemplarische Organisten-Probe*, containing forty-eight figured bass exercises in all keys, would have served as a further spur to Bach's organizing his own teaching pieces along similar lines; Mattheson's work was published in 1719, just before Bach presented CB to his son.

The order of keys in CB is slightly different for the two sets of pieces, but in both cases it involves an ascent upwards from C major (C, D minor, E minor, etc.), followed by a descent back to C minor (E, E♭, D, C minor). The fair-copy autograph (P 610) substitutes a simple ascent (C, C minor, D, D minor), which has the advantage of making it easier to find each piece within the book.[51] In addition, P 610 gives the pieces their now-familiar titles. As in the *Orgelbüchlein*, Bach also added a general title expressing his pedagogic intentions for the work as a whole. Like Bach's other fair copies, P 610 eventually acquired new corrections and revisions, but these never became as extensive or numerous as the ones visible in CB. Two Bach pupils, Heinrich Nicolaus Gerber and Bernhard Christian Kayser, made early copies with additional ornamentation.

Both sets were frequently copied by members of the Bach circle. Forkel (1802, 38/NBR, 453) explained that the Inventions (as well as the "Six Little Preludes") had been drafted "during the hours of teaching" as substitutes for the tedious finger exercises that Bach supposedly gave pupils prior to their study of "his own greater compositions." The report that Bach subjected his students to mechanical five-finger exercises, although accepted by proponents of a similar approach to keyboard pedagogy, is suspiciously in keeping with the nineteenth-century taste for technical studies. But other aspects of Forkel's account are supported by E. L. Gerber (son of the Bach student), who reported that Bach's pupils worked on the Inventions before continuing to the suites.[52] Many of his pupils might have made copies of the Inventions and Sinfonias at the beginning of their studies, as Gerber and Kayser did (Gerber's copy, in NL DHgm, is dated 1725). The pieces would have served as both exercises in performance and models for composition; the deep impression that they made on Bach's pupils is evident from Friedemann's and Emanuel's keyboard sonatas, which include movements written in imitation of both inventions and sinfonias.[53]

Bach's general title (in P 610) makes clear the works' pedagogic function, opening with the words (in large letters) "Candid Instruction."[54] The long title is worth considering in some detail, as Bach evidently chose his words with care. He addresses both *Liebhabern* and *Lehrbegierigen*: lovers of music as well as those eager for instruction. The latter—his pupils—would not have been beginners, having already studied simpler pieces; some would have grown up in musical families or had several years' experience as choristers. Thus, the teaching of Bach's peculiar style of keyboard polyphony would not have started out in a stylistic vacuum, as is too often the case today.

Both the two- and the three-part pieces are meant to teach *inventio*, meaning not a type of piece but the invention of motivic material. These *inventiones* will not only be interesting in their own right but will be "developed," an expression also employed in the general title of the *Orgelbüchlein*. In modern German, Bach's term *Durchführung* can refer to both the working out of motives (as in a Classical sonata form) and the exposition of a fugue subject. For Bach, however, the word may have meant nothing more than "worked out polyphonically"; the same word appears in the title of the *Orgelbüchlein* in reference to chorale melodies.[55]

Bach adds that the pieces are meant "above all" (*am allermeisten*) to teach a "singing" (*cantabile*) manner of performance and to provide a preview of *Composition*, which probably means what we would call counterpoint.[56] It is hard to know what precisely to make of the term *cantabile* in instrumental works such as these. Walther gives two definitions for a "cantabile" composition; one is simply the common sense of possessing a "fine melody," whereas the other, evidently referring to a capella polyphony, signifies that every part is capable of being sung. Bach's notion of cantabile style was evidently broad enough to include both the sighing half steps of the F-minor Sinfonia and the rapid arpeggios of the Invention in G or the Sinfonia in B minor. Hence, the word cannot imply the predominance of legato articulation or "expressive" dynamic nuances, although it may remind us that hardly anything in these pieces goes beyond what was considered suitable for the voice in the early eighteenth century.

The original title *Praeambulum* for each of the inventions reflected their similarity to presumably earlier, imitative preludes like BWV 930 (CB 9). The title *Fantasia* for the three-part pieces might have been an arbitrary label to distinguish them from the ones in two parts, or it could have pointed to their tendency toward even more rigorous, fugue-like counterpoint. Although Bach had written one rigorously contrapuntal fantasia in three parts (BWV 917), the same title could mean other things, as in BWV 903 and 904. It is unlikely we shall ever know why Bach used the rhetorical term *inventio* for the revised versions of the two-part pieces or the more strictly musical expression *sinfonia* for the three-part ones; both groups of pieces demonstrate "invention" according to his title. Neither term seems to have been used previously as a title for keyboard pieces. But Bach knew Francesco Antonio Bonporti's *Invenzioni da camera* for violin and continuo (op. 10, Bologna, 1712), which he used at just this time in the teaching of figured bass.[57]

Perhaps Bach's new titles reflected his realization that here he had created two essentially new genres of keyboard music. Like all of Bach's collections, these are less uniform than they seem at first, but the general preoccupation with contrapuntal development of engaging musical ideas, as implied by the general title, is clear enough. Not mentioned explicitly in the title, but equally important, is the attention to cogent formal design and varied tonality. Not only are the pieces in different keys, but all contain sophisticated yet compact modulating schemes comparable to those of Bach's larger works.

The modern habit of referring to the Sinfonias as "three-part inventions" goes back at least to Forkel.[58] But Bach's distinction is worth maintaining, for the pieces differ significantly. The entire collection is available in several dependable editions, including that in NBA V/3 (Dadelsen, 1970). At this writing, the editor's critical report for the latter still has not appeared, more than thirty-five years after its publication, but a summary can be found in the preface to the publisher's "practical" offprint of the volume.[59] More accessible to English-speaking readers is the excellent edition by Richard Jones,[60] although pupils will need to be reminded not to take literally the rhythm of the editorial realizations of ornaments, or to follow the pianistic fingerings, which, as in other piano editions, rely unnecessarily on finger substitution. Both editions include ornamented versions of several of the sinfonias, taken from the copies by Gerber and Kayser, as does the edition by Ratz and Füssl.[61] Ratz's analytical essay will be helpful to pupils in need of a measure-by-measure commentary, but a discussion of ornamentation in the same volume is outdated.

The Inventions

Unless one studies all of them, one may not realize the considerable differences between individual inventions. Table 10.2 indicates some distinctions, listing the Inventions in the earlier order of CB, which may correspond more closely to the order in which they were composed.[62] Subjects range in length from two beats to four measures; some pieces fall into clearly articulated bi- or tripartite designs, whereas others are through-composed, their formal divisions less distinct. Although most are abstract, predominantly in Italian instrumental style, one or two represent recognizable French dance types. All are imitative, and although none is a full-fledged fugue, several resemble double fugues insofar as the two parts open by simultaneously stating subject and countersubject, afterwards exchanging their material at the dominant.[63] Several inventions treat their subjects more in the manner of free sonata-style development than in fugal fashion; on the other hand, one or two others are so strictly imitative that they resemble canons.

In general, the inventions with short (half-measure) subjects and relatively free forms may have been composed first, those with longer subjects and more clearly articulated sonata- or fugue-like forms coming later. The pieces that Wilhelm Friedemann copied, or that Sebastian entered into CB as fair or revision copies, tend to be more like older preludes: relatively improvisatory in design and, in the inventions in C, G, and A minor, based on the free development of one or two motives, not resembling fugues despite the imitative treatment of the brief

Table 10.2 The Inventions

Number in CB	P 610	Key	Meter	Length of subject (mm.)	Initial imitn. (intvl.)	Type	Form	Length (mm.)	Restatement at (m.)	Recapitulation medial at (m.)	Recapitulation final at (m.)	Copyist in CB
1	1	C	C	1/2	8	free	tripartite	22	7	11**	19	JSBf
2	4	d	3/8	2	8		tripartite	52	18		42	JSBf
3	7	e	C	1/2	8	free	multipartite	21****	7			WFB
4	8	F	3/4	1	8	canonic	rounded bipart.	34	12		26**	WFB
5	10	G	9/8	1	5	gigue	rounded bipart.	32	14			WF+JSB
6	13	a	C	1/2	8	free	tripartite	24****	6b		18+	WFB
7	15	b	C	2	5*	dbl. fugue	rounded bipart.	22	5b		18	WFB
8	14	Bb	C	3	5*	dbl. fugue	through-comp.	20				JSBc?
9	12	A	12/8	2	5*	dbl. fugue	through-comp.	21		14b**		JSBc
10	11	g	C	2	5		tripartite	23	7		16b	JSBc
11	9	f	3/4	4	8*	legato	rounded bipart.	34	17	21***	29	JSBc
12	6	E	3/8	4	8*	chromatic	sonata	62			43	JSBc
13	5	Eb	C	4	5*	dbl. fugue	tripartite	32		12	27	JSBr?
14	3	D	3/8	2	8		multipartite	59			43	JSBf?
15	2	c	C	2	8	canonic	rounded bipart.	27		13	23	JSBc

JSB = J. S. Bach
WFB = W. F. Bach
c = composing score
r = revision copy
f = fair copy
*Two subjects in invertible counterpoint
**Recapitulation is of other than opening passage
***After double bar
****Expanded by several measures in P 610
+in P 610 only

(half-measure) subjects. Pieces that Bach appears to have been composing as he wrote them into CB are more elaborate in design. These include the double-fugal inventions in A and B♭ as well as the Invention in E, which although involving two subjects is the sole instance of an explicit rounded binary or sonata form (with central double bar). These apparently later pieces also contain more substantial passages of recapitulation (transposed restatement), although only in the Invention in A do these passages have a clearly episodic function as in so many of Bach's fugues. Otherwise the recapitulations are of opening material, or of passages using the main thematic material (often with the counterpoint inverted).

The counterpoint in the Invention in E♭ is especially refined, although the counter-intuitive passing dissonances in m. 25 were a second thought; Bach first wrote something far less challenging. One can imagine a bright ten-year-old pupil expressing dismay at the harsh dissonances on the second and third beats, only to have the teacher demonstrate how these are products of contrary motion toward the consonant major third on the fourth beat. Something similar could be said for the invention in E, whose chromatic lines in contrary motion might have been suggested by the numerous sharps (crosses) in the key signature.

The order of the pieces in CB resulted, generally speaking, in progress from simple to complex, free to rigorous.[64] This pattern is absent in the autograph, whose ordering merely leaves the impression of continuous variety. Formally the pieces resemble Bach's larger works, but realized on a smaller scale, so that a single phrase here corresponds to an entire section elsewhere. For instance, the inventions in C major and A minor share a tripartite design comprised of three phrases of roughly equal length; the second phrase begins by restating the opening in a new key and in inverted counterpoint, and the final phrase is to some degree a recapitulation of a portion of the first one. On the other hand, the proportions of the Invention in F minor are bipartite, with a cadence to the dominant and subsequent restatement at the exact center (m. 17); a sonata-like return near the end (m. 29) provides a degree of rounding. In the Invention in E, the expansion of each phrase into a period and the insertion of an actual double bar created a genuine sonata form.

Although several other inventions besides the F-minor possess nearly exact binary or ternary proportions (1:1 or 1:1:1), it is unlikely that these should be ascribed to a preliminary plotting out of the work according to a geometric or numerological pattern. Bach possessed a fine sense of musical proportion—one fine enough to recognize that numerically precise proportions could lead to musically unsatisfying results. Thus, in the inventions in E minor and A minor, Bach broke the nearly exact threefold symmetries of the original versions by expanding the third section. The early versions of these pieces lack a clear-cut return, that is, a restatement of the opening of the piece in the tonic at the beginning of the final section. A return is still absent in the revised version of the E-Minor Invention. But, by adding a return in the A-Minor Invention (m. 18), Bach put it into something like sonata form, and the phrase in mm. 14–7 (expanded from mm. 14–6 of the original) became a genuine retransition. The assimilation to later sonata forms may be fortuitous, but tonal design took precedence over measure counting.

Except in the two cases just mentioned, the versions of the autograph (P 610) differ from those of CB only in details. The most extensive revision is that at the end of the Invention in G minor, which is effectively half a measure longer in the final version.[65] Numerous smaller changes are visible within the composing scores of CB. In no case did these involve the large structure; Bach seems to have had a clear design in his head even while writing the most hastily drafted composing score. But in several instances he later changed the main thematic material. After finishing the C-Minor Invention, Bach altered the subject, probably to avoid an open fifth in m. 3 and elsewhere (see Example 10.11).[66] The subject occurs only six times in this piece, and always in the same canonic context, so the change had little effect on the counterpoint elsewhere. Not so in the G-Minor Invention, where Bach changed the subject while composing and only then added the countersubject, which does not fit the original subject (Example 10.10). But he probably left the treble at the opening unchanged until after the piece was finished. By then the original form of the motive (the mordent-like figure g′–f♯′–g′) had been worked into the counterpoint of mm. 5 and 12, where it remains as an echo of Bach's first thoughts.[67]

Since the Inventions are the first introduction to Baroque keyboard playing for many pupils, it is appropriate to add a few words on special performance problems in these pieces. In the C-minor Invention the short trills of the countersubject consistently create parallel octaves with the subject (Example 10.11). This has led to suggestions that one should start these trills from the main note (e.g., Neumann 1978, 316). But it is just as logical to conclude that Bach took no notice of "forbidden" parallels involving ornamental tones.[68] Bach tolerated more

Example 10.10 Invention in G Minor BWV 782, mm. 1–2: (a) original version (without bass); (b) final version.

orig.: c′

Example 10.11 Invention in C Minor BWV 773, m. 3.

obvious parallelisms in certain contexts,[69] and the present ones will go unnoticed unless the upper tone is prolonged excessively. Normally the upper note of a trill is a dissonant appoggiatura bearing an implicit accent, but in the C-minor Invention the upper note is often consonant (as in Example 10.11; both notes are consonant in mm. 15, 16, and 26). Yet this is no reason to alter the melodic shape of the trill, which can be reduced to a single quick appoggiatura if weak fingers or a sluggish action make it too hard to play the full ornament cleanly.[70]

Regardless of how one plays the trills, unisons between the parts in the C-Minor Invention cause the hands to collide in m. 13. One could play the piece on two evenly matched manuals. But Bach writes unisons in other pieces where two-manual performance is impossible, and the hand crossings in the B-minor Sinfonia were evidently meant to be played on a single manual. Hence it would be wrong to insist on dividing the parts between two keyboards for the sake of a few momentary unisons or voice crossings. Besides, divided manuals mean a quiet registration of just two eight-foot stops on most harpsichords, yet many of these pieces benefit from stronger registration. This is not to say that harpsichord is the ideal instrument for these pieces; the clavichord was probably the instrument most often used by eighteenth-century pupils, although some pieces, such as the E-major, would have been awkward on a fretted instrument.

Slurs pose editorial problems, and therefore questions of interpretation, in the inventions in D major and F minor. Bach added the slurs only when making the fair copies in P 610, where they are hastily and somewhat imprecisely drawn. Precisely because he did not take care to place them over well-defined groups of two or three notes, Bach is likely to have meant the slurs to apply to long groups of four, six, even eight sixteenths. Such long slurs, which are relatively unusual, do not signify a continuous or unbroken legato, for articulations would still have been assumed to fall before and after each slur. Even in these cases, the notes beneath each slur represent but a single harmony (except in m. 4 of the F-minor). Each slurred figure can still receive a single rhythmic impetus or, to put it another way, be played as a single graceful gesture. This suggests playing the D-Major Invention "in one," each slurred group of six sixteenths filling a measure of 3/8 time, which therefore constitutes a single long beat.[71]

Example 10.12 Invention in C, m. 1: (a) BWV 772; (b) BWV 772a.

Written-out ornaments and embellishments in several copies of the Inventions (and Sinfonias) suggest that one of the uses for these pieces was instruction in ornamentation. Gerber's manuscript gives unique flourishes at various points; one at the end of the B-Minor Invention seems to create parallel fifths with the bass. But a listener is unlikely to notice the parallels when the embellishment is played with appropriate panache, and in any case the notated rhythm should probably be interpreted freely. Bach himself added embellishments to each entry of the subject in the fair copy of the opening invention in C, producing the triplet version BWV 772a (Example 10.12). This provided a lesson in motivic consistency (and in triplet playing), but the systematic filling-in of just about every melodic third belabors what was originally a light and graceful theme.

The Sinfonias

The Sinfonias are less familiar to most players than the Inventions, as they are too difficult for beginners and therefore less often studied. As a group the Sinfonias are less diverse, and they tend to run a bit longer than the Inventions (see Table 10.3). Eleven of the fifteen—those in C, D, d, E, e, F, f, G, A, a, and B♭—are modeled on the type of fugal allegro (or andante) found in the early eighteenth-century trio sonata. This means that the upper voices open with imitation over a non-thematic bass, the latter voice then making the third entry. Yet there remains great diversity of both character and design. Fewer than half the pieces have regular countersubjects, and only the D-major Sinfonia systematically presents all six permutations of its subject and two countersubjects, each possible combination appearing once. Two other fugal devices absent from the Inventions, stretto and inversion, are employed here, but only in a few pieces (inversion in the Sinfonias in C and E, stretto in those in F and B♭). Bach probably composed these after the Inventions; they are represented in CB only by composing scores in Bach's own hand.

Like the Inventions, the Sinfonias are a new genre that in individual cases may resemble a fugue or a sonata movement. As in the Inventions, a design based on alternating expositions and episodes is rare, appearing most clearly in the Sinfonia in A (the same key in which it is manifested in the Inventions).

Table 10.3 The Sinfonias

Number in		Key	Meter	Length of subject (mm.)	Initial imitations (pts.)	(intvls.)	Counter-subjects	Type	Form	Length (mm.)	Recaps. (m.)
CB	P 610										
1	1	C	C	1	SMB	5, 8			bipartite	21	8b, 17b*
2	4	d	C	1	SMB	5, 8	1		double bipart.	23	22b*
3	7	e	3/4	2	SMB	5, 8	1	andante	double bipart.	44	
4	8	F	C	1	MSB	5, 8	1		rounded bipart.	23	15b*, 19b*
5	10	G	3/4	2	SMB	5, 8			rounded tripart.	33	16*, 27*
6	13	a	3/8**	4	SMB	5, 8	2***	minuet?	through-comp.	64	49
7	15	b	9/16	3	SB	8	1	free	rounded bipart.	38	20*
8	14	Bb	C	1	MSB	5, 8			tripartite	24	
9	12	A	C	2	SMB	5, 8		violin	fugue w/episodes	31	
10	11	g	3/8	1	SMB	5, 8		andante	bipartite	72	65
11	9	f	C	2	MSB	5, 8	2	chromatic	bipartite	35	20
12	6	E	9/8	1	MSB	5, 5		gigue	rounded bipart.	41	27*
13	5	Eb	3/4	1	SM	5		sarabande	multipart. (DC)	38	30
14	3	D	C	2½	SMB	5, 8	2		double bipart.	25	
[15]	2	c	12/8	2	SM(B)	8, 8			double bipart.	32	13b*, 28*

S = soprano
M = middle part
B = bass
*Episode or closing phrase
**Notated in double measures (2 × 3/8) in CB
***Never used simultaneously

Otherwise, episodes are short or indistinctly articulated, not surprisingly since the small dimensions that are a defining feature of these pieces would not permit lengthy episodes. More common are forms based on division of the whole into roughly equal sections, including a bipartite type in which each half is subdivided by a medial cadence or other articulation. Symmetry is carried farthest in the F-minor and A-minor Sinfonias, where much of the second half is comprised of recapitulation (in inverted counterpoint). This is so despite the otherwise antithetical character of these two pieces, the F-minor being severely chromatic, the minuet-like A-minor often falling into *galant* parallel thirds and sixths.

Three Sinfonias, in E♭, G minor, and B minor, largely abandon imitative counterpoint in favor of idiomatic keyboard writing. The first of these is a *galant* duet with bass; the G-minor is almost in *style brisé*. The B-minor is a special case, as much of it is really in just two parts; the middle voice has only one full statement of the subject, and this not until the second section. In addition, the initial imitation is at the octave, as in the Inventions. The latter is also true of the C-minor, which is further distinguished by the lack of full participation in the counterpoint by the bass. These features do not weaken the two pieces, which rather are among the most engaging in the set, but they demonstrate the flexibility with which Bach interpreted his general title.

It is harder here than in the Inventions to see a relationship between the order of entry into CB and the pieces' musical characteristics. Two of the "anomalous" Sinfonias, in E♭ and in C minor, come at or near the end of the series,[72] but the other two, in B minor and G minor, are nos. 7 and 11 in CB. The D-major Sinfonia, the last extant in CB and the only fully permutational piece with two countersubjects, immediately follows the non-contrapuntal one in E♭ major; the *galant* A-minor Sinfonia comes just before the B-minor, but these are sandwiched between the rigorous F-major and B♭-major, the only two to use stretto in a significant way. The very first piece in both autographs, the C-major, includes a complete series of entries using the inversion of the subject, but only the E-major comes close to repeating this variety of "demonstration" counterpoint. Hence there was no clear musical progression in the order of pieces in CB, and there is none either in P 610 apart from the key scheme; both arrangements, like the final ordering of the Inventions, merely follow the principle of diversity.

Bach took as much trouble over the less complex sinfonias as he did in the more rigorously fugal ones. The composing score of the Sinfonia in E♭ contains particularly numerous alterations, and most of the ornaments and embellishments here and elsewhere were later additions. NBA V/3 provides a "Concordance" of the ornamented versions of the Sinfonia in E♭ as copied by Gerber, Kayser, and Bach himself (in P 610). Although these differ only in details, they suggest that (1) considerable ornamentation was considered essential to an expressive performance of the piece, and (2) there was no single approved way of playing it.[73] The alterations include embellishments in small note values that appear in some editions as ordinary thirty-seconds; these were originally inserted as *petites notes* after the dotted eighths and rests in mm. 9, 10, and elsewhere. Hence a mathematically exact subdivision of the beat is probably inappropriate for these figures. Especially in their ornamented versions, the Sinfonias in E♭ and G minor are among Bach's most exquisite *pièces de clavecin*. The density of ornament signs approaches that seen in Preller's copies of earlier works, but here the placement of the signs is logical and systematic, with restatements of a given motive usually receiving the same ornaments. Copies of the English and French Suites by Bach's pupils show similar attention to performance details (see chaps. 13 and 14).

Ornaments are not the only French element in the E♭-major Sinfonia. Despite the dotted rhythms, the piece has nothing to do with an overture; it rather resembles a sarabande in three voices, a type found in several of Bach's suites (e.g., the G-Major Partita). The sarabande character does not necessarily imply a slow tempo, but finding a suitable pace is not easy. It is probably best to judge the tempo from the plainer version in CB; the ornamentation of the final version ought not hold back the tempo too much. As elsewhere in Bach's keyboard music, the appoggiaturas can be understood as short French *coulés* and *ports de voix* (*accents*); the piece loses its dance-like swing if these are performed as long ("variable") appoggiaturas of the type described three decades later by C. P. E. Bach (1753–62, i.2.2.8). On the other hand, the appoggiaturas probably ought not be so short as to be crushed against the main tone, like modern "grace" notes. Nor should they precede the beat; either way the effect of a gentle momentary dissonance would be lost. Careful attention to ornaments will deepen the expressive character of the piece, whose moderately elegiac tone is due in part to the early move to the subdominant (m. 3). This modulation also makes possible the wonderfully effortless return to the tonic near the end. The middle section (mm. 13–29) concludes in the subdominant, but the recapitulation of the opening phrase follows immediately (mm. 30ff.). The harmony of m. 1 is thus reinterpreted touchingly as V of IV, before the tonic has been fully re-established.

Although Gerber and Kayser preserved heavily ornamented versions of five Sinfonias, two additional opportunities for embellishment remain unrealized in all known copies. These are the fermatas that fall at climactic moments near the ends of the Sinfonias in E major and B minor. Fermatas often imply improvised cadenzas in eighteenth-century music. Yet Bach left comparable fermatas unembellished in WTC2 (fugue in E minor) and in the third movement of the D-minor Harpsichord Concerto BWV 1052; in each case the arrival on the dominant comes just before the concluding passage. The same is true here, suggesting that the fermatas be left alone.

Performance issues of a different character arise in the brilliant B-minor Sinfonia, whose most notable feature is a recurring flurry of thirty-seconds. The penultimate appearance of this motive involves a difficult sort of hand crossing

(m. 28). As in the Concerto BWV 973, raising the wrists and straightening out the fingers may make it possible to play the passage on a single manual. Friedemann Bach probably practiced the piece assiduously; his Fantasia in C (F. 14) contains similar writing.

Of the more rigorously contrapuntal sinfonias, the F-minor is often discussed on account of its chromaticism, which is intensified by the "rhetorical" pauses in its subject. In his fair copy, Bach placed slurs over the three-note motives in the theme, but Gerber and Kayser ornamented these with a slide (*Schleifer*) that forces a break in the slur. Played on the harpsichord, the ornament is the equivalent of an expressive crescendo to the higher second note (Example 10.13). The piece has inspired much speculation, in part because the subject incorporates the B-A-C-H motive, initially transposed (ab´-g´-bb´-a♮´) but later in its "original" form (m. 17). One thing that is certain about the piece is that it has the most schematic design of any of the Sinfonias, foreshadowing the fugue in F♯ of WTC2. Much of the first half (mm. 9–19), which modulates to A♭ and C minor, is later recapitulated a fifth lower (mm. 22–32). This takes the music deep into "flat" territory; the most remote point is reached with the e♭♭´ in m. 25—that is, the flat second degree (Neapolitan) of D♭.[74]

The considerable amount of near-literal repetition, varied only by permutation of the counterpoint, creates a danger of monotony, but four entrances of the subject in major keys introduce a vital change in color. These were spuriously "corrected" (perhaps by Forkel) at two points, making the entire piece seem monochromatic for the unsuspecting user of older editions.[75] Nevertheless the piece's prevailing color is very dark, established at the outset by harsh dissonances and the empty fifth on the fourth beat of m. 1 (which "resolves" to a tritone, the fifth being part of an implied 6/5-chord). The underlying progressions are perfectly conventional, but they are rarely spelled out in full, and odd intervals like the bare augmented fifth on the downbeat of m. 8 are "explained" only as the measure unfolds. As in other highly chromatic works (e.g., the prelude in A minor of WTC2), the piece's expressive essence lies in the tension between the almost geometrical regularity of the formal design and the bold dissonance and tortuous melody at the level of detail.

Example 10.13 Sinfonia in F Minor BWV 795, mm. 1–3a, with ornaments from copies by Kayser and H. N. Gerber.

Such boldness is a hallmark of Bach's style, something to which his pupils would have quickly grown accustomed. They must also have grown accustomed to the difficulties of his keyboard idiom. If the B-Minor Sinfonia presents the worst of this, the Sinfonia in B♭ is not far behind. The technical difficulties in the latter do not stem from any schoolbook rigor in its counterpoint, for it is the freest of the contrapuntally oriented sinfonias in the treatment of its subject. The subject is treated with particular freedom in two stretto passages that occupy most of the last third of the piece (mm. 17b–22, which constitute the climax). Difficulties arise for the player because Bach was unwilling to permit considerations of keyboard technique to dictate the voice leading; for instance, he revised mm. 19–20 so as to require a stretch of a tenth.[76] Yet Bach did make concessions to the exigencies of keyboard playing in m. 3, where both autographs show a tie joining tones that belong to two different voices; this illustrates a principle later codified by Emanuel Bach (1753–62, i.3.18).[77]

A final point of notation and performance is to be observed in the A-minor Sinfonia, whose short measures of 3/8 are grouped into pairs in CB. There full barlines occur only after each pair of measures; we might term these "double measures." Hence, as in several other similarly notated pieces (e.g., the first passepied of the English Suite in E minor), the true meter is compound. Notation in normal 6/8-time might have implied too quick a tempo; some rhythms involving thirty-seconds (m. 36) would seem rushed if taken too quickly. Double measures evidently signify a restrained tempo in which each measure of 3/8 is nevertheless counted "in one."

11

The *Well-Tempered Clavier*, Part 1

The *Well-Tempered Clavier* (WTC) is probably Bach's most famous keyboard work. This was already true during the half-century after his death; dozens of manuscript copies survive from that period, and the publication of three editions at the beginning of the nineteenth century was one of the first manifestations of the so-called Bach Revival.[1] No doubt the work's novel organization and its usefulness as a sort of textbook in composition and keyboard performance furthered its popularity at a time when manuals on fugue and other theoretical writings on music were being issued with increasing frequency. Bach's personal fame as a keyboard player as well as that of his pupils must also have encouraged the work's dissemination; other Bach keyboard works were available, but the WTC may have seemed a sort of official compendium of examples by a player of unparalleled ability and a master of the arcane art of strict counterpoint.

Of course the WTC is much more than a compendium of contrapuntal devices, a role belonging more properly to the *Art of Fugue*. As useful as both the preludes and the fugues may be as exercises for students, their importance (and their real usefulness in teaching) lies in the richness and variety of their musical content. For the WTC is a diverse set of keyboard pieces united only by their descent from the old multisectional *praeludium*, now composed of two distinct movements. Within this format, Bach provided examples of almost all the keyboard forms and styles available to him: dances, virtuoso improvisations, quasi-vocal pieces in *stile antico*, even sonata movements.

Writers have stressed the "educational" and "private" character of the WTC (e.g., Rosen 1990, 50), in contrast to the "public" character of the preludes and fugues for organ. It is true that many movements lack an outwardly virtuoso character. A few relatively brief preludes and fugues recall earlier pedagogic collections, and other movements evoke the learned contrapuntal works of seventeenth-century composers like Frescobaldi and Froberger. Indeed, echoes of Frescobaldi's *Capricci* of 1626 occur with sufficient frequency that one suspects that that volume—a genuine compendium of contrapuntal pieces in different genres (ricercars, canzoni, and capricci)—was a direct inspiration for the WTC.[2] But some of the great organ *praeludia* (e.g., the Toccata and Fugue in F, BWV 540) also contain learned fugues in archaic style; on the other hand, individual movements in WTC1, such as the fugue in G, are as flashy as anything in Bach's concertos. That the work is useful for pedagogy has been confirmed by nearly three centuries of experience by teachers and pupils. Yet, against the common assumption that Bach's pupils would have studied the WTC diligently, Beißwenger (2002, 11–4) points out that the extant complete manuscript copies made by Bach's pupils were probably not for their own use, but rather for Bach's (that is, for sale); pupils might have copied for themselves only individual movements that they were studying. Bach's title for the work mentions not only its usefulness for pupils but its suitability for "those those already skilled in this study."

Largely because of the WTC, we take for granted that the "prelude and fugue" was an established genre for Bach and his contemporaries. But the WTC did not necessarily begin as a collection of preludes *and* fugues, nor one that encompassed all twenty-four keys. The expression "preludes and fugues" in Bach's title does not explicitly refer to pairs of movements, although titles for suites and other such works, going back to the seventeenth century, also failed to specify how movements were grouped.[3] There were few exact precedents for the type of prelude and fugue found here: two musically independent movements of roughly equal length and complexity, probably too long to serve a genuine preludial or interludial function (as in church), most too difficult for any but advanced pupils. Bach's organ *praeludia* of this type were relatively recent works, and few of Bach's early clavier pieces are comparable. Of the fugues previously considered, the revised version of the "Albinoni" fugue BWV 951 comes closest, and it may date from the same period as WTC1, perhaps even having been considered for inclusion. Especially in WTC1, the prelude is often shorter than the fugue, but even in Part 1 the relationship between the two movements is sometimes reversed, the prelude being equal to or larger than the fugue. Even when short, the prelude remains a self-contained composition; eleven of the preludes appeared separately in the *Clavier-Büchlein vor William Friedemann Bach* (CB), albeit in distinct early versions. It is possible that the preludes were drafted as a separate series, joined only later to fugues which likewise might have been composed independently.

In assembling these collections, Bach would have had in mind earlier sets of keyboard pieces, some of which had been organized according to mode or tonality. The work's most immediate relative, formally and chronologically, was Fischer's *Ariadne musica*, containing twenty preludes and fugues in different keys.[4] Bach apparently borrowed several subjects from Fischer, but since Fischer himself might have borrowed, one cannot be sure that he was always Bach's source.[5] At least the plan of Fischer's work is likely to have influenced Bach, who might have taken from it the original ordering scheme for the WTC. Fischer placed each minor key (except for C) prior to the corresponding major key; a similar arrangement was used for three of the pairs of preludes and fugues in an early copy of WTC1.[6]

Other forerunners included manuscript collections, such as the one preserving the prelude and fugue BWV 895 together with works by Pachelbel and his pupils (see chap. 6). The latter are close to what has been termed a "verset tradition" (Ledbetter 2002, 52): fugatos on liturgical subjects, going back to Frescobaldi and earlier. But musically the WTC differs greatly from Fischer's collection and older "verset" sets. The didactic or liturgical function of these works is evident in the brevity of the individual pieces and the simplicity of the fugue subjects, sometimes chant-derived. But the movements of the WTC possess greater dimensions, and although Bach avoids an ostentatiously virtuoso style, he also avoids a condescending didactic tone. Verset collections might have furnished Bach with good concise subjects, as well as with the idea of a tonally organized series of pieces, but they could not offer models for the great variety of formal schemes and idiomatic keyboard textures used in both preludes and fugues.

Indeed, another distinction between the WTC and its predecessors is the sheer diversity of its individual pieces. No doubt deliberately intended, the diversity may also reflect the history of the work. Besides the separate transmission of some of the preludes, evidence for the independent composition of some movements has been seen in the archaic style of certain fugues, suggesting a relatively early date of composition. Most of the pieces had already undergone some degree of revision by the time Bach wrote out the famous autograph of Part 1 (P 415), which bears the date 1722; further revisions followed.[7] Hence, although 1722 is usually given as the date of WTC1, the collection must have existed for at least a short time previously, if not as an integral work, then as a group of separate preludes and fugues. This was certainly the case with Part 2, for which Bach apparently never prepared an integral fair-copy manuscript (see chap. 12).

Whatever its exact history, Bach's compilation of WTC1 proved to be part of the same ongoing project that included the assembly of the *Orgelbüchlein* at Weimar and the fair copy of the Inventions and Sinfonias at Cöthen. As in those works, Bach prepared an explanatory title page:

> The Well-Tempered Keyboard [*Clavier*], or Preludes and Fugues through all tones and semitones, including those with a major third or Ut-Re-Mi as well as those with a minor third or Re-Mi-Fa. For the profit and use of musical youth desiring instruction, and for the particular delight of those who are already skilled in this discipline, composed and prepared by Johann Sebastian Bach.[8]

Bach's title emphasizes the work's use of all available tonalities. Although his way of explaining this seems unduly verbose, Bach had to be precise about what he meant by "all" keys, since earlier collections like Fischer's had excluded certain rarely encountered tonalities (e.g. C♯ major). It would not have been obvious to every musician that such keys even existed; they had been unknown prior to the Baroque. By Bach's day, the number of modes had been effectively reduced to two, but the number of major and minor keys in frequent use had expanded considerably, and Bach's inclusion in the WTC of all twenty-four theoretical possibilities was a logical step. Bach's own music modulates to every available key, but outside the WTC the most "remote" tonic keys used in his keyboard music are those with signatures of four sharps or flats.[9] Organists had to contend with more difficult keys, since the organ was treated as a transposing instrument at Leipzig and elsewhere; a cantata movement in C minor would have an organ part in B-flat minor.

At the time of WTC1, Bach was not alone in his concern with providing players with examples of music in "all" keys; Mattheson's *Exemplarische Organisten-Probe*, published in 1719, contained two figured bass exercises in each tonality. It is sometimes supposed that such collections were made possible by the recent invention of "well-tempered" tuning systems for keyboard instruments. But these had long been known, at least theoretically; a better explanation lies in the increasing use generally of "remote" keys during the early eighteenth century, as composers of ensemble music broadened the range of tonalities to which recitatives, arias, and sonata and concerto movements modulated.

The word *wohltemperierte* was used mainly in connection with keyboard temperament, referring not to a particular way of tuning, such as equal temperament, but to any system that left all tonalities usable. Efforts have been made to prove that the WTC calls for one well-tempered system or another, but arguments tend to rely on dubious "internal evidence" and debatable assumptions.[10] Some movements in Part 2 were transposed from their original keys, and there are indications that this was also the case in Part 1; Bach is unlikely to have done this had he expected transposition to alter the sound in a significant way (due to an "unequal" temperament) or to elicit different affective associations. Williams (2003a, 66) asks whether "a composer of such unimaginable musical grasp had the slightest interest in temperament per se." Bach would have had to decide how to tune his instruments, but his decisions are more likely to have been based on pragmatic than theoretical grounds. Ledbetter (2002) argues that, by the time of WTC2, Bach had probably settled on equal temperament, and there is evidence from only a few years after his father's death that C. P. E. Bach favored such tuning for solo music played on the clavichord (see chap. 2).

Nevertheless, a keyboard tuned in equal temperament creates intonation problems for Baroque strings and winds that it accompanies. Whatever tuning Bach used for the WTC was not necessarily the same one employed for playing continuo. Other well-tempered systems retain subtle distinctions between keys, leaving "remote" tonalities like C♯ major and E♭ minor with relatively sharp major thirds. Continuo players were advised to omit out-of-tune thirds (see Schulenberg 2003), but in solo keyboard music even the tonic triad sounded rougher or less sonorous in certain keys, creating distinctions that were valued by some theorists and probably some musicians.

"Temperament" is not the only word in the title requiring interpretation; *Clavier* is equally ambiguous. Here the word probably refers not to a particular instrument but to the keyboard itself, tuned in a certain way. Certainly the translation "Well-Tempered *Clavichord*" is incorrect, reflecting at best a special usage of the later eighteenth century, when the word could indeed mean the clavichord specifically. WTC1 could have been played on the unfretted clavichords that are known to have existed as early as 1693, and in Saxony by 1716 (see Koster 2005); Loucks (1992, 58) has shown that only a few passages in the WTC are "genuinely unplayable" on a fretted clavichord. But on such an instrument many passages could be played only if one took liberties with note values or abbreviated ornaments. No doubt some players were forced to do just that. But Bach addressed the work not only to pupils but to experts, who are likely to have possessed suitable instruments.[11] Williams (1983a) argued convincingly that the harpsichord is the one instrument most suitable for *all* movements of the WTC, even if individual pieces may seem appropriate to clavichord or fortepiano. Either of the latter instruments—or the modern piano—can be used to shape beautifully the melodic line of, say, the prelude in G♯ minor of Part 2 or the C♯-minor preludes of both books. But neither clavichord nor fortepiano is as effective for clearly articulating inner or lower voices in a contrapuntal texture.

The organ has also been suggested as a possible instrument, although to play all movements of the WTC it would have to be well-tempered, perhaps still a rarity during Bach's lifetime. The simple pedal parts in Fischer's *Ariadne musica* may imply use of the organ, but most are optional or easily transferred to the left hand. An early copy of WTC1 (P 401) includes the word *manualiter* in the titles of most of the pieces, and Marshall (1986) took this as an indication for organ use—but it is not found in the autograph. At least one piece exists in an apparent organ version,[12] and in WTC1 the pedal point at the end of the A-minor fugue cannot be sustained as written without organ pedals. But there are long pedal points in other works surely meant for harpsichord, and use of organ pedals would not solve all the performance problems in this particular movement.

Pianists may be inclined to agree with Rosen (1990, 50) that theirs is the instrument that "will deliver Bach's original conception to the public most adequately." But this presupposes "public presentation in large halls"—and even pianists rarely play the WTC nowadays in anything larger than a recital hall. Rather than be overly concerned with which instrument is best suited to the music, pianists might, as in other works, emulate the better qualities of harpsichord

204 • The Keyboard Music of J. S. Bach

performance: clean and thoughtfully worked out articulation, expressive (not mechanical) ornamentation, and disciplined rhythmic freedom.

The Styles of the *Well-Tempered Clavier*

Although the two parts of the WTC were assembled at different times, their heterogeneous content makes it difficult to characterize their style in general terms or to find clear stylistic distinctions between them. Efforts that have been made since Forkel (1802, 55/NBR, 467–8) to find one book superior or more consistent in quality than the other seem arbitrary. Still, some differences are readily apparent. Part 1 contains only a single prelude in binary form (that is, with a central double bar), whereas Part 2 contains ten. There are more four-voice fugues in Part 1—four being the traditional number of voices for a learned keyboard ricercar or canzona—and only Part 1 contains fugues (two) in five voices. Probably a greater number of movements in Part 2 refer to the fashionable *galant* style, but several fugues in Part 1 already contain prominent *galant* elements—dance rhythms, expressive "sigh" motives, and so forth—and only Part 1 includes a fugue in the minimum number of voices possible (two).

Although Bach may have experimented with different ordering schemes, there is no evidence that the pieces were ever arranged according to features other than tonality. Williams (2003, 144) raises the interesting question of why C major came first. It may not yet have had the canonic status of first or simplest tonality, but Kuhnau's suites of 1689 provided a precedent, and their title might have suggested the way in which Bach articulated the idea of "all keys" in the title of WTC1, both referring to the ancient hexachord system that started on the note C (ut). Certainly it is no coincidence that the volume opens with a relatively simple prelude and closes with one of the longest and most profound of the four-part fugues. No such plan is evident in Part 2, however, and in both volumes the pairings of some movements seem incongruous. In WTC1 the A-minor fugue is inordinately long for its prelude, whereas the prelude in E♭ is an imposing four-voice composition with two subjects, dwarfing its fugue, which has just three parts and one subject. In Part 2 the prelude in B♭ similarly outweighs its fugue, but through its greater length and its unique use of hand crossings, not through contrapuntal elaboration. Such examples might have arisen when Bach brought together pieces that had been composed separately, as he is known to have done in WTC2. In WTC1 he may also have had to transpose pieces in order to fill in gaps (as he certainly did in Part 2). On the other hand, resemblances within each book between pieces in related keys—in Part 1, the preludes in C♯ and G♯ minor, and the fugues in C♯ and F♯ major—could reflect their having been composed in rapid succession specifically for inclusion in the WTC.

Attempts have been made to classify the preludes and fugues according to their use of a particular musical character or contrapuntal technique. But only a few movements systematically employ specific contrapuntal devices, and most fail to conform to any one well-defined genre. A number of the preludes of WTC1 open with passagework composing out a standard harmonic progression, a type of writing descended from improvisatory arpeggio preludes, like the one prefacing the Fugue in A Minor BWV 944.[13] Here the arpeggiation is always written out, and the motives used in the arpeggiation are usually developed later in the movement. But most of the preludes depart from the arpeggio model; some resemble Bach's inventions or sinfonias. Many of the binary-form preludes of WTC2 are in effect sonata movements. Even the basic distinction between prelude and fugue is blurred by two preludes (E♭ in WTC1, C♯ in WTC2) that are really self-contained preludes with fugues.

The fugues are traditionally distinguished by the number of voices, as Bach himself did in the movement headings in the autograph of WTC2. This is less arbitrary than it may seem, as the fugues in four and five parts tend to be more conservative in style than those in two or three, and are more likely to work out the contrapuntal possibilities of the subject in inversion, stretto, and so forth, reflecting the traditional four-part ricercar or fantasia. There are exceptions, however: in WTC1 the three-part fugue in D♯ minor is very severe and archaic, whereas the four-part fugues in A♭ and B are relatively light and modern in style. Kunze (1969) sought to place the fugues in more precisely drawn categories, distinguishing "ricercar" fugues, *fugae patheticae*, *fugae graves*, and other types. The terminology comes from Walther (1732, 265–67), but the expressions are not widely attested and may not have been well defined or in general use.

In any case, Walther's terms describe only the musical surface and have no bearing on the large structure. The fugues of the WTC draw on the full range of formal designs used in Bach's earlier fugues, excepting only da capo and ritornello forms. A surprising number join many of the preludes in incorporating elements of sonata form, by which is meant not the full-fledged sonata-allegro design of the Classical style but the simpler type that was being composed routinely by Bach's younger contemporaries (including his sons) by the 1720s. Essentially an expanded version of the rounded binary forms used in dances and other pieces, or of the parallel-section design used in through-composed preludes and other pieces, this type of sonata movement usually lacks a distinctly articulated "second subject." But there is usually a distinct closing passage of some sort at the end of each major division; a middle section modulating more remotely than the others; and a strongly articulated return of the subject in the tonic at the beginning of the final section, which also contains some amount of recapitulation.[14]

Whereas more preludes in WTC2 than in WTC1 employ some variety of sonata form, Part 1 contains a greater number of *fugues* adopting elements of sonata form. Evidently by the time of Part 2 Bach was more attracted to fugues emphasizing contrapuntal work as such, and was less interested in assimilating fugue to a type of formal design that was rapidly becoming the norm in other types of composition. Although a few fugues in both books are organized by the use of a particular contrapuntal technique (inversion, stretto, etc.) in each section, these form a small minority. Even in these pieces it would be a mistake to base an analysis solely on the contrapuntal devices employed; formal design in Bach's fugues goes deeper than that.

Text, Sources, and Editions

Few of Bach's keyboard works have histories as well documented as that of WTC1. Although Bach's composing scores are, as usual, lost, several manuscripts give texts predating the fair-copy autograph, and other copies were made prior to Bach's final revisions. Hence, scholars have been able to reconstruct a detailed history of the revisions made in each movement. A good start on this was already made in the nineteenth century, and Kroll's edition of both parts of the WTC in BG 14 remains a remarkable piece of scholarship.[15] But early editors, including Kroll, were hampered by the unavailability of many sources (e.g., CB) and the confusion of copies with autographs.[16] Most subsequent editions were based on Kroll's. The nineteenth-century variorum edition by Hans Bischoff,[17] like Kroll's still available in modern reprints, is somewhat more arbitrary than the BG and often fails to distinguish between authentic and inauthentic variants. Not until Dehnhard (1977–83) was there a true modern critical edition, followed shortly afterwards by those of Dürr (for the NBA) and Jones.[18] The latter is the most practical choice, especially for those without German, not least for its incorporation of the commentaries from Tovey's 1924 edition, which although dated in many respects showed greater awareness of historical issues, including performance practice, than many more recent writings. Not an edition, but almost as indispensable, is the thought-provoking study by Ledbetter (2002).[19] Groocock (2003) provides a systematic analysis of all the fugues, as well as a useful annotated bibliography of older analytic studies.

All the editions mentioned follow the autograph as the main text for WTC1.[20] Each also gives a selection of earlier readings, and Dürr even gives separately the complete text of WTC1 in its earliest known version.[21] Table 11.1 lists the most important sources, indicating the version or versions preserved in each.[22]

Bach's revisions in WTC1 are interesting not only for their own sake but because they help explain oddities in a number of pieces, particularly those preludes that were expanded for the version of the fair-copy autograph.[23] These preludes betray traces of revision in a change of texture or material at the beginning of an interpolated passage, but the problem, if it is one, is hardly noticeable. Elsewhere Bach's revisions affected only details, but like his revisions in other works, they reveal his continual effort toward perfecting his texts.

Table 11.1 WTC1: Stages of Revision and Chief Sources

Stage	Source	Copyist, Date	Comment
α1	Konwitschny ms.	2nd half (?)18th cent.	Entries by Forkel; formerly owned by Franz Konwitschny (1901–62), now lost
α2	CB**	WFB, JSB, 1720–1	Preludes: C c d D e E F
α3	CB**	WFB, JSB, 1720–1	Preludes: C# c# eb f
α3	P 401	Kayser, 1722–3	Later altered to give readings of A1
A1–4	P 415	JSB, 1722, revised 1732, 1736 or later, 1744	Revisions fall into 3 main layers; dates uncertain
A1*	P 1074	J. G. Walther(?), 1730s	Some readings pre-A1
A1	NL DHgm 69 D 14**	Meissner, ca. 1727 or later	Latter (but earlier) portion of composite ms.
A1	US BER	H. N. Gerber et al.	
A2*	P 202	AMB, Agricola (1740), C. H. E. Müller (ca. 1800)	Müller replaced missing portion of original ms.
A2	Hs MB1974	2nd half 18th cent.	Includes WTC2 (titles of Parts 1 and 2 exchanged)
A2	LEm Poel. 34	1st half 18th cent.	autograph(?) entry in prelude in G
A2	NL DHgm 69 D 14**	1st half or mid-18th cent.	Initial portion of composite ms.
A3	LEm Scheibner 6	ca. 1800	
A3*	P 402	Altnikol, 1755	Includes WTC2
A4	AmB 49	Anonymous 403	(?) owned by Kirnberger
A4	AmB 57/1	Anonymous 402	Analytical entries by Kirnberger

AMB = Anna Magdalena Bach
JSB = Johann Sebastian Bach
WFB = Wilhelm Friedemann Bach
*Contains mixed, arbitrary, or erroneous readings. Walther's copy P 1074 bears the date 1722, but the handwriting is late and Walther probably copied the date from his exemplar (Beißwenger 1992a, 29)
**Incomplete

Prelude and Fugue in C, BWV 846

WTC1 opens with what is now a familiar prelude, one that probably would not have seemed very challenging musically or technically to users of the volume in Bach's day. But like most Bach works the prelude contains its share of counter-intuitive harmonic turns, and although it is constructed mainly from repetitions of a single motive, the recurrences of the latter and the underlying voice leading are not quite as regular as a first glance might suggest. The fugue is a more challenging piece and therefore less familiar; even an accomplished player who could sight-read the prelude readily would do the same in the fugue only with stumbling and difficulty. For many of Bach's contemporaries that would have been enough to convince them that the WTC was no simple "delight" as his title might have suggested.

The prelude was not necessarily intended to be delicate, an impression conveyed today by its position at the head of what some have been taught to call the Well-Tempered "Clavichord." It is in five voices (as is clearer in its original notation), and the fugue is in four; both types of texture call, on the harpsichord, for a strong registration, and the prelude can be played energetically, enough to make the little flourish at the end sound brilliant. In the earliest version the arpeggiation was not written out. But the care with which Bach wrote every note in the final version suggests that his notation should be taken at its word. Harpsichordists today customarily hold out notes of an arpeggio, but here the rests, at least, might be observed literally, leading to a distinct articulation of each harmony. Pianists might consider playing without pedal, since the latter can reduce the figuration to a vapid blur.

Despite its apparent simplicity, the prelude cost Bach some trouble. It exists in at least two distinct versions, the earliest of which was probably the one Friedemann Bach copied in CB (erasures obscure the original reading). He and his father both made alterations in this copy, but its text was never brought fully into line with that of the autograph or later manuscripts. Thus, what looks like an intermediate version in CB may actually be only an incompletely updated copy of the early version.[24] The most important revision, not entered into CB, was the extension of the dominant pedal point in the final version.[25]

Because this type of prelude seems to consist of nothing more than a series of broken chords, its phrasing—that is, its form, understood as a series of modulating phrases—rarely receives due attention. Elided phrase endings in the middle of the piece make analysis somewhat ambiguous; table 11.2 shows one possibility. Although the outlines of this form are already evident in the earliest version, the structure is more clearly articulated in the final version. The arrival on the dominant pedal at m. 24 was strengthened by the insertion of m. 23, and the pedal point itself was lengthened.[26] The final tonic harmony was also extended, forming a short coda (mm. 32–5). Two earlier arrivals (on G and C, respectively) were strengthened by the insertion of mm. 11 and 19, which eliminated the elided phrase endings originally found at those points.

The insertion of m. 23 introduced an ambiguity, since this is the only measure in the main body of the final version that contains a passing tone. But which of

Table 11.2 Structure of the C-Major Prelude (WTC1)

Version of . . .	Number of Measures in Each Phrase						Total
Konwitschny ms.	4	5	7	3	4	1	24
CB (after correction)	4	7	8	3	4	1	27
P 415	4	7	8	4	8	4	35
Key or cadence:	C	→	G→	C→	C:V→	I	
Measure no. (P 415):	1	5	12	20	24	32	

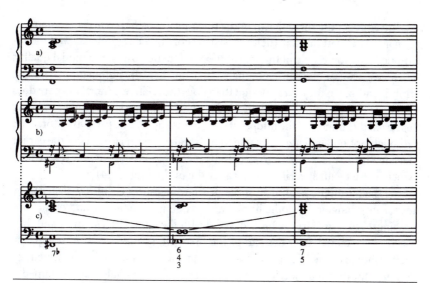

Example 11.1 Prelude in C, BWV 846/1, mm. 22–4: (a) earliest version; (b) final version; (c) analysis of final version.

the five pitches in the measure is the passing tone? If c′, then the harmony is a diminished-seven chord (6/4/2+); if b, the harmony is a suspended supertonic (II-6/4/3, ex. 11.1).[27] At the late stage of revision at which Bach added m. 23, he was probably writing out the arpeggiation of each measure, not leaving the notation in the form of five-part chords. If so he would not have had to decide which pitch is the passing tone, and the ambiguity might have been deliberate (as argued in Cone 1968). The ambiguity is a neat way of sidestepping a problem of voice leading: In the added m. 23 there is no graceful way to maintain the prevailing five-part texture without introducing a momentary unison doubling (see Example 11.1c). But a five-note chord, without doublings, is necessary if the rhythmic pattern of the arpeggiation is to be maintained.[28]

Bach also revised the fugue, but only after copying it into P 415. The subject originally moved in eighths and sixteenths, and the dotted rhythm on the third beat is the result of a revision that Bach extended throughout the fugue.[29] Marpurg quoted the subject in its original form in his *Abhandlung von der Fuge*, showing the first two entries as an example of a subject that does not leave the tonic (Example 11.2).[30]

Example 11.2 Fugue in C, BWV 846/2, early version, mm. 1–4a.

The almost pure diatonicism of the opening exposition reflects the status of C major as a "natural" key (neither "sharp" nor "flat"), recalling as well the restrained harmonic style of the *stile antico*. The fugue possesses a modal quality, or at least a weakened sense of tonality, inasmuch as the dominant plays a less prominent role in the overall design than does the relative minor. Nowhere does the fugue make a strong arrival on the dominant, the only strong cadences being to the relative minor (at the midpoint) and to the supertonic (m. 19b). Moreover, although not notated *alla breve*, the fugue recalls certain ricercars of the earlier Baroque in its preoccupation with a given contrapuntal device—here, stretto, which is used with special intensity after the midpoint (m. 14).

Yet the harmonic neutrality of the first few measures is quickly dispelled by increasingly angular melodic lines, harsh passing dissonances, and odd chord spacings. There are already hints of these with the tenor entry in m. 4, and they reach a first climax near the end of the first half, in mm. 12–3. Although the melodic logic of the individual voices is indisputable, some of the writing is so counter-intuitive that one wonders whether even Bach could have imagined it without knowing the ricercars from Frescobaldi's *Capricci*, which include equally unconventional exercises in an ostensibly archaic, quasi-vocal style.

Although not quite as vocal in quality as a true *stile antico* fugue, this piece raises similar interpretive questions. How detached or legato should one play the subject? The latter somewhat resembles the subjects of Bach's choral fugues on biblical texts; since Bach usually sets such subjects syllabically, the analogy to choral writing suggests an articulate approach, not legato (Example 11.3). Tempo might also be judged in vocal terms, a good pace being one that permits singing the subject in one breath (i.e., at least to the e′ on the third beat of m. 2). A slow legato presentation can be ponderous; Bach's alteration of the rhythm, perhaps meant to improve the voice leading (e.g., in mm. 4 and 18), also makes the subject lighter and the embellishment of the falling half step (f′–e′) more graceful. The closing phrase (mm. 26–7) employs an ascending formula also used in the fugue in G (BWV 860/2) and the organ chorale *Allein Gott in der Höh' sei Ehr'* BWV 663. This does not mean that the fugue has any religious significance but rather that it shares some of the chorale's festive character and should not be interpreted too severely.

Da - zu ist er - schie-nen der Sohn Got - tes,

Example 11.3 *Dazu ist erschienen der Sohn Gottes* BWV 40, first movement, mm. 29–30 (tenor).

Prelude and Fugue in C Minor BWV 847

The second prelude is again essentially a series of arpeggiations, but the motive used to compose out each harmony incorporates numerous neighbor tones, and the underlying voice leading is more often varied. The rushing two-part counterpoint and the cadenza-like passages in the final section make this a busy piece, but surely one to be played with some freedom, not as an anticipation of twentieth-century machinery. As in the C-major prelude, the phrases into which the apparently seamless surface is organized are not hard to discern. Even on the harpsichord certain dynamic effects can be expressed; for example, one can dwell momentarily on the downbeats of mm. 6, 8, and 10, where each bass note is a dissonant suspension resolving on the following downbeat. The design is similar to that of the previous prelude: an opening four-measure cadential phrase to the tonic, then modulations to the relative major (m. 14), later dominant and tonic pedal points.

Most of the coda (from m. 25), including the cadenza-like passage at m. 28, was the product of revisions.[31] Bach added or lengthened cadenza-like passages at the ends of at least four other preludes; as in the prelude in E minor, one of the passages bears the tempo indication *presto* (m. 28), and the others are marked *adagio* (m. 34) and *allegro* (m. 35). The word *adagio* in the midst of a quick piece, as at m. 34, might have signified rhythmic freedom rather than a particular tempo.[32] But does *presto* mean a faster tempo than at the opening, which has no tempo mark? The word *presto* was an all-purpose quick tempo mark for some earlier composers, but Bach evidently drew a distinction here between *presto* and *allegro*, writing the latter for the concluding four measures. These return to the broken-chord texture of mm. 25–7, implying that *allegro* is the basic tempo, presumably somewhat slower than *presto*. This is not to say that the *presto* marking signifies a sudden, mechanical shift to breakneck speed. Large leaps in both hands (mm. 29, 30, 31) require time, implying some tempo flexibility within the *presto* phrase, and the remainder of the piece can be somewhat less rapid and even more nuanced.

The fugue is in the relatively light style that Bach favored for the three-part fugues of the WTC, especially in the episodes. There are four of these, and although very short they are distinct, clearly articulated sections; the first episode (mm. 9–11) is eventually recapitulated a fifth lower (mm. 22–3). Just before the latter, the subject re-enters in the tonic with some of the force of a sonata-form return; the passage (mm. 20–1) restates mm. 7–8 with the three contrapuntal lines redistributed. Bach must have recognized the structural significance of this entrance, for in the revised version he made it more impressive by transposing the bass to the lower octave.[33]

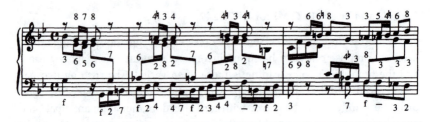

Example 11.4 Fugue in C Minor BWV 847/2, mm. 7–8, from P 401.

The fugue has been a favorite for analysts, perhaps including Bach's pupil Kayser, who was probably responsible for analytical markings in his copy P 401 (Example. 11.4).[34] The entries include numerals in the upper voice that indicate vertical intervals from the bass, as well as the letter "f" in the lowest voice to mark the local tonic note (*finalis*?) of each passage. Numbers attached to other notes in the lowest voice indicate their distance from the "*finalis*." The concern with tonality represents a step beyond Penzel's reduction of several preludes (including the C-minor) to a figured bass in P 1075; even the more sophisticated reductive analysis published by Kirnberger fails to engage with tonality.[35]

All these analyses remain focused on the local context, providing little clue to how Bach or his contemporaries viewed the larger structure of such fugues. Despite the clear alternation here between expository and episodic passages, any parallel to concerto design (emphasized by Ledbetter 2002, 158) is at best inexact. Other formal symmetries in this fugue have led to its being analyzed as both binary or ternary, depending on which articulations are taken to be most powerful and which passages are understood as being parallel to one another.[36] The recapitulatory design favors a tripartite interpretation, with divisions at mm. 11 and 20, but the fugue can also be divided in half at the cadence to the dominant in m. 17.

In fact the elided phrasing characteristic of fugues—as opposed to dances or sonata forms—makes the distinction between bipartite or tripartite form arbitrary or subjective, in the absence of decisive articulations. Evidently Bach did not keep a distinct formal plan in mind when composing a fugue of the present sort, for he apparently recognized the importance of the "return" at m. 20b only after writing it. Notwithstanding the clear plans of some pieces, his compositional process typically may have been improvisatory, a logical, clearly articulated form emerging only in the course of composition. Siegele (1989) has attempted to reconstruct "'the steps Bach took' in composing the [present] work," but each step in the reconstruction is doubtful, beginning with the initial assumption that Bach planned the order of entries prior to composing. Where we possess distinct early versions of Bach's fugues, we find that he sometimes added whole sections, as in the fugue in A♭ in WTC2. Even the opening exposition could be a later addition, as in Contrapunctus 10 from the *Art of Fugue*. The highly symmetrical form of the present piece may seem to leave little possibility of ever having been fundamentally altered. But it is possible to imagine a hypo-thetical early version skipping from the downbeat of m. 20 to the bass entry in m. 26—that is, lacking the recapitulation and ending with the tonic arrival now in the middle of m. 29.

Prelude and Fugue in C#, BWV 848

The prelude in C# at first looks like another one composed largely of broken-chord figuration, but this is true only of the latter part (mm. 63ff.), almost all of which was a later addition; up to there the piece is a two-part invention, with two distinct subjects that are regularly exchanged between the hands. To be sure, the main subject is simpler, closer to the violinistic Italianate concerto style, than that of the formally similar Invention in E♭. The two-voice texture might suggest a light registration, but the full-voiced chords at the end (already present in the earliest version) indicate on the contrary that, like the prelude in C, this piece is not delicate or quiet. A full registration may be in order, the lightness appropri-ate to the opening sections being achieved through crisp articulation—in both parts—though not a uniform staccato, which would sound mechanical. Pianists might again hold back on the pedal.

In addition to inserting the long arpeggio passage (mm. 63–98), Bach altered the opening motive, exchanging of the first and fourth sixteenths in m. 1 and parallel passages (editions in which the prelude opens on g#´ give the earlier reading).[37] Unlike the corresponding prelude in WTC2, this one was not, so far as is known, originally in a simpler key (C). Its very design seems calculated to force the player into increasingly difficult keys, opening with what is essentially a sequence moving about the circle of fifths, first upward from C# to A# minor (m. 31), then downward to F# (m. 47). The added passage (mm. 63–98) is a greatly extended prolongation of the original dominant pedal, using new figuration; without the interpolation the piece falls into four nearly equal sections (these begin at mm. 1, 17, 31, and 47).

The fugue is not only one of the liveliest and most *galant* in WTC1, but it includes one of the most extensive sonata-style recapitulation sections. That is to say that most of the final quarter of the piece (mm. 42–53) is drawn from the first section (mm. 1–11), altered only by a brief insertion that shifts the tonal goal from the dominant back to the tonic (m. 48a). This creates an impression of neatness and clarity that is in keeping with *galant* sonata style, and for this reason it might be regarded as one of the most modern pieces in the WTC.

Prelude and Fugue in C# Minor BWV 849

The C#-minor pair is one of the most imposing in the WTC. Although based on a dance rhythm, the prelude—the first example in WTC1 of what might be

Example 11.5 Prelude in C# Minor BWV 849/1, early version (BWV 849a/1), mm. 14–5 (corresponding to mm. 14–7 of later version).

termed an "arioso" type—has the same spaciousness and grandeur as the fugue, which is one of the two in five parts.

Despite its arioso melody, the prelude is polyphonic in texture, its design again close to that of the inventions. It opens with exchanges of a subject between treble and tenor, and its essentially binary design was originally articulated by a restatement of the subject in the tenor at the beginning of the second half (Example 11.5). The underlying rhythm is that of a siciliano, a slow gigue. But the convolutions of the melodic lines obscure the dance character, and the periodic phrasing of the dance is replaced by long lines that avoid cadences. The coda, a later addition (though already present in CB), begins with a deceptive cadence (m. 35) that holds off the final cadence for an additional four measures.

The tension inherent in the prelude's long phrases is likely to dissipate if the tempo is too slack, whereas a true andante (a "moving" tempo) allows the underlying dance meter to be felt. Most of the ornaments and appoggiaturas were written down only as revisions to P 415; there is not a single ornament sign in the copy in CB. The puzzling arpeggio sign on a two-note chord in m. 34 may mean that a passing tone should be inserted.[38]

In the fugue, the stark subject and the *alla breve* notation recall seventeenth-century ricercars, especially one in the same key by Froberger.[39] Ladewig (1991) notes the resemblance between the present fugue subject and that of Frescobaldi's Recercar I and finds further parallels between the two works, which can both be described as triple fugues.[40] Bach clearly meant to compose a monumental work in the old tradition, and the result stands alongside the organ fugue in F (BWV 540/2) and the second Kyrie of the B-Minor Mass among Bach's efforts in *stile antico*. As in the organ fugue, Bach eventually adds a livelier theme (at m. 36). But only the main subject is treated strictly. Both the second theme and a third one introduced later (tenor, m. 49) are better described as countersubjects, rarely used except in combination with the original subject.[41]

To be sure, when the new countersubject first enters in m. 35, it sounds as if a genuine second subject is being introduced, announced by the preceding full cadence and subsequent reduction in texture. But from this point onward the plan seems improvisatory, lacking the clear sectional divisions typical of Bach's fugues with multiple subjects (compare BWV 904/2 or the fugues in C# minor and G# minor in WTC2). The music never leaves the tonic for very long, and because the original subject is never long absent, it cannot make a dramatic re-entrance. A statement in the bass at the very bottom of Bach's *Clavier* (m. 73) might mark a second major division, giving the piece a tripartite structure overall. But any analytical division into sections is somewhat arbitrary after m. 35. Despite this, the fugue never gives the impression of wandering aimlessly, and the final page achieves urgency through the combination of stretto and some compelling chromatic progressions (mm. 94ff.).

Like the introduction of the second subject, the strettos create the impression of rigorous counterpoint. But Bach's notation of the voice leading in the stretto is ambiguous, and in the autograph it is impossible to trace the path of all five voices through mm. 94–100 without positing voice crossings and rests that Bach failed to make explicit. What matters here is the dramatic effect of stretto, not rigorous contrapuntal technique as such.[42] Despite its quasi-vocal character, the fugue remains true keyboard music, not an ersatz ensemble piece.[43]

Pedal markings in two copies may have indicated use of the organ.[44] But many older organs, including those in the two main Leipzig churches, lacked the low C# so crucial in m. 73.[45] In any case, organ style does not imply legato, and the diminished fourth in the subject (B#–e) might be marked by an especially distinct articulation of both notes. That Bach assumed such performance is evident from m. 15, where the soprano, stating the diminished fourth in the subject, leaps at the same time as the two inner voices, all played by the right hand. Legato would be impossible except with the aid of pedals (or, on piano, the damper pedal).

Prelude and Fugue in D, BWV 850

The prelude in D is again harmonically inspired, and like the preludes in C and C minor it opens with a variation on a simple cadential formula. But the harmony and the implied voice leading soon grow quite complex. Although the figuration might have been conceived as a five-finger exercise for the right hand, to toss it off at breakneck speed is to ignore, among other things, the regular alternation between short, dissonant pedal points representing stasis (e.g., mm. 8–9) and easy-going modulating sequences that move forward (mm. 10–11a).

The prelude was significantly revised, and only in the later version are the opening measures restated in the subdominant (mm. 20–4). From a formal point of view the revisions are the most substantial in any piece of WTC1, since the interpolation in the subdominant represents the insertion of an entire key area, not merely the extension of a dominant pedal point. As in other preludes, the closing dominant pedal (from m. 27) was prolonged to include a cadenza-like passage (mm. 30b–34), with an implicit *adagio* at m. 33. Bach also added the arpeggio sign on the first chord in m. 34; there was no space for a similar sign on the next chord, but it was probably understood that all four chords in this penultimate measure were to be arpeggiated. Two other Bach preludes end in a similar manner; although lacking arpeggio signs, the final measures of the D-minor prelude of WTC1 and the prelude of the D-minor cello suite (BWV 1008) would be more in character with the rest of each piece if played with broken chords.

Bach's fascination with the dotted overture style, which can be traced back to the early suites BWV 820 and 822, led to his incorporating it into cantata choruses as well as the present fugue. Although undeniably grand, this is a relatively unpretentious piece, despite the incessant dotted rhythms and energetic figures in thirty-seconds. It is also one of the least rigorous fugues in the WTC, abandoning the subject (save for its initial motive) two-thirds of the way through, after the cadence to E minor in m. 17. The absence of fugal rigor is no weakness, and the piece ends with a splendid series of flourishes in thirty-seconds—actually a stretto of the opening motive.

As in other dotted pieces, it is not always clear how to interpret the rhythmic notation. Mathematically exact "double dotting" was a twentieth-century practice, not an eighteenth-century one, but any extra lengthening of the dotted eighths raises questions about how the dotted rhythms should be played against steady sixteenths in another voice, as in the two episodes (at mm. 9 and 17). A working hypothesis for Bach is that what is written as a simultaneity should be played as one; that is, in the last half of m. 9 one should strike the three notes at the end of each beat as a chord. This does not rule out lengthening the dotted eighths and dwelling momentarily on the first sixteenth in each group. On the other hand, where a group of three thirty-seconds follows a dotted eighth, as in m. 3, the latter might be lengthened further and the thirty-seconds rushed; Bach would later find two different ways of writing what was probably meant to be the same rhythm (see Example 16.1).

Some of the apparent rhythmic conundrums may be products of modern misunderstanding of the tempo. As in any overture, a relatively quick pulse brings the dotted rhythms to life, even if played as written or with only slight over-dotting. The trick is to interpret the dot more as a rest, that is, a small articulation before the following shorter note or notes. It is also helpful to observe that the dotted figures usually come in pairs—that is, on alternating strong and weak beats—and that the flourish of thirty-seconds that opens the subject is an upbeat. Unfortunately, the latter is difficult to project on the harpsichord, and listeners will probably always hear the initial figure as a downbeat. The ornaments found in some editions on beats 3 and 4 might aid in defining the meter, even though probably not authentic.[46]

Prelude and Fugue in D Minor BWV 851

The prelude in D minor is again of the arpeggio-based type, and as in the D-major prelude the active line is that of the right hand. But the bass, which begins as a pedal point, gradually grows more independent, becoming expressive in mm. 10–1, where it contains a series of "sigh" motives. The annotations in P 401 note the presence of 4/2-chords on the even-numbered beats of these measures,[47] and the dissonances might be brought out by slurring the "sigh" figures in the bass—for example, a–g and F–E in m. 10. This is especially effective if the bass elsewhere is somewhat detached.

The early version ends with a chord on the downbeat of m. 15 (D/f#/a/d'). The added coda gives the left hand more to do, expanding the counterpoint to three parts (and more) in the last seven measures. Like the "cadenza" in the Fifth Brandenburg Concerto, the coda culminates in a descending series of broken diminished chords—perhaps a favorite improvisatory formula of Bach's.

The fugue makes much use of stretto and inversion, giving it the appearance of one of those that systematically explore the contrapuntal possibilities of the subject. But in fact it involves a free, kaleidoscopic permutation of three or four motivic fragments (as noted by Daverio 1992). Many of the stretto and *inversus* statements are incomplete or inexact, and instead of having a "contrapuntal" design this is one of the clearest examples of a fugue following the bipartite version of early sonata form. There is a central arrival in the dominant (m. 21), and the phrase that closes the first half returns to end the piece in the tonic (mm. 16–21 || 38–43). The introduction of the subject in stretto just after the central cadence (m. 22) recalls the similar procedure in the fugue in C. But by using the inversion of the subject at this point, Bach also alludes to binary-form dances, especially gigues, that invert the subject in the second half (to be sure, the inversion has already been heard once before, in m. 14).

Despite its quasi sonata form and three-voice texture, this is one of the more severe pieces in the WTC, not at all *galant* in style. The sixteenth-note motives in the subject and countersubject insure a high level of passing dissonance, since the first note of these figures is often an appoggiatura. Yet because the subject is essentially the elaboration of a mere two-chord progression (I–IV, sometimes V–I or V–II), the harmonic character of the fugue as a whole is somewhat static. Moreover, the only lasting modulation is the move to the dominant at the end of the first half. Such a piece may be most meaningful at a relatively slow tempo, which permits each passing dissonance to make an impact. The rhetorical quality of the subject, with its momentary pause in the second measure, will then also be more deeply felt.

Articulation needs to be particularly precise at a relatively slow tempo, but readings of slurs and dots are unusually problematical here, as are ornament signs. In the autograph, the slur in the second measure of the subject is almost certainly meant to cover all four sixteenths, but one source specifies a more mannered variety of articulation, with a staccato stroke on the first note and the slur over the next three. The same source, which Dürr believes could come directly from the Bach circle, gives many other unique indications for articulation and trills.[48] These are placed with care and in an internally consistent manner throughout the fugue. Although this version was considered sufficiently plausible for inclusion in NBA V/6.1 (as appendix 3), the aptness of some of the markings must be questioned. Substituting trills for turns in mm. 9–11 is consistent with the subject but makes the passage harder to play; such consistency is suspiciously pedantic.[49] Equally suspicious are the slurs plus staccato marks added on the sixteenth-note figures in mm. 4–5; these figures are more readily understood as written-out turns, slurred in groups of four notes rather than 3 + 1 as the more detailed markings direct. The more obvious articulation is not necessarily the right one, but Bach rarely ends a three-note slur on a non-chord tone, as becomes the case when the 3 + 1 pattern is applied on the downbeat of m. 5. It seems a mistake to repeat the same pattern mechanically on each recurrence of the motive through the remainder of the piece, regardless of the harmony.

Prelude and Fugue in E♭, BWV 852

The pair in E♭ opens with what is perhaps the greatest prelude in the volume, certainly the only one that eclipses its fugue in length and seriousness. This does not mean that the fugue is insignificant, but its function is something like that of a gigue at the end of a suite, a relatively light concluding movement rather than the main event.

The prelude falls into several distinct sections, including what is often described as a toccata-like opening. But the form is that of a double fugue, introducing separately two ideas that are then combined. The relatively short "toccata" section (mm. 1–9) is gentler and more contrapuntally conceived than the virtuoso improvisations that open Bach's earlier *manualiter* toccatas, recalling instead Fischer's prelude in D; this leads to an old-fashioned four-part fugato in ricercar style (m. 10). Thus, the first two sections constitute a little self-contained prelude and fughetta of the sort cultivated in the Pachelbel circle,[50] and perhaps at some early stage of its history the piece was just that, ending around m. 25 (Example 11.6). But the earliest surviving version already presents the piece in essentially its familiar form, save for the absence of mm. 3–4.[51] At m. 25 the principal motivic ideas of the two preceding sections are converted into full-fledged fugue subjects (or subject and countersubject), which are now presented simultaneously as in the final section of a double fugue.[52] The two rising

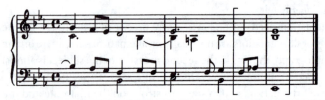

Example 11.6 Prelude in E♭, BWV 852, hypothetical early version: final cadence (corresponding to mm. 23–5 of later version).

fourths in the second subject give it a surging quality that is most completely realized in the final section. Beginning in a low tessitura (m. 49b), the section gradually climbs to the top note on Bach's *Clavier* (m. 59). The resulting splendid effect recurs in other fugues that climb to a high point shortly before the final re-entrance of the bass (cf. the fugue in F minor).

The prelude is not easy to play, and it is difficult to find a single tempo suitable for the two very different opening ideas. But any change of tempo (as called for in Keller 1965, 72) damages the piece's coherence and contradicts a remark added—in an unidentified hand—in the autograph at m. 10. According to this remark, the second section is not an *alla breve*; that is, one should not speed up at that point, shifting the pulse to the half-note.[53] The prelude ends after a climbing stretto for the upper two parts (mm. 64–7); the soprano here happens to quote the subject of the C#-minor fugue (mm. 66–7). This is no doubt a coincidence, as is the fact that the soprano's chromatic descent to the final chord (D♭–C–C♭–B♭) recurs in the alto at the end of the fugue (m. 37). But the chromaticism helps join together the two otherwise dissimilar movements.

The fugue, although in three parts, is not all lightness and *galanterie*, for chromaticism enters as early as the bridge between the last two entries in the first exposition (mm. 4b–5). A "rhetorical" rest that divides the subject into two halves may at first seem flippant, yet it becomes a dramatic event in the final statement of the subject (m. 34), when all three voices momentarily halt at this point. The fugue comes remarkably close to da capo form, falling (unlike the C-minor fugue) into a clearly tripartite design. The central ("B") section comprises an exposition in minor keys (mm. 17b–22), framed by two episodes. The third section (from m. 26) is, like the first, firmly in the tonic, much of it consisting of untransposed recapitulation (mm. 29–35a ‖ 6–12a, with voices exchanged).

Prelude and Fugue in E♭ Minor BWV 853

Like the Prelude and Fugue in C# minor, this pair in another "difficult" key immediately declares itself to be one of the more ambitious in WTC1. The prelude is an embellished adagio; the fugue, although in only three voices, is the first in the volume to apply various contrapuntal techniques systematically to the subject.

Prototypes for the prelude can be found in the slow movements of the Italian concertos transcribed by Bach (see chap. 8). Nevertheless, the opening harmonic progression is the same one employed in many other preludes (e.g., in C), and the form is bipartite. As in the prelude in C# minor, Bach expanded the original version by interpolating a coda, here after a deceptive cadence (m. 29). Friedemann Bach copied the later version, or rather as much as he could fit onto three pages in CB. But the unusual number of corrections in his copy suggests that he was reading from a heavily revised autograph, where embellishments might have been sketched without unambiguous indication of their rhythms (as in the autograph of the Sinfonia in E♭ in P 610). Indeed, the notation of the last beat of m. 13, containing one of Bach's most characteristic melodic embellishments, remained ungrammatical even after correction in the autograph.[54]

Such notation not only points toward rhythmic freedom in the prelude but is also a warning against too slow a tempo. Embellishments cease to be embellishments if the half-note pulse is subdivided with mathematical precision, as is likely to happen when the speed drops below a certain minimum. In both Friedemann's and Sebastian's copies the sixteenths are generally not broken up into groups of four, as in modern editions, but are beamed in units of eight, implying that each group remains a single unbroken gesture. Played with an undivided half-note pulse (and a tempo about double that under which the piece often languishes), the prelude ceases to be merely a dolorous arioso and can achieve real tragic grandeur.

Bach notated the fugue in D♯ minor, perhaps to facilitate transposition from an earlier version in D minor.[55] In the hypothetical D-minor version, the ascending scale in m. 15 would have ascended to c′′′ instead of faltering on a suspension. The latter would have become necessary only when the transposition took the top note of the scale (c♯′′′) above the upper limit of the *Clavier* used in the WTC.[56] The fugue falls into three main sections of almost equal length; these present the subject in its prime form, then in inverted (m. 30) and augmented (m. 61b) forms. Each section is subdivided into ordinary and stretto expositions.

A curious irregularity in the first two strettos proves to be of great formal significance. Each section contains one anomalous entry, an incomplete statement of the subject in a sort of quasi-augmentation. The first two of these quasi-augmented entries (m. 24, middle voice; m. 48, treble) anticipate the true augmentation of the subject in the last section. The fugue achieves its culmination when the prime, augmented, and quasi-augmented forms are all combined in stretto (m. 77).

The process is an abstruse one, unlikely to be sensed by the listener no matter how valiantly the performer attempts to bring it out. In many Bach fugues the introduction of more sophisticated or complex contrapuntal procedures coincides with increased chromaticism or rhythmic motion, resulting in a heightening of tension, but not so here. Nor are there episodes to provide relief from the rigorous counterpoint of the expositions. Instead, there is an unalloyed emphasis on austere "demonstration counterpoint," perhaps to the detriment of the fugue as a piece of music. This is unusual in a mature work of Bach; so too is the awkward way in which the piece lies under the hands, despite being limited to three voices. Much of Bach's music is difficult to play, but this piece is truly unidiomatic, with inaudible voice crossings in mm. 45–7 and stretches of a ninth required in mm. 21 and 51; in the latter one would have had to stretch a tenth were it not for another suspension, probably a stopgap to keep the passage playable.

Such a fugue appeals chiefly to those who can enjoy the details of the counterpoint, such as the cross-rhythms that arise in the strettos as the subject enters on different beats in different voices (e.g., mm. 24ff.). Such entries are of the type Marpurg called *per arsin et thesin*, that is, with the strong and weak beats displaced in the answer.[57] A pianist can indicate this through stress accents, but even then few listeners will get the point. Nor will manipulations of registration on the harpsichord (or organ) make such music more palatable to listeners who are simply not interested in it. As in other lengthy polyphonic works, the contrapuntal intricacies, especially the entries in augmentation in the last quarter of the piece, are probably clearest to the *Kenner* and least boring to the *Liebhaber* when the piece is played lightly and at a moderately quick pace. But a trill—with closing turn—added in P 415 on the eighth note b♯ in m. 74 suggests that by the 1740s (when the addition was made), Bach had a relatively slow tempo in mind; otherwise there is no time to play the ornament.

Prelude and Fugue in E, BWV 854

The Prelude and Fugue in E is one of the less imposing pairs. The prelude is a concise sonata form (or a large "three-phrase" form), the last section consisting of a recapitulation of the entire first section (mm. 15–22a ‖ 1–8a) transposed a fourth upwards. The meter and the figuration at the opening suggest a gigue, although the pedal point at the outset—a standard opening gesture for a prelude—implies one with a gentle, pastoral character. The close in each of the outer sections touches on the minor, including a few somewhat surprising chromatic lines (mm. 7b–8a, 21b–22a); these require a moderate tempo to fulfill their expressive potential.

The fugue is likewise small in scale and is clearest at a moderate tempo, though the omnipresent running sixteenths seem to invite greater speed. This fugue is of the same basic type as the little Fugue in C BWV 953 (in CB), also in three parts and suggesting quick violin writing. One can imagine Bach composing the present fugue (like BWV 953) quickly, almost improvisatorially; he made few subsequent revisions except in the last six measures, where the bass line underwent several changes. Here Bach may have originally aimed at achieving a subtle climax through a bass line that made scalar descents first through a fifth (mm. 24b), then through an octave (m. 27). But the stepwise motion in the bass created fifths with the upper parts. Although tolerable, since in each case one of the fifths is diminished, they evidently had become unacceptable to Bach by the 1730s, when he probably made the alterations in mm. 24 and 27 (a change in m. 26b belong to a later layer of revisions).

The scale originally in m. 27 had had the effect of broadening the motion of the closing measures; the same effect is achieved in a different way through the short series of bass suspensions in mm. 25–6. The suspension motive originates in the second countersubject and can be traced through the entire fugue; only at the end, however, does the idea lead to a *chain* of suspensions. The chain remains a short one, containing only two links—four if one counts the subsequent suspensions in the middle voice. But, given the small scale of the fugue, this is enough to bring the suspension idea to its logical development, signaling the end of the piece.[58]

Prelude and Fugue in E Minor BWV 855

Because the E-minor fugue is in only two voices, it is easy not to take this pair as seriously as it deserves. That it ought not be taken lightly is suggested by Bach's considerable expansion of the prelude in the revisions of 1722. The earlier version of the prelude lacks the coda (mm. 23ff.) as well as the arioso melody; this version is essentially an arpeggio prelude, comparable to those in D major and D minor although placing the figuration in the left hand. The addition of the melody, with its written-out embellishment, turns the piece into an Italianate adagio and was a particularly apt demonstration of "composition by variation" (Example 11.7). Bach's procedure would find a nineteenth-century echo in the *Ave Maria* by Gounod, who superimposed a "sugary tune," as Fuller Maitland (1925, 1:12) put it, onto the prelude in C.[59]

The coda serves as a sort of recapitulation, since its first four measures (mm. 23–6) repeat the opening bass a fourth higher. But formally the entire presto section is a long plagal cadence, and the V–I cadence at the end of the original portion (mm. 20–1) remains the formal close of the piece. Both original and added sections depend heavily on descending bass lines; the bass of the first section can be seen as descending through two and a half octaves if one disregards registral transfers (from e in m. 5 to B in mm. 19–20). The presto continues where the first section left off, its bass dropping through another two octaves (from a in m. 23 to A and B in mm. 40–1).

The presto marking at the beginning of the coda raises the question of tempo. The early version grows dull at less than a moderate allegro, but the ornate melody of the later version implies a slower tempo in the opening section. Too slow a tempo, however, makes it difficult to sustain the long notes of the melody (even

Example 11.7 Prelude in E Minor BWV 855/1, mm. 1–2, (a) early version (BWV 855a/1; bass omitted); and (b) later version.

on the piano) and, as in the prelude in D♯ minor, reduces a passionate piece to prettiness. The opening section, moreover, retains the short (eighth-note) chords in the inner voices on the accented beats; these can produce a certain vehemence when not held out beyond their written values.[60] Despite the presto marking in the coda, a vulgar acceleration through mm. 21–2 (as suggested in Keller 1965) ruins the striking effect produced as the bass line sinks against the sustained e˝ in the treble. A modest ritard is preferable in these measures, although on most instruments it will be necessary to restrike the e˝ on the downbeat of m. 22.

The fugue is a surprisingly dramatic little piece, the prickly chromaticism of its subject implying non-legato. This does not mean a uniform staccato; the notes in the subject that form a descending chromatic line (d♯˝–d˝–c♯˝ . . .) can be brought out by being held ever so slightly longer than the others.[61] This is not Bach's only two-part fugue; we have already seen the C-minor Fughetta BWV 961, and two of the duetti in the third part of the *Clavierübung* can also be considered true fugues. The present fugue resembles BWV 961 in that the answer constitutes a real modulation to the dominant, not a temporary excursion "on" the dominant. The same happens in the B-minor Invention, which like the present fugue is a symmetrical rounded bipartite form. The symmetry here extends to the subdivision of each half into two similar quarters. The second half (from m. 20) is essentially the same as the first with the parts exchanged and transposed; a minuscule alteration in m. 29 permits the piece to end in the tonic, shifting the interval of transposition from a fifth to a fourth. The symmetry is announced by the passage in octaves at the end of each half (mm. 19, 38), the second time introducing a restatement of the subject in the upper voice.

In the revised version of the fugue the final chord has the value of a mere eighth note, and its arpeggiation is written out (Example 11.8). This brusque ending is more in character with the rest of the piece than the original block chord, held out for the value of a dotted half, and it resonates with the two octave passages. These octaves, unusual in a fugue, call to mind the rage aria of eighteenth-century opera, which often opens with a ritornello played by the orchestra in unison. That Bach should have included such passages in one of his most geometrically designed movements reflects the same eighteenth-century aesthetic as the da capo aria: a passionate affect is contained within a rational design.

Example 11.8 Fugue in E Minor BWV 855/2, mm. 41–2, with endings from (a) early version (BWV 855a/2) and (b) later version.

Prelude and Fugue in F, BWV 856

The Prelude and Fugue in F is another relatively straightforward pair. The prelude retains vestiges of arpeggiando improvisation, including the common opening harmonic formula over a tonic pedal. Bach must have intended the prelude to be played brilliantly, for the autograph specifies that most of the long trills, indicated in earlier versions by the abbreviation *tr*, are to be played as *Doppelt-Cadenzen*, that is, trills prefixed by a turn from below or above.[62] No other piece by Bach repeatedly demands this difficult ornament, and the prelude is therefore a study for both hands in playing the latter. In the final cadence, even the bass receives a trill, and although Bach left it with the original *tr* sign, one might add a prefix from above to the trill on B♭ (m. 18).

Fischer's *Ariadne musica* provided the outline for the fugue subject and perhaps the countersubject as well (Example 11.9). But Fischer's fugue has the skipping rhythm of a French gigue and, although barred in 3/4, is effectively in 6/4 or even 12/4, as the measures fall regularly into groups of four. Bach smoothed out Fischer's dotted rhythms, halved the note values, and, by extending the second entry by one measure, threw off the four-square regularity of Fischer's opening measures.

The fugue is bipartite, divided precisely in half by an arrival on V of D minor (m. 36). The second half is very different from the first; the easy-going imitations of the first two expositions, which simply alternate between tonic and dominant, give way to three-part strettos in D minor (m. 37), then G minor (m. 47). The

Example 11.9 a) Fischer, *Ariadne musica*, Fuga no. 10, mm. 1–8; (b) J. S. Bach, fugue in F, BWV 856/2, mm. 1–9.

subject returns only once more in the tonic (soprano, m. 65), there embellished by the expressive half step eb´´–d´´ that is so prominent in the G-minor stretto.

Prelude and Fugue in F Minor BWV 857

The first half of WTC1 concludes with one of the most imposing pairs. The prelude, whose sonorous texture combines *style brisé* with contrapuntal writing, is quite up-to-date, whereas the fugue is archaic in several respects, though as usual this is not necessarily an indication of an earlier origin.

The prelude resembles the one in C# minor in its bipartite design and Bach's later addition of a coda (mm. 16b–21a). The theme, which at first appears to be an improvisatory arpeggiation of a conventional progression, is developed imitatively, as in an invention; the left hand repeats it at m. 2b and later in the relative major, at what was originally the halfway point (m. 6b). The theme is played over-legato, that is, with consonant tones held out, as indicated by extra stems and ties in the revised version. This careful notation (cf. the prelude in C) makes it advisable not to hold out additional notes or to disregard the written note values, as would happen if one used the damper pedal, which is likely to render a clear texture opaque. A steady andante tempo also helps; anything slower makes it hard to sustain the long lines of the theme. Even then it is probably necessary to restrike the closing pedal point once or twice (e.g., on the downbeat of m. 19 and the last quarter of m. 20), regardless of the instrument used.

The fugue opens with a stern chromatic subject in quarters, to which the countersubject adds *figure corte* and so-called *suspirans* figures that occur on practically every beat for the rest of the piece.[63] A downward leap of over an octave within the countersubject seems awkward and is not maintained after the first exposition; perhaps it is the product of a revision, although the alternative is banal and the note after the leap initiates the first *suspirans* figure, which can be delayed expressively.[64] If the figuration seems archaic, so is the absence of a clear division into expositions and episodes; instead, the fugue consists of individual entries of the subject joined by bridges, which are sometimes quite extensive but never articulated as distinct passages. Although the counterpoint is conceived permutationally, not all possible combinations of the subject and its three countersubjects are used. But even the bridges are freely permutational, the first two (mm. 10–3, 16–9) providing the material for all but one of the remaining five. Measures 37–40 form an exception, drawing material from the first countersubject.

As in the prelude, too slow a tempo makes an already somber piece unbearably dreary; the long chromatic notes of the subject are more imposing in a tempo quick enough for the *figure corte* of the countersubject to sound fleeting. The penultimate half note of the subject constitutes a small interpretive problem; should it bear a trill? In the fugue in B minor, a trill is marked at the end of a similar subject. But the autograph shows no trill here, and the ornament signs in several other sources may not be authentic.[65] Even if the ornament in the initial statement of the subject was "probably an understood performance practice" (Dürr, NBA V/6.1, preface), there is no reason to play the ornament in every statement of the subject. A full trill with termination is impossible to play in some cases, although a short trill can point out the presence of the subject in an inner voice (as in m. 36).

Prelude and Fugue in F♯, BWV 858

Few preludes and fugues in WTC1 seem as well paired as these two movements, both of which are light in texture and exceptionally good-natured. The prelude is essentially a two-part invention, similar in form and material to the Invention in G. Here Bach pays less attention to imitative counterpoint as such than to developing the syncopated motive first heard in m. 2. The motive forms what is essentially a conventional chain of suspensions, embellished through escape tones and other somewhat irregular passing notes (Example 11.10). These ornamental tones are drawn in part from an implied second upper voice; d♯˝ on the third beat of m. 2 moves implicitly to c♯˝ on the fourth beat. But not everything is spelled out on the surface; the piece is somewhat elusive in character. The prelude was originally two measures shorter; the early version (unknown except through the Konwitschny manuscript) employs a different form of the theme, dividing it into subject (m. 1) and countersubject (m. 2; see Example 11.10a).[66]

The fugue is similar to the one in C♯, suggesting that Bach might have written both while completing the "sharp" part of the scheme of WTC1. Both fugues have vivacious subjects beginning on off-beats, even livelier figuration appearing in the first episode. In this case the new figuration (see m. 7a, soprano) is eventually incorporated into a second countersubject, introduced during the second exposition (mm. 12ff.).

Example 11.10 Prelude in F♯, BWV 858/1, mm. 1–3: (a) early version (BWV 858a/1), upper part; (b) later version; (c) implied upper voice leading.

Sonata-form elements are abundant as also in the fugue in C♯. Here they delineate a bi- rather than a tripartite design. The first half ends with a cadence to the dominant (m. 17), and most of the second exposition, including a bridge between its two entries, recurs a fifth lower at the end of the piece (mm. 11b–17a || 28–33); as usual the upper voices are exchanged. This gives the fugue the neat, symmetrical quality of many pre-Classical sonata forms, but without seeming pat or schematic.

The trill on the dotted figure in the subject again poses technical as well as interpretive questions. It is a "long" trill, with written-out termination, and it is difficult to imagine the subject without it.[67] Yet the statement of the subject beginning in m. 11b lacks both ornament and termination, which would not only be hard to play here but would clash with the lower parts. Trill and termination are difficult to play in two other statements of the subject (mm. 15, 28), and in both cases a short trill at the beginning of the note will suffice.[68]

Prelude and Fugue in F♯ Minor BWV 859

The F♯-minor pieces are less closely matched than those in E or F, raising the possibility that they were composed separately. The first half of the prelude again resembles a fairly lively two-part invention. But the fugue, in four parts, is serious and severe, lacking episodes or passagework and permeated with expressive "sigh" motives.

Actually, the prelude changes character in the latter half, and this could be seen as a transition in the direction of the fugue. Shortly after the midpoint (m. 12b) the theme is presented in a somewhat varied, inverted form, and a bit later this begins to be accompanied by short three-part chords (mm. 15ff.). One might suspect from the altered character and texture of the passage that it is a later addition, like the interpolations in some of the other preludes, but there is no evidence for this. The chords are a development of the tenor line in the opening measure, and the thickening of the texture in the latter portion of the prelude could have been part of the original conception; it implies a strong registration throughout.

The fugue, although not exactly in *stile antico*, is vocal in inspiration. As in the C-major fugue (likewise in four parts), the quasi-vocal style suggests playing the subject in an articulate, "speaking" manner, the hemiola in m. 2 (perhaps also in m. 3) clearly marked. To a listener the meter will at first be unclear, since the subject moves independently of the barline. But it contains a built-in acceleration—the note values of the suspensions on a, b, and c♯′ diminish successively—and the meter becomes clear when the answer is combined with the countersubject.

The insistent "sigh" motives of the countersubject might make this an example of what Walther called *fuga pathetica*, as is also implicit in the melodic chromaticism of the subject. But despite the local chromaticism and a high frequency of passing dissonance, in terms of modulation this proves to be one of Bach's least adventurous mature fugues. The subject enters only on tonic and dominant, and although the inversion is introduced at the midpoint (m. 20b) there is only one further *inversus* entry; both inverted entries are buried in the lower voices. The only substantial lightening of the texture occurs in the middle of the second half (m. 28), where tenor and bass briefly drop out and a portion of the first half is repeated in the topmost register (mm. 28–31 || 7–10 an octave higher).

The archaic form suggests that this is a relatively early piece. But even if this is true, Bach would have known how to make it more interesting had he wished to do so, and its severity was surely intentional. Weighing down the first note in each "sigh" motives may prove quite expressive, but it is important to observe that the two-note groupings always begin on the second (or fifth) beat. Phrases and smaller rhythmic units tend to end on the stronger first and fourth beats, and a rising half step on the downbeat (as in m. 5, lower part) is not a sigh but a phrase division, with a new gesture beginning on the second note.

Prelude and Fugue in G, BWV 860

The prelude in G is the last in WTC1 of the arpeggio type, and also the last to survive in a shorter early version. Perhaps Bach failed to carry out a planned expansion of the preludes beyond this point, as Dürr suggests (1984, 66–7). But none of the remaining preludes is of the arpeggio type, and all are conceived on a somewhat larger scale than the preludes that Bach apparently composed before compiling the WTC. The four measures interpolated here (mm. 7b–8a and 14b–17a) do not substantially expand the prelude, which remains quite short in relation to the fugue. They do turn two modulating phrases into sequences (mm. 6–8 and 14–16a), and they introduce a third, entirely new sequence (mm. 16b–17) whose figuration is especially lively, making it the climax of the revised version.[69]

A few collisions between the two parts suggest the use of two manuals (mm. 2–3, also m. 7 in the later version). But on most harpsichords this would mean playing each voice on a single eight-foot rank. A more brilliant effect can be achieved by playing on one strongly registered manual and putting up with the occasional inconveniences of Bach's counterpoint.

The fugue has much the same virtuoso character as the prelude. Indeed, it comes closest of all the fugues in the WTC to the concerto-like pieces discussed in chapter 9. Yet it also has the contrapuntal type of design used in the fugue in D# minor. The second exposition (m. 20) treats the subject in inversion, and strettos occupy the central third of the piece (mm. 38–61a), though none is carried out strictly. As in the fugue in F#, a motive introduced in an episodic passage (m.

10) eventually combines with the subject, though only once and in inversion, just before the end (m. 80). The motive, which imitates violinistic bariolage, also dominates the episodes, which consequently sound like solos in a concerto.

Prelude and Fugue in G Minor BWV 861

The opening of the G-minor prelude bears a vague resemblance to the type of scoring that Bach used in his Leipzig cantatas when he wanted to imitate the sound of funeral bells. The bells are signified in the cantatas by repeated sixteenth notes, and although a solemn expression is doubtless appropriate, the tempo is not necessarily slow.[70] Here the common-time signature indicates that the pulse falls on the quarter note, and the figures in sixteenths and thirty-seconds should retain their integrity, without becoming subdivided, as is likely to happen if the pulse shifts to the eighth-note.[71]

The apparently homophonic texture of the opening is in fact contrapuntal; the three voices of m. 1 present distinctive rhythmic ideas that are later redistributed in free invertible counterpoint. The simplest idea is the long trill in the soprano, which might begin on the main note, like a *ribattuta*. By starting the trill slowly, gradually accelerating, and then decelerating, a harpsichordist can approximate a singer's *messa di voce*, a swelling of the voice followed by a diminuendo on one long note. This is not easy, especially when the other hand is playing steady sixteenths, but the prelude can serve as a good exercise in this useful technique.

The fugue subject can be traced to the one in E♭ from Fischer's *Ariadne musica*. Friedemann Bach quoted the same subject somewhat more precisely in his D-minor Fantasia F. 19 (Example 11.11).[72] Like Fischer, Sebastian Bach uses a tonal answer, and, as in the Fischer work, the climax of the fugue is a three-part stretto just before the close (mm. 28ff.). But Bach also has a regular countersubject, as well as an episode (mm. 24b–27) whose flowing sequences provide a moment of relief prior to the rigors of the final stretto.

The plan is clearly articulated by arrivals to VI (m. 12) and V of iv (m. 20). The one episode comes late in the piece, and there is no recapitulation; together with the sparing use of real four-part writing, these features suggest an early date, especially as there are some awkward moments: occasional voice crossings and odd doublings, and two tenths that the right hand must span in m. 18. Both subject and countersubject contain *figure corte*, and the fugue ends just as the

Example 11.11 Fugue subjects from (a) Fischer, *Ariadne musica*, Fuga no. 5; (b) J. S. Bach: fugue in G Minor BWV 861/1; and (c) W. F. Bach: Fantasia in D Minor F. 19 (mm. 33–35a).

tenor completes the last entry of the subject (another borrowing from Fischer). Unlike some of Bach's early fugues, however, this one is very concise, and the finely conceived formal plan makes it one of the most satisfying in the WTC.

Prelude and Fugue in A♭, BWV 862

As in the B-Minor Invention, which uses similar material, the opening two measures of the A♭-major prelude could have come from the allegro of a *galant* violin sonata. So too could the figuration in the modulating passage that begins in m. 9, where the resemblance to violin passagework was even stronger before Bach rewrote the upper voice (mm. 9–12 originally used the same motive as mm. 13–5). Like the Invention in B Minor, the prelude is divided in half by a strong cadence near the midpoint (m. 18). But there is also a coda (from m. 35), the latter evidently having been an original part of the prelude, not a later addition as elsewhere in WTC1.

The subject of the fugue, like that of the prelude, uses leaping eighth notes, but rather than evoking *galant* violin music these allude to the canzonas and ricercars of the seventeenth century.[73] One is initially tempted to take a lively tempo, yet the dense four-part texture and frequent dissonances within each hand create technical challenges, and the many refined details are more easily heard if the tempo is quite moderate. Restraint in speed also makes it easier to project the metrical shape of the subject, which, as in the D-major fugue, begins on the second beat. The true position of the downbeat may not be entirely clear to the listener until the cadence that ends the first exposition (m. 8, first beat). Nevertheless, the meter ought to be clear in the player's mind by m. 3, where prepared dissonances begin to fall on the odd-numbered beats, forming a chain of suspensions; the latter actually begins with a b´ on the last beat of m. 2, where it is embellished by a turning figure.

Prelude and Fugue in G♯ Minor BWV 863

The prelude in G♯ minor, like the one in C♯ minor, combines imitative texture with arioso style, in a siciliano rhythm. This is a gentler piece, lacking the urgency of the C♯-minor prelude. Except for a few brief passages it is in three real parts throughout, and the second half (from m. 14) even contains several *inversus* entries of the subject.

The fugue subject again starts on the second beat; harpsichordists must shorten the initial quarter note if it is not to sound like a downbeat. Because of its difficult tonality and dense four-part writing, players are likely to avoid this fugue, which may seem dry and archaic, like the four-part fugues in F minor and G minor. Yet a relatively late date is implied by the variety of keys through which it passes, as well the frequent if short episodes, two of them recapitulated (mm. 28–9 || 21–2, and 30–1 || 13–4). Moreover, the subject reveals an abstruse wit, for its latter half is the bass line of a standard cadential formula (IV–V–I), developed sequentially in the episodes.[74]

Wit is evident as well in the subject's tonal ambiguity, which leads to a near-reversal of the usual roles of subject and answer. The subject is of the type that is usually said to modulate to the dominant; thus, it requires a tonal answer to avoid a further modulation to v of v. But the answer, theoretically on v, is so altered as to appear to be on iv; every note except the first is a step lower than one would expect it to be.[75] Hence statements of the subject are often not in the key they seem to be, or they receive an unexpected modulatory twist at the end. Even the final entry (soprano, m. 37b) is a "real" statement on iv, yet the fugue ends just a few measures later with a perfectly satisfactory full cadence in the tonic.

Prelude and Fugue in A, BWV 864

The Prelude and Fugue in A is among the high points of WTC1, though rarely recognized as such. Perhaps it seems too cheerful, or the subject of the fugue too eccentric, to be taken seriously.

The prelude resembles a three-part invention. But unlike any of the fifteen sinfonias, it opens with the principal subject (in the soprano) already combined with the two countersubjects. There are six entries in all, forming three expositions joined by two brief episodes (mm. 6b–8a, 14b–17a). In theory the subject could combine with the two countersubjects in all six permutations, but only four are used, perhaps because the remaining ones lie awkwardly on the keyboard. Despite its schematic design the piece never sounds studied, and it ends with an exuberant little outburst in the soprano, ascending a two-octave scale.

The fugue, also in three voices, likewise falls into three symmetrically arranged sections, though these are much longer than those of the prelude, with a different sort of organization. The first is a rhythmically perverse gigue; the second (at m. 23) introduces a running countersubject in sixteenths. The third section (from m. 42) serves somewhat like a recapitulation of the first.

The initial section is one of Bach's wittiest efforts. The subject opens with a lone eighth note followed by a long rest, seemingly a caricature of the "rhetorical" pauses in some of Bach's early fugue subjects (as in the C-minor Toccata). The subject then continues as a sequence that permits numerous strettos; the second entry (alto, m. 2) is already a stretto entrance. The leaps in the subject give the counterpoint some of the character of Frescobaldi's *Recercar obligo di non mai di grado*, in which stepwise motion is entirely avoided.[76]

The most engaging aspect of the subject is its metrical playfulness. The last fugue of Corelli's op. 3—also in A, in the collection of trio sonatas from which Bach borrowed the subjects of the B-minor organ fugue BWV 579—is similarly permeated with hemiolas and cross-accents, but this fugue surpasses it. The first section is pervaded by syncopations and by metrical shifts from the indicated 9/8 to 2/4 or 3/4. The three voices are often effectively in different meters; for

Example 11.12 Fugue in A, BWV 864/2, mm. 6–9, with rhythmic analysis.

example, in m. 6 the bass (stating the subject) might be heard in either 2/4 or 3/4, whereas the soprano and alto suggest 6/8 and 3/4, respectively (Example 11.12). Other interpretations are possible, and for this reason a performer need not bring out any one metrical scheme to the exclusion of others. The metrical ambiguity is such that the three voices rarely move together to the downbeat; even at the cadence in m. 9, which marks the approximate midpoint of the first section, only treble and bass arrive together.

The introduction of running sixteenths in the second section, after a short bridge (mm. 20–2), gives the piece the design of a double fugue. But, as in the otherwise very different fugue in C♯ minor, the running figuration is more a rhythmic motive than a regular countersubject. The sixteenths disappear at the beginning of the last section, only to return near the end, where fragments from both preceding sections are recapitulated. The fugue concludes, like the sonata-form fugues in D minor and B♭, with a restatement of the closing phrase from the first section. But this is disguised by the addition of a running bass, hence alluding to the second section as well.[77]

Prelude and Fugue in A Minor BWV 865

The A-minor pair is the most problematical in the WTC. The fugue, much longer than the prelude, has an impressive design organized according to various contrapuntal manipulations of the subject, and it contains many attractive details; the closing section (from around m. 73) is particularly compelling. Yet both movements have a pedantic quality, the prelude because of the repetitious motives used to fill out the long measures of 9/8, the fugue due to the uncompromising working out of its contrapuntal design. Played with sufficient brilliance, both movements might achieve considerable power. But the fugue lies under the hands in a way that is extraordinarily ungrateful even for Bach, making it a challenge for the performer to avoid giving the impression of long-winded monotony.

In both movements the main material includes a sort of written-out mordent. In the fugue this takes the form of a simple *figura corta*, but in the prelude the figure is extended to three repercussions (bass, m. 1). The motive recalls the first movement of the First Brandenburg Concerto, which, like the prelude, not only begins but ends with the same figure. This is one of several features suggesting a Weimar origin for both movements, which have long been suspected of being early.[78]

The fugue is the longest in WTC1 in terms of measure-count. Its organization according to contrapuntal devices makes it the four-voice counterpart of the fugue in D# minor. In fact it is even more systematic, introducing the *rectus* and *inversus* versions of the subject in separate expositions (mm. 1, 14b), then treating each in separate stretto expositions (m. 27b for the prime form, m. 48 for the inversion). But there are no augmented or otherwise varied entries, and, because the two forms of the subject cannot be combined in their entirety without considerable contrivance, the final section (from m. 64b) is largely confined to presenting *rectus* and *inversus* entries in rapid alternation.

The fugue is by no means a dry working out of inversions and strettos. The last section is beautifully conceived, opening with stretto entries for the two lowest parts. It then ascends gradually into the top register during the episode at m. 71, the second of only two in the piece (the first is at m. 40). After two dramatic pauses (mm. 80, 82), the fugue culminates in a canonic coda that expands to five parts and, at the very end, nominally to seven. Nevertheless, the rhythmic homogeneity, the absence of lasting or compelling modulations, and the dearth of episodes make the piece wearying. The somewhat similarly planned fugue in Bb minor of WTC2 is more obviously interesting, thanks in part to its rhythmically and melodically more diverse subject. Here the subject has a simple tertian structure that outlines the ascending line A–C–E–G#–B–D; this simplifies the task of writing strettos but rules out variety in harmony or rhythm, as each note in the underlying line occupies half a measure.

To be sure, the actual subject considerably embellishes its underlying line, and there is a "rhetorical" rest in the middle of m. 2, preceded by the French formula of the falling third (*tierce coulée*). But the latter becomes an embarrassment when the subject is turned upside down, for the descending *tierce* is unidiomatic when inverted; the same is true of the leap of a diminished seventh that immediately precedes it. Nevertheless, Bach skipped over several impressive fugues in A minor—those of BWV 944, 965, and 904—in order to include this one in WTC1 (as Keller 1965, 112 noted). The harshness of the inverted subject is concordant with the general harshness of the harmony, which includes an unusually high density of passing dissonance. Some dissonant passing tones arise in connection with the zigzag motive in m. 3 of the subject, where they serve as rising appoggiaturas (as in m. 39). Other dissonances are almost inexplicable in terms of conventional counterpoint (e.g., m. 24, last two chords; mm. 38–9), and there are also some near-objectionable parallel fifths (mm. 38–9 again, also mm. 55 and 59, all involving tenor and bass). Although the real dissonances, that is, suspensions, usually resolve normally, the harmony shows a purposeful irregularity approaching that of Frescobaldi's *Capriccio cromatico con ligature al contrario*, in which every suspension resolves upwards.[79] Such a piece would have provided a model for counterpoint that explicitly broke traditional rules but followed its own internal logic.

The audacious roughness of the counterpoint must reflect a love of dissonance for its own sake, as well as a delight in demonstrating how "incorrect" counterpoint and dissonance treatment can establish their own sense. Heavy, slow, careful playing might make some of the tortuous melodic writing and voice leading clearer to a careful listener. But quick, light playing, although almost impossible to achieve, is more likely to make the lines comprehensible as lines and the numerous clashes more cogent.

The closing pedal point has been taken as an indication for use of the organ, since it cannot be sustained without pedals (see, e.g., Marshall 1986, 234). But the thick four-part writing and wide gaps between the voices at earlier points remain difficult to negotiate regardless of the instrument used.[80] Since the bass elsewhere was clearly not intended for pedals, the ending seems to be a genuine example of "demonstration counterpoint" that players were not expected to execute precisely as written. Except in the final pedal point, both movements are as idiomatic to the harpsichord as any other instrument; non-organists (including pianists) might simply leave out the low A after m. 84.

Prelude and Fugue in B♭, BWV 866

The pieces in B♭ are understandably among the most popular in the WTC, thanks to their brevity and their lively material. The prelude is the closest thing in the WTC to an improvised free fantasia; it is composed almost entirely of types of figuration also used in the solo passages and cadenzas of Bach's concertos. Preludes by Handel and other contemporaries use similar figures, so Bach presumably drew on the common property of keyboard players. But he may also have drawn specifically from Fischer's *Pièces de clavecin* of 1696, whose prelude no. 6 opens with the same motive and later employs full-voiced chords in dotted rhythm (as in m. 11 here).

Despite its improvisatory style, the prelude falls into two nearly equal halves, divided by the cadence to the dominant on the downbeat of m. 10. The latter therefore might be marked by a slight pause, although it falls in the middle of figuration in thirty-seconds. The rhythm throughout the prelude is as precisely notated as in the rest of the WTC, but it can be interpreted rather freely, especially in the cadenza-like passages of the second half. Bach's pupil Kayser wrote *adagio* at m. 11; as in the prelude in C minor, this probably implies rhythmic freedom as well as a relaxed but not necessarily very slow tempo.

This freest of preludes leads to one of the most regular of the sonata-like fugues in three voices. There are three expositions separated by two episodes (mm. 19–22 and 30–5); the second episode and most of the concluding exposition recapitulate earlier sections.[81] In addition, the fugue has a permutational element, since most entries of the subject are accompanied by both countersubjects.

Prelude and Fugue in B♭ Minor BWV 867

The two pieces in B♭ minor invoke very different types of ensemble music, but they form one of the most impressive and well-matched pairs in WTC1. The prelude is a sort of arioso, orchestrally conceived. Fuller Maitland (1925, 1:34) compared it with "Passion Music," probably having in mind the opening chorus of Bach's Saint Matthew Passion, which begins with somewhat similar motivic material, also over a tonic pedal point. The fugue, like the other five-part fugue in WTC1 (the C♯-minor), is an evocation of large-scale vocal polyphony in *stile antico*.

The prelude is in up to seven nominal voices, but these make up just three distinct strands. Bass and melody are the most prominent, but there is also a two-note rhythmic figure, which, like the short chords in the E-minor prelude, corresponds to a type of staccato accompanimental figure often assigned to strings or winds (Example 11.13). This figure is largely confined to the inner voices and is prominent only at the beginning of each of the three statements of the theme (mm. 1, 7b, and 20). But it contributes greatly to the sense of an inexorable march-like rhythm, which harpsichordists can mark by detaching the unstressed eighths at the ends of the second and fourth beats, breaking the chords on the following strong beats. The prelude is bipartite, divided precisely in half by a cadence to the dominant. In the brief episode at the beginning of the second half, the two-note rhythmic figure is transferred to the bass (mm. 13–4).

The fugue comes closer than any other in WTC1 to the pure *stile antico*; unlike the fugue in C♯ minor, it has no quick countersubject. Yet it could hardly be mistaken for Renaissance polyphony, and the declamatory subject is characterized by its wide leaps and "rhetorical" pause. There are no substantial episodes, only two sequential bridges (mm. 6, 42), and these are canonic, like the episodes

Example 11.13 Prelude in B♭ Minor BWV 867/1, mm. 1–2.

in some of the stricter fugues of WTC2 (e.g., in D and B). Canon also provides the climax of the fugue: the five-part stretto near the end that starts with the soprano entry in m. 67. Prior to this, at the beginning of the final section, Bach employs a contrapuntal device that he would use to climactic effect in several later works as well: simultaneous or paired statements of the subject by two voices in parallel motion (m. 55).

Prelude and Fugue in B, BWV 868

The prelude in B is one of the shorter ones, but it is not lightweight, being composed largely in three real parts. It broadens to four parts at the end, thus (like the F♯-minor prelude) preparing the fugue. There are three brief sections; the three-part texture of the opening is freely inverted at the beginning of the second part (m. 6).

The fugue, although in four voices, is lively and almost *galant* in character. It is, moreover, the only four-part fugue in the volume to have something like the rounded binary form employed in so many of the three-part fugues. Like the D-minor fugue, it reaches the dominant at about the midpoint (m. 18); an exposition using the inversion of the subject follows. Unfortunately, the inversion is melodically unattractive, for much the same reason as in the A-minor fugue: a leap in the subject, here a downward fifth, becomes awkward when inverted, and this may be why the inversion is dropped after just two entries.

The key of B major, with its five sharps, suggests difficult or thorny music, and the piece does not lie comfortably under the hands. But the counterpoint seems intended to sound effortless. Much of it consists of scalar figuration, derived from the countersubject, which reaches a climax with a two-octave descent in the bass (mm. 24b–25a). This happens just before the last recurrence of the piece's one episode (mm. 26–28a || 9–11a || 13b–15), which prepares the return of the subject in the tonic (m. 29).

Prelude and Fugue in B Minor BWV 869

WTC1 closes with a masterpiece. The key of B minor is associated with special efforts by Bach; one thinks immediately of the first Kyrie of the B-Minor Mass and the flute sonata BWV 1030. But early versions of both works might have been in other keys, and they almost certainly remained to be composed in 1722. Nevertheless, by that date Bach had already written one very fine three-part fugue (BWV 951) in the same key. Yet he left that one out of WTC1, as he also did several fugues in A minor, perhaps because it was based on a borrowed subject, or perhaps because he wished to close the volume with a four-part fugue.

Instead he may have composed the present movements specifically to bring WTC1 to an impressive ending. Both movements differ in important respects from others in WTC1, indicating that they were among the last ones written. For instance, both prelude and fugue have tempo markings, *andante* and *largo*, respectively; this may seem a superficial element, yet no other movements in either book of the WTC bear tempo indications, which perhaps signal special generic or expressive associations.[82] The prelude, moreover, is WTC1's only binary form with repeats. The same design would occur often in WTC2, but not in conjunction with the present style and texture, which derive from the contrapuntal type of trio sonata found in Corelli's first four *opera*. The latter, although all published before 1700, might have still seemed up-to-date at Cöthen in 1722. Certainly this was true of the fugue subject, whose "sigh" motives (marked by slurs) and stark chromaticism would have been understood as highly expressive. In the autograph, the first page of the fugue bears an unusual number of corrections, suggesting that, as he neared the end of his fair copy of WTC, Bach was still undecided about the text of the last movement.[83]

In the prelude, the walking bass and chains of suspensions are only the most obvious borrowings from Corelli. Though longer than most of Corelli's sonata movements, the prelude resembles many of them in its use of a "Phrygian" cadence at the end of the first half, in place of a true modulation to the dominant. The second half introduces new thematic material, never precisely restating that of the opening.[84] The tempo mark would have confirmed the piece's Italian style, although Corelli rarely used the word *andante*. For Bach the word probably meant literally "walking" or "moving" (not "slow"). Dense chromaticism in the final phrase prevents this from being an *andante allegro*, like several movements by Handel; it is closer to what Corelli called an *andante largo* in the Concerto Grosso op. 6, no. 2.

With the chromaticism of the coda, Bach's own style comes to the fore, pointing toward the fugue. The latter's *affetuoso* subject is hardly comparable to the themes of the other four-part fugues in WTC1 (especially those in minor keys: c♯, f, f♯, a). Key, tempo mark, the half-steps and other expressive intervals in the subject, and the shifting tonality (due in part to the modulating sequence within the subject) all seem premonitions of the opening movement of the B-Minor Mass. Both works achieve impressive dimensions, although the keyboard fugue lacks the clear structure of the Mass movement. Indeed, it possesses few strong formal articulations of any type—the only emphatic cadence is the final one—and, although it gives the impression of containing a great deal of recapitulation, hardly anything is restated literally except for two relatively brief episodes. Yet only in a poor or thoughtless performance does the fugue grow monotonous. There is enough subtle variety of rhythm, texture, and tonality to maintain interest, and when the polyphonic texture clears for a moment just before the end (m. 73), the brief soprano solo there is no less dramatic than the coda of the A-minor fugue or the improvisatory finales of earlier fugal works.

The material in the more important of the two recurring episodes has been traced to a vocal duet by Francesco Durante (Keller 1965, 128, citing Riemann 1912, 275). But the idea in question is a conventional sequence that any late-Baroque composer might have used; the same formula even appears briefly in the prelude (mm. 23b–24). The very conventionality of the episode provides relief from the rigors of the expositions, although the subject makes a curious false entry halfway through the first episode, the first three notes being stated by the alto (m. 19; the effect is repeated when the episode recurs a fifth lower in mm. 26–9). Perhaps this was the result of a fortunate error made during the composition of the piece; Bach might have begun to bring in the subject, realized that to do so at this point was premature, but left the three notes to stand. The contrived voice leading in m. 19, where the tenor leaps up by an eleventh, crossing the alto, suggests that Bach indeed made some sort of interpolation or alteration at this point.

A second, unrelated, episode makes two appearances near the center of the fugue (mm. 34 and 41), where it frames a bass entry that begins at the exact midpoint (m. 38). This episode is a sort of stretto based on the first measure of the subject, and thus furnishes hardly any contrast to the expository passages. But the second statement of this episode leads to the piece's one excursion into major keys—D and A, in mm. 44–50. By this point the rhythm, initially consisting of eighths, has given way to sixteenths that have been maintained unbroken since m. 31 in at least one voice of the texture. Hence, although the fugue can seem almost formless, the second half possesses greater momentum as well as greater tonal variety than the first, and this drives the music with increased urgency toward its conclusion.

This fugue is second only to the one in A minor in the number of problematical fingerings and voice crossings that it contains. One could avoid several awkward repeated notes by introducing discreet ties similar to those allowed by Bach elsewhere.[85] In addition, a few suspensions that are difficult to hold (alto b′ and a′ in mm. 36–7) might be released early, especially if they have ceased to sound on one's instrument.

12
The *Well-Tempered Clavier*, Part 2

For as long as two decades there was only one *Well-Tempered Clavier*, the set of twenty-four preludes and fugues whose fair-copy manuscript Bach had assembled at Cöthen in 1722. The compilation of a companion volume belongs to a much later stage in Bach's career. But because of its similarity to Part 1, and because at least a few of its movements may actually antedate those of the earlier volume, Part 2 is considered here rather than among the other late works.

Bach came to Leipzig in 1723. During his first few years there the preparation of new church cantatas (an average of more than one per week) and other duties associated with his new position would seemingly have left little time for composing new keyboard music. Yet Bach also managed to get the Partitas into print (starting in 1726), and not only these but the French Suites were composed or at least revised during the same period. Whether or not he was also composing new preludes and fugues during the 1720s and 1730s, in those years Bach revised WTC1 at least twice. By the end of the 1730s, he had evidently decided to gather together a second such set of pieces.

Bach seems never to have prepared an integral fair-copy autograph for WTC2 as he did for WTC1. Instead, Part 2 apparently remained a collection of small manuscripts, each containing one prelude and fugue.[1] The surviving sources and the tradition of Bach's sons and pupils leave little question that Bach was responsible for the compilation of WTC2 (and for its title). But if Bach indeed failed to prepare a definitive fair copy, it would not be surprising. The period around 1740 saw a series of large keyboard works printed, copied, or drafted: Part 3 of the *Clavierübung* (CU3, published 1739), the Goldberg Variations (published 1741), and the *Art of Fugue* (early version drafted by 1742 or so), as well as further revisions to WTC1. All this was in addition to work on WTC2, the largest and most heterogeneous of these collections, raising the question of whether Bach intended to publish it alongside the other keyboard works of the period. Its size meant that publication would have been enormously expensive and certainly unprofitable; it made better sense to leave to others the task of making manuscript copies of WTC2 from Bach's working scores.

Bach nevertheless must have devoted considerable time and energy to intensive work composing or revising the music of each set. At least a few movements in WTC2 go back in some form to the first few years at Leipzig, or even earlier. But these are substantially altered, above all the fugue in A♭, which was originally in F major and only half as long (as BWV 901/2). It would be hazardous to attempt to identify, from the final versions alone, other movements that might have been reworked from lost early versions. But WTC2, like WTC1, contains archaic movements, as well as a few seemingly mismatched preludes and fugues and one or two arguably inferior pieces. This implies that Bach drew certain movements from a heterogeneous group composed well before the compilation of the volume as a whole.

In general, however, the contents of WTC2 may well be late in origin—that is, after 1735 or so. There are real differences in style, or at least stylistic tendency, between the two books. The preludes of WTC2 tend to be longer, more nearly matching the fugues in length and weightiness, than their counterparts in WTC1. No fewer than ten preludes in WTC2 are sonata movements, with central double bars, reflecting the fact that, by the time WTC2 was assembled, the keyboard sonata had emerged as a major genre; Emanuel and probably Friedemann Bach had already written important examples.[2] Even preludes lacking central double bars show elements of sonata form, such as a division into two or three main sections, of which the last contains substantial amounts of recapitulated material. Bach had evidently distanced himself from the tradition of the prelude as a free, improvisatory piece; only the prelude in C♯ is clearly of the arpeggio type, so well represented in WTC1. A few other preludes in WTC2, such as those in C and F, can also be related to this tradition, but the broken chords are heavily embellished and the figuration is fitted into a sonata-form mold. One genre no longer represented at all is the embellished adagio, an Italian type that may not have seemed as fashionable by the 1740s as it did twenty years earlier.

The fugues include fewer four-part pieces than in WTC1, and there are none in five voices, nor in two. But the three-part fugues include some of the longest and most ambitious in the volume, among them two double fugues and one triple fugue. Fewer of the fugues show the borrowings from sonata style so evident in Part 1. Exact restatements or recapitulations of episodic material are less frequent, and episodes are more likely to involve short canons or strettos, as in the last two minor-key fugues of WTC1. In a few instances, notably the fugue in D, imitative or permutational polyphony is as pervasive in the episodes as in the expositions. Such writing reflects the interest in pure counterpoint that led Bach to compose the first version of the *Art of Fugue* during or shortly after the compilation of WTC2. Yet Bach also included the two *galant* fugues in F and in

F♯—both of which contain extensive amounts of recapitulation—as well as the dashing little fughetto in G and the fugue in C♯, which is virtually a burlesque of strict counterpoint. These last two old pieces were practically rewritten for WTC2; thus, during the same period in which he was creating some of his strictest fugues, Bach was bringing some of his freest ones to their final form.

Sources, Versions, Editions

Because there survives no complete autograph for WTC2, its text and textual history have proved more difficult to establish than for Part 1. Many small points in the evaluation of the manuscripts and the determination of Bach's final intentions about the text remain uncertain. The complexity of the endeavor may be judged from table 12.1, which lists only the most important sources. Kroll's edition in BG 14 was, like his edition of Part 1 in the same volume, one of the great achievements of nineteenth-century Bach scholarship. But it was done without knowledge of important sources—including the so-called London autograph—and, more than for Part 1, it is now obsolete, as are subsequent editions that were based on it. Kroll's work has nevertheless been superseded only recently, in the editions of Dehnhard (1983), Jones, and Dürr.[3] In addition, Tomita (1993) has produced a massive *variorum* edition, unusable at the keyboard but enlightening insofar as entire pages are devoted to showing the variant readings for just a few measures. Jones's edition is the most practical, especially for those without German. His lucid descriptions of the manuscripts and their relationships—together with his reconstruction of the history of the London autograph (Jones (1991a and 1991b)—will provide the necessary orientation for readers planning to plunge into the bewildering assemblage of data presented by Dürr and Tomita.

One reason for difficulty in editing WTC2 is that the London autograph is an incomplete set of individual manuscripts, one for each prelude and fugue.[4] A few of these are actually copies by Bach's second wife, Anna Magdalena. Many of these manuscripts include later revisions in Bach's hand, but his final readings for most, if not all, movements occur only in other, non-autograph, manuscripts that were apparently copied from a second set of lost autographs. The London set lacks a collective title page, but the familiar title does appear in several dependable early copies.

The London autograph dates from 1740 and later, but a few movements belong to an earlier group of little preludes and fughettas (BWV 899–902) discussed in chapter 10.[5] Two dependable copies of WTC2 have title pages giving the date 1742, perhaps transcribed from a title page in a lost autograph; this has led to the supposition that Bach considered the work finished by that date. Later readings are found, however, in a copy by Bach's son-in-law Altnikol dated 1744 (P 430), and further revised readings of uncertain date exist for some movements. Hence, even if Bach did not make major revisions after 1744, he may never have

Table 12.1 WTC2: Selected Sources

Source	Copyist, date	Comments, Including Contents If Not Complete (letters = movements, e.g., "G" = prelude and fugue in G)
Early versions		
P 804/5	Kellner, 1726–7	G: early version of fugue (BWV 902/2). Date from Stinson (1989a, 23)
P 804/38	Kellner, 1727	C: early version (BWV 870a). Date from Stinson (1989a, 24) or later
P 1089	Vogler, 1726 or later	C, d (prelude), G (fugue), A♭(fugue): early versions (BWV 870a, 875a, 902/2, 901/2 [in F]), with BWV 899–901/1, 902/1. Date: see NBA V/6.2, KB, 345–6
SBB 10490	J. H. Michel (1768 or later)	C, G (fugue), A♭ (fugue): early versions (BWV 870a, 902/2, 901/2) in cycle including BWV 899–901/1
P 563	J. H. Michel	C♯ (fugue): early version in C (BWV 872a/2), with prelude BWV 933
P 595/5	Agricola, 1738	c, d (fugues); C♯ (fugue): intermediate version in C (BWV 872b/1); E♭ (fugue, in D). Date: NBA V/6.2, KB, 399
P 226	AMB, ca.1739–40 or earlier	C♯ (prelude): early version in C (BWV 872a/1); d: prelude, intermediate version (BWV 875b). Date from Kobayashi (1988, 46)
LEm Go.S.19	Boineburg, late 18th cent.(?)	d, G (preludes): early versions. Date: see NBA V/6.2, KB, 398
Surviving autographs and related sources		
London, British Library, Add. ms. 35021	AMB, JSB, 1740–2	Separate manuscripts constituting 3 groups. Group 1: c, d, E♭, E, e, F, f♯, G, g, A, a, b; uses title *Praeludium*. Group 2: C♯,d♯, F♯, g♯, B♭, b♭, B; uses title *Prelude*. Group 3: C, A♭. Autograph revisions occur in all groups; three pieces are missing (c♯, D, f)
P 416	Anon. Vr (= Anon. 12), ca. 1742	Separate copies, some lost or in other libraries. Date from Jones (edition, 1994) and NBA V/6.2, KB, 57. Copied from Add. 35021
SPK P 274/4	JSB, ca. 1743–6	A♭ (fugue, alternate version). Date from Kobayashi (1988)
Copies derived in whole or part from other (lost) autographs		
SPK P 430	Altnikol, 1744 (+ autograph entries)	Gives later versions than Add. 35021 (and P 274) for many pieces; alterations (listed in NBA V/6.2, KB, 84) sometimes correct earlier readings to later ones; some alterations by unidentified hands
SPK P 402	Altnikol, 1755	Independent of P 430, but deriving from the same lost autograph; some singular readings. Includes WTC1
SPK AmB 57	Anonymous 402	Known as Kirnberger's *Handexemplar*, with his annotations. Includes WTC1. Text from Add. 35021, as edited by Kirnberger on the basis of P 430 or other sources
Hs MB1974	Two copyists, 2d half 18th cent.	Includes WTC1; title page gives date 1742. Mostly in one hand, text from Add. 35021, some corrections corresponding to P 430; two pairs (C, A♭) in second hand, text as P 430

JSB = J. S. Bach
AMB = Anna Magdalena Bach

considered the work finished, adding embellishments and refinements of detail to the end of his life.

The chronology of the work has been sharpened by reconstructing the "copying-out process" of the London autograph. A division of its component manuscripts into three groups or "layers" (see Table 12.1) emerged in scholarship published during the 1980s, especially that of Kobayashi (1988) and Franklin (1989b). Their work has been refined in the more recent editions by Tomita, Jones, and Dürr. In addition to distinctions in the forms of titles and in handwriting and paper type, pieces in each layer tend to have similar dimensions and to employ similar forms and compositional techniques. For example, the first layer contains most of the pieces in the simpler keys, and stylistic features in some of these pieces, such as those in G minor and A (discussed below), also suggest relatively early dates. It is difficult, however, to fix precise dates of composition for any of the pieces, despite the existence of parallels between, say, the B-major fugue of WTC2 and Contrapunctus 10 from the *Art of Fugue*, which might place both movements around 1740. It is just as easy to draw parallels to works from earlier periods—for example, between the A-major prelude and the prelude of the First English Suite, probably a Weimar work.

Because the London autograph gives the latest version for only certain movements, editors have had to determine which other manuscripts give later readings. Since the time of Kroll—if not Kirnberger—editors have recognized two main textual traditions, those of the London autograph ("Fassung A" in NBA V/6.2) and of the 1744 manuscript copy by Bach's pupil Altnikol ("Fassung B").[6] But version B is not always the later one; the chronological relationship between the two traditions varies from movement to movement. Hence editors have traditionally selected one tradition or the other as giving Bach's latest reading for each movement. In most cases the choice either is obvious, as in the addition of a coda to the fugue in E minor, or trivial, involving only matters of detail. Dürr, however, gives complete texts for both versions in separate sections of NBA V/6.2, choosing between the two traditions only in the "practical" offprint published by Bärenreiter (Kassel, 1996).

For some movements, the two traditions represent distinct versions. But in other cases they are essentially identical, providing little evidence for Bach's having revised the movements in question except for adding an occasional trill or refining the notation of ties or accidentals.[7] One cannot be certain whether it was Bach or someone else who made such small adjustments, which may involve only the addition of signs for a few ornaments that players would have added as a matter of course. Whereas Dürr refrains from mixing readings from the two traditions, even in his "practical" offprint, Jones does so explicitly. The result is probably a more accurate representation of how Bach would have expected each movement to be played. Only in a few cases is there real uncertainty as to which readings are later or more correct, and none of these involves musically critical aspects of the score.[8]

244 • The Keyboard Music of J. S. Bach

Prelude and Fugue in C, BWV 870

It is possible that Bach considered opening WTC2 with a relatively simple arpeggiando prelude (see below on the prelude in C#). But instead he chose an imposing prelude in four strict parts. The decision, together with the subsequent revisions of both movements, seems to indicate a more monumental conception for WTC2, which, like CU3, opens with a relatively massive piece—not with a modest, obviously pedagogical movement, as did WTC1.

The polyphonic notation of the present prelude does mask an arpeggiated texture. But the counterpoint is real and includes striking dissonances and chromatic voice leading.[9] Both prelude and fugue were originally shorter, part of a set of preludes and fughettas known to date back to at least 1727.[10] Perhaps, having decided to include the latter in WTC2, Bach found both movements too slight and expanded the closing section of each. He also rewrote the middle section of the prelude, and by adding the lower octave (C) to the opening pedal point added further weight to what would be the opening movement of his most ambitious collection of keyboard music. This is, then, a "big" piece requiring a full registration, and the thirty-second notes, added at a still later stage over the opening pedal point and elsewhere, imply a vigorous affect.

The prelude is preserved in no fewer than six textual states or versions (see Table 12.2). Two of these, copied by Vogler and W. F. Bach, respectively, give relatively insignificant variants, and the fingerings and ornaments in Vogler's copy may not even stem from Bach. Other variants document three distinct layers of revision; the crucial elements in the expansion of the original prelude occurred in the first layer of revisions. These are worth tracing in detail as they illustrate a type of compositional revision that is more profound and ingenious than that seen in WTC1.[11]

In WTC1, the revised preludes were expanded mainly by the addition of a coda. Bach did the same here, adding a closing pedal point on the tonic to balance the opening one. But he also inserted a new recapitulation section and a bridge passage leading up to it. Bach was dissatisfied with his first attempt at a revision, and he eventually replaced most of the bridge, or rather substituted a heavily rewritten version of it.[12]

The seams do not show. Nevertheless, the prelude remains a singular piece. It was already so in the early version, which obeys the aesthetic of the improvisatory prelude by avoiding exact repetitions, regular phrasing, and sequences. For example, after a weak arrival on the dominant (m. 7) there is a sequence that would normally have confirmed the modulation just made. But the passage veers off toward the relative minor (A minor) and the supertonic (D minor), never returning to G.[13]

In a sonata-allegro movement, such a modulating scheme would leave a nebulous impression, but it is entirely appropriate to the more relaxed ambience of a

Table 12.2 Prelude in C

Versions, Sources, Editions

BWV	Principal Source	Page no. in NBA V/6.2	Remark
870a	P 1089	307	
870a	P 1089	310	additional fingerings and ornaments (Vogler's?); facsimiles in Brokaw (1989), Lindley (1989a)
870b	Add. 35021	342	as originally entered in the ms. (= first layer of revision)
870b	Add. 35021	2	as revised in the ms. (= second layer of revision)
870b	I B DD70	6	minor compositional variants (copy by W. F. Bach, prelude only, with fugue in A♭)
870	P 430	156	further compositional refinements (= third layer of revision)

Layers of Revision

Layer of Revision	Alterations
1: original text of Add. 35021 (= BWV 870b)	revision of melodic lines and voice leading (mm. 1–14, 30)
	extension of bridge (mm. 15–9 inserted)
	addition of recapitulation (mm. 20–9 inserted)
	expansion of final chord into pedal point (mm. 32–3 inserted)
2: alterations in Add. 35021	revision of bridge (mm. 14b–19 replaced)
3: text of P 403, P 402, et al. (= BWV 870)	embellishment (32ds added in mm. 1–3, 6, etc.)

Formal Design

Version	Corresponding Measures						
Early (BWV 870a)	1–12	13–14	—	—	15–16		17
Late (BWV 870b, 870)	1–12	13–19 (bridge)	20–28a* (recap.)	28b–29	30–31 (final cadence)		32–34 (tonic pedal)
Tonal plan:	C→	d→	F→	g→	C————————————		

* = mm. 5b–13, a fifth lower

prelude to emphasize minor keys on the "flat" side of the tonic, without firmly articulating the dominant. This aspect of the prelude was strengthened in the final version, whose main articulations are the cadence to D minor at m. 13 and the arrival in the subdominant at m. 20. Both phrase endings are elided, with suspensions in the upper voices. Yet m. 20 is the beginning of a "subdominant reprise" (Jones, edition, 159)—that is, a recapitulation of the type later favored by Schubert, in which the opening section is restated a fifth lower. Normally such a recapitulation leads from the subdominant back to the tonic. But because of the unusual tonal design of the first section, the present recapitulation reaches the unexpected key of G minor just a few measures before the end.[14] From here it took great ingenuity to modulate swiftly and convincingly back to the tonic.

Bach does so through a chromatic descent in the soprano, which now echoes the similar descent in the revised bridge, mm. 18–9. The return to C major at m. 30 coincides with a return to the material of the original version.[15]

The London autograph preserves no trace of any compositional difficulties that Bach might have had in bringing the revised version of the prelude to a conclusion. But the bridge, also inserted in the first layer of revision, presents another story. As first entered into the London autograph, the bridge contained some weak voice leading (e.g., doubled Fs at the end of m. 14). In addition to correcting this, Bach added the chromaticism in mm. 18–9; as a consequence, the return to familiar material at the beginning of the recapitulation (m. 20) coincides with a return to diatonicism.

The fugue is of the *galant* type in three parts common in WTC1; it is also close to the little violinistic fugues BWV 952 and 953, also in C. Bach seems to have drafted the revised version while writing out the London autograph, but the essential revisions were limited to the addition of a coda (mm. 68–83). The latter helps the fugue balance the more heavily scored prelude; the texture thickens to five parts in the last few measures, and a few athletic figures in the left hand (mm. 76ff.) reach down to low C, which has not been heard since the opening of the prelude.[16]

Bach also changed the time signature from C to 2/4, halving the length of each measure. Comparable alterations in the B-minor prelude and the *Art of Fugue* show that Bach was concerned during this period with the implications of his metrical notation, although it is not entirely clear what those implications are. In a later view, pieces in 2/4 should be lighter and, presumably, quicker than those in 4/4. But Williams (1993, 620) argues that for Bach 2/4 time can imply a "stately" quality, and a certain deliberateness is implicit in the complexity of the subject, which incorporates *figure corte*, a rhetorical pause, and a zigzag motive. These old-fashioned gestures hint at a certain "stateliness" that accords with the grand conception of the revised version.

The copy by Vogler gives fingerings for early versions of both movements. Vogler was a pupil of Bach and his successor as court organist at Weimar. Vogler's fingerings follow the same general principles as those given by Bach in CB (see chap. 10), but the copies date from after Vogler's studies with Bach. The choice of fingers does not always seem well thought out, although some of the less likely ones found in modern editions of the pieces are misreadings.[17]

Prelude and Fugue in C Minor BWV 871

The second prelude and fugue belongs to the oldest layer of the London autograph and was in fact copied by Anna Magdalena Bach. It seems not to have received any subsequent revisions and must have been among the first pieces in the volume to achieve its familiar shape.[18]

In binary form, the prelude recalls the Inventions in its predominantly two-part writing and the use of voice exchange at the outset of each half (and elsewhere). The fugue also looks backward, recalling the C-major fugue of WTC1 in certain respects. Subject and countersubject share a restrained character reminiscent of the *stile antico*, and the form is distinctly bipartite, introducing a new contrapuntal technique after the midpoint (m. 14), where the subject is presented simultaneously in rhythmic augmentation and in its original values. Almost immediately the inversion appears as well (m. 15), albeit in a fairly free form. But although strettos are prominent from here to the end, rigorous counterpoint as such is less important than the dramatic effect achieved by the piling up of stretto entries.

The texture is limited to three parts until m. 19, where the bass enters with the subject in augmentation.[19] This might be taken as a sign of an early date, but the organ fugue in C, BWV 547/2, delays the entrance of its last (fifth) voice for similar reasons and until much the same point in the piece—almost exactly two-thirds of the way through. The bass entry in the organ fugue can be made to sound very impressive on an instrument with a strong pedal division. The present fugue might also benefit from organ performance, not only in the first entry of the bass but also in the earlier augmented entry in the tenor (m. 14). But this bass cannot be a pedal part; it ascends to d′ (m. 21) and has unidiomatic figuration in the coda (m. 26). Moreover, the detached pedal point in the coda—eighth notes separated by rests in mm. 23–5—is a device that Bach used elsewhere in the absence of a real pedal part, as at the end of the Chromatic Fantasia. Elsewhere, learned counterpoint mingles with *brisé* writing that seems especially idiomatic to the harpsichord (e.g., mm. 9, 11–3). The final chord even bears an arpeggio sign; could this imply a double or triple breaking of the chord (upwards, downwards, and upwards again)?

Prelude and Fugue in C♯, BWV 872

The prelude in C♯, like the prelude in E♭ of WTC1, is a self-contained prelude and fughetta. In its earliest known form (BWV 872a/1) it stood alone, in C, as did the fugue; both are substantially revised in WTC2. That the prelude was relatively early is clear from its sources and from the fact that its opening section is of the arpeggio type, otherwise not represented in WTC2. None of the arpeggiation was written out in the earliest version, which was notated (like the early version of the C-major prelude in WTC1) as a series of five-part chords.[20] By the time of the London autograph the chords had been resolved into a three-strand texture, with repeated eighth notes making up the middle strand. These are suggestive of orchestral textures that incorporate bow vibrato (cf. the lower string parts of the opening movement of Cantata No. 82).

Bach revised this middle strand as well as the voice leading of the three-part fugato that follows. In particular, he added chromaticism to the inner voice in mm. 44–6, which now echo the chromaticism at the end of the first section (mm. 23–4). Bach also added the *allegro* tempo mark, but the fugato retains a French quality, thanks to the *port de voix* in the subject.[21] This suggests that the fugato should have the relaxed character of a minuet or passepied, and the sixteenths might be played slightly *inégales*.

Such a manner of performance would create a welcome contrast with the fugue proper, which opens with an incisive staccato subject. The fugue is one of Bach's wittiest compositions, and unlike the G#-minor fugue of WTC1 it makes its humor evident to any reasonably attentive listener. The subject can be understood as extending to the middle of the second measure, making the opening exposition a stretto. But Bach abandons the latter portion of the subject before the piece is half over; the last full statement is the inversion in the soprano at m. 15b. The remainder is a fantasia on the triadic motive comprised by the first four notes. All of the expositions are actually strettos, and most (including the first) incorporate *inversus* entries. But this is to make the piece sound more rigorous than it really is. It is better understood as a series of phrases that each introduce one or two new thematic or rhythmic wrinkles, such as the running idea in sixteenths at m. 8 or the entries *per arsin et thesin* at m. 11. The running figuration grows less inhibited with each phrase, and the piece concludes brilliantly.

This plan is already visible, albeit in shorter and more restrained form, in the earliest version (BWV 872a/2). Like the C-major prelude, the piece was expanded several times, almost doubling in length; here the expansion was by way of the extension or outright replacement of most passages (see Table 12.3).[22] Already in the earliest version, each successive phrase increases in length and brilliance, so that the fugue, which begins like a dry contrapuntal exercise, ends as a virtuoso improvisation. In revising it, Bach must have had contrapuntal elaboration on his mind even if he did not take it very seriously; diminished and augmented entries (mm. 19 and 25, respectively) are among the interpolations.

Prelude and Fugue in C# Minor BWV 873

The two movements in C# minor form a particularly satisfying pair. Both have ambitious dimensions and are worked out strictly in three parts, and each has a clearly articulated structure: the first a sort of sonata form, the second a double fugue whose two subjects are introduced separately, then combined. Each

Table 12.3 Fugue in C#, Early and Revised Versions

Version	Corresponding Measures						
Early (BWV 872a)	1–4a	—	4b–6	7–9a	9b	10–17a	17b	18–19
Late (BWV 872)	1–4a	4b–7a	7b–10	11–14a	14b–17	18–25a	25b–31	32–35
Cadences	C#	G#	(C#)	a#:V	(C#)	C#:V		V I

movement is also a type of gigue; the prelude is akin to the siciliano, the fugue a quick *giga* in 12/16.

In texture the prelude somewhat resembles the Sinfonias. But the first imitative entry (in the alto, m. 7) comes late, after the voice carrying it has already served in a filler capacity. Although starting in the tonic, the ensuing phrase reinterprets the theme harmonically in order to move toward the dominant. Among the models for this type of writing is a variety of *galant* trio-sonata movement in which the upper voices alternate as in a duet, rather than combining in real counterpoint.[23] The bass here is an independent part, and the subtle harmony and intricately ornamented melodic lines would be echoed in the opening movement of the trio sonata in the *Musical Offering*. The theme is absent from the middle section (mm. 17–32), but its return in the subdominant at the beginning of what is in effect another "subdominant reprise" (m. 33).

The expressive melodic decoration makes for long measures of 9/8 time, and it is hard to find a satisfactory tempo. Few keyboard instruments will adequately sustain the longer tied notes in the bass and upper voices, yet it would be wrong to rush the music in an attempt to bring out the underlying siciliano rhythm, which may be best felt as an almost imperceptible lilt. The similarity to the so-called *empfindsamer* style now associated with Berlin suggests performing some of the small notes as what C. P. E. Bach termed "variable" appoggiaturas, taking half the value of the following note. Indeed, the Altnikol sources explicitly dictate this interpretation in a few spots (Example 12.1). Unfortunately, the loss of the autograph from the London set compounds the usual difficulty of ascertaining exactly what Bach actually wrote. The Altnikol tradition preserves an independent set of ornaments that sometimes coincide with, sometimes depart from, those in sources close to the London autograph.[24]

The fugue is, with those in F♯ minor and G♯ minor, a three-part one in a "difficult" key with multiple subjects; perhaps all three works were composed at about the same time. Kirnberger took the time signature of 12/16 as an indication for a most lively tempo.[25] Yet the fugue is serious in character, and the first subject eventually combines with a chromatic second subject that enters in stretto at the midpoint (m. 35). Each half of the piece is subdivided, the first by

Example 12.1 Prelude in C♯ Minor BWV 873/2 (upper staff), mm. 16–7; readings of (a) P 416; (b) P 402.

the *inversus* exposition beginning at m. 24, the second by the combination of the two subjects at m. 48.[26] The final (combined) exposition includes a demonstration of counterpoint invertible at the twelfth, as shown by the entries in mm. 48–9 and 55–6. Between them comes a single statement of the first subject alone, in inversion (mm. 53–4). That Bach was aware of some awkwardness in the passage is suggested by his revision of m. 54b, which returns to the tonic rather abruptly. Here the leaping upper and middle parts of the Altnickol sources, which give the later readings, reinforce the need for a moderate tempo.

Prelude and Fugue in D, BWV 874

The prelude in D is one of the most magnificent harpsichord pieces in WTC2, thanks to its exuberant theme and brilliant subsequent figuration. Of the four or five preludes of WTC2 in full three-part sonata form (i.e., with a complete recapitulation section), it comes closest in style and dimensions to some of the large sonata movements composed during the 1740s by Emanuel and Friedemann Bach.[27]

Like the first movement of Friedemann's D-major Sonata (F. 3, published in 1745), the prelude is still conceived contrapuntally—predominantly in three parts. Thus, mm. 1–2 are immediately repeated with exchange of material between the upper parts, and a large portion of the first section (mm. 1–7) is eventually recapitulated with the upper parts again exchanged (mm. 41–7). Such contrapuntal play was a way for Bach to impress a personal stamp on the new sonata style, avoiding a literal restatement of opening material.[28] In other respects as well the recapitulation, although corresponding measure-for-measure with the first section, departs from an exact restatement. The bass, which at first failed to take up the theme, now has an inverted stretto entrance (m. 43). In the last half of the recapitulation (from m. 52), the individual lines are varied to produce even greater rhythmic exuberance than before. Similar outbursts occur at the ends of the fugues in F and G, making the final section a culmination rather than a simple rounding-out of the form, as it is in many pre-Classical sonata movements.

The double time signature (¢–12/8) seems to convey special information of some sort, but exactly what is uncertain. The sign must reflect the presence of occasional duplet figures alongside the more frequent triplets; it cannot be a random survival of the proportional signs still employed, as a vestige of Renaissance rhythmic theory, in some late-Baroque works (e.g., some of Fischer's preludes and fugues). But the sign has no obvious bearing on the question of whether the duplets—pairs of equal eighths—should be interpreted literally or "assimilated" to the triplets. The issue cannot be settled by examining Bach's counterpoint, for both literal and "assimilated" readings produce parallel fifths at different points in m. 18 (Example. 12.2).[29] Evidently Bach overlooked the fifths, regardless of how he played the rhythm. "Assimilation," however, would

Example 12.2 Prelude in D, BWV 874/1, m. 18; (a) as notated, (b) with "assimilated" rhythm.

trivialize the contrast between the lively gigue figuration of m. 1 and the softer "sigh" figures of m. 2, which are notated as pairs of eighths. Hence it seems best to play the duplets literally throughout. It is disappointing that mm. 18 and 20 are the only ones in which the two meters are combined; for a more extensive exploration of conflicting meters one must look to no. 26 in the Goldberg Variations. The dotted rhythms appearing throughout the present piece (from m. 5) pose less of a problem; there is no reason to think that these are anything other than the usual shorthand for triple rhythms.[30]

The prelude overshadows the fugue, but the latter is also one of the more impressive pieces of WTC2. Allied to the *stile antico*, it nevertheless has a modern structure based on alternation between expositions and episodes, and the design is tonally conceived, the most important articulations being the arrivals to A (m. 20b) and F♯ minor (m. 27b). The latter is followed by an immediate return to the tonic , as in many early sonata movements. But what follows is not a recapitulation but a series of close strettos, the last containing entries for all four parts that cascade downward from highest to lowest (m. 44b).

The episodes, unlike those in the more *galant* fugues, are canonic in texture, hence not very different in style from the expositions. Such episodes might have made for a very plain piece, especially as all are based on the same five-note figure, drawn from the second half of the subject. In the course of the fugue, however, the motive grows from six notes (m. 7) to eight (m. 16), culminating in a two-octave descending scale in the bass (mm. 38–40)—a remarkable gesture in a piece derived from the restrained style of antique polyphony.

Although the fugue is notated *alla breve*, the prevailing note values are quarters and eighths (not halves and quarters), suggesting lively performance. As in other alla breves, players may fear that a quick tempo makes it impossible to bring out details of the counterpoint. A slow tempo, however, makes it harder for individual notes to be heard as parts of lines. In a lively tempo the three repeated eighths at the beginning of the subject form an incisive "speaking" motive, and the gesture stands out even in the overlapping stretto entries of the final section.

Prelude and Fugue in D Minor BWV 875

The prelude in D minor is another relatively early piece that underwent several reworkings. The angular quality of the fugue suggests that it too might be relatively early, but there is no documentary evidence for this, and the uneasy way in which its duplet and triplet phrases alternate may rather be an example of the harshness that Bach admitted in CU3 and the chorale fughettas BWV 696–9 et al., all works apparently of the late 1730s. The prelude and the fugue share an intense, vociferous quality, due to the packing of so much vigorous counterpoint within their concise frames.

Bach's revisions in the prelude can be traced very clearly. From the start, the piece was a fiery *moto perpetuo*, perhaps inspired by Vivaldi. The violinistic character of the figuration is clearest in the original version, which lacks the thirty-seconds added later (mm. 22, 24, etc.). The revisions enlarged the piece from forty-three to sixty-one measures, but the basic design remained bipartite, the theme being restated in the dominant at the beginning of the second half (m. 26; see Table 12.4).[31]

Like the theme of the *Musical Offering*, the fugue subject has a dualistic structure, opening with diatonic triplet sixteenths, then shifting to chromatic eighths. As a result, the fugue shifts constantly between duplet and triplet rhythms. The two rhythms combine only once, as if by accident (m. 9b). But the piece derives a special quality from the unresolved tension between the flowing triplets and the chromatic eighths, the two never becoming reconciled or "integrated" as they might have been through contrapuntal combination (see below on the prelude in F minor). The antithesis might be marked in performance by distinctly non-legato articulation of the chromatic steps in the second part of the subject, although these need to be played tenuto to carry weight.

Table 12.4 Prelude in D Minor BWV 875

Version	Corresponding Measures											
1. BWV 875a	1–5	—	—	6–14	15–19	—	20–21	—	22–25	26–32	—	33–34
2. Add. 35021, orig. reading	1–5	6–9	10	11–19	20–24	25–28	29–30	—	31–34	35–41	42	43–53
3. Add. 35021, first revision	1–5	6–9	10–16	18–25	26–30	31–34	35–36	37–38	39–42	43–49	50	51–61
Cadences:	d	d	d:V	a	a		(g)	(F)	d:V			d

The chromaticism of the subject might have led to rigorous counterpoint, but the fugue is closer to a virtuoso improvisation than an example of "demonstration counterpoint." It contains a sufficient number of partial strettos, quasi-inversions, and other manipulated entries for Marpurg to have selected it for measure-by-measure analysis in his *Abhandlung von der Fuge* (1753–4, 1:141–3). Yet most of these entries break off before the complete subject has been stated. Although not one of the great movements of WTC2, the piece might have been a personal favorite, or at least it incorporated a few favorite formulas; Bach seems to quote it in both CU3 (BWV 689) and the three-part ricercar from the *Musical Offering* (see chap. 17).

Prelude and Fugue in E♭, BWV 876

The Prelude and Fugue in E♭ is one of the less closely matched pairs in WTC2. The prelude is a lightly scored, gigue-like piece comparable to the lute prelude in the same key (BWV 998/1, discussed in chap. 15). The fugue, in four parts, imitates *a capella* style, although it has no preoccupation with contrapuntal technique as such. The differences in style might reflect different dates of composition; in the London autograph the prelude has the appearance of a first draft, whereas the fugue is virtually a fair copy. It is preserved with earlier versions of three other fugues in Agricola's copy.[32]

The prelude resembles the lute piece—which might be contemporary—in key, motivic material, and texture.[33] Both wait until the last phrase to bring the opening theme back in the tonic. And both are related to the arpeggiated type of prelude, although the underlying harmony is occasionally composed out in a rather allusive manner. Some corrections that Bach probably made while writing out the London autograph made the harmony even less straightforward. For example, simple whole steps in the bass of m. 34 were altered retrospectively to agree with the bass of m. 37, turning into descending sevenths; the leaps became ninths in m. 39. Such leaps enrich the implied voice leading, since the top note of a leap usually suggests a distinct line in the underlying polyphony (Example 12.3).

The fugue has some of the character of Bach's biblical choruses, though it is not in as pure a *stile antico* as the following fugue in E. Nor is it as learned as another quasi-choral fugue, the one in D, for both counterpoint and form here are simpler despite the presence of strettos in the last two expositions. The emphasis is rather on the straightforward working-out of the subject, and the *alla breve* notation implies a vigorous tempo, with leaps and syncopations well marked; one might compare the *turba* chorus "Wir haben ein Gesetz" from the Saint John Passion.

Example 12.3 Prelude in E♭, BWV 876/1, mm. 34–40: (a) final version; (b) earlier readings (bass, mm. 34–5); (c) analysis of m. 34; (d) analysis of m. 39

Prelude and Fugue in D♯ Minor BWV 877

Both movements of this pair, like the D♯-minor fugue of WTC1, might originally have been in D minor, the key in which Marpurg (1753–4) quotes the opening of the fugue. The autograph preserves a few possible traces of a D-minor version; both movements would have been easier to read and play in that key and might have been easily transposed through the addition of sharps to the original (lost) autograph. The archaic style of the fugue and its similarities to several fugues in WTC1 suggest an early date. But stylistic evidence of this sort is equivocal inasmuch as WTC2 was assembled at a time when Bach was interested in archaic types of fugal composition—including the *Art of Fugue*, which opens with several stylistically comparable quasi-vocal movements in D minor.

The prelude is a two-part invention in sonata form, like the Invention in E—but on a larger scale. One suspects that many of the figures involving thirty-seconds were products of revision, as in the C-major prelude, but the sources bear this out in only a few passages. Together with the intricate counterpoint (and the difficult key), the thirty-seconds urge a restrained tempo, although this may grow wearying due to the somewhat schematic design and unvarying texture.

The key alone would make the fugue among the least-played in the WTC. Its appeal is further limited by the dense four-part texture and somewhat diffuse structure. The basic model again lies in *a capella* style, the subject having the same freedom from the barline that characterizes the subject of the F#-minor fugue in Part 1. Thus, although the fugue is notated in common (rather than cut) time, it is austere and archaic in character; there are few episodes, and, as in Renaissance polyphony, entries of the subject usually overlap cadences in a manner calculated to eliminate obvious articulations. But a half cadence near the exact center (to V of IV, m. 24) articulates a bipartite form, and the sole episode of the first half (mm. 11ff.) is fleetingly echoed in the second (bass, mm. 35bff.). The climactic event, as in several four-part fugues of Part 1, is an ascent into the upper register during this second episode. This is answered, as in the F-minor fugue of WTC1, by the final entrance of the subject, a quasi-*pedaliter* entry in the bass (m. 40b).

The piece could end there and conceivably did so in some lost version; codas were later additions in three movements of the *Art of Fugue*. The present short coda, in which the subject and its inversion are stated simultaneously (m. 43b), seems somewhat out of place, as neither the inversion nor any type of paired entry has been heard previously. Perhaps Bach made a belated discovery of the possibility of combining subject and inversion, writing it into the piece as an afterthought. That the coda is indeed the culmination of the piece is indicated by the presence in the penultimate measure of the rare German sixth chord in root position (#IV$^{7/5/3b}$).[34]

Prelude and Fugue in E, BWV 878

The E-major prelude is again in binary form, but unlike the previous prelude it is in three voices. Both the opening pedal point and the gentle character recall the prelude in G, BWV 902/1. This, however, is a more sophisticated piece; the upper parts, for example, are more genuinely contrapuntal, exchanging material in the second phrase (m. 5). Nevertheless, the two-part notation of the right hand might in some passages originally have been written as a single voice (e.g., mm. 18–20).

The London "autograph" is actually in the hand of Anna Magdalena; numerous corrections suggest that she copied from a nearly illegible composing score that already contained corrections and revisions. Sebastian himself copied the last two measures on an extra system added in the lower margin, yet one passage was left uncorrected: the first beat of m. 50 was later altered in an unidentified hand, but other sources provide two alternate readings, and it is difficult to say which, if any, is correct.[35]

The fugue is the purest example in the WTC of the *stile antico*, signified not only by the long measures of 4/2 time but by the use of a traditional subject traceable to chant.[36] Actually, Bach seems to have taken not only the subject but most of the first six measures from the E-major fugue in Fischer's *Ariadne musica*. Bach continued to follow the general outline provided by Fischer up to the cadence on the dominant in m. 9.[37] By that point Fischer, working on a smaller scale, had already begun using the theme in stretto, which Bach reserves for the following section (mm. 9–16). This fugue is, then, an example of "demonstration counterpoint," a new device being introduced after each cadence: a new type of stretto (m. 16), varied and diminuted forms of the subject (mm. 23, 27), combinations of different forms (mm. 30, 35). Cadences are more frequent than in Bach's models, and the modulations range more widely than in music by either Fischer or the ultimate model, Palestrina.

As usual, too slow a tempo fragments the melodic lines, making it difficult to perceive such things as the shape of the penultimate phrase in the treble, which forms a long arch that rises to the highest note in the piece (a´´, m. 38) before descending through more than an octave. The descent continues in the final phrase, which echoes several chorale melodies whose closing phrases have similar outlines. This descent is derived from the end of the subject, and its extension into a complete scale just before the end is another example of a process observed previously in the fugue in D.

Prelude and Fugue in E Minor BWV 879

The E-minor belongs with the D-minor to the earliest layer of the London autograph, and it shows signs of being a relatively early composition as well. The prelude is a long invention somewhat resembling the prelude in D# minor. But the voices here are somewhat less equal—the bass often moves in eighths like an ordinary continuo part—and although there is a double bar there is no return. Such points do not make this a weaker piece. But reminiscences of the Inventions (especially the one in D minor) do support a relatively early date, and the rather dogged playing out of several not particularly compelling sequences makes the prelude seem long, particularly if both repeat signs are observed.

Four long trills raise the question of whether the upper note should be sharp or natural. No one in the Bach circle seems to have indicated such things notationally until Emanuel. Bach began to do so some time after 1750. A rule that seems to work in music by J. S. Bach is that it is best not to introduce notes from outside the natural scale of the currently tonicized key. Hence, in the first two trills, where the key is B minor, the upper note would be g (not g#) in m. 29, and c#´ (not c´) in m. 33. This is so despite the cross-relations that arise in mm. 30–2 as the treble twice strikes g#´ against the bass trill on f#.[38]

The fugue subject is long and rhythmically heterogeneous, mixing triplets, sixteenths, and dotted rhythms. Such a subject does not invite strict contrapuntal treatment, and the fugue is quite free, with a countersubject that it is less a line than a texture, sometimes written as arpeggiando figuration in one voice (e.g., at m. 7), sometimes divided between two parts in *brisé* style (m. 13). The rhythmic heterogeneity of the subject is more notational than real; the sixteenths are written-out ornaments (turns), and the dotted figures are surely to be assimilated to the triplets, as in the D-major prelude.

The fugue originally ended with a full cadence in mm. 70–1, as in the London autograph. The coda, preserved in the Altnikol group, includes a full statement of the subject in the tonic (m. 72). This corrects a possible flaw in the original version, where the last entry of the theme is in the subdominant (m. 60). The original ending was abrupt but dramatic; the idea of closing with a dramatic gesture is preserved at m. 70 by the sudden fermata, which might be understood as applying not to the note on the second beat but to the rest following it. The same syntax—fermata, then coda—recurs in the three-part mirror fugue of the *Art of Fugue*; it is even repeated within the present coda, a second fermata occurring in m. 83. As in the revised preludes of WTC1, there is a subtle change in style at the beginning of the coda, which is more free and exuberant than the rest of the fugue; the variation of the countersubject in mm. 72–3 includes leaps of a tenth. But the tempo need not change until m. 83, where the Kirnberger copies indicate *adagio*. This word might apply not only to the notes immediately surrounding the second fermata but to the remaining three measures, whose dense harmony seems to require a more deliberate tempo.[39]

Prelude and Fugue in F, BWV 880

The F-major prelude has a spaciousness that contrasts sharply with the nervous gigue rhythm of its fugue. Much of the figuration in the prelude is a rhythmicized version of that found in the unmeasured preludes of d'Anglebert and other seventeenth-century French composers. This figuration is essentially of the arpeggio type, despite numerous stepwise passing tones; often it suggests the so-called *style brisé*, although, as in the somewhat similar prelude in C, the counterpoint is by no means merely notational, and there are as many as five real voices.

The 3/2 time signature points to the broad underlying motion in half notes. The eighths at the surface in m. 1 are slurred in groups of four, confirming that there are just three pulses in the measure. Even these need not be strongly articulated, as the harmony generally changes only at the barline.[40] The prelude has some sonata-like elements, including a recapitulation (in the Classical sense). But it falls into four sections, rather than the usual two or three, and the greater portion of the second section (mm. 17–28) simply restates the first twelve measures in the dominant.

The fugue is in the rare meter of 6/16, which would normally imply a somewhat more rapid tempo than 6/8, according to Kirnberger (1771–9, 2/1:119). But the bursts of thirty-seconds shortly before the end require that the tempo not be overly quick. Moreover, the rhythm of the subject is not so straightforward as it first seems; a controlled tempo makes it easier to grasp the metrical shape of the subject as well as the apparent shifts in the placement of the downbeat. The subject begins in the middle of the measure, and if this is heard incorrectly, as a downbeat, the climax of the melody will seem to fall on a weak beat.[41] It helps to lengthen the climactic f´´ (m. 4) ever so slightly, slurring it to the following e´´. But some ambiguity in the subject is unavoidable and even desirable, pointing toward the hemiolic passage in mm. 9–14 that is effectively in 9/16.

Thereafter the meter settles down. But the fugue has an unusual design, dominated by a single long episode at the point where one might have expected a second exposition (mm. 29–52). Composed largely of strettos and sequences based on a motive from the subject, the episode has the function of a development section, and the subsequent re-entrance of the complete subject in the tonic (m. 52b) serves as a return. But this return is hidden in the inner voice, and the piece's formal proportions are not those of a sonata movement, since at this point it is little more than halfway over. The subsequent section quickly sinks to the subdominant (m. 58) and dwells for a while in the tonic minor before reaffirming F major with ecstatic figuration (mm. 89ff.). Perhaps one or more sections, or at least the thirty-seconds, were additions made in the course of a revision. There is no evidence for this in the sources, but the fugue ends somewhat unexpectedly with a recapitulation of the unassuming phrase that closed the first section (mm. 94–99a ‖ 24–29a).

Prelude and Fugue in F Minor BWV 881

Another well-matched pair, the F-minor movements are both in three parts, with strong references to *galant* style. Indeed, the prelude opens with what is almost a caricature of a *galant* or *empfindsamer* theme, replete with sighs in parallel thirds and sixths.[42] This theme alternates with and eventually is largely replaced by figuration in sixteenths. Since, however, the opening motive is later used to accompany the figuration (mm. 49ff.), one might, following Hofmann (1988, 54), speak of the "integration" of the two basic ideas. Formally the prelude resembles a sonata movement, but the return at m. 56b (or is it at m. 49?) is intensified by melodic variation and new counterpoint. Hence, despite the apparently simple periodic phrasing, the form is cumulative rather than symmetrical, as in the D-major prelude. The prelude ends with a surprisingly emphatic variation of the original closing phrase (compare mm. 66b–70 with 24b–28a).

The metrical structure of the thematic material is easily misunderstood. The opening theme begins on an upbeat, like a gavotte; the "sigh" motives fall on downbeats and ought to receive an expressive accent or a little extra time. One might be tempted to shift to a louder manual for the subsequent figuration, but when the two ideas are combined they need to be equally strong. Despite the expressive opening, this is not a delicate piece, and the dramatic closing gesture—in which the figuration in sixteenths is interrupted by two full chords (m. 70)—calls for a sturdy registration on the harpsichord.

The fugue is also of the *galant* type, alluding to a texture of parallel thirds or sixths in a sequential episode that occurs no fewer than four times. Equally *galant* is the tendency toward symmetrical, periodic phrasing, not only in the episode but in the expositions, where successive statements of the subject twice form eight-bar periods (at the opening and in mm. 25–32). The straightforward phrasing reflects the harmonic simplicity of the subject, which merely alternates between I and V, the dominant occupying mm. 2–3. These characteristics have led to the fugue's being perceived as simple, even cheerful (as in Keller 1950, 167). But the dominant prolongation is doubled in length in mm. 13–6, where the treble poignantly draws out the half step d♭′′–c′′ already present in the subject (m. 3). A more extended and dramatic dominant prolongation begins with the pedal point of mm. 50–2, continuing through m. 64. The drama does not reach Beethovenian heights, but it is enough to make the last third of the piece darker and more intense than one might have expected from the beginning. Here one might note the development of the simple idea of three repeated eighths, from the subject, which *is* something that would be characteristic of Beethoven.

The loss of the autograph again raises questions about textual details. Some copies give ornaments on the first downbeat of each movement—a trill and a mordent, respectively. Although reasonably well authenticated, the ornaments are hardly necessary.

Prelude and Fugue in F♯, BWV 882

The prelude in F♯ again alternates between a *galant* theme and harmonically inspired figuration, which provides a tenuous echo of the old arpeggio prelude. But up to the last two measures the texture is in two parts—one can imagine it scored for flute and continuo—and although the theme might be suitable for a sarabande, it is accompanied by a dotted bass line that propels it forward. The propulsion is fairly gentle, however—the 3/4 meter shows that this is not an overture—and when the arpeggiated figuration begins in m. 4 it gains a certain poise as a result of the continuing dotted figures in the bass. Although there is no double bar, the form is that of a sonata movement in three spacious sections plus retransition (mm. 45–56).

As in the prelude in C♯ minor, some of the ornaments and melodic figures have the slightly mannered quality of the mature *galant* style—particularly the appoggiaturas, including one on the second beat of m. 1 which is, however, an addition not found in the London autograph and other early sources. Despite the late style, it is unlikely that any of the appoggiaturas should follow C. P. E. Bach's rules on length, except perhaps in the cadences at mm. 44 and 67 (second beat).

These include a formula which, when it recurs in the final cadence, incorporates an appoggiatura written out as a quarter note.[43]

The fugue, in three parts, comes even closer than those in F or F minor to the texture of a *galant* trio sonata, thanks to the extensive use of "sigh" motives in parallel thirds and sixths during the episodes (e.g., mm. 24b–32a). The subject starts in the middle of the measure, as in a gavotte. The opening trill motive is not characteristic of the dance, but the periodic phrasing and the placement of "sigh" motives on downbeats are typical of the French dance, implying that the fugue should be played with some of the latter's gentle gracefulness. The trill at the outset is not developed as a motive, and although it focuses attention on the implicit chromaticism within the subject (E♯/E♮), the latter never becomes explicit; there is not a single direct chromatic half step in the piece.

The fugue has perhaps the most schematic design of any of Bach's three-part fugues, comparable to that of the E-minor fugue of WTC1 and the four Duetti. It is built around three expositions (at mm. 1, 33, and 65) composed permutation-ally, using the four possible combinations of subject and two countersubjects.[44] The expositions alternate with two lengthy sections, primarily episodic (mm. 12b–32a and 44b–64a); the second of these sections recapitulates the first. Each of these sections includes a single statement of the subject (at mm. 21 and 53); hence, expository as well as episodic passages are included in the recapitula-tory scheme, and the fugue gives the impression of a tidy geometric design. In keeping with this constructivist quality is a recurring canonic episode (mm. 12b–20a) similar to the ones in the learned D-major fugue. But here the "sighs" of the countersubject provide a conventionally expressive element that would have pleased proponents of the *galant* style.

Prelude and Fugue in F♯ Minor BWV 883

The Prelude and Fugue in F♯ minor are one of the high points of WTC2, and despite the difficult key and the complex form of the second movement (a triple fugue) they are more accessible to listeners and easier to play than one might expect. Unlike most of the other movements in such keys, they belong to the earliest layer of the London autograph, implying a relatively early date.

The prelude could be described as a monodic arioso, the melody being play-able on a separate (louder) manual despite the imitations in the inner voice at the beginning of each of the three main sections (mm. 2, 13, 31). The three-part texture is maintained strictly throughout, even when the voice leading of the lower parts becomes a notational fiction.[45] The structure is that of a concise tripartite sonata form, including a distinct retransition phrase (mm. 21–9); this distinguishes it from several preludes of similar texture in WTC1 (e.g., C♯ minor) whose forms are bipartite.

Example 12.4 Prelude in F# Minor BWV 883/1, mm. 6–8a (rhythmic notation from P 402 above staves)

The prelude alternates frequently between duple and triple rhythms, but the two appear simultaneously only once (m. 15b). Questions about the interpretation of Bach's rhythmic notation arise in mm. 7–8, where Altnikol's copies have triplets; here the autograph has *figure corte*, implying that the latter might have been shorthand for triplet performance (Example 12.4).[46] Yet elsewhere (mm. 15, 18, 25) the autograph shows compositional revisions, not mere renotation; would Bach have written a sixteenth and two thirty-seconds when he meant triplets (as in the tenor of m. 7)? Perhaps he instead intended to sharpen the rhythm in places like mm. 7 and 8, assuming that the thirty-seconds would be played freely, like other written-out embellishments.

The second movement is the WTC's only full-fledged triple fugue, with three subjects that are each presented separately and then combined. The first subject is serious and declamatory, invoking choral style; its syncopations later become dissonant suspensions, as in the fugue in D# minor. The two subsequent subjects are shorter, livelier, and more regular in rhythm; if the second subject is still "vocal" in character, the third is "instrumental" as those terms are understood today. The overall rhythmic design resembles that of the C#-minor fugue of Part 1, which begins in *stile antico* and grows more fluid with the introduction of the second subject (or countersubject). But the present opening section is not as severely archaic, and the ending is more up to date, resembling the allegro of a contrapuntal trio sonata.

The three subjects are systematically combined only in the final section (m. 51).[47] This contrasts with the two triple contrapuncti in the *Art of Fugue*, which more thoroughly investigate the combinatorial possibilities of their material. Here, contrapuntal demonstration is less important than the "integration" of the contrasting themes; the process is characterized by a gradual evolution in the nature of the rhythm. The expositions of the first two subjects include many short-winded, sometimes overlapping motivic gestures in the three voices; the second subject is even introduced in stretto.[48] The third subject, on the other hand, comprises flowing sixteenths that can be extended indefinitely through sequence. In fact the first subject also is sequential—it is an elaborated chain of suspensions—but the point is obscured by the fragmented rhythm of the accompanying voices in the first section. The sequence underlying the opening subject becomes explicit in the last section, where the halting motion of the first subject becomes subsumed within a texture dominated by the long, effortless lines of the third subject.

Prelude and Fugue in G, BWV 884

The prelude in G is one of three that were associated at different times with the fugue, which originally belonged to the group of pieces from which Bach drew the pair in C and the fugue in Ab. The little prelude BWV 902a must have seemed too short for inclusion in the WTC, and perhaps too similar to the D-minor prelude to be worth expanding; both are short pieces in 3/4 based on concerto-like figuration. Bach did expand the fugue slightly, but it remains one of the shortest and liveliest pieces in the WTC. For this reason the relatively lengthy arioso prelude BWV 902/1 must have seemed inappropriate, especially as it resembled the one in E. The prelude that was eventually included retains a few points in common with the other (earlier?) ones, but the similarities may be fortuitous. As in BWV 902a the material consists of violinistic figuration; and, as in BWV 902/1, a double bar follows the first section, each half opening with a short pedal point as well as an exchange of material between upper and lower parts.[49]

The fugue subject consists of arpeggios in running sixteenths, recalling early pieces such as the A-minor Fugue BWV 944. Although this alone cannot be a criterion for dating, the rather simple early version (BWV 902/2) could date from the Weimar period. Its expansion was limited to the interpolation of one passage (mm. 53–64), and the fugue retains its original dashed-off quality. But Bach refined the original counterpoint, which consisted of little more than chords played against the entries of the subject. He also eliminated the free entrance of a fourth voice in some of the chords, although a fourth voice remains implicit in some of the *brisé* figuration of the final version (e.g., mm. 16–9, right hand). The chordal writing in the original, although rare in Bach's surviving fugues, might have reflected the type of counterpoint that arose when fugues were improvised, or when *partimento* fugues such as BWV 907 and 908 were realized (see appendix A).

Whereas the substitution of figuration for staccato chords might have reflected a preference for greater elegance during the *galant* 1730s and 1740s, Bach's changes toward the end of the fugue added fire, or rather humor. The variation of the last two measures takes the form of a downward scale in thirty-seconds, a surprising and much more dramatic close than the conventional final cadence of the original. The new ending remains perfectly in character with the rest of the piece; anything but the merest ritard will ruin its effect.

Prelude and Fugue in G Minor BWV 885

Although the G-major pair is a delight, the G-minor pieces are among the more forbidding in the WTC. The key in itself poses no special problems, but the complex polyphony of the fugue would be difficult in any tonality, and both movements have harsh, angular lines with much passing dissonance. The impression created by the prelude might be somewhat different if it lacked the persistent dotted rhythms and the tempo indication (*Largo*); in that case it would resemble more closely the elaborated arpeggio preludes in C and F. In fact both the tempo mark and the dotting might have been later additions.[50] In any case, as in Contrapunctus 2 of the *Art of Fugue*—which may have undergone similar revision—the dotting is probably not that of an overture but a sort of written-out inequality, to be performed lightly, without emphatic articulation. Persistent over-dotting could grow wearying and transform the "broad" (*largo*) common time into a fussy 8/8.

The fugue is archaic in its rhetorical, repercussive subject and often dense contrapuntal texture. At times it is almost as awkward to play as the A-minor fugue of Part 1, which it resembles in its emphasis on "demonstration counterpoint." There are no episodes to offer any relief, unless one counts the coda beginning at m. 75. Nevertheless, the counterpoint here has fewer rough edges, and the chief contrapuntal device illustrated is rare in Bach's earlier work, one that will be termed "paired entries."[51]

Marpurg called this a double fugue, since there is a regular countersubject.[52] Indeed, the countersubject accompanies every statement of the subject, even in the stretto that opens the fourth and final section (m. 67). "Paired entries" are the topic of the last of the three regular expositions (mm. 45–66), where the subject is doubled in parallel thirds or sixths (Example 12.5). Paired entries are closely related to invertible counterpoint at the tenth—indeed, their presence is a demonstration that the counterpoint between subject and countersubject is invertible at that interval. The relationship between paired entries and invertible counterpoint must have been familiar to learned musicians of the generation or two before Bach, who might have discovered the technique in works by Scheidt or Buxtehude.[53] Yet although invertible counterpoint had long been a favorite topic of writers on fugue, its use at intervals other than the octave is fairly rare even in Bach's late works, appearing systematically only in the B-major fugue of WTC2 and Contrapuncti 9 and 10 of the *Art of Fugue*. Paired entries are equally

Example 12.5 Fugue in G Minor BWV 885/2, mm. 45–7.

rare, and their appearance here could be another manifestation of Bach's late preoccupation with strict counterpoint, indicating that the fugue is not as old as the style of the subject might suggest.

The technique of paired entries has a self-contradictory musical effect. It is impressive intellectually, and it is important in the design of this fugue, since it is reserved for the last regular exposition. Yet its effect is to simplify the texture, since it reduces the number of rhythmically independent parts. Thus, when the demonstration of contrapuntal technique reaches its climax—the simultaneous paired entries of both subject and countersubject at m. 59—there is actually a lightening of the texture and thus a weakening of tension. This impression is reinforced by the sequential character of the subject, which makes the passage sound like an episode. The musical climax occurs a few measures later in one of the most thrilling crescendos in Bach's keyboard music, as the two strands of the texture become more densely interwoven (mm. 62–5).

Prelude and Fugue in A♭, BWV 886

To create the pair in A♭, one of the more imposing in WTC2, Bach joined one of the last-composed preludes to one of the earliest fugues included in the volume. The autograph of the prelude dates from around 1741 (Kobayashi 1988, 46); the style suggests that the music is roughly contemporary with another equally late, spacious movement, the prelude in F♯. As in the latter, there is a pervasive but fairly gentle dotted rhythm, which is combined with triadic figuration. The form is another expansive sonata type, again without double bar, although here the recapitulation begins in the subdominant (m. 50). The closing phrases of the two preludes are very similar, this one exceeding the other in intensity by moving to the Neapolitan (m. 74); the same harmony appears prominently near the end of the fugue (mm. 45–6).[54] In other respects as well the prelude follows a tonal trajectory similar to that of the fugue, touching on the remote regions of B♭ minor and E♭ minor (mm. 42, 53) as well as the more conventional relative and subdominant.

The fugue was originally a short piece in F major, BWV 901/2. Both subject and countersubject represent traditional types, but the canzona-like diatonicism of the subject and the "chromatic fourth" in the countersubject are so different that they are rarely found together in the same piece.[55] The inclusion of the chromatic motive in what is clearly *not* a lament might be explained by Williams's (1997, 5) distinction between "objective" and "subjective" uses of the chromatic idea, only the former occurring here. Monelle (2000, 199) questions the validity of this distinction, which raises the issue of what is objective, and for whom. But it can hardly be controversial to say that in any such combination of diatonic and chromatic *topoi*, neither retains all of the associations that might elsewhere attach to each.

Except for its transposition, the original fughetta remains largely intact, right up to the final chord on the downbeat of m. 24. Yet the expansion changed a relatively simple piece into something profound—perhaps the most impressive instance of Bach's recognizing that more could be done with the material of an earlier work. To judge from the chronology of the London autograph, after copying out most of WTC2 Bach was left without a pair of pieces in A♭. Perhaps he turned to BWV 901 intending to expand both movements to adequate dimensions, but, finding it possible to do this only for the fugue, wrote a new prelude. To the original fugue Bach added twenty-six measures, disguising the seam by adding a fifth entrance of the subject at the end of the second exposition. Thus, one could hardly tell that the point at which the fugue veers off to F minor (m. 24) was originally the end.[56]

The new portion restates a short episode from the first section (mm. 27b–30 || mm. 10–13a). But otherwise the new second half differs considerably from the first. It makes greater use of all four parts; the original was in three voices except in the final phrase, and the appearance of a four-part opening exposition in the revised version remains largely a notational fiction.[57] In addition, the modulations in the second half range farther than in the first, reaching E♭ minor (m. 32).[58] These modulations realize the implications of the countersubject, whose chromaticism signified the potential of remote modulation and expressive voice leading but remained largely decorative in the early version, where the subject enters only on tonic and dominant.

Contrapuntal technique as such is not the focus of either half of the fugue. But the new section includes an entry *per arsin et thesin* (bass, m. 37), as well as a double stretto involving both subject and countersubject (m. 41). The latter occurs here in a variation that turns it into a chain of suspensions, intensifying the passage in which the tonic returns. As in the E-minor fugue, the added music also includes a fermata, followed by a quasi cadenza (mm. 46b–47). This leads to a concluding restatement of the subject, bolstered by an additional voice—a heightened form of the ending used in the original fughetta.

Prelude and Fugue in G♯ Minor BWV 887

Had the prelude in G♯ minor been written a half step lower (as it might have been originally; see NBA V/6.2, KB, 250–1 and 320), it would surely be one of the more popular pieces in WTC2. It is a fiery sonata movement surpassing the one in the related key of D♯ minor in vigor, dimensions, and richness of material. In the opening theme, *galant* "sighs" in parallel thirds are set against violinistic figuration; similar ideas occur in the F-minor prelude, but here they are combined contrapuntally from the start. Both are extensively developed; it is odd, therefore, that Bach does nothing with the echo at m. 3, the *piano* there and the subsequent *forte* being the only dynamic indications in the WTC.

There is more to wonder about in the following movement, a long double fugue in three voices whose two subjects are introduced separately, then combined. The first subject is that of a gigue, but its monotonous rhythm (all eighths) and simplistic sequential phrasing (2 + 2 measures) give it a static quality reminiscent of Reinken's gigue themes, such as the one adopted by Bach in the last movement of the Sonata BWV 965. The second subject is chromatic, forming an antithesis with the first subject similar to that seen in the fugue in A♭, or in the much earlier A-minor double fugue BWV 904/2. But the present second subject is oddly banal, merely descending from the tonic through a fourth and then climbing back up.

The weaknesses of the subjects are reflected in the fugue as a whole, which is unusually monochromatic for a mature Bach work. Entries of the subject in the first section are limited to tonic and dominant, and the only significant modulation to a major key (E) is brief and late (m. 111). An episode in the second section (mm. 82–93) moves halfway around the circle of fifths, but like the second subject it winds up where it started, on the tonic. Hence, the fugue compares unfavorably with the other double fugue in three parts, in C♯ minor. One possible explanation is that the present fugue was an early effort, presumably transposed from G minor; the absence of any significant differences between the autograph and Altnikol's texts would support this. Yet the episodes show what seems to be a mark of Bach's later fugues, the disciplined canonic or permutational treatment of motives derived from the first subject.[59]

To reduce the risk of monotony, harpsichordists can vary the registration of the three sections. On a two-manual instrument (already required by the prelude), one can play the first section on one keyboard, the second section on the other, and the third section with the two keyboards coupled.[60] There is no evidence that Bach would have changed registration in the middle of a harpsichord fugue, but this is precisely the sort of work in which it can be done convincingly today.

Prelude and Fugue in A, BWV 888

From his youth Bach evidently associated the key of A with closely worked imitative counterpoint, as witness the early fugues BWV 896/2 and 949. In the WTC, both A-major preludes are three-part sinfonias, as is the prelude of the First English Suite, also in A. The latter is particularly close to the prelude in WTC2, as both pieces are moderately paced gigues in 12/8 and share many other features besides (for a possible model, see chap. 13). The present prelude adopts a sort of sonata form; the middle section (mm. 9b–16) uses the inversion of the theme, but the prime form returns at the beginning of the retransition (mm. 16–9). The two forms alternate at the beginning of the last section, which is largely a recapitulation of the first (mm. 22–30a ‖ 1–9a). The restated material is somewhat disguised; in addition to being transposed down a fifth, with upper voices exchanged, the passage introduces a few small alterations that are sufficient to transform one measure, originally planted firmly on the tonic (m. 3), into a wistful glance toward B minor (m. 24).

The fugue is reminiscent of the one in E from Part 1. Both are in three voices, with light, airy figuration. Both are also short, of exactly the same length although differently organized. This fugue can be divided into three segments of about ten measures each, although the absence of clearly articulated episodes makes it hard to find unambiguous formal divisions. A restatement of the subject in the bass at m. 16 may seem the most important articulation of the piece, but at some point Bach undercut it by deleting two sixteenth notes (AA–E) on the downbeat.[61] The rare low AA, an impressive sonority in the present context, appears in some relatively early works, including the First English Suite. Its deletion not only brings the keyboard compass of the piece into conformity with that used elsewhere in the WTC; it clarifies the form, for arguably a more crucial moment is the entry of the subject at m. 20. This marks the start of a "subdominant reprise," preceded by the most dramatic two measures in the little piece.

Prelude and Fugue in A Minor BWV 889

The Prelude and Fugue in A minor is another short one, on paper. But the repeats in the prelude double its length, and the vociferous character of its fugue makes it seem bigger than it really is.

The prelude has a symmetrical, mosaic-like construction recalling that of the C-Minor Invention and the E-minor fugue of WTC1, here comprising units of one measure rather than two. Parallels could also be drawn to the four Duetti, which were at least roughly contemporary and at times use equally harsh chromatic counterpoint. The symmetry is very nearly exact, but Bach as usual breaks it at a crucial point. The double bar divides the piece into two equal halves, the second opening as a nearly exact inversion of the first. Each half is further subdivided, and the two divisions of the first half are virtually identical, save for the exchange and transposition of the two voices. But symmetry is replaced by free composition toward the end of the second half, where the established pattern of one-measure units grouped in pairs is interrupted by three measures in which the right hand has regular sequential figuration (mm. 27–9). Within the present context, this is a dramatic event, and as such it prepares the final cadence.

To be sure, the prelude remains something of a mathematical game, but this is a characterization that only the innumerate will find derogatory. The pervasive chromaticism is part of this game; this is not the "subjective" chromaticism of, say, the B-minor fugue in WTC1, but an intellectually playful "objective" variety related to the speculative or abstract chromaticism of many early Baroque ricercars and similar pieces. This is not to say that one should not articulate the individual chromatic intervals and dwell expressively on certain dissonances. But although chromaticism is associated with strict counterpoint *and* extreme pathos in some pieces, this does not seem to be one of them. The numerous accidentals raise some textual problems, but the allusive nature of the two-part harmony makes it difficult to settle them by analysis.[62]

The fugue subject opens with the same four-note motive as the choral fugue "And with His Stripes" in *Messiah*. But as the latter was written in 1741, Bach could only have drawn on the same common tradition as did Handel.[63] Nor can the pieces have anything like the same expressive character: Handel's is a strict fugue alluding to *stile antico*, whereas Bach's is one of the freest in the WTC, and its mercurial style—especially the brusque ending—suggests that it should not be taken too seriously.

The thirty-second notes in the countersubject might once have been staccato eighths, a continuation of those at the end of the subject.[64] But the flying thirty-seconds are aptly juxtaposed against the four stentorian quarters that open the subject, and they extend the acceleration in surface rhythm that begins within the subject itself, whose initial rhythmic motive is repeated (after a pause) in half the original values. The acceleration culminates with the trill that is first heard in m. 4, thereafter as a distinct motive developed in sequence in mm. 18b–21b and in the novel final cadence. The latter cleverly transfers the conventional cadential trill from the soprano to the alto and finally to the bass.

Prelude and Fugue in B♭, BWV 890

The prelude in B♭ is the longest of the sonata-form preludes of the WTC. Its opening measure could have been suggested by several preludes in Fischer's *Ariadne musica*, especially the one in G. As a whole the piece is particularly similar to Bach's C-minor fantasia (BWV 906/1), another sonata movement with a hand-crossing passage in each half.[65] The prelude is more relaxed than the slightly frenetic C-minor fantasia, again suggesting that for Bach the 12/16 signature does not indicate particularly rapid motion. Although the central section ("development") is of roughly the same length in both pieces, the outer sections here are more expansive. Exceptionally for music of this date, they contain distinct subdivisions analogous to the first and second theme-groups of Classical sonata form (mm. 21, 65). Yet the hand-crossing passage is recapitulated not in the final section but in the central one, with the roles of the two hands reversed, as in the fantasia.

Example 12.6 Prelude in Bb, BWV 890/1, (a) mm. 12–4; (b) analysis

Even if the tempo is the same as in the gigue-like fugues in C# minor and F—notated in 12/16 and 6/16, respectively—the slower harmonic rhythm and the opening pedal point make this more of a pastorale. The hand crossings do not contradict this impression, for in each case they grow naturally out of the texture of the preceding phrase; they do not open up new registers but represent continuations of the underlying voice leading (Example 12.6). Indeed, these passages, unlike the corresponding ones in the C-minor fantasia, could be played without crossing the hands, although this would require dividing the running triplets between them.

The fugue is short relative to the prelude, but it shares the latter's relaxed character, thanks to the slow harmonic rhythm, generally just one harmony per measure. The form is close to that of a sonata movement, and the phrase that brings the first section to a close in the dominant (mm. 29–32) returns at the end in the tonic. This little tag, with its bass of repeated notes, is particularly close to homophonic sonata style. Its appearance at the end is a little sudden, like the closing phrase in the F-major fugue, but it is graceful and unpretentious.

The copy in the London autograph belongs to the second layer, which often gives later readings. But Bach subsequently rewrote several passages, including the first countersubject, which originally moved in quarters (Example 12.7b).

Example 12.7 Fugue in Bb, BWV 890/2: (a) mm. 5–8; (b) mm. 5–6, early version (bass)

Example 12.8 Fugue in B♭, BWV 890/2, mm. 87–90, (a) early version (upper staff); (b) later version

Another revision casts light on an odd embellishment of the alto in the closing phrase. The figuration of the later version was a way of reconciling the original four-note chord with the prevailing three-voice texture (Example 12.8). Bach renotated the entire phrase, making explicit some of the polyphony latent in the original, although the two-part writing for the right hand remains something of a notational fiction.

Prelude and Fugue in B♭ Minor BWV 891

The pieces in B♭ minor occupy a position analogous to that of the B-minor prelude and fugue in WTC1, since they are the last "big" pair of Part 2, perhaps even its crowning moment. The prelude, though not as exact an imitation of trio-sonata style as the B-minor prelude of Part 1, is a three-part sinfonia, the longest and most substantial that Bach wrote. The fugue is a mature version of the rigorously contrapuntal yet expressive type that Bach had attempted in the D♯-minor fugue of Part 1.

The cut time of the prelude distinguishes it from the earlier B-minor prelude, which was marked andante. The tempo here must be closer to that of the fugue in F♯ in Part 2, for a less flowing tempo would cause the many suspensions and especially the dominant pedal point near the end (mm. 73–6) to lose tension. A recapitulation starts in the subdominant at m. 55, but there is no central double bar, and formally the movement is closer to some of the larger fugues than the sonata-form preludes: expository passages based on the material of the opening measures alternate with canonic episodes.

The fugue is a large-scale demonstration of stretto and inversion. Prime and inverted forms of the subject are introduced in distinct expositions (mm. 1, 42) and strettos (mm. 27, 67) before being combined (m. 80). Use of the augmented form of the subject is essentially ruled out by the piece's triple meter. As a climactic gesture Bach instead plays the trump card previously glimpsed in the G-minor fugue: paired entries, here applied to a close canon between *rectus* and *inversus* forms of the subject. The subject is one of Bach's most distinctive, punctuated by rests into four rhythmically diverse fragments. Dots added in Altnikol's copy P 430 on the first two notes reinforce the subject's declamatory quality, so long as they are understood to mean accentuation and separation, rather than staccato in the modern sense. Two tritones in the subject (mm. 2, 4) foreshadow the chromaticism of the countersubject, which is inverted along with the subject in the *inversus* exposition at m. 42. The countersubject plays no part in the strettos; still, Marpurg would have considered this a double fugue.[66]

The fugue returns to the tonic at the beginning of each major division, save for the last. Yet it is far from monochromatic, reaching G♭ major and A♭ minor during the *inversus* exposition (mm. 42–62). There is even an augmented sixth in m. 59, in the course of a statement of the inversion in A♭ minor, about the furthest modulation from the tonic. By contrast to the G-minor fugue (or the D♯-minor fugue of WTC1), which concentrates almost single-mindedly on the contrapuntal development of the subject, episodes—or, at least, bridges—play an essential role here. Their sequential, generally diatonic, character furnishes a respite from the expositions, though they too are canonic or permutational. No two of these passages use exactly the same material, but three (at mm. 31, 77, and 84) are related by their use of hemiola, being effectively in 4/4 time. This idea perhaps grew out of the strettos, which are at the interval of a half note, thus producing cross-rhythms against the underlying meter (3/2).

The fugue was originally written in 3/4, in half its present values.[67] But Altnikol copied it in 3/2, and it may be that his lost exemplar contained a verbal indication directing copyists to double the note values, such as occurs in the autograph of Contrapunctus 8 in the *Art of Fugue*. Bach's apparent uncertainty as to the best way to notate such pieces could reflect changing conceptions of the tempo, which might have slowed down in response to the dense counterpoint found especially in the later sections.

Prelude and Fugue in B, BWV 892

Bach's strictest contrapuntal exercises are usually in minor keys. But the fugue in B is a major exception, and with its prelude it forms one of the most impressive pairs of WTC2, on the same high level as the preceding one. The two movements of the B-major pair, unlike those in B♭ minor, are of virtually opposite types. The prelude, the freest in WTC2, has a roughly ternary design whose central section (mm. 12–36) is a sort of improvisation in concerto style. The fugue is in *stile antico*, with notable parallels to the *Art of Fugue* in its learned counterpoint, which is somewhat more abstract than elsewhere in the WTC (e.g., with more numerous voice crossings that cannot be made readily audible).

The first section of the prelude resembles the corresponding passage in the A♭-major prelude of Part 1; either might have served as the opening section of a sonata movement. After reaching the dominant, however, the B-major prelude passes through a delightful series of short-lived changes of texture, twice introducing a third voice, then soloistic arpeggiation of the type found in the solo sections of Bach's harpsichord concertos. Motion in sixteenths is virtually the only factor common throughout the prelude, although the "Alberti" bass at m. 23b can be traced to a motive from the first section (m. 3, beat 2). Eventually there is a recapitulation, largely reworked, that begins at m. 37. Perhaps the closest parallel in Bach's work is the last movement of the D-major gamba sonata (BWV 1028), whose penultimate section includes soloistic passages for each of the two players. Preparing the recapitulation is an emphatic pause on the dominant, preceded by eight repeated, dissonant chords in the left hand (m. 35). The same formula occurs in the C-minor fantasia, where it seems less appropriate as it comes at an earlier and less critical juncture in the form.[68]

The following movement deserves to be called a double fugue, even though the second subject, introduced at m. 28, is presented on its own only twice, elsewhere always accompanying the first subject. Butler (1983b, 296–7) suggests that the odd melodic leaps in the subject reflect the tradition of the contrapuntal *obligo*, in which the composer follows some rule governing the counterpoint or voice leading; the rule here would be to avoid motion by step.[69] If so, however, Bach abandons the *obligo* after the third measure, and despite its angular subject the fugue as a whole has some of the most serene four-part writing in WTC2, in this respect resembling Contrapuncti 4 and 10 of the *Art of Fugue*.

Contrapunctus 4 is relatively late, but Contrapunctus 10 belongs with Contrapunctus 9 to the first layer of the *Art of Fugue*; these as well as the B-major fugue might have been drafted around 1740. All three pieces are double fugues concerned with combining two subjects in particular types of invertible counterpoint; the B-major fugue involves counterpoint invertible at both the octave (m. 27) and the twelfth (mm. 42–5, 53–8).[70] By changing the time interval between the two entries of the two subjects, Bach later combines them in a third way (mm. 60–3). Even a sharp listener is unlikely to recognize the different types of invertible counterpoint without a score. But each variety of counterpoint places certain constraints on the intervals used in combining the two subjects, and this has an audible effect on the harmony. Fifths, for example, must be avoided in counterpoint at the twelfth, since they produce dissonant fourths upon inversion. In this case the combination of the two subjects embellishes what is essentially a series of parallel thirds.

The episode in mm. 64–74 stands out for its departure from the general emphasis on "demonstration counterpoint." The episode, which serves as retransition,[71] involves only the three upper parts, yet it makes a modest departure from the fugue's prevailing restraint in matters of harmony and rhythm, even introducing sixteenths during the climbing sequence in mm. 68–70. The subsequent re-entry of the bass with a statement of the subject (m. 75) therefore has some of the same effect as the concluding entries in the F-minor and B-minor fugues of WTC1, while serving as a sonata-style return.

Prelude and Fugue in B Minor BWV 893

Although WTC1 closes with one of its most impressive pairs, WTC2 does not. This might be a problem if either volume was meant to be played through in order. But of course this is not the case, and though light and a bit quirky the present B-minor pieces are by no means inferior or disappointing. The prelude is of the invention type, composed mainly of two equal voices, and for this reason one might wish to play it as a duet, on two lightly registered manuals. But the closing passage grows suddenly demonstrative, including a few full chords that imply a strong registration on a single manual. There are no signs that the closing section was a late addition, although Bach certainly revised the prelude; both Altnikol's 1744 copy (P 430) and the London autograph contain corrections showing that they were copied from an earlier version written in common time, using half the present note values. As in the fugue in B♭ minor, Bach's ideas about tempo must have evolved, and in this case he was clearly responsible for a tempo mark (*allegro*) added to the version in larger note values. In his 1744 copy (P 430) Altnikol also added staccato marks on the chords in m. 64; these make it clear that the outer voices of the two chords, although moving by half step, do not form slurred appoggiaturas such as appear in the soprano in the previous two measures.

Emanuel Bach presumably knew this prelude. His "Württemberg" sonata in the same key at one point comes to rest on the same diminished chord, graced by the same appoggiatura, as appears under the fermata in m. 57.[72] The sonata dates from 1744, and its closing movement in two voices also resembles an invention; these aspects of the sonata could have been inspired by his receiving a copy of WTC2 around this time, as suggested by Franklin (1989b, 276).

The octave leaps in the fugue subject give it a jolly character, but they pose problems of practicability in keyboard writing, as Bach would have known from his experience in earlier works (e.g., the Capriccio BWV 992). Thus Bach knew he was compounding the problem in the second exposition (mm. 27ff.), where he abandoned the first countersubject in favor of a new one whose wide leaps suggest violinistic string crossings. This second countersubject accompanies each of the remaining statements of the subject, despite the repeated voice crossings that result when the two subjects are placed in the same register (mm. 57–9). This would be frowned upon in a school fugue, but it serves very well as pure keyboard figuration, and the voice crossings are more easily seen on paper than heard in performance.

The dissonant appoggiaturas on the final chord are a later addition, absent from the London autograph.[73] Although they call to mind the ornament on the final sonority of the Saint Matthew Passion, they probably should not be taken as seriously nor held as long. The last phrase (mm. 97–100) is a partial stretto based on the first five notes of the subject, and the final entry (soprano, m. 99) is embellished. The fugue closes by converting its opening gesture into a final cadence—an understatedly witty way of ending the volume.

13
The English Suites

Bach's Later Suites

Next to the *Well-Tempered Clavier* and the inventions, Bach's best-known keyboard works are the suites that he composed, or at least collected and revised, during the 1720s and early 1730s. The twenty-one works in question include the six English Suites, the six French Suites, and the seven large suites (six partitas and an *ouverture*) published in Parts 1 and 2 of the *Clavierübung*. In addition there are two suites (BWV 818 and 819) that can be considered in conjunction with the French Suites, as well as three compositions for lute that resemble suites and were probably played on the lute-harpsichord and other keyboard instruments.

The suite is often viewed as the early eighteenth-century harpsichord genre par excellence. In Germany such music must often have been played on the clavichord, but by Bach's day suites were often specifically designated as harpsichord pieces, and the closeness of Bach's idiom to that of contemporary French music for harpsichord leaves little doubt that the latter was the preferred instrument. A more significant question is whether a suite was seen as anything more than a collection of pieces in a common tonality. Unlike earlier variation-suites, none of Bach's mature suites shows a significant amount of thematic material shared between movements; at most, the movements of a given suite may be generally similar in texture or character (e.g., the light, *galant* manner of French Suite no. 6). Certainly Bach planned the tonalities and contents of the three collections with some care. No set repeats a key, and with few exceptions each suite includes one each of what had become by the early eighteenth century the four standard movements (allemande, courante, sarabande, gigue). With each set, the variety and colorfulness of the individual dance movements increased, reflecting general trends, although unlike Rameau or François Couperin, Bach never (or almost never) composed named character pieces. He retained the traditional, abstract dance titles even as he left conventional dance types increasingly far behind.

Bach's suites were used for teaching, according to E. L. Gerber (BD 3:476 [item 950]/NBR, 322). But whereas Bach's extended titles for WTC1 and the Inventions stressed the works' pedagogic value, the printed title pages for the Partitas indicate that they are for the "spiritual delight" or "refreshment" of amateurs.[1] Nevertheless, Bach might have viewed his suites as lessons in style or, to use the eighteenth-century term, good taste (*le bon goût*)—a concept that, within the realm of the keyboard suite, was virtually synonymous with the French style of composition and performance.

Indeed, Bach's suites document his mastery of the French style of the day, as well as his incorporation of "German" harmony—that is, imitative counterpoint—into the predominantly homophonic tradition of the *pièce de clavecin*. Bach had begun to accomplish these things in the early suites considered in chapter 4, but those would have seemed outmoded by the 1720s. Except for the lute suite BWV 996—which seems relatively late and could be contemporary with the English Suites—the early suites appear to have been modeled on French or German compositions of the previous generation. The later suites reflect Bach's knowledge of more recent French harpsichord music—certainly that of Dieupart, whose suites Bach copied at Weimar between 1709 and 1716, and probably Couperin as well.[2]

In most of these works—especially the A-Minor Suite BWV 818 and individual movements from the English Suites—one senses a tension between Bach's impulses as a keyboard virtuoso and contrapuntist, on the one hand, and the niceties of the French *pièce de clavecin* on the other. Moreover, Bach, not content to imitate individual models, tended to mix styles and genres. The preludes in five of the English Suites are in concerto style, that is, the style of Italian orchestral music. On the other hand, two later opening movements take the form of a French overture, and the dances as well often suggest inspiration from French-style orchestral music. Still, Bach tended to replace the French *courante* and *gigue*, normally written in 3/2 and 6/4, with the Italian *corrente* and *giga*, respectively; although ostensibly dances, some of these are indistinguishable from binary-form or sonata movements in 3/4 and 6/8. The full harmony in some of Bach's sarabandes continues a tradition found in earlier German examples and a few of Couperin's. But in some sarabandes Bach also wrote out Italianate embellishment, making these movements resemble an ornamented adagio. He also extended imitative technique—traditionally present in the gigue—to the other dances, especially allemandes and courantes.

The language used for the title of a movement sometimes indicates the prevailing national style.[3] But Bach was inconsistent in this regard, and the essential ethos of the suite remains French. Even in heavily Italianized dances, the basic rhythmic schemes usually derive from the music of French court and theatrical dance. So do many melodic formulas—ornaments above all, but also distinctive cadential gestures like the *tierce coulée*, a formula used in metrically weak phrase endings. Moreover, Bach's suites, like all his mature keyboard works, follow the French tradition of precise notation. In their latest versions, all essential ornaments are indicated by signs or written out in notes, and every detail of the *style brisé* is made explicit through the pseudo-polyphonic notation developed during the seventeenth century to spell out the broken chords of idiomatic harpsichord writing.

German musicians such as Bach must have been conscious at all times of the imported nature of the suite. Players would have deliberately applied everything they knew about current French performing practice, including the use of *notes inégales* (which can soften the sometimes harsh voice leading of these pieces). Yet some German musicians explicitly aimed to create a distinctive style of their own. This emerges from the prefaces to Kuhnau's published collections of suites, from which Bach borrowed the title *Clavierübung* for his first keyboard publication. The selection and ordering of movements in Bach's suites may have depended more on the examples furnished by Kuhnau, Fischer, and other German composers than on French works. Bourrées, passepieds, and even gigues are by no means as common in French suites as they are in Bach's. Moreover, German examples of the dances tend to avoid—whether intentionally or not—the more elusive stylistic characteristics of their models, instead favoring sequences and other types of regular patterning, such as thematic parallelisms between the two halves of a binary form. The greater formal regularity of the dance movements in German suites, particularly the allemandes and courantes, makes them more accessible for modern musicians and listeners than their French models, which can seem formless and even irrational. Conversely, the Bach dance movements least likely to appeal to modern taste are those closest to the style of d'Anglebert or Couperin, like the two courantes of the First English Suite.

The ability to recognize the dances from their rhythms and melodic shapes, and to infer from the latter the tempo and general character of a given dance movement, would have been taken for granted by any European musician of Bach's generation. It is not possible to give a full account here of the individual dances. In general, each is associated not only with a particular meter and tempo but with specific patterns of stressed and unaccented beats, and in some cases particular motives or textures, such as the arpeggiations associated with the keyboard allemande. Not every piece designated as a dance possesses all of the features identified with the dance named in its title. But most dance movements reflect the geometric character of eighteenth-century choreography in their construction from clearly delineated phrases of four or eight measures, often arranged in a symmetrical binary form. There is usually a double bar at the center, and although few dances are full-fledged sonata forms with distinct recapitulation sections, many are in rounded binary form, that is, with a reprise of the opening phrase in the tonic somewhere toward the end of the second half. A few dance movements were even composed for sonatas (see chap. 15 on Partita no. 6). Their inclusion within a suite represents a blurring of the distinction between dance and sonata—that is, between French and Italian styles—also seen in keyboard pieces by Bach's best contemporaries, notably Handel and Rameau, and even in Corelli's violin sonatas and concerti grossi.

The suite as a whole, that is, an ordered series of dances and other movements in the same key, emerged as a distinct genre only during Bach's youth. Bach, like Kuhnau, avoided the term in his published works, using instead the word *partita* and specifying on the title page that each consisted of "preludes, allemandes, courantes... and other gallantries."[4] Hence Bach may still have regarded his suites primarily as collections of individual movements; the adoption of a standard order (allemande, courante, sarabande, gigue) in most manuscript and printed sources of the time does not mean that composers composed suites as such, nor that performers played them.[5]

This is evident from the manner in which some of Bach's suites grew through the addition of minuets and other movements. Some of the suites, like some of Bach's preludes and fugues, may have been assembled in part from previously existing material, although this can be proved only in the case of the Sixth Partita. By the same token, the grouping of most of Bach's suites into three neat half-dozens can be traced back only to the mid-1720s or so. Bach appears to have juggled several suites into and out of the collection now known as the French Suites, finally arriving at a more or less rational ordering scheme based on tonality, as in the WTC. Such a scheme can also be detected in the Partitas, but not in the English Suites, whose arrangement may reflect either the order of composition or the increasing difficulty and complexity of the individual suites.

As with most of Bach's keyboard works the loss of autograph material leaves the early history of the suites far from clear. Bach was once thought to have written most of the keyboard suites, together with the orchestral suites and the suites for unaccompanied violin, cello, and flute, at Cöthen, that is, between 1717 and 1723. But considerations of style and transmission imply that the English Suites are earlier, dating back to the Weimar period. What appear to be composing scores for portions of the French Suites survive from the Cöthen years; the Partitas are known only from later sources. Composers like Kuhnau and Couperin had used published suites as a means of bringing their music to a wider public, and at some point Bach is likely to have begun envisioning publication for his own suites. But practical considerations—the absence of a patron, or the dim prospect that such long, complex works as the English Suites would find buyers—evidently forced him to postpone publication until 1726, when he began to issue the Partitas. Nevertheless, the two earlier sets, although circulated only in manuscript, represent ideal publications of the sort that Bach might have issued had circumstances permitted.

Publication, real or ideal, did not prevent Bach from revising the suites in the same ways as the WTC. Bach continued to add ornaments and other small revisions even after the works had been widely copied or, in the case of the Partitas, printed. Copyists must have made their own additions, some perhaps on the basis of oral tradition, including lessons with Bach. Manuscript copies of the English Suites preserve a relatively uniform text. But since we possess no fair-copy autographs for either the English or French Suites in their final versions, it is difficult to verify individual ornament signs, slurs, and other textual details in these pieces. The critical editions of these works by Alfred Dürr (NBA V/7–8), although immensely valuable, necessarily leave many details open to question; for those without German, the more recent editions by Dehnhard for the English Suites (Wiener Urtext, 1998) and Jones for the French Suites (Associated Board, 1985) provide useful summaries in English.[6] Reprints of the BG and other old editions remain available but cannot be recommended. The BG actually contained two separate editions of the French and English Suites; the first, in BG 13, was so poor that the works were re-edited in BG 45 (see Becker 1953). Dover unfortunately reprinted the version of BG 13, but even the later BG edition mixes readings from different versions and is therefore unreliable.

The English Suites

The English Suites stand midway between the French Suites and the Partitas in length and in the demands they make on the player. Yet they are probably the earliest of the three collections, composed during the second decade of the eighteenth century.[7] The five preludes in concerto style have clear affinities not only with Bach's concerto transcriptions but with his large virtuoso preludes and fugues and the Brandenburg Concertos, all of which may have originated at Weimar. The dance movements, especially the allemandes and courantes, also suggest an early date, inasmuch as they still reflect the style of older German and French keyboard dances. Several allemandes open with what appear to be rhapsodic improvisations recalling Froberger. The courantes are all of the French type (in 3/2 or 6/4), even when attached to an Italianate walking bass, as in Suite no. 6. Only one movement, the gigue of Suite no. 1, contains dynamic markings, although these are perhaps implicit in the concerto scoring of the preludes, some of which might incorporate manual changes, implying that a large double-keyboard French harpsichord is a possible medium.

Bach's incorporation of a substantial amount of imitative counterpoint into so many movements of a keyboard suite had few precedents. But the allemandes in Dieupart's suites had a significant contrapuntal element, which might explain Bach's interest in them.[8] One consequence of the emphasis on counterpoint, however, was writing that is occasionally awkward or unidiomatic. Bach must have been aware of certain rough spots—for example, the stuttering repetition of the sixteenth note b′ in the allemande of Suite no. 2 (m. 2)—but tolerated them because they were justified by the voice leading and by the strength of the underlying musical thought.

The intensive counterpoint, although contrary to the character of the dances as received from the French, might have been a response to the apparent form-lessness even of polyphonically conceived dances such as Marchand's, which, however impressive their voice leading and local harmony, lack logical designs of the types found in these Suites. In Bach's later suites, counterpoint as such is less of an issue, and the writing is more obviously idiomatic to the keyboard; the style is more *galant*, with singing melodies and more transparent textures. Hence, the French Suites and the Partitas give the impression of being more polished than the English Suites, which, even on their own terms, may not be entirely successful. For example, the gigue of Suite no. 1 contains rather too many sequences of running sixteenths in two voices—a favorite device in Bach's early fugues and in the concerto transcriptions. At the risk of sounding like Scheibe, one may also complain that, especially in the courantes, the contrapuntal en-richment of the texture does not always compensate for the lack of an engaging melody. Thus, in the courante of Suite no. 6, what may seem a good idea in the abstract—the combination of French melody and Italian walking bass—proves dull in the realization.

The first suite differs from the others not only in the style of its prelude—which resembles a sinfonia (three-part invention) rather than a concerto—but in the presence of two courantes, the second being accompanied by two doubles. Its key, A, does not fit into the descending sequence of the others (a–g–F–e–d), and it is the only one of the English Suites to survive in a distinct early version, BWV 806a. Of the remaining suites, no. 2 is simpler in style and sparer in texture than the rest, at least in the outer movements. It is possible that no. 1 on the whole is later, no. 2 earlier, than the others, but all six suites may contain individual movements that were composed at various dates. On the whole, with the excep-tion of no. 1 these suites give the impression of a consistent style that departs imaginatively from the norms of the genre as Bach knew it. This is clearest in the most ambitious movements: the lengthy Italianate preludes, the harmonically adventurous and sometimes darkly expressive sarabandes, and the gigues, which although rigorously contrapuntal rarely involve more than two real voices and are therefore relatively transparent.

The sources show that Suite no. 1 was probably not an original member of the set, whose contents were probably fixed only after 1725 (see Table 13.1).[9] If Bach had any general title for the set, it was probably something straightforward and pragmatic: "suites with preludes" or the like.[10] The familiar designation as "English" suites does not occur in any early source, but it was already known to Forkel, who called the pieces "Six great suites…known by the name of the English Suites because the composer made them for an Englishman of rank."[11] Forkel wrote as if the title was already well known, having previously referred

Table 13.1 English Suites: Chief Early Sources

Ms.	Copyist, Date	Contents (Suite Nos.)	Comments
P 803, pp. 265–85	Walther, after 1712	BWV 806a	Sole source for early version of Suite no. 1
P 1072	Kayser, ca. 1717–25	1–6	Suite no. 1 originally separate, up to courante 2 earlier than rest. Basis of BG; formerly considered autograph
HAu 12 C 14–17	Gerber, 1725	1, 3, 5–6	Copied from P 1072; some unique (later?) readings. Group included French Suite no. 6, with prelude from WTC1
P 803, pp. 365ff.	J. T. Krebs	2, 6	No. 6 copied from Gerber ms.
AmB 489	Anon. 436 + Agricola	1–6	Gives later readings. Additions by Agricola, 1738–40. Later entries by Kirnberger
P 419	Kittel + Michel	1–6	Kittel copied Suite No. 1, part of Suite no. 2; made alterations in the rest
Private ownership	C. F. C. Fasch	1–6	

to the "English" suites without further identifying them (Forkel 1802, 28/NBR, 445). His explanation for the name would be more credible if we had evidence that Bach had ever given a copy to a visiting Englishman. There is nothing English about the music itself; suites published in England by Dieupart and Mattheson include preludial movements of various sorts, but this trait was by no means uniquely English.[12]

English Suite no. 1 in A, BWV 806

Bach might have made the A-major suite the first of the "suites with preludes" because of the brevity of its prelude. By then he probably had revised the suite to essentially its familiar form.[13] The early version (BWV 806a), preserved by Walther, gives a slightly shorter version of the prelude. It also lacks one of the two doubles or variations for the second courante, as well as the second bourrée. Besides adding these movements, the later version shows many small refinements in voice leading, ornamentation, and articulation, especially in the prelude, the courantes, and the sarabande.[14]

The prelude is not the only movement to differ stylistically from those of the other English Suites. The second courante is not at all imitative, whereas the sarabande, even in the early version (BWV 806a), is somewhat more heavily embellished than the sarabandes of the other suites. The gigue, though in principle imitative, is relatively simple in texture, closer in this respect to the gigues of the French Suites and the E-minor lute suite. Hence, there is reason to suspect that even the early version was composed after the remaining English Suites. Even if so, BWV 806 remains closer to them than to Bach's later suites. The concern with variation, seen in the two doubles for courante 2, recurs in the *agrémens* and the double attached to sarabandes in three of the other English Suites.[15] Courante 1 has the same invention-like imitations as the courantes of Suites nos. 2, 4, and 5, and the second double for courante 2 combines a French type of courante melody with a walking bass, like the courante of the sixth suite.

The prelude, however, is close to the A-major Sinfonia and the two A-major preludes of the WTC, especially that of WTC2, with which it shares its 12/8 time and the use of a short (half-measure) subject that is later inverted. The passages added in the revised version (mm. 10, 16b–17a) strengthen the most crucial articulations, the arrivals on the dominant (m. 9b) and the relative minor (m. 16b).

The brief flourish that opens the prelude (and the collection) recurs in the organ chorale *Vom Himmel hoch* BWV 738; the common use of an improvisational formula supports dating both works to Bach's Weimar years. The main subject of the prelude also occurs elsewhere; it is close to the themes of two gigues, also in A, by French composers whose music Bach probably knew when he composed the piece. One gigue is that of Dieupart's first suite, which Bach copied; the other appears in Gaspard Le Roux's *Pièces de clavecin* (Paris, 1705).[16] The pitches in Bach's theme come somewhat closer to Le Roux's, but the rhythm is more like Dieupart's (Example 13.1).[17]

Example 13.1 (a) Dieupart, *Première Suite*, gigue, mm. 1–6; (b) Le Roux, Gigue, mm. 0–3; (c) English Suite no. 1 in A, BWV 806, prelude, mm. 3–5 (lower voices omitted in each).

Whatever Bach's source, the parallels between the three pieces are too extensive to have arisen by chance.[18] The parallels suggest that the prelude should be understood as a gigue—and not, for example, as a gentler pastorale. They also have some bearing on the interpretation of the ornament sign first seen at the end of m. 3. Dieupart calls for a trill with a concluding turn, a complex ornament that cannot be played cleanly if the tempo is too quick. The most authoritative Bach sources add to that sign a preliminary turn from above, but even at a moderate tempo (not inappropriate for a French gigue), there is no time to play the resulting *Doppel-Cadenz*.[19] Perhaps what the copyists took to be an initial turn was meant to be a simple *appuy* (a lengthening of the initial, upper note of the trill); it may be more practical to reduce the ornament to a simple turn.

The allemande's opening pedal point and broken-chord figuration place it in the Froberger tradition. Yet the figuration is not as rhapsodic as it first appears. The texture is contrapuntal, and there are usually at least three real parts; the opening phrase contains an expressive rising scale in the tenor. The opening thematic material recurs at several points, particularly in the four-measure closing phrase of each half (over a dominant rather than tonic pedal). These restatements, and the almost verbatim repetition of mm. 9–10a at m. 12, impose a degree of thematic unity on the traditional improvisatory model. That in turn implies a disciplining of the rhythmic freedom appropriate to older allemandes, though not so much as to lead to stiffness.

The courantes are in a purer French style, demonstrating Bach's mastery of the sophisticated rhythm of the dance. A French courante typically comprises a succession of small gestures whose various rhythmic shapes can be projected through subtle effects of timing and articulation. Hemiolas—shifts from 3/2 to 6/4—are the best known of the dance's metrical quirks, but in both courantes Bach confines them to the final measure of each half. Elsewhere the metrical play is more subtle. For example, the first phrase of courante 1 (mm. 1–5) consists of a series of gestures beginning on the downbeat, or rather on the preceding eighth-note upbeat (Example 13.2). But the first gesture in the following phrase begins with c#′′ in the middle of m. 5, ending with the embellished *tierce coulée* on the downbeat of m. 6. The next gesture begins squarely on the second beat (f#′′). This sequence of events—a *tierce coulée* followed by a new gesture starting on a higher note—is a common French formula, recurring in mm. 12 and 16.

Example **13.2** English Suite no. 1 in A, BWV 806, courante 1, mm. 0–7, melody only (braces indicate gestures; overlapping braces indicate elisions).

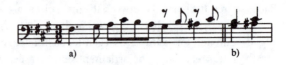

Example 13.3 English Suite no. 1 in A, courante 1, m. 6, left hand, from (a) BWV 806a; (b) BWV 806.

As in the prelude, some ornament signs raise questions, particularly a slant-ing line drawn between the two lower voices (Example 13.3).[20] In the sarabande (m. 1) the sign seems to mean an acciaccatura, that is, a passing tone included in a rapid arpeggiation of the chord.[21] But the same sign can mean a measured breaking of a two-note chord, such as Walther wrote out in mm. 6 and 16 of courante 1 (Example 13.3a).[22] Walther was copying the early version, and it would be odd for Bach to have used the less explicit notation only when revising. Perhaps the notation of BWV 806a was Walther's own "resolution" of shorthand employed in Bach's score.

This is the only Bach suite with two courantes, but older French composers sometimes provided whole series of courantes in the same key. The second cou-rante is rhythmically more straightforward than the first, and it lacks the latter's imitative texture; both features made it more suitable for variation. The variations applied to Baroque dance movements tended to take a heterogeneous texture and replace it with flowing eighth notes. Bach's technique is more imaginative than the mechanical arpeggiation found in doubles by less distinguished contemporaries. Yet one still senses the underlying aesthetic of rhythmic homogenization, even as Bach complicates it here or in the variation of the sarabande in Suite no. 6 (also in the four doubles in the B-minor *Partia* for solo violin). BWV 806a lacks the first double, and it reverses the order of double 2 and courante 2. Perhaps double 2 originated as a revised version of courante 2; Bach, after some hesitation, then decided to include both as illustrations of variation technique, together with an additional movement that became double 1.[23] This sequence of events would explain why double 1, which introduces sixteenths into both outer parts, is more brilliant than double 2, where the bass is turned into walking eighths but the melody is largely unaltered.

Like double 1, the sarabande is more florid than one would expect in the French style. Yet the Italianate embellishment of both treble and bass never obscures the dance rhythm or the regular four-bar phrasing. Bach must have invented this type of movement while improvising embellishments for simpler pieces. But there is no evidence that this particular movement originated in that way; the written-out embellishments appear to be essential parts of the melodic writing, not additions to a simpler original. Still, in a few passages Bach embel-lished his own embellishments, especially in m. 24, which prepares the return of the opening theme (Example 13.4).[24] The full chords make this a grand, sonorous movement; the occasional figuration in thirty-seconds implies that it was meant to be played with considerable fire.

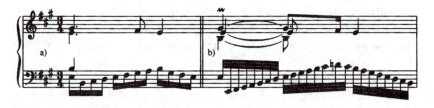

Example 13.4 English Suite no. 1 in A, sarabande, m. 24, from (a) BWV 806a; (b) BWV 806.

The two bourrées are longer and more contrapuntal than the bourrées in Bach's earlier suites, or in their models by composers like Fischer. Both can be played as duets on two keyboards. The revised version refines the articulation of bourrée 1, if Walther's copy of the earlier version (BWV 806a) can be trusted. Walther's unvarying two-note slurs preserve the underlying quarter-note rhythm of the dance. The later version distinguishes "sigh" motives slurred in twos from four-note *tierces coulées* and other figures. Both versions use slurs on repeated notes to imitate bow vibrato (bass, m. 30). The latter technique, which involves pressure on the string of a violin or cello to rearticulate the note without any break in the sound, cannot be literally imitated on the harpsichord. The slur implies that each note is to be held as long as possible before being restruck.[25] In Bach's keyboard music the notation seems to be confined to bass lines and was probably suggested by the use of bow vibrato in continuo parts, as in the opening sonatina of the *Actus tragicus* BWV 106.

The subject of the gigue resembles that of the prelude and, like the latter, is inverted in the second half. The closing phrase of each half is marked piano, serving like the *petite reprise* at the end of a French piece: an extra repetition of the closing phrase, usually indicated by a "Dal Segno" and played piano. The present closing phrase does not actually repeat the previous one, but it is sufficiently similar that it could have been suggested by written-out echoes in sonata movements by Corelli; the *giga* in the latter's op. 5, no. 10 has echoes at the ends of both halves, as in the present movement. *Piano* is already marked in BWV 806a, so it is apparently an original part of the text. But the sources differ on precisely where the change of dynamic level should take place, some manuscripts showing inconsistencies between the two passages.[26] On the harpsichord the change of manual is awkward wherever one takes it; best may be on the note after the downbeat in each voice.

English Suite no. 2 in A Minor BWV 807

The Second English Suite is relatively simple in texture, its melodic lines more angular and occasionally somewhat more awkward (especially in the first four movements) than those of the other suites. Yet the two bourrées are as assured as any of Bach's examples of this dance, and the gigue is a successful imitation of the Italian *giga* that closes some of Corelli's violin sonatas. Indeed, it so closely resembles a violin sonata movement that it would come as little surprise to find that it was a transcription. As such it forms an appropriate conclusion to a suite that opens with a large prelude in concerto style.

The genre that we recognize as the concerto was in the process of formation at the time Bach composed these suites. Although allied stylistically with the concertos that Vivaldi and other Italian composers were composing during the second decade of the eighteenth century, formally the preludes of Suites 2–6 are not particularly close to the ritornello designs that were becoming typical of quick concerto movements. The da-capo form of these pieces recurs in several of Bach's concerto movements, but also in other compositions, including fugues.[27] Nor do the opening sections of these preludes resemble a typical ritornello; the prelude of Suite no. 2 opens like an invention, and that of Suite no. 5 is a genuine fugue. All five preludes include arpeggiated passagework reminiscent of that found in the episodes of a solo concerto, but similar figuration occurs as well in solo and trio sonatas and other types of Italian ensemble music.

As in the first movement of the Fourth Brandenburg Concerto—also a da-capo form—only the B section of the present prelude contains distinctly articulated episodes. The A section is fifty-five measures long—exactly the same as the B section, and too long to be considered a ritornello. The B section opens by introducing a new idea, as part of what can be considered a "solo" episode (mm. 55–9); the latter can even be played on a quieter manual (see Example 13.5).[28] Passages employing this new idea alternate with others using the theme of the A section, seemingly imitating the syntax of a concerto although also coming close to that of a fugue. As in some early concertos, the "solo" episodes are somewhat less virtuoso in style than the "tutti" passages; with its appoggiatura (discussed below), the B idea is expressive or *affetuoso* in character. On the other hand, the A section includes much violinistic passagework, especially in a long dominant prolongation that generates considerable dramatic tension (mm. 36–46). Such writing is as likely to occur in the tutti sections as the solo episodes of early concertos; Bach imitated it in other keyboard pieces probably composed during the same period, such as the A-minor Fugue BWV 944.

In the first BG edition, the hooks or commas with which Bach indicated the appoggiaturas of the episode idea were mistaken for slurs (e.g., mm. 56–9). The editor compounded the error by extending it to what he considered to be parallel passages. The result was a series of two-note slurs from upbeat to downbeat, a common enough type of articulation in Classical or Romantic music but rare in Bach's (Example 13.5). The editor's slur produces an agogic accent on the upbeat, but the whole point of the intended appoggiatura is to create an articulation by repeating the note played on the upbeat. The result is an *accent*, an expressive *port de voix*.[29] The effect is intensified when the ornament becomes an acciaccatura within a dissonant chord, in mm. 96 and 98 (Example 13.6).

Example 13.5 English Suite no. 2 in A Minor BWV 807, prelude, mm. 55–7, (a) as in BG 13; (b) as in NBA V/7.

Example 13.6 English Suite no. 2 in A Minor BWV 807, prelude, mm. 95–6.

The allemande, as in Suites nos. 3–6, has an invention-like imitative structure. The bass of m. 2 imitates the treble of m. 1—or, rather, the *brisé* writing first assigned to the right hand is transferred, with idiomatic adjustments, to the left. The process is repeated after the arrival on the dominant, with voices exchanged (m. 6b). The second half of the movement works similarly, using a free inversion of the subject. Bach's critics might have found this procedure pedantic in an allemande, and in this instance they might have been right. The angular treble line at the outset of the second half is, like other such Bach lines, quite expressive and invites rhythmic freedom. Yet it cannot be played so freely when it is transferred in the next measure to the bass and combined contrapuntally with a treble line also moving in sixteenths. In short, the incorporation of expressive melodic material into a densely woven contrapuntal fabric leads to stiffness. The courante runs the same danger, especially as the rhythmic gestures traditional for this dance (which occur so idiomatically in the courantes of Suite no. 1) tend to be replaced, or rather embellished, by running eighths in both hands.

The sarabande is the first of two for which Bach wrote a separate set of *agrémens* or ornaments. The idea, and even Bach's original manner of notating the embellished treble line, apparently came from Couperin's *Premier Ordre*, in his first book of *Pièces de clavecin* (Paris, 1713). There several pieces are accompanied by an embellished version of the melody, printed on an extra staff at the bottom of the page.[30] It is often assumed that Bach (and Couperin) intended the ornamented version of each half to be played in alternation with the plain version, as a varied reprise. But this is far from certain; the ornamented version, like the original, includes repeat signs and might have been intended as an alternative to the main text, serving as an illustration of "composition by variation." Bach included varied reprises in one movement from the Vivaldi transcriptions (BWV 975). But the practice of varying the repeated halves of a binary form may not have become widespread until later in the century, when C. P. E. Bach described it (1753–62, i.3.31). Still, there can be no harm in applying the practice here.

Bourrée 1 has a fluid accompaniment figure in eighths whose originality is easily overlooked because of its superficial similarity to an Alberti bass. If one were to reduce the bass to quarter notes, the opening bars would not be very different from bourrées by lesser German contemporaries. The moving bass intensifies the contrast with the second bourrée, in A major; the three-part texture of the latter might have been inspired by the French double-reed trio of oboes and bassoon.

The gigue contains a curious indication that suggests that Bach was not shy about repeating movements that he liked. To accommodate players wishing to repeat the entire movement, at the end of the second half Bach provided a second ending that leads back to the beginning; there is a third ending with which to conclude. Similar indications occur in dance movements by d'Anglebert.

English Suite no. 3 in G Minor BWV 808

Suite no. 3 is distinguished by its formally rigorous prelude, a dark, beautifully embellished sarabande, and the appealing gavotte and musette that follow. The prelude, more concise and more clearly articulated than the others, comes remarkably close to being a textbook ritornello form. The three voices in the "solo" episodes (at mm. 33, 99, and 125) correspond to the two violins and continuo used in the solo sections of works such as Vivaldi's op. 3, no. 11 (basis of the organ transcription BWV 596) and in Bach's own "double violin" concerto BWV 1043.[31] The ritornellos are more heavily scored, and for this reason it is unnecessary to point out the form by using a quieter manual for the episodes; phrase elisions at the points of articulation would in any case make this awkward (e.g., on the downbeat of m. 33). Although it is customary to view Vivaldi as the inspiration for movements of this type, Williams (2000) notes a non-Vivaldian "spaciousness" and absence of caprice here; perhaps this reflects not only Bach's own musical personality but that of other Italian composers who furnished models or inspiration, such as Albinoni.

The key and the thematic matter of the prelude have parallels in the Fantasie that opens Suite no. 5 in Mattheson's *Pièces de clavecin*. Bach's movement is more sophisticated and much longer. Its unusually regular formal symmetry involves not only the recurrences of the ritornello but also the close parallelism between the first and third episodes (mm. 125–61 || 33–67). But the symmetry is broken by a dramatic retransition passage (mm. 161–80), which replaces the simple pause found at the end of the middle section in most da capo forms, including the prelude of Suite no. 2. The three remaining preludes also have retransition passages at this point, but none is as exciting or as elegantly conceived as this one, which prolongs the dominant through several measures of passagework (mm. 176–9) before falling with unslackened energy into the opening of the ritornello. The latter is modified to allow a smoother join, and this caused Bach some trouble. One copy preserves an earlier reading, and Kayser's manuscript contains an autograph entry at this point—the only certain autograph material surviving for the English Suites. Perhaps Bach wrote out the crucial measures because they had become illegible through revisions in his own score.[32]

In the earliest copy the prelude is barred in "double measures" like the A-Minor Sinfonia. It remains effectively in 6/8, the chief arrivals falling on the downbeats of odd-numbered measures, as do the dissonant 7- and 9/4-chords in mm. 9–13—but not those in mm. 16–20.[33] The discrepancy, which results from a phrase elision, would have been a reason for abandoning the notation in double measures—if indeed Bach authorized its abandonment in later copies.

The allemande is exceptional in that the main thematic idea appears first in the bass; it is this theme that is repeated in mm. 6 and 7 and inverted after the double bar. This allemande flows more easily than that of Suite no. 2, its more relaxed stance being evident in parallel octaves that Bach makes no effort to hide. The parallels arise naturally as two parts descend in parallel motion to a bare octave C♯ on the downbeat of m. 11. One can imagine Bach, a glint in his eye, pointing out the octaves to his pupils as the sort of things that "offended every beginner in composition, but afterwards soon justified themselves," as Forkel (1802, 27/ NBR, 444) put it. Bach's refusal to be bound by rules or pedantic consistency is also evident in the pragmatic fingerings given by two pupils, Kayser and Gerber. Whereas "4" in mm. 15 and 16 reflects the modern type of scale fingering, "3" in the inversion of the theme (m. 18) implies an older one (Example 13.7).

The courante is rhythmically the most complex in the English Suites, rivaling that of the D-major Partita in this respect and going well beyond the subtle metrical shifts normally encountered in French examples of the dance. The most extreme metrical play begins in the treble just after the *tierce coulée* in m. 9, resulting in a passage that is effectively in 4/4. The bass then introduces its own cross-rhythm when it enters in the latter part of m. 11 (Example 13.8). In the closing phrase of the second half (mm. 30–1), effective 4/4 measures in the outer voices coincide, forming a *hemiolia major* (three measures of 4/4 replace two of 3/2).

Example 13.7 English Suite no. 3 in G Minor BWV 808, allemande: (a) mm. 15–16a; (b) mm. 18–19a.

Example 13.8 English Suite no. 3 in G Minor BWV 808, courante, mm. 9–12.

The sarabande is one of the most original and impressive examples of the dance by any composer, unique for both its pedal points and the enharmonic progressions taking place over them. These give the piece the same mysterious or romantic quality found in sections of the Chromatic Fantasia; the effect is deepened by the embellishments, which rise to levels of improvisational fire exceeded only in the sarabande of the Sixth Partita. The initial tonic pedal, notated as being held for seven measures, must be restruck—perhaps several times—in order to be heard. Frescobaldi permitted this, and Bach must have done so as well in a piece expressly for the harpsichord.[34] It is also necessary to restrike treble eb´´, sustained through mm. 13–6 over a moving bass in a texture that recalls the adagio of the First Brandenburg Concerto (cf. mm. 9–11). Wide gaps between the parts (especially in m. 19) are neither the first nor the last points in the suite where a literal reading of the notation seems to require pedals. Although one can release a few notes early without ill effect, this piece, like the early versions of the Chromatic Fantasia and the Aria variata, might have been written for an instrument equipped with a short octave or simple pedalboard.[35]

The gavotte is more energetic than most French examples; it is also rhythmically more complex. The first half-measure is an upbeat, as usual in gavottes; one group of sources emphasizes this by placing an *accent* in the treble on the first downbeat (bb´´). Yet it is difficult to hear the proper metrical structure, even though cadences, long notes, and critical harmonies (such as the tritone in m. 11 or the diminished seventh in m. 25) are correctly placed on downbeats. The player can help by accenting the downbeats, not so much dynamically as by phrasing into them and stretching them rhythmically; this is facilitated by expressive gestures such as the written-out *tierces coulées* on the downbeats of mm. 12 and 14.

Nevertheless, some ambiguity is built into the music; one tends to hear an accent on a low bass note or when a new motivic figure is introduced, even when these occur in the middle of the measure (as at the opening or in m. 10). The same is true in the odd retransition phrase that begins over a drum-like pedal point (mm. 18b–26a); one is likely to hear the first two drumbeats as marking the beginning of a measure, especially if they are played with the mordents that they bear in the two earliest sources.[36] A departure from the gentle character of most French gavottes, this drumming must have been inspired by the *tambourin*, a dance (named for a drum) that could take the rhythmic form of a gavotte, as in the example from Rameau's *Pièces de clavecin* of 1724.

The sources designate the following movement *Gavotte II*, some copyists adding the qualifier *ou la musette*. Like the tambourin, the musette is named for an instrument, a small, gentrified sort of bagpipe. Not all pieces called musettes use gavotte rhythm, and the title here probably includes a programmatic element. The pedal point representing the bagpipe drone will have to be restruck from time to time, perhaps at the beginning of each four-measure phrase.

The gigue is a true fugue, with distinct subject and countersubject. Both themes are inverted in the second half. Despite the promising beginning in each half, there is a dropping off of inspiration in the second half, coinciding with the thinning of the texture from three to two parts. The gigue is unusual in returning to the *rectus* form of the subject in the final entry (bass, m. 43), preceded by an unfortunately workman-like sequential bridge (mm. 37b–41a).

English Suite no. 4 in F, BWV 809

Suite no. 4 is the only one of the original group of five suites in a major key. Bach generally favored minor keys for his most serious music, and although no weaker than the others, the F-Major Suite is the shortest and perhaps the most popular in style.

The prelude is a brilliant piece containing numerous references to orchestral style. The idea of opening the ritornello with a measure for treble alone might have came from Vivaldi's Concerto op. 3, no. 3 (arranged by Bach as BWV 978); the transcription, like the present piece, is in F and has an imitation in the bass in its second measure.[37] Although the style is predominantly Italian, the countersubject (treble, m. 2) is French, especially when played with the ornaments attached to it in some copies. Similar countersubjects occur in the fugal part of the overture to Dieupart's B-Minor Suite and in the overture to Bach's C-major orchestral suite BWV 1066.[38] The most striking parallel to an ensemble work occurs in the "solo" episodes, which employ the same motives as the first solo in the allegro of the Fifth Brandenburg Concerto.

The time-signature ₵, found in the earliest copies and also used in the Fifth Brandenburg Concerto, indicates a lively tempo, as does the additional indication *vîtement*. Some late copies place staccato strokes on all of the sixteenth-notes in the initial statement of the theme. This could imply unusually vigorous articulation, but it might have been simply a warning against slurring them or applying rhythmic inequality.[39]

The allemande anticipates the one in the G-Major Partita; both are brilliant pieces using both ordinary and triplet sixteenths. But this allemande quickly loses steam; the triplets drop out by the third measure in each half, and although they return there is a subsequent shift to the minor mode in both closing phrases (mm. 10b, 22b). It is as if Bach was not quite ready to abandon the traditional expressive style of a German allemande, and as a result the movement alternates uneasily between brilliance and pathos.

The allemande is imitative; the treble of m. 2 becomes the bass of m. 3. The courante contains comparable imitations at the beginning of each half. Yet although the phrases are somewhat longer than in most French examples, the upper line in the courante is rather too obviously composed of one-measure fragments, and it cannot be counted among Bach's more successful.

Like the courante, the sarabande is relatively short and rather plain by comparison with the corresponding movements in the other suites. Through m. 16 it is, in a sense, a version of the corresponding movement of Suite no. 1, shorn of its *agrémens* but following much the same rhythmic and harmonic plan.[40] Unless the tempo is unduly slow, little ornamentation is necessary beyond the normal breaking of the chords. Pianists, who might be inclined to see the movement as a quiet chorale like that in the Chopin *Fantaisie*, should remember that the full chords imply strong attacks and a rich sonority on the harpsichord.

Minuets almost by definition are unremarkable in style, and those of the present suite amble along with few complications. Both, however, are longer than most minuets of the time, and the active bass lines represent, as in the courante, Bach's attempt to invest the dance with some contrapuntal substance.

The gigue seems at first less a fugue than an invention. But if one ignores the first bass entrance, which is in the tonic (m. 1b), one discovers a normal three-part fugal exposition. Thereafter one never hears more than two voices at a time. A stricter working-out, however, might have been fatal to the piece's lively hunting character, implicit in the horn fanfare that opens the subject. The subject's octave leap, developed in the second half (mm. 30ff.), recalls the post horn motive found in several early works. These brass references might have been suggested by the key, the usual one for horns in Bach's music.

English Suite no. 5 in E Minor BWV 810

The suite in E minor, like the one in A minor, is somewhat rough around the edges, but after the D-minor suite it is the most ambitious of the set and perhaps the most satisfying of all. There are no weak movements; the courante, the least successful movement in other suites, is genuinely exciting, and the sarabande represents a new type, *galant* rather than intensely expressive yet *affetuoso* all the same (as pointed out by Eppstein 1986, 212).

The prelude is a true fugue in da-capo form—the only example among Bach's harpsichord works, apart from the prelude of the next suite, although there are also examples for organ, lute, and violin. As in those pieces, the episodes borrow the style of a solo concerto, using a violinistic idea that recalls the first solo in the Fourth Brandenburg Concerto (m. 40). Another "solo" passage (mm. 60–5) resembles figuration in the last movement of the Third Brandenburg Concerto. The form is an expanded and somewhat clearer version of that used in the prelude of the A-minor suite, the middle section falling into two closely parallel halves (mm. 40–73 largely correspond with 82–107). As in the suites in A minor and D minor, the prelude makes repeated use of pedal points, something the composer was evidently exploiting at this time for dramatic effect; the pedal note may be either tonic (mm. 14ff.) or dominant (mm. 74ff.). On some scale of demonic intensity, the pedal-point passages here rate higher than those in the A-minor prelude, lower than in the D-minor—but this prelude is the most polished of the three.

The allemande has the same earnest fugality as that of Suite no. 2 but is even more severe. The two hands could play on separate keyboards, which would solve the slight problem caused by voice crossing in mm. 5–6. The thematic material is unusually angular even for Bach, and its inversion in the second half (bass, m. 13) produces one of the harshest passages in his keyboard music (Example 13.9).[41] The passage bristles with passing dissonances and nearly simultaneous cross-relations, yet the contrary motion of the outer voices is clear, even if the precise voice leading of the implied inner parts is a matter for debate.

In the courante Bach discovered that he could write a more effective piece by inventing a distinctive rhythmic motive and developing it throughout the

Example 13.9 English Suite no. 5 in E Minor BWV 810, allemande: (a) mm. 15–17a; (b) analysis of mm. 15–6.

composition, rather than by imitating traditional French formulas. Departing from its models, the piece has a vituperous character, reinforced in some sources by a staccato mark on the last note of m. 1 and parallel passages. The rhythmic consistency, although appealing to modern taste as the working out of an easily remembered idea, might have seemed a weakness to those expecting the characteristic rhythmic play of the dance. Instead there is a playful flexibility of texture, as when the largely two-part counterpoint is relieved by a *galant* phrase on a dominant pedal (mm. 6–8, 18–9, etc.).

Galant style is also evident in the homophonic three-part texture and regular rhythmic patterning of the sarabande. The traditional rhythm of the dance is not immediately evident, but often the melodic line turns or the harmony changes on the second beat. In the opening measure and elsewhere one might be inclined to slur the eighths in pairs to produce "sigh" motives. But staccato dots were added here in one manuscript, and although probably not Bach's they are a good idea if taken to indicate a light separation rather than detached accents.

The first passepied is in the form of a rondeau, which was common in contemporary French keyboard music but rare in Bach's.[42] Musically, a passepied resembles a minuet with an upbeat; it is often written in 3/8. The earliest copy of the present movement gives it in double measures, like the prelude of Suite no. 3. The moderate tempo and flowing sixteenths of both passepieds make them good candidates for the use of *notes inégales*, although the latter might well have been expected throughout these suites, as in French music of the period generally.

The gigue continues the trend toward increasingly strict fugues in these closing movements; begun in the A-minor suite, this tendency reaches its climax in Suite no. 6. Here, three real parts are present for most of the time, not just during the opening exposition, and the first half comprises two complete expositions separated by a short episode. The subject maintains the suite's tortuous character with its angular chromaticism and built-in pedal point, recalling the figuration of the prelude. The second half perhaps slackens, falling after m. 65 into a series of sequences that are almost routine, at least for Bach. But it rouses itself at the end, concluding with a phrase that Bach must have remembered as he was finishing the gigue of the Sixth Partita, in the same key.

English Suite No. 6 in D Minor BWV 811

The last suite is the largest and was surely meant to be the crowning member of the set, though it was not necessarily the last composed. The first indication of its special character is the presence of a separate introductory section in the prelude, making the latter a self-contained prelude and fugue. In this it resembles an overture, but the introduction is in arpeggio style, lacking dotted rhythm. It bears no tempo mark, but it is in the same 9/8 time as the latter part of the movement. Hence the opening was probably meant to be played as an allegro; the latter tempo is marked explicitly in most copies after the adagio at the end of the first section. There is an old tradition of taking the entire first section at a substantially slower tempo (see Schulenberg 1999c), but this makes the cadenza-like passage in mm. 15–8 seem interminable.

The fugue alone is longer than any other prelude in the English Suites; the A section contains forty-nine measures, and the 9/8 meter makes these long despite the quick tempo. The mesmerizing figuration gives the movement the same intensity found in the A-minor Fugue BWV 944, another *moto perpetuo* from about the same time. But here the subject is short and simple, comprised of a few readily developed scalar motives; the inversion is introduced early in the A section (mm. 49ff.). The first answer (m. 39) is at the subdominant, not the dominant, a procedure that might seem anomalous had the dominant not received early and lengthy tonicization in the opening section (mm. 9–24). The A section instead moves quickly toward the relative major; A minor is the goal of the first part of the B section.

Motives from the subject saturate the texture so thoroughly as to give the impression that the same material is being constantly recycled. But apart from the repeat of the A section, there is little verbatim recapitulation. The B section again falls into two halves (mm. 86–112 and 113–43), but they are only roughly parallel with one another. There is also a distinct retransition (mm. 143–6), as in the prelude to Suite no. 3. Short pedal points of various types appear from time to time, as in the prelude to the E-minor Suite. In one type the right hand repeatedly arpeggiates the same chord while the bass moves (as in mm. 44–5), producing an effect somewhat like the "obstinate" figures in Bach's early works, but less ponderous because of the quick tempo.

The allemande is of the same prickly variety as that of Suite no. 5, with a melodic cross-relation in m. 1 as the treble moves from c#′′ to c♮′′. This is repeated in a different harmonic context in m. 5, where the bass restates the opening theme at the dominant (Example 13.10).[43] The last beat of m. 5 is rendered especially

Example 13.10 English Suite no. 6 in D Minor BWV 811, allemande: (a) m. 1; (b) mm. 5–6a.

surprising by the f´ in the inner voice, which leaps by a diminished fourth rather than to the expected e´. The awkward melodic intervals are among the piece's essential ideas, developed to a climax in m. 20, where the outer voices leap in opposite directions by a major sixth and a diminished seventh, respectively, as they compose out a diminished-seventh chord.

The courante is less inspired. Although in theory it was a good idea to combine a French-style melody with an Italianate walking bass, the latter diffuses the energy of the former, evening out its rhythmic irregularities. Perhaps the existing movement is a variation of an earlier one with "simple" bass, like double 2 in Suite no. 1.

The time signature of the sarabande (3/2) may signify a slower tempo than usual. But the movement need not lack fire, which can be attained through a steady tempo, a strong registration, and added ornamentation (e.g., trills on beat 2 in mm. 4 and 5). It goes without saying that many chords, especially those on the second beat, will be broadly arpeggiated, sometimes with acciaccaturas. The tempo is presumably the same as in the following double, where it can be determined from the flowing eighth notes. Given a moderate (not slow) half-note pulse, the double can generate considerable intensity, especially in the hemiolas—unusual for a sarabande—toward the end (mm. 21–2).

With its walking bass, the gavotte resembles one or two examples by Corelli.[44] The usually clear four-bar phrasing of the dance is replaced by asymmetrical phrase groupings after the double bar,[45] and by m. 14 the dance's normal meter seems to have vanished. Proper meter and phrasing are restored by the time the theme is restated in the tonic (m. 24b). But the dance's customary rhythm is brusquely rejected in the final cadence, whose staccato half notes are unprecedented in a gavotte. Gavotte 2, like that of Suite no. 3, is based on a tonic pedal point. Only one late source has the rubric *ou la musette*,[46] but the trill in thirds (mm. 14b–16a) is surely an imitation of rustic music-making.

In the gigue the collection's preoccupation with imitation and inversion reaches its culmination. Large portions of the first half of the movement are inverted almost verbatim in the second half, leading to mirror writing on a scale surpassed only in the *Art of Fugue*. The compositional virtuosity is reflected in that required of the player; the time signature 12/16 indicates a rapid tempo, and many of the long trills must be sustained while a second moving part is played simultaneously in the same hand.

Bach's precise intentions regarding the ornaments are somewhat unclear, especially on the long pedal notes in the second half. On these notes the NBA consistently places the sign for a long mordent—Couperin's *pincé continu*. But the sources show a confusing variety of signs (to judge from the table in NBA V/7, KB, 180). Some of the readings do suggest that the trill used in the first half of the gigue is to be inverted as a mordent in the second. But although the melodic material, and indeed the entire contrapuntal texture, is inverted, it is by no means clear that this should be the case with the ornaments themselves.[47] A mordent is not, in any case, an exact inversion of a late-Baroque trill, as the latter normally begins on the upper note. One might, however, wish to begin the trills in the first half of the gigue on the main note, to simplify performance and to avoid the harsh accented dissonances that would otherwise appear (mm. 11, 20). Perhaps Bach expected the player to simplify the trills further by converting them to measured figuration of the sort used in variation 28 of the Goldberg Variations; this, however, would reduce their bite, and there is no indication for it in the sources.

How Bach understood the compositional process of this movement can be gleaned from several examples of mirror counterpoint that he later transcribed from a treatise by Seth Calvisius.[48] To produce the inverted counterpoint after the double bar, the first note of each voice was transposed to a new pitch level; the following notes were then produced by turning each melodic interval upside-down. Thus the initial treble d′ became bass e′, and the next note in m. 25 was a half step higher (f′) rather than lower (c♯′).

Yet Bach must have understood that this purely melodic way of understanding counterpoint was insufficient for producing a coherent piece of tonal music. His subjects are harmonically conceived, and their implied harmonies must make sense upon inversion; so must the harmonic progressions spelled out by the polyphonic texture as a whole. As later in the *Art of Fugue*, the present subject outlines a D-minor triad. The first note of the subject is the tonic, and therefore the inversion must start on the fifth degree of the scale; the half step between leading tone and tonic becomes, on inversion, an expressive appoggiatura between the flat sixth and the fifth scale degrees. Bach, looking beyond the first note of the subject to its harmonic context, would have understood the first entry after the double bar as outlining an A-minor triad, in place of D minor at the beginning of the piece. Where the first three fugal entries follow the customary tonic-dominant pattern (d: i–v–i), those in the second half form a plagal pattern (a : i–iv–i).

Bach abandoned strict mirror counterpoint after the initial exposition of the second half. In m. 32 the top two voices are freely composed, but a measure later the soprano takes up the bass line of m. 9 (in inversion). Where the soprano originally made its second entry on the dominant (m. 8), there is now a bass entry on the subdominant (m. 32). The alteration is necessary in order to preserve a tonal design; had Bach maintained strict mirror inversion, the bass entry in m. 32 would have been in the tonic, beginning on the note a, and the piece would have ended in G minor, the wrong key. The process is summarized in Table 13.2. Although the construction of the movement is less strict than that of the later mirror pieces, in working out the gigue Bach would have gained insights into the relationships between counterpoint and tonality that would serve him well in his later researches into fugue. Bach would have remembered the complementary

Table 13.2 Inversional Structure of the Gigue BWV 811/8

Passage in Second Half (mm.)	Source Passage in First Half (mm.)	Source Voice(s) in First Half	Voices Generated in Second Half by Exact Inversion
25–31	1–7	BTS	STB
32–34	8–10	S	B
33–34	9–10	B	S
35–36	11–12	TS	TB (except for tenor a′)
37	13	BTS	STB (except for tenor a)
38–40	14–16	B	S (except for last three notes of m. 40)
41–43	17–19	S	B
44–46	20–22	BTS	STB (except for first and last notes in T; S an octave higher)
47–48a	22–24a	S	S

relationship between the two halves of this movement when he wrote the three-part mirror in the *Art of Fugue*, another virtuoso gigue whose two versions show complementary tonal schemes (see chap. 18).[49]

The closing passage of the first half could not be inverted to produce an entirely satisfactory final cadence, and Bach abandoned the plan after m. 47. The movement ends by instead combining the two forms of the subject, as in the prelude BWV 900/1 and some fugues of the WTC—a fitting climax to the series of suites in which Bach demonstrated the compatibility of *galant* dances with strict counterpoint.

14
The French Suites

The French Suites are the later but smaller pendant to the six English Suites, lacking the preludes included in the latter. The autograph score containing portions of French Suites nos. 1–5 is thought to date from about 1722—the year of the fair copy of WTC1—but the autograph of Suite no. 5 was not completed until some time after Bach's arrival in Leipzig in 1723. The suites cannot have been assembled into the now-familiar set of six until around 1725, perhaps simultaneously with the creation of the set now known as the English Suites. By then most of the French Suites had undergone at least one systematic revision, and Bach continued not only to refine details but to shuffle movements into and out of the set; parallels to the Partitas and even WTC2 suggest that the process continued into the 1730s. Closely related to the French Suites are two further suites, BWV 818 and 819, which Bach may for a time have considered including in the collection of "suites without prelude." They are similar enough to the French Suites in style and dimensions to be discussed with them in this chapter.

The designation as "French" suites, whatever its origin, has nothing to do with the style of the works, which on the whole are probably somewhat less French by contemporary standards than Bach's English Suites. Although slighter than the latter, the French Suites would not have been considered particularly short or simple, and the absence of preludes was hardly unusual. Still, the French Suites seem to reflect a conscious turn toward a relatively simple, more popular, more accessible style. If so, however, Bach's shift in style was a gradual one, for the first three French Suites—in this case, the numerical ordering does seem to reflect chronology—are old-fashioned by comparison with the last three. Although none of the allemandes is as severely contrapuntal as those of the English Suites, the courantes of Suites nos. 1 and 3 are still of the French type (notated in 3/2), and that of Suite no. 1 has the same imitative texture employed in the English Suites. In addition, the sarabande of Suite no. 1 has the unembellished, chorale-like appearance of several sarabandes in the English Suites, and the gigue of Suite no. 1 is an archaic version of the dance in duple time.

Still, none of the French Suites stands apart from the others to the degree that the A-major work does from the other English Suites. Especially in the last four French Suites, Bach achieved a suaveness rare in his earlier keyboard music. Although these works are not devoid of counterpoint or virtuoso display, they concentrate—especially in Suites nos. 4–6—on cantabile melodies and idiomatic keyboard writing. Perhaps Bach, recognizing that complicated contrapuntal music was not the best means of introducing himself to the public, or to pupils, aimed at a keyboard style that would be sufficiently *galant* to make for a saleable publication, without being devoid of musical substance. The last three suites, especially Suite no. 6, are clearly approaching the style of the Partitas, which would be Bach's first actual keyboard publications. Although lacking the large dimensions and unabashed virtuosity of that set, the French Suites reveal the same inventive approach to keyboard figuration and the same free treatment of the traditional dance-types. For example, no two of the allemandes or courantes are of quite the same sort, and several introduce types of keyboard writing unprecedented for these movements.

Bach may never have given the collection a distinctive title. As early as 1762, Marpurg referred to the six works as Bach's "French" suites,[1] possibly reflecting a tradition within the Bach circle. But the title remains as misleading as that given to the English Suites, whose dance movements on the whole are somewhat closer to Bach's French models than are those of the French Suites.

Sources, Versions, Editions

The autographs of Suites nos. 1–5 make up most of the first *Clavier-Büchlein vor Anna Magdalena Bach*. This manuscript (P 224), dated 1722, was the first of two that Bach dedicated to his second wife, whom he married at Cöthen late in 1721. The 1722 manuscript is distinct from the second one of the same title, dated 1725 (P 225), which is well known as the source of many familiar little teaching pieces. Most of these, however, are not by Bach and need not concern us here (see appendix B).

The earlier manuscript is thought to have been a wedding gift from Bach to his new wife; because the suites make up most of its surviving contents, it has been supposed that the pieces were written for her. A professional singer, Anna Magdalena is likely to have had some keyboard ability. But although portions of the five suites (especially the first) appear to be fair copies, others are rougher revision autographs, and the manuscript contains Bach's fragmentary composing scores for two other works.[2] At some point, then, Bach evidently began to use the manuscript as his own workbook, and this might be why he gave his wife a second Little Keyboard Book.[3]

The textual history of the French Suites after their initial entry in the 1722 book is complicated, for as many as five distinct versions survive for each piece. The revisions ranged from the insertion of ornament signs and other changes of detail to the addition and elimination of whole movements. Substantial compositional changes affected the voice leading and even the length and form of individual movements. Similar revisions took place in BWV 818 and 819.

Bach's revisions in these works may have been no more numerous or substantial than those made in other pieces whose composing scores do not happen to survive. It is remarkable, however, that the apparently simple French Suites should have undergone as many substantive changes as they did. The expansion of the allemande and courante of Suite no. 2, each in several stages, was apparently a response to what were perceived as real problems in the earlier versions, not merely a desire for greater length. Likewise, the frequent alteration of melodic lines, inner voices, and basses represents more than traditional embellishment or the refining of small details. In the English Suites, the logic of the counterpoint was sufficient to justify unidiomatic, even ungratifying details, just as in Bach's fugues. But the more homophonic style of the French Suites, where technical demands on the player had to be kept relatively light and the norms of the harpsichord idiom more closely observed, may, paradoxically, have posed greater challenges. Evidence of Bach's difficulties can be found in passages that were revised not once but twice, not simply by embellishing or intensifying a simpler reading but by improving awkward voice leading or unidiomatic keyboard writing.[4]

Bach made most of his changes not in the surviving autographs but in other scores now lost. Their revised readings must be reconstructed from copies made by pupils and other members of the Bach circle. The sequence of alterations, and even Bach's final intentions about certain details, cannot always be determined with certainty. There are many manuscript copies, not all containing the complete set of six suites, and the same manuscript may give later readings for one piece and earlier ones for another.

For this reason, the discussion of each individual work below is preceded by a summary of its principal sources and versions, as in chapters 4–7. Although most players will want to use the later versions, study of the earlier versions is, as always, instructive. But the relatively sparse indication of ornaments in the early versions may be illusory. It is likely that in adding ornament signs, Bach was merely specifying, for the benefit of his pupils, the types of ornaments that a good player would have used anyway.

The six French Suites have traditionally been edited alongside BWV 818 and 819. Nineteenth-century editions, such as those in BG 13 and 45, tended to mix readings belonging to different versions. Bischoff usually guessed right about which were the latest readings, and he reproduced the most important early readings in footnotes. But all such editions were superseded by that of Dürr in NBA

V/8 (1980), which was based on a far more complete and accurate investigation of the sources. Unfortunately, the format of the NBA edition makes it cumbersome to compare early and late readings. A subsequent edition by Richard Jones (Associated Board of the Royal Schools of Music, 1985) contains useful, concise accounts—in English—on the principal sources and the history of the text. Jones also gives suggestions for the realization of ornaments and other points of performance practice, although some are debatable. Less adequate, but presenting a cleaner text, is the edition by Hans-Christian Müller (Vienna, 1983).

As in his editions of the WTC, Dürr presents two distinct versions for each of the French Suites, as well as for BWV 818 and 819. The two versions of the French Suites are designated "A" and "B," but these do not correspond in every case with the very earliest or latest versions; the autograph drafts in the 1722 *Clavier-Büchlein* predate version "A" and were edited separately in NBA V/4.[5] Also given separately, but in an appendix of NBA V/8, are alternate versions of Suites nos. 3 and 4. Although Dürr designates version "B" as the "later, ornamented" (*verzierte*) version, in Suites nos. 1–5 the differences between "A" and "B" extend well beyond the more numerous ornament signs of "B." On the other hand, in Suite no. 6 the "A" and "B" texts are virtually identical, and one can hardly speak of distinct versions for this suite, which was the last composed.

Version "A" is based on a single source, a copy by Altnikol of what Dürr believes was a lost autograph of around 1725 (NBA V/8, KB, 54). Version "B," on the other hand, combines readings from various sources that are thought to give later texts. This leads to occasional discrepancies; in the loure of Suite no. 5, the "B" text gives an early reading crossed out in the autograph in m. 14. Moreover, because the ornament signs in text "B" were collected from different sources, all were not necessarily meant for a single performance, even if all stem from Bach (which is by no means certain). Hence, players need not feel obliged to realize every ornament in version "B" exactly as indicated.[6] Other editions give a single version corresponding more or less with NBA version "B," but, as in the latter, players should beware that not every detail of the text is necessarily Bach's; in cases of doubt, critical commentaries must be examined carefully.

Suite in A Minor BWV 818

Sources: P 418 (Kayser; no. 4 in set); LEm Go.S.9 (Gerber, as no. 2). *Editions*: BG 36; Dadelsen (1975); NBA V/8.
Later version (BWV 818a): *Sources*: LEm ms. 8 (Mempell); P 804/36 (later copy by Mempell). *Editions*: same as for BWV 818 (BG gives BWV 818a in appendix).

The A-minor suite falls stylistically between the English Suites and the First French Suite. Lacking a prelude, it might for a time have been regarded as part of the later set. One of the earliest copies, by Bach's pupil Kayser, includes BWV 818 together with BWV 819 while omitting the later French Suites nos. 5 and 6. Kayser revised his copy to include a number of ornament signs. But he did not add the three movements, including a prelude, that are present in the alternate version BWV 818a. The latter could have been a short-lived experiment to convert the work into a "suite with prelude"; the movements unique to BWV 818a are considered below after the discussion of BWV 818.

Although firm dates are unavailable for either version, sources and style point to a relatively early origin for BWV 818. It is certainly earlier than the last two French Suites, and it could go back to the time of the English Suites or even before. Both allemande and courante are imitative, as in the English Suites, and the sarabande has a double, as in English Suite no. 6. The gigue uses a trill motive (mm. 4ff.) that seems to have interested Bach in several movements of the English Suites, especially the gigue in A.

Several things cause one to look back farther still, toward the time of the early suites treated in chapter 4, even though the present suite is more sophisticated than those. The allemande and the courante are shorter by at least a few measures than the corresponding movements in most of the other mature keyboard suites. The double of the sarabande is of the same type as the one in the Praeludium et Partita BWV 833, breaking the chords of the "simple" version into scalar passagework, not arpeggios. The gigue has a very simple subject, although it is worked out carefully in three real voices. An attractive work, the suite nevertheless is somewhat tentative when placed beside those in the English or French sets. Hence, it is not surprising that Bach apparently abandoned it around 1725, but not without first attempting to bring it up to date in the version BWV 818a.

The allemande opens with an apparent quotation from *La Couperin*, the French composer's self-portrait in allemande style. The resemblance is probably fortuitous, as the Couperin piece was not published until much later (Example 14.1).[7] The revisions in BWV 818a refine the voice leading, in one passage

Example 14.1 (a) Suite in A Minor BWV 818, allemande, mm. 1–2a; (b) Couperin, *La Couperin*, mm. 0–1a.

eliminating some clunky sonorities by reducing the original three voices to two (mm. 19–20a).

The courante, with only eight measures in each half, has the concision of many seventeenth-century examples of the dance. For just this reason it may be more successful than some of the longer courantes in the English Suites. A modulation to the subdominant occurs as late as three measures before the end, but the tonic is re-established convincingly through the unusual progression in mm. 14–5, where one 6/4/2-chord resolves to another. The successful negotiation of this modulation within a compact, perfectly symmetrical movement proves to be one of the abstruse charms of this suite.

The *Sarabande simple* consists mainly of embellished apreggiation; the same type of sarabande occurs in the Fifth Cello Suite, and as the double of the sarabande in the Sixth English Suite. The present double substitutes two-part counterpoint, or rather embellishes what is implicit in the original sarabande: the two voices follow the outlines of the original treble and bass, retaining their exchange of material after the double bar. That Bach never quite finished this version of the suite is evident from the vagueness concerning the repetition of the second half of the double; the only explicit sign for a repetition is the indication of a *petite reprise* of the last four measures. The presence of such a reprise, rare in Bach's music, could be why neither copy provides a way to go back to the beginning of the second half, for a repeat of mm. 9–24. Dürr suggests transposing the bass of the existing first ending (m. 24A) upward by a third, in order to connect back to m. 9 (NBA V/8, KB, 158). But the second ending (m. 24B) is perfectly suitable for this purpose, as well as for ending the movement.

The short, rather prosaic subject of the gigue made it possible to employ all the artifice of a serious three-part fugue without the effect of overkill that arises from the long-winded subjects of some of Reinken's fugal gigues. The counterpoint is simple enough to retain its transparency even at the climax of the contrapuntal working-out, when *rectus* and *inversus* versions of the subject are combined in the middle of the second half (mm. 33ff.). But strict counterpoint is not the main issue here. The dramatic climax of the movement is the scale that begins at the top of the keyboard in m. 29b and sweeps down to low C by m. 32a, after passing through all three voices. Similar scale gestures occur at crucial moments in a few of Bach's early fugues (e.g., BWV 954, m. 80), another indication of the suite's closeness to relatively early works.

The alternate version, BWV 818a, adds a prelude and a minuet and substitutes a single sarabande for the sarabande and double of BWV 818. Oddities in the prelude have raised suspicions about Bach's authorship of this version, as has its survival only in two copies by Mempell, a rather late, peripheral copyist. But style gives no reason to question Bach's responsibility for the two new dance movements, or the revisions in the three movements common to both versions.

The minuet is a mature work of Bach, alternating between ordinary and triplet sixteenths in the up-to-date manner also found in the minuet of the D-major

Partita, published in 1728. Despite its brevity, the minuet is the most impressive movement of the entire suite, although its *galant* singing melody and flexible keyboard idiom (e.g., broken octaves in m. 15) distinguish it stylistically from the other movements. It nevertheless possesses a contrapuntal element, transferring the opening theme to the bass after the double bar.

The sarabande is in the Italianate idiom with expressive written-out embellishment and chromatic harmony that Bach used in the Partitas (especially the last, in E minor). But the texture here is a little thinner, and some striking details are not entirely worked out. A chromatic scale fragment in sixteenths (alto, m. 18) sounds unmotivated, despite being a sort of diminution of an earlier chromatic bass line in eighths (m. 14). Each chromatic step has a real harmonic function, but the chromaticism verges on the ornamental when the note values are reduced; Bach writes like this only in a few relatively late works such as the C-minor fantasia BWV 906/1. The dotted rhythm in the opening measures is old-fashioned; Bach had used it in the sarabande of the early *Partie* BWV 832. But he returned to it in the corresponding movements of Partitas nos. 1 and 6, and one wonders whether this movement (as well as the minuet) might have been considered for inclusion in the A-minor Partita, whose early version Bach entered alongside Partita no. 6 into the 1725 *Clavierbüchlein*. The copyist Mempell would not have known that the present movement is a variation of the sarabande of BWV 818—or perhaps both rework a simpler original. Performers of BWV 818 might as well play all three versions of the sarabande, together with the minuet.

The first movement, lacking a title in the sources but evidently a prelude, is a different story. Dürr (NBA V/8, KB, 74–5) rightly calls it "primitive" in some respects. The texture is simplistic for a Bach work of the mid-1720s, and the tempo mark *Fort gai* is likewise unusual. Even odder is the frantic passagework first heard in m. 15, where the broad *alla breve* meter of the opening is effectively replaced by a nervous common time (Example 14.2). Some of the voice leading, including the melodic augmented seconds of both voices in m. 16, is also

Example 14.2 Suite in A Minor BWV 818a, prelude: (a) mm. 1–3; (b) mm. 15–6.

peculiar. Yet the opening theme is original and striking,[8] and the formal design resembles the bipartite form used in several preludes in WTC1 (e.g., in A♭). Perhaps like the sarabande this is a piece from Bach's workshop that was never quite finished. Although not as original as the praeambulum of Partita no. 5, it has the same light, freewheeling keyboard idiom, another apparent link to works of the mid- and late 1720s.

Suite in E♭, BWV 819

> *Chief sources*: P 418 (Kayser; no. 6 in set); LEm Go.S.10 (Gerber; as no. 3).
> *Editions*: BG 36; Dadelsen (1975—allemande only; the remainder of the edition is of BWV 819a); NBA V/8.
> Later version (BWV 819a): *Sources*: P 418, with later additions (Kayser); P 420 (Vogler). *Editions*: BG 36, appendix (allemande only); Dadelsen (1975); NBA V/8.

It is easy to think of BWV 818 and 819 as a pair standing between two well-known groups of six suites. But the suite in E♭ is much closer than the one in A minor to the style of the French Suites, especially the three last ones. French Suite no. 4 is in the same key, and BWV 819 might have been dropped to avoid including two suites in E♭ within the same set. Yet Bach's pupils Kayser and Vogler both copied the two E♭-major works into their collections of six suites "without prelude," and at some point Bach prepared a revised version, as he did for the others.

The later version (BWV 819a) substitutes a different allemande, but otherwise the alterations are minor by comparison with those in BWV 818 or some of the French Suites.[9] As in BWV 818, Kayser's and Gerber's copies of BWV 819 contain additional ornaments. Dadelsen (1975) gives these ornaments in small type; the NBA places them in the main text for BWV 819 but not BWV 819a, which consequently is less fully ornamented than the earlier version.

The original allemande bears a striking similarity to that of French Suite no. 6, both allemandes resembling a sonata movement for flute or violin with continuo. Neither allemande contains much imitative counterpoint, but both use the same violinistic figure, which is eventually transferred from the upper voice to the bass.[10] The new allemande of BWV 819a is more distinct and might have been composed in an effort to salvage the suite for inclusion among the "suites without prelude." This allemande could date from the same time as BWV 818a, whose sarabande is likewise a new movement elaborating an older one.

The same technique of composition through variation that produced the new sarabande of BWV 818a was the basis of the new allemande in BWV 819a. The latter demonstrates in particular that sophisticated double counterpoint could emerge from the composing-out of a harmonic skeleton, foreshadowing the Goldberg Variations. As in the original allemande, the bass imitates the initial treble at the distance of half a measure, and the two parts exchange material at m. 9. But beyond this point the new version is more chromatic, and Bach introduces further contrapuntal tricks as well. Measure 5 is a mirror inversion of m. 3; this is possible because the harmonic progressions in the two passages are in a mirror relationship (I–IV and I–V, respectively). In mm. 16–7, where the original allemande presented two different composings-out of the same progression (V–I in F minor), the second measure is now a nearly exact repetition of the first, but with the two parts in inverted counterpoint at the octave.

Some of the writing, such as the mirror reflection of the two halves of m. 22 (treble only), is a bit contrived, but no more so than in the canons of the *Art of Fugue* and other late polyphonic works.[11] Like the duets of the Goldberg Variations, the later allemande can and perhaps should be played on two manuals. Its two halves were surely not meant to serve as varied reprises for the original allemande. Vogler's copy lacks the earlier movement, indicating that he understood the latter to have been replaced by the new one. Kayser, however, inserted the new allemande into his existing copy of BWV 819, and players would be justified in treating it as a double.[12]

The courante, although notated in 3/2, is largely in compound duple meter (6/4), like the courante of Rameau's A-minor Suite. The right hand's eighth notes are beamed inconsistently in the sources, not always reflecting the actual meter. Perhaps this is because Bach's view of the meter changed; the only substantial revision in the movement (m. 10) coincides with the one clear shift to triple meter (3/2), which the revision was presumably meant to clarify.[13]

The sarabande recalls the Sinfonia in the same key, thanks to its dotted rhythm and trio-sonata texture; the resemblance is strengthened by the numerous appoggiaturas in the copies of both pieces by Gerber and Kayser. As in other *galant* pieces (e.g., the F#-major prelude in WTC2, the sarabande of Partita no. 5), the proper length of the appoggiaturas is not obvious. "Long" performance would create exposed fifths in m. 10 (between alto and bass) and harshen the already sharp dissonances in m. 19; hence, as usual with Bach, "short" or "invariable" appoggiaturas seem best. The repeated notes in the bass are another *galant* touch, rare in Bach's music; as a strongly articulated drum bass would be out of character here, a quiet, fairly smooth touch is implied.

The bourrée is a more athletic version of the dance than occurs in the English Suites, the quarter-note pulse of older examples being broken into arpeggiated figures. One striking harmonic progression echoes a bourrée from the older set,[14] and the opening motive is reminiscent of that in the gavotte of French Suite no. 4.

Perhaps Bach never completed the present suite, or perhaps he originally composed a single series of dances in Eb, then sorted them into two suites. In any case, there is no gigue for this suite. It was not unusual for contemporary suites to end simply with a minuet or two, as this one does, but Bach's only other mature suite to lack a gigue (Partita no. 2) concludes with a large capriccio whose contrapuntal design makes it a substitute for the missing gigue. The pedal point at the opening of minuet 1 is a pastoral idea, and together with the repetitious melodic writing might have reminded listeners of the musette (mm. 3–4 contain a variation of mm. 1–2). Minuet 2 is designated *Trio* in the sources and is, like the sarabande, a *galant* piece in three parts. It is Bach's only keyboard piece outside the WTC in E♭ minor, and one wonders whether it was originally in another key, like the trio of BWV 814a (see below).

French Suite no. 1 in D Minor BWV 812

> Earlier readings: *Chief sources*: US Wc (Altnikol); P 224 (autograph fair copy, beginning of allemande and end of gigue lost); P 418 (Kayser; no. 1 in set); P 1221 (Gerber; as no. 1). *Editions*: NBA V/4, first part (after P 224 and P 418); NBA V/8, first part (version "A," after US Wc).
> Later readings: *Chief sources*: P 225 (A. M. Bach); P 420 (Vogler). *Editions*: NBA V/4, second part (after P 225); NBA V/8, second part (version "B," including ornaments from P 1221).

Suite no. 1 is distinct in style from the remaining French Suites, resembling the English Suites in the relatively strict counterpoint of all movements. It is for connoisseurs of Bach's version of French style; even the gigue is relatively severe, and its employment of a pervasive dotted rhythm (in duple time) leaves the suite without a truly quick movement. The suite might have been composed earlier than the rest of the collection; Bach's entry in the 1722 *Clavier-Büchlein* was a fair copy and already contains a few revised readings.[15] Subsequent alterations were limited to refinements of detail and the addition of ornaments.

The opening movement resembles the corresponding movement of the First English Suite in evoking the improvisatory allemandes of earlier German composers such as Froberger. As is often the case in such movements, phrases are held together by scalar descents in the underlying bass line—for example, from d′ to d in mm. 2–5 and again in mm. 5–9. The actual bass, however, alternates between pedal points, walking eighth notes, and motivic writing in smaller note-values, including the French dotted figures in mm. 4, 6, and elsewhere. Hence, some measures languish, others push forward—features that might be reflected in performance; the pace quickens in the approach to each cadence. A descending scale in sixteenths, introduced without fanfare in m. 10, proves to be a motive of some importance. In m. 18 the inversion of the idea, in the soprano, moves in contrary motion against a descending scale in the left hand; the two voices land on a tritone on the downbeat of m. 19, marking the restrained climax of the piece.[16]

The courante is the only one in the French Suites to use the meter traditionally employed in the French version of the dance (3/2). Its plan is similar to that of the courantes in the English Suites, stating a short *thema* in imitation at the beginning and inverting it in the second half. The opening pedal point and the surprise Neapolitan harmony in the closing phrase (m. 22) are shared with the allemande, but the two movements do not form a variation pair.

The sarabande is in four parts without florid embellishment, as in English Suite no. 4. But the counterpoint here is more dissonant, and the inner parts and bass have more life of their own. The bass even restates the first five measures of the opening treble line at the beginning of the second half, two octaves below the original pitch level, with the harmony considerably altered.[17] The full chords and the numerous ornaments (especially in Gerber's copy) imply a graver tempo than in other sarabandes, although no slower than many pianists continue to consider normal for the dance.

The first minuet opens in free triple counterpoint, the opening phrase recurring in two further permutations (the only ones that are practical on the keyboard). The abbreviation *tr* in the later statements of the theme (mm. 9, 21) might be realized as a simple turn—likewise in the alto in mm. 1 and 6. The second minuet is in da-capo form, a design that Bach used in several early suites (see chap. 4) and still in gavotte 2 of the Sixth Cello Suite. Bach would have regarded this as a simple *rondeau* design, following models like the little *menuet rondeau* that ends Marchand's G-minor suite, published in 1702. No copyist is reported to have written out the da capo, and therefore the fermata in the last measure is a *fine* indication that does not imply any special lengthening of the last note. Presumably the first minuet is to be repeated afterwards, although most sources do not specify this.

It is unusually difficult to find an effective tempo for the gigue, or even to determine its basic character. It is one of two by Bach in dotted duple time, the other being that of the E-minor Partita.[18] Duple rhythm is common in seventeenth-century gigues; Froberger had used it for about half of his examples of the dance.[19] That the tradition remained alive in the eighteenth century is clear from an example in Mattheson's suites of 1714, which Bach surely knew. The present example resembles several by Froberger in its pervasive dotted rhythm. It is unknown how closely the character or performance practice of such pieces was expected to approach that of a French overture, whose notation is similar. But there is little evidence for converting such pieces to triple time, despite recurring speculation to that effect. Silbiger (1993, 16) argues convincingly that alternate versions of Froberger's gigues represent reworkings of the pieces in different meters, not a written-out performance practice. If, nevertheless, some such performance practice was applied in Bach's music, players would have had to follow undocumented notational conventions that cannot be unambiguously reconstructed, despite the arguments of Ferguson (1975, 92–3) and McIntyre (1965).

The complex rhythm and numerous ornaments of the present gigue, especially in Gerber's copy, require a fairly moderate pace, despite the *alla breve* notation in the autograph.[20] The pervasive dotting implies energetic articulation, yet the numerous appoggiaturas and other ornaments demand elegance; a tempo of quarter note = 60 strikes an effective balance. The incorporation of such a movement in a suite of this date was a striking gesture, calling attention to the movement's strict counterpoint and symmetrical design. There is even a presentiment of a moment in the *Art of Fugue*, composed some twenty years later: an impressive "Phrygian" cadence, with trill in the bass, marks an important formal juncture (m. 22; cf. Contrapunctus 8, m. 93). Here it prepares the combination of *rectus* and *inversus* forms of the subject in the final section. Unfortunately, the incessant dotted rhythms can grow monotonous; the appearance of continuous sixteenths in the closing phrase of each half (mm. 11, 26) is in principle dramatic but perhaps too subtle to have much effect.

French Suite no. 2 in C Minor BWV 813

Earliest readings: *Sources*: P 224 (fragmentary autograph, minuet copied separately by A. M. Bach); P 418 (Kayser; no. 2 in set). *Edition*: NBA V/4, first part (after P 224 and P 418).
Somewhat later readings: *Sole source*: P 1221 (Gerber; as no. 5).
Intermediate readings: *Chief source*: US Wc (Altnikol). *Edition*: NBA V/8, first part (version "A," with alternate versions of allemande and courante from P 1221).
Later readings: *Chief sources*: P 225 (A. M. Bach, first three movements); P 420 (Vogler, with second minuet BWV 813a). *Edition*: NBA V/4, second part (after P 225 and P 420).
Latest readings: *Sole source*: P 418, revised text (Kayser). *Edition*: NBA V/8, second part (version "B," including minuet BWV 813a).

Although the surviving autograph of Suite no. 2 dates from about the same time as that of Suite no. 1, here Bach was either revising or composing as he wrote. Whether or not this makes the suite a somewhat later work, it has more of the *galant* character that is typical of the remaining works of the set. It adds several new types of movements to those previously found in Bach's keyboard suites: a courante in 3/4, an arioso-like sarabande, an air (unrelated to the one in the early suite BWV 833), and a skipping gigue in two voices.[21] Despite its relatively simple textures, the suite, especially the first two movements, cost Bach considerable trouble; few works survive in a more extensive array of early and revised readings.

Allemande and courante both exist in multiple versions (see Table 14.1). In each case the earliest known version is divided exactly in half by the double bar; later versions break the symmetry, inserting new material after the cadence that subdivides the second half. The result in both movements is to make the return

Table 14.1 Revisions In French Suite No. 2

Version*	Chief Sources	Edited in	Distinctions From Final Version
Allemande			
1	P 418, orig. text	NBA V/8, KB, 92	Measures 12b–13 in simpler form. Lacks mm. 14 and 15b–16a. Simpler bass in mm. 15a, 16b–18a
2	P 1221	NBA V/8, "A," alternate ending	Simpler bass in mm. 15b–18a. Different treble in m. 16a
3	US Wc, P 225, P 420	NBA V/8, "A"	Simpler bass in mm. 16–18a
4	P 418, corr. text	NBA V/8, "B"	(= final version)
Courante			
1	P 224; P 418, orig. text	NBA V/4, 1st part	48 measures. In place of mm. 38–50: 4 measures using same motivic material as mm. 46–9 of final version
2	P 1221	NBA V/8, "A," alternate ending	51 measures. In place of mm. 38–50: 7 measures
3	edition by Forkel	NBA V/8, "A," with variants listed for source Y2	54 measures. In place of mm. 38–50: 10 measures
4	US Wc, P 225, P 420	NBA V/4, 2d part; NBA V/8, "A"	Like version 3, with small variants in mm. 38–43
5	P 418, orig. text	NBA V/8, "B"	57 measures (= final version)

orig. = original
corr. = corrected (i.e., revised)
*Numbers correspond with *Varianten* as enumerated in NBA V/8, KB, 92–94

to the tonic less direct (or more dramatic). But in neither movement did Bach insert a full-fledged return or recapitulation section, as he would do in the A-minor Invention, composed at about the same time.

The courante closely resembles some of Bach's preludes, especially the "Six" (BWV 933–8), in being essentially a sonata movement, its texture more that of a work for violin and continuo than a *pièce de clavecin*. Bach could have found models for this type of Italian corrente, based on arpeggio motives in continuous eighths, in works at least as early as Corelli's op. 4 trio sonatas (1694). Bach's revisions here were more extensive than in the allemande, but all five versions retain the idea of ending with a restatement of the closing phrase from the first half, always after a climactic ascent to c‴, the highest note used in the French Suites. In the original version the ascent to this note was swift and direct, immediately following the cadence to the subdominant (m. 38).[22] In version 2 Bach inserted a new passage after the cadence, postponing and intensifying the eventual climb to c‴. Subsequent versions represent efforts to perfect the inserted passage, versions 3 and 4 being marred by a clumsy leap of a tenth in m. 44.[23]

Like the courante, the sarabande departs from French style, but in this case it is hard to find a model in the Italian repertory. Although the second beat often receives some sort of emphasis, through harmony or melody, this is essentially a free aria, like the opening movement in the Goldberg Variations. The texture is that of the "monodic" keyboard chorale, a genre represented in all three Little Keyboard Books (see chap. 10). Thus the sarabande can be played on two manuals, the two lower parts quieter and confined to the left hand. Despite the florid embellishment of the melody the tempo need not be any slower than usual, allowing one to play "in three" without subdividing the beats. This will help bring out the underlying sarabande rhythm in mm. 3, 7, et al., where the last two beats comprise a florid arpeggiation of a single harmony.

Bach might have applied the word *air* to the fourth movement as a generic term for a piece that, unlike the two preceding movements, could not be plausibly identified with any dance. The opening theme is inverted at the beginning of the second half, where the autograph shows that Bach originally considered having the bass imitate the treble (Example. 14.3a). Although he immediately changed his mind, he evidently had to resist the impulse to incorporate imitative polyphony even in a fairly simple piece such as this. He nevertheless gave the theme in its original form to the bass at the return (m. 13). There a first attempt to preserve the harmonic pattern of m. 1—with a VI^7 chord on the third beat—led to a near-simultaneous cross relation. Bach therefore simplified the harmony, making the type of compromise between rigor and euphony that he had been reluctant to accept in the English Suites (Example 14.3b).

In most copies of the suite there is only one minuet. Even this was absent from Bach's original draft in the 1722 *Clavier-Büchlein*, but a rubric in Sebastian's hand directs the player to the minuet copied by his wife near the end of the volume. A second minuet (sometimes designated BWV 813a) occurs in a few later sources, and its addition brought the suite into conformity with Suite no. 1. Both minuets might have been teaching pieces that Bach added to the suite as an afterthought. The NBA gives the slurs for minuet 1 differently in versions "A" and "B," the slurs in version "A" implying fussier and more detailed articulation. Some of the differences seem deliberate, such as the change in m. 3 from three two-note slurs to a single six-note slur. Others might be due only to the imprecise placement of long slurs meant to cover an entire measure.[24]

later reading: G   G

Example 14.3 French Suite no. 2 in C Minor BWV 813, air: (a) m. 5, canceled reading of autograph; (b) m. 13.

The gigue is the only one in the set to employ the dotted figures typical of the *canarie*, one of several French varieties of the dance. Although written in 3/8, it could have been notated in 6/8 or 12/8, and in the autograph the barlines after mm. 4 and 8 were altered to form four-measure groups.[25] Kirnberger would write that 3/8 implied a lively tempo, but with accents on every beat (unlike 6/8 or 12/8); hence, as in the gigue of the first suite, the player is being asked to find a happy medium between two mutually exclusive extremes. The skipping rhythm is heard almost without a break, and there is a danger of rhythmic monotony and atomization if accents come too strongly and regularly. Running sixteenths provide some rhythmic variety and acceleration toward the end of the second half, but they also require that one not take too quick a tempo at the beginning. A moderate tempo may actually help reduce the danger of monotony, allowing the player to introduce expressive rhythmic nuances and to make the ornaments more meaningful, for example by distinguishing a rapid mordent used for accent (mm. 1, 10) from a slower one used to sustain a long note (m. 12).

French Suite no. 3 in B Minor BWV 814

Earliest readings: *Source*: P 224 (fragmentary autograph; minuets separately). *Edition*: NBA V/4, first part (after P 224 and P 418).
Somewhat later readings: *Chief sources*: US Wc (Altnikol), P 418 (Kayser; no. 3 in set). *Edition*: NBA V/8, first part (version "A," after US Wc).
Intermediate readings: *Source*: P 1221 (Gerber; as no. 4).
Later readings: *Chief sources*: P 418, revised text (Kayser); P 804/49. *Editions*: NBA V/8, second part (version "B").
Intermediate (?) version (BWV 814a), with alternate second minuet: *Sole source*: P 514 (gigue fragmentary). *Editions*: BG 36, NBA V/8, appendix.

Suite no. 3 opens with the most delicate of the allemandes in the French Suites but closes with one of the most brilliant gigues. As in Suite no. 2, one senses the influence of *galant* chamber music, now even in the allemande, which has little to do with older examples of the dance (at least those for keyboard; ensemble examples might be found). The suite exists in at least four distinct versions, but none of the movements underwent changes as substantial as did the allemande and courante of Suite no. 2. Even the substitution of a different second minuet in the alternate version BWV 814a was accompanied by only a few changes in the other movements. The uncertain provenance of the one copy preserving this version, moreover, raises the possibility that this version of the suite is by someone other than Bach.[26]

One could imagine the allemande scored for flute and continuo. Because the two parts are so nearly equal, they could be played on separate manuals, probably single eight-foot stops, since this is an unusually delicate allemande for Bach.

Example 14.4 French Suite no. 3 in B Minor BWV 814, allemande, mm. 0–2.

Virtually every beat contains a statement of the opening motive, which consists of an upbeat of three sixteenths moving to an accented note that is often marked by a *port de voix*, as in m. 1 (Example 14.4). Hence, throughout the movement gestures end on the beat. Even when the accented note is a mere sixteenth, it can be lengthened ever so slightly and separated by a small articulation from the following gesture. This is fussy by later standards of phrasing and gesture, but it is appropriate in a movement that comes particularly close to the "speaking" quality of the music of Bach's French contemporaries.

The courante at first seems uniformly in 6/4, a type that Rameau would use for his A-minor suite (published ca. 1729–30). Hemiolas occur frequently, but often in only one of two or three voices, as in the treble of mm. 4, 8, and 17. The sarabande is another example of the arioso type seen in Suite no. 2, less "monodic" as the bass and even inner voice share thematic material. Nevertheless one can play it on two manuals, albeit with the inner voice crossing from the left to the right hand (mm. 13–5, 19–20). As in the air of Suite no. 2, Bach revised a passage in which the theme returns in the left hand (mm. 21–2). A variant at this point in BWV 814a may stem from an attempt to improve the upper part (Example 14.5). Yet the result is not clearly an improvement; it may be an intermediate reading that was rejected prior to the final reading of version "B."[27]

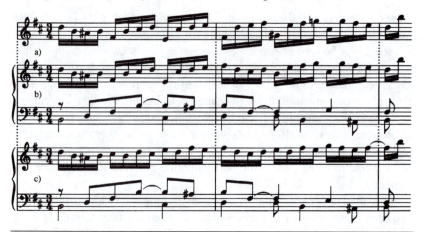

Example 14.5 French Suite no. 3 in B Minor, sarabande, mm. 21–23a: (a) BWV 814, version "A"; (b) BWV 814, version "B"; (c) BWV 814a.

The next movement, in most sources, is the anglaise, which seems originally to have been called a gavotte although lacking the latter's half-measure upbeat.[28] The time-signature "2" is a French equivalent of cut time, used for gavottes as well. The sturdy *mouvement* in quarter notes and the four-square phrases, many cadencing in the middle of the measure, give the piece the rustic flavor supposed to characterize this not very well-defined dance type.

As with Suite no. 2, the minuets were written separately in the 1722 *Clavier-Büchlein*, and if Bach ever indicated their proper position it was through a rubric written on a page now lost. In most copies the minuets come at the end of the suite, but Altnikol and Gerber placed them between anglaise and gigue, which corresponds with the position of minuets in Bach's other suites. Minuet 1 underwent the most extensive revision of any movement in the suite. A new bass line for the last eight measures was the most prominent change, a chain reaction set off by a relatively minor alteration of the treble in mm. 29 and 31. In the autograph, Bach gave minuet 2 the heading *Menuet-Trio*; it is in three parts throughout, resembling the first minuet of Suite no. 1 in its suggestions of triple counterpoint (inverted after the double bar).

For minuet 2, BWV 814a substitutes a version of the similarly named but smaller *Menuett Trio* BWV 929, attached in CB to the suite in G minor by Stölzel. Both versions of this little trio probably derive from one now lost; the version in BWV 814a is unlikely to be the original, if only because it descends to low BB, a note otherwise not found in the French Suites.[29] But the rich sonority of this minuet (a sixth lower, not a third higher, than BWV 929) makes an effective contrast to minuet 1; perhaps Bach thought of using it in the B-minor *Ouverture*, which likewise tends toward low sonorities in this key. Both trios are notated in "3," as opposed to 3/4; if this implied a slower tempo, it would be appropriate to their more expressive character.

The gigue, like the allemande, is essentially a binary sonata movement in two voices, showing few signs of the traditional dance rhythm. What seems like new material at the beginning of the second half is actually an embellished variation of the subject. Bach inserted mm. 11–2 and three parallel passages (mm. 29–30, 47–8, 61–2) only after completing the autograph; this made symmetrical eight-measure phrases (e.g., mm. 9–16) out of what had been six-measure ones.

French Suite no. 4 in E♭, BWV 815

Earlier readings: *Chief sources*: P 224 (autograph); US Wc (Altnikol); P 418 (Kayser; no. 6 in set); P 1221 (Gerber; as no. 6). *Editions*: NBA V/4, first part (after P 224), NBA V/8, first part (version "A," after US Wc).

Later readings, including minuet: *Chief sources*: P 418, revised text (Kayser); P 420 (Vogler). *Edition*: NBA V/8, second part (version "B").

Alternate (?intermediate) version (BWV 815a): *Chief sources*: P 289/13 (Michel); US NHy LM 5024 (Rinck). *Editions*: BG 36, NBA V/8, appendix.

With Suite no. 4 the French Suites move into major keys and take on a more popular style, and echoes of pieces by Froberger, d'Anglebert, and other seventeenth-century composers grow fainter. Hence this suite looks forward to the Partitas, perhaps already being drafted during the same period; the first two movements show stylistic parallels with those of Partita no. 1. The allemande still uses the arpeggios traditionally associated with the genre, but the arpeggiation now falls into regular motivic patterns, as in Bach's preludes, avoiding the expressive irregularity cultivated in earlier keyboard allemandes. The courante is mainly in two voices, written in 3/4 with triplet eighths, which is typical of neither the French courante nor the Italian corrente—evidently a new invention, used again in Partita no. 1.[30]

The sarabande has some of the traditional dance rhythm, but its texture has little to do with that of earlier sarabandes. One would hardly have expected the graceful opening gesture of the right hand and the walking bass line accompanying it to change places, yet they do so when the counterpoint is inverted in m. 3 and elsewhere. Like the sarabande, the gavotte is a relatively gentle version of the dance, at least for Bach, lacking the emphatic upbeat of two quarters and the metrical ambiguities of those in the English Suites. Like many French gavottes, it can be played expressively, in a moderate tempo, as implied by the two-note slurs which the later version sets over the first few drooping "sigh" figures. The air is almost a variation of the gavotte, containing the same number of bars and even opening in the middle of the measure. There is also a brief, somewhat elegiac minuet, found only in a few later copies and thus absent from many editions, but a worthwhile addition to the suite.[31]

The gigue is a true fugue, though mainly in just two voices, hence resembling the gigue of the Fourth English Suite, to which it is also related by the horn calls in its subject. The subject is even closer to that of the fugal gigue in the Telemann suite found in CB. Friedemann's copy of the Telemann piece has been placed around the beginning of 1723, the same time when Sebastian was copying the present suite into the 1722 *Clavier-Büchlein*. The possibility of Telemann's influence on Bach is obvious; the two pieces even contain similar ornaments, since both subjects were later graced by mordents.[32] Bach made only one substantial revision in the gigue: in mm. 35 and 37 the leaps in the main motive were stretched from thirds into tenths, imitating the overblowing of brass instruments.

The suite exists in a considerably altered version (BWV 815a) containing a prelude and a second gavotte but no minuet or gigue. The movements that this version shares with the familiar one also contain a few changes, not all of which seem to be improvements.[33] Nevertheless, the relatively good provenance of this version—the copyist Michel worked closely with C. P. E. Bach—and its musical style leave little reason to doubt Bach's authorship. Like BWV 818a, it might be an experiment of the mid-1720s, although parallels with movements in WTC2 suggest a later date.[34] Performers might well combine movements from both versions.

The prelude opens with a series of chords marked *arpeggio*, leading to a simple fughetta. This is the same design found in the early version of the C#-major prelude of WTC2 (BWV 872a/1),[35] although the latter lacks the return to arpeggio style at the end, in a four-measure coda. Despite the shorthand notation of the arpeggiando passages, the fughetta is fully worked out, the voice leading precisely notated. There is even a distinct closing phrase (mm. 22–3), recapitulated at the end to give the fughetta a bipartite form.

The second gavotte is also fully worked out, and at much greater length; indeed, it is Bach's longest and most intricate example of the dance. Any qualms about playing it are set aside by its exquisite counterpoint. As in the gavottes of the English Suites, the second half has an episode of irregular meter and phrasing (mm. 36–50a), normal movement being restored with the restatement of the theme in the bass.

French Suite no. 5 in G, BWV 816

> Earlier readings: *Chief sources*: P 224 (autograph); US Wc (Altnikol). *Editions*: NBA V/4, first part (after P 224); NBA V/8, first part (version "A," after US Wc).
>
> Later readings: *Chief sources*: P 1221 (Gerber; no. 8 in set); P 420 (Vogler); LEm ms. 8 (Mempell). *Editions*: NBA V/8, second part (version "B").

The suite in G, one of Bach's most elegant harpsichord works, is even more popular in style than the preceding one, placing greater priority on singing melody and idiomatic treatment of the instrument while further reducing the role of imitative counterpoint. Not surprisingly, it appears to be a later composition; although Bach sketched out the first few measures of the allemande in the 1722 *Clavier-Büchlein*, he did not complete the score until coming to Leipzig.[36] Later revisions were insignificant, apart from an important variant in the sarabande.

Both allemande and courante make graceful use of violinistic figuration; the latter even appears in the bass of the allemande, as in mm. 8b–10a, where the treble has an arioso melody. The two movements, as well as the loure, follow similar symmetrical binary plans, the courante and loure having exactly the same cadence structure as the aria of the Goldberg Variations. The courante is effectively a two-part invention, inverting first the counterpoint after the double bar, then the theme itself in the last phrase (from m. 24).

The sarabande is another example of the arioso type, performable on two manuals. The ornaments are an essential part of the melodic line and (exceptionally) are present in the autograph. The movement may be Bach's longest sarabande in number of measures, though not in real time, as it lacks the florid embellishment of other examples and can be played andante or even faster. Bach later varied the final phrase, giving it a more ornate form that soars to high c‴ three measures before the end. This gives the sarabande a more satisfactory conclusion than the original version, which reached its peak (b″) in the previous phrase (m. 35).

The forthright melodies of the gavotte and bourrée make them favorites with players and audiences, so it may be necessary to point out that neither is entirely typical of the respective dances. The strongly accented rhythm of the gavotte is rare in French examples. In the bourrée, Bach has softened the dance's vigorous quarter-note pulsation, producing an arioso melody accompanied by what appears to be an Alberti bass; a closer parallel, however, would be the lively cello writing in certain Bach arias.[37]

The loure, mislabeled as bourrée 2 in some sources and older editions, is absent from the most authoritative sources of the later version of the suite, implying that Bach decided to omit it.[38] Still, it is worth playing as one of only two examples of this dance by Bach (for the other, see chap. 16 on BWV 1006a). A loure is essentially a slow gigue, but Bach's examples are more motile than suggested by Walther's (1732, 372) description of the dance as being performed "slowly and with gravity." The basic rhythm here is close to that of a French courante; the dotted rhythms gain a dance-like spring by lengthening each dotted quarter and leaving a small silence after it—and by not dwelling on the appoggiaturas. The flourishes in sixteenths were afterthoughts, squeezed into already completed measures in the autograph.[39] They may not have been a good idea, for the combination of florid embellishment with counterpoint in the closing phrase of each half is a little stiff, in the manner of the English Suites; the player needs to find a way to make the sixteenths glide smoothly without slowing the basic pulse.

On paper the gigue is the longest in the French Suites, but the 12/16 time signature implies a very lively tempo. With the gigue of Suite no. 1, it is one of the set's two most fully worked-out fugues, with two expositions in each half. But otherwise the two gigues have nothing in common, and the repeated arpeggios in the present subject lead to the most brilliant keyboard writing in the entire set. The movement is not easy to play, and some passages are maddening to learn (mm. 34–5, 40–1). Once one has mastered them, it is all too tempting to play the piece as a *moto perpetuo*. But there are plenty of opportunities for expressive rhythmic nuances, as at the seven-chord on the downbeat of m. 42, on which one might dwell for a split second before attacking the following cadenza-like passage.

At the end of the 1722 *Clavier-Büchlein* stands a minuet in G, BWV 841, which has been suggested as a possible addition for Suite no. 5. The piece had been previously copied into Wilhelm Friedemann's Little Keyboard Book, where, however, it is the simplest of three G-major minuets. It might make for a nice contrast after the bourrée, but no source incorporates it into the suite.

French Suite no. 6 in E, BWV 817

> Earlier readings: *Chief source*: US Wc (Altnikol). *Edition*: NBA V/8, first part (version "A").
> Later readings: *Chief sources*: P 1221 (Gerber, with prelude BWV 854/1); P 420 (Vogler). *Edition* NBA V/8, second part (version "B").

The Sixth French Suite was almost certainly the last composed, perhaps as late as 1725. The NBA distinguishes two versions, but it would have taken Bach only a few moments to make the few small revisions that distinguish "B" from "A."[40] Like the E-major *Partia* for unaccompanied violin—in the same key, and likewise closing a set of six—this is the lightest work in its collection. Some of the inner movements—the gavotte, polonaise, and minuet—are unusually slight for Bach, but the four main movements are imaginative, especially the courante, and the suite as a whole continues the trend of Suites nos. 4 and 5 toward fleet writing and spare textures (compare, e.g., successive courantes and bourrées). The thin counterpoint and singing melodies make this suite more suitable than most for the clavichord, although the key would have challenged pupils trying to play it on small fretted instruments.

Gerber's copy opens with the prelude in E from WTC1 and thus belongs not with the French Suites but with the "suites with preludes"—that is, the English Suites. If this was Bach's idea, it might have been another short-lived experiment that occurred to him in the course of planning the *Clavierübung*, like the suites BWV 818a and 815a. Bach's failure to publish the present suite (with or without a prelude) might have reflected a decision to print only music that was more monumental in scope and more challenging in style and technique.

The allemande resembles the corresponding movement of BWV 819, but it contains more varied material while avoiding the repetitions of one- and two-measure units that make the allemande of the Eb-major work somewhat square. The courante may be the most delicately scored of all of Bach's keyboard dances, almost monophonic at times. It has even less in common with traditional courantes than those of Suites nos. 4 and 5, yet its descent from earlier movements of this type is evident in the inversion of the opening gesture at the beginning of the second half. Although the courante gives the impression of being a tossed-off improvisation, even details such as the values of the detached bass notes are precisely indicated. Holding notes beyond their written values (e.g., in the arpeggios) will increase the sonority, but at the risk of weighing down the gossamer filigree.

The next few movements show less inspiration, perhaps having been conceived as undemanding pieces for not very advanced pupils. The sarabande is too regular in its rhythms and phrasing to rival Bach's more ambitious examples of the dance. It is remarkable for the divergent ornaments given by Vogler and

Gerber, conveniently set out on parallel systems in NBA version "B." These ornaments might be products of aural tradition, deriving not from any autograph but from different ways in which Bach played the piece for each pupil.[41] Both ornamented versions are effective, and no one set of ornaments need be regarded as definitive.

As in Suite no. 4, the gavotte is characterized by parallel thirds and sixths and an occasional expressive "sigh" figure; the detached pedal point in the first two measures gives it a pastoral quality. The polonaise is equally *galant*. Bach wrote only two other examples of this dance, both orchestral,[42] but the polonaise—or *polonoise*, as it was then spelled—was popular throughout the eighteenth century, especially as an easy type of keyboard piece. The 1725 *Clavier-Büchlein* contains examples by other composers, including (probably) Emanuel Bach. Musically, most eighteenth-century examples resemble minuets; Gerber designated this one *Menuet poloinese* [sic], "Polish minuet." It has little in common with nineteenth-century polonaises, apart from the triple meter and the placement of cadences on the second beat.

The bourrée, Bach's last, is also his most lively, although the bourrée of BWV 819 uses similar motivic material. The even more lively gigue opens with imitations at the octave, avoiding the traditional fugal answer used in the other gigues of the set. This gigue was later the basis for Kirnberger's demonstration of how to compose a "sonata" movement as a variation of an existing piece.[43] Even if the method came from Bach himself, Kirnberger's sonata does not speak well for his sensitivity to his teacher's music. His "sonata" is a clumsy pastiche, far less imaginative than Sebastian's demonstrations of variation in the allemande of BWV 819a or the sarabandes of BWV 818a.

A few late sources put the minuet directly after the polonaise, where it serves as a pendant to the latter, like a trio. But this ordering may be anachronistic, reflecting a later perception that a suite must end with a relatively long quick movement. There is apparently no manuscript authority for placing the minuet immediately before the gigue, as in some editions. Altnikol, Gerber, and Vogler all place it last, after the gigue, as Mattheson did in all four of his published suites that contain both types of movement.[44] The "little minuet," as Gerber called it (*Petit minuet*), is somewhat pallid, constructed like the sarabande in two-measure units. These can grow monotonous, but perhaps the idea was to challenge the player to make something out of the unrelenting alternation between monophonic and homophonic measures.

15

Clavierübung, Part 1

The Six Partitas

In the six Partitas Bach continued in the direction marked by his French Suites, favoring new approaches to traditional keyboard dances, new types of keyboard texture, and further use of *galant* idioms as opposed to imitative counterpoint. Some movements are close to those of the French Suites, especially no. 6. But in general the Partitas are larger, the style freer and more variegated, and the technical demands on the player greater. The keyboard range is wider, extended from four octaves to over four-and-a-half (GG to d′′′ in Partita no. 5). Most of the dances are longer and diverge farther from traditional models; the preludes, each of which in principle represents a different sort of opening movement (overture, toccata, etc.), are original forms, only the overture of Partita no. 4 adhering closely to the genre to which it ostensibly belongs.

The Partitas were Bach's first keyboard publications, and their content and style reflect the circumstances of their publication. Bach had arrived in Leipzig in spring 1723. Three and a half years later he announced publication of the first of what would be six large suites with preludes.[1] These suites, that is, the Partitas, were first issued separately, then re-issued in a collected second edition in 1731. Bach would repeat the title of this first collection, *Clavier Ubung* [*sic*] or "Keyboard Practice," for three further publications. Volume 3 is primarily for organ; the others represent Bach's crowning achievement in genres associated with the harpsichord: suite, variation, and quasi-transcriptions of a concerto and an *ouverture* (orchestral suite).

The entire series is unlikely to have been fully planned, let alone composed, by 1726, when it began to appear in print. But Bach would certainly have been thinking long before that date about publishing keyboard music; Couperin's *Troisième livre* (1722) and Rameau's *Pièces de clavecin* (1724) would have provided immediate spurs, if they had reached Cöthen and Leipzig. Printing music was expensive, the production and sale of printed matter complicated and time-consuming. Some previous composers, such as Kuhnau, served in effect as their own publishers, arranging for the private engraving and printing of works which they sold from their own homes. Some keyboard publications bore dedications to prominent figures who might have subsidized the costs of commercial publication. Bach would have had to decide whether to aim at pleasing a single patron or a larger public, and whether to share the tasks of editing and selling his work with an established publisher or to take on most of the production process and sales himself. He would have been under pressure to issue something short, easy, and fashionable—*galant*, in the language of Bach's time. Yet at a time when few could actually hear him play, and performers' reputations were based on music that they composed, he must have felt compelled to issue something worthy of his reputation as Germany's greatest keyboard player. WTC1 and the English Suites were probably too long and by 1726 too old fashioned. The French Suites, on the other hand, might may have seemed too insubstantial, although variant versions (including the suites BWV 818a and 819a) dating from these same years may reflect rejected drafts of pieces Bach considered publishing, especially before the final scheme of six (or seven) partitas had emerged.

It is possible that the Partitas were composed at Leipzig expressly for publication.[2] In any case, writing the pieces probably took far less time and effort than seeing them through the process of engraving, printing, and publication. Bach may have shifted his priorities precisely in order to do this, for by March 1725 his production of church cantatas, composed on a weekly basis for the preceding two years, had slackened. During the months preceding the publication of Partita no. 1 in November 1726 he composed relatively few new church works, in some cases performing instead works by his Meiningen cousin Johann Ludwig Bach. He did, however, present several new cantatas containing concerto movements and arias with solo organ, works that would have revealed Bach to the Leipzig public, perhaps for the first time, as a player of fashionable keyboard music.[3] By then Bach had probably already composed at least three of the Partitas, for the 1725 *Clavier-Büchlein* for Anna Magdalena opens with autograph copies—not first drafts—of Partitas nos. 3 and 6. Partita no. 2, not published until 1727, is relatively conservative in style and has a fairly restricted range (BB♭–d♭′′′); it too might have been composed several years earlier.[4]

Despite their difficulty and the unprecedented transformations of traditional movement types, the Partitas appear to have proved relatively popular, surviving in a greater number of printed copies than do Bach's subsequent publications (Talle 2003, 5–6). Either because he lacked a patron or because he wished to control every aspect of production, Bach was his own publisher, overseeing the engraving and printing of each volume. His initial publication of the Partitas in installments would have avoided the risks and costs associated with a larger volume. That he was eventually able to publish four large collections of keyboard music, and was planning a fifth (the *Art of Fugue*) when he died, suggests that his enterprise was more successful, his works more highly prized, than one might have expected, considering their expense and the unfashionability of much of the music.

In issuing a collection of keyboard suites, Bach followed the model of Johann Kuhnau, his predecessor at Leipzig, who published four volumes of keyboard music (two containing suites) between 1689 and 1700. Kuhnau had called his suites *Parthien*, presumably a German equivalent for Italian *partita*; both words appear on the title page of the suites published in 1697 by Johann Krieger. The Italian word could mean "variation," as in Bach's chorale partitas, but despite occasional vague thematic parallels between movements, Bach's partitas are in no sense variation-suites. Bach had used the similar term *partia* for his three suites for unaccompanied violin; as Williams (2001, 15–6) points out, the headings of the present suites might have meant that each was a "part" or "division" of the complete volume. Even if all these words had simply become equivalents of "suite," it is curious that Saxon and Thuringian composers preferred Italian titles for published music that is in many respects French in inspiration; was this a way of reflecting the mixed style of their music, or did it express antipathy toward French music or musicians? Graupner's partitas of 1717 are largely Italian in style, seemingly modeled on the *sonate da camera* of Corelli's op. 5, and Jones (1988, 71) argues that by 1725 "the Italian style was at least as important as the French" in Bach's conception of the keyboard suite.

In any case, Bach's terminology reflects his consciousness of earlier publications, especially Kuhnau's *Clavierübung*. The latter expression is roughly equivalent to the Italian *Essercizi* and the English *Lessons*, used for keyboard publications during the first half of the eighteenth century. Taken literally, these terms imply that the music was primarily pedagogic, but the words might have meant nothing more specific than our *pieces*. Bach's full title added that the music was to "refresh the spirits of music-lovers," omitting the pedagogic implications of the "Candid Instruction" that headed the title of the Inventions and Sinfonias.[5]

How extraordinary these pieces are becomes clear when one compares their movements with preludes and dances by Bach's contemporaries or in his own earlier suites. Williams (2003b) points at a superficial level to such features as the use of hand crossings and 2/4 meter, not previously used by Bach in a keyboard suite. At deeper levels he suggests the possibility of an "anxiety of influence," in the sense that the partitas borrow ideas from but then "swerve away" from works not only by minor composers such as Kuhnau and Mattheson but more imaginative ones like Couperin and especially Rameau. Indeed, Cole (2000) shows that at least one movement, the courante of the C-minor Partita, seems to elaborate upon the opening idea in the courante from Kuhnau's suite in the same key. Williams also points to the set's "systematic variety," whereby hardly any two instances of a given dance are of the same type. There were already signs of this in the French suites and WTC1, but in a published work Bach might have been even more "anxious" to outdo other composers by offering a comprehensive set of *exempla* of a particular type of composition: here preludes and dances, later (in the *Art of Fugue*) "contrapuncti" and canons. The order of tonalities is systematic as well, more so than in his two unpublished sets of suites, although the "wedge" organization of keys is not immediately apparent (Bb–c–a–D–G–e, continuing with b and F in Part 2).

One might suppose that in published works Bach would have been unable to make the revisions that he was in the habit of carrying out in his earlier un-published ones. But the copper plates used for music printing could be and were altered, especially to show new ornaments; many such changes were made for the collected edition of 1731.[6] Moreover, some printed copies show hand-written corrections in ink; one copy of the 1731 edition contains numerous autograph alterations and for this reason has been regarded as Bach's *Handexemplar* (per-sonal copy).[7] Four other exemplars contain similar alterations, but it is unclear whether these can be traced directly to Bach.[8] Nevertheless, many of the read-ings are stylistically plausible and, like the ornaments in pupils' copies of the English and French Suites, might be played even if Bach never notated them himself. Revisions from the supposed *Handexemplar* are incorporated into the editions in NBA V/1 and by Klaus Engler (Wiener Urtext, 1993), but one must scan the critical reports of both editions to find corrections and additions from the other altered copies. For this reason, and because of a number of debatable editorial emendations (some discussed below), neither edition can be recom-mended without reservations. Early versions of Partitas nos. 3 and 6 appear in NBA V/4 (facsimile in Dadelsen 1988); there are several facsimile editions of the 1731 print.[9]

Partita no. 1 in Bb, BWV 825

The opening work in the *Clavierübung* (CU) is not particularly large (e.g., by comparison with the English Suites) and is relatively light in texture. By the stan-dards of the day, however, its dimensions were ambitious, its technical demands high. Considering these potential impediments to the work's popular success, Bach must have placed his hopes in its novelty. Indeed, those who opened the first installment of the *Clavierübung* in 1726 not knowing Bach's previous music might have been amazed by his treatment of some of the traditional keyboard dances. The allemande opens with fantasia- or concerto-like arpeggiation, only later coalescing into more regular writing. The corrente—called here by its Italian title—is in effect a sonata movement in 9/8, as in French Suite no. 4. The final movement, a giga with hand crossings, seems to be without precedent.

The praeludium is essentially a sinfonia or three-part invention. Musicians unfamiliar with Bach's Sinfonias might have thought of it as a type of fantasia

(Bach's first term for the Sinfonias) and might have been surprised when the theme, accompanied in simple part-writing in mm. 1–4a, is imitated at the dominant by the bass, as in a fugue (mm. 4bff.). From modest beginnings the movement gradually broadens out, first in register, then in texture, expanding to five nominal voices in the last phrase, whose final chord spans four octaves. At the close the left hand even doubles the bass in octaves. Not only the magnificent ending but several short pedal points give the movement a grandeur not encountered in the Sinfonias; except at the outset, the pedal tones are not held but rather touched lightly by the left hand, which then leaps to take the inner voice (mm. 9, 12, 19–20)—a quasi-pedaliter keyboard idiom that Bach used previously in the Chromatic Fantasia.

The pedal idea continues in the opening and closing phrases of the allemande. The largely monophonic arpeggiation that starts each half extends to the allemande the free-wheeling writing found in the courante of the Sixth French Suite. As in the praeludium, the texture thickens as each half proceeds; perhaps the style also grows a little less unconventional (for an allemande). Yet there is much about the oddly fragmented melodic line of mm. 12b–16, all over an implied dominant pedal point, that seems unprecedented and not a little strange. Also odd is the prominence of the minor mode in both halves (g and f, then c), which gives the ostensibly delicate piece a dark undertone, especially when the bass unexpectedly plunges to GG (m. 28). The corrente is more heterogeneous, similar to but longer than the courante of French Suite no. 4, not far in style from the gigue of Partita no. 4. The latter, however, is in 9/16, its melodic gestures more straightforward; this corrente moves more deliberately. Brief pedal points again play a role, notably in a dissonant passage that includes three "obstinate" leaps of a major seventh in the bass (m. 43)—perhaps a deliberately humorous effect.

The sarabande employs written-out embellishment similar to that which Bach gave separately as *agrémens* in the English Suites. Like the sarabande of BWV 818a, this movement might have originated as a simpler piece,[10] and it is a useful analytical exercise to reduce the existing melodic embellishment to a simpler version. This makes it easier to see the four-measure phrasing and traditional sarabande rhythm underneath the florid surface. Embellishment of simple underlying lines is, however, such a basic element in Bach's mature style that there is no reason to assume that the movement ever existed in a substantially simpler form. Much of this Partita is composed over simple scalewise basses; for example, the first half of the sarabande closes (mm. 9–12) over a descending bass also used at several points in the corrente (e.g., mm. 18ff.).

The minuets are surprisingly simple, perhaps added (like those in the French Suites?) to give beginners something to play in Bach's first keyboard publication. The second is striking for the reduction of texture and rhythm to mostly quarter notes, in mostly four-part harmony; Bach had written a similarly minimalist "trio" movement in bourrée 2 of the Cello Suite in E♭, and perhaps the idea was to sound like a woodwind group (hence the numerous suspensions). These are the only movements in the Partitas for which there is some evidence of their having been composed separately, like the minuets of the French Suites. They survive in slightly more rudimentary versions in a manuscript collection of pedagogic pieces dating from perhaps the 1740s; Bach might have composed the two minuets in the early 1720s.[11]

The giga is unique not only for its hand crossings but for their use in every measure of the piece, which in its harmonic conception is closer to an arpeggio prelude than either a French or an Italian jig. Since the print contains no verbal explanation for the use of hand crossing, Bach must have expected musicians to be already familiar with the technique. One source would have been Rameau's 1724 suites, whose preface describes the somewhat similar *batteries* in *Les cyclopes*. Hand crossings might have disarmed critics who found Bach's music overly serious. Certainly Bach plays a joke on the player, for it is not at all obvious which hand should cross over the other. Although one naturally expects the initial high note (f′′) to belong to the right hand, it may be more convenient to take this and all upward-stemmed leaping notes with the left. Stem directions, which in this type of figuration dictate division of notes between the hands, are inconsistent in the final measures of the two halves but can be interpreted as follows: note 1 (left), notes 2–4 (right), notes 5–7 (left).[12]

The movement evidently was widely known. Gluck seems to have based an aria on material from the opening section (see Buelow 1991), and the giga was practiced into the nineteenth century alongside other pieces thought to have an etude-like character.[13]

Partita no. 2 in C Minor BWV 826

The Second Partita was announced a little less than a year after the first, on September 19, 1727. Its minor key and the style of the opening sinfonia declare it to be a more serious piece. It is also more conventional, containing a relatively traditional allemande and courante as well as a rondeau, a form favored by Couperin and other French composers but treated sparingly by Bach. Yet these movements are conventional only superficially. The sinfonia, whose initial section looks like the dotted section of a French overture, changes after just seven measures to something quite different, though it does not have much to do with a typical Italian overture (*sinfonia*) either. Even the rondeau elaborates the conventional type in its extended form and contrapuntal texture. The partita closes with what Bach calls a capriccio, actually a sort of fugue in binary form. As there is also a fugue in the opening movement—and the courante, too, is consistently imitative—this partita made up for the absence of fugal writing in the first work of the series.

The short introduction of the sinfonia might have been suggested by the one that opens Mattheson's tenth suite of 1714; both are in essence the expansion of a single plagal cadence, unrelated to anything that follows except perhaps the dotted rhythms in the final cadence (mm. 90–1). The seemingly redundant tempo markings—*Grave adagio*—perhaps emphasize that this is not an energetic French overture but a weighty introduction, in which the dark sonority of each massive chord is fully felt. The impression is strengthened by the time-signature: C instead of the ₵ used in the overture of Partita no. 4. An ornamented version copied by J. G. Müthel, although not necessarily Bach's, shows how one of Bach's last pupils might have performed the piece around 1750.[14]

The introduction leads to an andante whose florid upper line resembles that of an adagio. But the treble, accompanied by a walking bass, lacks the improvisatory qualities of an embellished adagio (except in its closing passage) and moves somewhat faster. It ends by dissolving into a short written-out cadenza—that is, an ornamented cadence (m. 28); here someone added the word *allegro* in one of the altered exemplars of the 1731 print, followed by *adagio* a measure later (m. 29).[15] Similar markings were added in some of the preludes of WTC1, presumably for the benefit of pupils, since they are hardly necessary. The same exemplar, and another as well, also correct the ungrammatical rhythmic notation of m. 29. But the latter is unaltered in the *Handexemplar*, implying that Bach considered the notation of the print adequate. No doubt the notation was meant only to suggest the general shape that the free, improvisatory rhythm ought to take.[16]

The sinfonia closes with a real fugue—not an invention—in two voices. As in the E-minor fugue of WTC1, also in two voices, the figuration is so rich in harmonic implications that the two parts suffice to suggest an orchestral texture. (The same is true in the allemande, sarabande, and rondeaux, also mainly in two parts.) The fugue subject belongs to a type that is composed out of a single dominant chord; other examples occur in the Sixth English Suite and the Third Orchestra Suite. This is one source of the fugue's unusually urgent character; each statement of the subject serves as a dominant preparation for the following passage, rather than serving as a point of repose. The fugue is divided in half by the episode in mm. 24–34; most of the second half consists of recapitulation, although the symmetry is not so exact as in the E-minor fugue.

As in BWV 819, the allemande is in two severely contrapuntal parts. The closing phrase of each half echoes the toccata of Partita no. 6 (already composed in 1727), as do the "sighs" in mm. 9 and 10. But the latter are softer than those in the toccata, the trill sign being placed on the second note rather than the first, indicating a half-trill.[17] The courante is of the French type, in 3/2, but the motives in sixteenths, present in virtually every measure, give it a fiery character. The use of imitation recalls the courantes of the English Suites, but rhythm and texture here are more flexible; in m. 3, for example, the imitative counterpoint momentarily dissolves into an ornamented arpeggio.

The printed ornaments in the courante were supplemented with particular enthusiasm in the Washington exemplar of the print. The *Handexemplar* had

Example 15.1 Partita no. 2 in C Minor BWV 826, courante (ornaments in parentheses from US Wc): (a) mm. 1–2; (b) mm. 12b–13.

already added a mordent in m. 2, and the same ornament might be added in other statements of the theme as well, including the initial statement in m. 1. But the additional ornaments in the Washington exemplar, shown in parentheses in example 15.1, complicate the lines, making the movement as a whole less vigorous. The inversion of the theme after the double bar raises the same question that occurred in the gigue of the Sixth English Suite: when the theme is inverted, should the ornaments in the theme also be inverted? The print has mordents only in the inversion of the theme; and in no exemplar was the sign altered. Yet, at least in m. 13, a trill on g′ is plausible, and it would avoid a collision between the hands on the note f′.

On paper, the sarabande looks like the allemande; both are largely in two parts, moving in sixteenths. But the harmony changes in the sarabande on the first and second beats, not on the third (at least through m. 8). Some of the sixteenths bear carelessly placed slurs, each interpreted in NBA V/1 as covering an entire beat (four sixteenths). This is consistent with the piece's gentle, undemonstrative nature, but the more articulate interpretation occasionally found in BG 3 (e.g., 1 + 3 in m. 16) cannot be ruled out.

The rondeau (or *Rondeaux*—Bach gives the title in the plural) is an imitative duet, reminiscent of the "Fantasia on a Rondo" BWV 918 in the same key. The present movement follows a more conventional rondeau design, although the last two statements of the theme are varied (mm. 65, 97). The theme falls into the customary eight-measure phrases, subdivided into groupings of two measures apiece. But in the course of the second *couplet* (mm. 48–64) the two-bar "hypermeasures" grow fuzzy, and it becomes hard to distinguish accented from unaccented measures until the return of the theme. The theme itself is built around a

Example 15.2 Partita no. 2 in C Minor BWV 826, rondeau (with implied bass figures and realization): (a) mm. 1–5; (b) mm. 49–52.

sequence of leaping sevenths (mm. 3–6). These are derived from a conventional chain of suspensions, although suspensions are not present explicitly until the second *couplet* (Example 15.2). The ornament in the theme, given in m. 1 as a trill, is easier to play when shortened to a turn, and the *Handexemplar* indicates a turn when the theme comes back in m. 33.

In designating the last movement a capriccio, Bach might have remembered his early Capriccio in E, BWV 993, supposedly written "in honor of" his teacher and older brother Johann Christoph, who had died in 1721. The present piece is a much stricter fugue in three voices, the only irregularity being the presence of all three parts from the outset. Nevertheless it is one of Bach's more unbuttoned keyboard pieces, even though the 2/4 meter does not necessarily imply great speed (see Williams 1993, 616). The title, although it could allude to the old contrapuntal capriccio, might also reflect the wild leaps of a tenth in the subject. These are developed by the bass in a recurring sequential episode that must be one of Bach's most entertaining passages to play, once one has it under the fingers; Bach obligingly recapitulates it in the second half (mm. 81–6 ‖ 11–6). The two halves are exactly equal in length, but they are not exactly symmetrical; as in the gigue of the Third English Suite, the subject returns in its original form (bass, m. 87) after being used in inversion for most of the second half.

The leaps of a tenth have a parallel in the scherzo movement of a violin sonata in the same key by J. G. Graun (no. 2 in a set published at Merseburg, ca. 1726). W. F. Bach went to study violin with Graun in 1726, but without knowing the precise dates of composition it is impossible to say who might have borrowed from whom. On the violin, such tenths require a certain amount of deliberation, as also for keyboard players unaccustomed to playing Scarlatti sonatas that make similar demands. Hence Williams's argument that the 2/4 time signature calls for a certain "stateliness" could apply even here, in the sense that the movement should retain its poise.

Partita no. 3 in A Minor BWV 827

The Third Partita, announced at the same time as the second (September 1727), seems lighter in character, at least at the outset. It opens with a fantasia that is essentially a long two-part invention, and it includes two apparently comic movements, a burlesca and a scherzo. Yet these are fiery in character, and the allemande resembles the passionate example in Partita no. 6, with which it shares its flourishes in thirty-seconds (unusual in an allemande) and a nearly identical final cadence. Early versions of Partitas nos. 3 and 6 occur side by side in the 1725 *Clavier-Büchlein*, prompting views that these were composed at about the same time, even as a sort of pair. The narrower compass of the manuscript version, which twice avoids notes below C, has been interpreted as evidence that Bach adapted an existing suite for performance on a smaller instrument (clavichord?) belonging to his wife, but this seems unfounded (see Jones 1988, 68–9). The manuscript version lacks the scherzo; in preparing the work for publication Bach added two measures at the end of the fantasia (mm. 118–9) and revised many other passages, especially in the bass of the first three movements.

The first movement was originally designated *Prélude*. Bach had used the similar title praeambulum for the early versions of the Inventions; that the movement wound up with the title originally given to the *three*-part inventions (originally called fantasias) proves the interchangeability of all these titles. Presumably a familiar title such as *fantasia* was preferable to *inventio* in a published work.

Although opening very much like some of the Inventions—including the one in the same key—the movement is spun out at greater length. It reaches the dominant at m. 31, whereupon the first thirty measures are repeated at the new pitch level, with voices exchanged. This accounts for precisely half the piece (in the published version); the remainder includes a retransition (mm. 67–78) and a sort of recapitulation (mm. 79ff.), although the theme does not reappear at the beginning of the latter. The movement is a little pale beside the more demonstrative opening movements of the other Partitas, and this may account for the relative obscurity of Partita no. 3 as a whole. The fantasia's quasi-geometric design is less intriguing today than it may have seemed in the eighteenth century, but the movement can be surprisingly expressive if the player chooses to bring out (perhaps through a slur) the mildly dissonant double-appoggiatura in the theme: b′–gb′–a′ in m. 1. The motive recurs throughout the movement, which therefore need not be played as an unnuanced stream of sixteenths.

The allemande can be considered a preliminary study for that of Partita no. 6. The extravagant melodic figuration of both movements makes them energetic virtuoso pieces, not to be approached timidly. This in turn implies a fairly vigorous tempo, not one that will shift the pulse from the quarter to the eighth note. Even at a brisk tempo, listeners are likely to misunderstand the upbeat, unusual for an allemande, which lasts for a full beat.[18] The latter may sound like a downbeat no matter what the player does; in fact, throughout the movement, the differentiation between "strong" and "weak" beats is ambiguous, and cadences fall on the third beat, not the first. An odd ornament sign in m. 6, on the note g´´, appears in both BG and NBA as a mordent prefixed by a small half-circle. But the original notation indicates a trill that starts with a turn from below and ends with another turn; the complex ornament is not implausible in the highly embellished context.[19]

One can easily imagine the corrente scored as a sonata movement for violin and bass, as was the *Tempo di Gavotta* in Partita no. 6. As in that movement, Bach made many revisions in the bass but hardly any in the treble, which never descends below g (the lowest string on the violin).

The sarabande is of the trio type, as in the Fifth English Suite and BWV 819. But now virtually nothing remains of the traditional sarabande rhythm or character. Like the allemande (and the corrente) it begins with an unusual upbeat figure, and this recurs as an important motive throughout the movement. An essential element of the motive is the ornament on the second note, whose identity was obscured by the imprecision of Bach's engravers. In many places in the original print the ornament sign looks like a mordent and was so interpreted in BG 3. But Bach indicated a trill in the 1725 *Clavier-Büchlein*, to which the print adds a slash at the end of the sign to indicate a closing turn (*Nachschlag*). The often faulty or ambiguous placement of this slash in the print led to the misinterpretation of many of the signs as mordents. But Bach's intentions are clear, although the ornament is hard to play in the available time. One does not expect so brilliant and complex an ornament as the *Trillo und mordant* (the name given to it in CB) to be played on the third beat of a sarabande. But this is no ordinary sarabande, and a sturdy trill will not conflict with the piece's almost marchlike character.

Another notational oddity occurs in m. 8, where the print appears to have been corrected after originally omitting the top note of the right-hand chord c´´/e´´. The autograph has the same two notes separated by a slanting stroke, which evidently led the editor of NBA V/1 to read here two consecutive sixteenths (c´´ followed by e´´). There is no ornament sign in the print, but the apparent ornament sign in the autograph elsewhere signifies an acciaccatura, which may be the best solution here (i.e., thirty-seconds c´´–d´´, sixteenth e´´).

Bach originally called the next movement a *Menuet*, but the figuration in sixteenths is not characteristic of the dance, and the piece was published as a *Burlesca*. Perhaps the new title makes some unidentified allusion; perhaps it suggests playing with mock-heroic swagger. In any case, Bach revised only the title, not the musical text. The original title implies a fairly courtly tempo, which would also allow the rather odd voice leading in the closing phrase (mm. 14–5, 38–9) to sink in. The same is true at the climactic passage in octaves in the second half (m. 32), which one can imagine as a burlesque on the type of octave passage found in the E-minor fugue of WTC1, presumably a more serious piece.

The scherzo could have been an afterthought, added to bring the number of movements up to the seven of the other partitas, or to fill space left at the bottom of the last page occupied by the burlesca.[20] The title, which Bach might have taken from a movement in the Bonporti Inventions for violin, recurs in what is probably an early work of Friedemann Bach.[21] It has nothing to do with Haydn's or Beethoven's pieces of the same title, and Williams's (1993, 620) warning against a "scurrying" tempo in 2/4 time is very apt here; the staccato chords in the left hand rather imply two sturdy beats in each measure. The "joke" of the title might lie in the piece's brevity or in its almost crude keyboard texture: left-hand chords accompany a violinistic right-hand line, the sort of thing that would have arisen when violin sonatas were played as impromptu keyboard solos. Particularly notable is the simultaneous acciaccatura in m. 28 (g#/a), a borrowing from the Italian style of continuo realization, also imitated in Domenico Scarlatti's sonatas.

The gigue is the one example of the dance in the Partitas that comes close to the traditional German fugal type, looking back specifically to the Reinken sonata in the same key transcribed as BWV 965. As in the gigue of BWV 965, the subject consists of uninterrupted eighth-notes. There are also two countersubjects, at least in the first half, and each half contains two expositions, here separated by an episode. None of these elements is unusual in a Bach gigue. But could the piece reflect Bach's memory of the older composer? Reinken, who had praised him at Hamburg in 1720, had died in 1722, three years before Bach prepared the autograph of the partita.

As Wolff (1979) first showed, three of the altered exemplars of the 1731 print contain substantial changes in the second half of the gigue. These exemplars agree on certain changes in the *inversus* form of the subject but not on all of the resulting "chain-reaction" revisions (Example 15.3).[22] The changes were evidently motivated by an effort to render the inversion more literal. But it remains inexact, and another purpose might have been to make the inverted form of the subject easier to play by eliminating the need for finger crossing. Some of the "chain-reaction" alterations led to awkward details in the counterpoint; in two exemplars, thirds became open fifths and tritones in the central episode (Example 15.3b; see asterisks).[23] The final exposition required more extensive changes, and here each of the three exemplars gives a somewhat different version. These might be interpreted as successive revisions, but none appears in Bach's supposed *Handexemplar*. Jones (1988, 35–6), noting the "dissonance, false relations and

Example 15.3 Partita no. 3 in A Minor BWV 827, gigue (after copy in US Wc): (a) mm. 25–6; (b) 39–40; (c) 44–46a.

inconsistency" created by the alterations, concludes that they are best explained by imagining "that he [Bach] might have set the task of achieving a more strict inversion of the subject as a composition exercise for his pupils." Certainly Bach's pupils were not above tinkering with his counterpoint; Kirnberger did so in his "sonata" based on the gigue of French Suite no. 6, and perhaps also in variations found in his copy of the gigue of English Suite no. 4.[24]

Partita no. 4 in D, BWV 828

The Fourth Partita, whose original title page was dated 1728, is the most splendid of the Partitas and, with the possible exception of Partita no. 6, the longest. Three or four movements—the overture, courante, gigue, and perhaps the minuet— evoke orchestral style, but the remainder are intimate and highly expressive, above all the allemande, one of the longest and most profound ever written.

The overture is of the same type found in the orchestral suites of Bach and his contemporaries, and in chamber works like the Dieupart suites that Bach had copied at Weimar. Such movements are usually regarded as consisting of a slow dotted section followed by a fugue, but many can also be viewed as a somewhat peculiar sort of binary form. Often the second half is, as here, a fugue in concerto style having little in common with the first half. Yet the tonal structure is that of a binary form, the first half moving to the dominant, and there is no explicit change of tempo at the beginning of the second half, despite the change in meter and character. Thus, a movement of this type may be more unified than is sometimes thought, regardless of whether the dotted rhythm returns after the fugue. The most serious problems of performance practice arise in the dotted section, where a player focusing on the details of the rhythmic notation and the flurries of *tirate* (runs in thirty-second notes) may fail to project the long lines and simple underlying phrasing. The dotted section comprises just three long phrases, and these are the usual ones for a binary suite movement: the opening thematic statement, cadencing in the tonic (m. 5a); a modulating transition (mm. 5b–12); and a closing phrase leading to a firm cadence in the dominant (mm. 13–8).

Lingering controversy about over-dotting in such a movement (see chap. 2) still distracts attention from equally important interpretive issues, such as tempo and articulation. The tempo should surely be quick enough for the *ti-rate* to sound brilliant, as in other pieces with written-out embellishment. The time-signature is ₵, as in most French overtures, and although the movement is not an *alla breve* in the usual sense, it can be understood as having just two long beats in each measure. The most important dotted figure is a three-note upbeat (sixteenth–dotted eighth–sixteenth) that moves toward the next beat, not from the preceding one. The effect is best conveyed if the notes, especially the dotted ones, are somewhat detached. When this is done, at the right tempo, there may be little need for over-dotting as such, except on dotted quarters and in the combination of dotted eighth followed by three thirty-seconds (as in m. 7). Although Bach cannot have intended his rhythmic notation of the *tirate* to be interpreted absolutely literally, the rhythmic freedom taken should probably not be so great as to upset the vertical relationships between contrapuntal parts (e.g., in m. 10, treble g#′′ should presumably coincide with bass e).

The meter of the fugal section is a somewhat complicated 9/8 time, the eighths within the beat being grouped into anapestic patterns (weak–weak–strong) that reflect the organization of the beats themselves (Example 15.4). In its allusions to ritornello form, this section somewhat resembles the preludes of the English Suites, but Bach would make a cleaner distinction between "tutti" and "solo" sections in the B-minor overture of CU2. The lighter texture and the relatively plain motivic material at m. 34 suggest a lyrical solo episode, but heavy chords and brilliant scales in mm. 36 and 40 imply "tutti" interruptions. Yet at the next entrance of the subject (bass, m. 48), which presumably corresponds to a ritornello, the texture is limited to two voices. Such scoring will frustrate attempts to impose on the movement a registration scheme based on alternating fortes and

Example 15.4 Partita no. 4 in D, BWV 828, overture, mm. 18–20.

pianos, but it shows that Bach conceived the movement as idiomatic keyboard music, not an ersatz orchestral piece.

The first dance movement is arguably Bach's finest allemande, although Froberger or even Couperin might have been hard pressed to identify it as such. The embellished treble line makes this more a monodic arioso than the traditional arpeggio-based keyboard allemande, although the style of the latter emerges once in each half (mm. 18, 40–2), incidentally ruling out performance on two manuals. The voices of the accompaniment (usually two) are as essential as the top part and can serve as a guide for judging the right tempo. If one cannot hear the gradual rise of the tenor in mm. 5–6, the tempo may be too slow, preventing the individual gestures in the treble from cohering into larger phrases.[25]

Formally, the movement is distinct from most other allemandes in its close approach to ternary sonata form. There is no return, but, after reaching a cadence in B minor in the middle of the second "half" (m. 40), two simple but very beautiful measures of retransition lead to a partial recapitulation, opening in the subdominant (m. 42 || m. 5). Within each section the melodic figuration accelerates in a gradual, disciplined way from mainly sixteenths to a combination of triplets and thirty-seconds. As in many Bach pieces the crowning point in the figuration is a complete scale shortly before the final cadence of each half.

The movement deserves close analysis, which can be offered here for the first half. The opening thematic statement (mm. 1–4) accelerates from a plain chord to quietly moving figuration, most of it derived from arpeggiation. In its gradual acceleration this opening foreshadows the rhythmic shape of the movement as a whole, although the opening phrase comes to rest on f#′ (m. 4), the note on which it began. In the following modulating passage, the treble, having leapt into the higher register, gradually descends from f#′′ (m. 5) to b′ at the beginning of m. 16. The arrival on b′ is already implicit in m. 13, which marks the beginning of a beautifully prolonged dominant (V of V); the half-step c♮′′–b′, first heard in m. 12, recurs in m. 16, where the motive is repeated on each note of the chord (c′′–b′, f♮′′–e′′, a′′–g#′′). The dominant continues to be prolonged through the deceptive cadence at m. 18, which is followed by a six-measure closing phrase (expanded to seven measures when it returns at m. 50). The harmonic progression in m. 18 recurs in the retransition (mm. 40–1), where the echo of the earlier passage contributes to its delicate pathos.

Another source of pathos is the half-step c′′–b′, first heard in embellished form in mm. 2–3, where it constitutes an unexpectedly early deflection from the tonic. The motive returns in various harmonic guises at the movement's most crucial moments, sometimes in retrograde (b′–c′′): in mm. 12–6, as noted above; in the closing phrase of the first section (m. 23); as the second section approaches its final cadence (with the Neapolitan harmony in m. 37); and in the appoggiatura at the beginning of the third section (m. 42), where the progression occurs twice more (mm. 50 and 55). The motive does not merely unify the allemande; through its repeated emphasis on a tone outside the tonic scale (c♮′′) it ensures that an expressive tension is present throughout the course of this long movement.

The character of the courante is defined by the jubilant *figure corte* in the opening theme. One does not expect to find such writing in a courante, and although in principle following the French version of the dance, the movement uses few of the traditional melodic or rhythmic formulas. Even the metrical ambivalence associated with the dance is treated more playfully than usual, the two main thematic ideas, presented in double counterpoint in mm. 1–2, being inherently ambiguous in meter.[26] But the bass of m. 3 is clearly in 6/4, and when a new motivic idea is introduced by the treble in m. 9, it is imitated by alto and tenor at intervals of *five* quarter notes. Against the energetic motives in small note values are set some written-out examples of the expressive "long" appoggiatura, which would become a favorite mannerism in the *empfindsamer Stil* now associated with Berlin but for Bach probably identified with Dresden. Particularly characteristic are the instances where it is followed by a short trill, as in mm. 8, 11, and 15.

The same ornament forms part of the opening theme of the sarabande, which is repeated at the beginning of that movement's two subsequent sections (mm. 13, 29).[27] The sarabande theme is the product of a particularly fantastic transformation of the traditional dance type; the accent on the second beat is clear enough, but the figuration, which juxtaposes a languishing appoggiatura (m. 1) with a sudden arpeggio (m. 2), is unlike that of any other sarabande. The remainder of the movement recalls the allemande in the florid embellishment of the upper part. But the sarabande is a shorter and somewhat lighter piece, even though it is, like the allemande, a complete sonata form with return. The flurries of thirty-seconds, especially the quasi-cadenza in m. 34, can even achieve some brilliance if the tempo does not drag.

The aria preceding the sarabande may resemble a type of "Dresden aria" that Bach would hear a few years later in Hasse's *Cleofide*. But after the first phrase it becomes more clearly a short binary form in idiomatic keyboard style, like the air in French Suite no. 4. The idiom here is more refined, the keyboard texture treated more flexibly, even by comparison with the similarly conceived scherzo of Partita no. 3: the accompaniment in staccato chords is now combined with a pedal point (m. 4), later transformed into the quasi-pedaliter texture seen in Partita no. 1 (m. 41). The placement of a short air or aria before the sarabande in both Partitas nos. 4 and 6 led to the suggestion (Louwenaar 1982–3) that the order of movements in the print was merely to avoid a page turn within the sarabande, or for what Rameau, in the preface to his *Nouvelles Suites* (ca. 1729–30), called the "convenience of the engraver." In Partita no. 6, however, the aria is absent from the manuscript version, implying that Bach composed it for the print, perhaps specifically to fill in what would otherwise have been an almost empty page. The same might be true as well of Partita no. 4, where there seems little musical reason for playing the aria after the sarabande; doing so would place the two shortest movements of the suite side by side.

The minuet is even more likely to have been composed as a page filler, although it turned out too long for the space left at the end of the sarabande, and the last five measures had to be squeezed into the bottom margin to avoid a page turn. Yet the placement of the minuet is problematical, as it is practically in the same meter as the gigue. The gigue is in 9/16, the minuet in 3/4 with numerous triplets (like the one in BWV 818a). Presumably, the gigue should go somewhat faster. Dotted rhythms against the triplets, as in m. 7 of the minuet, should surely be "assimilated," but not the ordinary duplets in mm. 1–2, probably not even in m. 10 where they are heard against the triplets.

Despite its unorthodox meter, each half of the gigue opens in the traditional fugal manner. But the second half, instead of using the inversion, introduces a new subject, with which the original subject is combined once (m. 55), then dropped for good, except for the use of its main motive in the closing phrase.[28] This closing phrase touches briefly on the minor mode, an expressive gesture that echoes the close of the first part of the overture, just as the prominent c‴ in the subject points back to the allemande.

Partita no. 5 in G, BWV 829

Partita no. 5 was announced in May 1730, almost two years after Partita no. 4.[29] The new work was shorter than the preceding one, though still a very substantial piece by contemporary standards, with a big opening movement and an impressive fugal gigue. Partita no. 5 might have been composed at about the same time as Partita no. 4, for several distinctive passages in the first movement closely resemble the overture and the gigue of the previous suite.[30] Moreover, both gigues follow the unusual scheme of opening the second half with a new subject. As Partita no. 6 was written by 1725, this is probably the last work in the set to have been composed; it uses the widest keyboard range (GG–d‴). Williams (2003, 19–20) makes the curious observation that all movements employ some form of triple time, even the allemande (with its pervasive triplets).

The first movement is designated a praeambulum, but perhaps only because the term *fantasia*, which today would seem more appropriate, had already been used in Partita no. 3. The light, often monophonic, texture and the almost banal simplicity of the material give the impression of free fantasy, but Williams (2003b, 155) sees here an "uncanny" originality, implying tighter control and precision than one would find in a true improvisation. The opening passage functions as a sort of ritornello, but the movement is more succinct and less predictable than the preludes of the English Suites. It is probably another hand-crossing piece, like the gigue of Partita no. 1; the division of notes between the hands, indicated by the direction of note stems in mm. 5–16, calls for the right hand to cross over the left, reaching deep into the bass. Later the left hand gets to leap (mm. 73ff.), but this is another quasi-pedaliter passage without hand crossing.

The allemande returns to ideas from the corresponding movement in the Fourth English Suite: a short theme containing triplet-sixteenths is developed in two-part imitative counterpoint, then inverted after the double bar. Here Bach avoids decelerating to ordinary sixteenths after the first phrase, which had put a damper on the enthusiasm of the earlier allemande. But some duple rhythms do occur, provoking the usual question: which if any of the figures written in duple notation are to be interpreted literally? One assumes "assimilation" of the dotted rhythms that occur simultaneously with triplets. But what does one do with the dotted figure in the opening theme (Example 15.5)? Assimilation improves the counterpoint when the theme is transferred to the left hand, producing parallel tenths rather than a dissonance (f#/g′) at the end of the third beat of m. 1. Yet the passing dissonance is hardly noticeable, and when, in the last measure of the first half (m. 12), the dotted motive from the theme is set against a duple figure in the tenor, there is no evident need for assimilation. Nor is it clear how one would "assimilate" the written-out ornament on the downbeat of m. 25a.[31]

The corrente is another example of the dance that could have served equally well as a prelude or a sonata movement. Three times the treble makes a conspicuous climb to d′′′, a note used previously only in the scherzo of Partita no. 3; hence it is curious that the first two times it is a dissonant appoggiatura (m. 22) or part of a dissonant chord (m. 54).[32] Only the third time is it consonant, when the two hands move in contrary motion to the outer limits of Bach's keyboard compass at the close.

Example 15.5 Partita no. 5 in G, BWV 829, allemande: (a) m. 1; (b) m. 12a; (c) m. 25a.

Example 15.6 Partita no. 5 in G, BWV 829, sarabande: (a) mm. 0–2; (b) mm. 19–22a.

The sarabande is of the trio type, with numerous appoggiaturas, some notated as *petites notes*, others written out as regular quarters (Example 15.6).[33] The dotted rhythm and the numerous appoggiaturas are reminiscent of the Sinfonia in E♭—which also underwent further ornamentation in pupils' copies—and raise similar questions of tempo and rhythm. Here the written value of the *petites notes* varies, but there is little evidence that such distinctions had any meaning until after Bach's death, and appoggiaturas written as small notes were probably all meant to be fairly short.[34] Two appoggiaturas (both on b′, mm. 20, 22) are indicated by "hooks" or commas, probably not because they are meant to precede the beat, as Neumann (1978, 126) thought, but because in these instances the main note is approached from below; hence the appoggiatura in each case is a′, not c′′, which would create parallel fifths in m. 22.[35]

The crucial problem in this movement, to be solved before attacking the appoggiaturas, is that of tempo. As in the Sinfonia in E♭ or the loure of French Suite no. 5, the dotted rhythms and occasional flourishes are lifeless unless the movement is performed at least at a moderate walking pace. This seems to rule out, among other things, "pre-beat" performance of the appoggiaturas; there is simply no time for this, given the dotted rhythms. One presumably should double-dot the quarter notes; the double dots in some editions (e.g., BG 3) are not original, however.[36]

The thin texture and cryptic notation of the *Tempo di Minuetta* recall the giga of Partita no. 1. If the double stemming of every third note is meant to reflect the division of notes between the hands, then hand crossing occurs near the end (Example 15.7). In any case the double stemming visually reinforces a melodic contour that creates a hemiola throughout the piece.[37] The latter rhythm is uncharacteristic of the dance, and perhaps for this reason Bach called the movement *Tempo di Minuetta* rather than a minuet proper. The passepied that follows has more of the traditional minuet character. Several other hand-crossing pieces from the Bach circle are nevertheless termed minuets; perhaps this movement started a small rage in Leipzig for such things.[38]

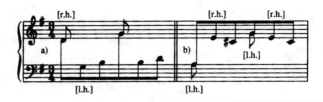

Example 15.7 Partita no. 5 in G, BWV 829, *Tempo di Minuetta*: (a) m. 1; (b) m. 33.

The gigue, trumping the one in Partita no. 4, is a full-fledged double fugue; the second subject is introduced after the double bar, then combined regularly with the first subject (from m. 46). There is also a little recurring episode or bridge (mm. 9–10a ‖ 48–49a ‖ 56a–57). The subjects complement one another well, leaping and resting at different moments to create an interlocking dialogue. But the piece is hard to play, in a way that anticipates the strange keyboard writing of Bach's late works, as when the middle voice leaps from right hand to left in mm. 46–7.[39] If Bach had intentionally kept Partita no. 1 relatively simple, in order to make it accessible to the public, he had abandoned most of the restraints on his challenging keyboard idiom by the time of the Fifth Partita.

Partita no. 6 in E Minor BWV 830

The Sixth Partita is the crowning work of the set and Bach's greatest suite. The allemande and the sarabande contain some of the most audacious and dramatic melodic embellishment ever written, and the work opens and closes with two particularly ambitious contrapuntal movements. It is easy to understand why Bach withheld it from publication until 1730 or 1731, although it was ready in 1725 for inclusion in the *Clavier-Büchlein* of that year.[40] The autograph is more heavily corrected than that of Partita no. 3 in the same manuscript, and the printed version shows many additional revisions, including the expansion of the opening toccata by the equivalent of three measures. As in Partita no. 3, an entire movement (the air) was added as well.

The toccata has little in common with Bach's earlier pieces of that title beyond the basic plan of a fugue framed by prelude and postlude. Prelude and postlude are in principle improvisatory, as before, but now they are integrated with the central fugue, which incorporates an important motivic idea from the prelude in the last episode (mm. 72–81). The fugue, moreover, ends in the dominant, the tonal circle being completed by the postlude. The latter is an abbreviated restatement of the prelude, omitting only the material already recapitulated in the fugue. The entire movement is notated *alla breve* and can be played in a single tempo, although the cadenza-like passages in the outer sections invite free rhythm.[41]

The fugue subject combines *galant* "sighs" with "rhetorical" pauses. The fugue, in three voices, resembles some of the more *galant* three-part fugues of WTC2 in its construction out of two- and three-measure phrases, reflecting the sequential character of the subject (cf. the fugues in F minor and F♯ major). But the harmony and voice leading are dissonant and chromatic; the first note in each "sigh" figure becomes a dissonant appoggiatura when combined with the countersubject, whose alternation between ascending and descending forms of the melodic minor scale regularly creates melodic cross-relations. Two long episodes provide diatonic relief from the chromaticism of the expositions; the second of these, starting in C (mm. 72–7), marks the farthest remove from the tonic.[42] From here, however, there is a swift and inexorable modulation from C major to the "sharp" regions of E minor and B minor, culminating in the return of the prelude in the latter key (m. 89). This is a magnificent moment; that it is in the parallel minor of the dominant, rather than the tonic, might have posed a problem for another composer, but Bach balances the strong arrival in B minor with a dramatic move to the subdominant shortly before the end (mm. 101–2).

The allemande is a heightened version of that found in Partita no. 3. Both movements, with their pervasive dotted rhythm and virtuoso figuration, somewhat resemble the ritornello of the aria "Komm, süsses Kreuz" in the Saint Matthew Passion.[43] Bach had written at least two earlier allemandes of this sort—in the Fifth Cello Suite and the First Violin Partita—and perhaps all can be traced back to a type found in French gamba music, as in the first allemande in B minor from Marais's second book of *Pièces de viole* (Paris, 1701). The scale figures and, in the second half, the arpeggiated *figure corte* (mm. 14b-16) make the present allemande a particularly vivid virtuoso piece; Friedemann Bach imitated it in the allemande of his Suite in G Minor (F. 24).

The corrente is one of two movements otherwise known from an early version of the Sonata in G for violin and obbligato cembalo BWV 1019. For Jones (1988, 71) this movement completes a process of increasing "rhythmic complexity and elaboration" in the Italian courantes of the French Suites (nos. 2 and 4–6) and the Third Partita. Like the movement that replaced it at the center of BWV 1019, it is a large sonata form, and neither the initial syncopated idea nor the figuration that follows is characteristic of either French or Italian courantes. Syncopation is present in some form or another in almost every measure, the *brisé* texture of the opening becoming elaborated into increasingly brilliant passagework.

That the corrente was first drafted for use in a violin sonata seems unlikely, for even in the sonata version it is designated *Cembalo solo* and lacks a violin part. It is the third of six movements comprising BWV 1019a, where it is balanced by a fifth movement for violin and continuo, called *Violino solo*; this became the Tempo di gavotta of the partita. The inclusion of the two "solos" in a sonata for violin and obbligato keyboard was an original idea, producing a novel variety in the sequence of movements. But it could have been a product of the same juggling of pieces, some new, some previously composed, that apparently produced other short-lived experiments such as the suite BWV 815a during the 1720s.[44] That Bach should have drawn on the sonata is not surprising, for the six sonatas for violin and cembalo are another collection that Bach seems to have assembled while completing the French Suites and planning the Partitas. The Sonata in G is the last in the set, and Bach would drastically revise it, replacing several movements. The final version lacks a "violin solo" but does incorporate a new central movement for solo keyboard. The latter, although less brilliant than the corrente of Partita no. 6, is again a large sonata form, comparable to some of the preludes of WTC2 (e.g., E minor, G♯ minor)—with which it is likely to be contemporary, as the final version of the violin sonata may date from the 1740s.

The three versions of the corrente show few differences. The first five notes of the melody in the sonata version were different, showing that it was the idea of syncopation or *brisé* style, not the precise melody, that was foremost in Bach's mind. The *Clavier-Büchlein* version is written in "double measures," that is, subdivided 6/8 time. Bach replaced this with simple 3/8 time, perhaps because phrase elisions shifted the "downbeat" from the odd- to the even-numbered measures at two points in the second half (compare mm. 29–43 and 90–104).

The air, even if it was prompted only by the need to fill a blank page, provides a breathing space between the corrente and the sarabande. It opens like a gavotte, on a half-measure upbeat,[45] as does the scherzo of Partita no. 3, another "filler" movement whose opening phrase uses the same accompaniment of staccato chords. Almost every subsequent phrase is based on a variation of the descending line found in the bass of the first two measures. This is true even of the closing phrase (mm. 24b–28a), which is further varied in a *petite reprise*.[46]

The sarabande combines the majesty of a French *sarabande grave* with the fire of an Italian adagio. The sarabande of Partita no. 1 can be thought of as a preliminary exercise for this one, although this could be the earlier piece. Both are highly embellished, and both open with a dotted figure, though the latter is now shifted to the upbeat and is worked into several hemiolas (e.g., in mm. 2–3 and in the closing phrase of each section). The embellishment is more florid than in Partita no. 1—so florid that it obscures the fact that this movement is a concise sonata form, with a genuine return at m. 29 preceded by a four-measure retransition phrase. That the climactic burst of figuration in mm. 28–9 indeed decorates a return is clearer in the simpler version of the autograph, which retains the dotted upbeat from the beginning of the movement (Example 15.8).[47]

The extraordinary embellishment poses greater interpretive challenges than in any comparable movement in Bach's keyboard music. As usual, the form and character of the sarabande are obscured if the tempo is too slow. Excessive rhythmic freedom has the same effect, although the rhythmic notation must be taken with a grain of salt. Often the first note in a group of thirty-seconds cannot but be lengthened, as in m. 17, where such a note is ornamented by a mordent.[48] But the underlying beat should not be greatly affected by such nuances, even though it will have to be stretched in the cadenza-like passage at the return.

The *Tempo di Gavotta* is another concise sonata form, arranged from the earlier version in the G-major Violin Sonata. Although the movement has little

Example 15.8 Partita no. 6 in E Minor BWV 830, sarabande: (a) mm. 0–1; (b) 28–9 (earlier version from P 225 on upper staff).

of the traditional gavotte character, the bass does open with the traditional upbeat of two quarters. In transforming the movement into a keyboard solo, Bach heavily revised the bass line.[49] He must also have made substantial revisions in the upper part, at least in mm. 23b–26a, where the bass of the violin version cannot be reconciled with the familiar treble line. Unfortunately, the original

Example 15.9 (a) Sonata in G for cembalo and violin BWV 1019a, Violino solo, mm. 23b–27a (reconstruction); (b) Partita no. 6 in E Minor BWV 830, Tempo di Gavotta, mm. 23b–27a; (c) same, autograph (P 225), m. 25a; (d) autograph, reading prior to correction, mm. 26–27a.

violin part is lost; Example 15.9a provides a reconstruction.[50] Throughout the movement, the conflicting duple and triple rhythms of the two parts present a problem for performance, at least in the surviving version for solo keyboard. Inevitably, there have been arguments for altering the written values (Collins 1966, 311–2), but, as in the allemande of Partita no. 5, "assimilation" is doubtful except where dotted rhythms fall directly against triplets. Presumably the groups of sixteenths can be interpreted freely.

The gigue is Bach's most profound movement composed under this title. Like the *Tempo di Gavotta*, it has been viewed as a rhythmic conundrum (e.g., by McIntyre 1965, 489), thanks to its dotted rhythms and its archaic meter-sign ₵, equivalent to 4/2. As in almost any piece notated in a persistent dotted rhythm, one can alter the written values to produce a more or less convincing version in triple meter, which would eliminate some of the movement's angularity. But the latter is an essential element—a rhythmic complement to the thorny chromatic voice leading. The version of the autograph, where the note-values are half those of the print, looks like Froberger's gigues in dotted rhythm or the gigue of French Suite no. 1, where literal interpretation seems best. Although the note values are doubled in the print, there is no good reason why that notation should not be interpreted literally as well.

The doubled values and archaic mensural sign associated the piece with the *stile antico* (see Wolff 1968, 45). But the first reason for the doubling of values might have been that the *figure corte*, introduced in m. 9, were an afterthought that Bach began to add only after he had begun writing out the autograph. Unforeseen when the piece was first drafted, the lively figuration in sixteenths and thirty-seconds became an important motive, not mere embellishment, and it became more appropriate to write it in larger values, which would also be more legible.[51]

Apart from the addition of *figure corte*, Bach made no effort to ameliorate the archaic contrapuntal style of the gigue. The subject, leaping through dissonant intervals, recalls passages in Froberger's abstract polyphonic pieces as well as his gigues.[52] The severe character of the counterpoint is reinforced by the absence of lasting modulations; the piece never really leaves the tonic, although there are brief, complementary modulations in the middle of each half—to the dominant in m. 15b, to the subdominant in m. 41b. The two halves form a nearly perfect binary symmetry, which might justify the omission of the repetitions when performing before a sleepy audience. But the second half is longer than the first, and just before the end, the subject, introduced in inversion after the double bar, returns in its original form (m. 49). Something similar happened at the end of the Third English Suite, but here it takes place in the upper voice, and the effect is repeated in a closing phrase that also alludes to the subject; this is clearer in the version of the autograph.

Especially with this movement, one can understand Williams's (2001, 20) view that the Sixth Partita returns to the "distancing thoroughness" of the English Suites. Yet for all its contrapuntal rigor and austerity, the suite as a whole, including the gigue, is simultaneously resplendent and full of pathos, exceeding the English Suites in that respect, at least when played with freedom and spirit. Certainly the shape and perhaps the meaning of the first volume of Bach's *Clavierübung* are profoundly affected by ending with this strange yet compelling movement, as far removed as one could imagine from the gigue of the opening work.

16
Clavierübung, Part 2, and Other Works

The success of the Partitas evidently led Bach to continue the series. During the 1730s and early 1740s he brought out three further volumes of "Keyboard Practice" (*Clavierübung*) while producing WTC2 and the first draft of the *Art of Fugue*. These years also saw the preparation of the harpsichord concertos and other ensemble works thought to have been for the Leipzig Collegium Musicum. Bach seems to have composed few new keyboard works apart from those included in the great collections. But he also composed or revised a few lute pieces that are more or less playable on keyboard instruments; two transcriptions (one fragmentary) for keyboard also probably date from this period.

These works are diverse in style and genre, making it difficult (and not very useful) to make general statements about them. Even within the *Clavierübung*, esoteric explorations of canonic counterpoint and chromatic harmony mingle with *galant* melody and rhythm. One senses increasing maturity as well as heightened freedom from conventions, even when Bach is ostensibly following the latter. But the accuracy of such perceptions depends on the chronology of the music, which is not well understood in the absence of first drafts or, in most cases, any autograph material at all.

Clavierübung, Part 2

In 1735, four years after the collected edition of the Partitas, Bach published part 2 of the *Clavierübung* (CU2).[1] The volume contained two works representing the two chief orchestral genres of the day: a concerto and an *ouverture*. Having taken over the directorship of the Leipzig Collegium Musicum in 1729, Bach is presumed to have led performances of works not only by such older composers as Vivaldi and Telemann, but by younger contemporaries like Hasse and the Graun brothers.[2] It is assumed that he also performed his own instrumental works, and although we have documentation only for performances of a few secular cantatas, the relatively small number of suites and concertos for instrumental ensemble that survive do so in versions that were probably created for performance by the Collegium. Would the performances also have included works for solo keyboard? No evidence for this survives, and one wonders how, at a time when there was no tradition of public harpsichord recitals, audiences would have reacted to the playing of long keyboard "lessons" (*Clavierübungen*) and ersatz ensemble pieces, especially if a real ensemble was present during the performances, waiting to play.

The two works in part 2 were meant, as the title page declared, to represent the *italiänischer Gusto* and the *französische Art*, respectively. By 1735 the rivalry between the French and Italian styles had become a cliché, although the distinction remained real. Both had evolved in response to the increasingly *galant* style of the times, and this is reflected in Bach's two works, particularly the concerto. The tonalities of the two pieces (F and b) are separated by the symbolically significant interval of a tritone, which also continues the "wedge" pattern of keys in CU1 (Bb–c–a–D–G–e). Bach had previously made the two national styles the basis of organization in his Six Solos for unaccompanied violin, compiled about 1720 as alternating sonatas and *partie* (suites). What such collections actually demonstrated was the existence of a German approach that integrated both styles. Even French composers had been self-consciously composing in a mixed style, as in Couperin's *Goûts réunis* (Paris, 1724), and Italians like Corelli had been doing so as well without making a fuss over it. Bach's keyboard works had, from the beginning, blended elements of the two styles in varying proportions. In both of the present works one can see French influence in the precise indication of ornaments and the requirement of a double-manual harpsichord. On the other hand, not only the concerto but the fugue in the *ouverture* has the fire and impetuosity associated with the Italian style, as well as the customary ritornello design.

Although one would never want to underestimate a work by Bach, it is possible that the novelty of the two pieces exceeds their intrinsic musical worth. Despite the irresistible vivacity of the concerto, neither work has quite the splendor of the D-major Partita or the depth of the Partita in E Minor. The concerto nevertheless deserves its popularity among pianists, for whose instrument it is better suited than most of Bach's harpsichord music. On the other hand, the *ouverture* is relatively little known even among harpsichordists; it is awkward to play and too long for most modern recital programs: like the Sixth French Suite it contains a few too many short dances. There are even signs of a certain carelessness in the production of the volume, for the indications for the use of two manuals—one of the special features of the publication, announced on the title page—appear to have been late additions and are not fully integrated into the musical fabric.

Many of the changes of manual are analogous to the tutti/solo alternations in a concerto. But forte does not always correspond with a "tutti" passage (i.e., a ritornello), nor does piano necessarily imply "solo" or "episode." In the first movement of the concerto, episodes are scored mainly for a forte upper line with softer accompaniment in the lower voices. But there is also a piano echo within a ritornello (mm. 67–8), and in the last movement both hands have forte passages within "solo" episodes. Occasionally it is unclear whether a passage is a ritornello or an episode, but this occurs in ensemble concertos as well. In any case, it would be a mistake to regard either work as a literal adaptation of an orchestral genre, or to see the changes of manual as direct imitations of ensemble scoring. The alternations of dynamic level add weight to alternations of texture and material that are already woven into the fabric; the use of two manuals is not formally essential in the way that it is in the organ sonatas or the Goldberg Variations.

What appears to be an early version of the first movement of the concerto reveals substantial variants, including a different version of the main theme and a complete absence of dynamic indications.[3] Some readings, including that for the main theme and other passages in the ritornello (m. 11), seem intended to avoid notes above a´´—implying adaptation (spurious?) for some non-standard keyboard instrument. But elsewhere this version credibly represents an early stage of composition, as in the much plainer left-hand accompaniment in mm. 15ff. (unlikely to be a subsequent simplification). Particularly notable is the presence of two extra measures whose elimination created regular four-measure phrases (after mm. 64 and 142). The figuration, where different from the familiar version, tends to be more conventional, as is typical in Bach's early drafts. Readings independent of those in the final version imply that Bach developed both from an even earlier draft.[4]

Preserved as an isolated movement, the early version would not necessarily have been conceived as part of a keyboard concerto. It is unlikely to date from as early as the preludes of the English Suites, which, although superficially similar, lack movements in 2/4 and are more contrapuntal, less *galant* as the term was understood by the 1720s. But the restricted range and relatively simplistic texture imply a date no later than 1725 or so, before the composition of the more imaginative and wide-spanning Partitas nos. 4 and 5.

Several other manuscripts preserve pre-publication versions of both works, but these differ only in detail from the published ones.[5] Even the transposition of the *ouverture* from C minor to B minor involved few substantive changes. The chief source of the C-minor version, a copy by Anna Magdalena Bach (in P 226), probably dates from around 1730; hence, the *ouverture* might have been the seventh partita mentioned in Bach's newspaper announcement of Partita no. 5.[6] Indeed, the *ouverture* is sometimes referred to as the Seventh Partita, but Bach did not use that title. Had it appeared as part of the earlier set, its opening movement (an overture) would have duplicated that of Partita no. 4, and its original key (C minor) that of Partita no. 2.

As in the Partitas, the existence of an authorized early edition does not eliminate all questions about the text. Bach had this work printed and published in
far-off Nuremberg, and the first edition was unusually faulty, despite corrections
made before and after printing. There was a second edition by the end of 1736,
and one corrected exemplar of the first edition has been identified as Bach's
Handexemplar.[7] Nevertheless, there remain many small problems in the reading
of ornaments and rhythms and the placement of dynamic markings. Unlike most
previous editions, NBA V/2 gives the two works together, as they were originally
published. It emends dynamics, ornaments, and the like, usually on the basis of
manuscript corrections in the *Handexemplar*. A few doubtful emendations are
discussed below.[8]

Concerto in F, BWV 971

CU2 opens with the Italian Concerto and not, as one might have expected,
with the French *Ouverture*. The presence of overtures at the center, rather than
the beginning, of CU1 and 2 (and of the Goldberg Variations) has never been
explained; in this case, perhaps Bach wished the shorter and in some respects
more up-to-date piece to come first. The concerto reflects not so much the style
of the early Venetian concertos that Bach had transcribed around 1713–4, nor
Bach's own concertos of perhaps a few years later, as it does the later works of
Vivaldi and the concertos of Bach's younger German contemporaries like Quantz
and the Graun brothers.[9] Indeed, the modern short title "Italian Concerto" is
a misnomer, for it is actually a German concerto after the Italian style, a point
implicit in Scheibe's praise of it as something that "will be imitated all in vain by
foreigners."[10] Certain features, such as the rather consistent four-bar phrasing
in the outer movements and the use of a distinct solo theme in the first movement—a lyrical theme graced by numerous "sigh" figures—may be more common
in concertos of the 1730s than those of twenty years earlier. Likewise, the regular
ritornello designs of the outer movements, nowadays so firmly associated with
the "Vivaldian" concerto, are less consistently present in earlier works than in
later ones. Even the slow movement, which was clearly meant to exemplify the
Italian style of melodic embellishment, may have a more direct connection with
other German compositions containing written-out ornamentation, relatively
rare in Italian works.[11]

   As published, the first movement lacks a tempo marking; allegro is therefore
implied, but following Williams (2001, 22) the 2/4 meter implies something
slower than usually assumed today.[12] The opening theme echoes that of a work
by Georg Muffat—perhaps an unconscious borrowing, since the movements
otherwise have nothing in common, but the similarity is too close to be accidental.[13] The ritornello form of the concerto movement is clear, the opening theme
being restated forte in C (m. 53), B♭ (m. 103), and the tonic (mm. 139 and 163).

One can readily imagine the episodes for divided keyboards in mm. 31–52 and 91–103 as solos scored for violin (forte) and accompaniment (piano); the latter would be furnished by upper strings in mm. 31–42, basso continuo thereafter. But mm. 61–72, which are largely forte, do not replicate ritornello material; is this a developmental passage for the "tutti"? The same question arises after the shortened entry of the ritornello theme in m. 103, despite the absence there of any original dynamic indications (see below). Hence, like Bach's orchestral concertos, the movement blurs the distinction between ritornello and episode.

Despite the quasi-orchestral genre, the keyboard writing is not closely modeled on that for instrumental ensemble, although Bach had used some of the same textures in the Vivaldi transcriptions. For example, the broken-chord accompaniment for the left hand in mm. 43–5 corresponds with a passage in BWV 976 (mvt. 1, mm. 8–11). Occasionally the left hand has an accompaniment in repeated notes, an apparent borrowing from orchestral style that is rarely seen in Bach's keyboard music. Similar accompaniments, however, are common in contemporary keyboard works by younger composers.[14]

The middle movement derives more directly from Vivaldi. Comparable scoring—a soaring melodic line accompanied by simple lower parts, without ritornellos—occurs in many of his slow movements, as does the simple bipartite form. Despite the florid embellishment of the upper part, this is not an adagio but an andante, like the second section of the sinfonia in Partita no. 2. A "walking" tempo, with steady motion in the lower voices, conveys fire to the melodic embellishment and makes it easier to perceive the phrase structure. The first half, for example, opens with a periodic theme (mm. 4–7, 8–12) followed by a sequential transition (mm. 13–8). A pedal point on the dominant of the relative major (mm. 19–25) then leads to a cadence in the new key (mm. 26–7). The theme consists not in the actual notes of the florid upper part, nor in some putative underlying melody divested of its embellishments, but in the underlying progressions.[15] Thus the first period (mm. 4–7) returns at the opening of the second half (mm. 28–31) with a substantially different right-hand melody but the same accompaniment; the transitional sequence of mm. 13–8 is recapitulated with both parts altered (mm. 32–5) and a new extension leading to a pedal point in the tonic (mm. 36ff.). Breig (1991, 297) points to the larghetto of Vivaldi's double-violin concerto op. 3, no. 8 (transcribed for organ as BWV 593) as a model; the two movements have much in common, including a quasi-ostinato bass.

The last movement seems originally to have been called an allegro, changed to presto in the print. Perhaps the *alla breve* notation normally conveyed something slower, but here Bach's first thought was for unabashed impetuosity, as evident in the ascending scales of the main theme. Formally the last movement resembles the first, with a similar key scheme (ritornellos in F, C, d, Bb, a, and F) and several nearly parallel passages.[16] But it makes a more thorough recapitulation of episodic material, beginning at m. 155, and this brings it somewhat closer to the through-composed sonata form common in *galant* concertos of the 1740s and later.[17] The ritornello is shorter and simpler from the point of view of phrasing, lacking the formality inherent in the first movement's sequential ritornello theme. Yet the ritornellos are more contrapuntal than those of the first movement, and at one point the main line shifts to the left hand (mm. 93–6). The episodes also take a distinct approach, treating the two hands as partners in a duo, each alternatingly forte and piano. For this reason both hands move frequently between manuals, an advance on the simpler dynamic scheme of the first two movements and one of several ways in which the finale presents the greatest technical challenge to the player. It is usually the simpler melodic idea that tends to be played forte, allowing it to be heard more clearly against the livelier filigree of the other part.

The sources seem to have omitted a few necessary dynamic markings in the outer movements; uncertainty as to how to supplement these markings may reflect their having been late, somewhat artificial additions to a completed composition. A forte should probably be supplied for the left hand at m. 104 of the first movement, as indicated in NBA V/2. Not only does the ritornello theme enter at this point, but in ensuing passages the left hand is at least the equal of the right, and there is a piano indication at m. 129. The NBA restricts this latter indication to the left hand, probably correctly although the print is ambiguous here.[18] Less certain is the addition of dynamic markings for the left hand at four points in the third movement. At first it seems implausible that Bach intended the left hand to remain forte throughout mm. 92–171, and the NBA adds alternating pianos and fortes in mm. 127, 141, 155, and 166. But consistency with parallel passages demands that the left hand stay forte at mm. 127 and 155, where, following the principle noted earlier, it has simpler but equal thematic material. The passage returning at m. 155 was originally played piano (mm. 77–80), but exact parallelism is maintained for only three measures, and there is no good place for the left hand to switch from loud to soft.[19]

Ouverture in B Minor BWV 831

The B-Minor *Ouverture*, like Bach's two early works of the same type (BWV 820 and 822), is dominated by the opening movement, a large French overture containing powerful dotted sections and a virtuoso fugue in concerto style (or a concerto-like section with fugal ritornellos). The proportions of the work, which is heavily weighted toward the front, are odd by later standards. But dance movements comprise a greater portion of this work than in many orchestral suites and *ouvertures*, and the dances, especially the very expressive sarabande, are more substantial than usual, even by comparison to those in Bach's orchestral suites. None of the dances requires any changes of manual, but the alternating dynamic levels associated with exposition and episode in the fugue return in the closing *echo* movement, giving the work as a whole a degree of cyclic closure.

The overture, unlike that of Partita No. 4, has a concluding as well as an opening dotted section. It is hard to say why one overture closes with such a section and another does not; in this case it cannot be because of any lack of finality at the end of the fugue. The latter is self-contained, beginning and ending in the tonic; it closes by recapitulating much of the initial exposition/ritornello (mm. 123b–143 ‖ 26b–46). The same is true in the overture of Partita no. 4, so the addition here of a final dotted section simply adds weight to the opening movement of the suite—unnecessarily, as the movement is already unusually long, even without the indicated second repeat.

The dotted portions of the overture were the subject of a bruising controversy over the interpretation of their rhythmic notation.[20] Frederick Neumann's argument against the "so-called French style," by which he meant over-dotting, rested in part on the differences between the present overture as notated in the print and in the manuscript copy by Anna Magdalena Bach. The latter gives the early C-minor version (BWV 831a), in which the outer sections of the overture are less heavily dotted.[21] But did the revisions for the print signify a change in the actual rhythm or merely in its notation? If the latter, it would be necessary to conclude that there was a convention of lengthening not only dotted quarters but also a quarter tied to a sixteenth, and even a single sixteenth followed by three more (Example 16.1). This is hard to believe. Yet it is possible that Bach, while actually altering some of the original rhythms, merely renotated others.[22]

In this view the changes in mm. 1 and 2 were real revisions: a relatively smooth rhythm involving sixteenths was replaced by more vehement motion in thirty-seconds. Even in the original version, however, thirty-seconds eventually appeared just before the double bar (mm. 17–20A).[23] As this made for an inconsistency between the opening and closing phrases in this section of the piece, it made sense to intensify the motion from the outset, sixteenths remaining only in mm. 13, 146, 148, and 158. This would have been a compositional change, but

Example 16.1 *Ouverture* in C Minor BWV 831a, overture, mm. 1–3 (rhythms from BWV 831 above and beneath staves).

Example 16.2 (a) *Ouverture* in C Minor BWV 831a, overture, mm. 8–9a; (b) *Ouverture* in B Minor BWV 831: same.

Bach also notated the lengthening of dotted quarters more precisely, replacing the simple eighth note in m. 3 and elsewhere with a sixteenth rest plus sixteenth note.[24] He also eliminated notational discrepancies of the sort originally found at the end of m. 8, where parallel motion in the outer voices was notated in both sixteenths and thirty-seconds (Example 16.2). The insertion of a rest between the trill and its termination appears only here and was probably not a normal element in long trills; it might have been a special practice that Bach used in pieces in dotted rhythm.[25]

One effect of the revised rhythm was to make a long piece more homogeneous, and the dotted sections run the risk of monotony, especially if taken too slowly. The fugue is likewise prone to monotony, thanks to its heavy reliance on recapitulation; the three "solo" episodes are all recyclings of the same material, and the outer ritornellos/expositions are essentially identical. The highly schematic structure points toward the great Eb-major prelude (BWV 552/1) in the third part of the *Clavierübung*, but the material here is less varied. The changes of manual, although helping to clarify the ritornello structure, evidently were afterthoughts, and in one passage they require the hands to leap between keyboards five times in as many measures (mm. 89–93). The player hardly needs the added distraction, for this is already the most difficult as well as the one really compelling passage in the fugue. It serves as the third ritornello, although it is based not on the subject but on a new theme derived from the countersubject; the latter enters in four closely spaced statements that mount upward, always forte, through the circle of fifths.[26]

Of the nine dances, the most distinguished are the two slowest ones, the courante and the sarabande. The former is of the French variety, but it opens with a tonic pedal point that tolls every four beats, articulating a hemiola; the

Example 16.3 *Ouverture* in B Minor BWV 831, sarabande, mm. 1–6. Slurs cut by a single vertical stroke are absent from the first (1735) edition; the slur and the tie cut by double vertical strokes were eliminated from the second (1736) edition; brackets indicate an addition in the NBA.

idea returns in the last phrase (mm. 20–1).[27] The sarabande forms the high point of the suite. Like the sarabandes of the English Suites, it is in four strictly maintained parts, but the individual voices have greater rhythmic independence than in the earlier chorale-like sarabandes. The dense counterpoint includes many harsh passing dissonances, and the movement is as difficult to play well as any fugue, testing the harpsichordist's ability to draw out the long lines of the melody (and inner voices) while softening the naturally harsh attacks of the instrument through the breaking of chords and the discreet use of over-legato.

The slurs in the sarabande are problematical (Example 16.3). Both original editions contained obvious errors; the second eliminated two ties, including a nonsensical one in mm. 4–5, and added some slurs, but the length of some of those remaining is inconsistent (compare the treble in mm. 1–2 and 5). Probably no slurs should cross the barline; those that do so might have been engraved that way by false analogy to the ties.[28] One might compare the slurs in the aria that opens the second half of the Saint Matthew Passion (preserved in autograph), which begins with a similar gesture (Example 16.4).

The smaller dances grouped around the sarabande contain many refined details (e.g., the accompaniment in gavotte 1, mm. 12–3) and ingeniously varied textures, sometimes exploiting the lower range of the harpsichord (as in bourrée 2, whose thin scoring suggests use of the mute or "lute" stop). But despite

Example 16.4 "Ach, nun ist mein Jesus hin," from Saint Matthew Passion, BWV 244, mm. 1–4 (violin 1 only).

their tuneful character they grow long in performance. Even the gigue becomes monotonous with its constant skipping rhythm, despite the development of a *tirata* motive reminiscent of that used in the overture.

The absence of regular echoes in the last movement is also a disappointment until one realizes that the title does not refer to antiphony in the traditional sense. Only twice is a complete phrase restated piano, and then not immediately as in the echo movement of the suite BWV 821.[29] Rather, the dynamic contrasts articulate little motivic gestures—what C. P. E. Bach would later call *Einschnitte* (cuttings or cesuras)[30]—perhaps in an allusion to the old Baroque echo aria, where the device can be touching and witty at the same time.[31] The fleeting dynamic alternations require quick jumps between manuals (see, e.g., mm. 29–30); in the last movement of the volume, these are the final development of a technique introduced in the opening work.

Formally the movement is not very different from some of the rounded binary preludes in WTC2; the last return of the theme (tenor, m. 62) is intensified by its combination with new counterpoint, as in the preludes in D major and F minor. From this point of view the manual changes are merely a somewhat capricious way of decorating a binary-form "aria"; the latter is comparable to the 2/4 movements in the A-minor and D-major partitas (note again the staccato articulation). More striking than the echo effects is the series of modulations immediately after the double bar. These turn swiftly toward the subdominant or "flat" side of the tonic, in a restatement of the theme whose individual phrases are transposed kaleidoscopically to new pitch levels (D–e–A–D–G). Equally kaleidoscopic is the swiftly changing texture, suggesting if not exactly imitating various ensemble scorings and making the *echo* an appropriate close for Bach's volume of quasi-orchestral harpsichord solos.

Transcriptions

Sonata in D Minor BWV 964, after Sonata no. 2 in A Minor for Solo Violin BWV 1003; Adagio in G, BWV 968, after Sonata no. 3 in C for Solo Violin BWV 1005, first movement

Chief source: P 218/2 (Altnikol). *Editions*: BG 42, Dadelsen (1975), NBA V/12.

Bach's much-reproduced fair-copy autograph of the Solos for unaccompanied violin (P 967) dates from 1720. As is well known, they belong to a tradition of harmonically self-sufficient works for unaccompanied string instruments. They require no supplementation or accompaniment, but, given the rarity of string players able to meet their considerable technical and musical challenges, they are a repertory waiting to be appropriated by players of the keyboard and other polyphonic instruments. Bach was probably making impromptu keyboard arrangements long before these two transcriptions were written down; Adlung commented in 1758 that the works for unaccompanied strings "can be very well played on the clavier."[32] This indicates that, although they may not have been heard frequently in their original medium, they continued to be performed by keyboard players, as Kellner's copies, made in the 1720s, attest (see Stinson 1990, 59ff.). As in most of Bach's keyboard arrangements, transposition by fifth brought the original into a tessitura more suited for keyboard instruments.

The two transcriptions are preserved together in a manuscript copy by Altnikol, who studied with Bach from 1744 until 1748. In a review published in 1775, another Bach pupil, Agricola, stated that Bach had often played the sonatas and suites for unaccompanied string instruments "on the clavichord," confirming Adlung's report and suggesting a more specific medium for the present works.[33] Altnikol's manuscript copy of the two transcriptions contains title and attribution only for the Sonata BWV 964, and this is in the hand of another Bach pupil, J. G. Muethel, who perhaps named Bach only as composer of the original work, not transcriber. Both arrangements contain surprises that have been seen as pointing to "the generation of the sons of Bach, especially Wilhelm Friedemann" (Dadelsen, 1975). Hence, Bach's responsibility for the arrangements has been questioned (e.g., by Eichberg 1975, 39), and they appear in the NBA in a volume of doubtful compositions. If indeed by Bach, BWV 968 probably dates from no earlier than the late 1720s, in view of its wide range (down to GG) and pseudo-pedaliter scoring; something like the leaping left-hand part at the opening occurs several times in the partitas (e.g., praeambulum of Partita no. 5, mm. 73–7). It is harder to place BWV 964 chronologically, but the chromatic scale at the end of its first movement, like that in the bass of BWV 968 (m. 32), has parallels in the Fantasia and Fugue in C Minor BWV 906 and the keyboard version of the Fourth Brandenburg Concerto, both works of the late 1730s.[34]

In fact it would be surprising if anyone but Bach had been responsible for the audacious keyboard writing of BWV 968.[35] In both works the filling out of the harmony, especially of the inner voices in the fugue (BWV 964, second movement), reveals nothing atypical of Bach. The one disappointment is the last movement of BWV 964, whose arpeggio figuration is, for the most part, simply divided between the hands; only a few bass notes are added. But this very restraint also points to Bach; similar textures occur in the lute pieces and in other keyboard works (e.g., the praeambulum of Partita no. 5). Altnikol was one of Bach's more talented students, and, as Bach's son-in-law, inherited part of his music collection; clearly he had access to things that were not widely distributed. It would not be surprising if, around the time of the quasi-transcriptions in CB2, Bach was also making actual transcriptions of pieces composed fifteen or twenty years earlier; at the same time he was also revising concertos from the same period.

Bach had added much embellishment and substantially amplified the harmony in his transcriptions of Reinken's ensemble sonatas (BWV 965–6). Such changes were unnecessary in his own violin pieces, which despite their solo scoring had a rich (if implicit) polyphonic texture; the slow movements were already heavily embellished. Bach did add new counterpoint in the fugue; for example, in one passage (mm. 18–9) the added bass forms a brief canon with the original bass line, now placed in the alto. Elsewhere the transcription process was confined largely to realizing what is implicit in the original, bass tones, inner voices, and suspensions now being held out for their full values.

Bach's three sonatas for solo violin are expansive *sonate da chiesa*, modeled after smaller Italian works for violin and continuo, especially Corelli's op. 5, nos. 1–6. Each opens with an adagio and fugue, followed by another slow movement and an allegro. In BWV 964 the opening adagio is in through-composed bipartite form; as in the similarly conceived andante of the Italian Concerto, the recapitulation (in the subdominant, at m. 14) is recognizable from the bass line, the upper parts being considerably varied. The fugue's closest relatives among the keyboard works are the preludes of English Suites nos. 5 and 6, but without a da-capo design or a ritornello it lacks the concerto allusions of those works. Nevertheless, there are episodes composed of idiomatic violin figuration (as in Corelli's sonatas) as well as others of a more contrapuntal nature, some using the descending chromatic line that serves as countersubject in the fugue in A♭ of WTC2.[36] The fugue was known to Mattheson, who expressed his admiration for Bach's ability to draw a long piece from so short a subject.[37] The overall form is somewhat rambling, but it has a roughly bipartite shape, the second half beginning with the introduction of the inversion (m. 125); each half is further subdivided by the chromatic episode (mm. 73, 232).

In the third movement, an andante in binary form, Bach further embellished one cadenza-like flourish (m. 9) but otherwise left the original essentially unaltered. The allegro is a much larger binary form consisting almost entirely of violinistic figuration. At the keyboard one is tempted to sustain the notes of the broken chords in order to increase the sonority, even to add occasional bass notes. Yet Bach seems to have been careful, as always, to indicate exactly what he intended, and it may be best to add nothing. The same goes for the echo dynamics suggested in the BG; these are present in the violin version but awkward to play on the harpsichord (they would, of course, suit the clavichord).

Bach seems to have approached the transcription of the third violin sonata (BWV 1005) with greater freedom than the second, as the arrangement of the adagio completely alters the texture and character of the original. Thus, it is a profound disappointment that Bach—or at least the copyist Altnikol—got no further than the first movement, which ends on the dominant. As there are no orphan fugues in G to go with it, one must couple it with something else, perhaps the G-major Toccata or the concerto transcription BWV 973.

BWV 968 opens with the same progression found at the beginning of the adagio in the oboe concerto by Alessandro Marcello (arranged as BWV 974).

But by m. 4 the conventional harmonies have been replaced by something more chromatic and unpredictable. As in the violin version, the texture quickly expands in a quasi-imitative way. The process is intensified after m. 5 by the addition of luxuriant counterpoint in sixteenths for the left hand. The leaping accompaniment in the first few measures, which will make pianists want to use the damper pedal, sounds clunky on a harpsichord played or voiced carelessly; this may lie behind the suggestion that the transcription was intended for lute-harpsichord (*Lautenklavier*) (Dadelsen 1975), where the notes would have rung undamped. The movement is another bipartite form, extended by a modulating coda; the second half begins (m. 15) with a brief reference to the opening.

The Later Lute Works

The lute and its repertory had exerted a profound influence on harpsichord music in the seventeenth century, but in Bach's works the inspiration flows in the other direction. Bach knew lutenists at Leipzig and owned a lute at his death, but he probably did not play the instrument with any facility. Nevertheless, he evidently composed a few works for the instrument during his Leipzig years. These are worth examining closely, not only for their intrinsic musical qualities but because they illustrate Bach's continuing interest in new instrumental media. They also form fascinating connections with other works, including the transcriptions considered above.

The surviving autographs of these pieces are written in keyboard score, as are the majority of the copies, whose titles indicate that copyists were usually unaware that the pieces might have been meant for lute. In fact the intended medium remains uncertain, for they are fully idiomatic to no one type of Baroque lute. They might have been played on various instruments, including German lutes of several different designs, the theorbo, and the lute-harpsichord or *Lautenklavier*. The few surviving copies in tablature notation are adaptations by individual lutenists for their own use.

There was a bewildering variety of lute-type instruments in Bach's day (and an equally confusing list of terms to describe them). Although no longer much heard in other parts of Europe, professional lutenists were employed at German courts well into the second half of the eighteenth century. Much has been made of the appearance of two virtuoso lutenists at Leipzig in 1739,[38] but the visit of Weiss and Kropffgans may have been remarkable only for having been recorded in a document that happens to survive. Bach had probably known Weiss long before then. A member of the Dresden court since 1717, Weiss, like his colleague Quantz, was a virtuoso and a gifted composer who also made innovations to his instrument. This has given rise to the idea that Bach could have composed one or more of his "lute" works for unconventional instruments, on which Weiss might have performed things now thought impossible. Of course, such a player could also have adapted works composed for an "ideal" lute to suit a particular instrument at hand, just as Bach apparently adapted portions of a work by Weiss to produce the sonata in A for keyboard and violin BWV 1025 (see Schröder 1995).

Two of Bach's lute works, the early suite BWV 996 and the prelude BWV 999, have already been considered (see chaps. 4 and 10, respectively). Five more are discussed below,[39] with an emphasis on the musical features of these works and their suitability for keyboard performance.[40] At his death Bach owned two lute-harpsichords, at least one of which was probably the instrument reportedly built around 1740 at Bach's suggestion.[41] The rather sketchy verbal descriptions of such instruments indicate that there was no standard model, but that the best ones sounded remarkably close to an actual lute, which they imitated through the use of gut strings and the omission of dampers. No historical examples survive, so the sound and musical capabilities of such instruments cannot be judged confidently from the diverse modern reconstructions that have been made and even recorded. But the sustained efforts of several German builders, including Johann Nicolaus Bach, to make such instruments imply that although unusual they were a recognized type. Having had such an instrument built, Bach surely would have used it, and Kohlhase (NBA V/10, KB, 98–100) argues that the lute-harpsichord should be regarded as a distinct medium in its own right, not a mere "ersatz instrument." But that Bach composed any music specifically for it is as unlikely as the suggestion that certain pieces were intended for the clavichord or the fortepiano. Like other "clavier" pieces, the works allegedly for lute-harpsichord contain nothing that would rule out other types of keyboard instrument.

All of the lute works are thin in texture, suggesting that Bach meant them to be playable in principle on some sort of lute. But many keyboard pieces, including the last movement of the Sonata BWV 964 and several movements of the B-minor *ouverture*, are not very different in style. Moreover, the lute pieces contain slurs and sustained notes that would be routine in keyboard writing but can hardly be made audible on the lute. The low tessitura of these pieces helps compensate for the light textures; in the resonant middle and low registers of a good harpsichord one is less likely to regret the absence of full harmony, and this would have been especially true on an instrument without dampers. Yet the pieces contain unidiomatic figuration and wide gaps between voices, implying that Bach did not consider a keyboard instrument the primary medium.[42] Pedals, which were present on some lute-harpsichords, would help the keyboard player in some passages but not others.[43]

Whatever the intended medium, the relatively late dates of the sources imply that the pieces originated, or at least were revised, at Leipzig. Three works, BWV 995, 1000, and 1006a, were arrangements, carried out at roughly the same time as other arrangements and revisions of solo and orchestral works. BWV 997 and

998 were substantial new compositions, probably composed in the late 1730s or early 1740s.[44] All presumably would sound best on a good lute, well played, for which neither the so-called lute-stop (really a mute) found on modern harpsichords nor the true lute-stop (a set of jacks plucking close to the nut) is an adequate substitute. But this music—especially the original works BWV 997 and 998—deserves to be played, and performance on harpsichord is no worse than on guitar, the usual modern alternative.

Suite in G Minor BWV 995, after Suite No. 5 in C Minor for Solo Cello BWV 1011

Sources: B Br 4085 (= Fétis 2910; autograph in score, 1727–31); LEm Becker III.11.3 (tablature). *Edition*: NBA V/10.

The six suites for solo cello have traditionally been dated to Cöthen, but Eppstein (1976) argued convincingly that they are Bach's earliest group of suites for non-keyboard instruments; a Weimar origin is therefore likely. Suite no. 5 is the most French of the group, opening with a French overture (designated *Prelude* [*sic*]). It is also the one suite in the set to call for a substantial amount of chordal playing, and therefore was perhaps the most appropriate choice for lute arrangement. In the original, the cellist is asked to tune the top string down a step, from a to g, and notes played on this string are written a tone higher than sounding pitch. This presented problems of legibility for a keyboard or lute player attempting a transcription at sight and might have been an additional reason for Bach's having made a transcription of this particular suite.[45]

Bach's manuscript of BWV 995 includes his note that the work was for a "Monsieur Schouster," probably the Leipzig book dealer and amateur lutenist Jacob Schuster (Schulze 1983, 247).[46] BWV 995 proper is the version of the autograph; a tablature version attributed to the Saxon lutenist Adam Falckenhagen is an arrangement for the common thirteen-course lute.[47] Bach, however, called for the type of instrument by the Leipzig maker J. C. Hoffmann with an extra bass course down to GG—the "new" note also used to striking effect in BWV 968 and in the Fifth Partita, here used to produce an impressive pedal-point effect at the opening of the prelude.

The counterpoint of the fugue was entirely implicit in the original version, indicated through leaps and arpeggios within a single line. Here the fugue retains its very light texture, only a simple bass being added in the expository passages. Not much is added elsewhere, although the dance movements took on more ornaments, especially appoggiaturas, and the dotted rhythms of the allemande were revised much like those in the overture of BWV 831, which dates from the same period.

Fugue in G Minor BWV 1000, after Sonata no. 1 in G Minor for Solo Violin BWV 1001

Chief source: LEm III.11.4 (Weyrauch; tablature). *Edition*: NBA V/10.

Two transcriptions are known of the fugue from Bach's first violin sonata, the present one for lute as well as an organ version in D minor (BWV 539/2). Williams (2003, 74) considers the authorship of both arrangements to be uncertain, since they do not sufficiently resemble anything else with a clear attribution to Bach. But it is hard to understand why anyone but Bach would have expanded the piece by the equivalent of two measures each time he transcribed it, especially as the additions and alterations do not occur in the same places in the two arrangements. The organ version is in five voices, with an independent pedal part. The simplicity of the added voices suggests that this version is earlier than the transcription BWV 964, where the added parts in the fugue make a significant contribution to the counterpoint. The lute version, although playable as a *manualiter* keyboard work, survives only as a tablature and therefore is likely to depart from any autograph score that may once have existed; keyboard players will want to make appropriate adjustments.[48]

Suite in E, BWV 1006a, after *Partia* no. 3 for Solo Violin BWV 1006

Chief source: Tokyo, Musashino Music Academy, Littera rara vol. 2-14 (autograph). *Editions*: BG 42, NBA V/10.

By the time Bach copied out the autograph of BWV 1006a, he had already arranged the first movement of the E-major violin *partia* as an organ solo with orchestral accompaniment in Cantata no. 120a, performed in 1729.[49] Hence there are good reasons for doubting that BWV 1006a, which is closer to the original violin version, could have been meant for a keyboard instrument.[50] Apart from the prelude, the suite is easily managed on a keyboard instrument, but the prelude is the most striking movement, and it cannot be played effectively on a keyboard instrument lacking pedals. Two hands are needed for some of the figuration involving repeated notes, which were originally intended for performance on alternate strings of the violin (e.g., in mm. 13–6). The combination of two-fisted *batteries* with simple pedal writing is reminiscent of the end of the early Praeludium BWV 921; perhaps one of Bach's lute-harpsichords had "pull-down" pedals like the ones that Johann Nicolaus Bach of Jena added to his instruments of this type (described by Adlung 1768, 2:162).[51]

With a little practice one can play all of the figuration with the right hand, but inevitably the *batteries* lose some of their effect. Still, the effort is worth it, as the prelude is one of Bach's most entertaining pieces, stylistically and formally without close parallels. The opening flourish suggests toccata style, but the thoroughgoing *moto perpetuo* is closer to the *capricci* or cadenzas in the Vivaldi concerto that Bach transcribed for organ as BWV 594. Formally the movement follows a sort of bipartite design: much of the first part returns after the midpoint (mm. 59–78 || 9–28), unusually at the subdominant, but the opening gesture never comes back. The dances are entirely idiomatic *manualiter* pieces. The loure is of particular interest as a more strictly fugal example than the one in the Fifth French Suite, although each half employs a different subject.

Suite in C Minor BWV 997

Chief sources: P 650 (Agricola; title: *Praeludium, Fuge, Sarabande und Gigue fürs Clavier*); LEm III.11.5 (Weyrauch, tablature, lacking fugue, double; title: *Partita al Liuto*). *Editions*: BG 45, NBA V/10.

The odd sequence of movements making up BWV 997—prelude and fugue, sarabande, gigue, and double—makes it seem a collection of miscellaneous pieces. But the uniformly mature style points to its having been conceived integrally, and it is Bach's strongest original lute work. The title "suite" does not occur in the chief sources, and the organization is closer to that of a *sonata da chiesa*. Many copies survive, indicating that the piece was popular; only one source uses lute tablature, most of the rest assigning the work to *Clavier* or *Clavicembalo*.

The keyboard sources give the notes in the top staff an octave above sounding pitch, except in the last movement.[52] The last movement, a double (variation) of the gigue, has too wide a compass to be playable on the lute; on the other hand, m. 2 (|| 38) is somewhat unidiomatic on the keyboard as written.[53] Such apparent carelessness might cast Bach's authorship of this movement in doubt, especially as it represents a thorough recomposing of the gigue, maintaining only its essential bass and harmonic outlines (as in the allemande of the Suite BWV 819a); but the style is entirely Bach's.

The first two movements are a prelude and fugue comparable in design, if not quite in dimensions, to the "Wedge" fugue for organ (BWV 548), pairing a ritornello-form movement in concerto style with a fugue in da capo form.[54] Although the proportions of the fugue are similar to those in the preludes of the last two English Suites—the A section is only slightly shorter than the B section—arpeggiated passagework is confined to the B section, as in the "Wedge." A further connection to Bach's later organ works occurs in the B section: this introduces a varied form of the subject whose oscillating figuration (m. 56) resembles motives used in both the "Wedge" and in the organ prelude BWV 552/1 from the *Clavierübung*.

The opening of the sarabande is famous for its resemblance to the theme in the closing chorus of the Saint Matthew Passion, which is in the same key; the resemblance is closer when one corrects an error in m. 18 of the edition in NBA

V/10.[55] The gigue has some of the same *empfindsamer* character, with appoggiaturas playing a prominent role in the motivic material. The initial phrase is composed over much the same bass as the opening of the prelude and is varied again in the double that follows.

Performing this suite on the keyboard requires somewhat more adjustment than the preceding works. But the changes do little damage to the musical substance, and whereas one might question the value of playing the previous lute works on the keyboard, doing so in this piece is eminently justified by the richness of the texture and the profoundly expressive style. Keyboard players will need to transpose and simplify small portions of the bass line; on instruments lacking high f´´´ most of the double can be played an octave lower than written.[56]

Praeludium, Fugue, and Allegro in E♭, BWV 998

Sole source: Tokyo, Ueno-Gakuen Music Academy (autograph). *Editions* BG 45, NBA V/10.

The customary title for BWV 998 (given above) is a variation on the label "Toccata, Adagio, and Fugue" that has become attached to the organ toccata in C (BWV 564). Bach gave the work no general title, merely labeling the first movement *Prelude pour la Luth. ò Cembal* [sic]; it could be viewed as a church sonata lacking a slow movement after the fugue. The heading in the autograph reflects the fact that, of all the "lute" pieces, this is the only one that is entirely playable as written at a keyboard instrument, without pedals.[57] Whether it is equally idiomatic for lute is another question; there are no contemporary tablatures.

The prelude is similar in meter, form, and texture to the prelude in the same key in WTC2, which the fugue also seems to quote.[58] The fugue subject is reminiscent of the chorale melody *Herr Jesu Christ, wahr'r Mensch und Gott*, the basis of Cantata no. 127 (first performed in 1725). As in BWV 997, the fugue is in da-dapo form, and again only the B section contains free figuration. This, however, is a somewhat less ambitious movement, perhaps also a less satisfying one, the opening section being marred by a few oddly prosaic passages (mm. 7–8, 13–5). The allegro, a large binary form, opens with the same gesture as the gigue of the earlier lute suite BWV 996. It shares that piece's perpetual motion in sixteenths, but instead of chromaticism and counterpoint offers galant fluidity and simplicity of texture.

17
The *Clavierübung* Continued

During the 1730s the focus of Bach's keyboard composing shifted from suites to other genres, including variation and canon, in which he had previously worked only sporadically. Besides the preludes and fugues of WTC2, the keyboard works of his later years include the Goldberg Variations, the ricercars from the *Musical Offering*, and the *Art of Fugue*, in which he combined canon, strict fugue, and variation in ways never previously explored. Integral to this group is part 3 of the *Clavierübung* (CU3), which, although comprised primarily of chorale settings for organ, includes pieces playable on other keyboard instruments.

Sources for these works survive from 1739 and afterwards, but only for the *Musical Offering* can any individual compositions be dated with precision. The focus on certain common compositional techniques, as well as occasional parallels in thematic content between works published in different collections, makes it likely that Bach worked on more than one of these projects at a time. But although most of this music was surely composed after 1735 or so, it is problematical to speak of these as "late" works or as representatives of a distinctive late style, since they cover a wide range, both stylistically and chronologically. Even the *Musical Offering* and the *Art of Fugue* include music as outgoing as anything from Bach's earlier years, proving that Bach in his old age did not quietly retreat into the contemplation of pure counterpoint. Yet there is a recherché quality to much of this music; the allusive harmony, tortuous melodic lines, and high tolerance for passing dissonance imply that, more frequently than before, the composing out of a predetermined contrapuntal design sometimes took precedence over other considerations.

One such consideration was practicality of performance. More than previous works, the *Art of Fugue* and the ricercars from the *Musical Offering* raise practical issues that will be considered in due course. The two last installments of the *Clavierübung*, although as difficult to play, are less problematical in this regard.

Clavierübung, Part 3

CU3, published in 1739, retains the dedication to *Liebhabern* (music-lovers) found on the title pages of the first two volumes but adds "especially for those knowledgeable in such things" (*und besonders denen Kennern von dergleichen Arbeit*).[1] The volume must have astounded even knowledgeable contemporaries, not only for its large size but for the borrowings from archaic genres and the consistently counter-intuitive, dissonant counterpoint and angular melodies. Although it contains many elements of the fashionable style *galant*, these are woven into textures and forms whose complexity and density were barely hinted at in volumes 1 and 2. CU3 can therefore be considered the first installment in a series of works that constituted Bach's systematic contribution to the tradition of speculative counterpoint, which extended back to the Renaissance by way of Frescobaldi and other predecessors.

Outwardly, CU3 is a practical anthology of pieces primarily, if not exclusively, for the organ. It has been supposed that the volume "displays something of the organization of a typically Bachian organ concert" (Wolff 1986b, 288), although it is unlikely that anyone would have played straight through the volume as a concert program.[2] The central portion of the volume consists of ten chorale melodies, each presented in a *manualiter* and a shorter *pedaliter* setting.[3] The chorales are framed by the two movements of the great *pedaliter* Prelude and Fugue in E♭ BWV 552; the fugue is preceded by four duetti for manuals only.

Like the WTC, the volume has been discussed at great length (e.g., by Williams 2003), and the present discussion is limited to matters of interest primarily to non-organists. Wolff (1986b, 287) and Butler (1990) have argued that the pieces need not all have been written shortly before publication in 1739, as has usually been assumed. Nevertheless, the collection marks a sharp change in direction from CU2. Superficial elements of *galant* style, including sigh motives, triplets, and "quasi-ostinato bass lines" (stressed by Butler 1990, 17–20), are present in several movements. But a number of the chorales, including the six settings of the Kyrie and Christe, are based on archaic melodies whose modal character is reflected in Bach's harmony, which is neither conventionally tonal nor genuinely modal. These settings avoid sequences, full cadences, and other types of formal articulation normal in eighteenth-century music. Often they end with a "modal" cadence that surprises the listener into the realization that these were meant to be not abstract, self-contained works of art but parts of a liturgical act. Even in movements characterized by *galant* melodic writing, the presence of canon (as in the *pedaliter Vater unser* BWV 682) or the avoidance of sequence and periodic phrasing (as in the *manualiter Allein Gott* BWV 675) are departures from *galant* style as it occurs in, say, the Partitas.

The title indicates that the work is "for the organ" (*vor die Orgel*), but there also exists a letter by Bach's amanuensis, Johann Elias Bach, written just before publication, that states somewhat more ambiguously that the new print contains "clavier" pieces that are "*chiefly* for organists" (emphasis added).[4] Bach may therefore have contemplated performance of some of the music on harpsichord and clavichord, with or without pedals. But it is unlikely that any of the music, except possibly the duets, was conceived primarily for stringed keyboard instruments. *Manualiter* pieces mingled with *pedaliter* ones in collections of organ music that served as models for the volume, such as Grigny's *Premier Livre d'orgue* (Paris, 1699).[5] Even by 1739, not all German organs had pedals, and certainly not all organists had any substantial pedal technique; many players would have welcomed the inclusion of *manualiter* chorales. In their avoidance of *brisé* writing, as well as their restrained use of ornaments and frequent inclusion of plain sustained tones even in the top voice, these settings differ from the "monodic" chorale preludes in CB and elsewhere that Bach probably did intend for clavichord or harpsichord.

Nevertheless, pianists and harpsichordists would do well to play this challenging music, which otherwise will be heard by few other than organ enthusiasts. The *manualiter* chorales provide a good survey of the various types of keyboard chorale setting, a genre that was never meant to be the exclusive domain of organists. Although the long notes of the alto cantus firmus in the first *Allein Gott* BWV 675 make the piece unidiomatic for stringed keyboard instruments, it is worth studying as a rare example of a chorale fantasia in ritornello form playable without pedals. By the same token, the cantus-firmus setting of the *manualiter Vater unser* BWV 683 provides a taste of Bach's so-called *Orgelbüchlein* style, a direct setting of the melody with a homogeneous contrapuntal accompaniment and no interludes.

More practical for recital purposes is the *manualiter* Kyrie-Gloria series (BWV 672–5), a tonally integrated sequence that can be extended to include the A-major fughetta—actually a compact double fugue—on *Allein Gott* BWV 677.[6] The three Kyrie movements, each apparently starting in a major key but ending on V of A minor, are examples of the quasi-modal style mentioned earlier, also alluded to in the *Art of Fugue* (especially in the early version of Contrapunctus 2). The first Kyrie is a little contrapuntal fantasia on the opening of the melody, especially the first three rising notes ("Ky–ri–e"). The Christe comes somewhat closer to being a conventional fughetta, although the subject in the treble, quoting the first six notes of the chorale, is accompanied at the outset by free writing in the lower voices (imitation begins with the tenor entry in m. 3). The second Kyrie begins, like the two *pedaliter* Kyries, with paired stretto entries, again based on the three rising notes from the opening of the melody. From m. 21 onwards it develops the motive from m. 3, which combines with itself in inversion in the last complete measure (cf. the fugue in d♯ from WTC2 and Contrapunctus 5 from the *Art of Fugue*).

Three of the remaining *manualiter* chorales are fughettas on subjects derived from their respective chorale melodies; each uses distinct styles and compositional techniques. The quasi-permutational counterpoint of *Christ unser Herr* BWV 685 has the intricacy of some of the Goldberg canons, but on the harpsichord or clavichord it is hard to project the long notes of the subject, which appears alternately in its *rectus* and *inversus* forms. On the other hand, with its lively repercussive subject and dance-like rhythm, the fughetta on *Diess sind die heil'gen zehn Gebot'* BWV 679 seems a natural harpsichord piece, as is *Wir glauben all'* BWV 681, whose pervasive dotted rhythm recalls the gigue of French Suite no. 1; the last bar of the much earlier gigue is practically quoted at the close. BWV 681 is, with the overtures in CU1–2 and variation 16 of the Goldberg cycle, another instance of the French dotted style initiating the second half of one of these volumes. Bach described the corresponding piece in the *Art of Fugue* (Contrapunctus 6) as being in "French style"; like the fugue in D minor in WTC1, BWV 681 drops the subject halfway through, in favor of free motivic development.[7] Despite the "Dorian" key signature, it is in the pure minor mode.

The last two *manualiter* chorales are larger, darker pieces. *Aus tiefer Noth* BWV 687 follows a six-part double-pedal setting of the same melody. Although not a *tour de force* like the *pedaliter* setting, this too is an austere, archaic fantasia in motet style (despite the 2/4 signature). Each phrase of the chorale melody is worked out imitatively in the three lower voices, the soprano then entering with the same melodic phrase in long notes. To play this well would be a good exercise for pianists, but it is unlikely to make much of an impression on the harpsichord no matter how sensitively its complex but relatively uninspired counterpoint is played. The last chorale setting is a full-scale four-part fugue on the first phrase of *Jesus Christus unser Heiland*, BWV 689. Its F-minor tonality (actually B♭ minor for long stretches) complements what would have been, given the tuning of many organs, the equally extreme F♯ minor of the previous *manualiter* setting. The subject is, from its initial entrance, worked out in strettos of various sorts; the same concern with canon surfaces in movements from the *Art of Fugue*, and one episodic passage (mm. 30–2) is reminiscent of the fugue in D minor from WTC2. Unfortunately, even more than in the *Art of Fugue*, it is difficult to project all of the this work's expressive details on the harpsichord; two climactic gestures, the bass entry at m. 50b and the augmented tenor entry at m. 57, require the sustaining powers of an organ.

Seven other *manualiter* fughettas on chorale melodies for Advent and Christmas are more idiomatic on, perhaps intended for, stringed keyboard instruments (BWV 696–9, 701, and 703–4). Once thought to be early works, their sophisticated counterpoint is now recognized as being nearly equal in ingenuity and expression with that of CU3, with which they must be roughly contemporary. In three and four voices, they range from "simple" fugues with regular countersubjects to what is actually a short fantasia on *Vom Himmel hoch* (BWV 701), combining lines 1–3 of the chorale tune in ways that parallel the Canonic Variations for organ on the same melody (BWV 769).[8]

The four duetti have been regarded as "clavier" pieces since the nineteenth century, although there is nothing in them unidiomatic to the organ, which had a long tradition of fugal *bicinia*. Butler (1990) argues that they were late additions to the volume, but Bach was working on other projects during the same period, and they could have been conceived as "clavier" pieces, even candidates for inclusion in WTC2. In each, a straightforward gesture at the beginning of the subject is contradicted later by irregular or otherwise "difficult" writing—unusual chromatic intervals, for example. In no. 1 the theme opens with a plain scale figure but ends with a series of twisting, seemingly clumsy gestures (mm. 5–6). Duetto no. 2 in F has an almost purely diatonic A section, the subject opening with a broken triad in quarter notes, implying detached articulation, but the middle section begins with a slurred motive containing an augmented second.[9]

Although the four pieces obviously resemble the inventions, a closer predecessor was the large two-voice fantasia that opens the A-minor Partita. Here the initial imitation is always at the dominant, and there are distinct episodes, making each piece more a fugue. Yet, more than in a normal Bach fugue, the designs tend toward the geometric, incorporating much recapitulation; the schematic form and the chromatic double counterpoint of no. 1 recall the prelude in A minor of WTC2. Number 2, in da-capo form, surpasses the two-part fugue in E minor of WTC1 in the complexity and exactness of its symmetry, at least in the B section. Yet these remain playful pieces. Duetto no. 3 introduces a telescoped variation of the subject at the return (mm. 28ff.), interpolating a few beats' worth of new material into the rests of the subject so that the latter can be used in a sort of pseudo-stretto.[10] Number 4 repeatedly reworks phrases from the opening section (mm. 1–16) in double counterpoint, somewhat like the canons in the *Art of Fugue*; the subject appears only in tonic and dominant. The humor is abstruse, but this is hardly the work of a contrapuntal pedant or a mystic obsessed with numerical symbolism.

The Goldberg Variations

The work known as the Goldberg Variations was published in 1741 under the title "Keyboard Practice, consisting of an aria with diverse variations for the two-manual harpsichord."[11] Today the work is usually regarded as part 4 of the *Clavierübung* series, but the title does not make this explicit and could be interpreted to mean that Bach "intended to separate this work at least to some degree from the preceding parts."[12] It is dedicated simply to music-lovers, without the suggestion of deeper mysteries contained in the title of CU3. But like other late works of Bach it has been the subject of numerous special studies, some finding esoteric special meanings in the music. Williams (2001) is a valuable commentary, going into greater detail than is possible here.

The modern title may be the result of a misunderstanding. Forkel (1802, 51–2/NBR, 464–5) reported that Bach wrote the work for Count Keyserlingk, a diplomat and patron of music then living at Dresden, who knew Bach and frequently visited Leipzig; according to Forkel, the work was to be played by Keyserlingk's harpsichordist Johann Gottlieb Goldberg. Williams (2001, 5) suggests that Bach actually composed the music for his son Wilhelm Friedemann, a great virtuoso, who was then also at Dresden and is known to have taught Goldberg; Friedemann later dedicated a keyboard sonata to Keyserlingk. But despite Goldberg's youth—he would have been only thirteen or fourteen at the time—Forkel's story remains credible inasmuch as Goldberg later gained the reputation of a virtuoso.[13] Forkel adds that Keyserlingk called the work *his* variations, and that Goldberg would play them for him during the Count's frequent sleepless nights—not, presumably, to put him to sleep, but to entertain him when sleep was impossible. Bach was in Dresden in November 1741 as Keyserlingk's guest, and, as with the English Suites, the popular title might stem from Bach's having given a noble connoisseur a special presentation copy (NBA V/2, KB, 113).

The circumstances of the work's actual composition remain obscure. In writing a large set of variations, Bach turned to a form that he had not used in a completed keyboard work since the early chorale partitas. But his contemporaries and immediate predecessors had hardly neglected variation form—Corelli, Handel and Rameau, among others, had published extended examples. By the 1740s, variation sets were turning into a simpler type of piece, often pedagogic in nature. Bach, however, evidently envisioned the Goldbergs within a tradition of large, encyclopedic variation sets for keyboard going back to the sixteenth century.[14] The title *aria* for the opening movement was also traditional, employed by Pachelbel and other German predecessors for short binary forms used as the basis of variations, although these sets were rarely as long or diverse as the present one.

Variations might serve not only as exercises in performance but as demonstrations of compositional technique. In Renaissance variations the most common technique was the addition of counterpoint to a cantus firmus sounding in long notes. By the seventeenth century, variations were often based on what we would term a harmonic progression, understood at the time as the realization of a figured bass line. The Goldberg set is built on a bass line whose first four notes were also the basis of a sarabande with twelve variations attributed to Johann Christoph Bach, usually identified as the Eisenach composer (1642–1703) of that name.[15] Such variations illustrated the same compositional technique as the doubles for the sarabande of BWV 818 and the allemande of BWV 819a, but on a more massive scale. The Goldbergs show that music belonging to practically any genre, including strict fugue and canon, could emerge as the realization of a single bass line or harmonic progression.

History and Design

The large structure of the work revolves around canons. Canon is the precise imitation of one voice by another throughout a composition (or at least a substantial portion of one). The imitation need not be exact, since it may take place at any interval and may involve alterations of note values and melodic shape (e.g., inversion), but any such changes must follow some regular rule. Until the late 1730s, Bach's interest in strict canon seems to have been limited to individual chorale settings and to brief compositions written as offerings to friends. Stimulated perhaps by the enthusiasm of learned amateurs such as Mizler for such things, in his late years he not only created all sorts of ingenious canons but, more significantly, integrated them into the plans of four large works: the Goldberg Variations, the Canonic Variations for organ BWV 769, the *Musical Offering*, and the *Art of Fugue*. The sequence in which these works were composed is unknown, as only printed editions and fair-copy autographs survive. But although much of Bach's earlier music (notably the Leipzig church cantatas) was apparently composed quite quickly, these works would have required long hours of preparatory sketching and experimentation on paper. Each, moreover, underwent significant revision, sometimes even after engraving and printing.

In the Goldberg Variations only every third movement includes a canon. Canonic movements alternate regularly with other variations that can be described as belonging to "duet" and "free" types. At the end, the initial aria is repeated (Table 17.1). Although broadly symmetrical, the plan contains irregularities. The three-movement pattern of canon, free variation, and duet emerges only with variation 3 and ends with variation 29. The overture, which, as in CU1–3, divides the work in half, falls in the middle of one of the threefold groups. Two canons in contrary motion (variations 12 and 15) occur in the first half; three variations in the minor mode (nos. 15, 21, and 25) fall toward the end. From such discrepancies, Breig (1975, 254) posited that the first twenty-four variations might have constituted an original core, organized around the first eight canons. The remaining variations might have been added later, certain movements—in particular the overture (variation 16)—perhaps being substituted for others among the original twenty-four. In any case it seems likely that the Goldbergs, like other Bach collections, grew by increments, the final arrangement emerging only after some experimentation.

The structure as we know it certainly produces effective juxtapositions between individual variations. For example, the overture forms a splendid contrast with the canon in the minor mode that precedes it; this makes the overture seem like a new beginning, appropriately at the outset of the second half of the work. But does the work as a whole constitute a true cycle, with a large structure that one can perceive in performance? Or is it more a series of pieces set out according to a rational plan like the movements of the WTC but not meant to be played straight through? Is the threefold pattern, like the series of widening intervals of imitation involved in the canons, merely an organizational device, intellectually satisfying but irrelevant to the way in which one plays or hears the work? Conceivably, in a complete performance the three-variation unit produces a large-scale rhythm or pattern perceptible to a careful listener. This pattern is defined especially by the canons, which tend to be relatively restrained in character, hence constituting

Table 17.1 Structure of the Goldberg Variations

Movement	Type	Manuals	Voices	Model	Remarks
Aria		1	(3)		
Var. 1	free	1	2		duo; hand crossings
Var. 2	free	1	3		trio; quasi-canon
Var. 3	**canon**	1	3		**at the unison**
Var. 4	free	1	4		
Var. 5	duet	2			
Var. 6	**canon**	1	3		**at the second**
Var. 7	free	1 or 2	2		*al tempo di Giga*
Var. 8	duet	2			
Var. 9	**canon**	1	3		**at the third**
Var. 10	free	1	4		*Fughetta*
Var. 11	duet	2			
Var. 12	**canon**	1	3		**at the fourth, by contrary motion**
Var. 13	free	2	3		embellished andante (sarabande)
Var. 14	duet	2			
Var. 15	**canon**	1	3	minor	**at the fifth, by contrary motion**
Var. 16	free	1	2–4		overture
Var. 17	duet	2			
Var. 18	**canon**	1	3		**at the sixth [*alla breve*]**
Var. 19	free	1	3		
Var. 20	duet	2			
Var. 21	**canon**	1	3	minor	**at the seventh**
Var. 22	free	1	4		*Alla breve*
Var. 23	duet	2			
Var. 24	**canon**	1	3		**at the octave**
Var. 25	free	2	3	minor	embellished *adagio*
Var. 26	duet	2			juxtaposes 18/16 and 3/4 time
Var. 27	**canon**	1	2		**at the ninth**
Var. 28	free	2			hand crossings
Var. 29	free	1 or 2			
Var. 30	free	1	4		*Quodlibet*
Aria					

regularly occurring points of repose. The work breaks out of this pattern toward the end, where the last half-dozen variations—all extraordinary in one way or another—serve together as a climax.

The sheer length of a composition can create the impression that it is transcendent in character, if only in the sense of transcending the normal temporal bounds of the style.[16] This alone might explain the special quality that one senses in the return of the aria after the last variation—a moment that inevitably reminds modern listeners of the da capo at the end of the variations in Beethoven's piano sonata Op. 109. But no retransition prepares the return of the opening theme as in the Beethoven work, nor has any material from the aria, other than the bass, recurred substantially in the variations. At most one hears an occasional echo of the aria, as in the underlying sarabande rhythms of variations 13 and 25 and again in variation 26, where the sarabande rhythm serves as one strand in a polymetric texture. Hence the cyclic aspects of the work are minimal, and it is easy to imagine re-ordering many of the variations without changing substantially the effect of the whole.[17]

Bach would have considered the question of cyclic form differently from later composers, as the work was presumably not intended for complete public performance. Few of the original purchasers would have regarded it primarily as something to be played from cover to cover; Goldberg's performances for Keyserlingk might have consisted only of favorite movements, ending if the latter did fall asleep. The chief principle governing the sequence of the variations, other than the canons, may well be local contrast, each variation being a self-contained recomposition of the underlying harmonic ground and phrase structure. Successive movements do not add increasingly florid embellishment to a recognizable "theme" or develop its motives in increasingly ingenious ways. Although the aria reappears at the end, the variations do not progressively move away from and then return to it (as they do in op. 109). Any tendency toward increasing brilliance in the duets and free variations is countered by variations of an increasingly restrained or serious nature, which culminate in the somber G-minor arioso of variation 25; from this point of view the only discernible general trend is toward greater extremes in both directions.

Text and Performance

Anna Magdalena Bach's copy of the aria in the 1725 *Clavier-Büchlein* was once assumed to date from long before the variations and thus to constitute evidence that the aria, like other pieces in the manuscript, had been borrowed from another, anonymous composer, possibly French. But the handwriting is now thought to date from near the time of the work's publication and thus has no bearing on the authorship of the aria.[18] The engraving and publishing were entrusted to Balthasar Schmid of Nuremburg, and as in CU1–3 some copies contain hand-written corrections. One copy, recognized by Wolff (1976) as Bach's *Handexemplar*, includes the composer's autograph of "various canons upon the first eight fundamental notes of the preceding aria" (BWV 1087).[19] Added neatly on the last (unprinted) page, these might have been composed preparatory to the Goldberg Variations. But they give the bass in a different rhythmic form, and two are known in slightly revised versions dated 1746 and 1747, respectively; the latter are listed separately as BWV 1076 and 1077.[20]

Although more or less playable on a solo keyboard instrument, these canons cannot be considered keyboard music; the first four are not even "music" as such, rather theoretical examples or demonstrations of how the bass line or its counterpoints might be treated canonically. The third of these examples is incorporated in its entirety into no. 13, becoming one of three strands in a *canon triplex à 6*. Bach's "musical thinking" asserts itself in the course of the set, and with no. 5 we suddenly face real music of considerable charm. Bach's impulse toward variety manifested itself not only in the diverse canonic techniques but in the chromaticism of nos. 6 and 11. His tendency toward increasing elaboration emerges in the more complex later numbers, culminating in a canon that combines augmented and diminuted versions of the theme, in both upright and inverted forms. Bach and his friends and family might have improvised ad hoc performances "both *vocaliter* and instrumentaliter," as he put it (*BD1*, item 23/NBR, item 152, p. 152). Any performance today is necessarily an arrangement, ranging from the relatively straightforward realization for strings and harpsichord by Reinhard Goebel to a neo-Baroque recomposition by Joel Feigin.[21]

Bach's corrections and additions to the printed text of the Goldberg Variations proper are incorporated into the edition in NBA V/2. Unfortunately, as in CU1–3, Bach did not rectify ambiguous ornament signs. The imprecision of the original print is exacerbated by modern editions in which hardly a single sign appears as Schmid engraved it. Schmid's signs for trills and mordents are longer than usual (they contain extra "wiggles"), and the vertical or oblique stroke that ought to be drawn at the center or at the beginning of the mordent sometimes stands too far to the right (Example 17.1). Only facsimile editions, of which there are several, can show the signs exactly as they appear in Schmid's print. Both BG 3 and NBA V/2 regularize Schmid's mordent signs to a form identical to that for the long trill with suffix (*Nachschlag*).[22] No doubt aware of the problem, C. P. E. Bach (1753–62, i.2.3.6) later warned of the potential for confusion between a carelessly drawn mordent and a trill with *Nachschlag*. In fact, in Schmid's print the vertical stroke is not always as badly misplaced as it is in the modern editions. Anna Magdalena Bach's copy of the aria makes it clear that the ornament first sign in m. 1 of the aria represents a mordent—likewise in mm. 2, 5, 8, and so on, and by extension elsewhere in the work.

Other ornament signs raise harder questions, especially in the overture (variation 16). Extensions at the beginnings of the trill signs in mm. 2, 3, 5, and elsewhere are represented in NBA V/2 by the straight diagonal stroke of the *tremblement appuyé*, signifying a lengthened first (upper) note.[23] These initial strokes are distinctly curved in the original, corresponding with the ornament

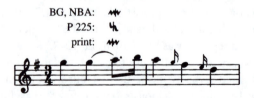

Example 17.1 Goldberg Variations BWV 988, aria, mm. 1–2 (upper staff).

Example 17.2 (a) Goldberg Variations BWV 988, variation 16, m. 2; (b) C. P. E. Bach, Versuch (1953–62), i.2.3.28, Tab. 4, Fig. 43c.

that Bach taught Wilhelm Friedemann to call a *Doppelt-Cadenz*, but which C. P. E. Bach called the "trill from above" (*Triller von oben*, 1753–62, i.2.3.26–8). Emanuel Bach illustrates it in a context close to the present one (Example 17.2): the ornament fills in a melodic falling third, a turn following. Since the time of WTC1 (see the prelude in F), J. S. Bach seems to have had a special fondness for this complex ornament. Slight irregularities at the ends of two of these signs (bass, m. 5, and treble, m. 8) have been cited as evidence for a "termination-by-hook" (Schwandt 1990, 68, citing Emery 1953, 64–5). But in m. 5 the termination or closing turn at the end of the trill might have been played anyway (C. P. E. Bach 1753–62, i.2.3.13). In passages like m. 8, where the trill precedes a descending figure, Emanuel Bach counsels against a termination or suffix (1753–62, i.2.3.16).

The most celebrated performance elements in the Goldbergs are the hand crossings and the use of two manuals. These must be considered separately, as variation 1, which employs hand crossings, is designated as being for one manual, whereas several variations containing only incidental hand crossings are for two manuals. The hand crossings were once assumed to reflect Domenico Scarlatti's influence, and Marshall suggested (1976a, 348) that copies of Scarlatti's *Essercizi* (London, ca. 1739) might have reached Leipzig in time to inspire the composition of the hand-crossing variations. But this can be no more proved or disproved than Rameau's suspected influence on the Partitas. By 1740 virtuoso hand crossings would not have been new to Bach. Any stimulation that he received from works of Scarlatti or Rameau might have led not to direct imitation of hand crossing or some other device, but rather to the "anxiety of influence" postulated by Williams (2003, 156). In this view, the hand crossings and the etude-like sequences built from simple motives in Scarlatti's *Essercizi* would have made Bach "anxious" to "surpass" the latter, through more rigorous and more extensive use of devices already familiar to both composers.[24]

In any case, to speak simply of hand crossing is to oversimplify. Of the ten variations with significant hand crossings, five (nos. 8, 11, 17, 23, 26) are true duets, virtuoso manifestations of the old *bicinium* or the traditional *pièce croisée*. Here the hand crossings are incidental products of voice crossings, that is, of polyphony whose independent parts are played by different hands in the same register. The five other hand-crossing variations (1, 5, 14, 20, 28) involve leaps of one hand over the other in order to strike notes in different registers. As in the prelude in B♭ from WTC2, the registrally isolated notes belong to separate implied voices in the polyphonic texture (see Example 12.6). In any given variation, most of the material is divided equally between the hands according to some symmetrical scheme. Thus, at the opening of variation 5 the left hand crosses over the right, the pattern being inverted after the double bar, as is the motivic material itself. In this way the crossing of hands, potentially the most vulgar of keyboard techniques, is integrated into the refined "architectonic" type of design that characterizes so much of Bach's music.

The need for two manuals was indicated on the title page, as in CU2. Only here, however, is the use of two keyboards integral to the music, used not to create incidental dynamic contrasts but to allow the free voice leading of equal, independent parts; for this the manuals must be uncoupled.[25] Only in variation 7, where Bach allows use of either one or two keyboards, and perhaps in the "monodic" variations 13 and 25, where a treble part is accompanied by two lower voices, could the movements designated as being for two keyboards have been conceived apart from double-manual performance. Variation 5, although indicated as being for either one or two manuals, is clearly a duet and is exceedingly awkward to play on one manual. Variation 1, on the other hand, contains hand crossings but is confined to a single manual, perhaps because the two voices, although sharing some material, are more distinct in character than in true duets; the lower part still bears some resemblance to a traditional basso continuo line. Bach again offered a choice of one- or two-manual performance in variation 29, whose *batteries* divided between the hands seem to call for a loud, brilliant effect achievable only when played on one manual. But a passage in the duet variation 23 (mm. 27–30), together with the C. P. E. Bach sonata cited below, suggests that Bach might have preferred the rapid alternation of quieter timbres produced by playing variation 29 on two independent manuals.

The indications for one- or two-manual performance do not specify how each variation is to be registered, but there can be little doubt that Bach expected a player to take full advantage of the capabilities of a given instrument. Organists normally changed registration for each setting in a series of variations. That harpsichordists might do the same is clear from C. P. E. Bach's registrations for a *cembalo* sonata composed in 1747 that ends with a variation movement.[26] As in other German sources of the period (e.g., Adlung 1768), the stops are referred to in the same manner as on an organ, as *Cornet*, *Flöte*, and so on. Emanuel specifies some surprising combinations; for figuration somewhat resembling that of variation 29 he prescribes muted *Cornet* on the upper manual, octave and coupler on the lower.[27] Most instruments have more limited registrational possibilities than the special one for which C. P. E. Bach's sonata was composed. But the latter shows that players need not be limited to two plain eight-foot ranks in playing the duets.

Pianists have dealt with the technical problem posed by double-manual variations in various ways, some honoring Bach's division of the notes between the hands, others pragmatically redistributing the notes. Whatever the solution, the musical problem is to maintain the integrity and equality of the crossing parts. Subordination of one part to another (e.g., through dynamics) would contradict the fact that the voices are usually of equal importance and based on the same material. Pianists sometimes try to imitate the registrational possibilities of the harpsichord through octave transpositions of parts, or by playing one voice legato, another staccato. Although novel, such devices do not produce anything analogous to actual harpsichord sound, where homogenous articulation is rarely used (see chap. 2). Simply playing each line as beautifully and imaginatively as possible, as one would do in any contrapuntal work, is more likely to project the counterpoint to an audience than contrived pianistic effects that distract the ear and the player from its musical content.

The Aria

Doubts about Bach's authorship of the aria appear to be unfounded (see Neumann 1985 and the reply in Marshall 1989, 54–8). Still, the almost excessively variegated style of the melodic embellishment is rare in Bach's output; its eventual evening out into steady sixteenths in the last phrase (from m. 27) is an idea previously used in the sarabandes of French Suites nos. 3, 4, and 5. The combination of a fragmented melodic surface with a slow harmonic rhythm would be characteristic of Emanuel Bach and other composers of the "empfindsamer" generation.

The framework for the aria and the subsequent variations is the bass line with its implied continuo figures—a background of simple four-part counterpoint rather than a series of harmonic progressions in the modern sense (Example 17.3). Neither aria nor variations ever gives the bass in what might be called its hypothetical original form; even in the aria the main tones of the bass—what Bach called the *Fundamental-Noten*—are embellished or altered (cf. Example 17.5). Elsewhere the underlying counterpoint is varied by chromatic inflections, above all in the three variations in the minor mode. Another sort of alteration occurs in the hand-crossing variations, where the *Fundamental-Noten* may be transferred from the left hand to the right (e.g., variation 5, mm.

Example 17.3 Goldberg Variations BWV 988, hypothetical *Fundamental-Noten* (with figures).

21–4). Occasionally the *Fundamental-Noten* are also displaced from their usual positions on the downbeats, but displacements by more than a beat, such as occasionally occurred in the old variation-suite, are rare except in the fugal part of the overture (variation 16).

Hence, the harmonic rhythm is consistent throughout the work, one principal harmony appearing in each of the aria's thirty-two measures, which correspond in number with the thirty-two movements (counting the repeat of the aria at the end). The measures fall symmetrically into phrases of four and eight measures, yet, as in most binary movements, the symmetry is inexact: the cadence at the end of the first phrase (m. 8) is still in the tonic, but the third phrase modulates from dominant to relative minor, making the tonal design tripartite. The periodic structure is retained in the individual variations; even in the fughetta (variation 10) the subject enters every four measures. Only the fugal section of the overture (variation 16) departs significantly from this pattern, and even there the overall dimensions of the second half—sixteen "double measures" of 6/8—are unaltered. Elsewhere, the elision of phrases prevents the music from becoming trapped in a periodic vise. Elided phrasing first occurs in variation 2 (at m. 24) and becomes the norm in the canons, where the periodic structure is hidden by the overlapping phrases of the individual canonic parts. Nevertheless, the underlying periodicity is less thoroughly disguised than in, say, some of Purcell's grounds.

Besides the problem of Schmid's irregular ornament signs, the aria raises the question of how to perform the many appoggiaturas indicated as small notes. "Pre-beat" performance has been advocated (e.g., in Neumann 1978, 142), but should one disregard advice that Emanuel Bach published just twelve years later? He shows an example in which third-spans (*Tertien-Sprünge*) are filled by appoggiaturas, just as in m. 2 (Example 17.4a; compare Example 17.1).[28] And he denounces the "odious after-beat [*hässlicher Nachschlag*]" (1753–62, i.2.2.25; see Example 17.4b), which reduces a series of appoggiaturas to innocuous passing tones.[29] Playing the appoggiatura in m. 4 before the beat would, moreover, create a stutter, as it immediately follows a sixteenth note on the same pitch. As m. 4 merely repeats m. 2 in embellished form, both appoggiaturas must be played on the beat.

At thirty-two measures (sixty-four with repeats), the aria is longer than the average theme of a Baroque variation set, and some of the individual variations are substantial compositions in themselves. It is harmless to omit some of the repeats, especially in very long movements such as variations 13 and 25, or those in which the two halves are very similar, such as variation 17.

Example 17.4 C. P. E. Bach, Versuch (1753–62): (a) Tab. 3, Fig. 9a, with realization; (b) from Tab. 4, Fig. 20a.

The Variations

The first variation opens the series with a bang. Hand crossings, which first appear in m. 13, are a development of the leaps in the bass of m. 1. These hand crossings do not contradict the direction for single-manual performance, for the texture remains that of a sonata movement, albeit one with unusually athletic violin and continuo parts.[30] The three-part texture of variation 2 accordingly imitates the trio sonata. It opens fugally; the initial two-measure interval between entries is reduced to a single measure in the stretto entries of the second half (mm. 24ff.), pointing toward variation 3, the first of the canons.

All but the last of the canons are also in trio-sonata texture—two canonic voices over a free bass—but they are necessarily somewhat different in style from any of Bach's earlier keyboard works in three voices, such as the Sinfonias. Writing canons is fairly easy; writing canons within the constraints laid down here is not. Bach's abilities were such that even the strictest constructive device did not dictate musical choices to him. Nevertheless, the practical requirement that the music must be playable by two hands on one keyboard led to writing that would seem odd outside a canonic context. In the first three canons the upper parts cross more often than would ordinarily be the case in keyboard music, due to the close interval of imitation. Moreover, the individual voices contain occasional odd melodic intervals or form peculiar vertical intervals, and are sometimes fragmented into uncommonly short phrases. Especially in the two canons by inversion, unusually rough passing dissonances are allowed. The same occurs in the Canonic Variations and the canons of the *Musical Offering*, and it would be fair to say that all this music is a bit contrived. Yet the bass, which is free and not bound by the rules of canon, shares motivic material with the canonic parts and borrows some of their distinctive melodic character. Whatever peculiarities may have been forced upon Bach by the use of canon and the limitations of ten fingers on one keyboard have been integrated into a distinctive but coherent style.

This style colors the non-canonic variations as well. Nothing comes as close to atonality as a strange moment in the Canonic Variations (no. 3, m. 19). But m. 9 of variation 2 is odd; not only do the upper parts momentarily double the third of the harmony, but they do so while forming a bare fourth with the bass (Example 17.5). In fact, bass f♯′ is a passing tone, and the underlying harmony is a G-major triad elaborated by a routine 5–6 progression, as in m. 1.[31]

Variation 4 consists of four-part imitative polpyhony. The declamatory three-note motive (b′–g′–d′′) suggests a motet sung rather deliberately, and one can imagine four vocal parts entering in descending order, accompanied by continuo; the vocal bass enters with the main motive in m. 4. Yet the time-signature (3/8) suggests a dance, perhaps a minuet. The leaps in the main motive imply detached articulation, as does the normal shortening of tones before suspensions in mm. 6, 7, and so on.[32]

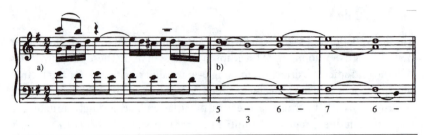

Example 17.5 Goldberg Variations BWV 988, variation 2: (a) mm. 9–10; (b) analysis.

Variation 5, the first of the duets, is designated "for 1 or 2 manuals." Williams (2001, 60) suggests that this could be a remnant of an early stage of composition. Like no. 1, this variation lacks the symmetry of some of the later duet variations; in mm. 9 and 17 the left hand takes up motives in sixteenths that are not quite the same as the right hand's. That may or may not be a sign of an earlier origin, but it makes performance on one manual only slightly less impractical than in subsequent duets. In m. 19 Bach added slurs in his *Handexemplar* (on the eighths e´´–c´ and a´–g´´); because of voice crossing the first slur is realizable only on two manuals.

In Bach's *Handexemplar*, variation 7 bears the added heading *al tempo di Giga*, surprising twentieth-century commentators who supposed gigues were always fast and fleeting. Despite the Italian terminology, this is a French gigue like the one in the *Ouverture* BWV 831. It need not go quickly, especially in view of the numerous short trills and appoggiaturas. The option to play the variation on two manuals makes it possible to subordinate the bass to the upper part and, if the keyboards are uncoupled, solves the problem of the unison on e´ in m. 24.[33]

Variation 8 is the first of the full-fledged duets. Its arpeggios and other virtuoso motives look as if inspired by not only musical but also technical considerations, making it an etude, although the genre did not yet exist. The two thematic ideas presented in the first measure by treble and bass, respectively, are developed with such single-minded intensity, and the two parts range up and down each keyboard with such freedom, that the writing would have seemed slightly deranged by mid-eighteenth century standards of decorum. In this, at least, the music recalls that of Domenico Scarlatti. Yet the two composers were living in a rational century, and the symmetrical exchanges of material between the two hands follow the same logical principles as in the Inventions or the Duetti. In the last four measures the sequential figuration of the right hand makes a downward plunge through almost three octaves; this precisely mirrors the writing for the left hand at the end of the first half.

Some editors alter a note in m. 3 in order to form a closer parallel with the following measure (Example 17.6). But no ambiguity or correction occurs in the original, and the two measures are not precisely parallel. The second note in m. 3

Example 17.6 Goldberg Variations BWV 988, variation 8: (a) mm. 3–4; (b) analysis.

(d′) can be understood as a dissonance that resolves (to c♯) on the third beat, the resolution being transferred to the bass. In modern terms, the dissonant harmony is ii[7]; the same harmony is involved in two later passages that also are sometimes emended.[34] But the printed text should stand, especially as Bach left these "errors" alone while correcting others in each of the variations in question.[35]

The fughetta (variation 10) is not very rigorous, all four parts sounding together only in the last four-measure phrase of each half. In his copy Bach added a mordent to the initial note of the subject; the engraver left out or misdrew the ornament in most entries. Presumably, the mordent (as well as the trill on the second note) can be extended to each statement of the subject.

Variation 11 is in 12/16 time, which according to Kirnberger (1771–9, 2/1:124) indicates a quick tempo. But Williams (2001, 64–6) questions whether this piece is any "less lyrical and more brilliant" than the gentle B♭-major prelude of WTC2, which uses the same time signature. Both contain broken chords that might be brilliant, but also descending scales that can be played delicately; on a two-manual instrument the frequent crossing of parts produces a subtle play of timbres that disappears at too quick a tempo. Still, delicacy may be out of place here, for both parts have several long *Doppelt-Cadenzen*, implying brilliance.[36] The best solution may be to compromise; harpsichordists might add the four-foot rank to one part, sacrificing the equality of the two voices for the sake of subdued brilliance and greater timbral contrast between the manuals.

Variation 12 is the first of the two canons by contrary motion. The prevalence of sixteenth-note figuration suggests a lively tempo, and although one rarely hears the variation played that way, Williams (2001, 67) recalls that Tovey found here a "droll capriciousness." The odd chromatic and augmented intervals, which start in m. 24, seem to imply "expressive" performance. Yet the chromaticism is of a quasi-ornamental character that Bach seems to have discovered in his later years, as in the sarabande of 819a and the Adagio BWV 968. In such cases the individual chromatic tones need not be articulated deliberately, as one might do in a chromatic line moving in larger note values. The inversional relationship between the canonic parts is most easily heard when the tempo is quick enough for each measure to be perceived as a unity; a lively tempo also helps the ear fill in momentarily empty sonorities like the open fifth on the third beat of m. 24.

If the canon by inversion were exact, the trill in m. 4 would be answered by a mordent in m. 5. But although slurs are added in both measures in the *Handexemplar*, there is no mordent. Perhaps this was an oversight; near the end, a trill in one part is answered by a mordent in the other (see mm. 29–30). But ornaments need not always be imitated exactly, even if this might be desirable in principle.[37]

The written-out turns found at one point in variation 12 (mm. 19–20) become the principal motive in variation 13. The latter could be described as an embellished andante, like the middle section of the sinfonia in Partita no. 2. But it is also an ornate sarabande; the dance rhythm of the aria emerges in the emphasized second beat of both melody and accompaniment. The upper voice is played on a separate manual, as is possible in those sarabandes from the French Suites whose "monodic" texture is adopted here. The solo line achieves considerable brilliance, ascending in the third phrase to what Bach seems to have regarded by this date as the normal upper limit in keyboard music (d‴ in m. 21).

With variation 14 (a duet) the trend toward increasing brilliance continues, but it is broken off in variation 15, the most lugubrious of the canons, which is also the first of the variations in G minor. The text of both variations is altered slightly in some editions, but the harmony suggests that Bach's readings should stand (Example 17.7). In variation 14, the addition of a sharp in m. 25 (right

Example 17.7 Goldberg Variations BWV 988: (a) variation 14, mm. 25–6; (b) variation 15, mm. 27–8 (each with analysis).

hand) is presumably prompted by the g♯ in the bass just a beat earlier. Yet in this measure the tonality is shifting back toward the tonic G major, and the substitution of g♯′ for g′ in the treble contradicts the modulation. In variation 15, the slur found in the print at m. 28 points out that the bass note g is an appoggiatura. There is no reason to think (as in NBA V/2) that the slur is a misplaced tie, such as occurs in the much less accurate print of the B-Minor *Ouverture*. The same appoggiatura, albeit without slur, recurs at the corresponding point in variation 25 (see Example 17.9 below).

The numerous two-note slurs and the somewhat convoluted chromatic lines of variation 15 invite slow, rhythmically free performance, as do the many "sigh" (or "dragging") motives. But the tempo mark *Andante*—the only tempo marking in the original print, unless one counts *Alla breve* in variation 22—could be a warning not to make the movement an adagio. *Con moto* would be the modern equivalent. The pulse is on the quarter, not the eighth, and, as in the previous canon (variation 12), the larger shape of the lines is obscured if they become too leisurely. The odd ending, with the upper part ascending to d′′′, resembles a gesture used in recitative to set questions (Example 17.8). Hence, although the variation marks the end of the first half, it has an open quality that leads toward the second.

Variation 16 opens with a tonic chord on the downbeat, like many orchestral overtures (e.g., in Bach's B-minor Orchestral Suite). The chord not only re-establishes the major mode but, with the scale in the right hand, fills in the middle register, which was left empty at the conclusion of variation 15. The first (dotted) section is, as usual, notated *alla breve*, implying a vigorous tempo. Dots on the sixteenths in mm. 8–9 may indicate both equal values (as opposed to *notes inégales*) and emphatic articulation. The fugue is ostensibly in four voices, but all sound together only for the value of a single eighth (in m. 23). Nevertheless, unlike the fughetta in variation 10, this section has the non-periodic rhythm and elided phrasing of a normal fugue. Only its brevity and the absence of a complete fugal exposition in the tonic betray the fact that it follows a pre-existent tonal plan. Within the first exposition the fugue moves from D to E minor, and although the ground bass is treated freely, the cadence to E minor arrives on schedule in m. 31, halfway through the section.

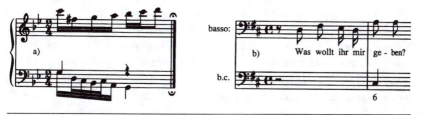

Example 17.8 (a) Goldberg Variations BWV 988, variation 15, m. 32; (b) *Saint Matthew Passion* BWV 244, recitative (NBA No. 7), mm. 4b–5a.

Variation 17 is another etude-like duet. Bach's first thought must have been the broken thirds, which climb without a break through two-and-a-half octaves in the first four measures (lower staff); to this he would have added the less regular counterpoint in the right hand.[38] Variation 18 is alone among the canons in its *stile antico*. Notated in cut time, it resembles the *Alla breve* (variation 22) not only in its rhythm and notation but in the use of a chain of suspensions as its main motivic idea. These two similar variations appear in close proximity among several relatively modest variations that follow the overture; they are broken up by the big duet no. 20 and the minor-mode variation no. 21, so there is no sense of redundancy when variation 22 beings. Variation 19 is sometimes regarded as an imitation of lute style and therefore played on the "lute" stop, but it has little in common with actual lute music. It uses an arpeggiated motive that may suggest a plucked string instrument, but this is only one strand in a three-part contrapuntal texture that is developed permutationally, as in the Sinfonias.

With variation 20 the work resumes the trend toward unabashed virtuosity, taking up the leaps, trills, and *batteries* introduced in variation 14. Indeed, from this point onward the duet variations abandon the decorum of ordinary two-part counterpoint. Unlike variation 14, which retained a basic symmetry, variation 20 moves to new and climactic figuration in its later stages, as do the next two duet variations. The penultimate phrase (mm. 25–8) abandons the pretense of two-part counterpoint altogether, dissolving into *batteries* of triplets.

But the following two variations are again restrained. Despite its minor mode and the chromatic inflection of several *Fundamental-Noten*, variation 21 does not aim for deep pathos. The motives in sixteenths have few rough edges, flowing relatively smoothly, and the tempo is better andante, as in an allemande, than adagio. The next variation is labeled *Alla breve*, pointing out that it is a four-part motet. By contrast with variation 18, which is a canonic duet with bass accompaniment, here the bass shares the main motivic material with the upper parts (mm. 9, 17, etc.).

Variation 23 may be the most difficult of the duets, but it is also one of the wittiest. Its material is the G-major scale, treated in close canon (mm. 1–7, 13–5) and in contrary motion against itself (mm. 9–12, 17–20). The idea of introducing climactic figuration in the last quarter is carried further than in the previous duet, for Bach now doubles the scales in thirds (m. 25) and sixths (m. 31) while again introducing *batteries* (m. 26). Emanuel Bach suggested that double scales should be played by repeating the same fingering for each dyad: "With many successive thirds…one does better in a quick tempo to continue with the [same] fingers, since crossing them is more difficult."[39] This advice is not entirely practical here, since the F♯s and C♯s fall awkwardly under the fingers, but following Emanuel one can assume a staccato rather than a legato touch.

Variation 24, the canon at the octave, might be a pastorale; the dance is suggested not only by the swaying rhythm but by the tonic pedal in the closing measure of each half. The design differs from that of the previous canons, since midway through each half the leading voice (*dux*) pauses and exchanges roles with the other canonic part (*comes*). This might be pointed out by a small articulation after the first note of m. 9, likewise after the third note of m. 24, where the mordent on the next note helps mark the new role of the treble as *dux*.

That Bach paid close attention to the connections between adjacent variations is clear at the start of variation 25, where the dyad g/b heard at the close of the previous variation is repeated with the substitution of b♭. This minimal change announces the last of the minor-mode variations, also the longest and most profound of the "free" settings. Although there could hardly be any doubt about the matter, Bach added the word *adagio* in his own copy, thereby indicating a need for expressive freedom, even virtuosity, in the performance of the piece's written-out Italian embellishments, and underlining the distinction between this and variation 13, also scored for florid treble accompanied by two slower parts on a second keyboard. As always, too slow a tempo causes the embellishment of the "solo" part to lose urgency; it also makes it hard to hear the very expressive writing in the two lower parts, whose main motivic idea, introduced at the outset by the bass, is a declamatory rhythmic motive consisting of an upbeat of three "speaking" notes followed by a "sigh." The motive is later taken up by the tenor (m. 9) and eventually treated in canon by both lower parts (m. 13); it is bracketed in Example 17.9.

Of course, the focus of variation 25 is on the embellished treble. The embellishments are thematic, not improvisatory, and the opening measures are recapitulated in the second half, making this variation more a sonata form than any other, although the recapitulation begins in the subdominant (m. 25). The most dramatic gesture occurs not at the beginning of the recapitulation, as one might expect, but two measures later, where the music modulates back to the

Example 17.9 Goldberg Variations BWV 988, variation 25, mm. 27–29a.

tonic. The passage contains an augmented sixth, marked by an asterisk in example 17.9. This interval, always an extreme harmonic gesture for Bach, had already occurred in m. 3, where its early appearance is a sign of this variation's special pathos. The same harmony has an even greater effect when, at m. 27, it reverses the previous modulation into "flat" keys. The subsequent return to the tonic (mm. 28–9) coincides with the melody's rapid ascent to d‴, an extraordinary gesture in a slow movement.

The bright major third at the opening of variation 26 fills the void left by the barren G at the end of the preceding variation. This is the last of the true duet variations, and it brings the idea of a divided texture to its most extreme development, introducing genuine polymeter as 3/4 time in one keyboard is juxtaposed against the rare 18/16 in the other. There is no reason to think that Bach intended rhythmic "assimilation" of the two lines. Kirnberger, who quoted the upper staff of m. 1 as an example of 18/16 time (1771–9, 2/1:129–30), does not mention any sort of rhythmic alteration. On the contrary, he lends support to the idea that the movement comprises two contrasting meters, explaining that the sixteenths form pairs, not groups of three. Groups of three sixteenths would correspond with eighth notes in the other staff; groups of two create a cross-rhythm (Example 17.10).

A less important question in variation 26 is whether the dotted rhythms are to be played literally or are to be adjusted by making the sixteenth in each dotted figure fall with the last sixteenth of the group of six (as in m. 2, first beat). What does matter is that the sarabande rhythm, always present in the parts notated in 3/4, be clearly heard as such. The variation in effect combines the French dance rhythm with a more or less Italianate virtuoso line; Bach had played with simpler versions of the same combination in the English Suites.[40] The dichotomy between the two strands of the texture is strengthened in Bach's *Handexemplar* by the addition of appoggiaturas to the passages in sarabande rhythm, as in the lower staff of example 17.10, m. 2.[41] The presumably are to be realized as short *ports de voix*.

Variation 27 is the one canon without a free bass, hence seemingly simple although the figuration is surprisingly awkward to play. The omission of a free part was encouraged by the wide interval (a ninth) between the canonic voices.

Example 17.10 Goldberg Variations BWV 988, variation 26, mm. 1–2.

It also provides a welcome clearing of the texture, making this the last variation in two parts (no regular duets have been heard since variation 17). From here the texture grows more complex, and also more unusual.

For a modern listener, the nearly continual trills of variation 28 recall the closing sections of several late piano works of Beethoven. The resemblance is only superficial, however, and variation 28 should probably not be interpreted as light, feathery, delicate, or however else one might describe the effect in Beethoven. Such trills in a harpsichord piece imply something forthright and brilliant, as do the leaps of up to a tenth in the bass and the chords in as many as five voices (m. 9). The piece could have been suggested by works of Frescobaldi and later composers in which written-out trills accompany motion in other voices, though none develop the idea so thoroughly or at such length as in this case.[42]

Written-out trills are also the predominant element in variation 29, where they take the form of parallel 6/3-chords played by alternating hands. Bach had used comparable motives in ensemble works, such as the Third Brandenburg Concerto (first movement). In a keyboard piece this would have been an extravagant virtuoso gesture, like hand crossing, and Bach uses it only here and briefly in variation 20.

Between variation 25 and variation 29 the work has proceeded from its most introspective to its most extroverted movement. The last variation, the quodlibet, provides a winding down preparatory to the closing restatement of the aria; its evocative title and musical quotations invite speculation of various sorts. Forkel (1802, 3–4/NBR, 424–5) reported, perhaps apocryphally, that members of the Bach family had improvised quodlibets at their annual gatherings, and a fragmentary example for voices and continuo survives by the young Bach (BWV 524). Both the latter and the quodlibet in the Goldberg Variations incorporate folktunes into contrapuntal textures usually associated with more serious matter. Hence, the somewhat pompous, stolid four-part texture of variation 30 is an affectionate if slightly mocking glance backwards at an older type of counterpoint. Each half closes by combining two phrases of a single tune (*Kraut und Rüben*); the same ingenious device, really a form of stretto, occurs at the end of the Canonic Variations. But the material reveals its folk origin in the incongruous nature of the melodies—especially the leaping figures heard after the double bar—and in the heavy-footed rhythms that articulate each quarter of each measure, even at the cadences.

At least six melodic fragments in the quodlibet are known to be or appear to be quotations (see Table 17.2 and Example 17.11). The most important, those heard in the upper part at the beginning and end of the first half, have been identified as coming from two folksongs (Schulze 1976, 68-9). One of these, *Kraut und Rüben*, had previously served, under the title *La Capricciosa*, as the basis of Buxtehude's thirty-two *partite* BuxWV 250, also in G and forming obvious parallels to the Goldberg Variations.[43]

Table 17.2 Quotations in the Goldberg Quodlibet

Melodic Fragment	Measures and Voice in Which Fragment is First Used	Source
a	0–1 (T)	*Ich bin so lang nicht bei dir g'west*
b	3b–4 (T)	quasi-inversion of A; part of same tune?
c	9–10 (S)	continuation of A?
d	13b–15a (A)	part of the same tune?
e	2–3 (A)	*Kraut und Rüben*
f	7–8 (T)	continuation of E

Example 17.11 Goldberg Variations BWV 988, melodic fragments in variation 30: (a) m. 1 (tenor); (b) mm. 3b–4 (tenor); (c) mm. 8b–9 (soprano); (d) mm. 13b–15a (alto); e) mm. 2–3 (alto); f) mm. 7–8 (tenor).

The direction to repeat the aria after variation 30 suggests that the aria is not really *the* theme of the work but another variation—one of an infinite number of possible realizations of the *Fundamental-Noten*. The print concludes with the words *e Fine* (and End). But in Bach's *Handexemplar*, at the bottom of the page on which he added the fourteen canons on the bass notes of the aria, he wrote the word *Etc.*, signifying that the series could, in principle, continue forever.

18

The *Musical Offering* and the *Art of Fugue*

Despite their dependence on archaic models and frequent use of *stile antico*, Bach's last published keyboard works are expressive and sometimes brilliant. Although difficult both technically and intellectually, they clearly were meant to be played, not merely contemplated. As in CU3 (*Clavierübung*, Part 3) and the Goldberg Variations, the music occasionally incorporates *galant* thematic ideas within learned contrapuntal designs, but no more than in those previous publications does it make concessions to fashion. It is inevitable, due to the unusual format of each work, that studies have tended to treat them as intellectual conundrums or monuments of Bach's contrapuntal skill. Yet the superficial devices of canon and fugue embodied in each movement are so closely integrated with the deeper musical content that it is impossible to consider one without considering the other.

The *Musical Offering* is dated to 1747 with a precision that is unique among Bach's major instrumental works. The *Art of Fugue*, on the other hand, grew by accretion through the 1740s. Its first conception and early drafts may well have taken place in the late 1730s, at the same time as CU3 and WTC2. Although the *Art of Fugue* was not published until after Bach's death, an early version was essentially complete by around 1742, and Bach had carried out at least the preliminary stages of its preparation for printing by late 1749. Thus the *Art of Fugue* is not, on the whole, as late as it was once thought to be. A few movements, including the fragmentary quadruple fugue, could date from as late as 1749, but it is possible that the two ricercars from the *Musical Offering* were Bach's last entirely new keyboard pieces.

The *Musical Offering*

As Bach continued to work on the *Art of Fugue* after the completion of the *Musical Offering*, the latter may be considered first. The *Musical Offering* was an outgrowth of Sebastian's visit in May 1747 to Potsdam, near Berlin, where Emanuel Bach served King Frederick II ("the Great") of Prussia as one of the royal keyboard players. Wolff (2000, 426), noting that the visit took place shortly after Prussian troops had lifted their occupation of Dresden and Leipzig (a result of the Second Silesian War), suggests that Bach went as an "ambassador of peace." But if so this was in an unofficial capacity, and Bach's fulsome praise of Frederick in the dedication of the printed work would not have pleased the Dresden court, perhaps instigating the Saxon prime minister's decision two years later to name his favorite as Bach's successor, while Bach was still living.[1]

Bach's visit to Potsdam was reported throughout Germany.[2] Evidently Bach was asked to improvise on the king's fortepianos, playing among other things a three-part fugue on a theme by the king himself. Doubts concerning the king's ability to invent the theme are unfounded, for the he was a highly accomplished amateur composer and flute player; many of his flute sonatas and several concertos survive. Later accounts of music at the Berlin court stress its *galant* character, but King Frederick II had studied counterpoint and probably knew similar fugue subjects by his teacher Quantz and perhaps Zelenka (see Oleskiewicz 1999, 85–6). Frederick would have known that his theme, comprised mainly of long notes with numerous chromatic melodic intervals, offered the potential for both contrapuntal elaboration and expressive harmony.

The Berlin newspaper reported that the king himself played the subject for Bach, "without any preparation," on the fortepiano. Such informality, which was characteristic of the king's demeanor within his private circle, might have seemed a gesture of respect toward the titular court composer of the king's arch-rival, the Elector of Saxony. It evidently made an impression on Bach, who referred to it in his dedication of the published work to Frederick. Within two months of his visit, Bach had composed the three-part ricercar, had it engraved and printed—as he had promised the newspaper correspondent he would do—and sent a special dedication copy to Berlin. The latter included several canons, and was probably meant to include the six-part ricercar as well; by September all thirteen items that constitute the complete work had been printed and advertised.[3] Within little more than a year Bach had sold or given away one hundred printed copies of the "Prussian fugue," as he called it, and was planning to have it reprinted.[4] Years later Emanuel Bach would write to Forkel that the work was easily obtainable in manuscript copies from publishers like Breitkopf.[5]

Because of the peculiar physical format in which the work was published—separate compositions in two-stave keyboard score, open score, instrumental parts, and puzzle-canon notation, all on different sizes of paper—discussions have tended to become mired in considerations of the proper order of its parts. Evidently Bach's initial idea of composing a single keyboard fugue had expanded quickly into a series of diverse examples of imitative composition. The complete work contains two fugues (called ricercars) in three and six voices, respectively; a trio sonata in four movements; and ten canons (or nine canons and a "canonic fugue") in two to six voices. But only the ricercars and two of the canons conform to the original idea of music playable on solo keyboard.

The canons, as well as the sonata, might have been envisioned for performance by Frederick and the small contingent of favored musicians who played with him in the intimate private concerts at Potsdam.[6] Burney's (1772–3, 3: 104ff.) famous account of one of these concerts depicts a rigid, musically sterile routine, but twenty-five years earlier they were probably more varied and less formal, with livelier interplay between Frederick and his musicians. Bach, perhaps advised by Emanuel, might have thought the canons an especially apt entertainment for such a musically and intellectually brilliant gathering. The work cannot have been intended for integral public performance, and there is no evidence that Bach had even an ideal ordering scheme in mind for its various components, which were printed in such a way as to be saleable separately rather than as a single unit.[7] The two ricercars and the sonata are the main elements, performable as self-contained pieces. As with the fourteen canons on the Goldberg bass, a concert performance of the whole is perforce an arrangement, into which the canonic movements must be fitted wherever they seem effective.

Although masterpieces, the ricercars do not achieve the supreme level reached by the Goldberg Variations or parts of the *Art of Fugue*. The great work in the *Musical Offering* is the sonata; the ricercars are too free in form to have concentrated Bach's powers of invention at the highest level. Some of the oddities of the latter stem from the nature of Frederick's theme, which is longer and rhythmically more homogeneous than most of Bach's subjects. Neither ricercar develops the theme in canon or in any of the other types of learned counterpoint that Bach had by that date fully "researched" in the *Art of Fugue*. Instead, the expository passages treat the subject somewhat like a cantus firmus, as a framework for more lively counter-material. The episodes develop fragments of the subject imitatively. Neither ricercar does much with its countersubject, although in each case a leaping motive from the latter is the basis of the final episode.

The Three-Part Ricercar BWV 1079/1

The term *ricercar* is most often used today to refer to an archaic, unusually strict keyboard fugue. The term was also used in the sixteenth and seventeenth centuries in the sense of a prelude, albeit often one in fugal style. Mattheson and Walther knew of this usage, and it is likely that Bach was aware of it as well.[8] Preludes were, in principle, improvised, and as the *Musical Offering* had its origin in an improvised three-part fugue, the present movement is often thought to be a record of Bach's actual improvisation on the royal subject at Potsdam. The six-part ricercar, on the other hand, is assumed to be Bach's later working out of the theme in strict counterpoint, away from the keyboard.[9] This would explain why only the six-part ricercar was set out in open score, like the ricercars of Frescobaldi and Froberger, whereas the three-part ricercar appeared in regular two-stave notation.

The three-part piece cannot precisely reproduce what Bach actually played at Berlin. Bach could not have remembered it perfectly, and one would not expect a genuine improvisation on an unfamiliar subject to contain the considerable quantity of nearly verbatim recapitulation found here. Yet improvising a three-part fugue on the long but rhythmically homogeneous subject would have been relatively easy for Bach. It would have involved the same much-rehearsed skills involved in playing a chorale fantasia, particularly where the subject employs long equal note values.

If the piece is not a faithful transcription of Bach's improvisation, it need not be regarded as peculiarly suited to the fortepiano.[10] Had it been conceived for the piano, one might expect it to include the dynamic indications already found in Emanuel Bach's Prussian and Württemberg Sonatas, published in the early 1740s. But the ricercar contains not even an occasional echo, let alone a pianissimo or any of the gradual changes of dynamic level that were indicated in works of the period by closely spaced pianos and fortes. Bach, in the dedication, says only that the king set forth the theme on a "clavier," and there is no instrumental designation in the score.

Williams (1986d, xii–xiii) nevertheless points to several features that would have suited the early piano. The subject, comprised chiefly of sustained notes, enters several times in a high tessitura, where it is unlikely to project well against the busier lower voices when played on the harpsichord; and the hocket-like figuration in m. 111 and at the end can sound clumsy on the latter instrument. Frederick's pianos were by Gottfried Silbermann, and Quantz had arranged for the purchase of one of them just a few weeks before Bach's arrival (see Oleskiewicz 1999, 98). Hence the king might have been eager for Bach to try them. To judge from modern reconstructions, these instruments had an exquisite tone and sensitive touch but less sustaining power and a smaller dynamic range than the Viennese fortepianos from later in the century. Frederick used them primarily for accompaniment, but their clear sonority and incisive attacks are effective in the thin contrapuntal texture of the three-part ricercar. Performing counterpoint on such an instrument would have challenged a harpsichordist or organist sitting down at one for the first time, but Bach had played Silbermann's instruments previously and might already have been serving as the latter's sales agent in Leipzig.[11] If Bach ever practiced his contrapuntal music on the clavichord, which seems more than likely, he would have cultivated the chord voicing and attention to "light and shade" that become necessary when playing on a dynamic keyboard instrument.

Not counting the opening exposition (mm. 1–30), the piece falls into two halves, the end of the first being marked by an arrival in the dominant minor (m. 109). The two halves are roughly equal in length but are formally self-contained and very different in character, reflecting the different character of the two halves of the subject itself. The first half has a symmetrical design in which three expositions alternate with two episodes; the second episode is a recapitulation of the latter part of the first (mm. 87–94 ‖ 38–45).[12] Despite this "architectonic" design, the texture often is only pseudo-contrapuntal. The triplets in the episodes fall into simple antiphonal exchanges between the upper parts—what Marpurg (1753–4, 1:13) called a "canonic sequence"[13]—and the bass entries at mm. 46 and 95 are accompanied in a sort of *brisé* style.

An immediate change takes place at the beginning of the second half. The first half of the piece is characterized by flowing, sequential motion, as in the triplet episode. Based on arpeggiation, the latter derives from the first half of the subject, whose opening notes furnish its bass line. The second half introduces "sigh" motives and makes greater use of harsh chromatic voice leading derived from the latter part of the subject. This becomes explicit at m. 115, which introduces a motive consisting of a chromatic scale-fragment in eighth notes, a rhythmic diminution of the latter portion of the subject.

If the first half is strict in design but free in detail, the reverse is true of the second half, whose chromatic counterpoint is spun out in a more discursive manner. The somewhat rambling episode at the beginning is interrupted by unexpected rests in the upper parts of m. 122; these call attention to a little *fuga per diminutionem* that starts there in the bass but is not pursued beyond the next measure. Shortly afterwards (m. 128), an outbreak of triplets quotes the subject of the D-minor fugue from WTC2—an equally free fugue whose subject falls into two halves related to one another like those of the royal theme. Although the somewhat arbitrary character of this section may reflect its origin in improvisation, Bach underscored the essentially binary form of the movement. The second half contains relatively little recapitulation, but it concludes with the same passage that ended the first half, producing the impression of formal closure (as in the F-major fugue of WTC2).

The Six-Part Ricercar BWV 1079/2 (formerly 1079/5)

In its greater number of voices and old-fashioned notation (an equivalent of 4/2), this movement comes closer to the usual modern idea of a ricercar. Both pieces, however, were described simply as fugues when Bach announced the work in September 1747 (BD 3:656 [item 558a]/NBR, 229), and neither makes a systematic exploration of contrapuntal technique as in the ricercars of Frescobaldi.

In the original print, the six-part ricercar, together with the puzzle canons, was headed by the contrived acrostic *Regis Iussu Cantio Et Reliqua Canonica Arte Resoluta* (A Composition By Order of the King, With Other Matter Worked Out in a Canonic Manner).[14] Bach had used his own theme to improvise a six-part fugue during the Potsdam visit; here Bach makes amends for not having used the king's subject.[15] Bach's autograph survives for this piece alone (in P 226); it is a fair copy, differing only in a few spots from the print, which invariably gives stronger and presumably later readings.[16] Only once, in m. 61, is the revised version somewhat unsatisfactory; having discovered parallel fifths in the original, Bach was forced to make an awkward passage even harder to play.[17]

The autograph shows that, despite the use of open-score notation in the print, Bach conceived the work as a keyboard piece, writing it on two staves as he also did the *Fuga a 3 soggetti* in the *Art of Fugue*. The ricercar is perfectly playable on the harpsichord, more so than on the fortepiano, where, as on modern piano, it is hard to keep the dense counterpoint in the lower register transparent (e.g., in mm. 29ff. and 79ff.). Bach's visit to Potsdam had included an organ recital (see BD 2:435 [item 554]/NBR, 224), and organ is possible here if a clear-sounding registration can be found, but pedals are not required. Voice crossings in several passages cannot be projected to a listener on any keyboard instrument (e.g., in m. 86).

The work is built around twelve statements of the subject, six forming the opening exposition, the remainder occurring singly, in alternation with episodes. The opening exposition is unavoidably long, constituting more than one-third of the work if one counts the extension of the exposition that leads to the first full cadence (m. 39b). As one would expect, this exposition culminates in massive polyphony in six parts, made more impressive by the fact that the last entrance is in the bass (mm. 25ff.). During the following sections, the texture lightens as momentum builds, leading to a brief trio-sonata episode over a walking bass at m. 70; this coincides with the modulation furthest from the tonic (B♭ minor in m. 71).

Elsewhere this work is more severe than the three-part ricercar, avoiding the latter's easy-going sequential episodes. The three largest episodes are fugatos on short themes derived from the subject, using counterpoint that is some respects in more rigorous than that of the expositions. In the second episode (mm. 52–8), three melodic ideas pass permutationally through all six parts. The last episode (mm. 90–8) is a double fugato combining leaping figures (from the countersubject) with sustained chromatic lines (from the subject); this makes it the climax of the piece.

Inevitably the six voices lack the rhythmic independence that they would have in an ensemble work. The end of the opening exposition (mm. 25–39) is the only extended passage to use all six voices, and it is essentially a ready-made sequential formula whose texture divides into two sets of three parts moving

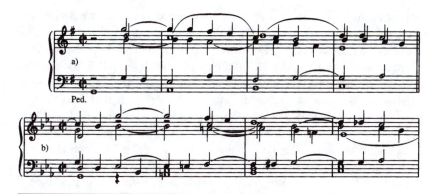

Example 18.1 (a) *Pièce d'orgue* in G, BWV 572, mm. 29–32; (b) Ricercar a 6, BWV 1079/2, mm. 29–30.

in contrary motion. Wolff (1968, 127) found a simpler version of the passage in the *Pièce d'orgue* BWV 572, probably composed at Weimar (Example 18.1). In the ricercar this is the one extended sequence and the only passage that is recapitulated (mm. 79–80 ‖ 29–30, varied and transposed).

The Canons BWV 1079/4a and 1079/4i (formerly 1079/3a and 1079/6)

Only the two canons designated *a 2* (in two parts) are playable on solo harpsichord. One, the first of the *Canones diversi super thema regium* (Various Canons on the Royal Theme), is a crab-canon that can be played as a *pièce croisée* on two manuals, as suggested in NBA VIII/1. The other is the first of two puzzle canons printed in the unused space at the end of the six-part ricercar; this bears the subtitle *Quaerendo invenietis* ("By seeking ye shall find," after Matt. 7:7 or Luke 11:9). The solution printed in the appendix of NBA VIII/1 and other editions is the most graceful, but the title invites the reader to look for alternate solutions.[18]

Like most puzzle canons, this is a perpetual canon, meaning that it repeats endlessly without ever reaching a final cadence. The longer compositions of this type in the *Art of Fugue* include codas that bring each piece to a musically satisfying conclusion. The fermata customarily added on the downbeat of m. 9 is only a stopgap, and the underlying harmonic progression hardly constitutes a satisfactory cadence.

The *Art of Fugue*

Alone among Bach's late keyboard works, the *Art of Fugue* was apparently planned from the beginning as a complete and systematic exposition of contrapuntal techniques. Nothing quite like it had been done before, certainly not with such rigor or on such a large scale. Clearly, Bach intended to make a substantial contribution to a repertory of learned keyboard fugues that went back to the time of Sweelinck and Frescobaldi. He may even have thought of the *Art of Fugue* as a treatise in the form of concrete examples, which is how C. P. E. Bach advertised the work about a year after his father's death.[19] The *Art of Fugue* thus took its place beside earlier encyclopedic musical textbooks, such as Fux's *Gradus ad Parnassum*, Rameau's *Traité de l'harmonie*, and Mattheson's *Vollkommener Capellmeister*, the last of which contains four substantial chapters on fugue, one of them directly challenging Bach to publish such a work.[20] Bach may also have envisioned the work as extending a "learned tradition" of counterpoint cultivated in northern Germany and preserved in such sources as the "Sweelinck" theory manuscripts (see Walker 2000, 204ff.). But Bach's teaching reportedly "omitted all the dry sorts [*trockene Arten*] of counterpoint given by Fux and others,"[21] and it is not surprising that his treatise on fugue eschews elementary examples and consists solely of actual compositions.

As with the *Clavierübung*, Bach's composition of the *Art of Fugue* may have reflected his wish to surpass other recent publications. Fux's *Gradus* (of which Bach owned a copy) had included, beside the numerous illustrations of species counterpoint, several complete pieces, among them Mass movements in *stile antico*. Walsh of London had published Handel's *Six Fugues or Voluntarys* in 1735,[22] and Hurlebusch's *Compositioni musicali*, containing five fugues alongside suites and variations, came out in (probably) the same year in Hamburg. Another Hamburg publication, Mattheson's *Wohlklingende Fingersprache* (2 vols., 1735–7) contains twelve fugues of various types, including several lengthy examples with multiple subjects.[23] In notation and style the *Art of Fugue* is more consistently allied than any of these with older representatives of the contrapuntal tradition. But it contains too many expressive, *galant*, even virtuoso elements to represent the pure *stile antico*.

This is not to say that the *Art of Fugue* is free from abstraction. Chromaticism in Baroque music is in principle expressive, yet certain works by other composers (such as Froberger's ricercars) seem to employ chromaticism for its own sake. The same may be true of the Augmentation Canon, whose bizarre chromaticism gives it a peculiar musical flavor not unlike that of several movements in the Goldberg Variations. Moreover, the prevailing retrospective style generally avoids musical symbols or gestures that by convention indicated expressivity in eighteenth-century music, despite occasional allusions to dance rhythms or the use of *galant* mannerisms in some movements. The absence of such clichés does not really mean that the music is inexpressive, yet its apparently neutral character is reinforced by the relatively uniform notational appearance and the printing in open score, with *alla breve* rhythm in the majority of movements.

More concrete echoes of older style include the suggestions of modal writing in some movements, and the preponderance of designs defined not by tonal considerations but by the introduction of different contrapuntal techniques or new subjects and countersubjects in each section. Many of the fugues lack clearly defined episodes, consisting of a nearly seamless contrapuntal fabric devoid of the clear structural articulations typical of eighteenth-century music. Even the overall form of the work—a series of imitative pieces based on rhythmic and melodic variants of the same subject—reflects archaic models, although the individual sections of Frescobaldi's and Froberger's capriccios, ricercars, and similar works are not so independent of one another as are Bach's *contrapuncti* and canons, each of which is a distinct composition.

There is one main theme, but it is varied in every movement. At first the theme takes simple, unembellished forms that resemble the types of subjects found in a late-Renaissance motet. Yet the present theme differs from a typical sixteenth-century subject in its triadic structure, which implies a harmonic alternation between tonic and dominant (tonic and subdominant when inverted). Hence the subject is tonal rather than modal, as are the pieces themselves; the modal ending in the early version of one fugue was a superficial local gesture. The subject's triadic structure also makes it readily capable of combination with itself and with other subjects even when inverted or otherwise altered. Bach treats the subject freely and does not insist on exact, canonic imitation except in the pieces actually designated as canons. Tonal answers as well as more radically altered forms of the subject are used whenever convenient—especially in the more complex fugues—and throughout the work Bach treats fugue as a fluid, sometimes even improvisational form, never as a mechanical exercise.

Given its unique character, it was perhaps inevitable that the *Art of Fugue* would be interpreted as the expression of various philosophical, theological, and even autobiographical ideas, the last arising because of the citation of the family name in two movements. Typically these interepetations disregard the work's counterpoint, treating the latter as secondary to the purported meanings drawn from the thematic material. But the work's musical effect is a product not of the thematic matter as such, but of how the latter is integrated into the whole composition, considered in all its contrapuntal complexity. The romantic search for cosmic truths and autobiographical references in the work, even when not based on equivocal evidence or anachronistic views of artistic self-expression, tends to devalue Bach's achievement. This is because it focuses on superficial aspects of the work while disregarding its practical demonstration of compositional technique—probably its chief aim in the composer's view—as well as its profoundly imaginative and expressive character.

Other scholarship has underscored the practicality of the *Art of Fugue* as solo keyboard music, and it is no longer uncommon for it to be performed or recorded as such. Yet the work's organization makes clear that it was intended to serve pedagogic and theoretical ends. Unlike the *Well-Tempered Clavier*, which is organized by key, the *Art of Fugue* eschews tonal variety, the order of movements being determined by the contrapuntal techniques illustrated in each. It does not offer lessons in a wide variety of keyboard genres, being restricted to "fugue," broadly defined. Although the *Art of Fugue* remains "clavier" music, Bach cannot have expected most purchasers to play it so much as to study it. Nevertheless, that they would have done so at a keyboard instrument was apparently self-evident; Mattheson implies as much in a brief 1752 report of the work (BD 3:13–4 [item 647]/ NBR, 377).

Title, Origin, and Ordering of Movements

The source of the title is uncertain. In the autograph, the words *Kunst der Fuga* [*sic*] are in the hand of Bach's son-in-law Altnikol. The use of the term *Kunst* has a parallel in Marpurg's *Kunst der Clavierspielen* (Berlin, 1750), suggesting that someone younger than Bach supplied the title; Marpurg wrote the preface for the reimpression of 1752.[24] Yet Sebastian had taken care over the titles of the canons, which were revised at his instigation.[25] Thus it is hard to believe that he did not decide on a title for the collection as a whole, although the autograph manuscript of around 1742 lacks one.

Regardless of who first attached it to the work, the word *Kunst* ("art") would have expressed a view of fugue as something higher than unreflective craft or technique. The term here has the sense still seen in the expression "arts and sciences," setting music on the level of a learned discipline like law or classical philology. The last word in the title also has a somewhat archaic significance, for the term *Fuge* here refers to both fugue and canon. For Mattheson (1739), "fugue" could still mean simply "imitation," not a genre of composition, and Marpurg continued to use the term in this way in his *Abhandlung von der Fuge* (1753–4), calling the two types of composition "periodic" and "canonic" fugue, respectively. Here Bach avoids using the term "fugue" as a label for an individual piece, employing instead the term *contrapunctus*. Even that may be less a title than a way of indicating that each piece illustrates a particular type of counterpoint, just as each of his inventions had illustrated the working out of a particular "idea" (*inventio*). Perhaps another reason for using the title *Contrapunctus* was that some of these pieces are not fugues in the usual sense. The opening measures of Contrapunctus 6, for example, combine different forms of the subject, all in the tonic, no voice entering in direct imitation of any other.

The composition and first edition of the *Art of Fugue* have been intensely studied, yet some questions remain unanswered and probably unaswerable. Discussions tend to focus on the work's posthumous publication, in an incomplete and probably inauthentic form, thereby distracting attention from an equally unique feature: it is the only major collection of Bach's keyboard music to survive in an early version in an integral autograph manuscript. Wolff (1975) pointed out that the latter preserves a distinct but internally consistent form. The basic conception is already clear, and those movements that are present do not differ fundamentally from subsequent versions. But many musical and notational details differ in the same ways that distinguished early versions of movements in the French Suites or WTC2, and perhaps in other works whose early versions are lost. Most striking is the renotation of more than half the movements in ways that suggest an evolving concept of the tempo and meter of each piece, or at least of how tempo and meter are best conveyed notationally.

Twelve fugues and two canons are found in the autograph (P 200), which was completed by about 1742, although individual movements could be significantly earlier, a few probably later.[26] Alterations were made in the autograph at least until 1749; some thought to be in the hand of Johann Christoph Friedrich Bach (Sebastian's second youngest son, then seventeen years old) were presumably made at a time when Sebastian's illness or blindness prevented him from entering them himself. The print reveals further changes, the most obvious ones involving the order of the individual pieces and the addition of several further ones.

Although the work is unlikely to have been completely engraved and printed until after Bach's death, the plates for some of the pieces may have been prepared under his direction. Like most of Bach's previous publications, it was engraved—more properly, etched—through a process by which the image of a specially prepared manuscript page could be transferred to a copper printing plate, which therefore preserved most details of the original.[27] This explains the autograph character of many pages in the original print, once thought to have been due to Bach's having carried out the engraving himself. Bach would have planned the entire publication in the same detailed manner as he had the *Clavierübung* and the *Musical Offering*, down to the placement of each page turn. But at some point the original plan was altered, probably because of the addition of new pieces, perhaps also because of the expansion of existing ones. It is far from certain that Bach had arrived at a firm conclusion regarding the organization of the print at the time of his death. In any case the form in which it appeared was not correct.

Efforts to discover Bach's intentions have yet to resolve all of the "ordering problems" in the *Art of Fugue*. What is clear is that the print contained several pieces that do not belong, and the quadruple fugue is incomplete. Some mistakes could have been due to misunderstandings by the editors—presumably Altnikol and C. P. E. Bach—and the engravers.[28] The elder Bach had left a large legacy, both musical and material, and at his death there would have been more pressing matters than the identification and proper ordering of the various portions of the work, some of them perhaps written on loose pages. Emanuel saw the work into print, despite the fact that by this time he was probably occupied with writing his own treatise (C. P. E. Bach 1753–62). It failed to sell even after Marpurg added his preface, and Emanuel advertised the plates for sale in 1756, when prospects of war were probably reducing the marketability of complex contrapuntal music and increasing the value of copper.

The ordering of pieces in the autograph, shown in Table 18.1, already presented a coherent arrangement, as Wolff (1983c) showed. The first four pieces (as yet untitled) developed the subject in *rectus* and *inversus* forms, first separately, then in combination. The style, initially quite severe, grew more flexible in the remaining fugues, which came in pairs, the last three pairs alternating with canons. As in the print, the work proceeded toward increasingly learned counterpoint, and the theme underwent greater melodic and rhythmic variation in the more complex pieces.

The relatively pristine scores of the first few pieces in the autograph imply that they had been composed previously. Stylistically these are the most archaic works in the collection, suggesting that Bach initially intended to write the entire work in pure *stile antico*, only gradually allowing more modern elements of style. Although the autograph was begun as a fair copy, alterations appear in increasing number as one turns the pages. Some appear to be corrections made by Bach while copying, others are probably later revisions, and still others were made by other hands, possibly even after the plates were engraved. Further revisions, never entered into the autograph, are found in the printed text. These included

Table 18.1 *Art of Fugue:* Contents of the Autograph (P 200)

P 200	BWV*	Description of Movement**
1	1	fugue, R
2	3	fugue with countersubject, I
3	2	fugue, R
4	5	counter fugue, R + I
5	9	double fugue, counterpoint at the 12th
6	10a	double fugue, counterpoint at the 10th
7	6	counter fugue with diminution
8	7	counter fugue with diminution and augmentation
9	15	canon at the octave—twice, first in "puzzle" notation
10	8	3-part triple fugue
11	11	4-part triple fugue
12	(14)	augmentation canon—early version, twice, second time in "puzzle" notation
13	12	4-part mirror fugue—R version written above I on 8-staff systems
14	13	3-part mirror fugue—I version written above R on 6-staff systems
(15)	(14)	augmentation canon (intermediate version)

*Numbering within BWV 1080; corresponds with the print for nos. 1–9, 11–13
**R = using *rectus* version of subject; I = using *inversus*

Table 18.2 *Art of Fugue:* Hypothetical Order, with Supplementary Pieces

Title (As In Print)	Numbering of Movement In ...			Remarks
	P 200	print	BWV	
Contrapunctus 1 [R]	1	1	1	Rebarred in 2/2 (not 4/2), new ending
Contrapunctus 2 [R]	3	2	2	Revisions as in no. 1
Contrapunctus 3 [I]	2	3	3	Revisions as in no. 1
Contrapunctus 4 [I]	—	4	4	Not in P 200
Contrapunctus 5 [R + I]	4	5	5	P 200: ¢. Print: C
Contrapunctus 6 a 4 in Stylo Francese	7	6	6	Changes in rhythmic notation
Contrapunctus 7 a 4 per Augment et Diminut:	8	7	7	
Contrapunctus 8 a 3	10	8	8	P 200: 2/4. Print: ¢, values doubled
Contrapunctus 9 a 4 alla Duodecima	5	9	9	Print: values doubled
Contrapunctus 10 a 4 alla Decima	—	10	10	= no. 6 of P 200 with new opening, values doubled
Contrapunctus 11 a 4	11	11	11	P 200: 2/4. Print: ¢, values doubled, much revised
Contrapunctus inversus a 4	12 (top)	12/2	12/1	P 200: 3/4. Print: 3/2, values doubled
Contrapunctus inversus 12 a 4	12 (bottom)	12/1	12/2	Print: alterations as in preceding
Contrapunctus inversus a 3	13 (top)	13/2	13/1	P 200: 2/4. Print: C, values doubled
Contrapunctus a 3	13 (bottom)	13/1	13/2	P 200: 2/4. Print: ¢ (error for C?), values doubled
Fuga a 3 Soggetti	—	20	19	Quadruple fugue. Autograph in P 200, Beilage 3
Canon alla Ottava	9	16	15	
Canon alla Decima [in] Contrapunto alla Terza	—	17	16	Not in P 200
Canon alla Duodecima in Contrapunto alla Quinta	—	18	17	Not in P 200
Canon per Augmentationem in Contrario Motu	15	15	14	Autograph in P 200, Beilage 1; no. 12 of P 200 is early version
Contrap: a 4	6	14	10a	Early version of no. 10
Fuga a 2 Clav:	—	19/1	18/1	Arrangement of no. 13/2; autograph in P 200, Beilage 2
Alio modo. Fuga a 2 Clav.	—	19/2	18/2	Arrangement of no. 13/1; autograph in P 200, Beilage 2
Wenn wir in höchsten Nöthen sein	—	21	(BWV 668a)	Early version of BWV 668

new endings for the first three fugues and a new opening section for the second double fugue. Bach also rewrote the Augmentation Canon and revised (or authorized the revision of) the rhythmic notation of many pieces.

The movements wholly lacking in the autograph must be relatively late. These pieces—a new fugue (Contrapunctus 4), the fragmentary quadruple fugue, and a second pair of canons—upset the original plan. Table 18.2 reconstructs the print as Bach might have intended it to appear; the table follows Butler's (1983a) suggestion that the work was meant to conclude with the canons rather than with the quadruple fugue.[29] All titles are given as they appear in the print, although some of these may be contrary to Bach's plan. The last four entries are the additional pieces whose inclusion was also probably contrary to Bach's intentions. The first three of these are alternate versions of pieces already present. The last, the chorale fantasia *Wenn wir in höchsten Nöthen sein* (BWV 668a), was included to compensate for the incompleteness of the last fugue, as the brief prefatory notice in the first edition (1751) explained.[30]

According to this notice, Bach dictated the chorale shortly before his death; the romantic speculation arising from this was put to rest by Wolff (1974). The chorale is usually traced to the shorter Weimar setting of the same melody in the *Orgelbüchlein* (BWV 641). But both compositions must go back independently to a simpler earlier version, lost but perhaps not very different from the present one. Exactly what Bach dictated is unclear, but in view of what Williams (2003, 384) calls the "old-fashioned" form and "commonplace" counterpoint, it might have been no more than the small alterations made by other hands in the autograph of the *Art of Fugue* proper. The archaic, chromatic style of the fantasia is not entirely unlike that of the fugues and canons, but it has nothing to do with their subject or tonality (it is in G major), and it requires pedals, albeit briefly (mm. 9–10).

As in most of Bach's other collections, the question of ordering is tangential to the music itself, since the pieces cannot have been meant for cyclic performance. Certainly the work is not a set of variations in the usual sense of the word.[31] It is possible that the first three or four fugues in the early version did form a closed, unified group (discussed below).

Performance and Editions

The early twentieth-century view that the *Art of Fugue* is best presented by instrumental ensemble has been largely abandoned.[32] A tradition of keyboard performance goes back at least to the beginning of the nineteenth century.[33] And the ranges of the individual voices, the publication in score (not parts), the absence of continuo figures, and the splitting of some voices into two or even three parts near the ends of several fugues all violate the conventions of eighteenth-century instrumental music. Inner voices sometimes have brief, fragmentary entries solely for the purpose of filling out chords, and occasionally the texture approaches that of the *style brisé*.[34] With the exception of the four-part mirror fugue, the fugues are no less idiomatic than Bach's other keyboard works in learned style, and they contain little that is particularly suitable to other instruments.

Although the keyboard character of the work becomes self-evident the more one plays it, it is difficult to find unequivocal evidence for the use of any particular keyboard instrument. C. P. E. Bach's 1751 *Avertissement* described the *Art of Fugue* as "expressly intended for the use of *Clavier* and organ,"[35] meaning both stringed and wind keyboard instruments. Mattheson's report of the following year mentioned the work as evidence for the superiority of German musicians in organ playing and fugue writing, but this does not mean that he took the *Art of Fugue* itself to be primarily an organ work. In any case, the fugues and canons are entirely playable *manualiter*, and their bass lines are not pedal parts. The range exceeds that of Bach's organ music; the Canon at the Tenth, which opens with long-sustained notes that might otherwise suggest use of the organ, extends upward to d′′′.[36] Although the organ—or the modern piano—can be used to advantage in many movements, the same considerations that point to the harpsichord as the primary medium in other collections (e.g., the WTC) apply here. No one player on one keyboard instrument can render with complete clarity the voice crossings found in some movements. But the whole idea of conveying to a modern audience the contrapuntal detail of this, or any, Bach keyboard work is chimerical; the best that can be hoped for is that listeners will glimpse the richness of the texture and the profound expression of most movements.

Regardless of the keyboard instrument used, the music is difficult to play, especially if taken at the relatively lively tempo implied by the *alla breve* notation of most movements. Like other late works of Bach, much of the *Art of Fugue* abandons the norms of idiomatic Baroque keyboard writing, making it impossible to sight read—one explanation for the work's original lack of success in an age when rehearsal in the modern sense was a rare luxury. As in many a twentieth-century piece—and in the six-part ricercar—it is necessary to work out fingerings with great care and to follow them religiously if one is to play without stumbling. The quasi-vocal style of the fugues might suggest a hyperlegato approach. But the more articulate manner of performance advocated here for comparable works (e.g., the C-major fugue in WTC1) will spare the player many finger substitutions and other unnecessary complications of nineteenth-century piano fingering.

Only the two mirror fugues require abnormally wide stretches of the hand; a single player might manage them more readily on an instrument with the narrow keys that Bach's pupil Agricola favored.[37] Otherwise these pieces are more easily performed by two players on two instruments, as Bach directed in his arrangement of the three-part mirror fugue. The arrangement includes an additional free fourth part, and although probably not meant for publication, it appeared in the print under the rubric *a 2 Clav:*. The latter must mean separate keyboard instruments, assumed to be harpsichords (*clavicembali*) in NBA VIII/2.1 but possibly clavichords according to C. P. E. Bach.[38]

The *Art of Fugue* has appeared in many editions, including no fewer than five dependable ones issued since the Bach tercentenary: by Williams (1986b), Wolff (1987b), Moroney (1989), Klaus Hofmann (NBA VIII/2, 1995–6), and Jones (2002). Hoke (1979) is a facsimile of the original (autograph and print). Williams's edition is in open score, whereas Wolff, Moroney, and Jones set out the work in two-staff keyboard score. Wolff, moreover, gives the version of the autograph in a separate volume, as does the NBA, which includes open- and keyboard-score arrangements of each. Of older editions, Czerny's keyboard reduction (Leipzig, 1838; many reprints) is inaccurate but remains interesting for the restraint with which Beethoven's most famous student added "expression" markings. Few today will want to use Tovey's edition in open score, but his commentary (1931) has not been surpassed.

Contrapuncti 1–5

The print opens with a pair of fugues using the *rectus* version of the subject, followed by a pair using the inversion. In the fifth piece the two forms of the subject are combined. Contrapunctus 4, the second *inversus* fugue, was a late addition absent from the autograph, as were the codas in each of the first three fugues. Moreover, the places of Contrapuncti 2 and 3 were reversed, and what is now Contrapunctus 2 originally ended with the dominant chord on the downbeat of m. 78. Such an ending might have been intended to form an unbroken connection between this and the following movement, which became Contrapunctus 4 (as argued in Bagnall 1975, 60). It must also have been meant to sound like the modal cadences that occur at the ends of all but one of the Kyrie and Christe settings in CU3, although the fugue otherwise is entirely tonal. Another link to the *pedaliter* pieces in CU3 is the autograph's notation of all three fugues in measures of 4/2, under a cut-time signature.

Although Bach eliminated those particular archaisms, the original group of four fugues remains relatively old-fashioned even within the *Art of Fugue*. Many passages lack the well-defined harmonic rhythm and strong sense of harmonic directionality that one expects in a late-Baroque work, and the modulatory range is very limited. There are few strong cadences, that is, with root motion in the bass; in Contrapunctus 1 the only full cadence is the one at the end. There are episodes, but they are short and differ little from other passages, avoiding sequence and other types of regular harmonic patterning as in antique polyphony; this makes each fugue an unbroken web of independently flowing voices.

Bach's tendency toward perceptible, rational structure reasserts itself in Contrapunctus 4, the fugue that was added in the printed version. This piece, although forming a pair with Contrapunctus 3—both use the inversion of the subject—is longer, and it has a relatively clear tonal design articulated by the regular alternation of expositions and episodes, the latter all constructed of sequences employing similar material.[39] The comparatively modern style of Contrapunctus 4 makes the next fugue seem like a stylistic regression. Yet the counter fugue Contrapunctus 5—so designated because it combines the upright and inverted forms of the subject—is the logical conclusion to the first group, explaining its grandiose coda in six voices (already present in the version of the autograph).[40]

Of the four original fugues in this group, Contrapunctus 1 is the simplest in style and the most accessible for modern audiences, becoming unexpectedly dramatic near the end with a few surprising pauses and full chords. How to treat these chords and rests (mm. 70b–72) is a performance problem, especially on harpsichord. Despite Bach's precise notation, one is tempted to stretch out some of the note values, adding an embellished breaking of the chords or even little cadenzas to fill in the rests. The earlier version ended on the downbeat of m. 74, having concluded with the long episode (or coda) that started in m. 60. The abruptness of the original ending (pointed out by Bagnall 1975, 59) was not necessarily to the piece's disadvantage. But most of the other contrapuncti revert to Bach's older practice of concluding shortly after a statement of the subject. The last five measures, added for the print, add such a statement in the tenor, bringing the first piece closer to the pattern that had become established as Bach composed the rest of the collection. In addition, the counterpoint in the upper voices contains the same rhythmic motive (with ties over the barlines) that characterized the countersubject in Contrapunctus 2 before it was converted to dotted rhythm. As in several subsequent contrapuncti (e.g., nos. 2 and 6), the structure of the first fugue is free, almost improvisatory; there are no lasting modulations, and the order of entries does not follow any obvious pattern. There is a recurring episodic passage, but only the material of two voices is recapitulated, the others adding free counterpoint (mm. 17–20 || 36–9 || 66b–70a).

Contrapunctus 2 is marked by its thoroughgoing dotted rhythms, but in both autograph and print these look like later additions. The four-note slurs were certainly added; they are present only in the print, and only through m. 21, but are presumably to be extended throughout the piece. The slurs imply that the dotting should be relatively gentle—as in *notes inégales*—not exaggerated as in an overture. The smoother interpretation would be in keeping with the primarily stepwise voice-leading, and would make more understandable the many suspensions consisting of a sixteenth-note tied over the bar-line—a weak enough rhythm without over-dotting.

For the published version Bach not only eliminated the quasi-modal ending but also revised one passage (mm. 38–42) rather heavily, adding the bass in mm. 40–2. Perhaps Bach recognized that the passage, which connects the second and third expositions, is a weak link, but the revisions do not eliminate the suddenness of the modulation from A minor to F within just three measures (mm. 42–4). The new coda again includes an additional statement of the subject; originally, the last entry was the syncopated one in the tenor at m. 69. Use of the subject in syncopation (*per arsin et thesin*) was one of the rarer fugal devices, and it might have been meant to serve as a sort of climax. But it is hidden in the tenor and does not involve any particularly compelling counterpoint; the coda makes for a more decisive ending.

Syncopated entries characterize the entire second exposition in Contrapunctus 3 (mm. 23–39). The variation of the subject here involves more than just syncopation, yet the new form of the subject still fits together with the original form of the countersubject. The subject is varied for a second time in the last section (at m. 58), where the countersubject undergoes variation as well (e.g., at m. 55). Although Contrapunctus 3 originally came second, the new order makes better sense. Not only does Contrapunctus 3 use more syncopation (or variation) than Contrapunctus 2; it is also the first movement with clearly articulated episodes and the first to maintain a countersubject throughout. It was perhaps another bit of quasi-modal thinking that put the initial statement of the subject (now inverted) on the dominant, in the form that would be appropriate in a tonal answer—that is, with a fourth instead of a fifth as the initial melodic interval. But the "real" form of the subject prevails from the second exposition onward.

The presence of a regular countersubject employed in invertible counterpoint means that Mattheson, Marpurg, and probably Bach himself would have called Contrapunctus 3 a double fugue. Some still use that terminology today, although the preferred expression here is "fugue with countersubject"; either way, it is anachronistic to describe this as a "simple" fugue (likewise Contrapunctus 4). The countersubject is the source of the material developed in the first two episodes (mm. 19–23 and 39–43). Moreover, the chromaticism of the countersubject gives the fugue a special character recalling that of some of the more tortuous ricercars of the early seventeenth century. This points to a slower tempo and, in general, less smooth articulation than would be appropriate in Contrapunctus 2.

The chromaticism helps make this the most compelling of the four original fugues. The piece makes the most remote modulations so far, passing within a ten-measure span from E minor, at the beginning of the third exposition (m. 43), to C minor at the beginning of the last (m. 51). The climactic moment occurs when the outer voices, moving by contrary motion, pass through an augmented sixth in m. 63. It is characteristic of the elusive style prevailing throughout the *Art of Fugue* that the expected dominant chord never quite materializes; indeed, it is hard to locate any final V–I cadence. The augmented sixth resolves normally to a 6/4-chord, but one must imagine the bass (A) of the latter chord prolonged through mm. 64–5, finally moving to d in the second half of m. 66.

Contrapunctus 4 opens with the "real" inversion of the subject that was avoided at the beginning of Contrapunctus 3. But the new fugue is more regular in design and less severe in style than the three original ones. Indeed, its design is the most symmetrical in the collection, coming closest to what might be considered "normal" for a Bach fugue. Besides the regular alternation between exposition and episode, there are complementary cadences to the dominant and the subdominant, respectively, at the middle of each of the two largest episodes (mm. 53, 103). In a remarkable exposition at the center of the piece (mm. 61–80), four ascending entries (bass, tenor, alto, soprano) form an ascending sequence (F–g–d–a); the passage moves from the "flat" to the "sharp" side of the tonic (F major to E minor). Bach had been familiar with such modulating expositions since the time of the early Capriccio BWV 992; here the device is the crux of the movement, not a self-contained gesture.

Notwithstanding the overall symmetry of the movement, Bach dramatizes the return to the tonic at m. 107 through the use of a climactic contrapuntal device. This last exposition opens with a pair of close strettos *per arsin et thesin*, first for the two lower voices, then the two upper, accompanied by the swirling motives of the countersubject. This can be an exciting moment in performance, a good example of how, even in a strict fugue, rhythmic, contrapuntal, and formal elements can combine to create a powerful musical effect.

Up to now each fugue has used either the upright or the inverted form of the subject. Contrapunctus 5 combines them in the opening exposition, the *rectus* form following the *inversus* at the distance of three measures. Hence, this is both a counter fugue, combining upright and inverted forms of the subject, and a stretto fugue, in which imitations begin at various time intervals before the previous statement of the subject has been completed. The strettos in the second exposition (mm. 17–30) are again at the distance of three measures, but the time interval changes in each of the remaining three expositions, imitations occurring at distances of two, six, and four quarter notes, respectively. One might have expected the smallest time interval to occur in the last exposition, and in a sense this is so, for the time interval diminishes to *zero* in the final phrase, producing a so-called *canon sine pausa*, in which the two forms of the subject occur simultaneously (as in the close of the D♯-minor fugue of WTC2). Otherwise, the closest strettos occur not in the expositions but in the two canonic episodes (at mm. 53 and 65). These, although derived from the subject, are variants of the venerable contrapuntal formula on which Bach constructed the little canon called *Trias harmonica* (BWV 1072), published by Marpurg (1753–4).[41]

The print gives the time signature as C. This looks like an error for cut time, found in the autograph, but inasmuch as Bach directed changes in the notation of other movements it could be a deliberate indication for a more moderate tempo. In the autograph, this is the first and only movement notated in measures of 2/2 rather than 4/2, thereby serving as a transition to movements more modern in notation and style.

The Two Large Counter Fugues: Contrapuncti 6 and 7

The next two fugues move away from the *stile antico*, although like Contrapunctus 5 both are counter fugues. The term (from German *Gegenfuge*) was used by Mattheson (1739, iii.20.6) to refer to the combination of the subject with itself, not in stretto—although these are also stretto fugues—but in inverted or rhythmically altered forms. These movements add diminished and (in Contrapunctus 7) augmented forms of the subject to those previously used. Combinations of the various forms are so pervasive that there is hardly a moment in either piece when one is not hearing at least two simultaneous statements of the subject, proceeding at different speeds or in different directions. Contrapunctus 6 employs four different forms of the subject, Contrapunctus 7 six; no given configuration of entries is repeated anywhere in Contrapuncti 5, 6, and 7.

As published, all three counter fugues are in common time (not cut time). Contrapunctus 6 adopts the dotted style of an overture, bearing the designation *in Stylo Francese* ("in French style"). Despite these "modern" elements, neither Contrapunctus 6 nor 7 has the clear formal articulations of Contrapunctus 5, which otherwise is closer to the *stile antico*. Moreover, although each section of Contrapunctus 5 employs a distinct type of stretto, the combinations of various forms of the subject in Contrapuncti 6–7 do not seem to fall into any particular order. The dense imitative fabric of the expositions in Contrapunctus 6 is relieved by several distinct episodes, whereas Contrapunctus 7 is anchored by the four entries of the subject in augmentation. But neither fugue has a clear modulating design, and the overlapping entrances of the voices prevent phrase-endings or cadences from occurring simultaneously in all four voices. Even the four augmented entries in Contrapunctus 7, although clear enough on paper, do not coincide with cadences or other articulations in the accompanying voices, which move in a nearly unbroken stream of quicker entries and free counterpoint in small note values. Hence the augmented entries fail to make the dramatic impact created by, say, the entries of the cantus firmus in a chorale fantasia, and both fugues can seem nebulous in performance.

This is not necessarily an aesthetic problem; rather it reflects a particular style of organization, and both pieces retain features that make them more than loosely connected contrapuntal combinations. Throughout Contrapunctus 6 there is a tension between dotted figures and running sixteenths. In the first half (through m. 38a or so) the running notes never last for more than three consecutive beats in any one voice. Thereafter one finds several more extended passages in sixteenths, of which the last two (mm. 59b–63 and 64b–68a) are also the longest. The increased momentum in the latter part of the piece propels it toward an impressive passage (mm. 68b–72) in which dotted rhythm again prevails, culminating in a homorhythmic build-up to a fermata (m. 73). Contrapunctus 7, with its more homogeneous rhythm, contains nothing so striking, but it concludes with an expressive free coda (mm. 58ff.) reminiscent of those in earlier works (e.g., the B-minor fugue of WTC1).

In the autograph both pieces were heavily revised—more so than the other fugues. Many alterations in Contrapunctus 6 involving the rhythmic notation were probably made not by Bach but someone else, possibly Anna Magdalena Bach (see NBA VIII/2, KB, 30). Most of the changes in Contrapunctus 7 are compositional in nature and were apparently entered by Sebastian himself. Some alterations in Contrapunctus 6 were not included in the printed version, perhaps because they were made in the autograph after the plates had been etched. It is unknown whether Bach authorized these changes; Moroney (1989, 115) observes that the decoration of the subject in m. 38 (soprano) would be the only instance of such embellishment in the entire movement. But it involved only the writing out of a turn in a common melodic formula (compare the overture of Partita no. 4, m. 8), and the embellishment of mm. 46–9 does not go much beyond that.

The greatest number of alterations in Contrapunctus 6 involved the notation of the dotted rhythms. These changes formed a precise parallel with the changes made for the printed version of the first movement of the B-Minor *Ouverture* BWV 831 (see chap. 16).[42] As in BWV 831, only some alterations point to real changes in rhythm, others being merely notational (as in m. 7). The substantive changes might have been triggered by the presence in different sections of the piece of flowing sixteenths, on the one hand, and jerkier motion elsewhere consisting of a dotted (or tied) note followed by three sixteenths or thirty-seconds. Motives apparently of the latter sort occur in both the subject (m. 3, soprano) and the episodes (e.g., mm. 13–4). The revisions left the sixteenths unchanged in the subject and passages derived from it (e.g., mm. 44–45a), but sharpened the rhythm elsewhere so as to involve thirty-seconds consistently (as in mm. 50–54a). Long runs of sixteenths in a single voice also were unaltered, most notably in the extended passages described above. Hence the revisions produced a more purposeful distinction between the two types of rhythm, strengthening the tension between the two; occasionally, however, one does hear the gears shifting (as in the middle of m. 54).

The dotted rhythms raise the issue of over-dotting, especially when normal and diminuted forms of the subject are juxtaposed (as in mm. 2–3). Both forms of the subject contain dotted rhythms, the one involving dotted quarters, the other dotted eighths. Literal interpretation would contradict the conventions of "French style," yet normal over-dotting would produce an inconsistency between the original and diminuted forms, the note after the dot becoming the same short value in both. Other inconsistencies are already notated, however, for in the diminuted entries the last five notes of the subject lack the dotted rhythm present in the initial entry (bass, m. 4). Thus it seems hard to object to the interpretation advocated here for other pieces in overture rhythm: over-dotting on quarters only, not eighths.

This conclusion applies only in Contrapunctus 6. A more rigorous rhythmic relationship holds between the three rhythmic forms of the subject employed in Contrapunctus 7. Perhaps to point this out, only in the latter piece is the contrapuntal device specified in a Latin subtitle, *per Augment[ationem] et Diminut[ionem]*. In the previous piece, literal interpretation of the note values would twice lead to consecutive seconds that are awkward to play and musically inconsequential, as they involve parallel motion (mm. 67, 78). Consecutive seconds arise only once in Contrapunctus 7, and they are hidden in the two lowest voices, moving in contrary motion (m. 39). The latter passage was a revised reading, implying that Bach did not accept the rough voice leading without first exploring other possibilities.[43] At any rate, here he apparently assumed literal interpretation of the note values.

The Double Fugues with Invertible Counterpoint: Contrapuncti 9 and 10

The autograph gives the two double fugues prior to the counter fugues, which the two triple fugues then follow; the seemingly less rational order of the print (see Table 18.2) might reflect considerations for conveniently placed page turns.[44] All four pieces were originally notated in half the values of the print; the smaller note values probably represented Bach's first conception of the tempo, which slowed during composition under the weight of contrapuntal elaboration and melodic embellishment.[45] When the double fugues were prepared for publication, the original common-time signature was retained; the triple fugues, originally in 2/4, appeared in cut time. The notation in 2/4 did not necessarily imply a particularly lively tempo, but it does suggest emphatic articulation of the second as well as the first beat, something that perhaps translates into a more deliberate, expressive type of performance for the two triple fugues. The latter share melodic material and can share a tempo as well, but the double fugues are distinct in character, and Contrapunctus 9 might go almost twice as fast as Contrapunctus 10.

The four pieces combine new subjects with the common subject of the *Art of Fugue*—which from this point on will be termed the *theme*. Although the new subjects are not always introduced in expositions of their own, each has a distinct identity and first appears in a clearly articulated section of the piece, unlike an ordinary countersubject. Exactly what Bach called such pieces is unknown, but they represent a type distinct from the "double" fugues seen in Contrapuncti 3 and 4, that is, "simple" fugues with regular countersubjects. Indeed, Contrapunctus 10 seems to have been revised with just this distinction in mind.

Contrapuncti 9 and 10 illustrate not only the use of multiple subjects but also double or invertible counterpoint at various intervals. For the print Bach added two canons employing the same varieties of invertible counterpoint. The latter is often explained in textbooks as the product of a mechanical process in which the composer avoids certain intervals between the two voices. Apart from reducing a delightful type of counterpoint to dry rules, such an explanation errs in being applicable mainly to species counterpoint in two voices, not to the harmonically generated polyphony of a Bach fugue. There, "forbidden" intervals can become permissible through chromatic alterations of the two parts, or by the addition of free parts. Although even a fugue can get along without it, invertible counterpoint is a necessity in the permutational designs that Bach and his predecessors followed in serious contrapuntal writing. More generally, it is essential for the exchange of material between voices, as in the recapitulatory schemes of the WTC and other works.

Double counterpoint at the octave involves being able to transpose one of two voices an octave (or two) above or below the other. Such writing is so fundamental to fugue that Bach did not bother to devote a contrapunctus to it specifically, although it can be seen in the relationship between, say, theme and countersubject in the opening exposition of Contrapunctus 3 (Example 18.2). The subjects of the two double fugues are combined in invertible counterpoint at the twelfth (or fifth) and tenth (or third), respectively (Example 18.3 and Example 18.4). In Contrapunctus 10 the two subjects also invert at the octave, and this makes possible the "paired entries" that serve as climaxes of the last two sections (Example 18.5).[46]

Neither movement was originally a full-fledged double fugue, and Contrapunctus 9 remains one only in Marpurg's sense, as the theme, introduced as the second subject, lacks an exposition of its own. Nevertheless each entry in augmented note values, resembling a cantus firmus, is a dramatic event. Bach might have found a model for this in pieces by Frescobaldi whose final section combines a new subject with the principal theme in long notes.[47] The first subject of Contrapunctus 9, whose virtuoso character is apparent in its initial octave leap and the running eighths that follow, is one of the longest in any of Bach's

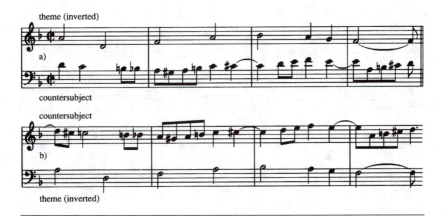

Example 18.2 *Art of Fugue* BWV 1080, Contrapunctus 3: (a) mm. 5–8; (b) mm. 15–8 (soprano and bass).

Example 18.3 *Art of Fugue* BWV 1080, Contrapunctus 9: (a) mm. 59–62 (alto and bass); (b) mm. 89–92 (soprano and bass).

Example 18.4 *Art of Fugue* BWV 1080, Contrapunctus 10: (a) mm. 44–7 (alto and tenor); (b) mm. 66–9 (soprano and tenor).

Example 18.5 *Art of Fugue* BWV 1080, Contrapunctus 10: (a) mm. 75–8 (soprano, alto, bass); (b) mm. 115–8 (alto, tenor, bass).

mature fugues—but it must be so in order to combine with the long notes of the theme as used in this movement. The new subject includes a prominent "sigh" motive in m. 5, and this is twice involved in chromatic progressions containing an augmented sixth (mm. 76–7, 102–3). But these are not moments of great pathos; indeed the piece demonstrates that the art of fugue need not be confined to pieces of a serious or pathetic character.

Contrapunctus 10 is a graver work. Originally, it opened with the exposition of the main theme (mm. 23ff.), which was combined only later (m. 44) with the new subject. This early version appears in the print as *Contrap[unctus] a 4* and used to be called Contrapunctus 14 (as in BG 25/1), a title better reserved for the fragmentary fugue. The exposition added at the beginning of the revised version is rather unusual, since its subject was conceived as countersubject to the main theme and is not suitable for a conventional exposition of its own. Hence, this is a stretto exposition, and its initial entries fall on I, IV, I, and V (D–G–D–A), in place of the usual tonic/dominant alternation. The last two of these entries are inverted, even though the inversion of the subject is never used in the main body of the fugue. It is not even easy to say where each statement of this subject ends; the last note of the first entry might be considered to be f♯′ in m. 4.

Perhaps in order to make the opening stretto exposition seem less incongruous, Bach added a partial stretto entry at the first entrance of the main theme as well.[48] Kerman (2005, 42), finding the new counterpoint of mm. 23–6 "crude and unlovely," doubts Bach's responsibility for the added parts. It is fair to ask how well the "join" between new and old material was made, for the passage provides evidence that Bach composed one section at a time, a method that could lead to clumsy transitions in the work of a poor or distracted composer. But Contrapunctus 10 was engraved from a plate apparently prepared under Bach's direction,[49] and the surging bass added in mm. 23–5 is not unrelated to what follows (e.g., soprano, mm. 28–30). The piece's incongruities are apparent only upon close analysis, and in its final form Contrapunctus 10 is as satisfying as any movement in the *Art of Fugue*.

The Two Triple Fugues: Contrapuncti 8 and 11

In the autograph the two triple fugues appeared together at the conclusion of the series of regular fugues. Each is longer and individually more compelling than any of the other completed contrapuncti; together they form an unparalleled pair of masterpieces. Their separation in the print seems inappropriate, as, more than any other pair, they provide *alio modo* illustrations, in three and four parts, respectively, of the same contrapuntal devices. The parallelism extends to the use of the same basic design and the same thematic material, including a version of the B-A-C-H motive that is incorporated into one of the subjects (Example 18.6). Both fugues contain a strong articulation near the midpoint,

Example 18.6 *Art of Fugue* BWV 1080, thematic material in Contrapuncti 8 and 11 (asterisks indicate sharps absent in the autograph): (a) Contrapunctus 8, mm. 1–5a (alto); Contrapunctus 11, mm. 27b–31a (alto); (b) Contrapunctus 8, mm. 39b–42a (alto); Contrapunctus 11, mm. 93b–96 (soprano); (c) Contrapunctus 8, mm. 94–98a; Contrapunctus 11, mm. 1–5a (alto).

and each ends with a climactic exposition containing simultaneous entries of all three subjects. These and other complementary relationships between the two contrapuncti are summarized in Table 18.3.

The three-part fugue is divided into two nearly equal halves, even possessing a sort of recurring closing theme in the form of a running figure that appears

Table 18.3 Complementary Designs of Contrapuncti 8 and 11

Contrapunctus 8			Contrapunctus 11		
mm.	thematic material*	cadence at end of section section	mm.	thematic material*	cadence at end of section
1–39a	a	d	1–27a	c	d
39b–93	a + b	d:V	27b–71a	a + cs (both later inverted)	a
94–124	c	a	71b–89a	c inverted	F
125–46	a + b	a	89b–146	a + b, also single entries of c and a (inverted, with cs)	C
147–88	a + b + c	d	146–84	a + b + c; c + its inversion	d

*Letters indicate subjects as shown in Example 18.6.
cs = countersubject

rather suddenly just before the final cadence of each half.[50] The bipartite division is less clear in the four-part fugue, thanks to its greater number of subdivisions, only the most important of which are shown in the Table 18.3. Contrapunctus 11 actually contains two substantial cadences near the center: that at m. 71, which is followed by an impressive entrance of the theme (in inversion), and that at m. 89, which is closer to the exact midpoint and immediately precedes the entrance of the third (B-A-C-H) subject. The four-part fugue is the more monumental of the two, and unlike Contrapunctus 8 it uses both upright and inverted forms of two of its subjects, one of which even possesses its own countersubject. Nevertheless, the two fugues are almost precisely equal in length, and the crucial moment at which all three subjects are first combined occurs at virtually the same point in each.

This moment is particularly dramatic in the four-part fugue, as it occurs (m. 146) in the midst of the most chromatic, most rapidly modulating section of the piece. Yet the passage combining the three subjects serves to prepare an even more crucial event, a simultaneous combination of *rectus* and *inversus* forms of the main theme (m. 158). The two forms of the theme had previously entered together in the coda of Contrapunctus 5. Here they occur in double counterpoint at the tenth (compare mm. 158–62 and 164–8), and the combination is integrated into the body of the piece, coinciding with the return to the tonic and thus marking the beginning of the final section.

This is a splendid moment, the culmination of the entire series of Contrapuncti 1–11. Yet the final section of Contrapunctus 11 maintains its tension to the end, through the surprising moves to the Neapolitan at m. 164 and to the submediant (B♭) just five measures before the end. Only in the final phrase does the soprano at last restate the theme in the tonic in its real, upright form. This entry is so perfectly prepared that there is no need for a conventional cadential formula, a final pedal point, or any other elaboration to make the close utterly compelling.[51]

Besides doubling the original note values of the two triple fugues, Bach raised the already high level of chromaticism by inserting accidentals in certain statements of subject *b*, including its first entry in Contrapunctus 8 (see Example 18.6b).[52] He also revised several passages in Contrapunctus 11. But although Bach himself was responsible for the engraver's copy of Contrapunctus 11, he did not add a single ornament sign to the text, unless one counts the c-appoggiatura on the downbeat of m. 57 (which represents the first note of subject *a*). On the other hand, in Contrapunctus 8—for which someone else prepared the engraver's copy—the autograph already gave a *Doppel-Cadenz* at the end of the first statement of subject *a* (m. 3). In the print this became a simple trill with termination, but it was extended to most of the remaining entries. The ornament is, however, virtually unplayable in several instances (e.g., m. 83). Perhaps Bach instructed the copyist verbally to add the trill into each entry of the subject, but was unable to see the results; the ornament can be abbreviated or omitted where it is impractical.

The Two Mirror Fugues: Contrapuncti 12 and 13

The two mirror fugues, so called because the entire contrapuntal fabric of each can be inverted, are, in a sense canons, since they employ a much more rigorous contrapuntal procedure than any of the previous pieces. This might explain why they came last in the autograph as originally constituted, and after the main sequence of contrapuncti in the print. As with the triple fugues, Bach chose to write complementary pieces in three (Contrapunctus 13) and four parts (Contrapunctus 12). But the two mirror fugues share no material apart from the theme, which appears in them in very different forms. Otherwise the pieces are as unlike as could be imagined, the four-part Contrapunctus 12 being unusually austere, the three-part fugue one of Bach's liveliest late works.

These pieces are in some ways the most problematical of all of Bach's late keyboard compositions; their origin, title, ordering, and performance practice all raise questions that can be treated here only summarily. For obvious reasons, mirror pieces have always been rare, but Bach probably knew two settings by Buxtehude of the chorale *Mit Fried' und Freud'* (BuxWV 76/1–2), published in 1674 at Lübeck. Although not fugues, each is designated a *Contrapunctus* and employs four-part counterpoint invertible at the octave; the second piece is written in mirror counterpoint.[53] Buxtehude's models in turn might have been hymn settings published in 1669 by Christoph Bernhard (extract in Snyder 1987, 217). Bach could have come across these as well during his visit to Lübeck or during his student years near Hamburg, where Bernhard was music director until his death in 1692. The gloomy and archaic Contrapunctus 12 might have been directly inspired by the Buxtehude pieces; the similarities in key, meter, and texture are striking.

Still, Bach's mirror fugues are very different from the Bernhard and Buxtehude works. Bernhard's settings are in a quite pure *stile antico*, and both older composers evidently wrote one voice (or rather one pair of voices) at a time. This is clearest at the cadences, which, as in sixteenth-century music, were conceived in terms of motion toward perfect consonances by pairs of voices. Hence the bass tends to move by step rather than from dominant to tonic, even in final cadences (Example 18.7). In addition, each movement is too short to have contained substantial modulations, which in any case one would not expect to find in a quasi-modal seventeenth-century work.

Long before writing the *Art of Fugue*, however, Bach had faced the problem of mirror writing in a tonal context, in the gigue of the Sixth English Suite. Although the two halves of that work are not perfect reflections of each other, they illustrate principles that are developed with greater rigor in Contrapuncti 12 and

Example 18.7 (a) Bernhard, *Prudentia prudentiana, partes* 1 and 2: mm. 26–8; (b) Buxtehude, *Mit Fried' und Freud'* BuxWV 76/1, mm. 12b–14; (c) Buxtehude, *Mit Fried' und Freud'* BuxWV 76/2, mm. 12b–15.

13. With these pieces the mirror principle extends to the deepest levels of tonal design, and the mirror fugues are, consequently, as much a study in the relations between keys as in invertible counterpoint. Upon inversion an authentic cadence becomes a plagal one, and a modulation from tonic to dominant is redirected toward the subdominant. Thus, in one version of the four-part mirror fugue, the initial imitation is at the dominant; in the other version, the second entry is on the subdominant. In the second episode of the three-part fugue (mm. 23–6), one version ascends by sequence through the circle of fifths (d–a–e–b), whereas the other descends (d–g–c–F). In addition, the three-part fugue illustrates the non-invertibility of the diminished-seven chord: both versions come to rest on the same harmony at the fermata in m. 59.

Mirror technique is not the only device illustrated in these pieces. Like

Table 18.4 The Two Versions of Contrapunctus 13

Version and Identifying Features	Voice	Form of Subject in Initial Entry	Corresponding Voice in Other Version
Contrapunctus inversus a 3	S	*inversus*	B
BWV 1080/13/1	A	*rectus*	S
top in autograph	B	*inversus*	A
second in print			
first note a´			
first entry *inversus*			
first three entries on d–d–a			
Contrapunctus a 3	B	*rectus*	S
BWV 1080/13/2	S	*inversus*	A
bottom in autograph	A	*rectus*	B
first in print			
first note d´´			
first entry *rectus*			
first three entries on d–d–g			

Contrapunctus 3, the four-part mirror fugue twice varies its version of the subject, embellishing the melodic intervals through small note values at the beginning of the second exposition (m. 21) and again, slightly differently, in the final entry (m. 50). In addition, each version of the three-part piece employs both *rectus* and *inversus* forms of the subject, although never simultaneously. Moreover, instead of simply inverting the entire texture—which would have meant keeping the same voice in the middle of both versions—for the three-part mirror Bach employed the more complex system of inversion illustrated in Table 18.4.[54]

Williams (1986b, xvi) considers it "logical" that the three-part mirror piece (Contrapunctus 13) should come first, just as the triple fugue in three parts precedes the one in four parts. Yet the four-part mirror (Contrapunctus 12) comes first in both autograph and print, perhaps reflecting the more sophisticated technique of the three-part fugue. More difficult is the question of which version of each fugue is to be considered the upright form and which the inversion. In the autograph, Bach wrote the two versions of each movement simultaneously on double systems of eight staves (Contrapunctus 12) and six staves (Contrapunctus 13).[55] The print, however, gives the two versions of each fugue separately, in each case reversing the order vis-à-vis the autograph; that is, the version placed second is the one placed on top in the autograph.

The confusion does not stop here. The print uses the title *Contrapunctus inversus* for both versions of the four-part fugue but only for the second version of the three-part one.[56] A further complication is that Contrapunctus 13 embellishes the theme in such a manner that its upright form *sounds* like an inversion: it opens with a downward leap from tonic to dominant (d´´–a´) rather than the other way around (Example 18.8). The NBA follows its two sources (print and

Example 18.8 *Art of Fugue:* theme as embellished in (a) BWV 1080/13/2 (theme in upright form); (b) BWV 1080/13/1 (theme in inverted form). Asterisks mark tones of theme in original (unembellished) form.

autograph) precisely, but other editions are maddeningly inconsistent in the titles and ordering used. Table 18.4 presents the relevant information as clearly as possible.

The whole issue is musically of little importance, but editors and performers have to decide which piece comes first and what to call each version. The NBA adds the editorial subtitle *forma recta* or *forma inversa* to each version as deemed appropriate, but these labels have no basis in the sources and apply properly to the initial form of the *subject* in each movement, not to the movement as a whole. These labels are essentially arbitrary in the three-part piece, a counter fugue employing both forms of the subject in each version. Because fugues normally go to the dominant before moving elsewhere, one might designate BWV 1080/12/1 and BWV 1080/13/1, respectively, as the upright forms, although the latter leaves the tonic only for the third entry.

The two versions of each piece were necessarily composed simultaneously and are virtually equal in musical quality, showing few signs of contrivance. Bach even took care that both versions of each fugue should conclude with something resembling a V–I cadence. Naturally the cadence cannot occur at the same point in each version. In the "top" version of the three-part fugue (BWV 1080/13/1), the bass moves to the tonic from the dominant on the downbeat of the penultimate measure; in the "bottom" version (BWV 1080/13/2) it does so within the penultimate measure. The situation is ambiguous in the more archaic four-part fugue, whose bass fails to move by direct root motion at the final cadence, just as in the Buxtehude pieces. Both versions, however, have reasonably well articulated bass A's near the end (in mm. 52 and 54, respectively).

These concerns would be nothing but pedantry if the ambiguities of order and title were not directly relevant to the demonstration of mirror technique, applied at the level of tonal design as well as local voice leading. If it was Bach's intention to obscure the difference between "upright" form and "inversion," he succeeded. He also succeeded in demonstrating that mirror technique could be applied to utterly different types of music. Contrapunctus 13 is by far the more engaging of the two, thanks to its lively gigue rhythm and clear harmonic directionality; the latter is particularly evident in the four sequential episodes. The four-part fugue, on the other hand, has neither episodes nor a distinctive tonal trajectory, and voice crossings make it a bit murky, especially in the "bottom" version (BWV 1080/12/2), which contains much parallel motion low in the bass staff. The piece can nevertheless come to life if the beat remains on the half note and the embellishments in eighths are played lightly. Unfortunately, few possess hands large enough to play the parallel sixths and occasional tenths with sufficient grace, lightness, and evenness. Performance by two players may be as necessary here as in the three-part mirror fugue, for which Bach prepared a two-keyboard arrangement.[57]

The arrangement (BWV 1080/18) at first provokes disappointment, as the added voice is free, not invertible. But an invertible part would necessarily have been fragmented, musically trivial, or both, defeating the purpose of the arrangement, which presumably was to give both players something interesting to do with each hand. Perhaps because it was not completely invertible, Bach apparently did not prepare the arrangement for printing, and it was published in an early version that does not reflect revisions made in the solo version. The notes of the arrangement remained in their original values—half those of the solo version—and m. 4 of the subject and all parallel passages use equal note values, without the later dotted notation. Evidently, Bach was unhappy with the resulting metrical ambivalence, as he eliminated it almost entirely in the revised solo version.

Perhaps he meant to eliminate it entirely. The dotted notation in the subject should certainly be understood as shorthand for triple "skipping" rhythms; the same may also be true of several other remaining examples of duple notation in the solo version as published.[58] But not so in m. 46a, which contains a run of six sixteenth notes—the only group of more than two sixteenths in the entire piece. The sudden change in rhythm underscores the structural role of the passage, which is to prepare the return of the theme in the tonic two measures later.[59]

The Fragmentary Fugue [Contrapunctus 14]

The famous "unfinished" fugue was apparently one of the four pieces that Bach decided to add to the *Art of Fugue* after completing the early version. Although not necessarily Bach's last composition, it is probably very late, composed after some of the other movements had already been prepared for engraving. Whether Bach actually left it unfinished or his heirs simply failed to recognize the sheet or sheets of paper containing its conclusion is unknown. It was included in the print as a *Fuga a 3 Soggetti* (Fugue with Three Subjects), a title usually taken as meaning "triple fugue" and therefore a mistake. But "three subjects" might mean those other than the "theme," which would constitute a fourth subject (as in the titles of BWV 574 and 917).

The fugue survives in an incomplete autograph, apparently a revising score. The print gave the fragment up to the half-cadence on the downbeat of m. 233; the autograph contains six more measures and part of a seventh.[60] A remark added in the autograph by Emanuel Bach explains that the composer died "over this fugue, where the name B-A-C-H is used as a countersubject."[61] This seems to mean that Bach died at the moment he combined the "Bach" theme with the first subject, but that, taken literally, is clearly impossible. Emanuel might have intended the remark as a concise if not entirely accurate way of alerting copyists to the fact that the piece was incomplete. Wolff (1975) points out that, on the contrary, Bach must at least have sketched out a combination of four subjects in quadruple counterpoint. But it is impossible to say whether the piece was completed in some form and whether it was meant to be the last fugue in the collection. Bach's obituary, to which Emanuel contributed, states that illness prevented the composer from fulfilling his "plan" (*Entwurf*) of completing the "penultimate" fugue and of working out a final quadruple mirror fugue.[62] Perhaps Bach indeed expressed such an intention at some point. But his plans for the work had already changed at least once, and there is no way of knowing what he had in mind for it during the last months of his life.

That the fragment was even meant for the *Art of Fugue* was once questioned, as the main theme of the larger work never appears in the extant portion of the fugue. But Gustav Nottebohm (editor of the Beethoven sketchbooks) demonstrated in the late nineteenth century that that theme could, with a few rhythmic alterations, be combined with the fugue's three other subjects.[63] Where Bach would have placed the completed fugue within the work is uncertain; editors have most often placed it last, but Butler (1983a) makes a strong argument for placing it before the canons.

Naturally, speculation has centered on how the fugue might have ended, and many completions have been offered. All add the main theme of the *Art of Fugue* as a fourth subject, but most are invalidated as reconstructions of Bach's possible intentions through improbable stylistic details—anachronistic harmonic progressions, faulty voice leading, or the need for organ pedals (never required in the extant movements). Virtually all reflect the view that the fugue must have been of enormous length, ending with a grand pedal point or a romantic apotheosis of the main theme—assumptions belied by the relatively unpretentious ending of Contrapunctus 11, which is the real high point of the work, at least as it stands. If Butler is correct, the loss amounts to less than a page of music, or about forty measures (see Table 18.5). This would yield about 280 measures for the complete fugue, keeping the piece within manageable limits, although forcing certain strictures on its content. What seems clear is that Bach composed the piece in sections, linking them by bridges that perhaps were worked out only during the writing of the surviving autograph. Corrections in the latter show that the closing passages of the first two sections underwent revision,[64] and Wolff (1975, 74) suggested that the final section was "already written down elsewhere."

Nottebohm's combination of the four subjects is not perfect, but a rhythmic alteration of the first subject makes it possible to combine the same four subjects in inversion as well as in *rectus* form (Example 18.9).[65] The last few measures in the autograph (omitted from the print) show that Bach, having introduced the first three subjects, was now combining them. Presumably the fourth subject, the theme of the *Art of Fugue*, would have entered soon afterward. The general procedure would not have been unlike that employed in Bach's other fugues with multiple subjects. But the structural proportions would have differed, since the sections would have been of diminishing length. The theme would not have

Example 18.9 (a) The four subjects of the fragmentary fugue BWV 1080/19 (three lower voices from mm. 233–39a); (b) same, inverted.

Table 18.5 Proposed Reconstruction of the Fragmentary Fugue

Subject(s) used	a	b	a + b	c	a + b + c	a + b + c + d
At measure	1	114	147	193	233	247
Length of section in measures		← 33 →	← 46 →	← 40 →	← 12 →	
	← 113 →	← 79 →	← 52 →	← 34 →		
Page breaks in original print	1	2	3	4	5	6
At measure:	1	47b	92	139b	186	233	(280)

been heard until near the end of the piece, as shown in Table 18.5 (largely after Butler 1983a, 56).

This is an unusual design, but the fragment is already huge and the possibility of some unprecedented sort of conclusion cannot be discounted. Bach had previously combined an opening in *stile antico* with more current types of material introduced in subsequent sections.[66] In its consistently austere style, the present movement is close to the Confiteor of the B-Minor Mass, which also must date from the end of Bach's life. The Confiteor is for the most part a double fugue in five voices, in form and proportions not unlike Contrapunctus 10. But its last section (m. 73) introduces a Gregorian cantus firmus—in effect a third subject—in long notes and in stretto. Hence, what is probably Bach's last choral fugue has a structure without precedent but perhaps resembling in some respects the design of his incomplete keyboard fugue.

Of the three extant sections, the first is a practically self-contained four-part ricercar. The subject has been traced to that of a *fuga reale* in Berardi's *Documenti armonici* (1687), but although belonging to a common tradition the two subjects are not identical, and Bach consistently avoids real answers in favor of tonal ones.[67] This section treats its subject with unusual thoroughness, including *inversus* and stretto expositions, but it has a somewhat rambling character and lacks the tautness of comparable pieces, such as the Bb-minor fugue of WTC2. With the entry of the second subject the piece virtually begins anew, the style changing in response to the new subject, a long running theme resembling the first subject of Contrapunctus 9.

The style shifts again with the introduction of the B-A-C-H subject in the third section, the easy diatonic flow of the second subject being replaced by harsh chromatic motion. Compared to the exposition of the second subject, that of the B-A-C-H theme is more thorough, incorporating inversion, stretto, and a regular countersubject. The tonality becomes tortuous, passing through remote keys in rapid succession; one remarkable passage contains the rare interval of the diminished sixth (m. 224, last beat). The restless modulations are an outcome of the subject's chromaticism, but not a necessary one; the combination of the three subjects at m. 233 (omitted from the print) is tonally stable, in character with the first two subjects. If one wishes to read the B-A-C-H exposition autobiographically, mere use of the chromatic motive (which occurs in other works) might be considered less significant than the difficult modulations (e.g., to E minor in mm. 205–6, repeated in 220–1), which perhaps represent the composer as obstreperous, or challenging, or audacious.

The proposed reconstruction leaves no room for an exposition of the main theme alone, which must enter as a cantus firmus–like countersubject, as in Contrapunctus 9 (or the Et exspecto). If the main theme was indeed to have appeared rather suddenly in the final section, this would have served not only as the piece's climax but also as a sort of explanation for the first three sections, their relevance to the *Art of Fugue* becoming clear as their respective subjects were combined with the theme of the work in the final summing-up. The acceleration of surface motion during the B-A-C-H section and the subsequent combination of the first three subjects would have been a way of building momentum toward this moment. Wolff suggests that at least the combination of four subjects must have been sketched somewhere, but the final page of the autograph trails off, the last measure unfinished. Even if Bach had completed a final quadruple exposition, he may have been undecided about how to connect it with the surviving fragment. Or perhaps Bach broke off work after deciding that fundamental changes were necessary; if so, these probably were never carried out.

To conclude a performance exactly where the fragment ends would be a dramatic gesture but one that invites a sentimental response. Although no completion can fulfill Bach's plan—whatever it was—it is better to conclude the piece in some manner. The completion in Example 18.10 follows the reconstruction of Table 18.5, incorporating the inverted combination of subjects from Example 18.9b.[68] Those who find such a reconstruction distasteful might consider the possibility of bringing the fragment to a quick, provisional cadence, as shown in Example 18.11. This draws on the original, canceled reading of mm. 112–4 at the end of the first section in the autograph.

Another solution occasionally heard is to return to Contrapunctus 1 after the half cadence on the downbeat of m. 233, repeating the first fugue either in its entirety or partially. But although the Goldberg Variations returns to its Aria, the corresponding procedure here would be anachronistically romantic. Transcendant complexity, not simplicity, is the goal toward which the entire work has been moving.

The Canons

It is anticlimactic to conclude a study of Bach's keyboard music with the canons of the *Art of Fugue*. But strict canon is traditionally the most learned if not the most sophisticated type of polyphony. The canons of the *Art of Fugue* are in just two

Example 18.10 The fragmentary fugue BWV 1080/19, mm. 233ff., with suggested completion.

Example 18.10 The fragmentary fugue BWV 1080/19, mm. 233ff., with suggested completion (continued).

Example 18.10 The fragmentary fugue BWV 1080/19, mm. 233ff., with suggested completion (conclusion).

Example 18.11 The fragmentary fugue BWV 1080/19: suggested provisional ending (mm. 239ff.).

voices, lacking the free bass lines found in the canons of the Goldberg Variations and the Canonic Variations for organ. Yet they are full-length compositions, not epigrammatic puzzles like most of the canons in the *Musical Offering*. In writing two-part canons that would also be substantial pieces of keyboard music, Bach set himself a task as unprecedented as the composition of a full-length three- or four-part mirror fugue. He carried it out with characteristic imagination; each canon follows different structural principles and has a distinct musical character, combining *galant* melodic formulas in varying proportions with the archaism and abstraction that color most of the *Art of Fugue*. All four canons operate within a fairly restrained tonal and harmonic ambitus, although the Canon at the Tenth and the Augmentation Canon contain a strong dose of local chromaticism. None is quite as regular in construction as the term *canon* might suggest. In particular,

Bach substitutes whole for half steps (and vice versa), applying a sort of *musica ficta* to create leading tones and define tonality unambiguously, whenever there is a danger that the harmonic vagueness implicit in techniques such as canon at the tenth might get out of hand.

Only two canons appear in the original autograph, and one of these (the Augmentation Canon) was so completely reworked that the printed version must be regarded as a new piece. Bach may first have planned to print the canons in the traditional enigmatic notation; the autograph gives the earliest version of each piece both as a puzzle canon in one voice and in its two-part solution. But in their revised versions, none but the Canon at the Octave could have been adequately represented in puzzle form. The other three depart from strictly canonic designs and had to be written out in two parts. Even so, two of the four remain perpetual canons, with repetitions that could theoretically go on forever, as in the much shorter canons in the *Musical Offering*.

In the print the order of the canons appears to have been confused, and although the Augmentation Canon was printed first it was probably meant to come last.[69] The first canon should be the one at the octave, which not only demonstrates the simplest type of canonic technique but also most clearly follows the design of a traditional perpetual canon. Its gigue-like rhythm makes it the most ingratiating of the canons, and the hand crossing in the final cadence makes it the most extroverted.

Each of the remaining canons is divided into sections somewhat resembling the expositions of a fugue, each division opening with some form of the main theme. The four sections in the Canon at the Octave begin with (1) the inversion, varied (m. 1); (2) the same, in a "tonal" answer (m. 25); (3) the theme in upright form, at the dominant (m. 41); and (4) the same, in the tonic, varied somewhat differently (m. 61). Hand crossing appears as the climax of what is labeled elsewhere as the *finale*, a coda after the double bar that ends the canon.[70] Except for the last five measures, the *finale* is essentially identical to the first quarter of the piece (mm. 5–23), which therefore falls into a sort of da capo form.

The Canon at the Tenth is a demonstration of invertible counterpoint at the same interval as in Contrapunctus 10, and its binary structure reflects this. In the first half, treble imitates bass at the interval of a tenth. The second half (mm. 40ff.) consists of the same music with the original bass transposed up an octave and the original treble down a tenth. This changes the interval of imitation from a tenth to an octave. As Yearsley (2002, 196–7) shows, the second half also substitutes "sweet" imperfect consonances for some of the "antique" or "severe" fifths and octaves of the original counterpoint. Yet the latter intervals remain prominent throughout the piece—not the only reason it possesses what Yearsley calls "a quality unusual for the music of the period." Rhythmically the canon is striking for the very gradual shift in each half from an exceedingly grave *mouvement* in long notes to an almost chaotic flurry of lively figures. Paralleling this is a gradual shift in register from the middle to the top of Bach's keyboard.

Several voice crossings in the second half make performance on two manuals advisable (as also in both versions of the Augmentation Canon). A few puzzling appoggiaturas (in mm. 37, 76) might have been late revisions intended to be played as ordinary sixteenths. Throughout, the original notation combines dotted and triplet rhythms, but triplet "assimilation" as assumed by Czerny and later editors is probably correct. The *finale*, however, shifts to duple rhythm, although there is no new tempo mark and no new time signature at this point (m. 79). Czerny evidently assumed that the notes of the theme kept their original durations, hence marking the passage Lento. A more intuitive reading of the notation is that each *measure* should take the same amount of time as before, effectively doubling the speed of the theme (in the bass).

The fermata in the penultimate measure indicates a cadenza over an implied 6/4-chord. Although something of a surprise in a canon, the idea of a cadenza in a solo keyboard piece was a familiar one in German sonatas of the 1740s. The cadenza should presumably be short and perhaps canonic, like those for two flutes given as models by Quantz (1752, 15.26–30). Example 18.12 provides a suggestion derived from a cadenza by Emanuel Bach for the slow movement of his two-harpsichord concerto of 1740.[71]

The Canon at the Twelfth is the shortest of the canons but the most intricate in structure, combining an essentially binary design with the theoretically infinite form of a perpetual canon. Certain passages are constructed so as to sound like a regular fugue, or at least a two-part invention. Although the second voice waits eight measures before entering, statements of the opening motive are then exchanged at half-measure intervals between the two voices (see mm. 9, 17, etc.). As in the Canon at the Tenth, the two halves of the piece are related

Example 18.12 C. P. E. Bach, cadenza from W. 120 (no. 54) for Double Concerto in F, W. 46, second movement, adapted for use in Canon at the Tenth BWV 1080/16.

by invertible counterpoint, the two voices exchanging roles at the center, beginning at m. 34.

The last canon has the most complicated title and uses what are nominally the most advanced contrapuntal devices. In fact the *Canon per Augmentationem in Contrario Motu* did not necessarily involve more difficult compositional problems than the others.[72] But it is the most chromatic of the canons and perhaps the most expressive, incorporating a jagged opening phrase, later *galant* "sighs" (mm. 23–4). The imitation is both inverted and in augmentation, as the title indicates. In addition, the leading voice (*dux*) contains varied statements of the theme in diminution (mm. 13b–15a, 17b–19a, 30, etc.). The most remarkable event is a series of slurred chromatic figures that reach a climax in the dizzying outburst of m. 29. It is hard to parse the precise tonal or harmonic significance of each accidental in this measure, but the underlying idea is a descending chromatic scale that has undergone melodic embellishment.[73] Rhythmically the passage prepares the differently varied statements of the theme that begin in the next measure, simultaneously in both voices (m. 30).

Neumann (1978, 135) noticed that on-beat performance of the appoggiaturas in mm. 23 and 75 leads, on paper, to hidden octaves. C. P. E. Bach (i.2.2.17) counseled players to avoid ornaments that disturb the "purity of the harmony" (*Reinigkeit der Harmonie*), yet Agricola (1757, 77) considered such parallels permissible when they were products of short appoggiaturas and inaudible. If one is bothered by the bare octaves produced by on-beat performance of the appoggiaturas, they can be avoided by the elegant pre-beat performance favored by Quantz.

The early version of the Augmentation Canon is a slighter composition, yet it would have been included in the original print with greater justification than the early version of Contrapunctus 10.[74] The Augmentation Canon survives in no fewer than four versions: (1) the initial entry in the autograph, probably a fair copy; (2) embellishments added to that, then abandoned; (3) the new composition, entered at the end of the autograph; and (4) the printed version, also preserved in the autograph engraver's copy. Bach's dissatisfaction with the first version is shown by some revisions entered early in the autograph (in mm. 3–5). But these led to consecutive fifths and octaves upon imitation (see Baker 1975, 68–9), and, rather than revise it further, Bach abandoned the early version entirely. The early version is more regular in its phraseology, as signaled by the sequential character of the first "countersubject," in mm. 3–4. It is also a little staid in its relatively conventional rhythmic and motivic patterns. Hence it is not surprising that Bach replaced it with the quirkier and less readily grasped printed version.

Both versions nevertheless follow the same general plan, concluding with a restatement of the main theme. In the earlier piece, the restatement is incomplete, and the *finale* (mm. 41–4) is a lively, self-contained mirror canon at the interval of a half-measure—a sort of stretto. In the printed version, the *finale* (mm. 104–8) restates the entire theme in the upper voice; there is no stretto, but the full statement of the theme gives the piece a more fully rounded design, closer to that of the other canons. It also echoes Contrapunctus 11, the climax of the fugues, which ends with a plain restatement of the theme in the top voice. This ending is modest yet forceful, serious and witty at the same time—qualities that we may suppose characterized Bach himself, and which he might well have wished to be present in his last published keyboard work.

APPENDIX **A**

Works of Uncertain Authorship

The previous pages have raised questions about Bach's authorship of certain works; there are many more for which these questions remain open. Ideally one would ignore questions of attribution and judge a composition strictly on its musical qualities. But the assignment of a work to Bach inspires us to examine it more carefully, perhaps to seek deeper meaning in it, and considerations of authenticity sharpen one's understanding of style. Even an inauthentic attribution can provide evidence about the influence or posthumous reception of Bach's music.

Decisions about attribution, although not wholly subjective, are susceptible to influence by personal temperament and prevailing scholarly fashion—whether it seems more exciting at a given moment to discover new attributions to Bach or to debunk old ones. In general, broad skepticism is in order, for otherwise decisions about the authorship of additional works, or views about Bach's style and its development, will be based on unproved speculation. In many instances it is impossible to reach a clear-cut decision about attribution, and one can say only that a work is "probably," "possibly," or "almost certainly not" by Bach. It is these cases, as opposed to clearly spurious works, that mainly concern us here.

Schmieder listed doubtful and spurious works in the appendix (German *Anhang*) of his BWV catalog, where they bear "BWV Anh." numbers. The 1990 edition of the catalog re-organized the Anhang and moved certain pieces to it from the main part of the catalog, but other dubious works continue to bear regular BWV numbers. Many works now regarded as doubtful or spurious were first published in BG 36 and BG 42 and have appeared in later editions as well, including the NBA.[1] Potential works of Bach continue to be identified both in newly accessible archives and as familiar sources are re-examined by new generations of scholars; such scrutiny led to the re-assignment of the Fantasia BWV 1121 to Bach (see chap. 6).[2]

433

Bach himself may have been responsible for some questionable attributions, as his personal collection of music contained anonymous pieces that were later taken to be his own (for examples, see appendix B). But the great majority of his keyboard works survive in signed autographs, attributed copies by close associates, or well-documented contemporary editions. Distinguishing true from false attributions has nevertheless occupied Bach scholarship from the beginning of the discipline. Decisions about authorship rest on many factors, but these fall into two main categories: the provenance and reliability of a work's sources, and its musical style. A composition must satisfy criteria in both categories to be accepted as Bach's. Even a work copied by Bach or a member of his family must be questioned if its style seems improbable, as in the case of the Telemann suite in CB. On the other hand, something that "sounds like Bach" cannot be accepted as his if there is no original attribution in the manuscript, or if the only surviving source is a nineteenth-century edition.

Views about sources can change; the identification of Yale's "Neumeister" manuscript as a possible repository of early Bach works increased the potential credibility of other sources that contain related compositions.[3] Among these is a manuscript from the lost Schelble-Gleichauf collection whose copyist might have had access to additional, otherwise unknown, early Bach works; attributions from this collection therefore must be considered seriously.[4] Judgments about style also are liable to change, and it is no longer possible to question the authenticity of large numbers of firmly attributed works, as Schreyer (1911–3) did, simply because they violate certain rules of counterpoint, some of them laid down after Bach's death. Opinions as to what sounds like Bach may be based on works whose own attribution is in doubt, a spectacular case being that of the famous "Toccata and Fugue" for organ in D minor BWV 565 (see Williams 1981); anything that sounds like the latter could well have been written by someone else!

Some questionable Bach attributions occur in late sources containing pieces whose style or level of craftsmanship clearly raises questions. Fugues on the B-A-C-H motive are prominent in this category, among them a fugue in B♭ (BWV 898) whose sources and almost Beethovenian style place it near the end of the eighteenth century. The same is true of the Kleines harmonisches Labyrinth BWV 591, which quotes the B-A-C-H motive while echoing the Art of Fugue.[5] Although competently composed, such pieces were not necessarily meant to sound like Bach, let alone be confused for his work.[6] They reflect elements of Bach's style (its chromaticism, its contrapuntal texture), but they remain remote from it and do not imitate any specific Bach compositions. BWV 591 has an imaginative ternary form, but it is small-scale and loosely constructed, and its inconsequential modulations between tonalities separated by a half step are uncharacteristic of Bach-circle composers.

Other pieces are stylistically less remote from Bach but equally unlikely to be his. Their sources are poor or unrelated to known Bach manuscripts, and the music suffers from sheer musical incompetence or lack of imagination. Among these is an inept *manualiter* toccata in F minor (BWV Anh. 85), most likely a pastiche by a later composer who probably knew works from the north-German repertory that Bach himself had studied.[7] Similar considerations apply to a number of pieces published as organ works in NBA IV/11. Mostly *manualiter*, they include three chorale partitas of variable quality and origin, as well as several fugues so unlike Bach's better-attributed works that there is little reason to consider them here.[8] For instance, BWV Anh. 97, despite its adventurous tonality (F♯ major), looks like a skillful school fugue from the later eighteenth century. Its chromatic subject is close to that of a fugue in E-flat by Johann Christoph Bach of Eisenach (BWV Anh. 177/2).[9] But the strict adherence to *stile antico* and the mature modulating scheme point away from Bach's early fugues, whereas the failures of imagination and occasional clumsiness are unknown in Bach's later music.[10]

Yet another group of questionable pieces consists of competent efforts in styles clearly belonging to the late seventeenth or early eighteenth century. Although they lack reliable attributions and contain details uncharacteristic of Bach's known works, one might argue that an inventive teenager, such as Bach presumably was, would have composed unique things in various styles. The problem with basing an attribution on such an assertion is that the argument can be neither proved nor disproved; in scientific language, the attribution is "unfalsifiable," there being no way to test it. For example, BWV Anh. 80 is an attractive, technically proficient suite in F. The style is close to that of Buxtehude; a few melodic passages in the allemande and courante and the partial variation relationship between the two movements recall Handel's Suite in E, HWV 430, which could date from as early as the composer's years in Hamburg (1703–5). Logically the work cannot be ruled out as Bach's, but there is no particular reason to assign it to him as opposed to, say, Reinken or even the young Handel. The sole manuscript copy of this work in fact bears an attribution to Bach, but the latter is in lighter ink and in a later hand than the rest of the manuscript, and may represent nothing more than an enthusiast's guess.[11]

Other pieces, including the "Neumeister" chorales, have a greater chance of being genuine Bach works, despite the absence of completely dependable attributions. Several have already been mentioned in the main text, either in entries of their own or in the course of discussing other works.[12] Others are treated below in roughly chronological order as determined by style. A few less likely pieces of special historical or musical interest are also included.

Sarabande con partitis BWV 990

Sources: Gb Scholz 5.10.1; lost copy, Schelble-Gleichauf collection; A Wn 5012. *Editions*: BG 42, NBA V/12.

BWV 990 would be a welcome addition to the short list of variation sets by Bach. Leonhard Scholz, the Nuremberg organist whose manuscript clearly attributes it to Bach, has emerged in recent years as an important Bach copyist who had access to rare and early works. Although the style of BWV 990 has been placed in the mid-seventeenth century (Eichberg 1975, 45–6), the wide-spanning scales and arpeggiation in several variations (here called *partitae*) are more likely to have been written in the 1690s or later. The same is true of the harmony in some of the more expressive variations (e.g., the Neapolitan in *partita* 12, m. 14). The sixteenth and last variation is a little gigue (*L'ultima partita o giguetta*) using the type of running figuration in 6/8 found in several of Bach's early gigues (e.g., in BWV 996). Although occasionally suggesting north-German organ style, the virtuoso writing seems calculated for the harpsichord, clavichord being a second choice; in this the work is distinct from the more modest variation sets by Pachelbel and his pupils, including older members of the Bach family.

The piece is surely German. The Latinizing title ("sarabande with variations") is reminiscent of that of BWV 833, and the opening *partita*, that is, the sarabande, is a German adaptation of the French dance. Its da-capo form recurs in north-German sarabandes, notably the famous one from Handel's Hamburg opera *Almira* that became the aria "Lascia ch'io piango" in *Rinaldo*. There is another sarabande of this type in the slightly doubtful Suite in F Minor BWV 823, whose opening measures contain a descending bass somewhat similar to the one here. The present bass line, together with the rhythm, would not be out of place in a chaconne,[13] and the style of some variations recalls Handel's early keyboard chaconnes. A few mannerisms, such as the slurred downward leaps in mm. 6 and 11 of the sarabande, recur in authenticated early Bach works, and the same motive plays an important role in the first variation (*partita* 2). Hence, if the present order of the variations is original, the composer's first thoughts included the development of an expressive "sigh" figure, not virtuoso showmanship.

The basis of the variations is not primarily the melody of the sarabande but its bass line. Despite the strict maintenance of da-capo form in all sixteen *partitae*, which may grow wearying, BWV 990 remains a very attractive work. The intense concentration on a few simple motivic ideas in *partitae* 2, 3, 5, and others—sometimes requiring considerable keyboard dexterity, as in *partitae* 6 and 10—points to an intellectually rigorous virtuoso such as Bach. A significant work, BWV 990 would considerably broaden our view of Bach's early style if it could be shown to be his.

Fantasia and Fugue in D Minor BWV 905

Sources: GB DRc E 24 (fantasia, mm. 1–15 only); lost copy, Schelble-Gleichauf collection. *Editions*: BG 42, NBA V/12.

BWV 905 comprises a short prelude in Corelli style and a fugue somewhat reminiscent of Bach's two longer fugues on themes by Albinoni (BWV 950–1). Its source situation at first seems dubious, but the Durham copy could derive from one brought to England by a distant cousin of Bach, and Bach's pupil Gerber may have owned a copy as well.[14]

A startling Neapolitan harmony in the opening measure of the prelude moves directly to the leading tone, and likewise in m. 19 of the fugue, implying that the composer shared with Bach an interest in "difficult" voice leading. This progression recurs only twice (prelude, mm. 4–5 and 10–1), but equally quirky, harmonically inspired writing occurs in the fugue (e.g., mm. 42–6). Again this points to a composer sharing Bach's harmonic invention and willingness to sacrifice melodic euphony in favor of challenging but logical voice leading. The rough passages are balanced by plain ones, several including successions of parallel sixths and thirds that are hard to play and continue for a few notes longer than one would expect in a mature Bach work. The prelude of the Suite BWV 821 contains similar writing, but that work too is somewhat doubtful.

Neither movement modulates very far, and entries of the fugue subject are confined to tonic and dominant. Together with some of the cadence formulas, especially the one at the end of the fugue, this is consistent with an early Bach composition. Weaknesses like the unidiomatic parallel motion, or the dropping out of the bass early in the prelude (mm. 3–4), are due to over-literal imitation of the trio-sonata idiom. Some lapses in the part writing—near-parallel fifths in the prelude (m. 17), an augmented second followed by an unprepared ninth in the fugue (m. 29)—resemble those occurring in better-attributed early works. A few audacious gestures, such as the opening Neapolitan or the dissonant scales in m. 52 of the fugue, are the sort of thing that Bach learned to tone down in later compositions.

> Substituting d′′ for b♭′ in prelude, m. 8, improves but does not entirely repair an awkward passage; in fugue, m. 41, e′ is better than c′ in the middle part.

Prelude in C Minor BWV 919

Sources: P 1229 (Preller); D Bim Mus. ms. J. B. Bach 1; lost copy by Kellner.
Editions: BG 36, NBA V/12.

The prelude BWV 919 (called a *Fantasie* in BG 36) opens with thematic material and a type of imitation reminiscent of the prelude of the Fourth English Suite. But thereafter it avoids that work's references to concerto style and is closer to the Inventions, which it resembles in its strict two-part texture, including a couple of voice crossings (m. 18) that make performance on two manuals appropriate.

Like the Invention in C Minor, it also includes a brief da capo of the opening exposition (at m. 23). But BWV 919 lacks that work's rigorous canonic design; instead, at a rather late point in the form (m. 15), it introduces a second subject that is never combined with the principal one.

Hence there would be good musical reasons for questioning Bach's authorship of the piece even if it were not attributed to "Bernhard Bach" in P 1229. There were several Bernhard Bachs, the best known being the composer Johann Bernhard of Eisenach and Erfurt, to whom Schulze provisionally assigned the piece (1984a, 80–1). Other possibilities are the Ohrdruf Bach of the same name (1700–43) and Sebastian's son Johann Gottfried Bernhard, who, like Preller, studied at the university in Jena.[15] Up to the cadence in the relative major (m. 15) the counterpoint has the logic and austerity characteristic of Sebastian's. But afterwards there is falling off of craft and invention. The new subject and countersubject are based on banal arpeggiation, and not only are the formal proportions wrong, but the return at m. 23 is clumsily prepared. Might Bach have composed only the first section, leaving the remainder to be completed by a pupil?

A somewhat similar invention-like piece appears in LEm ms. 8 in place of the final fugue of the D-major toccata; Wollny suggests an attribution to Bernhard Bach of Ohrdruf (NBA V/9.1, KB, 56). Longer and more engaging, but marred at one point by parallel fifths, this too looks like a capable pupil's work, incorporating echoes of Telemann and some modestly virtuoso figuration.

Fugue in E Minor BWV 956

> *Sole source*: P 804/8 (Leonhart Frischmuth; facsimile in Stinson 1989a, 131). *Editions*: BG 42, NBA V/12.

As the sole surviving copy of BWV 956 is by a student of Kellner, it might have been copied from a manuscript in Kellner's possession. Stinson (1989a, 130) suggests that Kellner himself could have been the composer, finding that the piece "betrays nothing of the experimental range of Bach's early efforts." But this is perhaps to overlook the chromatic counter-melody in mm. 25–6, the Neapolitan harmonies in mm. 48 and 49, and the well-handled acceleration of surface motion in the final section. There are also clumsy moments, including hidden fifths between the two lower parts (m. 21) and a banal lapse into parallel thirds (m. 28). But there is greater variety of texture, harmony, and voice leading, and more of a sense of drama, than in two fugues known to be by Kellner himself.[16] The latter also lack the vestiges of seventeenth-century style found here, such as the persistent *figure corte*.

The subject, as in BWV 905/2, is of the sequential type that Bach used in some early fugues but largely abandoned after his Weimar period. The fugue as a whole resembles those early efforts of Bach in which, after the initial exposition, single entries of the subject alternate with substantial episodes. The choice of modulations suggests some tonal planning, a move to the relative major falling near the exact center (m. 35b). The final entry, in the bass (m. 63), is prepared by an ascending sequence that moves to the tonic swiftly and surely from the fairly remote key of F, using clever if dissonant voice leading (mm. 57b–60a). In short, BWV 956 remains a "possible" early work of Bach's.

Fugue in E Minor BWV 945

Sources: Hauser collection (lost); P 315. *Editions*: BG 36, NBA V/12.

BWV 945 is less clearly a "possible" work, weaker in style and source situation. The lost copy from the Hauser collection was supposedly an autograph, but BG 36 did not describe it as such, and it lacked an attribution (Kobayashi 1973, 342, 388); the attribution in P 315 also is not original. The assignment to Bach might have depended on an enthusiastic guess by Robert Schumann, who first published the piece in 1839. In P 315—a late Viennese source according to Eichberg (1975, 14)—the fugue occurs anonymously alongside an Allemande and Courante in A (BWV 838) now assigned to Graupner. These have little in common musically with the fugue.[17]

The fugue nevertheless has a distinctive theme and a rational, clearly articulated design that falls into two halves, using sharply contrasting countersubjects. The second countersubject, introduced after the cadence at m. 34, is a lively, if old-fashioned, violinistic idea, and in the final phrase a sequence derived from it brings the piece to an impressive conclusion. The more restrained first countersubject is less well conceived, consistently forming weak passing dissonances (*échapées*). Moreover, the octave leaps in the subject produce passages that are awkward to play as well as weak contrapuntally, as when the alto leaps over the tenor in m. 22. Yet Bach's fondness for thematic material containing octaves is clear from BWV 992, 915, and other early works. Although this hardly constitutes evidence for his authorship, it cannot rule it out.

An oddity of this and several of the other doubtful fugues in minor keys (BWV 947, 958) is their somewhat unclear tonality, manifested in frequent wobbling between tonic, mediant, and dominant minor. This could reflect conscious archaism or the lingering hold of modality (a sign of an early date). Or it may signal the inexperience of a composer who knows that a fugue must introduce the subject in various keys but cannot quite reconcile the techniques of contrapuntal imitation and tonal planning. Such ambivalence is absent from Bach's authenticated works, save a few very early ones and some late ones where it is deliberate. But it is striking how few of Bach's well-attributed early "clavier" fugues are in minor keys, which raise special problems for tonal planning. A piece like BWV 945 could represent the early stages of grappling with those issues.

Fugue in A Minor BWV 947

Source: Edition by Griepenkerl (Leipzig, 1847). *Modern editions*: BG 36; Dadelsen and Rönnau (1970); NBA V/12.

The manuscripts that preserved BWV 947 are lost, and it is known only from nineteenth-century editions.[18] It is more homophonic than the other fugues examined here; it has a regular countersubject, but the last few statements of the subject are accompanied simply by chords, and the episodes consist of banal figuration with equally simple accompaniment. The composer was competent but unimaginative, incorporating two almost verbatim repetitions, something never found in a well-attributed Bach fugue (mm. 48b–53 ‖ 54–8 and 72–75a = 76a–80). In fact hardly anything in the piece resembles music known to be by Bach.

One of the few points of contact is the subject, whose repeated notes and simple conjunct motion recall the opening movement of the organ Fantasia in G, BWV 571. That work's authorship has also been questioned, but it has a much more respectable source situation, and its almost absurdly simple thematic material and counterpoint seem a deliberate ploy, reflecting its peculiar and rather appealing combination of fugue and ritornello-form elements.[19] The most attractive aspect of BWV 947 is its neatness, evident in the immediate repetitions of simple motives and the regular two-measure intervals between entries in the two main expositions (mm. 1–8 and 33–40). This is not characteristic even of Bach's earliest pieces, and BWV 947 is almost certainly not his work.

Fugue in D Minor BWV 948

Chief sources: D B Mus. ms. 10580; P 487; LEu N. I. 10338 (M. pr. Ms. 20[i]); US NHy LM 4941; Gb. *Editions*: BG 36; Dadelsen and Rönnau (1970), NBA V/9.2.

This is one of the stranger pieces in the Bach canon, excluding such obvious pastiches as the *Concerto e Fuga* BWV 909. Nevertheless it is included in NBA V/9.2 on the evidence of its sources, which fall into three independent groups all naming Bach (or at least "J. S. B.") as the composer. None, however, is by an identified copyist close to Bach, and the style, although seemingly from somewhere in his orbit, does not point unequivocally to him.

The work is claimed to be early and based on "norddeutschen Vorbildern" (NBA V/9.2, KB, 294), but there are no models for its bizarre coda in the works of Reinken, Böhm, or other north-German composers. Zehnder (1995, 332–3) groups the work with several others that he assigns to the period 1709–11. One of these, the organ praeludium in G minor BWV 535/1, includes the thing closest in Bach's output to the cadenza at the end of BWV 948, which takes it around the entire circle of fifths (cf. BWV 535/1, mm. 19–32). But the stylistic affinities between these pieces are superficial, even if the present subject, consisting of a short motto followed by sequential figuration, resembles others in Bach's early fugues. One full measure of the subject (m. 4) arpeggiates a single dominant-ninth harmony, a type of gesture that seems relatively late.

Odd things happen in the second half of the piece, where a near-verbatim recapitulation of the first exposition (mm. 45–52 || 6–9 + 11b–15a) is interrupted by a short, unmotivated cadenza in A minor (m. 53). Up to here the fugue has been in three parts, but a fourth voice now enters, seemingly requiring pedals; the new voice does not state the subject until m. 62b. Shortly afterwards comes a second, much more lengthy cadenza that passes mechanically through the circle of fifths on its way to a motivically unrelated close.[20] Even apart from the ending, the unimaginative counterpoint, which accompanies the sequences of the subject in routine eighths and quarters, would place Bach's authorship in doubt. Measures 65–6 are virtually unplayable even with pedals. It is conceivable that, like the prelude to the Suite BWV 815a, BWV 948 represents an experimental stage of a piece that was never brought to final form; perhaps it was finished by someone other than Bach.

Fugue in A Minor BWV 958

Source: P 291. *Editions*: BG 42, NBA V/12.

BWV 958 somewhat resembles the Italianate fugues BWV 905/2 and 947, discussed above. It occurs only in a late source, but like a number of Bach's earliest fugues it suffers from distant modulations placed too near the end: G major is reached at m. 50, E minor at m. 54, in a piece only sixty-two measures in length. Two other passages contain sudden, unmotivated changes of key or material (mm. 21–2, 43–6), and the piece fails to maintain the integrity of the three voices, a fourth part entering occasionally but never for more than a few beats.

Although the "repercussive" subject seems archaic, the first measure could have been suggested by the opening fugue in Handel's E-Minor Suite HWV 429 (fugue first published 1720). Other passages suggest an acquaintance with the fugue of Bach's E-minor Toccata.[21] Together with some simplistic broken-chord figuration (mm. 44b, 48), these points suggest that BWV 958 is a derivative work of relatively late date.

Fugue in E Minor BWV 960

Source: ABB (incomplete). *Edition*: BG 42.

This work also has little chance of being Bach's. Some passages recall the preludes from the English Suites, others the earlier fugue BWV 896/2. Direct octaves and

Example A.1 Fugue in E Minor BWV 960: suggested ending (mm. 143–7).

rough passing dissonances in mm. 9–11 are restated in mm. 72–4, a suspiciously literal recapitulation of music from the opening exposition. This occurs within a long section that modulates several times—that is, redundantly—to G major (mm. 48–91).

The piece was a late entry, lacking title and attribution, at the end of the Andreas Bach Book. The copy ends at the bottom of a page, where the indication *Verte* ("turn") suggests that more was to follow. But perhaps only a few measures are lacking; a satisfactory modulating design (essentially e–G–e) is complete by m. 115. A conclusion is suggested in Example A.1.

Fugue in A Minor BWV 959

Source: Dl Mus. ms. 2405-T-31. *Editions*: BG 42, NBA V/9.2.

Like BWV 948, this is more likely to be by a pupil or admirer of Bach than Bach himself. Both the melodic writing and the texture are inspired more by harmony than counterpoint. The bizarre subject suggests Zelenka or Friedemann Bach, not Sebastian, despite some possible echoes—again—of the E-minor Toccata (e.g., in mm. 11–2). Neither Bach is likely to have been responsible for the banal episodes in mm. 24–9 and 34–6 nor the overdramatic closing gestures in the last four measures.[22]

Sarabande in G Minor BWV 839

Source: "Notenbuch der C. F. Zeumerin" (lost, dated 1735). *Editions*: Kretzschmar (1910), NBA V/12.

This graceful and affecting little work is even more suggestive of Friedemann Bach. His authorship would not be ruled out by the title, *Sarrabando del Sig[nore] Bach Lips[ia]*, under which it was preserved in a lost manuscript collection of short keyboard pieces. The contents (according to Kretzschmar 1910, 67) included an aria, vivace, and gigue by "Görner," possibly J. G. Görner, with whom Bach disputed the directorship of music at the university shortly after arriving in Leipzig.

The piece's restless chromaticism is handled well except in the final cadence, where the text might be corrupt. Particularly characteristic of W. F. Bach is a recurring passage over a bass that oscillates between notes a half step apart (mm. 3–4, 9–10, 26–7).[23] The following piece, a *Courante di Bach* in G (BWV 840), is also harmonically adventurous but corresponds with a movement in an *ouverture* by Telemann (TWV 32:13).

> Consecutive fifths in the fourth measure from the end can be avoided by emending the upper staff: for treble d''–d'' read b♮'–c'', and for alto b♮'–c''–b♮' read g'–ab'–g'. The alto in the penultimate measure might also read a third lower.

Prelude BWV 923a; Scherzo in D Minor BWV 844; Andante in G Minor BWV 969; Presto in D Minor BWV 970

Sources: all movements in US NHy LM 4813b (Rinck?), Schelble-Gleichauf collection (lost); BWV 844a in P 563 (Michel, with other short pieces), CH Zz Ms. Car. XV 244, A8b (Nägeli, with BWV 815a/1); BWV 970 in P 683 (C. P. E. Bach, early version), P 804/39 and P 1184 (both: revised version Fk. 25/2, with Fk. 25/1). *Editions*: by Roitzsch (Leipzig, 1880); BG 42 (BWV 923a, 844, 844a, 969 only); NBA V/12.

At least one of these pieces is assuredly by Friedemann Bach; the set as a whole illustrates how later musicians adapted Sebastian's music. In the Yale manuscript the pieces form movements of a *Toccatina per il Cembalo* in D minor comprising the following pieces: BWV 899/1, BWV 900/2 (transposed to D minor), BWV 923a, BWV 844, BWV 969, and BWV 970.[24] Short transitions connect the movements into a continuous cycle, somewhat like the organ Pastorale BWV 590. Pastiches formed from disparate movements are not uncommon in sources from the second half of the eighteenth century.[25] The *Toccatina* is a relatively skillful example; Eichberg's (1975, 25) suggestion that the arranger belonged to the circle of the organist Kittel, one of Bach's last pupils, is plausible and consistent with a date of origin in the later eighteenth century.

BWV 923a seems to have been adapted from the prelude BWV 923, an apparently authentic if perhaps unfinished work (see chap. 10). Kayser's copy of the latter breaks off at the end of a page, in the middle of m. 15; is it coincidental that BWV 923a diverges from BWV 923 at nearly the same point (the end of m. 14)?[26] The ending in BWV 923a includes hand crossings of a type suggesting that the composer knew the C-minor fantasia BWV 906/1. But other figuration ties the hands up in ways that seem closer to Friedemann than Sebastian Bach.

A cadence on the dominant leads to BWV 844. This is evidently a revised version of BWV 844a, also designated a scherzo but in E minor. Both versions are similar in form and proportions to the scherzo of Partita no. 3, the probable "starting point" for the composer, who has been plausibly identified as Friede-mann Bach (Eichberg 1975, 26, primarily on the basis of style). The piece has some of his quirky wit and harmonic invention and is with BWV 970 the most successful of the group, especially in the more refined D-minor version.

BWV 969 is an attractive imitation of a fugal trio-sonata movement, with a recurring episodic idea reminiscent of a passage in the opening chorus of Cantata no. 7.[27] But the form—a modified da capo, the subject being entirely absent from the B section—is rare in fugues by J. S. Bach. Details like an unprepared tonic 6/4-chord (m. 8) seem to rule out his involvement.

BWV 970 is derived from an early work of W. F. Bach, one of several hand-crossing pieces apparently inspired by the *Tempo di Menuetto* in Partita no. 5.[28] The original Presto was revised and expanded by the composer to become the second of a pair of minuets in G minor (F. 25). The present version is an appar-ently spurious adaptation by someone who had access only to the early version, preserved in a copy by C. P. E. Bach. Although clearly not by J. S. Bach, BWV 970 illustrates how his invention of a particular type of keyboard figuration continued to inspire younger players later in the century. The crossed-hands figuration creates cross-rhythms against the beat (e.g., in mm. 7–10). This goes far beyond the mild hemiolas in the movement from the Partitas, recalling other keyboard works of Friedemann (e.g., the E-minor Fantasia F. 21, mm. 66ff.).

Fantasia and Fughetta in B♭, BWV 907; Fantasia and Fughetta in D, BWV 908

Chief Sources: P 804/18 (BWV 907), P 804/26 (BWV 908) (both Kellner; title of BWV 907/1: *Prelude*); P 485; AmB 531 (attribution to Bach crossed out); B Br Fétis 7327 (Gerlach). *Editions*: by Roitzsch (Leipzig, 1880); BG 42; BWV V/12.

These are in some ways the most interesting of the doubtful pieces, for both their notation and their content. They are *partimenti*, written on a single staff and largely in a single voice; the player fills in the harmony according to the figured bass notation, as in Example A.2.[29] Kirnberger altered the attribution of BWV 907 from Bach to "Kirchof," that is, the Halle organist Gottfried Kirchhoff, who had published a series of preludes and fugues of this sort. But Kirchhoff's publication does not include BWV 907 or 908, which are longer and more idiomatically conceived for keyboard instrument than the pieces in his *A B C musical* (Amsterdam, ca. 1734).[30] Hence it is impossible to judge the accuracy of the altered attribution in AmB 531, although the latter was apparently copied from a manuscript by the Leipzig organist Gerlach (Stinson 1989a, 129). Gerlach is thought to have been a pupil of Bach, who could have known the pieces and recommended them to his students.

Example A.2 Fugue in B♭, BWV 907/2, mm. 8b–10 with suggested upper voices: (a) simple; (b) more florid.

The keyboard partimento was a common teaching tool; Kirchhoff might have learned of it from his teacher, Zachow, whose better-known pupil Handel wrote similar things (edited in Ledbetter 1990). Bach is likely to have known the partimento fugue in the first volume of Niedt's *Musicalische Handleitung* (1700); the piece recurs in a manuscript collection of sixty-two partimento preludes and fugues that bears a very doubtful attribution to Bach himself (P 296, analyzed by Renwick 1999). "Half" of the pieces published by Kirchhoff are also in P 296 (Milka 2003, 257), apparently in early versions.

Unlike the exercises in P 296, BWV 907 and 908 are fully idiomatic keyboard pieces. Despite the incompletely realized notation, they are in every other sense finished compositions—distinctive, well-crafted pieces with clear tonal designs. They are longer and more sophisticated than most partimenti, and the initial exposition of each fugue is fully written out through the third entry of the subject. Several episodes contain arpeggio figuration which, like the passagework in the middle of the B-major prelude of WTC2 or the praeambulum of Partita no. 5, needs no filling out.

Regardless of the composer, if Bach copied these pieces or used them in teaching, he is likely to have revised or corrected them. The bass is fully and precisely figured, and the style hardly rules him out—insofar as one can discuss his style in a type of piece of which he left no authenticated examples. Each prelude, after opening with the traditional flourish on the tonic chord, proceeds, like many of preludes in the WTC, to sequential repetitions of a single motivic idea. Both the fugue in B♭ and the prelude in D reveal binary symmetries, with an episode of free figuration near the exact center of each.

The *Clavier-Büchlein vor Anna Magdalena Bach*

The two little keyboard books for Anna Magdalena Bach contain some of the best-known music associated with the Bach name. Although most of the minuets and other small pieces are not actually by Bach, they deserve mention here.

Bach presented his second wife with manuscript music books in 1722 and again in 1725; both are now in Berlin (P 224 and P 225). The 1722 book comprises mainly the early versions of the French Suites. The famous minuets and other teaching pieces are in the 1725 book, available in several modern editions.[1] The contents of both manuscripts appear in NBA V/4; Dadelsen (1988) is a facsimile of the 1725 manuscript. The numbering of pieces here follows the NBA.

Music continued to be entered into both books well after the dates on which Bach presented each to his wife. Bach himself wrote most of the surviving entries in the 1722 volume over the next three or four years. The 1725 book opens with his copies of Partitas nos. 3 and 6, but thereafter the pieces were entered mostly by Anna Magdalena, over a long period probably extending into the 1740s. Other members of the family, especially C. P. E. Bach, also entered individual pieces; Sebastian himself made only a few further contributions. From this, and from the heterogeneous but generally simple musical contents, one gathers that the book provided teaching material for the younger Bach children.

In addition to the French Suites the 1722 book contains a few short pieces, all discussed elsewhere: the minuets BWV 813/5, 814/5, and 841; the chorale BWV 728; and the fragmentary Air with Variations BWV 991. There is also a fragmentary organ fantasia in C, BWV 573.

The 1725 book contains, in addition to the two partitas and two of the French Suites, several vocal works and some two dozen keyboard pieces. Most of the little pieces are anonymous, but a few composers are named, and several pieces once assumed to be by Bach have proved to be by others. The anonymous pieces were listed in the appendix of BWV and thus bear "BWV Anh." numbers.

Most of the little pieces, whether or not bearing attributions, are simple binary dances in *galant* style. Bach might have brought back copies of such pieces from his trips to Dresden, intending to use them in teaching. Schulze (1979b, 64) suggests this was the case with two of the best known of these pieces, the little minuets in G and G minor, nos. 4–5 (BWV Anh. 114–5). These are from a suite by Christian Pezold, organist at the Sophienkirche in Dresden, where Bach played in 1725. Also likely obtained in Dresden was the polonaise in G, no. 28 (BWV Anh. 130), otherwise known as a work of Hasse.[2]

Only a few other pieces have been identified. Number 29 is the C-major prelude from WTC2, and the untitled no. 26 is the aria from the Goldberg Variations. Number 6 (BWV Anh. 183) is a version of *Les bergeries* from Couperin's second book of *Pièces de clavecin* (1717).[3] A minuet copied by Bach with an attribution to "Mons. Böhm" (no. 21) seems too simple and *galant* in style to be by the well-known composer of that name. But Böhm lived until 1733, serving as Bach's Lüneburg agent for the sale of Partitas nos. 2 and 3 (see BD 2:169 [item 224]); who else would have been known in the Bach household as "Mr." Böhm?

The most extensive of the pieces for solo keyboard (outside the four suites) is the *Solo per il Cembalo* no. 27 (BWV Anh. 129), otherwise known as the first movement of a sonata by C. P. E. Bach.[4] Also possibly by Emanuel Bach is a series of four smaller pieces. Two of these, the marches nos. 16 and 18 (BWV Anh. 122, 124), have become well known, although only the two polonaises in G minor, nos. 17 and 19 (BWV Anh. 123, 125), show some inkling of the composer's later *empfindsam* style.[5] The second of these polonaises recurs as a movement of a keyboard sonata that bears an attribution to C. P. E. Bach in another manuscript copy.[6] The theme of one of the marches (no. 16) recurs in a movement from a flute sonata attributed to Franza Benda (see Dorfmüller 1989). Another march—no. 23 (BWV Anh. 127), one of the longer and more impressive of the marches and dances—bears an attribution elsewhere to C. P. E. Bach. Its theme resembles that of C. P. E. Bach's *Solo* and, less closely, the opening of Friedemann's Duo for two cembalos, F. 10. Possibly all these pieces are reworkings, by members of Bach's circle, of familiar melodies that provided ready material for composition exercises.[7]

It is conceivable that Anna Magalena Bach herself composed some of the anonymous pieces in the 1725 volume. Women composers in Germany were few and far between during this period, and some of her unattributed copies have proved to be of works by other composers. But, as a professional musician, Anna Magdalena would have possessed the necessary skills (see Marshall 1990, 193).

It is tempting to try to pick from the remaining pieces those that seem likely to be by Sebastian Bach. The long, somewhat asymmetrical phrases of the minuet in F, no. 3 (BWV Anh. 113), indicate a composer of distinction, as does the affecting shift to the relative major in m. 6 of the minuet in D minor, no. 36 (BWV Anh. 132).[8] Also relatively accomplished are the imitative minuet in A minor, no. 14 (BWV Anh. 120), and the chromatic minuet in C minor, no. 15 (BWV Anh. 121). Both have a Dresden air about them; as Dadelsen (NBA V/4, KB, 87) observes, they are likely to be by the same composer, whether or not Bach. Less distinctive are the minuet in G, no. 7 (BWV Anh. 116), and the two pieces that follow. But Bach might have had a hand in the two versions of the polonaise in F, nos. 8a–b (BWV Anh. 117). These relate to one another as do the two versions of the second courante—with "simple" and varied bass—in the early version of the First English Suite (BWV 806a). The two versions of the aria no. 20 (BWV 515, 515a) are in a similar relationship; Bach himself wrote the bass line for the second version (facsimile in NBA V/4: ix). This aria is really a minuet despite the text provided for it ("Erbauliche Gedanken eines Tobakrauchers"), which fits the melody rather poorly.

Bach is known to have composed only one polonaise for keyboard (in the Sixth French Suite), but this manuscript contains six, reflecting the contemporary popularity of the dance as an easy type of keyboard piece. Bach cannot be ruled out as composer except in the melodically arid polonaise in D minor, no. 24 (BWV Anh. 128). The polonaise in G minor, no. 10 (BWV Anh. 119), has some of the cocky poise that may originally have been characteristic of the dance but is replaced by fashionable elegance in most eighteenth-century examples.[9]

Certainly not Bach's is the untitled dance no. 32 (BWV Anh. 131), presumably a rigaudon. Apparently a composing score, it seems to be the work of Bernhard Dietrich Christian Ludewig, who taught the Bach children during the 1730s.[10] This is one of several hints that this book had ceased to serve for Anna Magdalena's private recreation (if it had ever done so) and was being used for teaching her children and step-children. A bar appears to be missing in the first strain, which has only seven measures. Another work uncharacteristic of Bach is the well-known musette no. 22 (BWV Anh. 126), whose ornamental chromaticism was probably meant to evoke a folk idiom. The title is erroneous, for this is actually a *murky*, an odd dance characterized by a bass in leaping octaves; C. P. E. Bach later wrote several equally eccentric examples.[11]

Chorales like nos. 12 and 13 (BWV 510–1) and the aria no. 33 (BWV 516) could have served as exercises in continuo realization. These and other settings for soprano and figured bass, like other eighteenth-century lieder, could also have been performed as keyboard solos or as songs in which the vocal line was doubled on the keyboard. The same is true of the songs in the Schemelli *Gesang-Buch* (Leipzig, 1736), for which Bach provided figured basses. Number 35 (BWV 514) of the present manuscript is a chorale setting similar to those in the Schemelli book. Bach was noted for his elaborate continuo realizations,[12] but in this type of piece a simple realization is best; the number of inner voices

Example B.1 *Schaff's mit mir*, Gott BWV 514, mm. 1–4, with suggested inner voices and ornaments

played by the right hand can be allowed to vary idiomatically (Example B.1). Surely it is unnecessary to turn the graceful little piece into an exercise in strict or elaborate four-part realization.

Notes

Notes for Chapter 1

1. An exception was C. P. E. Bach, who was known strictly as a clavier player, even admitting to Burney that he had lost the ability to play on the pedals, through lack of practice. Unlike many of Bach's pupils, he never held a position as organist.
2. Bach's Weimar cantatas date mostly from 1714–5, the Leipzig ones from 1723–7.
3. See BD 2:10 (item 7)/NBR, 40. Citations of latter type mean that an item appearing in the original language in *Bach-Dokumente* (BD) is translated into English in *The New Bach Reader* (NBR).
4. Activity on harpsichord as well as organ is implied by Bach's describing himself as entering both the ducal *Capelle* and "chamber music" (BD I: 1, item 1; NBR, 57). Rampe (2002b, 61–3) proposes that Bach would have led the Weimar court band as violinist, a possibility not ruled out by his designation in 1714 as *Concertmeister*, but not supported by any evidence either.
5. See BD 2:175 (item 232)/NBR, 136. The work was a special memorial composition, not a sacred cantata. Few scholars have accepted Dreyfus's argument (1987a, 23–32) that Bach frequently used harpsichord alongside organ in his regular Leipzig church cantatas; see in particular Kobayashi (2001, 99).
6. The two accounts mention only organ and "clavier" (see NBR, 79 and 301). That the event was to have taken place in the "home of a leading minister of state" suggests use of harpsichord, not organ and certainly not the more modest clavichord or spinet.
7. This statement applies to the keyboard works; many cantatas, in particular, survive in what appear to be first drafts. By "fair copy" I mean an autograph lacking extensive corrections and therefore seemingly providing a final, corrected text. "Revision copy," a term introduced by Marshall (1972, 1:5), refers to an "intermediate" score in which Bach made significant compositional alterations while copying from a first draft ("composing score").
8. There is no single catalog of Bach manuscripts, but Kast (2003) lists the holdings of the main Berlin library. The *J. S. Bach Quellendatenbank* <http://www.bach.gwdg.de/> is an online database, searchable by title, BWV number, and other fields, that lists sources for all of Bach's works.
9. Since the first edition of this book was published, Anonymous 5 has been identified as the Cöthen official Bernhard Christian Kayser (Talle 2003, 155–67), Anonymous 300 as the Berlin copyist Johann Friedrich Hering (Wollny 1995).
10. Works of all types discovered since 1950 have been added at the end of Schmieder's list, which originally concluded with the *Art of Fugue* (BWV 1080).
11. For full bibliographic information about each source mentioned, see the list of abbreviations at the head of the Bibliography.
12. Beißwenger's (1992a) chronology of Walther's manuscript copies supersedes the findings in Zietz (1969).

13. Among the anonymous pieces are BWV 939–42, 954, and 983; those with only a title in Kellner's hand include BWV 943, 955, 963, and 986–7.
14. See Synofzik (2001). The traditional dating of Preller's copies puts them as late as 1753 (see, e.g., NBA V/9.1, KB, 20).

Notes for Chapter 2

1. The dispute can be traced by reading Neumann (1965); Fuller (1977); Donington (1977); Neumann (1977); Neumann (1979); and finally O'Donnell (1979). Also relevant are Neumann (1974) and Fuller (1985).
2. On the generic "clavier" see Marshall (1986, 234); on "demonstration counterpoint" see Williams (1980–4, 3:191–2; 195).
3. Bach owned five *clavecins*, two lute-harpsichords, and a set of clavichords (BD 2:492–3; 504 [items 627 and 628]/NBR, 251–2; 256), but information as to their makers, styles, and so forth is lacking.
4. Bach's concern with sonority is evident in the instrumentation of many vocal works and in reports of his views on organ registration; see, for example, the selections from Adlung (1768) in BD 3:191–2 (item 739)/NBR, 364–6.
5. The "lute" pieces are discussed in this book as potential keyboard pieces. Another work possibly composed for a special type of harpsichord is the Aria variata BWV 989 (see chap. 6).
6. Harpsichords and clavichords could be equipped with pedalboards, as was apparently the case with a harpsichord acquired in 1722 by the Cöthen court, during Bach's presence there (see Hoppe 1998, 22–4). Such an instrument would have been convenient for playing otherwise unsustainable bass pedal points in the Third English Suite and the Fifth Brandenburg Concerto, as well as in several of Bach's early fugues.
7. As argued by Rampe (1998). Speerstra (2004), however, makes a strong case that these pieces were played on pedal clavichord.
8. The title page of Johann Krieger's *Musicalische Partien* (1697), a likely model for Bach's early suites, designates the music specifically for spinet or clavichord.
9. See Speerstra (2004). Rampe's claim (2002a, 94) that Bach owned *three* sets of clavichords with pedals seems a misreading.
10. Rampe (2002a, 91–100) asserts that the harpsichord was primarily a "court instrument," but see Koster (2005).
11. The idea of dividing Bach's keyboard music between organ and "clavier" seems to be first documented in the list of compositions included in Bach's obituary (BD 3:85–6/NBR, 303–4), which was in part the work of C. P. E. Bach.
12. As in Blood (1979).
13. Lehman's (2005) reconstruction of "Bach's" temperament is based on twelve ornamental swirls that Bach drew across the top of his title page for WTC1; although ingenious, the argument lacks documentary support (if the swirls were so important, why did Bach's students not copy them accurately, if at all?).
14. For contemporary evidence see BD 2:450 (item 575)/NBR, 336; also in Williams (1980–4, 3:188).
15. See Williams (1980–4, 3:118).
16. See Rasch (1986 , 294–300) on both Werckmeister and Neidhart's *Beste und leichteste Temperatur* (Jena, 1706), which describes equal temperament.
17. Kirnberger (1771–9, 2.3:185) listed "die verschiedene Characterisirung der Tonarten" among the advantages of his unequal circular temperament.
18. These instruments were equipped with sliding keyboards to accommodate different pitch levels. This device, found today on many harpsichords, requires something close to equal temperament if it is to be used for instantaneous transposition by half step, but the Prussian pianos were normally kept with the keyboard at its lowest playing pitch (see Oleskiewicz 1999, 98–9).
19. C. P. E. Bach (1753–62, i.introduction.14 and i.1.8).
20. For example, it appears that the organ prelude and fugue was normally performed on full organ (*organo pleno*); see Williams (1980–4, 3:171–2).
21. Variations in the last movement of a sonata by C. P. E. Bach (W. 69), composed in 1747 for a four-stop harpsichord, each employ a different registration.

22. See chap. 16; also Williams (1980–4, 3:180), quoting mm. 88b–95 of the overture.
23. Williams (1980–4, 3:171), quoting Stauffer (1980, 171).
24. Emanuel Bach (1753–62, i.3.22) prescribes holding single notes for half their written value; whether or not he meant this to be taken literally, it implies non-legato as the basic touch.
25. See especially chap. 6 in Quantz (1752). Butt (1990) surveys the articulation patterns used in Bach's music, especially the cantatas.
26. This function of the slur was recognized as early as 1925 by Schenker (1925–30, 1:43–60, especially 54).
27. Emanuel Bach (1753–62, i.3.18) refines this prescription, indicating the holding down only of notes that belong to one harmony.
28. Such slurs in some editions of English Suite no. 2 are a misreading (see chap. 10).
29. *Parthenia or the Maydenhead of the first musicke that ever was printed for the Virginalls* (London, c1612; facsimile, New York: Broude Brothers, 1972).
30. Emery (1953, 7) warns against relying on transcriptions when there is doubt as to the reading of a sign.
31. See, for example, the first two *couplets* of Couperin's *Les Moissoneurs* (*Second Livre*, Paris, ca. 1717), where the sign for the *unison* dictates "pre-beat" performance of the little note.
32. See the discussion in chapter 17 (Example 17.4). Neumann's (1978) argument for off-beat performance of many appoggiaturas in Bach depends on subjective arguments, e.g., that on-beat performance of certain appoggiaturas can "disturb the unity of rhythm" (147). The evidence presented by Jones (1991b, 607) for Bach's renotation of appoggiaturas in WTC2 (see Example 12.1) supports the present view.
33. See Williams (1990, 43) on a passage in the sarabande of Partita no. 6, where he assumes, probably correctly, the use of a "short" appoggiatura. Emanuel Bach is speaking of the long appoggiatura when he objects to appoggiaturas that "corrupt the purity of the voice leading" (1753–62, i.2.2.17).
34. For a succinct summary of Quantz's system, see Oleskiewicz (2004).
35. As early as the preface to his *Capricci* of 1624, Frescobaldi had made it clear that tempos were not determined by strict proportions.

Notes for Chapter 3

1. See Yearsley (2002, 232–3), citing Forkel and Alfred Burgartz, "Der preussische Stil in der Musik," *Die Musik* 26 (1931): 721–3.
2. "Die Schöpfung einer Ordnungswelt, die keiner romantischen Beseelung oder gefühlshaften Vermenschlichung noch bedarf" (Gadamer 1946, 15).
3. On various usages of the word *galant*, see Sheldon (1975; 1989–90).
4. The early version, BWV 535a/2, is present in MM in Bach's own hand and must have been written by 1707 or so. Zehnder (1995, repeated in 2001) assigns the revised version to 1709–11, Breig (2001 , 122–3) to a somewhat later period (on the basis of its two-flat key signature). Whatever the date, the denser counterpoint suggests a relatively mature reworking.
5. Many works of the type now known as the prelude and fugue appear in the sources under the heading *praeludium*. But the title "prelude and fugue" or its equivalent does occur in Bach sources and will be retained here for most such pieces.
6. Other composers shared this interest; Böhm's *ouverture* in D major is preserved in ABB, which, like other keyboard sources of the period, also contains direct transcriptions of orchestral works.
7. Forkel (1802, 18/NBR, 437) noted how few musicians of his own time understood the distinction between organ and "clavier" touch.
8. The letter, written January 13, 1775, to Forkel, was the chief basis for the latter's account of Bach's early development (Forkel 1802, 5–6); see BD 3:288–90 (item 803)/NBR, 398–400.
9. Suites in which the similarities between movements are limited to thematic material are sometimes considered variation-suites (e.g., in Godt 1990). Here the term will be used only where at least one movement is a full-fledged variation of another.
10. Edited in Hill (1991) as a work of Reinken's, and previously as a work of Böhm on the basis of an attribution added by Johann Christoph Bach to a copy in another hand in MM (no. 20). In fact Böhm may have never used this technique. Another suite, also once published as a work of Böhm, was left anonymous in MM (no. 14). Howard Schott included it as Suite no. 29 in his edition of Froberger's keyboard works (Paris: Heugel, 1989), but that attribution

is even less likely; an identification of the work as Froberger's "Wasserfall" suite (described by Mattheson) is contradicted by the discovery reported by Wollny (2003, 106–7). Hence there is no evidence that Bach knew, even anonymously, any variation-suites by the most important early proponent of the genre in Germany.

11. The French word *ouverture* (italicized) will be used here for keyboard suites in orchestral style; see chap. 4.

12. The autograph of the organ fugue BWV 535a/2, a very accomplished but somewhat archaic piece, can be dated to the end of the Arnstadt period (see Hill 1987, 4–5; 101; 132); the concerto transcriptions have been placed around 1713 (Schulze 1984a, 146–72).

13. Episodes in the form of short bridges connecting statements of the subject of course occur in earlier works, but in this book the term "episode" will be limited to longer, more distinctly articulated passages.

14. See Schulze (1984a, 18n.) and Stauffer (1993). The English Suites also suggest influences from within Germany, including suites by Mattheson and by J. C. F. Fischer. Two movements from the latter's *Pièces de clavecin*, published in 1696, appear near the end of ABB.

15. Friedemann received his *Clavier-Büchlein* at the age of ten in 1720, the date on its title page, but Forkel (1802, 38/NBR, 453) suggests that Bach's pupils studied for some time prior to receiving any written pieces.

16. But the only mature sonata movement per se for solo keyboard is the third movement (for harpsichord alone) of the Sonata BWV 1019 for violin and obbligato cembalo.

Notes for Chapter 4

1. Individual volumes of the *Neue Bach-Ausgabe* (NBA) are cited by series and volume numbers (roman/arabic, respectively). For editors' names and dates of publication, see the bibliography. "KB" (*kritischer Bericht*) indicates one of the commentary volumes.

2. Ornament tables in both ABB and MM derive indirectly from d'Anglebert's, via tables in other French publications.

3. Material in the first movement of Handel's Suite HWV 453 recurs in the overture to *Agrippina*; material from the Suite HWV 449 in the overture to *Il pastor fido*. The dating of Handel's early keyboard works, as opposed to his operas, is not much more certain than Bach's (see Best 1983). Williams (1989) compares keyboard overtures by the two composers.

4. Hill (1987, 254–5) discusses the possibility. The Pestel and Telemann works are edited in Hill (1991). The Telemann *ouverture*, which includes a colorful polonaise, might be one of the two hundred such works the composer reportedly wrote while working in Poland from 1705 to 1707 or 1708; if so, J. C. Bach would have copied it into ABB soon after its composition. Hill (1991) identifies the composer of the other work as Gottfried Ernst Pestel (1654–1732), following information in Gerber (1790–2). But ABB names him as "J. E. Pestel"; this corresponds with the entry for Johann Ernst Pestel (1659–1740) in Fétis (1878–80, apparently following information given by Mattheson). Both are identified as organists working at Altenburg, a Thuringian city with numerous Bach connections.

5. A flat on a′′ in m. 24 is an addition to the manuscript, presumably due to a misunderstanding of the phrase structure or the harmony; F minor, and therefore ab′′, should not be heard until after the downbeat of m. 25.

6. Compare, e.g., the toccata in the same key (BWV 915), mm. 160–4.

7. Compare m. 15 in the subject of BWV 820 with mm. 50ff. in BWV 822.

8. E.g., the end of Toccata XI in *Il secondo libro di toccate* (1627).

9. The closing echo of mm. 21–4, written out in NBA V/10, is indicated by signs in the manuscript and may have been intended only after the repetition of the entire second half (mm. 9–24). The copyist left out the second beat of m. 19; the emendation in NBA is plausible, but the tenor on the first beat of the measure might have been a misreading by the copyist of tablature letters intended for the treble on the second beat.

10. The barely hidden octaves at the cadences have parallels in the *Air pour les Trompettes* in the Suite BWV 832.

11. The Italian form of the title in BWV 833 may explain the stylistically impossible older attribution to Bernardo Pasquini (see Hill 1985, 250).

12. The work, in Bsa SA 4444, bears an improbable attribution to Froberger; intriguingly entitled "Der Naseweise Orgelprobierer" (The Wise-Guy Organ Tester), it was perhaps part of a tonally organized series of similar pieces bearing descriptive titles (details in Wollny 2003, 101).

13. Hill (1987, 418–20) places BWV 833 earlier than BWV 820. But the latter is among the earlier entries in ABB, and the stylistic differences between the pieces could be due to their belonging to somewhat different types.
14. The same notational quirk occurs in many lute tablatures and older keyboard suites.
15. Measures 21–2 of the courante correspond to mm. 11–3 of the allemande. Similar flexibility with respect to the durations of the ground notes occurs in variation-suites by Froberger, Reinken, and others.
16. Ornaments added in the manuscript but suppressed in the NBA and Hill (1991) strengthen the movement's French character; Example 4.2 shows these in parentheses, although the mordents in mm. 11, 13, and 21 are unidiomatic.
17. See, e.g., the opening aria in *Ne' tuoi lumi, o bella Clori* HWV 133 (1707), or the sequential opening of "Wann ich dich noch einst erblicke" from Keiser's *Janus* (1698), quoted in Harris (2001, 226).
18. Example 4.2 contained several errors in the first edition of this book; they have been corrected here.
19. Item 32/18 in Ruhnke (1984); the attribution to Telemann stems from Danckert (1924 , 122).
20. A fourth copy once owned by Forkel is in PL LZu Ms. Spitta 1752/3.
21. The Brussels manuscript once belonged to Fétis, who believed it autograph; see Dart (1970) and the reply in Dömling and Kohlhase (1971).
22. See ABB (no. 38/3), edited in Hill (1991).
23. The term *Cornet* was sometimes used for a nasal-sounding harpsichord stop (see Koster 1999, 67–9), presumably by analogy to the organ stop of the same name.
24. Triplets like those present here also occur in the trumpet aria of Cantata no. 20, first performed at Leipzig in 1724. There is no reason to "assimilate" the duplets to the triplet rhythm.
25. E.g., in the allemande, the "sighing" fifth in m. 9 and the "obstinate" figure in mm. 18–9.
26. Similar difficulties arise in the fugues BWV 946 (mm. 36–7) and BWV 954 (mm. 28–30, 48), and in BWV 993 (m. 69) when played without pedals.
27. Compare the cadences at the first double bar in the gaillarde in G and the arrangement of Lully's overture to *Cadmus*, both in d'Anglebert's *Pièces de clavecin*.
28. Much the same harmonic progression occurs near the close of the fugue in the Capriccio BWV 992. Stinson (1989a, 123–4) points out further stylistic parallels in the "Neumeister" chorales.
29. Stinson (1990, 24) assigns the copy to Kellner's "3, middle" handwriting phase, dated "after 1727."
30. This version cannot be by Bach, as Kohlhase shows (NBA V/10, KB, 119). Wiemer (1987) reports ornaments in Gerber's copy that suggest he studied the piece under Bach.
31. By Lutz Kirchhof (*J. S. Bach: The Works for Lute in Original Keys and Tunings*, Sony S2K 45858, 1990). Hopkinson Smith had previously found it advisable to record it in F minor (*Johann Sebastian Bach: L'Œuvre de luth*, Astrée E 7721, 1986), and North (1995) declares it to be "clearly keyboard writing and not lute music!"
32. Niedt (1700–17, vol. 2) prescribes such a flourish for the beginning of an improvisation, as does C. P. E. Bach more than half a century later (1753–62, ii.41.14).

Notes for Chapter 5

1. The sole evidence is furnished by the obituary, written partly by Emanuel Bach, and by the latter's letter to Forkel of January 13, 1775 (BD 3:288 [item 803]/NBR, 398–9).
2. Both MM and ABB, which include several of Bach's early clavier fugues, also contain isolated fugues belonging to the north German organ tradition, among them works by Reinken and Heidorn.
3. Corelli also provided material for the organ fugue BWV 579. The fugue of the E-Minor Toccata may also have been based on an Italian work (see chap. 7).
4. BWV 957, a setting of *Machs mit mir Gott, nach deiner Güt*, was included in BG 42 under the title "Fughetta"; it is edited in NBA IV/9 as one of the so-called Neumeister chorales attributed to Bach.
5. NBA IV/9 includes three *manualiter* fugues, BWV Anh. 42, 90, and 97, all regarded here as spurious. Williams 2003 gives convincing evaluations of the first two. The third seems, like Anh. 42, a school fugue from the second half of the eighteenth century, although less skillful.

Its attribution to Bach may be due to its chromatic subject, akin to that of the fugue in E-flat now attributed to the older Johann Christoph Bach (BWV Anh. 177/2).

6. This is especially apparent in some of the early organ fugues, notably BWV 533/2.

7. There would be no point in counting expositions as recapitulations, since the subject itself is continually "recapitulated."

8. MM was lost at the time Naumann prepared BG 36 from the copy by Mey (probably a student of Kellner). Wolffheim (1912) published the prelude as part of an article announcing the rediscovery of MM.

9. Suites, for example, are often headed simply *Prelude* or *Allemande* (referring to the first movement).

10. Dirksen (1998, 134) finds that the subject "seems to be based on" that of the gigue in Reinken's C-major fugue, but the relationship is a family one at best.

11. As in the sixteenth-note motive at the end of the subject (which is the basis of the episode at m. 14), and in the treble in mm. 60–1. Compare Kuhnau's Biblical Sonata No. 1 (David and Goliath), third movement, mm. 8–11, and the opening of the sixth movement (*La gioia degl'Israeliti*).

12. The young Bach seems to have had a greater fascination with "sharp" than with "flat" keys; the only deep plunge into flat areas in Bach's early keyboard works is the excursion in the overture of BWV 822.

13. A passage in the allemande of Corelli's Op. 2, No. 3 prompted a famous controversy over the composer's tolerance of barely hidden fifths. Bach writes similarly in BWV 896/2 (mm. 38–9), 954 (m. 19), and 951a (mm.20–1).

14. Presumably Carlo Francesco Pollarolo (1653–1722). As Silbiger (1987, x) points out, the capricci in ABB are stylistically distinct from the more fluent pieces attributable to this composer in Bologna, Civico Museo Bibliografico Musicale MS DD/53 (facsimile in Silbiger 1987). Pollarolo's operas were, however, known in Hamburg (see Roberts 1986, xi), and perhaps Bach obtained the pieces during his student years at Lüneburg.

15. Preller's copy (P 1087) has a pedal marking for the last bass entry (m. 112). P 409, by an unidentified copyist, has pedal markings in mm. 67 and 121; only the last is likely to be authentic.

16. In P 247 this is part of a passage whose bass is assigned to the pedals (pedal markings appear in mm. 27, 40, and 48). Most of the ornaments, including the appoggiatura in m. 2 of the subject, occur only in copies of the later version.

17. It is possible that *di Erselio* is in the hand of the main copyist, but like other attributions in this manuscript it was added after the original entry of the title. The words *Organist in Freiberg* in the same heading are an even later entry by Georg Poelchau (see Heller 1995, 131).

18. The reference in Schmieder (1990) to a copy in the "Neumeister" codex at Yale (LM 4708) is erroneous. The copy of BWV 954 in P 804 is on different paper from that used for the copies of BWV 965 and 966.

19. Through a misunderstanding, the BG named the source as "Sonata VI." For more on Reinken's originals, see chap. 6. ABB contains a fugue by Peter Heidorn (edited in Hill 1991) on a similar subject, said to be Reinken's but unidentified.

20. Something similar happens in mm. 49–50 of the B-minor "Albinoni" fugue, but only in the revised version BWV 951; could BWV 954 have undergone a comparable revision that left no traces?

21. Hill (1987, 444–46) argues that BWV 949 is also derived from an Albinoni trio-sonata (op. 1, no. 7), but the fleeting resemblances are not conclusive. Albinoni's fugues often employ similar subjects; another trio-sonata fugue by Albinoni (*So* 21 in Talbot 1990, 280; ed. F. Polnauer [Bryn Mawr, PA: Presser, 1977]) has a subject like that of BWV 946. Bach may not have been the only German composer to borrow from Albinoni; the theme in the fugal ritornello of the Concerto BWV 985, Bach's keyboard arrangement of a work by Telemann, resembles that of the fugue in Albinoni's op. 1, no. 11.

22. Talbot (1995, 142) reports first identifying the model in his 1968 dissertation.

23. From the second movement of Albinoni's op. 1, no. 3.

24. The middle voice in mm. 24, 44, etc., comes from m. 8 of Albinoni's first violin part. Also borrowed is the motive in mm. 32–3 (treble), heard earlier in m. 5 (middle voice) and in m. 13 of Albinoni's first violin part.

25. Kellner's version is edited in NBA V/9.2, KB, pp. 339–43; Stinson (1989a, 57–8) gives a facsimile and dates the copy "before 1725?"

26. Kellner provides sharps in mm. 21, 23, 25, and 32, the last of which is confirmed by the parallel passage in the Albinoni model (second movement, m. 26).

27. The model was the second movement of Albinoni's op. 1, no. 8.

28. The only other early fugue usually thought to have undergone as radical an overhaul is the organ fugue in D, BWV 532/2. Williams (2003, 44–5) finds the shorter version (BWV 532a) "unlikely to be authentic," but, as in the somewhat comparable case of the fugue in the toccata BWV 914, one must wonder why, if BWV 532a is a later abbreviation, the editor also altered many passages, including the subject, in a stylistically consistent way.

29. One copy containing both versions, AmB 606, was presumably made for Kirnberger, who was also aware of the existence of different versions of pieces in the *Well-Tempered Clavier*.

30. Hill (1987, 432–3) reproduces a fantasia in B minor that is paired with BWV 951a in the copy at Durham Cathedral. The fantasia, in the style of a late seventeenth-century violin piece, is not unskillful, but its conventional harmony and simple texture (usually one moving part with simple two-part accompaniment) are uncharacteristic even of Bach's early works, unless the A-minor fugue BWV 947 is his.

31. Titles in P 801 and ms. 8 specify *Clavicembalum*. Other relatively early fugues designated as harpsichord pieces in dependable copies include BWV 894, 903, and 944, all discussed in chap. 9. Preller's copy, unusual for him, transmits the text without added fingerings and ornaments.

32. The other work is the very early organ fantasia BWV 563.

33. Corelli's op. 3, no. 4, was published in 1689, five years before Albinoni's op. 1, no. 8.

34. Example 5.3b shows the ending of BWV 951a as preserved in a group of later sources. Two earlier copyists, including Johann Christoph Bach, gave an alternate ending that is a measure longer; although the NBA regards this as the original, it could equally well be later. Five manuscripts substitute B for D# in m. 87, perhaps to accommodate instruments with a short octave (without D#). The latter note is also missing in the longer version, which may represent a more artistic solution to the problem of the short octave. In BWV 951, Bach reverted to the rhythm of the more forceful shorter ending; he also preserved Albinoni's ascent to high b′′ just before the final cadence, which now falls properly on the downbeat.

35. Practically the same passage occurs in BWV 954 (m. 11).

36. Measures 93–5 correspond with mm. 29–31. For the latter, BWV 951a gives a diminished chord, which is less compelling than the Neapolitan of BWV 951.

37. The superficially akin Allabreve BWV 589 is a very different sort of piece, clearly requiring pedals and probably much later in date, although also likely composed as retrospective stylistic "research."

Notes for Chapter 6

1. Dürr (1986a) and Williams (2003, 541–5) offer sensible reservations with respect to Bach's authorship of the pieces copied by Neumeister.

2. Number 41, edited in Schneider (2002, 127); its clumsiness makes it unlikely that Bach wrote it. Buxtehude, Flor, and others composed more competent pieces of this type.

3. This holds for both the well-authenticated partitas of BWV 766–8 and 770 and the shakily attributed BWV 771, as well as three more doubtful works edited in NBA IV/11. Of the latter, BWV Anh. 77 and 78 are stylistically plausible and occasionally inventive; e.g., *vers* 4 of Anh. 78 is a chromatic *bicinium*, alluding in a quirky way to two rarely combined seventeenth-century types. Williams (2003) provides detailed coverage of these and other chorale works.

4. Compare Forkel (1802, 23/NBR, 441) on those whom Bach (according to Forkel) called "clavier hussars."

5. The alternate title "Fantasia" in BG 36 was evidently editorial.

6. The use of a short octave is unlikely due to the presence of F# as well as D in the piece.

7. The same one observed in the suite BWV 821; see Stinson (1989a, 123).

8. Compare the *batteries* at the opening of BWV 922 with those at the close of BWV 921, and the *perfidiae* of both pieces (BWV 922: mm. 14–31; BWV 921: mm. 8–26).

9. Compare mm. 96ff. with BWV 533/1, mm. 20ff. BWV 533a is a *manualiter* version of the better-known BWV 533; accepted in the first edition of this book as a possible early "clavier" work, BWV 533a is as likely to be a later simplification (see Williams 2003, 47–8).

10. Krebs treated the two title words in the same way in his copy of the Chromatic Fantasia and Fugue BWV 903, also in P 803.

11. Could the introduction have suggested the similar threefold opening of the doubtful toccata and fugue in D minor BWV 565?

12. The term *figura corta* (plural *figure corte*) is used here for motives consisting of two sixteenths and an eighth.

13. The titles of both pieces are quoted here from Johann Christoph Bach's copies; BWV 574 appears in ABB.

14. It is therefore unlikely that BWV 895 ever belonged together with the preludes and fugues BWV 870a, 899, 900, 901, 902, as suggested by Dehnhard (1973, vi), even though the tonic A of BWV 895 would complete a hexachord begun by the five others (which are in C, d, e, F, and G, respectively).

15. The tuning instructions are from Werckmeister's *Die notwendigsten Anmerckungen und Regeln wie der Bassus continuus, oder General-Bass wohl könne tractiret werden* (Aschersleben, 1698); edition, translation, and commentary in Barte (1995, 226ff.).

16. Williams (1980–84, 3:101) finds stylistic parallels in the opening chorus of the Weimar cantata BWV 61.

17. Compare the choral entrance "Ich harre des Herrn" on an E♭-major chord after the preceding duet has ended on G, in BWV 131. Kuhnau, in his preface to a set of cantata libretti published in 1710, recommends the use of "a new key [*tonus*]" where the text contains a *conjunctio adversativa* such as "but" (*sondern*; see Richter 1902, 152).

18. The word *thema* is apparently a synonym for *fuga*, as in the D-minor toccata (see Edler 1995, 92); the plural (*themata*) would be necessary if the word "theme" was here equivalent to "subject," but the two birds are imitated by distinct subjects.

19. Poglietti's *Compendium oder kurtzer Begriff, und Einführung zur Musica* (ms. dated 1676) includes examples of short fugues based on various birdsongs and other extra-musical references; see Federhofer (1958, 267).

20. The *Ursprung der musicalisch-Bachischen Familie* (BD 1:255–61 [item 184]/NBR, 283–94) describes Jacob as an oboist. But he also studied flute with Buffardin, according to a later entry by C. P. E. Bach, and the term could be applied to players of various instruments (see Protz 1957, 407n.). Hill (1991, xxiii) considers BWV 992 "one of the first copies" entered into MM, the "likeliest date of composition" being "the end of 1703."

21. Autobiographical pieces by Baroque composers are rare; Bach might have known of several by Froberger (see Wollny 2003 for a recently identified example).

22. The additional heading *Arioso* is a later addition in MM, according to NBA V/10, KB.

23. Opus 1, no. 12 (mvt. 1, m. 18).

24. The indication *adagio poco* in the BG derives from late sources and is erroneous.

25. Albinoni's op. 1, no. 12, also opens with a downward octave leap.

26. The correct title is *Fuga all'imitazione di posta* (given wrongly in BG). I have not found a documented military trumpet signal particularly close to the subject.

27. Walker (1989, 23) distinguishes between the true "permutation fugue" and the "strict double fugue" found in Reinken's *Hortus musicus*.

28. The most thorough investigation (Beißwenger 1992a) places the copy of BWV 965 most likely between 1714 and 1717—which would not rule out composition at an earlier date. Heller (2002, 323–3) reviews the dating history of these pieces.

29. A few traces of an earlier version survive in the Łodz source, especially a simpler reading for the countersubject (fugue, m. 5, sop.) whose echoes persist in mm. 9 and 14. I am grateful to Christoph Wolff for making his microfilm copy of this source available to me.

30. Example 6.2 follows the original notation of the courante in measures of six beats; a superfluous sharp in the bass figuration for the first note of the example is omitted.

31. The gamba part, although notated separately from the continuo, only rarely functions as an independent fourth voice.

32. Compare mm. 64–5 of the fugue with mm. 41–2 in the third movement of BWV 1043. An even closer parallel occurs in the "Dorian" toccata for organ, BWV 538/1 (mm. 21–2), which contains an important parallel with BWV 966 as well (see below).

33. The courante in this particular set is a new piece, not a variation of the allemande.

34. The same progression occurs in the organ concerto BWV 595, m. 33 (this measure not present in the *manualiter* version of the same movement, BWV 984).

35. But conceivably by Bach's older brother, as suggested by Schulze (1985, 77–8) and affirmed by Melamed (1999), or by one of the other members of the family bearing the same name.

The title *Aria variata*, given to this anonymous work in the modern edition by Peter Dirksen (*Johann Christoph Bach (1642–1703): Werke für Clavier*, Wiesbaden: Breitkopf und Härtel, 2002), is absent from the piece's only source. But the words *Aria... variata* appear in the original title of the *Aria Eberliniana*, which is very similar and hence likely by the same composer.

36. Williams (1999, 197–8) suggests that the presence of tempo markings—implying a different speed for each variation—would have seemed a significant Italianism when the piece was new.

37. Hill (1987, 368–71) argues that the Krebs/Kellner version is earlier, but see below. The NBA presents the theme twice, based on the copies by Krebs and J. C. Bach, respectively.

38. Williams (2003, 579) notes the presence of the rubric *la prima alla maniera* in versus 1 of the doubtful chorale variations BWV Anh. 77, copied by Krebs, suggesting that Krebs meant "in the Italian manner." But there Krebs may have been indicating performance on two manuals, as suggested also by the texture (ornamented melody for the right hand accompanied by two parts in the left hand) and the presence of dynamic indications within the right hand part.

39. Krebs omits variation 9, and Kellner omits both variations 8 and 9, placing variation 10 after variation 4.

40. E.g., how to connect back to m. 5 when taking the second repeat in variation 9; the first ending shown in BG 36 is an editorial conjecture.

41. Similar notation occurs, in a somewhat similar context, in the ABB copy (no. 22) of a toccata by Pachelbel. See also the discussion of BWV 806a in chap. 13.

Notes for Chapter 7

1. B Br 4093, a somewhat mysterious mid-eighteenth-century collection of some of Bach's most important early keyboard works (see NBA V/9.1, KB, 15–6), contains all seven toccatas (BWV 916 in G appears under the title *Partita*). LEm ms. 8 contains four toccatas, but only two of these, BWV 910 and 913, are in the same hand and on the same paper.

2. It is not certain which Gerber, father or son, copied the lost Gerber manuscript of BWV 916. Wollny (2002, 249) points out that the watermark of H. N. Gerber's copy of BWV 914 implies that it was *not* made during the latter's Leipzig studies with Bach.

3. Dirksen (1998, 135) points to the presence of recitative-like passages in the D-major and E-minor toccatas as evidence for a special relationship between them and a doubtful toccata in A (BWV Anh. 178). But all seven of Bach's firmly attributed toccatas include at least short passages that could be characterized as resembling recitative.

4. Landowska (1924, 131) provided her own de-embellished version of the adagio of the Italian Concerto for study, but it is better for pupils to begin with an example by Bach himself.

5. The BG divided the toccatas between vols. 3 and 36. Other recent editions are by Tamás Zászkalicky (Budapest: Könemann, 1998) and Christian Eisert (Vienna: Wiener Urtext, 2000), the latter based on a textual study (Eisert 1994). Earlier editions by Heinz Lohmann (in his complete edition of the organ works, Wiesbaden: Breitkopf und Härtel, 1968–79) and Rudolf Steglich (Munich: Henle, 1962) did not include a thorough evaluation of all sources.

6. Hill (1987, 624) places all three toccatas within the last of three "phases" in the compilation of ABB.

7. The relationship of the Brussels source to Bach remains unknown, and its order for the remaining toccatas appears to be arbitrary.

8. The flourish is one of three passages shown in footnotes in NBA V/9.1, from a group of sources emanating from Bach's Weimar circle. Even if Bach's, these readings look like later rationalizations of the *stylus fantasticus*, which would have seemed increasingly foreign to later musicians: mm. 51–2 were made to coincide exactly with m. 96, and the flourish after m. 107 "explains" the latter's chromatic embellishment of the fifth scale degree, a seventeenth-century mannerism. The flourish is less incongruous tonally if one adds sharps on d´´, a´, and a.

9. Although Bach did not know Keiser personally (according to C. P. E. Bach, BD 3:289 [item 803]/NBR, 400), he might have heard such pieces during his Lüneburg years. Cf. the overtures to Keiser's *Adonis* and *Janus*, both in *Handel Sources*, vol. 1 (New York: Garland, 1986).

10. Compare mm. 138b–39 with mm. 13–5 of the cantata chorus. Bach later used essentially the same bass in the opening movement of Cantata no. 78, in which the ostinato line is treated much as a fugue subject, migrating into the upper parts and even undergoing inversion.

Krummacher (1991, 191–2) makes a further connection between the closing movement of the cantata and Buxtehude's D-Minor Passacaglia BuxWV 161, which likewise contains a modulating ostinato.

11. Similar formulas recur later in the Chromatic Fantasia (mm. 63–4) and even the toccata of the E-Minor Partita.

12. Compare mm. 12–5 of BWV 532/1 with mm. 78–80 in BWV 912. The fugue of BWV 532 includes at its center entries in F♯ minor and C♯ minor (mm. 64b, 80).

13. Similar figures occur in three of the four movements of an anonymous D-minor suite (no. 20 in MM; see chap. 3, note 10), serving there as in BWV 912 as a unifying motif.

14. The idea that the ties are somehow related to an original assignment of the piece to organ is unconvincing, for they are a basic element of the so-called *brisé* style associated with lute and harpsichord. But the possibility that they were deliberately removed cannot be dismissed; comparable figures occur in BWV 913 (mm. 7, 29–30, 117–8) without ties in any sources.

15. An additional motivic link between the various improvisatory sections is the descending-sixth "sigh," used in E minor in both the first bridge (mm. 71–3) and the second (mm. 116–7).

16. Quantz (1752, 9.2–4) would later proscribe trills in thirds, "except, perhaps, upon the bagpipe."

17. The voice crossing is overlooked in the NBA. For corrected readings for the edition of BWV 912a in Hill (1991), see Schulenberg (1994).

18. The title, *In honorem delect[issimi] fratris Christ. Bachii*, was reported in an announcement of the first edition (see NBA V/9.1, KB, 78).

19. Compare mm. 13–14 with BWV 989, variation 9, m. 7.

20. Compare mm. 291–3 (Example 7.2) with BWV 965, allemande, mm. 24b–26. In revising the toccata, Bach varied the original bass in much the same way he had embellished Reinken's, converting stepwise eighths to arpeggiation in sixteenths (cf. Example 6.3).

21. The Brussels manuscript labels the section *un poco presto*, a credible early reading given the frequent use of *presto* (rather than *allegro*) in tempo marks from before the second decade of the eighteenth century.

22. Compare mm. 63–8 with BWV 922, mm. 14–30.

23. Pestelli (1981) gives a legible facsimile of the fugue as it appears in Naples, Biblioteca del Conservatorio, Ms. 5327, fols. 46v–49r; Eisert 1994 includes an edition of this fugue, attributed to Marcello.

24. The short version of the fugue has never been printed in integral form and is disregarded in NBA V/9.1, making comparison of the two versions difficult; BG 36 reported only selective variants. The sources for the shorter version are late and clearly erroneous in some details, but substantial, musically plausible variants in mm. 117–8, 123, and 130 cannot be rejected outright. Parallels to the Italian fugue in mm. 82, 87–9, 107, 111b–114, and 133ff. imply that Bach reworked some of the material that the two pieces have in common.

25. Nineteenth-century editors knew two other manuscripts, now lost.

26. A parallel occurs in the praeludium and capriccio that open Buttstett's *Musicalische Clavier-Kunst* of 1713; both movements end with the same ten measures and were perhaps conceived as forming a single work.

27. Wollny (2002, 252–3) suggests of the fugue of BWV 915 that "for long stretches it is nearly a permutation fugue." But, to follow Walker's distinction between permutation fugues and strict double fugues, this is an example of the latter (see chap. 6, note 27).

28. The dotted notation of the subject is presumably to be "assimilated" to the triplets of the countersubject.

29. It would have been possible to state the upright and inverted versions of the subject simultaneously, as Bach would do in WTC1 at the close of the fugue in D♯ minor.

30. Compare mm. 158–60 with 91–3. Harrison (1990) analyzes the fugue as a musical equivalent of the "rhetoric of persuasion."

31. A copy in US NHy LM 5025 has pedal indications in the "tutti" sections despite the presence of the word *manualiter* on the title page.

32. E.g., trill on b′ (16th) in m. 57. NBA V/9.1 prints both Preller's and Christoph Bach's versions as appendices, including as well the latter's ornamented version of the third movement.

33. Williams (1980–4, 3:236–41) discusses further examples of such endings.

Notes for Chapter 8

1. The duchy of Weimar was shared during this period by two co-reigning dukes, Wilhelm Ernst and his nephew Ernst August; Johann Ernst was the younger half-brother of the latter.

2. A distinction is sometimes drawn between the terms "arrangement" and "transcription," the latter implying something closer to a verbatim copy or reduction of the original. No such distinction will be made here, since the lines are too hard to draw; for example, some of the works in question would have to be considered arrangements in one movement, transcriptions in another.

3. "[L]ehrte ihn [Bach] musikalisch denken" (Forkel, 1802, 24/NBR, 442); Wolff (1988c) singles out this phrase and interprets it in terms of the "Ordnung, Zusammenhang, and Verhältnis" that, according to Forkel, Bach found in Vivaldi's music.

4. Forkel (1802, 24/NBR, 441) says that Bach transcribed "all" of Vivaldi's concertos, but this probably means only those "which were then just published," that is, Vivaldi's op. 3. Forkel apparently did not know that Bach had arranged works by composers other than Vivaldi, nor does he seem to have had access to the transcriptions themselves, for otherwise he would not have mistaken the solo part of Bach's own D-major harpsichord concerto (BWV 1054) for one of the transcriptions (see Schulze 1984a, 146–7).

5. Hill (1987, 255) noting the existence of other transcriptions in ABB, questions the need for invoking an Amsterdam practice as an influence on Bach (see Schulze 1984a, 155–6).

6. See Butler (2003) on later concerto arrangements by Scheibe and Gerber, as well as Stinson's (1992) edition of transcriptions by Scheibe and others of works by Vivaldi, Telemann, and Tartini.

7. Particularly problematic are BWV 983, which is anonymous in its earliest source (P 804/35), and BWV 592a, found only in one late manuscript that also happens to be the only other source for BWV 983. No fewer than nine of the *manualiter* transcriptions are *unica*.

8. P 280, Bernhard Bach's copy, includes as a twelfth piece the organ transcription BWV 592. The title page (facsimile in Schulze 1984a, 197), declaring all twelve originals to be Vivaldi's, is in the hand of Bernhard's son Johann Ernst, who studied with Sebastian beginning in 1737. Although seemingly dependable, this source contains a number of doubtful readings (notably in BWV 977; see Example 8.5). These might reflect Bernhard Bach's uncertainties in copying from a not always legible autograph draft.

9. For Walther, see the editions by Max Seiffert (DDT, 26–7 [Leipzig, 1906]) and Tamás Zász-kaliczky (Budapest: Editio Musica, 1976). One reason for supposing that his arrangements preceded Bach's are the relatively early dates of the composers whose works Walther transcribed.

10. The NBA text requires emendations, e.g., read e♭′ (for e♮′?) in BWV 982, mvt. 2, m. 4, 2d beat, and similarly in mm. 28 and 30; d♯′ (for b♮?) in BWV 987, mvt. 1, m. 29. The consecutive octaves in BWV 982, mvt. 3, mm. 74–5, and the parallel fifths in BWV 981, mvt. 4, mm. 26–7 are in the source, but the direct fifths in BWV 972a, mvt. 1, m. 27, must reflect an error (read b′ for a′ on beat 2?). Those in m. 15 of the same movement are less objectionable; arising through the embellishment of Vivaldi's bass line, they are absent from the familiar version.

11. Bach did rewrite a solo passage employing repeated notes in BWV 978 (third movement, mm. 56–9) and a short phrase for the tutti in BWV 985 (third movement, mm. 15–16a).

12. The device was sometimes used by strings in conjunction with or in imitation of the organ tremulant (see Carter 1991). It involves no cessation of sound and is thus distinct from modern portato (or, as it is often called, portamento).

13. E.g., in BWV 972 (mvt. 1, mm. 42ff..), 976 (mvt. 1, mm. 50ff.), and 981 (mvt. 3, mm. 37ff.., and mvt. 4, mm. 41ff.).

14. See, e.g., BWV 975 (mvt. 1, mm. 23–30), 976 (mvt. 2, mm. 9, 15, etc.), 981 (mvt. 3, m. 10), 982 (mvt. 1, m. 53), and 592a (mvt. 1, m. 91). The examples in BWV 976 and 981 result from verbatim copying of the originals.

15. E.g., the flying octaves of BWV 982 (mvt. 1, mm. 76–8) and the rapid arpeggiation in BWV 980 (mvt. 2, mm. 13ff.), taken unaltered from the original.

16. The note d‴ occurs in BWV 974 (mvt. 3, m. 49) and 975 (mvt. 1, m. 50). Only one of three sources has the note in BWV 974, but in BWV 975 it is preceded by c♯‴, so d″ cannot be

considered "isolated" (Marshall 1986, 231–2). Low BB occurs in BWV 979 (several times), low BB♭ in BWV 982.

17. In BWV 973 (mvt. 1, m. 25) and 980 (mvt. 1, m. 31) the transcription fails to ascend to d‴ where the latter would correspond with the original. In BWV 975, the note d‴ is not "avoided" (Marshall 1986, 231–2); it simply happens to occur only once.

18   The organ concerto BWV 595 also uses manual alternations within the opening ritornello; since the original has not been found, it is impossible to say whether these corresponded with solo/tutti alternations.

19. See, e.g., BWV 972 (mvt. 3, mm. 57–8 and 73–4). Here and elsewhere the breaking of six-teenth-note beams in BG 42 was editorial, although Bach is known to have used this notation in later works where changes of manual occur (e.g., in the *Clavierübung*).

20. That Bach cultivated such a technique is apparent from a comparable passage in the B-Minor Sinfonia BWV 801, which was surely intended for a single keyboard; see chap. 10.

21. Compare mm. 35–37a here with mm. 65ff. in the first movement of BWV 809.

22. See mvt. 1, mm. 14–5 and 20–4, and mvt. 3, m. 95. Also earlier is the simpler notation of the accompaniment in mvt. 1, mm. 15–6 and 24, and mvt. 2, mm. 20 and 27.

23. For instance, the simplistic tenor part in mvt. 1, mm. 1–3, or the evident error of c♯‴ for a′ in mvt. 1, m. 49, might have arisen through misreading of a cramped autograph.

24. This assumes that the otherwise undocumented version of the concerto arranged by Bach had the same scoring and dynamics as the one published in op. 4. The BG inserted editorial "tutti" and "solo" indications but omitted a "solo" indication at m. 23, perhaps because the latter is a solo passage *within* the ritornello.

25. So-called varied reprises are now associated with C. P. E. Bach, but they also occur in the Triple Concerto BWV 1044 and in the *Jigg* of an early Handel suite (HWV 438). On the *doubles* and *agrémens* in the English Suites, see chap. 13.

26. Compare first movement, mm. 45b–51a, and third movement, mm. 88–103.

27. The title in P 280 is *La Stravaganza Op. IV. Concerto I. pag. 2. trasposto da b. in g.* (NBA V/11, KB, 29).

28. Ryom (1986, 473) reports that the theme recurs in an aria in Vivaldi's opera *Orlando finto pazzo* (1714).

29. Mey could have been a student of Kellner; see Stinson (1989a, 31).

30. A transposition downward by a third (as in BWV 976) is not impossible but would place the original adagio in C♯ minor, ending with a quite unusual chord of G♯ major.

31. A similar melodic line occurs in the *fantasia* movement of Bonporti's Invention op. 10, no. 5, published in 1712; a copy annotated by Bach dates from around 1723 (NBA IX/2, 214).

32. Example 8.5 follows P 804 except as follows: in mm. 30b through first beat of 32, the treble in P 804 reads a third higher; in m. 32, the tenor in P 804 reads c′–f′–f′–f′–c′. The text in BG 42 is that of P 280 with the addition of a flat on tenor e′ in m. 31. NBA follows BG 42 but without the latter's sharp on f′ in m. 32.

33. SW Mus. ms. 3530 identifies the composer as "Marcello"; errors in the manuscript suggest that the transposition to C was the copyist's work, as Manfred Fechner argues in his edition (Leipzig: Peters, 1977). The C-minor version is item Z799 in Selfridge-Field's (1990) catalog of the works of the Marcello brothers; the published version in D minor is D935. The concerto is cited in *Anonimo veneziano* (Milan: Rizzoli, 1971), a "testo drammatico" by Giuseppe Berto that served as the basis of a film by Enrico Maria Salerno (1970).

34. In m. 49, DS 66 gives the last two notes as b″–a″, corresponding to the printed edition of the concerto. That Bach later altered the passage is suggested by the apparent misreading a″–f″ in P 804.

35. The athletic left-hand part in mvt. 2, mm. 16–8, could be a product of revision, or else was later simplified; Heller shows the alternate versions (NBA V/11, KB, 103–4) but leaves open the possibility that the differences are due to Walther, not Bach.

36. A reconstruction of the original solo concerto, by Ettore Bonelli (Padua: Zanibon, 1964), disregards Bach's version and adds anachronistic performance markings, including a "realiza-tion of the double bass and Cymbals [*sic*]."

37. See NBA V/11, KB, 100, where both fragments are edited, and cf. the flourish after m. 107 in J. L. Krebs's copy of the F♯-minor Toccata (shown in NBA V/6.2, p. 9fn.).

38. A copy in Lund (Sweden) attributes the work to Vivaldi, but a manuscript from the Este collection (now in A Wn according to Ryom 1969, 82) assigns it to Torelli; see Haas (1927,

entry 143a). Both copies call for five ripieno string parts (including two violas), a sign of an early date.

39. The second of these passages is marked *andante* in BWV 979, perhaps a deliberate alteration by Bach.

40. Walther began teaching the Prince in 1707 and continued when the latter returned from his university studies in 1713.

41. On Frederick's affinity for mournful adagios, see Oleskiewicz (1999, 89).

42. "[E]in verschwiegener Gruss in die Ewigkeit" (Schering 1902–3, 241).

43. See the edition by Siegfried Kross in *Georg Philipp Telemann: Musikalische Werke*, vol. 23 (Kassel: Bärenreiter, 1973). The work is designated TWV 51:g21.

44. Opus 1, no. 11 (ed. Walter Kolneder, Mainz: Schott, 1959), second movement.

45. Williams (1984) argues that BWV 1029 originated as a concerto.

46. Bach omits most of the slurs and the bass figures, but these might have been absent from the early version of Telemann's score.

47. For a substantial quotation from the allegro as published in the Prince's op. 1, see Schering (1903–4, 567). I am grateful to Joshua Rifkin for sharing copies of both the print and the manuscript parts for the original concerto in ROu Mus. ms. saec. xvii.18 51.39a; the latter include a second solo violin part.

48. Bach transcribed R. 208a for organ as BWV 594. Similar themes occur in the third movement of a concerto that Walther wrongly attributed to Meck, and in the first movement of a *Concerto e Fuga* (BWV 909) bearing a spurious attribution to Bach (ed. in BG 42).

49. Compare the cadential formula in mm. 50–1 (also found in BWV 983, mvt. 2, mm. 7–9), with BWV 808, mvt. 1, mm. 31–3. The texture and material in mm. 52–4 and elsewhere are also reminiscent of the suite movement.

50. BWV 595 repeats, perhaps unnecessarily, the statements of the ritornello theme in C (mm. 1, 7b), G (9b, 16), E minor (25, 31b), and D minor (33b, 50). The modulation between the two last keys includes a jarring juxtaposition of the chords of B major (e:V) and G minor (d: iv) about which Bach may have had second thoughts, even if today "one might rather find this the highlight of the movement (Williams 2003, 219–20).

51. But Vivaldi's op. 3, no. 12 (= BWV 976) also has an imitative slow movement, and there is an *Ecco* movement composed of continuous forte/piano alterations in Bonporti's op. 10, no. 10 (not one of the pieces copied in P 270).

Notes for Chapter 9

1. Theodor Leberecht Pitschel (1716–43), in NBR, 333–4.

2. Marchand failed to show up; see the accounts of Birnbaum (NBR, 79) and Forkel (1802, 7–8/NBR, 427–8).

3. On the doubtful fantasias and fugues BWV 905, 907, and 908, see Appendix A.

4. Another piece quite similar to the fantasia of BWV 904 is BWV 539/1, a short *manualiter* prelude in D minor paired in a few sources with the organ arrangement of the fugue of the violin sonata BWV 1001. Bach's responsibility for both movements (and their pairing) has been questioned and stylistic weaknesses in both pointed out (e.g., by Williams 2003, 72). Despite its faulty formal proportions, BWV 539/1 contains so many Bach fingerprints (the ingenious voice leading of mm. 11–2, the cadence formula used in mm. 23 and 43, the climactic scale descending through an octave and a half just before the end) that it is hard not to see it as Bach's own preliminary version of BWV 904/1. Lacking an unattached *manualiter* fugue in D minor (other than the doubtful BWV 948), harpsichordists must leave it for organists.

5. The manuscript P 320, previously ascribed to Kittel, is now thought to be by his pupil Gebhardi, working from his teacher's copy (NBA V/9.2, 181).

6. See fantasia, mm. 87–8, 92–4; fugue, mm. 16, 26–32.

7. E.g., the outer movements of BWV 1046a (the early version of the First Brandenburg Concerto) and the preludes of English Suites nos. 3 and 5.

8. At m. 53, in the middle section, the treble has the inversion of the opening motive of the principal subject. But this leads to nothing and has no significance in the overall design.

9. The second subject also has its own sharply contrasting countersubject, an arpeggiated idea; the combination of the two at m. 41 is reminiscent of the third episode of the fantasia (mm. 81ff.).

10. For further discussion, see the end of this chapter. Liszt realized the prelude in a Romantic version of Baroque style.

11. Keller (1950, 82) thought that the subject resembled that of the first allegro of the Torelli work transcribed as Concerto No. 8 (BWV 979), but the running sixteenths of that theme are mostly Bach's, not Torelli's.

12. BWV 1044 adds orchestral ritornellos at the beginning and end of each movement and inserts other ritornellos as well. This accords with mid-eigtheenth-century views of concerto form (see Stevens 1971, 89), but it ignores the ritornello structure already built into the prelude. Also atypical of Bach is the extended keyboard range (to f''''), which points to a late date. For arguments on both sides, see NBA VII/3, KB, 47–8.

13. See m. 53b in BWV 894/1, m. 109 in the first movement of BWV 1052.

14. The arranger of BWV 1044 must have been conscious of the underlying progression, for the new ritornello composed for the last movement is based on a harmonic reduction of the original fugue subject.

15. See m. 90. At the corresponding point in the concerto (mvt. 3, m. 120) there is a ritornello—the only substantial ritornello in this movement apart from those added at beginning and end.

16. Compare mm. 84–5 of the fugue with m. 22 of the prelude, and the bass in m. 133 of the fugue with m. 10 of the prelude.

17. First adequately described by Lee (1988), C. P. E. Bach's Fantasia in E♭ (H. 348) has finally been edited in CPEBCW I/8.2.

18. The embellishments for the recitative were reprinted as "variants" in the old Bischoff edition; apparently representing aural rather than written tradition, they are stylistically foreign to W. F. Bach's known works.

19. Bent (2005, 99–103) shows how Schenker created the edition by marking up pages from BG 36.

20. Stauffer (1989) presented research up to that date; Wolf (2003) summarizes the current state of knowledge, based on the author's critical commentary for NBA V/9.2. Particularly important is his re-evaluation of P 421, which had been accorded undue significance in earlier studies due to a date (1730) attached in the manuscript to another piece and therefore irrelevant.

21. The intermediate version of P 803 differs from the familiar one in giving a shorter form of the cadenza in mm. 21–5.

22. None of the analyses of the passage in Schenker (1984) is entirely satisfactory. My analytic sketches are intended only to illustrate the melodic shape of the bass and upper voices; they should not be understood as "Schenkerian" reductions.

23. Measure 37 appears in various ways in the sources. The startling harmony (g♭/b♭/c'/e♭'/ b♭'/d♭'') on the second beat is a passing sonority prolonging the diminished-seven chord on the downbeat.

24. As in Friedemann's Fantasia in E minor, F. 21, and Emanuel's first "Prussian" Sonata, W. 48/1.

25. Bach used the version of the concerto found in Vivaldi's autograph (R. 208), not the version published as op. 7, no. 11 (R. 208a). The relationship between the Vivaldi work and Bach's fantasia was previously noted by Schleuning (1969, 78) and Tagliavini (1986).

26. Because the bass notes are never sustained beyond what can be conveniently managed by manuals alone, the suggestion that the work was conceived for an instrument equipped with an actual pedalboard (BG 36:xlii) is not convincing. However, the use of a pedal instrument remains an obvious possibility, as also in the "cadenza" of the Fifth Brandenburg (in mm. 189–94) and a few other works probably composed at Weimar (see chap. 13 on English Suite no. 3).

27. NBA V/9.2, following the sources, shows a♮' on the second beat of m. 50, although writing the note as b♭♭' would be more correct. Schenker, following Forkel, gave the pitch as b♭', justifying this incorrect reading in a polemical analysis (Schenker 1984, 38–9; further discussion in Bent 2005, 127–8).

28. Schenker noticed the sequential character of mm. 49ff., but his analytical sketches (in Schenker 1984, 37 and 83, also Bent 2005, 127) insist on the faulty reading in m. 50.

29. See the fantasias in E♭ and in A, W. 58/6–7, published in 1785.

30. For example, the juxtaposition of arias in C major and B minor symbolizes the Incarnation in Cantata no. 121 (see Dürr 1999, 143). As late as 1751, in his opera *Armida*, C. H. Graun symbolized the heroine's sudden shift of affections, first hating then loving Rinaldo, in a recitative that passes swiftly from B♭ minor to B minor (act 2, scene 2, in SBB AmB 202).

31. See Quantz (1752, 14.9) and C. P. E. Bach (1753–62, i.29), for whom the terms are analogous to piano and forte.
32. See Heinse (1903, 59), quoted in Schleuning (1973, 279).
33. Schenker (1984) contains a chart showing all the variants of the subject.
34. The Bethlehem autograph has been dated to 1729, but as Wolf (NBA V/9.2, KB, 199) observes, the paper is too rare to be sure when precisely Bach used it. For similar reasons the Dresden autograph also cannot be exactly dated.
35. Rameau's rondeau *Les Cyclopes* was published in 1724, fourteen years before Scarlatti's *Essercizi.*
36. Emanuel's earliest keyboard sonata was composed in 1731, according to a list of works that he prepared in the 1770s (Bsa SA 4261). No such list exists for W. F. Bach.
37. Interruptions also occur at the repeats in the Dresden autograph, but the Bethlehem autograph gives first endings that maintain the motion in triplets. It is unclear why these are absent in the Dresden autograph.
38. A similar notational convention seems to be assumed in Altnikol's copies (P 402 and 430) of the prelude in F♯ minor of WTC2 (mm. 7–8); see chap. 12.
39. The convention of adding an accidental to an ornament sign to indicate the precise notes of the ornament already occurs with Couperin, but it seems to have been unknown in the Bach circle prior to Emanuel Bach. See C. P. E. Bach (1753–62, i.2.3.19, especially the additions of 1787).
40. For the original reading, see NBA V/9.2, KB, 202.
41. E.g., the "Wedge" for organ BWV 548/2, the fugue in the C-major solo violin sonata BWV 1005, and the fugues in the lute works BWV 997 and 998 (discussed in chap. 16).
42. Thus Dadelsen and Rönnau (1970), repeated in NBA V/9.2.
43. The completion in Example 9.6 derives almost all of its material from the extant fragment; its length is based on the assumption that the fugue would have filled the bottom of folio 3′ in the Dresden autograph, as well as one face of a now missing sheet originally attached to folio 1 (see Schulze 1984b). Completions by Moroney (1992) and by Michel Philippot (described in NBA V/9.2, KB, 227, not seen here) avoid a da-capo ending.
44. For example, C. P. E. Bach (1753–62, i.3.26) calls for a single upward and a single downward arpeggio for chords of unspecified "long" note values. But later, referring to half-note chords in his D-Major Fantasia W. 117/14, he directs that each chord be "twice broken" (*im Harpeggio zweymahl vorgetragen*, ii.40.14), without specifying the direction of the arpeggiations. Other sources show both practices; Griepenkerl advises breaking each chord up and down only once, and this is the approach taken in P 551. But Stauffer (1989, 161) shows an illustration from a Salzburg copy of BWV 903 implying that each chord in the arpeggio passage is to be rolled twice.
45. See the elaborate realization of C. P. E. Bach's D-minor Fantasia W. 114/7 by J. C. F. Rellstab (1759–1813), reproduced by Karl-Ernst Schröder in Rampe (2002, 216–8). Liszt's version of the fantasia BWV 944/1 may have been a continuation of the same living tradition, although it is too worked-out to come across as a spontaneous improvisation.
46. It has been proposed that the copyist of P 551, who signed his name "Gebhardt," was identical to Ludwig Ernst Gebhardi; the latter's brother Johann Nicolaus studied with Kittel (see NBA V/9.2, KB, 129n. 12, and 132).
47. Griepenkerl recognizes the incongruity of this, defending his view with the assertion that "here no respect at all can be paid to the bar lines."
48. As in an example from a relatively late source, shown in Hogwood (1988, 152).

Notes for Chapter 10

1. CB is now at the Yale University library in New Haven; Herz (1984) gives a detailed description, supplementing that in NBA V/5, KB. Most of the dates and identifications of handwriting given below are from these two sources. NBA V/5 is the only critical edition; there is also a facsimile edition by Ralph Kirkpatrick (New Haven: Yale University Press, 1959). An old popular edition by Herrmann Keller (Kassel: Bärenreiter, 1927), still the basis of reprints, is riddled with errors.
2. The extended title of the organ book (P 283) makes clear its pedagogic purpose: *Orgel-Büchlein worinnen einem anfahrenden Organisten Anleitung gegeben wird, auf allerhand Art einen Choral durchzuführen...* (see BD 1:214 [item 148]/NBR, 80).
3. The Pastorale consists of four very different movements played in unbroken succession;

only the first requires pedals. As such it resembles pastiches like the Toccatina discussed in appendix A, a posthumous compilation of movements by Bach and his sons. The second and fourth movements of the Pastorale might have originated as separate clavier pieces; the second movement is a compact sonata form in *cantabile* style, and the fourth, in binary form, could have served as the gigue of a suite (cf. Stinson 1989b, 461).

4. CB numbers correspond with the numeration of the pieces in NBA V/5. The pieces are not actually numbered in the manuscript.

5. Even C. P. E. Bach, a strong advocate of the clavichord, uses the word *Clavichord* in his famous treatise (1753–62) when he wishes to specify the instrument; the word *Clavier* in the title refers to keyboard instruments generally.

6. There are no sources for BWV 924, 924a, 925–6, 928, or 930–2 independent of CB, and of these only BWV 926 and 928 appear in composition or revision autographs, guaranteeing Bach's authorship. BWV 927 exists anonymously in both CB and P 804/53, and in later sources; BWV 939–42 are preserved only in anonymous copies in P 804/53.

7. F mus. Hs. 1538; facsimile in Stauffer (1993, 92). The table in d'Anglebert's *Pièces de clavecin* (Paris, 1689) appears to have been the model for that in Dieupart's *Six Suittes de Clavessin* (Amsterdam, 1701), which Bach also copied (see Schulze 1984a, 18; Beißwenger 1992, 191). The ornament tables in MM and ABB are edited in Hill (1991).

8. One nineteenth-century editor was badly confused by this notation; see the discussion of English Suite no. 2 in chap. 13.

9. The *veränderlicher Vorschlag* (C. P. E. Bach 1753–62, i.2.2.11). Emanuel's rule, that the appoggiatura takes half the value of the main note (two thirds if the latter is dotted), was a response to the new *galant* style of composition and performance; see Schulenberg (2003).

10. Neumann (1978, especially 127–32) presents an unnecessarily polemical argument to prove the same point. His argument for "pre-beat" performance of appoggiaturas in Bach's music (132–49) depends on questionable assumptions about "harmonic logic" and "rhythmic logic."

11. An overly literal reading of d'Anglebert's table suggests that his *cadence* is a trill preceded by a turn (as in Neumann 1978, 392).

12. *Triller von unten* and *Triller von oben*; see C. P. E. Bach (1753–62, i.2.3.22–8).

13. The same is true of the prelude BWV 930 = CB 9; these are the only two pieces with fingering assuredly by Bach.

14. LeHuray (1981) makes a similar observation about Byrd's music.

15. See mm. 22–3 and 39 (right hand), 34–5 and 38–9 (left hand).

16. The widely reproduced portrait, said to be of W. F. Bach, is often attributed to a non-existent "Wilhelm Weitsch," following the 1962 *Katalog zu den Sammlungen des Händel-Haus in Halle* (p. 2:9). An earlier catalog (*Deutsche Bildnisse 1500–1800* [Halle: Staatliche Gallerie Moritzburg, 1961], 120) reported a signature reading "F. Weitsch Fec.," but this was not visible when I viewed the portrait at the Halle Händel-Haus in 1995. Friedrich Georg Weitsch was well-known as a portrait painter; his sitters included King Frederick the Great (1780), Meyerbeer, and the writer Eschenburg, whose portrait resembles the one in Halle in style and in the subject's elegance and lively expression.

17. Edited in BG 40:151. The source, P 285, also contains a similar reworking of the chorale BWV 683a (given in NBA IV/4, KB, 51).

18. Another source (P 1149) attributes BWV Anh. 73 merely to "Bach"; the independent pedal part is not typical of C. P. E. Bach's fully authenticated organ works, but the style of the added portions does not rule out his authorship. For a facsimile from R 25, see NBA IV/1, KB, 122–4. The work derives from the *Orgelbüchlein* setting BWV 639.

19. BWV 1044 is based in part on BWV 894 (see chap. 9). BWV 668 is related to the prelude *Wenn wir in höchsten Nöthen sein* BWV 641 in the *Orgelbüchlein*.

20. Dates are from Herz (1984) and Stinson (1989a).

21. The same movement appears in BWV 814a (a version of the Third French Suite); see chap. 14. Bach's entry in CB looks like a rough draft, implying that BWV 929 is the original version.

22. In the source, the lower staff of m. 9 repeats the reading of m. 8. The simpler emendation found in many editions (a–b–c′) is that of BG 36.

23. Plath (NBA V/5, KB, 54) dated the first entry to 1722–3, the completion to 1725–6.

24. In CB the piece is labeled *Praeludium 2*, but the digit is a later addition.

25. It is not certain that the final revision is in Bach's hand, but the omission of necessary ac-

cidentals implies that whoever made the entry was composing, not copying from another source.

26. BWV 931 has been taken to be the work of an unidentified "French composer" (as in Herz 1984, 93). Wollny (1993, 443, entry for Fk.-Add. 206) lists BWV 931 with BWV 924a, 925, and 932 as works of Friedemann Bach. The entry that follows BWV 931 in CB (after a blank page) is an untitled bass line resembling the ritornello for a continuo aria. Corrections by the unidentified copyist imply that it is a first draft.

27. BWV 943 was excluded from NBA V/9.2 on the same grounds as BWV 939–42. It will apparently be issued in a projected volume of doubtful organ works, although the only features conceivably pointing to the organ are its four-octave compass and concluding pedal point.

28. All six preludes occur, albeit in a different order, in P 528, by a copyist who may have worked for C. P. E. Bach. P 885 (Kittel) and P 540 (Forkel) give the six preludes in the traditional order.

29. NBA V/9.2, KB, 35, raises the possibility of C. P. E. Bach's involvement; the *prallender Doppelschlag* in BWV 933, m. 4, is an ornament typical of his but not his father's music. Like other details in the text, it could have been introduced by any number of later eighteenth-century copyists; many ornaments in the NBA text could be Kittel's.

30. The resemblance is especially close when one considers the earliest version of the courante; see table 14.1.

31. Originally the soprano might have rested in m. 38, entering in m. 39 with an exact (downward) imitation of the alto of m. 37. Hofmann finds traces of revisions in the texts of nos. 1 and 5 as well.

32. Kellner's copy specifies lute as the medium; the suggestion that the piece is "for lute or keyboard" was Spitta's (1873–80, 2:646, quoted by Kohlhase, NBA V/10, KB, 156).

33. Kellner uses a key signature of two flats, which could have been used for either key; Bach continued to use "Dorian" signatures until around 1723. In CB he still uses the two-flat signature for both the Invention and the Sinfonia in C minor, but these are notated with three flats in the revised version of 1723.

34. BWV 872a/1 was incorporated into WTC2 as the prelude in C♯; it occurs as an independent piece in P 226 (see chap. 12).

35. As Williams (2004, 86) points out. The use of treble clef for the top stave, unique in the volume, might point to optional performance of the melody on the violin, as in Dieupart's suites.

36. See (Maul 2004, 111); whether or not a transcription of an orchestral work, the *Partia* is too simple in texture to be by Bach.

37. Dadelsen (1975, 133) speaks of BWV 841–2 as "composition exercises of the young Wilhelm Friedemann that J. S. Bach corrected [*verbessert*]."

38. P 648 and P 1094 both preserve BWV 952 together with BWV 923 (see below) and 951. BWV 952 also occurs in two other late copies, one of them, LEm ms. 2a, perhaps from the sphere of C. P. E. Bach. The work is edited in BG 36:184, Dehnhard (1973), and NBA V/9.2.

39. See, e.g., the second part of the overture in A by Dieupart, copied by Bach.

40. Bach employs a comparable technique in the central section (mm. 33–58) of the opening movement in the B-minor flute sonata BWV 1030.

41. Dürr admits the impossibility of proving Bach's hand in the compilation of the set (NBA V/6.2, KB, 370).

42. It is unclear why BWV 899 is listed among doubtful and spurious works in both NG and NG2. Stinson (1989a, 127) noted the unusual order of the first three fugal entries but saw no reason to take this as a mark against Bach's authorship; the formal parallelism between the two movements might point toward rather than against Bach's authorship.

43. Compare the subject of "Himmelskönig, sei willkommen" in Cantata 182, as well as the chorus "And with his stripes" in *Messiah*, which opens with a similar motive in the minor. A more exact parallel, in the same key of F major, occurs in the last movement of a Sonata by Telemann for five-part strings, TWV 44:11, preserved in manuscript copies by Pisendel and several others (including Quantz), in Dl 2392-Q-14 and 14a.

44. In the 1692 organ book of Pachelbel's pupil Johann Valentin Eckelt, where the attribution is a later addition (Belotti 2001, 9–10)

45. Also notable is the final cadence, which recurs in the Domine Deus of the *B-Minor Mass*, probably a reworking of an earlier duet in da capo form.

46. No fewer than eight manuscripts transmit the two movements together. But apart from an ornament in m. 55 and a passing tone in m. 73 (the 32d a´´; see NBA V/9.2, KB, 243), no substantive differences distinguish the versions of the fugue as transmitted singly and with BWV 923. Hence the fugue was not reworked at the time it was attached to the prelude, as we might expect to have been the case were Bach responsible for joining the two movements.

47. Compare mm. 6–7 with BWV 903/1, mm. 33–4; and mm. 24–5 (or 27–8) with BWV 903/1, mm. 36–7. Measure 20 also recalls solo figuration from the D-minor concerto BWV 1052 (first movement, mm. 46ff.).

48. Pachelbel is named as composer in one extant manuscript and in an early print (Berlin: Trautwein, 1826). Whatever confusion gave rise to the misattribution, it also extended to the fugue (BWV 951), which is assigned to "Pachelbel" in Bsa 4726.

49. Seen here was the edition by Hans Joachim Moser and Traugott Fedtke (*W. H. Pachelbel: Gesamtausgabe der erhaltenen Werke für Orgel und Clavier* [Kassel: Bärenreiter, 1957]).

50. A hypothetical reconstruction is available on the author's website at <http://www.wagner.edu/faculty/dschulenberg/bachcomp.html>.

51. Kayser's copy P 219 gives a possible intermediate arrangement, in which each invention is immediately followed by the sinfonia in the same key.

52. BD 3:476 (item 950)/NBR, 322. Gerber's account does not mention the Sinfonias, but these are perhaps to be understood among the Inventions.

53. See, e.g., movement 2 of Friedemann's Sonata in D, F. 3, and movement 1 of Emanuel's First Prussian Sonata W. 48/1.

54. The initial word is *Auffrichtig*, not *aufrecht* ("upright") as one might guess from NBR, 98, which gives a translation and facsimile of the complete title page (for the German, see BD 1:220–1 [item 153] or NBA V/3, p. 1).

55. On the meaning of *durchführen*, see Sachs (1980, 138–40), who points out the close line-by-line parallelism of the extended titles of both collections.

56. Cf. Walther's (1732, 178) definition of *Composition*: "die Wissenschaft, *Con*- und *Dissonanzen* also zusammen zu setzen."

57. P 270 contains Kayser's copies of four of Bonporti's inventions, to which Bach added some basso continuo figures. Kobayashi (NBA IX/2, KB, 214) dates the copy to 1723; these versions of the sonatas were edited in BG 45 as possible works of Bach. Facsimiles of Kayser's copies appear in the edition of Bonporti's op. 10 by Roger Elmiger and Micheline Mitrani (Biblioteca Musicale Trentina, 6/1–2; 2d ed., 1984).

58. Forkel refers to the Sinfonias as inventions in the title that he added to his copy, P 220; cf. Forkel (1802, 55/NBR, 467).

59. Kassel: Bärenreiter, 1971; rev. ed., 2002. The only thorough textual commentary remains that of Landshoff (1933).

60. London: Associated Board, 1984.

61. *Johann Sebastian Bach: Inventionen und Sinfonien*, ed. Erwin Ratz and Karl Heinz Füssl (Vienna: Wiener Urtext Edition, 1973). Less adequate is the edition by Rudolf Steglich (new edition, Munich: Henle, 1979) with a cursory editorial commentary, whose English translation contains errors that will baffle students, e.g., a reference to "triplets" (for *Triospiel*, i.e., writing in three voices) in the Sinfonia in E♭. Among other elementary analytical studies are J. N. David (1957) and, on the sinfonias, Johnson (1986).

62. Table 10.2 includes information about the interval at which the initial imitation takes place; the presence of a second exposition ("restatement"); and the location of recapitulated passages both within the body of the work ("medial") and toward the end ("final"). "Type" and "form" as shown in the table are imprecise and subjective and are meant only to give a general characterization of each piece.

63. This type of opening is disguised in the B-minor Invention, where the continuo-like bass of mm. 1–2 is embellished by the treble in mm. 3–4.

64. Derr (1981) discerned a grouping of the original praeambula into "triptychs," groups of three distinguished by details of form and compositional technique. Some of Derr's criteria, such as the supposed need for two manuals to perform pieces of the third "triptych," are problematical. But as the order in CB corresponds with the approximate order of composition, it is not surprising to find common features in adjacent members of the set: conjunct motion in the themes of Praeambula 1–3, disjunct motion in nos. 4–6, longer subjects, possessing distinct countersubjects, in nos. 7–9.

65. The alterations began with the bass of m. 21b and led to an extended closing phrase, which reaches the final cadence on the third beat rather than the downbeat of the last measure.

66. The fifth note of the subject was originally c′′, with parallel readings in each subsequent statement. In Example 10.11, in addition to the change indicated, bass f was originally g.

67. The treble of m. 5 shows alterations in both CB and P 610 to correspond with the revised version of the subject, but neither is assuredly by Bach. The original reading for the second note of m. 5 is d′′, not bb′. The changes might have been elicited by a desire to make the subject more distinct from that of the C-minor Invention.

68. Schleuning (1979, 33–60, especially 59–60) surveys twentieth-century opinions on the problem.

69. See, e.g., the cadential formula at the end of the four-part chorale *Jesu, meines Herzens Freud'* BWV 361 or in m. 2 of *Freuet euch, ihr Christen alle* (BWV 40/8, as "Jesu, nimm dich deiner Glieder").

70. As allowed by C. P. E. Bach (1753–62, i.2.3.18); this explains the substitution in some sources of appoggiaturas for short trills in the subject of the Fughetta BWV 961.

71. The staccato dots in some editions of the D-Major Invention are all erroneous, stemming from a "chance ink-spot" in m. 5 (Dadelsen, preface to the offprint from NBA V/3, vii).

72. The C-minor Sinfonia is absent from CB, but Forkel's manuscript P 220 provides a basis for a reconstruction of Bach's early version, as also for the missing second half of the original Fantasia in D (see NBA V/5).

73. Bach himself entered the ornaments and embellishments into Gerber's copy, perhaps relying on memory, since these differ from the readings in Kayser's manuscript (where the ornaments are also a later addition).

74. In P 610 Bach writes the note as d♮′, which may be less correct but is more readable than the single flat on eb′ used in CB to signify the same note. In P 610 Bach used a single large flat for the bb b′ in the same measure.

75. BG 3 gives Gb and Cb in mm. 13 and 26, respectively; these notes bear no accidentals in CB or P 610.

76. In CB the bass of mm. 19–20 originally ascended, rather than falling to D. In theory one could avoid the stretch by exchanging the held f in the middle voice between the hands, but this is impractical. A tenth is also required in the penultimate measure of the E-minor Sinfonia.

77. The relevant discussion at the end of the paragraph was added only in the 1787 edition.

Notes for Chapter 11

1. The editions were by Forkel (Leipzig, ca. 1801), Schwenke (Bonn, 1801 or 1802), and Nägeli (Zürich, 1801).

2. Frescobaldi's 1626 volume (reprinted in 1628 and 1642) incorporated his earlier *Recercari, et canzoni franzese* (1615) together with his capricci published in 1624. There is no direct evidence that Bach knew any of these collections, but see below for apparent allusions to specific pieces within them. C. P. E. Bach documented his father's admiration for Frescobaldi in the Obituary and later writings.

3. In Bach's manuscript, the word *Praeludia* is written much larger than the word *Fugen* and is on a separate line (see the reproduction in NBR, p. 96).

4. *Ariadne* includes separate pieces in E minor and in the Phrygian mode (also on E). Exemplars are known of the 1713 Vienna edition and the 1715 Augsburg edition; Walther (1732, 246) mentioned a 1702 edition. The best modern edition remains that of Ernst von Werra, *Johann Kaspar Ferdinand Fischer: Sämtliche Werke für Klavier und Orgel* (Leipzig: Breitkopf und Härtel, 1901).

5. The subject of Fischer's fugue in E, also used by Bach, resembles a traditional Gregorian motive; the subject of the E-minor fugue also occurs in Buxtehude's Praeludium BuxWV 142 in the same key. Ledbetter (2002) finds parallels to subjects by other composers, if not direct borrowings, in the fugues in G# minor (Kerll), C# minor (Muffat), and A major (in the anonymous *Wegweiser*, Augsburg, 1668), all in WTC2—the last two with further parallels to Corelli as well.

6. P 401, copied by Kayser. The copies of the preludes in CB show traces of a similar ordering, and changes in the numbering of a few pieces in the autograph of WTC2 suggest that there, too, some minor-key pairs might have once preceded the corresponding ones in the major.

7. The date 1722 appears to have been altered, making its original reading ambiguous, but most manuscript copies give that date.

8. For the German text, see BD 1:219 (item 152) or Ledbetter (2002, 2), whose translation I have followed in part.

9. One exception, the trio for the closing minuet of the Suite BWV 819, is in E♭ minor.

10. For example, Barnes (1979) assigned "prominence" values to individual major thirds on a largely subjective basis, asserting, for example, that because the prelude in C♯ of WTC1 is "a fast-moving piece in two parts...the ear has no chance to judge whether the major thirds are good or bad" (49, 51). More recently, Lehmann (2005) argues that twelve ornamental loops drawn across the top of the title page in the autograph P 415 represent coded instructions for an unequal temperament. If so, Bach's pupils were unaware of this; Kayser in P 401 drew ten rather than twelve loops, and other copies omit the decoration entirely.

11. Koster (2005) casts grave doubt on arguments for the rarity of harpsichords in Germany (as in Rampe 2002a, 91–100).

12. Agricola's copy of the fugue in E♭ from Part 2 (in P 595) contains pedal indications, but this is an early version of the work, in D.

13. Hofmann (2001, 159) refers to such a movement as a *Klangflächenpräludium*.

14. The term "recapitulation," it will be recalled, is used here for any episodic passage that is restated, including restatements that are transposed or in inverted counterpoint.

15. Kroll first edited the work for Peters (1862–3).

16. Older literature refers to a "Fischof autograph," actually the copy by Kayser (P 401); a "Zürich autograph," in fact a copy by Bach's student Meissner (now in NL DHgm); and a "Müller autograph" predominantly in the hand of Anna Magdalena Bach (P 202). The actual autograph (P 415) was referred to as the "Volkmann-Wagener autograph."

17. Berlin: Steingräber, 1884.

18. London: Associated Board of the Schools of Music, 1994.

19. Dürr also has written a useful handbook, at this writing available in German only (1998, revised 2000).

20. The pages bearing the fugue in F♯ and the beginning of the prelude in F♯ minor are missing from P 415, but the text can be reconstructed from copies.

21. See NBA V/6.1, Appendix 1. This version, designated α1, is preserved in photocopies at LEb of the lost "Konwitschny" manuscript, whose readings are usually close to those of Forkel's edition (the "Forkel version" of the older Bach literature). The eleven preludes in CB represent a slightly later stage of revision and can be consulted in NBA V/5.

22. The chief source for the information in Table 11.1 is NBA V/6.1, KB.

23. All the preludes were expanded or significantly revised in some way save for those in E, F, F♯ minor, G♯ minor, B♭ minor, and B minor. The fugues in G and B♭ minor were also slightly expanded, and the ending of the fugue in B♭ was rewritten.

24. For this reason the score in NBA V/5 bears a footnote indicating that its text, transcribed literally from the CB, may be "nicht authentisch." Riedel (1969, 93–6) refers to this text as a "conflated version."

25. Measures 28–34 are absent in the earlier versions.

26. The early edition by Schwenke gave an additional measure prior to m. 23; this reading recurs in some later editions. The insertion was not necessarily Schwenke's invention; see NBA V/6.1, KB, 181.

27. Schenker (1969, 37), among others, opts for the diminished-seven chord, as the alternate interpretation would have the suspension c′ ornamented by its own resolution (b).

28. In the earlier versions Bach was less careful about voice leading, allowing octave doublings (e.g., in m. 12) as he did in arpeggio passages in other pieces, including the Chromatic Fantasia.

29. Bach later made an additional rhythmic change to improve the voice leading in m. 15; this, as well as a late alteration in m. 12, is omitted in most editions prior to NBA V/6.1.

30. Marpurg (1753–4, vol. 1, *Tab.* X, *Fig.* 1).

31. The early version has just two measures in place of the last thirteen (from m. 26), lacking the passages marked *presto*, *adagio*, and *allegro*. An intermediate version (in appendix 2 of NBA V/6.1) has a somewhat simpler version of the *adagio* measure and three instead of four measures of closing *allegro*.

32. Praeludium 15 in Fischer's *Ariadne musica* shows a similar alternation between presto and

adagio. In Frescobaldi's *Fiori musicali* (Venice, 1635), which Bach knew, the preface already directs the use of "adasio" (= adagio) at *trilli* (cadences?) and *passi affetuosi*.

33. A corresponding alteration is visible in the copy in P 401, reproduced in Dürr (1986).

34. Dürr (1986) gives facsimiles of the relevant pages. He allowed the possibility that the markings were by Bach, but see Talle (2003, 163). Errors in similar markings in Kayser's copies of the D-minor and B-minor preludes led Deppert (1987) and Lester (1992, 86–7) to question Bach's involvement in the annotations; particularly telling was the failure of the annotator to recognize a copying mistake in the D-minor prelude.

35. Kirnberger (1771–9) reduces the prelude in A minor and the fugue in B minor to a figured bass, somewhat along the lines of Rameau's fundamental bass but without the latter's implied analysis of harmonic functions.

36. Lester (2001, 68), cites analyses in the older literature that find both binary and ternary divisions.

37. Bach also embellished the eighth notes at the end of the countersubject (bass, m. 8), which became sixteenths, but the original motive remains in mm. 33–46.

38. The same would be true in m. 29, if the slash visible in the facsimile of the autograph represents an acciaccatura between the notes b♯ and d♯′; it is absent from the NBA and most other editions.

39. Adler no. 6 (i.e., no. 6 in Froberger's autograph collection of 1658).

40. Another partial concordance is the versus Et misericordia from Magnificat II in Kerll's *Modulatio organica* (Munich, 1686), to which Ledbetter (2002, 211) also traces the fugue subject in G♯ minor; Kerll too could have derived his idea from Frescobaldi.

41. Marpurg (1753–4) used the term *Doppel-Fuge* for any fugue with a regular countersubject, but the term is misleading in cases such as this, where the second subject is never passed systematically through all five voices.

42. Some editors clarify the voice leading by altering the f♯″ in m. 96 from a whole-note to a half-note, but this has little justification in the sources. The other five-part fugue also contains some ambiguous voice leading (at m. 37); see Kroll's discussion of the fugue in B♭ minor (BG 14:237–8).

43. An instrumental arrangement would have to clarify the voice leading; one source for the "correction" in m. 96 is P 204, by Schwenke, who like Mozart arranged some of the pieces in WTC for string quartet.

44. Reported in NBA V/6.1, KB, 428. One of these copies is also a source for the ornamented version of the D-minor fugue, discussed below; in mm. 42–3 of the present fugue this copy includes an attractive embellished reading for the treble, adopted in some of the early editions and possibly authentic.

45. The Weimar organ compass is uncertain; see Williams (1980–4, 3:125). Bach's Leipzig organ parts avoid low C♯ (see Marshall 1986, table 4).

46. The mordent on the third beat and the trill on the fourth come from the manuscript in NL DHgm, but not the portion of that manuscript copied by Bach's pupil Meissner.

47. Facsimile in Dürr (1986). The indication *c.e.* on the second beat of m. 11 might mean *chorda elegantior* (Walther 1732, 160), referring to the accidental in the upper voice (e♭″), but if so the same indication should also have been placed in m. 10.

48. See NBA V/6.1, KB, 171. The source, the copy in NL DHgm, is a composite manuscript, one portion of which was copied by Meissner. The D-minor fugue is in the portion by an unidentified copyist.

49. Virtually unplayable ornaments were also added to Bach's original text in the printed version of the three-part triple Contrapunctus 8 in the *Art of Fugue*; this might have been authorized by Bach, but the *Abklatschvorlage* (see chap. 18) for this piece was not in his hand.

50. See, e.g., BWV 895 (chap. 6), which is preserved with somewhat similar pieces by older composers associated with Pachelbel.

51. This slightly shorter version is edited in appendix 1 of NBA V/6.1—apparently for the first time, as the prelude is not in CB. Also little known is Bach's late revision in m. 34 (substituting tenor g for e to avoid a cross relation).

52. The bass in mm. 18b–20 anticipates the full form of the second subject. Kerman (2005, 65) disapproves of the present characterization of the subjects, perhaps because of their free treatment later in the movement. But Bach treats them no more or less freely than the first two subjects of the fugue in C♯ minor, which have a similar relationship to one another although

introduced in reverse order (the more lively idea there coming second). The combination of this archaic subject with a running motive has a fortuitous parallel in the chorus "Wretched Lovers" in Handel's *Acis and Galatea* (HWV 49a), composed around 1717.

53. The pencil entry (illegible in facsimiles) reportedly reads "nicht Allabrevemässig sondern wie der 1ste Tact gewesen, fortgespielt." A similar remark in another eighteenth-century copy (P 208) suggests that the warning not to change tempo goes back to a member of the Bach circle; see Dürr (1988b, 97).

54. After the dotted eighth, P 415 has four thirty-seconds followed by a sixteenth; the first two thirty-seconds were later altered (not necessarily by Bach) to sixty-fourths. P 401 and several other early copies give a grammatically correct reading, which most editions follow.

55. In Mattheson's *Exemplarische Organisten-Probe*, each of the two *Probestücke* in this key are printed in *both* D♯ minor and the enharmonically equivalent E♭ minor.

56. For arguments for and against a D-minor original, see NBA V/6.1, KB, 188. Marpurg (1753–4, vol. 1, *Tab.* XI, *Fig.* 2) quotes the opening of the fugue in D minor, but most of his quotations from pieces in "difficult" keys are transposed up or down a half step and do not necessarily reflect alternate versions of the pieces.

57. Marpurg 1753–4, 1:8. Walther (1732) uses the same term for an *inversus* answer.

58. Forkel, in a passage that led contemporaries to doubt his musicality, argued for what is in fact a completely erroneous reading of mm. 25–6, eliminating the suspension while creating parallel octaves with the treble (see Forkel 1802, 27/NBR, 444).

59. The Gounod parallel was noted by Riedel (1969, 337).

60. A number of Bach's ensemble movements with arioso melodies include a similar chordal strand, assigning it either to the string or woodwind chorus (First Brandenburg Concerto, adagio) or to continuo alone (Cantata no. 202, opening aria).

61. For other views on how to articulate the subject, see Williams (1983, 338–9).

62. Some editions place a slash through the end of the trill sign, signifying a terminating turn (suffix). Although this suffix should certainly be played (see C. P. E. Bach 1753–62, i.2.3.13 and i.2.3.23), the slash is not in the autograph.

63. The *suspirans* is a figure entering after a short rest or "breath."

64. Conceivably the lower voice originally had c′ (8th), c–d (16ths) on the third beat of m. 4.

65. The sign was present in the Konwitschny manuscript (the source of the early version) and is a later addition in P 202.

66. Measures 17–8 are absent in the early version. In m. 1 the autograph lacks the trill, but the ornament is present in P 401 and other copies. The autograph does have the ornament in mm. 7 and 12 (left hand).

67. The relevant pages of the autograph are lost, but the dotted figure is already present in the version of the Konwitschny manuscript. Although the latter entirely lacks trill signs, these would have been understood.

68. Kayser's copy (P 401) shows a trill in m. 28 and a mark in the corresponding m. 15 that is probably also a trill sign.

69. Bach slightly expanded the fugue as well, turning the final measure into two.

70. Compare, for example, Cantata no. 127 (*Herr Jesu Christ, wahr'r Mensch und Gott*), third movement, mm. 31ff.

71. As in the G-major fugue, one suspects the thirty-seconds to have arisen as embellishments of figures in simple sixteenths. But the Konwitschny manuscript preserves only a few such readings, e.g., in mm. 16b–17a.

72. The prelude preceding Fischer's E♭-major fugue opens somewhat like the Praeludium in the same key (BWV Anh. 177) by Johann Christoph Bach (1642–1703). The latter is likely to be earlier than the Fischer work.

73. Compare the subject of Canzona I in Frescobaldi's *Secondo libro di toccate* (Rome, 1627).

74. Compare the thematic use of a cadential formula in the first movement of Haydn's D-Major Quartet op. 50, no. 6 (described by Rosen 1972, 128).

75. As Marpurg (1753–4, 1:46) puts it, the answer is "borrowed" (*entlehnet*) from the subdominant (*der Quarte*). This is a common feature in modal counterpoint, including Bach's chorale settings, e.g., the *manualiter* fughetta on "Allein Gott" BWV 677 from Part 3 of the *Clavierbüchlein*.

76. Recercar 8 in the 1615 and 1626 volumes.

77. Measures 46–8 ‖ 17–9 transposed; 49–50 ‖ 29–30 transposed; treble of 51–4 ‖ alto of 17–20.

78. See NBA V/6.1, KB, 190, although Dürr elsewhere (1984, 63) argues against assuming an "allzu frühe Entstehung."
79. Capriccio 7 in the 1626 volume.
80. See mm. 16, 43, 48, 69, etc. One would have to use *two* feet on the pedals to save the hands from having to stretch a ninth during the final pedal point (m. 86).
81. Measures 30–4 are derived from mm. 19–21; mm. 37–44 ‖ 9–16, with transposition and voice exchange. The first two measures of the coda (45–6) originally repeated mm. 15–6, transposed by a fifth, but Bach later exchanged the two upper parts.
82. Both movements lack tempo markings in the Konwitschny manuscript.
83. For example, the fourth note of the tenor entry in m. 4 was originally c#′, not d′; this is confirmed by the earlier copy P 401.
84. Compare the final allegro of Corelli's op. 3, no. 7. Both the texture and the opening thematic material of Bach's prelude also have a close parallel in the *bizzarria* movement of Bonporti's op. 10, no. 7 (not one of the movements in P 270).
85. Between tenor and bass f# on the fourth beat of m. 13 and between alto and soprano g′ in m. 44. Compare m. 3 in the Sinfonia in B♭.

Notes for Chapter 12

1. Actually, Bach prepared at least two distinct sets of scores, each probably containing all movements; only the "London" set, described below, survives, and it is unknown why it does not contain all of Bach's later revisions. Despite speculation that Bach in fact did prepare a revised fair copy (now lost), there is no firm evidence that such a manuscript ever existed.
2. Emanuel's earliest sonatas can be securely dated back to 1731 (see Berg 1979); those of Friedemann are not so easily datable, but two mature works were published in the 1740s.
3. The edition by Richard D. P. Jones is published by the Associated Board of the Royal Schools of Music (London, 1994). Dürr's edition (NBA V/6.2, 1995) is reviewed in Schulenberg (1999b).
4. Facsimile in Franklin and Daw (1980), reviewed by Wolff (1983b). Three pairs are missing from the London autograph.
5. NBA V/6.2 includes not only WTC2 but "Five Preludes and Fugues" and "Four Fughettas," as well as five individual preludes. Each group of pieces is thought to include early versions of movements later incorporated into WTC2; in some cases the variants are quite minor. It is not entirely clear whether Bach was responsible for these groupings of pieces or for all of the variants. I am grateful to Joshua Rifkin for an advance copy of his article (n.d.) that proposes a redating of the first layer of the London autograph from 1739 to 1740–1.
6. Throughout this chapter, references to the "Altnikol" copies mean not only P 430 and P 402 but others in the same group (Jones's group "D," NBA's group "B").
7. Essentially identical in both traditions are the pairs in c, D, d, f, G, g#, a, B♭, b♭, and B.
8. Only in nine movements do Dürr and Jones disagree on significant points: the preludes in F# and f#, the fugue in b, and both movements in c#, g, and A.
9. But it is hard to see the piece as a Frescobaldian *toccata di durreze e ligature* (Keller 1965, 136–7), which would be quite different in rhythm and design.
10. The earliest form of the work is known as BWV 870a; the subsequent version entered into the London autograph is known as BWV 870b. The prelude has some points in common with the allemande and courante of a variation-suite in D by Johann Georg Kreysing, published in Telemann's *Getreuer Music-Meister* (1728, p. 25). Bach is likely to have seen the publication, but given the date of publication Kreysing probably did not furnish a model for Bach.
11. On the compositional history of this movement, see Breckoff (1965), Franklin (1989a), and Brokaw (1989), as well as the editions of Tomita, Jones, and Dürr.
12. Jones (1991a, 442) argues that Bach drafted these changes in a now-lost manuscript, then transferred them to the London autograph.
13. For a more conventional sequence using similar motivic material, see the Concerto for two harpsichords BWV 1061, first movement, mm. 5–6.
14. See m. 27b, corresponding with m. 13 in the first section. In the present context, G minor functions not as dominant but as ii of IV, just as D minor at m. 13 is ii of I.
15. Measure 30 corresponds with m. 15 in BWV 870a.
16. The low C in the prelude was also a revision. Other sources show later refinements, e.g., a rewritten right-hand part in mm. 67–70.
17. See Lindley (1989a). Lindley seems to agree with Faulkner (1984, 23) that the fingerings

in Vogler's copy "transmit Bach's intentions," but what Lindley calls the "remarkable 1–1–1 fingering" for the alto in the final cadence of the prelude makes it impossible to hold the quarter-note d′. LeHuray (1990) gives a judicious evaluation of Vogler's fingerings.

18. An early version of the fugue, preserved under the title *Fugetta* in Agricola's copy P 595, differs only in details (distinctive readings of this version are listed in NBA V.6.2, KB, 417–8).

19. Some editors see a new (tenor) voice entering in m. 14, but there remains only one middle part through m. 18. The eighths in m. 16 (eb′–c′′–bb′–c′′) are beamed together in the London autograph, not divided between tenor and alto as in some editions.

20. For the earliest version of the prelude, see NBA V/6.2:344 (or BG 14: 243).

21. The ornament, already present in the early version, is notated as a c-appoggiatura (not a small eighth note) in the early sources; it should probably be played quite short. The word *allegro* (uncapitalized) occurs over the second beat of m. 25 in the autograph.

22. For the nineteen-measure early version, see NBA V/6.2:358 (also in BG 36:225). The intermediate version, which lacks mm. 25–9 (as well as much of the embellishment in thirty-seconds), is in NBA V/6.2:352.

23. See, e.g., the Siciliana movement of Quantz's trio sonata in G minor QV 2:34, or the opening Larghetto of QV 2:17 in E♭ (both edited by Mary Oleskiewicz in *Johann Joachim Quantz: Seven Trio Sonatas* [Middleton, WI: A-R, 2001]).

24. This is one of the movements in which it is not clear which tradition gives later readings. The Altnikol group preserves at least one seemingly earlier variant (m. 49, bass), although elsewhere it "resolves" appoggiaturas, as in Example 12.1.

25. Kirnberger (1771–9, 2/1:124) quotes the subject of the present fugue alongside that of BWV 961 (in 12/8) to demonstrate that the latter is slower.

26. The first four (chromatic) notes of the second subject are foreshadowed in m. 20, and by the chromatic figure used repeatedly as counterpoint to the first subject in the *inversus* exposition.

27. Franklin (1989b, 269–70) sees all ten preludes of group 2, to which the D-major belongs, as employing a "reprise"; five have a "large three-part structure." But the late appearance of the reprise in some of these (e.g., F minor) distinguishes them from full-fledged sonata forms.

28. Friedemann also avoids a literal return in the first movement of F. 3.

29. Bach's tolerance of such easily overlooked parallel fifths, created by ornamental figuration, is also documented in the G-minor fugue (m. 63).

30. That is, a dotted eighth followed by a sixteenth is to be executed as a triplet quarter followed by a triplet eighth.

31. The early version of the prelude, designated BWV 875a, is one of the preludes and fughettas copied by Vogler in the 1720s; the London autograph gives the "most fully developed state" (NBA V/6.2, KB, 206).

32. P 595/5 gives the fugue in D, as one of four fughettas (in NBA V/6.2:352–7). The three entries of the subject in the bass were assigned at some point to the pedals, not necessarily by Bach (see NBA V/6.2, KB, 418).

33. One might add the prelude to the list of pieces from WTC2 that Franklin (1987, 459) regarded as possibly meant for the lute-harpsichord.

34. Some copies have b♯′, not b♮′, on the last eighth of m. 45, but this makes little sense; Bach had known of the extraordinary effect of this chord since the time of the early Praeludium BWV 921, perhaps via Kuhnau (see Williams 2003, 89). Here he deploys it more sensibly as a dramatic closing gesture.

35. The original reading of the London manuscript, b–a–g♯, is clearly wrong; the later correction g♯–f♯–e creates hidden octaves with the treble (A–G♯). Altnikol's reading b–g♯–e makes little sense motivically; Kirnberger's c♯′–b–a is strongest even if it is his own "conjectural correction" (Jones, edn., p. 172).

36. Marpurg (1753–4, vol. 1, *Tab.* 20, *Fig.* 4) quotes a subject and a countersubject that are both similar to the present themes, save for their mode (Phrygian); these are from Froberger's Fantasia 2. Froberger, like Bach, introduces the subject in diminution shortly after the halfway point. Bach may have known the fantasia; Kirnberger and Forkel owned manuscript copies.

37. Bach's m. 9 is m. 19 for Fischer, who bars the piece in 2/2, as did some copyists of WTC2. The London "autograph" and other copies use short barlines to divide certain measures in half, a practice extended to the entire piece in the editions by Jones and Dürr.

38. The prefixed trills in mm. 29 and 86 (*Triller von unten* and *von oben*, respectively) sound odd with a sharp upper note, less so the ordinary trills in mm. 33 and 89. Dürr and Jones read the sign in m. 86 as a regular long trill, which is possible (or it could be a *tremblement appuyé*); Dürr sees the turn element as a later addition in m. 29.

39. In Bärenreiter's "practical" offprint from NBA V/6.2, the tie that should cross the barline between mm. 69 and 70 is transposed to another point within m. 69, in agreement with "Fassung B." Bach probably intended both ties (Jones's reading), the first one being understood by the convention described by C. P. E. Bach (1753–62, i.3.18). The second tie, included in the earlier text of "Fassung A," is also a later addition in Altnikol's 1744 manuscript, among other copies.

40. Williams (1983, 337) nevertheless counsels against playing the opening of the prelude "smoothly," and indeed the slurs imply articulation of each half-note beat. In mm. 10 and 11 the first two beats are slurred together, perhaps reflecting the rhythm of the bass (dotted half, quarter). The slurs were probably late additions and are absent from the NBA's "Fassung B" and some other editions.

41. The subject of the last movement of the Fifth Brandenburg Concerto has a similar metrical shape and is equally subject to misunderstanding.

42. Virtually the same theme appears as an episode in the fugue of BWV 998, constituting a second link between WTC2 and that unusual lute piece.

43. In place of appoggiaturas on the second beat in mm. 44 and 67, the autograph has signs for the *tremblement appuyé*.

44. The second countersubject cannot be used in the bass, as this would produce parallel fifths.

45. As in the *brisé* writing of m. 15 and the exchange of material between bass and tenor in mm. 23 and 25. Measures 15 and 25 are notated somewhat differently in the earlier version transmitted in the Altnikol copies.

46. Another such case occurs in the three-part mirror fugue of the *Art of Fugue* (see chap. 18).

47. The first subject enters twice toward the end of the second section (mm. 29, 34b), but neither entry is combined with a full statement of the second subject.

48. Not every entrance contains the complete second subject; the alto does not state the latter in full until m. 22b.

49. An early version of the prelude (edited in NBA V/6.2: 350) differs only in the simpler bass of mm. 23–4 and 43. As Jones notes, the preservation of this version alongside the early version of the D-minor prelude makes possible an origin "at least as early as the 1720s."

50. Altnikol's copy in P 402 lacks the tempo mark, and rhythmic variants in the Altnikol copies (mm. 20–1) suggest that the sixteenths were not originally dotted throughout.

51. There seems to be no generally accepted term for this device; Dürr (1998, 368) uses the German equivalent *paariger Einsatz*, and it is also sometimes termed a *canon sine pausa*, that is, a canon with no rest between the two entries.

52. More precisely, Marpurg (1753–4, 1: 140) calls this a "canonic" double fugue, since the countersubject is a continuation of the subject within a single musical "breath" (*Pneuma*)—but this is true only for the three entries of the countersubject in the first exposition.

53. See Snyder (1980, 549–53) for a passage from Werckmeister's *Harmonologia musica* (1702) that draws a connection between canon and "gedoppelt *Contrapunctus*."

54. The close of the prelude seems to have made an impression on Friedemann Bach, who appears to quote it in his Fantasia in C Minor F. 16 (m. 54).

55. A subject nearly identical to that of BWV 901/2 (and in the same key) occurs in Telemann's *Sonata a 5* TWV 44:11.

56. A second autograph of the fugue (P 274) represents an independent and apparently rejected version containing a few changes beyond those found in the London autograph. This text, printed as a "Variante" in NBA V/6.2:108, recurs in several copies, including one by W. F. Bach (I B DD70). The Altnikol copies give what are probably still later readings, notably in mm. 53–7 of the prelude and 14 and 32 of the fugue.

57. See m. 8, where the two autographs find different ways of maintaining the appearance of four parts.

58. Not v but perhaps ii of IV; still, Monelle (2000, 202) is right to call attention to the rarity of the "dominant minor" in fugues in major keys. A parallel occurs in the organ fugue in F, BWV 540/2, where the second subject enters in C minor (m. 119); is it a coincidence that the latter work also combines chromatic and diatonic subjects?

59. E.g., in mm. 23–32; the technique is used with particular intensity in the incomplete fugue in C minor BWV 906/2.
60. If one cannot engage the coupler while playing, the first section can be played on the coupled eight-foot ranks, the second section on the upper keyboard, and the third section on the lower keyboard with the addition of the four-foot rank (drawn by the left hand while resting in m. 95).
61. The low notes are in the London autograph, the eighth rest in the Altnikol copies. Bach also revised the end of the B-minor fugue to avoid a note below C, although BB occurs twice in the B-major prelude.
62. As Jones points out (1991b, 609), altered readings in Altnikol's copy P 430 produce a more regular sequence in mm. 23–4, and in m. 30 they make the latter consistent with parallel passages in mm. 1, 17, and 26. Yet neither Jones nor Dürr (NBA V/6.2, KB, 326) can trace these changes unequivocally back to Bach, and the reading of the London autograph may be superior in m. 24, where the dominant chord on the third beat (V of VII) sounds stronger than Altnikol's ii^7 of III.
63. Larsen (1972, 143) refers to Seiffert (1899, 206–7) for comparable themes by Pachelbel, Buxtehude, and others.
64. E.g., starting on beat 3 of m. 3: e–e′–a–c′ | f♯–a–d♯–f♯.
65. Marshall (1976b, 6) points out formal similarities, as well as the use of similar notation to indicate hand crossing in the autographs of the two pieces.
66. Marpurg (1753–4, i, *Tabulae LIV–LV*) quotes the subject in combination with its inversion as an example of double counterpoint. But he gives the subject in D minor, and his first example shows it in an altered form never used in the actual fugue. Whether or not the latter corresponds to an actual early version, it is possible that Marpurg's way of illustrating double counterpoint—two lines of music, one of them repeated on a third stave an octave lower—corresponds to the way in which Bach initially sketched this type of combination.
67. It appears thus in the NBA's version "B," together with the tempo mark *Adagio*, found only in one late copy (LEm PM 5697, by Gotthard Fischer, a pupil of Kittel).
68. In the Altnikol copies an eighth rest replaces tenor g♯ on the downbeat.
69. As in the *Recercar ottavo, obligo di non uscir mai di grado* in Frescobaldi's capricci of 1626, also alluded to in WTC1 (see chap. 11). Butler sees Bach's countersubject as an example of *contrapunto alla zoppa*, a "rhythmic obligo."
70. Although the combination of the two subjects in the B-major fugue is invertible at the octave, Bach never inverts the counterpoint of mm. 27–30 at that interval.
71. The fugue, though hardly a sonata form, does have a sonata-like tonal design. Cadences in the dominant (m. 27) and subdominant (m. 60) mark the ends of the "exposition" and "development," respectively.
72. See W. 49/6, first movement, m. 64.
73. Jones (edition, 196), thinks that Bach might have added them himself in P 430.

Notes for Chapter 13

1. See, e.g., the title page for Partita no. 1 in NBR, 129 (facsimile, p. 130).
2. On the date of Bach's Dieupart copies, see Beißwenger 1992, 282 (including a sample facsimile). A piece published by Couperin appears in the second Little Keyboard Book for Anna Magdalena Bach; see also the discussion below of the *agrémens* for the sarabande in the Second English Suite.
3. In the sources of Bach's suites the term *gigue* is sometimes spelled *gique*, no doubt reflecting the local pronunciation of the French form of the word (the Italian would be *giga*). Walther (1732, 281) gives the alternative spelling *Gicque*. Gigue will be used here throughout.
4. Kuhnau had used the word *partie*, evidently an exact equivalent for *partita*. Walther (1732) left the word *suite* undefined, though he used it in the definition of the word *Ouverture*.
5. The familiar order was recognized as normal by the late seventeenth century; in at least three cases, Roger's posthumous print of ten Froberger suites (Amsterdam, 1698) disregarded the composer's disposition of the movements, putting the gigue last instead of second.
6. But Colin Tilney's "suggestions for performance" for the English Suites (included in the Dehnhard edition) contain some questionable assumptions, e.g., applying C. P. E. Bach's rules on appoggiaturas to his father's *accents* (see below).
7. Dehnhard, in the preface to his edition, cites good source-critical evidence for placing the English Suites "earlier than previously assumed, namely before 1717" (p. xi).

8. Dieupart's suites could be performed not only on solo keyboard but as ensemble works; Bach's manuscript copy includes a note to this effect (see Beißwenger 1992, 200–1), as does Walther's copy in P 801.

9. The copy of BWV 806 in P 1072, by Bach's pupil Kayser, was prepared over an extended period, begun around 1717 but completed as late as 1724 (Talle 2003, 156–7). Titles in Kayser's copies, including numbers for the individual suites, were altered or added later, indicating that the original ordering differed from that first found in Gerber's copies, which date from 1725 (NBA V/7, KB, 16ff.).

10. P 1072, in its final state, is entitled *Six Suittes avec leurs Preludes* [sic] *pour le Clavecin*. Walther gave a similar title in his copy of BWV 806a.

11. Forkel (1802, 56/NBR, 468). The words "Fait pour les Anglois" in one eighteenth-century source are a later addition in an unidentified hand, possibly Johann Christian Bach (NBA V/7, KB, 29; see facsimile in NBA V/7).

12. Dieupart's suites (Amsterdam, 1701) were dedicated to the Countess of Sandwich, and the composer reportedly spent much of his career in England. Mattheson's *Pièces de clavecin*, published in 1714 in both English and German editions, present direct parallels with Bach's works (see below on Suite no. 3). But d'Anglebert, Dandrieu, and Rameau, among others, published suites at Paris containing preludes.

13. Kayser's copy of the revised version in P 1072 was completed before the title was changed.

14. BWV 806a is edited in NBA V/7. Although an adequate dating for Walther's copy is not available, it is preserved alongside other relatively early works likely to have been copied while Bach was still in Weimar; Beißwenger (1992a) assigns Walther's hand in these copies to "Schriftstadium III."

15. The suite BWV 818a contains another instance of Bach's composing a new movement as a variation of an existing one (see chap. 14).

16. P 801 includes Dieupart's A-major suite in Walther's hand.

17. As David Fuller noted in NG 5: 473.

18. Jaccottet (1986, 198–9) points out additional thematic parallelisms between BWV 806 and the Dieupart suite. Some less convincing parallels are drawn in Dannreuther (1893–5, 1:138).

19. Neither BG nor NBA accurately reproduces the ornament sign found in the principal source, P 1072; throughout both editions, the vertical stroke within the ornament sign is displaced to the left, as in the sign for a mordent.

20. See mm. 1, 6, 13, and 16. In some editions these signs (present in P 1072) are replaced by undulating vertical lines, indicating a broken chord; BG 45 had both indications.

21. Thus Neumann (1978, 595–6).

22. See Walther (1708, 37, para. 87), where the sign is used to indicate the breaking of pairs of eighth notes moving in parallel thirds. In the next paragraph, however, the same sign indicates an acciaccatura.

23. Walther's title for courante 2 is *Courante précedent* [sic] *avec la Basse Simple*; this movement corresponds with double 2 of the revised version, but there are substantial variants between the two. Mempell omitted courante 2 in LEm ms. 8; perhaps there was some ambiguity in Bach's material as to which movements were to be copied.

24. Several copies preserve what may be an intermediate version for m. 24 (see NBA V/7, KB). In Example 13.4a, NBA V/7 gives alto e′ as a dotted half, but the notehead may have been filled in, to judge from the copy of P 803 seen here. The sharp on bass d suggested by the NBA in the same measure has no basis in the source.

25. Staccato dots, present in addition to slurs in BG 13, are absent from the extant sources of this work and were not used in the Bach circle for notating this effect, although they occur elsewhere.

26. In Kayser's copy, the word *piano* starts beneath the third sixteenth note in m. 12, between the first and second notes in m. 36.

27. Concertos: first movements of the first and fourth Brandenburg Concertos; fugues: "Wedge" in E minor for organ BWV 548/2, second movement of Sonata in C for violin BWV 1005, last movement of the Fifth Brandenburg Concerto. Butler (2004) describes the prelude of Suite no. 3 as "not cast in da capo form at all," which is true in the limited sense that its A section is relatively short, and when it returns its first four measures are modified to join with a preceding retransition phrase.

28. Possible piano passages: from m. 55/note 2 through m. 59/1 (left hand: to 60/1); 62/2 to 66/1; 70/2 to 78/1; 80/2 to 82/1.

29. These *accents* are likely to have been played short, sometimes even before or straddling the beat.

30. P 1072 and several other early sources give the *agrémens* in this form. The version on two staves, which includes alterations in the inner voices in mm. 15–6, 19, etc., apparently derives from the lost copy by Gerber (see NBA V/7, KB, 77).

31. That the present work dates from the period of Bach's close involvement with Venetian concertos is confirmed by the use of a cadence formula rare in later works but used in the same key in the second movement of Concerto no. 12 (BWV 983), mm. 8–9. The third movement of the same concerto (mm. 41–4) is practically quoted in the gigue of Suite no. 4.

32. Dürr reconstructs the earlier reading for mm. 181–7; this was erased in AmB 498, a copy owned by Agricola and Kirnberger (see NBA V/7, KB, 138).

33. The dissonances in mm. 9 and 11 were overlooked by most copyists, as well as the editors of BG 13 and 45.

34. Frescobaldi: preface (*Al lettore*) to the first book of toccatas (Rome, 1615). Bach: title of P 1072 (see note 10).

35. Cf. prelude, mm. 46, 50, etc., and the musette.

36. Kayser and Gerber placed mordents on bass g–g in mm. 18, 20, and 21; the Agricola/Kirnberger copy (AmB 498) transfers these ornaments to the following downbeats.

37. An echo of the same idea occurs in the prelude BWV 894/1.

38. The motive might be what led Dannreuther (1893–5, 1:138) to claim this piece as further proof of Dieupart's influence on Bach.

39. Staccato strokes appear in AmB 489 and related copies. A few late copies, e.g., that by Fasch, omit the tempo mark and have common time in place of cut time.

40. The late source AmB 489 contains a few additional ornaments—not found in most editions prior to the NBA—as well as signs that may represent further "diminutions" that were never written out (as Dürr suggests, NBA V/7, KB, 153).

41. The figuration resembles that in the little prelude BWV 900/1, also in E minor.

42. Bach uses rondeau form in the gavottes of the early Suite BWV 822, the violin partita BWV 1006, and the flute suite BWV 1067.

43. The mordent in the theme, placed editorially on bass g in Example 13.10b, appears on the alto or tenor note in the sources (NBA V/7, KB, 172).

44. Cf. the gavotta in Corelli's Concerto Grosso in F, op. 6, no. 9.

45. Measures 12b–20a constitute an eight-bar phrase but cannot be evenly divided. Gavotte 1 in Suite 3 also departs from normal gavotte phrasing after the double bar with a six-measure phrase.

46. LEm ms. 26, a copy by Penzel, who studied at the Thomasschule.

47. In the *Art of Fugue*, both *rectus* and *inversus* versions of the four-part mirror fugue have trills in mm. 11 and 23. There, and in the two-harpsichord arrangement of the three-part mirror fugue, a few other ornaments are present only in the *rectus* or the *inversus*, not in both.

48. See Werbeck (2003), especially the example designated *Secundus quando Bassus ascendit . . .* on pp. 93–4.

49. Siegele (1960) gives a detailed account of the present gigue.

Notes for Chapter 14

1. In a discussion accompanying his own *Clavierstücke* (Berlin, 1762); see BD, 3:173 (item 715).

2. The organ fantasia BWV 573 and the air with variations BWV 991 (see chap. 10). There might have been many more sketches or drafts, but about forty leaves were removed, probably in the eighteenth century (NBA V/4, KB, 26).

3. The 1725 volume contains two of the French Suites as well as two of the Partitas, but otherwise it is of relatively little importance as a source of Bach's own music.

4. See, for example, the revisions in Suite no. 3: allemande, m. 10; sarabande, mm. 21–2; Suite no. 4: allemande, mm. 7, 9, 14; gavotte, m. 5; Suite no. 5: allemande, mm. 7, 21. The changes are most easily studied by comparing versions "A" and "B" in NBA V/8 (discussed below).

5. Anna Magdalena's copies of two suites in the 1725 *Clavier-Büchlein*, also edited in NBA V/4, are essentially identical to Dürr's version "B."

6. Dürr admits (NBA V/8, KB, 58) that the readings for version "B" are a collation, at least as far as performance signs are concerned.

7. *La Couperin* appeared in the composer's *Quatrième Livre* of 1730. A copy of the rondeau *Les bergeries* in P 225 is distinct from the version printed in Couperin's *Second Livre* (1717), but it is uncertain whether the differences are due to Bach's having come across an early version transmitted in manuscript.

8. Measures 2 and 4 contain echoes of the first movement of the D-minor harpsichord concerto BWV 1052 (mm. 62ff.); Bach's version of the latter for organ and orchestra opened Cantata no. 146, first performed in 1726 or 1728—another possible link between this suite and the mid-1720s.

9. The BWV number 819a, originally applied only to the new allemande, now seems to have been extended to the entire suite as given by Vogler.

10. Compare BWV 819, mm. 3–4 and 9–10, with BWV 817, mm. 1 and 9. The two movements also share a syncopated motive, used in the second half of each (BWV 819, m. 20; BWV 817, m. 22b). Both turn to the relative minor just after a cadence to the tonic (BWV 819, m. 7; BWV 817, m. 5).

11. Dürr describes the chromaticism of the new allemande as "somewhat artificial" (NBA V/8, KB, 76).

12. Kayser is the only copyist to give both allemandes. Talle (2003, 157) dates his copy of the later allemande "around 1730," some five years after the original entry. Dürr places Vogler's copy no later than 1729.

13. Perhaps in m. 10 there ought to be a tie between the first two notes of the bass, in both versions.

14. Compare mm. 25–8 with English Suite no. 2, bourrée 2, mm. 17–20.

15. E.g., the dotted rhythms in the bass in allemande, mm. 7, 15, where the Altnikol copy gives apparently earlier readings.

16. Compare m. 20b in the allemande of English Suite no. 6.

17. The bass also has the melody after the double bar in the sarabande of the Sixth English Suite, but for only two measures.

18. The note values of the gigue in the partita were doubled when it was published; both movements were originally notated in the same fashion, mainly in dotted eighths and sixteenths.

19. Eleven of Froberger's twenty gigues are in duple meter (four of the pieces occur in both duple- and triple-time versions). Rhythmic notation similar to that of a duple-time gigue also occurs in sections of Froberger's canzoni and capricci, and in the *manualiter* setting of *Wir glauben all' an einen Gott* BWV 681 in CU3.

20. Cut time appears to have been the norm in seventeenth-century duple-time gigues. The NBA's version "B" has common time, but Jones reports in his edition that P 418, P 420, and Gerber all give cut time.

21. Related types of courantes and gigues appear in the suites for cello and violin; at least the cello suites are probably earlier (see Eppstein 1976, 47).

22. Corrections in P 224, as well as a shift in the appearance of Bach's notation, suggest that in mm. 38–44 he was composing a new ending to replace a still earlier reading, now lost (see Seidel 2002, 226–8, including facsimile).

23. Seidel (2002, 230) describes version 2 as Bach's shortened revision of version 4. But as version 2 was copied only by Gerber, in 1725 (see NBA V/8, KB, 40–1), it is unlikely to represent a revision of an earlier text preserved in several later copies.

24. Anna Magdalena's hasty writing of slurs is evident in the facsimile in NBA V/4: viii. Slurs in her copy of the gigue from the first cello suite (in P 269) are equally imprecise.

25. Bach normally drew barlines separately for the upper and lower staves of each system, but after m. 4 and m. 8 someone (not necessarily Bach) added heavy barlines between the staves. The copy breaks off after m. 12, at the end of a page, so it is unclear whether this notation continued.

26. Except for the alternate minuet and an important variant in the sarabande (see Example 14.5), the text of BWV 814a differs only in small details from that of NBA version "B."

27. That BWV 814a stands between versions "A" and "B" is also implicit in m. 23 of the anglaise, where Kayser first changed and then restored the original reading; BWV 814a retains the rejected note d′ in place of bass a♯.

28. The relevant page of the autograph (P 224) is lost, but copies read "Gavotte" (NBA V/4, KB, 32).

29. Curiously, the low note is avoided in the first ending (m. 16A), and one must emend the d in m. 9 to D upon repetition.
30. In both courantes, dotted rhythms are presumably to be "assimilated" to the triplets.
31. The NBA gives the minuet only as part of version "B"; Kayser inserted it into his copy around the same time as the allemande of BWV 819a (facsimile in NBA V/8).
32. At least some of the mordents in CB appear to be later additions. Those in the subject of the gigue in French Suite no. 4 appear only in Kayser's and Gerber's copies.
33. See bass of allemande, mm. 17–8; courante, 11–2 and 32; gavotte [1], 13–5.
34. See below on the prelude. In gavotte 2, mm. 26–8 recall the prelude in F minor and the fugue in F♯ of WTC2.
35. Michel also copied BWV 872a/1; see chap. 12.
36. Facsimile in Dadelsen (1958, plate 8), transcribed in Marshall (1972, sketch 167).
37. E.g., "Mein gläubiges Herze" in BWV 68, or the duet "Wir eilen mit schwachen doch emsigen Schritten" in BWV 78.
38. As Jones suggests (edition, p. 8).
39. In mm. 5 and 6, left hand; see facsimiles in NBA V/4 and the separate edition of BWV 816 by Hans-Christian Müller (Vienna: Wiener Urtext, 1983).
40. Gerber already had the revised version available for his copy, made in 1725 or soon afterward. The only revisions that involved changing any notes appear to be those in the bass of the courante, m. 29, and of the polonaise, m. 2.
41. Cf. Forkel (1802, 38/NBR, 453–4) on Bach's habit of playing pieces for pupils before they studied it.
42. The *polacca* in the First Brandenburg Concerto and the polonaise in the suite with flute BWV 1067.
43. On Kirnberger's *Methode Sonaten aus'm Ermel zu schüddeln* (Berlin, 1783), see Newman (1961), which includes the first half of Kirnberger's derived sonata.
44. There is no reason to think that Mattheson's minuets were engraved out of order to fill up unused space, for in several cases an entire gigue and minuet fall on one page. The NBA puts Bach's minuet last.

Notes for Chapter 15

1. For the announcement of Partita no. 1 in the November 1, 1726, issue of the Leipzig *Post-Zeitungen*, see NBA V/1, KB, 9.
2. Jones (1988, 67–77) argues that the Partitas were composed almost entirely at Leipzig, in the order 3, 6, 1, 2, 4, and 5.
3. The cantatas in question are BWV 170, 35, 169, 49, and possibly 47.
4. Partita no. 3 also is restricted to a relatively narrow range in the version of the *Clavier-Büchlein*; low AA in the allemande occurs only in the printed edition, d‴ only in the scherzo, which is absent from the manuscript.
5. The full title, repeated in essentially the same form in each installment of the Partitas, begins: *Clavier Ubung* [sic] *bestehend in Praeludien, Allemanden, Couranten . . . und anderen Galan-terien; Denen Liebhabern zur Gemüths-Ergoezung verfertiget von Johann Sebastian Bach.*
6. Two subsequent issues of uncertain date contain a small number of musically insignificant changes. For details of the work's publishing history, see Jones (1988) and NBA V/1, KB, 9ff.
7. GB Lbl Hirsch III.37 (cited in NBA V/1, KB, as exemplar G23).
8. Wolff (1991b, 215, 218) finds that exemplar G25 (in US Wc) contains markings of "autograph character" and "may have served for performance and instruction in Bach's presence." But Jones (1988, 33–4) argues that alterations in exemplars G24 (SPK), G26 (US U), and G28 (A Wn-h), although showing similar handwriting, are unlikely to be Bach's on account of "the many discrepancies between them and the dubious character of some of the alterations."
9. Wolff (1984) reproduces an exemplar in Leipzig; facsimiles of the the supposed *Handexem-plar* have been published by Gregg Press (1985) and Fuzeau (1991, rev. 1995). Performer's Facsimiles (New York, n.d.) has issued a facsimile of G25, the Washington exemplar.
10. Jones (1988, 67–8) points to the crowding of triplets in the sarabande of Partita no. 3 (mm. 16–9, in the autograph P 225) as evidence that Bach was adding melodic embellishment as he wrote that movement. But the triplets are not clearly inserts and do not replace earlier entries.

11. The early forms of the minuets are edited in NBA V/1, KB, 72–3, from SPK P 672 (Michel).

12. The original confused the issue by omitting a rest in m. 16; in emending this NBA V/1 also changed the direction of several stems.

13. The giga is preserved alongside C. P. E. Bach's F-minor *Probestuck* (W. 63/6/1), also containing hand crossings, together with the latter's so-called Solfeggietto (W. 117/2) in the nineteenth-century manuscript SPK N. Mus. ms. 10480.

14. Müthel's copy (P 815), transcribed in NBA V/1, KB, Nachtrag, 15, contains some stylistically implausible details, such as a stuttering repetition of the thirty-second f'/g' in m. 6.

15. In the Washington exemplar (G 25).

16. Jones (1988, 34–5) argues that conflicting alterations of the passage in exemplars G25 and G26 cast doubt on the reliability of both.

17. The *Pralltriller* of C. P. E. Bach (1753–62, i.2.3.36).

18. An upbeat figure lasting a full beat also occurs in the allemande of the Reinken suite arranged as BWV 965—which perhaps inspired the gigue of BWV 827.

19. The autograph shows a similar sign; neither NBA V/4, KB, 74, nor NBA V/1, KB, 60, reproduces it exactly.

20. To avoid an awkward page turn, the gigue starts at the beginning of the next page. This left three systems free after the conclusion of the burlesca.

21. The scherzos from Bonporti's *Inventioni da Camera* (Bologna, 1712), edited in BG 45, bear no particular resemblance to this one, nor to one attributed to Bach as BWV 844 (probably by W. F. Bach; see appendix A).

22. The exemplars, with their sigla from NBA V/1, are those in US Wc (G25), US U (G26), and A Wn-h (G28). Their variant readings were first published in Wolff (1979, 74), subsequently in the *Nachtrag* to NBA V/1, KB, and in the edition by Engler.

23. These alterations occur in G25 and G28. The open fifths in mm. 39–41 could have been avoided by also altering the bass, as was done in m. 27.

24. In AmB 489 (readings in NBA V/6, KB, 156). For the sonata, see Newman (1961).

25. I owe this insight, gained in the course of an audition, to Ralph Kirkpatrick, who made me sing the middle part.

26. The upper line in m. 2, like the bass of m. 4, is an elaboration of the tenor in m. 1.

27. A mistake in the original print led to misreadings for the slur and ornament in mm. 1, 13, and 29 in BG 3 and other editions prior to NBA V/1.

28. The second half of the gigue also includes (in mm. 70–3) a quasi-inversion of a passage from the first half (mm. 21–4).

29. The delay might have been related to Bach's assuming the directorship of the Leipzig Collegium Musicum in April 1729; another possibility is that the engraver, Bach's student J. Gotthilf Ziegler, had been unavailable (Butler 1986, 15–6).

30. Compare overture, mm. 41–3, and praeambulum, mm. 37–8; gigue of Partita no. 4, mm. 33–6, and praeambulum, mm. 32–6. There is also a resemblance between the main theme of the praeambulum and that of movement 1 in the sixth sonata (also in G) from the ca. 1726 set by J. G. Graun.

31. For evidence elsewhere that may favor assimilation, see the discussions of the F#-minor prelude in WTC2 (chap. 12) and the three-part mirror fugue in the *Art of Fugue* (chap. 18). Additional evidence supporting assimilation can be found in Bach's manuscript copy of Handel's cantata *Armida abandonnata* (HWV 105); see the foreword to Chrysander's edition (HG 52/1: ii) and the variants illustrated there for movement 4, especially mm. 32–5.

32. The note d''' occurs also once in the praeambulum (m. 87).

33. Müthel, who preserved an ornamented version of the sinfonia of Partita no. 2, also copied a version of the present movement that supplements the original ornaments, edited in NBA V/1, KB, Nachtrag, 18–9. Most of the same ornaments appear in the exemplar in US U (G26), but this does not increase their credibility.

34. The passage in C. P. E. Bach (1753–62, i.2.2.11) arguing for meaningful distinctions in the written values of appoggiaturas was added only in the third (1787) edition; Emanuel's own early works make no such distinctions.

35. These appoggiaturas are absent from NBA V/1 but appear correctly in BG 3. In m. 20 the sign in the print is distinctly beneath the main note (see Example 15.6b), at least in the exemplar of the 1731 print (at LEm) reproduced in Wolff (1984).

36. The quarters in mm. 24, 26, etc., are followed by sixteenth rests, the latter being effectively equivalent to a second dot. In the print, single eighths and sixteenths in different voices that follow dots (e.g., m. 9, third beat) are consistently aligned vertically with one another.

37. Williams (2003b, 150) relates the hemiolic figuration to that found in Rameau's *Les tricotets*, which appeared in Rameau's *Nouvelles suites*, not published until 1729 or 1730. In Rameau's earlier minuet *Le lardon* the left hand jumps around and crosses the right, in a manner that might have inspired the present piece.

38. See the hand-crossing minuets by C. P. E. Bach (W. 111, engraved in 1731; see Butler 1986, 12–5; facsimile in Berg 1985, 5:103) and W. F. Bach (F. 25/1–2), as well as movements in two suites or sonatas in G edited as early works of C. P. E. Bach in CPEBCW I/8.2 (no. 68, mvt. 4, and no. 70, mvt. 2;).

39. Cf. mm. 22–3 in variation 16 (the *Ouverture*) in the Goldberg Variations.

40. The E-minor Partita was first printed separately, like the others in the set, but no exemplars survive of the first edition, whose existence is inferred from manuscript copies, from contemporary references to it, and from corrections in the 1731 print.

41. This integration of prelude and fugue, previously glimpsed in the prelude in E♭ in WTC1, is further developed in the massive organ prelude (BWV 552/1) that opens part 3 of the *Clavierübung*.

42. The manuscript version lacks mm. 74–5; in revising the work for publication, Bach lengthened the C-major "plateau."

43. The early version of the aria, in BWV 244b (probably dating from 1727), uses lute rather than viola da gamba; Bach might have written it with the possibility of keyboard performance in mind, as he did the lute movements in the Saint John Passion.

44. That BWV 1019a dates from Cöthen, as proposed by Rempp (2001, 181), would be hard to prove; the sole source dates from 1725 (Schulze 1984a, 115–6), and the piecemeal copying of the movements there implies that they were composed separately (Talle 2003a, 74ff.).

45. Thus, the air would seem redundant if played after the sarabande, immediately before the *Tempo di Gavotta*.

46. NBA V/1 emends m. 30 "by analogy to mm. 10 and 26," changing treble e′′ to d′′ and bass e′ to d′. But the *Handexemplar* retains the printed text without alteration, and the departure from the pattern established in m. 26 is not necessarily a problem.

47. Further analysis in Schulenberg (1999a, 114–6). In both versions the trill sign in m. 29 extends to the third beat (contrary to BG 3 and NBA V/1). This implies that the figure on the third beat should be played as a continuation or termination of the trill.

48. The ornament in m. 17 is not on the eighth note a′ (as it appears in the NBA) but on c′′ in both the print and in the autograph; the latter also places a mordent on g′ at the corresponding point in m. 19.

49. Corrections in P 225 (e.g., in m. 7) confirm that the version in BWV 1019a is earlier, though not necessarily the earliest. Further revisions were made for the print.

50. Eppstein (1964) first offered a reconstruction; another appears in *J. S. Bach: The Music for Violin and Cembalo/Continuo*, ed. Richard D. P. Jones (Oxford: Oxford University Press, 1993), 67–8. Both follow the version of P 225 more closely than the imaginative, if speculative, reconstruction in Jones's dissertation (1988, 128–9), which even offers alternate solutions more idiomatic to the violin in a few measures.

51. The passing notes and the beams signifying sixteenths (originally, thirty-seconds) were insertions in mm. 9 and elsewhere in the autograph. A similar process may have occurred in the B-minor prelude of WTC2.

52. See, for instance, the subject of Canzon 1.

Notes for Chapter 16

1. The date is based on an autograph entry in Walther's personal copy of the *Lexicon* (Walther 1732); see NBA V/2, KB, 15–6.

2. Glöckner (1981) reconstructs the repertory of the Collegium Musicum from the few surviving sources.

3. Beißwenger (1995) includes a complete facsimile of the sole source, Scholz's manuscript copy in Gb.

4. For example, in mm. 16 and 18 the alternate version has scalar figuration for the right hand, instead of repeating the arpeggios of the previous measure; where the familiar version pauses on held chords in mm. 27–8, the other continues with figuration in sixteenths.

5. Most important is Oley's copy of BWV 971 (in US Bp, source A in NBA V/2, KB). This agrees with the copy in Gb in the simpler reading of mm. 37–8 of the first movement, and elsewhere preserves traces of an intermediate version, later erased and replaced by that of the print.

6. According to this announcement, two more partitas would follow; see BD 2:202 (item 276).

7. Lbl K.8.g.7, designated source G in NBA V/2, KB. The engravers of the print are identified in Butler (1980).

8. Other debatable readings include the placement of dynamic markings in the last movement of the concerto (mm. 33 and 53); some slurs (mm. 47–8, 77–88) and rhythms (m. 152) in the overture; and the addition of an appoggiatura in the second passepied (downbeat of m. 17) and a trill in the gigue (m. 22).

9. Butler (2003) notes the imitation of this later style in compositions by several of Bach's pupils.

10. Scheibe's review appeared in late 1739, two years after his notorious criticism of Bach's vocal works. See BD 2:373–4 (item 463); the translation in NBR, 331–2, is from the expanded version published in 1745.

11. Written-out embellishment is especially common in the Dresden string works of Pisendel (see, e.g., Fechner 1980).

12. Williams suggests that the three movements of the concerto "seem to have been calculated and notated so as to have the same pulse" (i.e., on the quarter, quarter, and half note, respectively), an intriguing possibility although not dictated by any known notational convention of the time.

13. Schering (1902–3, 243) noted the resemblance to the theme of the final section of the *symphonie* that opens the ballet *Impatientia* in Muffat's *Florilegium primum* (Passau, 1696; ed. in DTÖ 2 by Heinrich Rietsch [1894]). The resemblance is less marked in the presumed early version of the movement, which bears the tempo mark *All[egro] moderato* as opposed to Muffat's *Presto*; the latter might, however, have been an all-purpose "quick" tempo indication for the older composer.

14. In the alternate version, repeated notes are first heard in m. 15 of the ritornello; this was presumably the origin of the idea not present until m. 30 of the published version.

15. A "Dekolierung" by Landowska (1924, 131, reproduced in Schleuning 1979 and elsewhere) eliminates only the most superficial layer of melodic embellishment.

16. Compare mm. 97–100 and 132ff. with mm. 69–72 and 112ff., respectively, in the first movement.

17. The return in m. 152, following almost immediately upon a cadence to A minor, sounds like the da capo of an aria and has parallels in sonata and concerto movements from the same period, e.g., the first movement of C. P. E. Bach's A-major concerto of 1741, W. 8; Schulenberg (1984, 134).

18. At m. 129 the print has only the word *piano* and a bracket that seems to indicate that the dynamic applies to the upper stave. But the bracket may have been meant to point to the lower staff (as suggested in NBA V/2, KB, 61); elsewhere in the movement, the repeated-note accompaniment heard in mm. 129ff. sounds piano against a forte melody, and *forte* at m. 139 is placed between the staves at the beginning of the measure—which makes sense only if the right hand is already forte. In any case, *piano* in m. 129 cannot apply to the a′′ on the downbeat and must have been misplaced to the left by half a beat.

19. The NBA's piano in m. 155, lower stave, occurs in the middle of a motive.

20. The most relevant article here is Neumann (1974); see also Neumann (1965; 1977; and 1979) and Fuller (1977; 1985).

21. BWV 831a is edited separately in NBA V/2. It lacks many of the ornaments of the printed version, but the only substantial difference involving notes occurs where straightforward downward transposition from C to B minor would have produced an FF♯ (bourrée 2, m. 12). A second copy of BWV 831a, in LEm ms. 8 (Preller), includes the copyist's usual excessive ornamentation.

22. Both Neumann (1974) and NBA V/2, KB, 50–1, cite against the view adopted here the many additional ornaments in the Preller copy (partly transcribed in NBA V/2, KB, 87–8). As in other heavily ornamented Preller copies, the ornaments, which are probably Preller's own (see Schulze 1984a, 85), require a slow tempo, but this does not necessarily reflect Bach's practice around 1730. Neumann supposed that Preller's copy was "written probably in the

1730s," but it can hardly have been copied much before 1750, as Preller was born in 1727 (Schulze 1984a, 76–7).

23. Thirty-seconds also appear in the early version in mm. 8, 11, and 12 (left hand); 153 (first beat); and 160–1.

24. In the earlier version some dotted rhythms were already notated in this manner, e.g., in m. 4.

25. See C. P. E. Bach (1753–62, i.2.3.6) on the normal long trill with suffix or turn, and on not playing an additional turn when, as in this case, one turn is already written out (i.2.3.16, example d).

26. The first entry is that of the soprano in m. 89.

27. The first courante in the *Pièces de clavessin* (Paris, 1687) of Elizabeth Jacquet de La Guerre opens in a vaguely similar way; there is no reason to think that Bach knew the piece.

28. The first edition likewise placed an erroneous slur on the tenor in passepied 2, mm. 1–2, by false analogy to the tie in the bass. The errors in the passepied and sarabande were perpetuated in BG 3 and other editions.

29. This is a point in favor of the authenticity of BWV 821, since the latter is clearly *not* a later and therefore spurious imitation of the echo movement in BWV 831.

30. See the second movement, subtitled "L'Einschnitt," in his keyboard sonata W. 52/6 (composed in 1758).

31. See, e.g., the aria "Flösst, mein Heiland" (mm. 43b–45) in part 4 of the Christmas Oratorio (BWV 248/4); also mm. 1–2 in the first movement of the Concerto in C minor for two harpsichords and strings BWV 1060, known in modern arrangements for oboe and violin.

32. ". . . lassen sich aber auf dem Clavier sehr wohl spielen" (BD 3:124 [item 695]).

33. "Ihr Verfasser spielte sie selbst oft auf der Clavichorde" (BD 3:292–3 [item 808]).

34. In the concerto (BWV 1057), see mvt. 2, m. 69, where a "Phrygian" cadence like that of BWV 964 is embellished by an added chromatic line in recorder 1.

35. BWV 968 lacks m. 17 of the violin version, indicating that it could derive from an earlier draft of the latter.

36. The same countersubject occurs in the fugue of the Third Violin Sonata BWV 1005.

37. The subject is quoted in Mattheson (1737; see NBR, 328); as Mattheson does not mention the remarkable scoring for solo violin, he might have known the work from a transcription or an impromptu keyboard performance.

38. Documented in the letter by Johann Elias Bach in BD 2:366 (item 448)/NBR, 204.

39. Bach also included obbligato lute parts in early versions of his two surviving Leipzig passions: in the arioso "Betrachte, meine Seele" in the first (1724) version of the Saint John Passion, later played alternatively on organ and harpsichord (or lute-harpsichord?); and in the aria "Komm, süßes Kreuz" in an early version of the Saint Matthew Passion (BWV 244a), later replaced by viola da gamba.

40. The differing views cited in chap. 4 on the practicality of BWV 996 as a lute work are typical of what has been published to date and will not be further pursued here.

41. According to Agricola's note in Adlung (1768, 2:139, = BD 3:195 [item 744]/NBR, 366).

42. Final chords in BWV 995 (courante) and BWV 997 (prelude) are easily adjusted for the keyboard, as is the chord in BWV 997, sarabande, m. 3, second beat. In the fugue of BWV 997, bass notes unplayable at the keyboard must be tranposed up an octave in mm. 48, 63–4, 79 (|| 101), 87, and 96–7. The fugue of BWV 998 has an unplayable stretch at m. 15, in a passage where Bach clearly sacrificed a cogent treble line for playability on a non-keyboard instrument.

43. Unidiomatic figuration occurs in BWV 995: gavotte 1, mm. 17–18; BWV 997, prelude, mm. 40, 42, 44; sarabande, mm. 6–7; double, m. 2. Figuration in the first movement of BWV 1006a, mm. 17–28, which Bach had previously rewritten for organ (presumably with pedals) in BWV 29/1, is left in a form unidiomatic for a keyboard instrument.

44. Kobayashi (1988, 65), however, dates the autograph of BWV 998 to "around 1735."

45. The problems are evident in the errors and corrections in the copy of the original suite (P 804/40) by Kellner, who attempted to resolve the *scordatura* into normal notation (see Stinson 1989a, 60).

46. Facsimile of the autograph with introduction by Godelieve Spiessens (Fontes musicae bibliothecae regiae belgicae, vol. I/1, Brussels: Bibliotheca Regia Belgica, 1981).

47. Radke (1964) compares the two versions; Schulze (1983, 246) tentatively identified the copy-

ist, whose tablature is reproduced in NBA V/10, KB. Rifkin (1995, 134–6, especially note 56) further considers technical aspects of BWV 995 and its dedicatee.

48. E.g., in m. 5, f′ on the second half of beat 2 can be changed to d′ to give the soprano an unaltered statement of the subject.

49. The sinfonia is better known from its re-use in Cantata no. 29 (1731). Swanton (1985) discusses the organ part of the cantata, reproducing the first page of the autograph (St 106); there are no explicit pedal indications, but use of pedals is implied by the notation in mm. 13ff.

50. The figuration in mm. 17–28 of the prelude, rewritten idiomatically for keyboard in BWV 29/1, follows the original; only the sustained trill on mm. 82–5 of the gavotte requires a keyboard instrument.

51. Agricola, in his annotation for an earlier passage (2: 139), fails to mention the presence of pedals on the lute-harpsichord with three ranks of strings that Bach acquired around 1740. But pull-down pedals would not sound their own strings, hence there would have been no reason to mention them in a passage where Agricola is describing the lute- and theorbo-like sounds that the Hildebrandt instrument was capable of producing.

52. The octave notation of the first four movements, retained in BG 45, led to unfounded suggestions that the work was for flute (or violin) and continuo (see NBA V/10, KB, 143). This notation might have stemmed from an indication in the lost autograph for octave transposition in case of keyboard performance, as in "Betrachte, meine Seele" in the Saint John Passion. The abandonment of this notation in the double implies that the latter was composed separately.

53. Measure 2 is not difficult to play, but the figuration would be more idiomatic if g′′ were assigned to the top voice instead of the bass. The note f′′′, which occurs in m. 8, is found in no other Bach keyboard works apart from the Triple Concerto BWV 1044, another problematical late composition.

54. The earliest source of the "Wedge," according to Stinson (1989a, 24), is a joint copy by Bach and Kellner (P 274) dated "after 1727."

55. Weyrauch's lute tablature (reproduced in NBA V/10, KB) provides naturals on A in m. 13 (bass) and a′′ in m. 18. In addition, e in m. 44 of the double must be natural by analogy to m. 12 and to the corresponding measure in the gigue *simple*.

56. A few bass notes must be played at written pitch, and at some point in the final phrase the treble must also jump up to notated pitch (perhaps on written c′′ in m. 42). For adjustments in the fugue, see note 42 above.

57. Only m. 15 of the fugue requires a momentary stretch greater than an octave, and if one cannot manage the latter, then tenor f can simply be shortened from a quarter to an eighth. Anyone troubled by the blatant parallel fifths in m. 46 of the prelude can eliminate them by substituting f for e♭ in the first chord.

58. At mm. 66–7; compare the prelude in F minor.

Notes for Chapter 17

1. The antithesis between music-lovers or amateurs (*Liebhabern*) and connoisseurs (*Kenner*) would be a familiar one in the later eighteenth century, repeated in the titles of six famous sets of keyboard pieces published by C. P. E. Bach in the 1770s.

2. The non-circulating temperaments on many organs would have made the complete list of pieces an ideal rather than a realizable concert program in many places (see Wolff 1991b, 417, "Postscript").

3. One melody, the German Gloria *Allein Gott*, appears in three settings, of which the first is not explicitly designated as being *manualiter* or *pedaliter*; it is usually taken to be *manualiter* although it is possible to play its chorale cantus firmus on the pedals.

4. "... einige *Clavier* Sachen, die hauptsächlich vor die Herrn *Organisten* gehören" (BD, 2:335 [item 434]/NBR, 202).

5. Wolff (1984, 30) points to Grigny's possible influence on the structure of Bach's volume; Bach had copied out the Grigny work at Weimar between 1709 and 1712 (Beißwenger 1992, 194–5).

6. These four movements (like their *pedaliter* counterparts) constitute a Lutheran organ mass; the following chorales represent the catechism or declaration of belief. Butler (1990, 51ff.) argues plausibly that the Kyrie group was originally meant to be played *attacca*, the final chord of the Christe and the initial rest in Kyrie 2 being later additions. If so, these form a parallel to the first three movements in the early version of the *Art of Fugue*.

7. Williams (2003, 414) finds the notes of the chorale melody in the top line of mm. 11b–14.

8. Dirksen (2002, 182) makes a case for including the New Year's chorale BWV 702 in the set. Its counterpoint is complex (stretto, counterpoint at the twelfth), but apart from lingering questions about its textual integrity and authorship (see Williams 2003, 441–2), it differs from the others in being a double fugue on lines 1–2 of the chorale, and it requires pedals for the last phrase.

9. Yearsley (2002, 103–4) sees here a response to Scheibe's criticism of Bach's "turgid" style; other works in the volume could be interepreted similarly, e.g., the combination of canon with *galant* triplets in the *pedaliter* fantasia on *Vater unser* BWV 682. Zelenka and other composers had been juxtaposing "galant" with chromatic ideas for as long as Bach, however.

10. Something similar occurs often in the recapitulations of certain trio-sonata movements by J. G. Graun and C. P. E. Bach, where alternate phrases of the returning theme are divided between the upper parts. J. S. Bach does the same in the first movement of the B-minor flute sonata BWV 1030 (mm. 35ff.).

11. *Clavier Ubung bestehend in einer ARIA mit verschiedenen Verænderungen vors Clavicimbal mit 2 Manualen.* For the date 1741, rather than 1742, see NBA V/2, KB, 94, and Butler (1988).

12. Marshall (1976a, 342–3). Another possible explanation is that the engraver Schmid, not Bach himself, was the publisher for this volume (Wolff, NBA V/2, KB, 109).

13. Forkel probably learned the story from Friedemann, who surely would have mentioned the fact if the work had been written for him. Goldberg is often described as a pupil of J. S. Bach, whose influence is palpable in several compositions, including a trio sonata in C long attributed to Bach as BWV 1037. But even if Goldberg spent time as a boy in Leipzig (which is not established), his teacher there might have been not Sebastian but Friedemann. The latter took over the teaching of Nichelmann around 1730.

14. Composers of such sets include Byrd, Bull, Sweelinck, Frescobaldi, Poglietti, and Buxtehude. The fragmentary Air with Variations BWV 991 in the 1722 *Clavier-Büchlein* is more likely to have been of the simple pedagogic type.

15. Another possibility is Bach's older brother of the same name (Schulze 1985, 77–8). The sarabande (without its variations) is edited in NBA V/2, KB, 110, the complete work in *Johann Christoph Bach (1642-1703): Werke für Clavier*, ed. Pieter Dirksen (Wiesbaden: Breitkopf und Härtel, 2002). This work is considerably simpler than two other variation sets usually attributed to Johann Christoph Bach of Eisenach, making it plausible that this is an imitation by a younger namesake of the latter. A somewhat similar bass line occurs in the first three movements of Reinken's C-Major Suite (MM, no. 15).

16. Breig (1982, 115) makes a similar observation on the length of the *Art of Fugue*, as compared to Quantz's ideal proportions for a concerto or sonata.

17. Bach re-ordered the Canonic Variations either before or after printing, and the copies of the early chorale *partite* give the individual variations in differing orders. There is no evidence of any such tinkering with the Goldberg Variations.

18. Small differences in the ornaments and especially in the rhythm of m. 24 show that Anna Magdalena's manuscript copy probably stems from a prepublication autograph; see NBA V/2, KB, 101–2.

19. "Verschiedene *Canones* über die ersteren acht Fundamental-Noten vorheriger Aria. von J. S. Bach." Facsimile (from Bach's *Handexemplar* in F Pn) in NBA V/2, which also includes Wolff's edition and solutions to the canons.

20. Bach holds a copy of BWV 1076 in Haussmann's well-known 1746 portrait.

21. "14 Canonic Variations by J. S. Bach (BWV 1087)," for two pianos (1995).

22. The regularized ornament signs are explained in NBA V/2, KB, 114, as corresponding with the "main version" (*Hauptform*) of the sign as found in the print.

23. The term *tremblement appuyé* is d'Anglebert's; the sign is not shown or named in either of the main Bach sources on ornaments, CB and C. P. E. Bach (1753–62).

24. For example, compare variation 17 with *Essercizi*, no. 18 (K. 18), mm. 28–9.

25. The keyboards must be uncoupled to permit the sounding of unisons.

26. On changing registrations between individual variations on a chorale tune, see Williams (1980-4, 3:157). The contract offered to Bach in 1713 at Halle required him to "change the…stops at each verse" (BD 2: 50 [item 63]/NBR, 67). For the C. P. E. Bach sonata (H. 53 = W. 69), see the facsimile of a manuscript copy with autograph additions in Berg (1985, 3:319). The copy is by Schlichting, who worked for Emanuel around 1750 (see Rifkin 1985, 160n.), although the autograph entries dictating the registrations could be later.

27. In variation 3 of the last movement of W. 69.

28. C. P. E. Bach does not actually show the bracketed realization of Example 17.4a, which is based on the description in his verbal text (1753–62, i.2.2.14).

29. Or was this practice "odious" because Emanuel Bach was jealous of his privileged colleague Quantz, who favored it (1752, 8.6)?

30. Bach was already writing similar continuo parts in his Weimar cantatas, not coincidentally at a time when he is also thought to have produced the cello suites; cf. the continuo duet "In meinem Gott" from Cantata 162.

31. As printed, the slurs in mm. 9 and 11 appear to be on the first three sixteenths, not all four as in BG 3. Either reading is possible, but a four-note slur is more likely, given the imprecision with which slurs appear elsewhere. The longer slur clarifies the function of all four sixteenths as an *accentuirte Brechung* ("broken chord with acciaccatura," Kirnberger 1771–9, 1:217).

32. As Schwandt (1990) points out, the sharp in m. 32A is editorial; it seems unnecessary.

33. BG 3 and other editions contain an error: read b′ for a′ on the downbeat of m. 25.

34. See variation 16, m. 21, where the last note in the alto is sometimes changed from e′′ to f♯′′; and variation 26, m. 14, where the second note of the alto is usually changed from d′′ to e′′ to avoid an innocuous cross relation. The alteration for variation 16 appears in four exemplars of the original print—but not Bach's (according to NBA V/2, KB). On transferred resolution, see Arnold (1931, 840–55), especially his Example 7, taken from C. P. E. Bach (1753–62, ii.13.2.4—Example 358c in Mitchell's translation). Another example of transferred resolution occurs in the last measure of variation 9, where tied b′ in the alto resolves as a′′ in the soprano.

35. Two errors were, however, left to stand in the *Handexemplar* in variation 25; both involve missing accidentals, which are supplied by other exemplars (m. 2: flat on a; m. 13: sharp on f).

36. As in variation 16, the reading of several of these ornaments as *tremblements appuyés* in NBA V/2 does not seem to correspond with the original.

37. Compare the discussion of the trills in the gigue of English Suite no. 6 (chap. 14).

38. Williams (2001, 73) suggests that here Bach remembered a passage in the Vivaldi transcription BWV 973. NBA V/2 reads g on the downbeat of m. 29, following a *custos* at a page break in the print; this is stronger than the printed b and corresponds with the bass of the aria.

39. "Bey vielen hinter einander vorkommenden Tertien…setzt man bey geschwindem Zeit-masse lieber mit den Fingern fort, indem alsdenn das Abwechseln schwerer fällt" (1753–62, i.1.69).

40. Fux did so more literalistically in Partita no. 7 of his *Concentus musico-instrumentalis* (Nuremberg, 1701), edited in DTÖ 47 (1916) and as "Nürnberger Partita" by Adolf Hoffmann (Wolfenbüttel: Möseler, 1939).

41. Williams (2001, 84) gives a helpful example showing just the 3/4 portion of mm. 1–8, rewritten on two staves with a simple bass line and "harmonized as a sarabande."

42. Possible sources for the idea include several pieces in the *Aggiunta* added to the 1637 edition of Frescobaldi's *Toccate d'intavolatura* (Bk. 1), and the chaconne that closes Fischer's *Pièces de clavecin* (ABB no. 47; example in Williams 2001, 87).

43. Williams (2001, 91) suggests that both allude (independently?) to the older *Bergamesca* theme, treated by Frescobaldi among others.

Notes for Chapter 18

1. In June 1749 Count Heinrich von Brühl forced the Leipzig city council to grant Gottlob Harrer an audition and a promise to be appointed "Capell-Director" upon Bach's death (NBR, 240).

2. The chief documents, listed in NBA VIII/1, KB, 102, are contemporary newspaper reports (see BD 2: 434–5 [item 554]/NBR, 224); Bach's printed dedication to Frederick, dated two months later (BD 1:241–2 [item 173]/NBR, 226–8); Bach's obituary (BD 3:85 [item 666]/ NBR, 302–3), written by Agricola and Emanuel Bach; van Swieten's 1774 letter describing a conversation with the King (BD 3:276 [item 790; facsimile opposite page 224]/NBR, 366–7); and Forkel's account (1802, 9–10/NBR, 429–30), evidently based on a vivid retelling of the story by Friedemann Bach (who Forkel says had been present).

3. This scenario follows Butler's (2002) reconstruction of events, based on close examination of the paper and engraving of the printed work.

4. Letter of Oct. 6, 1748, to J. E. Bach (BD 1: 49/NBR, 234). The letter is often interpreted as

referring to the complete *Musical Offering*, but Butler (2002, 325) shows that it refers specifically to the three-part ricercar. In calling the latter the "Prussian" fugue, Bach followed the same convention that has turned C. P. E. Bach's publication of 1742, dedicated to the king, into the "Prussian" sonatas (W. 48).

5. Letter of Sept. 15, 1774; no. 69 in Clark (1997, 65).

6. Most of the court musicians mentioned in modern accounts (e.g., Wolff 2000, 427) probably played only at the Berlin opera; Frederick's concerts at the Potsdam Stadtschloß and later at Sansouci are likely to have involved no more than four or five string players, a keyboard player, and occasionally a bassoon (Mary Oleskiewicz, personal communication based on the court *Capelletats* and *Schatoulle-Rechnungen*, now at the Geheimes Staatsarchiv, Berlin-Dahlem).

7. Butler (2002, 329–30), following a suggestion of Michael Marissen, points to Bach's newspaper announcement of Sept. 30, 1747 (BD 3: 656 [item 558a]/NBR, 229) as establishing an order of (1) ricercars, (2) sonata, and (3) canons. This, however, merely lists the contents by genre, and modern editions follow diverse orders. On the arbitrary nature of the parallels drawn by U. Kirkendale (1980) between Bach's purported ordering of this work and a Latin oration in the manner of Quintilian, see Wolff (1991b, 421–2, with relevant quotations from Williams 1983a, 236, and Williams 1985b, 276).

8. On the ricercar as prelude, see W. Kirkendale (1979). Walker (2000, 288–90) quotes Mattheson's discussion (1713, 175–6) of terms used for preludial movements, most of which occur in Mattheson's 1713 *Pièces*. Wolff (1991a, 330–1) relates Walther's definition (1732, 525–6) to Bach. Both Mattheson and Walther derived their definitions of relevant terms from Brossard.

9. C. P. E. Bach, in his letter to Forkel of Jan. 13, 1775 (BD 3:289 [item 803]/NBR, 399), mentioned that Bach's works not based on an improvisation were composed "without instrument" (*ohne Instrument*).

10. According to Williams (1986d, xii), Thurston Dart made this suggestion in the 1950s.

11. See Wolff (2000, 412–3) on Bach's sale of such an instrument to a Polish nobleman in 1749, and on Agricola's report that Bach had tried out Silbermann's instruments in the 1730s.

12. Substantial portions of the second and third expositions also restate previous passages with little change (mm. 80–6 ‖ 65–71 and 95–101 ‖ 41–52).

13. This type of sequence is a prime technique of "*galant* counterpoint" (Marpurg 1753–4, 2: 94), especially the simple diatonic imitations found in duo and trio sonatas by younger Berlin composers such as C. H. Graun.

14. In the dedication copy sent to Berlin (AmB 73), this acrostic appears across the first page of the *three*-part ricercar, to which it more strictly applies inasmuch as the latter represents the piece Bach actually played for the king.

15. That Bach used his own subject for the improvisation in six parts is indicated in the Obituary (NBR no. 306, p. 303; BD 3:85) and repeated by Forkel (1802, 10/NBR, 430).

16. NBA VIII/1, KB, 91–4, discusses all ten revised passages, presenting the alternate versions on parallel staves.

17. A note (f) is missing in m. 61 of the later version as given in NBA VIII/1 (cf. NBA VIII/1, KB, 92, Example 3).

18. Four further solutions from early sources are given as *Beispielen* 11–4 in NBA VIII/1, KB, 141–3. The first, however, incorporates a misplaced repeat sign, and the second and fourth have improper dissonance treatment in mm. 19 and 5–6, respectively.

19. "Die Kunst der Fuga, in 24. Exempeln," from the notice of May 7, 1751 in the *Critische Nachrichten aus dem Reiche der Gelehrsamkeit* (NBR, 256–8); a shorter announcement using the same phrase appeared in the *Leipziger Zeitungen* (BD, 3:8–9 [item 639]/NBR, 258).

20. "As far as anyone knows, no engraved prints of double fugues with three subjects have appeared other than my own work entitled *Wohlklingende Fingersprache*...but one might very much wish to see something similar published by the famous Mr. Bach of Leipzig, who is a great master of fugue" (Mattheson 1739, iii.23.66). "Double fugue with three subjects" is Mattheson's term for a triple fugue employing invertible counterpoint. The E♭-major fugue in CU3 contains three subjects, but they are never all combined simultaneously; several triple fugues in the WTC (even if composed by 1739) were never engraved and published. Attention to Mattheson as a stimulus to Bach was drawn almost simultaneously by Butler (1983b) and Stauffer (1983).

21. C. P. E. Bach, letter of Jan. 13, 1775 to Forkel (BD 3:289 [item 803]/NBR, 399).
22. Bach might not have known that the Handel fugues included at least one very early piece, and some may have been unauthorized arrangements.
23. This is the work that Mattheson cited in his own 1739 treatise. Haffner of Nuremberg published a reprint of both volumes in 1749 under the charming but meaningless title *Les doits parlants*. Despite glimmers of imagination, the work seems barely competent, and one wonders sadly if this is a reflection of the composer's deafness.
24. This preface replaced a brief notice in the 1751 edition apologizing for the unfinished fugue; the music was unchanged.
25. This is evident from a remark entered by Friedrich Bach into the autograph *Abklatschvorlage* of the Augmentation Canon.
26. The triple fugues, the mirror fugues, the end of the Canon at the Octave, and the two versions of the Augmentation Canon appear in what may be a later portion of the manuscript; opinions vary as to the precise date of this portion, ranging as late as 1746. Hoke (1979) contains facsimiles of both the autograph and the print; the latter includes hand-written corrections corresponding to the errata list (in C. P. E. Bach's hand) on the back of page 4 of Beilage 3 of P 200.
27. The manuscript, which was written on one side only and then soaked in oil to render it transparent, was then traced in reverse onto the prepared plate. Such a manuscript is called an *Abklatschvorlage*; an autograph example for the Augmentation Canon survives (facsimile in Hoke 1979). The process is described in Koprowski (1975).
28. The traditional identification of the engraver as J. G. Schübler was challenged by Wiemer (1977, 40ff.), who instead named Schübler's younger brother. Butler (personal communication, Sept. 23, 2003) has confirmed the traditional identification of Johann Georg as engraver of "the majority of the plates" of the *Art of Fugue*, despite the existence of "strong grounds for identifying Johann Heinrich . . . as the engraver of the *Art of Fugue*" (see Boyd 1999, 466 and 441).
29. Butler's order is based in part on what he takes to be traces of altered page numbers in the print. Although this aspect of his theory has not been universally accepted, his ordering is more logical than the traditional one.
30. Even this work was presented imperfectly, since at least the first twenty-five measures evidently existed in a slightly improved version, the fragmentary BWV 668. The latter is preserved (under the title *Vor deinen Thron tret' ich*) at the end of the manuscript of the "Eighteen" organ chorales (P 271).
31. Forkel (1802, 53; see NBR, 466) was the first to describe the *Art of Fugue* as a variation work.
32. The most influential of many arrangements was that of Wolfgang Graeser, who wrote a study (Graeser 1924) and orchestrated the work for a celebrated performance conducted by the Thomaskantor Karl Straube in 1927.
33. See lists of editions in Dedel (1975, 53–4) and of performances in Kolneder (1977, vol. 5).
34. See, for example, Contrapunctus 1, mm. 36–47, and the tenor in mm. 60–3.
35. "zum Gebrauch des Claviers und der Orgel ausdrücklich eingerichtet" (quoted in Wilhelmi 1992, 102; translation in NBR, 257).
36. The treble rises to e′′′ in the three-part mirror fugue, and the bass consistently extends upward to d′—to e′ in the four-part mirror fugue.
37. See Agricola's commentary in Adlung (1768, 2:23–24; also in BD 3:193 [item 742]/NBR, 365).
38. His *Avertissement* (see note 34) describes the duet versions of Contrapunctus 13 as "zwey Fugen für zwey unterschiedene Claviere oder Flügel," implying a distinction between clavichord (*Clavier*) and harpsichord (*Flügel*). It does not follow, however, that the word *Clavier* elsewhere in the same *Avertissement* points specifically to the clavichord.
39. The episodes follow cadences to D minor (m. 23), A minor (43 and 53), C (87), and G minor (103).
40. Wolff (2000, 434) and others group Contrapunctus 5 with the two following counter fugues.
41. Facsimile in NBR, 222 (solution in NBA VIII/1: 3).
42. As it was Anna Magdalena who copied the early version of the *ouverture*, she might have been especially familiar with changes that Sebastian wished to make in the notation of Contrapunctus 6, hence the (postulated) presence of her hand there.

43. The revised reading, present in the autograph as well as the print, is "probably" in the hand of J. C. F. Bach (NBA VIII/2, KB, 35).

44. See Wiemer (1977, 50ff.) and Butler (1983a, 52–3). Possibly someone thought Contrapunctus 11 was a quadruple fugue, as its second subject has also a distinct countersubject (m. 27b). But this would not explain why the first triple fugue, Contrapunctus 8, precedes the double fugues Contrapuncti 9–10 in the print.

45. An autograph verbal entry in the manuscript indicates how Contrapunctus 8 was to be notated in the print.

46. On "paired entries," see the discussion of the fugue in G minor from WTC2 in chap. 12. This is another form of the so-called *canone sine pausa* used at the end of Contrapunctus 5.

47. See, e.g., the canzona *La bergamesca* in Frescobaldi's *Fiori musicali*.

48. The earlier version opened with the soprano entry in m. 23; the voices accompanying this entry, including the partial stretto entry in m. 24, were added later.

49. According to Wiemer 1977, 18–9, the hand matches that of a copyist who worked with Bach on P 65, a manuscript score of Cantata no. 195.

50. Measures 178–80 constitute a quasi-inversion of mm. 91–3.

51. Even the trill on the penultimate chord in the Czerny edition is inauthentic and unnecessary.

52. Especially mm. 22b–24a, 81b–83a, and 144–46a.

53. Although the pieces include verbal texts, Snyder (1987, 216–8) considers them examples of learned keyboard music. Dennis Collins (1996) traces the "forerunners" of Bach's mirror fugues back to accounts by Zarlino in the sixteenth century and Brunelli (1610) and Bononcini (1673) in the seventeenth; each gives rules that Bach is likely to have known in some form.

54. Bach allowed several departures from strict mirror inversion in order to avoid a series of implied 6/4-chords. In mm. 14 and 16, the middle voice would have read d′ not c′, and e′ not d′, respectively, had BWV 1080/13/2 reflected the other version exactly. Two other small differences, in mm. 15 and 48, involve what are both essentially embellishments having no essential impact on the harmony or voice leading.

55. This notation is transcribed literally in NBA VIII/2.2 (pp. 58ff.; facsimile, p. xiii).

56. Wiemer (1977, 33–5) suggests that the term *inversus* in the titles indicates the use of mirror technique itself, not the upright or inverted status of the individual versions.

57. To accommodate players with "smaller hands," Moroney (1989, 118) suggests transposing the alto up an octave in BWV 1080/12/1 (beginning on the second note of m. 24); this eliminates the parallel tenths but not the other difficulties. The one truly unmanageable stretch in the three-part fugue, on the fermata in m. 59 of the "top" version, could be finessed by inserting a cadenza or by freely arpeggiating the chord under the fermata.

58. See mm. 19, 21, and 49. Notational discrepancies between the various versions of this movement in mm. 21 and 49 suggest that Bach was revising these passages in the direction of triple interpretation, as in the F#-minor prelude in WTC2.

59. No source for any version has dots in m. 46a. The facsimile of the autograph (Hoke 1979) shows a smear possibly indicating that Bach blotted out a dot after the first note in the alto (bb ′) in the "bottom" version. The print seems to call here for skipping triplet rhythms in the bass, but these occur only in the "top" version, where they are notated without dots, and the note values of the treble fail to add up properly. The thirty-seconds in the treble here might have arisen when Bach, in preparing the *Abklatschvorlage*, erroneously copied the unreduced original values.

60. The autograph (Beilage 3 of P 200) is on the same type of paper used for the engraver's *Abklatschvorlagen*; the significance of this was pointed out by Wolff (1975, 73).

61. "NB. Ueber dieser Fuge, wo der Nahme B.A.C.H. im Contrasubject angebracht worden, ist der Verfasser gestorben" (NBA VIII/2, KB, 54).

62. Hofmann (NBA VIII/2, KB, 96n. 59) suggests that Mizler added this comment to the obituary without having any precise knowledge of the work; another plausible suggestion (Bergel 1985, 2: 40) is that by "fugue" the report means what we would call a section or exposition, not a complete piece.

63. Nottebohm's solution, published in *Musik-Welt* 20 (1881): 232–6, is quoted in the preface of Williams (1986b) and in Wolff (1975, 73).

64. Measure 111 was inserted and the next three measures reworked; the lower staff at the end of the second section (mm. 190–2) also shows corrections. The revision of Contrapunctus 10 also provides evidence for this working method.

65. Bach already alters the rhythm of the first subject once (m. 158) to combine more smoothly with subject 2.
66. As in the C#-minor fugue of WTC1 and the F-major organ fugue BWV 540/2.
67. Ledbetter (2002, 96) describes the fragmentary fugue as beginning with Berardi's subject (through an apparent editorial error, the sentence in question reads "Mattheson" for "Bach"). The view that Bach might have made a copy of Berardi's treatise depends on a nineteenth-century catalog reference to a lost manuscript (Beißwenger 1992, 341)
68. For another completion along similar lines, but without the inversion, see Moroney (1989, 69).
69. See Wiemer (1977, 52–3) and Butler (1983a, 51–4).
70. The term *finale* occurs in the autograph of the first version of the Augmentation Canon and in the print of the Canon at the Twelfth.
71. Example 18.12 is based on a cadenza in B Br Ms. U5871 (page 18, number 52) for the Concerto in F, W. 46. The cadenza probably dates from well after 1740.
72. The title, like the piece itself, underwent changes; the title given here is that of the print.
73. All but the first accidental in m. 29 appears to have been a later addition in the earlier of the two autograph scores (P 200, page 38). Even later are the slurs in mm. 15–6, 22, 28–9, etc., added in the autograph *Abklatschvorlage* (Beilage 1 of P 200).
74. This version of the Augmentation Canon is edited in Wolff (1987b, vol. 1), Williams (1986b), and NBA VIII/2.1: 54 (repeated in modern clefs on p. 126).

Notes for Appendix A

1. The NBA has already published several works here considered dubious; vol. V/12, planned for imminent publication as this is written, will include other works of doubtful authorship.
2. I have not seen an anonymous praeludium in G minor in Leipzig, Univ. Bibl., N.I. 10338 (*olim* M. pr. Ms. 20^i), which Wollny (2002a, 52) suggests could be by Bach.
3. Wolff (1985c) argues for the authenticity of Neumeister's Bach attributions; Dürr (1986a) and Williams (2003, 541ff.) are more guarded.
4. BWV 957, published in BG 42 as a "Fuga" in G on the basis of the Schelble-Gleichauf manuscript, also occurs in "Neumeister," which reveals it to be a chorale fughetta on the melody "Machs mit mir, Gott, nach deiner Güt." Neumeister copied a later version (or at least a more complete and accurate text) of the piece that makes Bach's authorship even more plausible.
5. Compare mm. 31–2 with Contrapunctus 11, mm. 122–3. BWV 591 is edited in NBA IV/11.
6. This is certainly true of the Fugato in E minor BWV 962, part of a collection published at Berlin in 1780 by the Viennese composer Albrechtsberger.
7. Evidently no source ever attributed BWV Anh. 85 to Bach; the name Dobenecker, also attached to the work, was probably that of an owner, not a composer (Spitta 1873–80, 2: 650–1). Morana (1993) argues for Bach's authorship, but the work suffers from incompetent counterpoint and its lapses cannot all be explained as products of faulty copying or editing. It is edited in NBA V/12.
8. See Williams (2003) on the chorale partitas BWV 758 and Anh. 77 and the fugues BWV Anh. 42 and 90 (in F and C).
9. The same theme appears in a fugue in C identified as a work of Johann Ludwig Krebs (NBA, KB, 108–9). The earliest source for BWV. Anh. 177 (LEm III 8.5) attributes it to "Signori Joh.: Christoph. Bachio Org: Isennaci." The work (edited in BG 36 and NBA V/12) provides the best evidence that this Johann Christoph Bach was a significant composer of keyboard music—and an audacious one, as a chromatic piece in E♭ would have been extremely rare for a seventeenth-century composer. See Melamed (1999) for a re-evaluation of other attributions to this composer.
10. For instance, the music comes to a momentary halt after arriving on the dominant in m. 126; this way of announcing the return of the tonic (and the begining of a stretto) is characteristic of Classical-era fugues, not Bach's. As in BWV Anh. 42, the last entry is in the tenor, not the bass, and the piece ends with a short, motivically irrelevant tonic pedal point.
11. The source is wrongly claimed as a Bach autograph in van Patten (1950, 9); the attribution, on the first page, is not visible in van Patten's facsimile. The subject of the gigue bears a family resemblance to that of a clumsy fugue in G that follows the concerto BWV 974 in P 804. But the latter has nothing demonstrable to do with Bach. The work appears in NBA V/12.
12. Among these are the suites BWV 821 and 823; the preludes BWV 539/1, 923, and 943; the fugue BWV 955; and the fugue arrangement BWV 1000.

13. See, for example, the Passacaille in the same key by Louis Couperin.
14. The Erfurt keyboard player Johann Christoph Bach (b. 1676) is thought to have emigrated to England; this might explain the presence of BWV 905 in a manuscript collection that also includes BWV 951a and the toccata BWV 913 (see NBA V/9.1, KB, 40). The estate catalog of E. L. Gerber listed a copy of a "Fantasia con Fuga aus D♭," possibly BWV 905.
15. Bach's son, born in 1715, died in Jena in 1739, more than a decade before Preller's arrival.
16. BWV Anh. 180 in D minor, edited in BG 36 as a work of Bach, and Fk. n. v. 39 in C minor, available in several editions as a work of W. F. Bach. See Stinson (1989a, 172n. 26).
17. BWV 838 appears in BG 42; for the complete suite, see *Johann Christoph Graupner: Acht Partiten*, edited by Lothar Hoffmann-Erbrecht (Leipzig: VEB Brietkopf und Härtel, 1953).
18. Griepenkerl based his edition on two manuscripts owned by Forkel, one of them supposedly in the hand of Kellner. Even if these sources survived today, the attribution of the work would remain cloudy.
19. The sources of BWV 571 include P 287 (Kellner) and B Br Fétis 2960 (II 4093), an important source of the *manualiter* toccatas and other major early works.
20. The BG set off this passage as an "extended ending" (*verlängerter Schluss*), since it can be viewed as an interpolation inserted after the diminished chord in m. 66b; it is, however, present in all sources. Curiously, the next piece in the Yale manuscript (a fugue in C by "J. Krieger") does have two alternate endings, although neither is a cadenza.
21. Compare mm. 43 and 57 with the subject and mm. 138–9 of the fugue in the E-minor Toccata.
22. The coda of the longer fugue BWV 950 is equally dramatic (as noted in NBA V/9.2, KB, 319), but that of BWV 959 is disproportionate to the simplicity and brevity of the piece as a whole.
23. Compare the polonaise in C minor (F. 12/2), mm. 21–2, or the polonaise in D minor (F. 12/4), mm. 9–12 (= Sonata in G [F. 7], second movement, mm. 17–20).
24. Naumann, editor of BG 42, was unaware of the Yale manuscript and failed to include BWV 970. All four pieces appeared in the Supplement to the nineteenth-century Peters edition of Bach's keyboard works.
25. Other likely pastiches are the Fantasia in G Minor BWV 920 and the Praeludium and Fugue in A minor BWV 897, both also edited in BG 42 from the Schelble-Gleichauf collection. Many passages in these pieces are clumsy, and there is little reason to think that either contains material from the Bach circle; the prelude of BWV 897 is from a concerto for solo harpsichord by C. H. Dretzel (see Ahlgrimm 1969).
26. NBA V/9.2, KB, 250 suggests that the two versions are similar beyond this point, but the two versions differ in how they continue the sequence that begins at m. 12b. There is nothing in BWV 923a to correspond with the concluding passage of BWV 923, written as block chords but presumably played as arpeggios.
27. Compare mm. 12–3 with BWV 7, first movement, mm. 3–4. Slow movements in trio-sonata style (perhaps suggested by Sebastian's sinfonias) occur in keyboard sonatas by W. F. and C. P. E. Bach from the 1740s.
28. The history of BWV 970/Fk. 25/2 as reconstructed by Wollny (1993, 85–7) is more convincing than that of Morana (1990, 23–5), who argues for the involvement of J. S. Bach.
29. BG 42 renotated both pieces on two staves, with modernized clefs. The Supplement to the old Peters edition includes both the original notation and a pianistic realization by Czerny; another realization, equally pianistic in style, occurs in PL LZu Spitta Ms. 1658 (for BWV 908 only).
30. Kirchhoff's publication was long considered irretrievably lost, and accounts relied on a description by Marpurg (1753–4, 1:149f.). A copy in St. Petersburg has been reported by Milka (2003), but I have been unable to see a promised facsimile edition.

Notes for Appendix B

1. For an annotated edition of the keyboard pieces unique to P 225, see *J. S. Bach et al.: The Anna Magdalena Bach Book of 1725*, edited by Richard Jones (Associated Board, 1997), which is excellent save for its pianistic fingerings.
2. Viertel (1977, 38) shows a variant version in F that appears as a movement of a sonata in SBB Mus. ms. 9640 (a reported concordance in GB Lbl Add. 32075 has not been confirmed). The pieces by Richter in Friedemann's keyboard book may also stem from Dresden (see chap. 10).

3. The simplified left-hand part and other alterations in the Couperin work are considered unlikely to stem either from an authentic early version or from Bach (discussion in NBA V/4, KB, 81).

4. On Emanuel's sonata W. 65/7, see Schulenberg (1984, 122–5); a few errors in the latter are corrected in Horn (1988, 85n.). Later versions of the sonata are published complete in Berg (1985, 3:196–204).

5. Glöckner (1981, 53) dates C. P. E. Bach's handwriting in the four pieces to 1732. Dadelsen assigns all four pieces to C. P. E. Bach (NBA V/4, KB, 37–8), as does Jones in his edition, but they are anonymous in the manuscript and the attribution cannot be regarded as certain, despite their inclusion in CPEBCW I/8.2 (nos. 61–4).

6. The sonata, not listed by Wotquenne (1905), is mentioned in entry 1 in Helm (1989, 3) and edited in NBA V/4, *Anhang* 1, and in CPEBCW I/8.2:123.

7. Leisinger and Wollny (1993, 146–51) reproduce and compare three versions of the march BWV Anh. 127. See also the entry in BWV (1990) for Anh. 40, a song from Sperontes' *Singende Muse an der Pleisse* (Leipzig, 1736), whose incipit is similar to that of W. 65/7/1 and F. 10. BWV Anh. 40 is accepted (on slender grounds) as a work of J. S. Bach in BC (entry H 3).

8. Rust (BG 20: xv) observed the similarity of the incipit to that of the aria "Fromme Musen" in the secular cantata *Tönet ihr Pauken* BWV 214, first performed in December 1733 and parodied a year later as "Frohe Hirten" in the Christmas Oratorio.

9. BWV Anh. 119 is also preserved in a 1729 Leipzig manuscript under the title *Taniec* (Polish "dance"); see Hlawiczka (1961). That is a slightly less refined version for treble instrument and bass; does its existence imply that this example of the dance is of popular origin?

10. See Wollny (2002a, 33–6). Schulze (1975, 48) had previously identified the hand as that of the young Johann Christian Bach.

11. See the character piece entitled L'Aly Rupalich W. 117/27, edited in CPEBCW I/8.2; facsimile in Berg (1985, 5:196).

12. E.g., by Mizler; see BD II, item 432/NBR, 328.

Bibliography

Abbreviations

For library and manuscript sigla, see p. 497.

Acta   *Acta musicologica*
AMw   *Archiv für Musikwissenschaft*
BACH   *Bach: The Quarterly Journal of the Riemenschneider Institute*
BC   *Bach-Compendium* (full citation below)
BD 1   *Bach-Dokumente I* (full citation below)
BD 2   *Bach-Dokumente II* (full citation below)
BD 3   *Bach-Dokumente III* (full citation below)
BG   Bachgesamtausgabe (full citation below under Bach, Johann Sebastian, 1851–1900; volumes cited are listed below)
BJ   *Bach-Jahrbuch*
BJHM   *Basler Jahrbuch für historische Musikpraxis*
BMw   *Beiträge zur Musikwissenschaft*
BuxWV   catalog number of work by Buxtehude in Karstädt (1974)
BWV   Wolfgang Schmieder, *Bach Werke-Verzeichnis* (full citation below under Schmieder 1990)
CB   *Clavier-Büchlein vor Wilhelm Friedemann Bach* (see chapter 10)
CM   *Current Musicology*
CMS   *College Music Symposium*
CPEBCW   *Carl Philipp Emanuel Bach: The Collected Works* (Packard Humanities Foundation, 2005–)
CU   *Clavierübung*
DDT   *Denkmäler deutscher Tonkunst*
DTÖ   *Denkmäler der Tonkunst in Österreich*
EKJ   *Early Keyboard Journal*
EKSN   *Early Keyboard Studies Newsletter* (Westfield, Massachusetts)
EM   *Early Music*
F.   Catalog number of work by W. F. Bach, listed in Falck (1913—see below)
Fk. n. v. Catalog number of work attributed to W. F. Bach, listed in Kast (2003—see below), not in Falck (1913)
H.   Catalog number of work by C. P. E. Bach, listed in Helm (1989—see below)
HG   *Händelgesamtausgabe* (full citation below under Händel, Georg Friedrich, 1858–85)
HWV   Catalog number of work by Handel, listed in *Händel-Handbuch* (full citation below)
JAMS   *Journal of the American Musicological Society*
JM   *Journal of Musicology*
JMR   *Journal of Musicological Research*

JMT	*Journal of Music Theory*
Mf	*Die Musikforschung*
ML	*Music and Letters*
MQ	*The Musical Quarterly*
MT	*The Musical Times*
MTS	*Music Theory Spectrum*
NBA	*Neue Bach-Ausgabe, Notenband* (full citation below under Bach, Johann Sebastian, 1954–; list of volumes cited below)
NBA, KB	*Neue Bach-Ausgabe, Kritischer Bericht* (full citation below under Bach, Johann Sebastian, 1954–; list of volumes cited below)
NBR	*New Bach Reader* (full citation below)
NG, NG2	*The New Grove Dictionary of Music and Musicians*, first and second editions (full citations below)
RIM	*Rivista italiana di musicologia*
SIMG	*Sammelbände der Internationalen Musik-Gesellschaft*
SJ	*Schütz-Jahrbuch*
TWV	Catalog number of work by Telemann in Ruhnke (1984—see below)
W.	Catalog number of work by C. P. E. Bach in Wotquenne (1905—see below)
WTC	The *Well-Tempered Clavier* (see chapters 11–12)

BG and NBA: Volumes Cited

BG vol.	Date	Editor	Contents
3	1853	C. F. Becker	BWV 772–801, 910–1, 944, *Clavierübung*
13/2	1863	Franz Espagne	BWV 806–17
14	1866	Franz Kroll	WTC
20/1	1872	Wilhelm Rust	BWV 81–9
25/1	1878	Wilhelm Rust	BWV 1080
30	1884	Paul Graf Waldersee	BWV 141–50
31/2	1885	Alfred Dörffel	BWV 1079
36	1890	Ernst Naumann	individual keyboard works
38	1891	Ernst Naumann	free organ works
40	1893	Ernst Naumann	organ chorales
42	1894	Ernst Naumann	keyboard arrangements, etc.
43/2	1884	Paul Graf Waldersee	Little Keyboard Books for A. M. Bach
45/1	1895	Ernst Naumann	BWV 806–17 (revised edition)
45/2	1897	Alfred Dörffel	BWV 996–98, CB, etc.

NBA vol.	Date	KB	Editor	Contents
IV/1	1983	1987	Heinz-Harald Löhlein	organ chorales, partitas
IV/4	1969	1974	Manfred Tessmer	*Clavierübung*, Pt. 3
IV/5–6	1972, 1964	1978–79	Dietrich Kilian	organ preludes and fugues
IV/7	1984	1988	Dietrich Kilian	miscellaneous organ works
IV/9	2003	2003	Christoph Wolff	"Neumeister" chorales
IV/11	2003	2004	Ulrich Bartels	miscellaneous organ works
			Peter Wollny	chorale partitas
V/1	1976	1978	Richard Douglas Jones	*Clavierübung*, part 1 ("Nachtrag," 1997)
V/2	1977	1981	Walter Emery	*Clavierübung*, part 2
			Christoph Wolff	BWV 988, 1087
V/3	1970	—	Georg von Dadelsen	Inventions BWV 772–801
V/4	1957	1957	Georg von Dadelsen	*Clavier-Büchlein* for A. M. Bach
V/5	1962	1963	Wolfgang Plath	*Clavier-Büchlein* for W. F. Bach
V/6.1	1989	1989	Alfred Dürr	WTC1
V/6.2	1995	1996	Alfred Dürr	WTC2
V/7	1979	1981	Alfred Dürr	English Suites BWV 806–11
V/8	1980	1982	Alfred Dürr	French Suites BWV 812–9
V/9.1	1999	1999	Peter Wollny	toccatas BWV 910–6
V/9.2	1999	2000	Uwe Wolf	miscellaneous "clavier" works

V/10	1976	1982	Hartwig Eichberg	miscellaneous "clavier" works
			Thomas Kohlhase	lute works
V/11	1997	1997	Karl Heller	transcriptions
V/12	[2005]		Ulrich Bartels,	doubtful works
			Frieder Rempp	
VII/3	1986	1989	Dietrich Kilian	BWV 1041–4
VIII/1	1974	1976	Christoph Wolff	*Musical Offering*, canons
VIII/2.1–2	1995	1996	Klaus Hofmann	*Art of Fugue*
IX/2	1989	—	Yoshitake Kobayashi	*Die Notenschrift Bachs*

Library and Manuscript Sigla

Note: Library names and collection locations are subject to change. Names and sigla given here are those used in recent literature. The "country" element is omitted from sigla for German libraries, since these are so numerous.

A Sd — Salzburg, Dom-Musikarchiv
A Wn — Vienna, Österreichischer Nationalbibliothek
A Wn-h — Vienna, Österreichischer Nationalbibliothek, Sammlung Anthony van Hoboken
ABB — Andreas Bach Book (LEm III.8.4; see "Some Major Manuscript Sources for the Early Works" in chapter 1)
AmB — Amalienbibliothek (the library of Princess Anna Amalie of Prussia, now part of the SBB)
Bim — Berlin, Staatliches Institut für Musikforschung
B Bc — Brussels, Conservatoire Royal de Musique
B Br — Brussels, Bibliothèque Royale Albert 1ᵉʳ
Bsa — Berlin, Sing-Akademie zu Berlin, Notenarchiv (on deposit in SBB)
CH Zz — Züurich, Zentralbibliothek
DK Kk — Copenhagen, Det Kongelige Bibliotek
Dl — Dresden, Landesbibliothek
DS — Darmstadt, Hessische Landes- und Hochschulbibliothek
F — Frankfurt-am-Main, Universitäts-Bibliothek
F Pn — Paris, Bibliothèque National
Gb — Göttingen, Johann-Sebastian-Bach-Institut
GB Drc — Durham, Cathedral Library
GB Lbl — London, The British Library
HAu — Halle, Universitäts- und Landesbibliothek
Hs — Hamburg, Staats- und Universitätsbibliothek
I B — Bologna, Civico Museo Bibliografico Musicale
LEb — Leipzig, Bach-Archiv
LEm — Leipzig, Musikbibliothek
LEu — Leipzig, Universitätsbibliothek
MM — Möller Manuscript (SBB Mus. ms. 40644; see "Some Major Manuscript Sources for the Early Works" in chapter 1)
NL Dhgm — The Hague, Gemeente Museum
GB Ob — Oxford, Bodleian Library
P — SBB (see below), Mus. ms. Bach P (followed by shelf mark; used for manuscript scores, including keyboard works)
PL Lzu — Łodz, Biblioteka Universytecka
ROu — Rostock, Universitätsbiblitohek
SBB — Staatsbibliothek zu Berlin (Berlin, Staatsbiliothek Preussischer Kulturbesitz, Musikabteilung mit Mendelssohn-Archiv)
St — SBB (see below), Mus. ms. Bach St (followed by shelf mark; used for manuscript performance parts)
SW — Schwerin, Wissenschaftliche Allgemeinbibliothek
US BER — Berea, Ohio, Baldwin-Wallace College, Riemenschneider Memorial Bach Library
US Bp — Boston Public Library
US Nhy — New Haven, Yale University
US U — Urbana, Illinois, University of Illinois
US Wc — Washington, D.C., Library of Congress (used in chapter 14 for the manuscript US Wc ML 96.B186)

Literature

Adlung, Jacob. 1768. *Musica mechanica organoedi*. Edited by Johann Lorenz Albrecht, with additional material by J. F. Agricola. Berlin: Friedrich Wilhelm Birnstiel. Facsimile, edited by Christhard Mahrenholz, Documenta Musicologica, 1/18. Kassel: Bärenreiter, 1961.

Agricola, Johann Friedrich. 1757. *Anleitung zur Singkust*. Berlin: Georg Ludwig Winter. An annotated translation of Pier Francesco Tosi, *Opinioni de' cantori antichi e moderni*. Bologna, 1723. Facsimile edited by Kurt Wichmann. Wiesbaden: Breitkopf und Härtel, 1994. English translation by Julianne Baird as *Introduction to the Art of Singing*. Cambridge: Cambridge University Press, 1995.

Ahlgrimm, Isolde. 1969. "Cornelius Heinrich Dretzel, der Autor des J. S. Bach zubeschriebenen Klavierwerks BWV 897." *BJ* 55:67–77.

Ansehl, Peter, Karl Heller, and Hans-Joachim Schulze, eds. 1981. *Beiträge zum Konzertschaffen Johann Sebastian Bachs*. Bach-Studien, 6. Leipzig: Breitkopf und Härtel.

Arnold, F. T. 1931. *The Art of Accompaniment from a Thorough-Bass as Practised in the XVIIth and XVIIIth Centuries*. Oxford: Oxford University Press.

Bach, Carl Philipp Emanuel. 1753–62. *Versuch über die wahre Art das Clavier zu spielen*. 2 vols. Berlin: Christian Friedrich Henning (vol. 1), Georg Ludwig Winter (vol. 2). Facsimile, with a *Nachwort* by Lothar Hoffmann-Erbrecht and a supplement containing the additions from the edition of 1787–97 (Leipzig: VEB Breitkopf und Härtel, 1981). Translated by William J. Mitchell as *Essay on the True Art of Playing Keyboard Instruments* (New York: Norton, 1949). Most citations to this work take the form i.2.3.4, referring to volume, chapter, subchapter, and paragraph number, respectively, in the first edition. Mitchell's translation groups the forty-one short chapters of volume 2 into seven.

———. 1773. [Autobiography]. In Burney 1772–3, vol. 3. Translation in Newman (1965); facsimile in Newman (1967).

Bach, Johann Sebastian. 1851–1900. *Werke*. 46 vols. Edited by the Bach-Gesellschaft. Leipzig: Breitkopf und Härtel. Numerous reprints. For editors and dates of individual volumes, see the list of volumes cited (above).

———. 1954–. *Neue Ausgabe sämtlicher Werke*. Edited by the Johann-Sebastian-Bach-Institut, Göttingen, and the Bach-Archiv, Leipzig. Kassel: Bärenreiter. *Kritische Berichte* (editorial reports) appear in separate volumes. For editors and dates of individual volumes, see list of volumes cited (above).

Bach-Compendium: Analytisch-bibliographisches Repertorium der Werke Johann Sebastian Bachs. 1985–. Edited by Hans-Joachim Schulze and Christoph Wolff. Leipzig and Dresden: Peters.

Bach-Dokumente I: Schriftstücke von der Hand Johann Sebastian Bachs. 1963. Edited by Werner Neumann and Hans-Joachim Schulze. Kassel: Bärenreiter.

Bach-Dokumente II: Fremdschriftliche und gedruckte Dokumente zur Lebensgeschichte Johann Sebastian Bachs. 1969. Edited by Werner Neumann and Hans-Joachim Schulze. Kassel: Bärenreiter.

Bach-Dokumente III: Dokumente zum Nachwirken Johann Sebastian Bachs. 1972. Edited by Hans-Joachim Schulze. Kassel: Bärenreiter.

Bach-Fest Buch. 1975. Program book for the Third International Bach Festival of the German Democratic Republic (Leipzig, Sept. 16–23, 1975).

Bach Reader, The. 1966. Edited by Hans T. David and Arthur Mendel. Rev. ed. New York: Norton. See also *New Bach Reader* (below).

Bagnall, Anne. 1975. "The Simple Fugues." In "Seminar Report" (see Wolff 1975), *CM* 19:59–61.

Baker, Thomas. 1975. "Bach's Revisions in the Augmentation Canon." In "Seminar Report" (see Wolff 1975), *CM* 19:67–71.

Barnes, John. 1979. "Bach's Keyboard Temperament: Internal Evidence from the *Well-Tempered Clavier*." *EM* 7:236–49.

Barte, Paul Thomas. 1995. "The Keyboard Manuscripts of Johann Christoph Bach, Cantor in Gehren." D.M.A. diss., University of Rochester.

Becker, Heinz. 1953. "Ein unbekannter Herausgeber der Bach-Gesamtausgabe." *Mf* 6:356–7.

Beißwenger, Kirsten. 1992a. *Johann Sebastian Bachs Notenbibliothek*. Catalogus musicus, 13. Kassel: Bärenreiter.

———. 1992b. "Zur Chronologie der Notenhandschriften Johann Gottfried Walthers." In Beißwenger et al. (1992), 11–39.

———. 1995. "An Early Version of the First Movement of the *Italian Concerto* BWV 971 From the Scholz Collection?" In Melamed (1995, 1–19).

———. 2002. "Rezeption und Verbreitung des Wohltemperierten Klaviers I zu Lebzeiten Johann Sebastian Bachs." In Rampe (2002, 7–25).

Beißwenger, Kirsten, et al., eds. 1992. *Acht kleine Präludien und Studien über BACH: Georg von Dadelsen zum 70. Geburtstag am 17. November 1988.* Wiesbaden: Breitkopf und Härtel.

Belotti, Michael. 2001. "Johann Pachelbel als Lehrer." In Kaiser (2001, 8–44).

Benstock, Seymour, ed. 1992. *Johann Sebastian Bach: A Tercentenary Celebration.* Westport, CT: Greenwood Press.

Bent, Ian. 2005. "'That Bright New Light': Schenker, Universal Edition, and the Origins of the Erläuterung Series, 1901–1910." *JAMS* 58:69–138.

Berg, Darrell. 1979. "Toward a Catalog of the Keyboard Sonatas of C. P. E. Bach." *JAMS* 32:276–303. Reviewed in Schulenberg (1987).

———, ed. 1985. *The Collected Works for Solo Keyboard by Carl Philipp Emanuel Bach 1714–1788.* 6 vols. New York and London: Garland. Facsimiles of eighteenth-century sources.

Bergel, Erich. 1985. *Bachs letzte Fuge: Die "Kunst der Fuge"—ein zyklisches Werk: Entstehungsgeschichte—Erstausgabe—Ordnungsprinzipien.* Bonn: Brockhaus.

Berke, Dietrich, and Dorothee Hanemann, eds. 1987. *Alte Musik als ästhetische Gegenwart: Kongressbericht Stuttgart 1985.* 2 vols. Kassel: Bärenreiter.

Best, Terrence. 1983. "Handel's Harpsichord Music: A Checklist." In Hogwood and Luckett (1983, 171–87).

Bingmann, Anke, Klaus Hortschansky, and Winfried Kirsch, eds. 1988. *Studien zur Instrumentalmusik: Lothar Hoffmann-Erbrecht zum 60. Geburtstag.* Frankfurter Beiträge zur Musikwissenschaft, 20. Tutzing: Hans Schneider.

Birtel, Wolfgang, and Christoph-Hellmut Mahling, eds. 1986. *Aufklärung: Studien zur deutschfranzösischen Musikgeschichte im 18. Jahrhundert—Einflüsse und Wirkungen,* Band 2. Annales Universitatis Saraviensis: Reihe Philosophische Fakultät, 20. Heidelberg: Carl Winter Universitätsverlag.

Blood, William. 1979. "'Well-Tempering' the Clavier: Five Methods." *EM* 7: 491–7.

Blume, Friedrich. 1963. "Outlines of a New Picture of Bach." *ML* 44:214–27.

Bodky, Erwin. 1960. *The Interpretation of Bach's Keyboard Works.* Cambridge, MA: Harvard University Press.

Boyd, Malcolm, ed. 1999. *J. S. Bach.* Oxford Bach Companions. Oxford: Oxford University Press.

———. 2000. *Bach.* The Master Musicians Series. 3d ed. New York and London: Oxford University Press.

Brainard, Paul, and Ray Robinson, eds. 1993 *A Bach Tribute: Essays in Honor of William H. Scheide.* Kassel: Bärenreiter, and Chapel Hill: Hinshaw Music.

Breckoff, Werner. 1965. *Zur Entstehungsgeschichte des zweiten Wohltemperierten Klaviers von Johann Sebastian Bach.* Tübingen: n.p.

Breig, Werner. 1975. "Bachs Goldberg-Variationen als zyklisches Werk." *AMw* 32:243–71.

———. 1976. "Bachs Violinkonzert d-Moll. Studien zu seiner Gestalt und seiner Entstehungsgeschichte." *BJ* 62:7–34.

———. 1982. "Bachs 'Kunst der Fuge': Zur instrumentalen Bestimmung und zum Zyklus-Charakter." *BJ* 68:103–23.

———. 1990a. "Die geschichtliche Stellung von Buxtehudes monodischen Orgelchoral." In Edler and Krummacher (1990, 260–74).

———. 1990b. "Textbezug und Werkidee in Johann Sebastian Bachs frühen Orgelchorälen." In Petersen (1990, 167–2).

———. 1991. "Das Ostinatoprinzip in Johann Sebastian Bachs langsamen Konzertsätzen." In Heidlberger et al., 287–300.

———. 2001. "'. . . das Fehlerhafte gut, das Gute besser und das Bessere zum Allerbesten zu machen': Zum Umarbeitungsprozeß in einigen Orgelkompositionen Bachs (BWV 535, 572 und 543)." In Staehelin (2001, 121–41).

Brokaw, James A. 1989. "The Genesis of the Prelude in C Major, BWV 870." In Franklin (1989a, 225–39).

Brown, Howard Mayer, and Stanley Sadie, eds. 1990. *Performance Practice: Music after 1600.* The New Grove Handbooks in Music. New York: Norton.

Brusniak, Friedhelm, and Horst Leuchtmann, eds. 1989. *Quaestiones in musica: Festschrift für Franz Krautwurst zum 65. Geburtstag.* Tutzing: Hans Schneider.

Buch, David J. 1985. "Style brisé, Style luthé, and the Choses luthées." *MQ* 71:52–67 and 220–1.

Buelow, George. 1983. "Johann Mattheson and the Invention of the *Affektenlehre*." In Buelow and Marx (1983, 393–407). Reprinted in *Eighteenth-Century Music in Theory and Practice: Essays in Honor of Alfred Mann*, edited by Mary Ann Parker (Stuyvesant, NY: Pendragon), 187–203.

———. 1989. "Expressivity in the Accompanied Recitatives of Bach's Cantatas." In Franklin (1989b, 18–35).

———. 1991. "A Bach Borrowing by Gluck: Another Frontier." *BACH* 22/1 (Spring/Summer):43–61.

Buelow, George J., and Hans Joachim Marx, eds. 1983. *New Mattheson Studies*. Cambridge: Cambridge University Press.

Burney, Charles. 1772–73. *Carl Burney's der Musik Doctors Tagebuch seiner musikalischen Reisen*. Translated by C. D. Ebeling (I–II) and J. C. Bode (III). Hamburg: Bode. Facsimile edited by Richard Schaale, Documenta Musicologica, 1/19. Kassel: Bärenreiter, 1959.

Butler, Gregory. 1977. "Fugue and Rhetoric." *JMT* 21:49–109.

———. 1980. "Leipziger Stecher in Bachs Originaldrucken." *BJ* 66:9–26.

———. 1983a. "Ordering Problems in J. S. Bach's *Art of Fugue* Resolved." *MQ* 69:44–61.

———. 1983b. "*Der vollkommene Capellmeister* as a Stimulus to J. S. Bach's Late Fugal Writing." In Buelow and Marx (1983, 293–305).

———. 1986. "The Engraving of J. S. Bach's *Six Partitas*." *JMR* 7:3–27.

———. 1988. "Neues zur Datierung der Goldberg-Variationen." *BJ* 74:219–21.

———. 1990. *Bach's Clavier-Übung III: The Making of a Print. With a Companion Study of the Canonic Variations on "Vom Himmel Hoch," BWV 769*. Durham, NC, and London: Duke University Press.

———. 2002. "The Printing History of J. S. Bach's *Musical Offering*: New Interpretations." *JM*:306–31.

———. 2003. "Toward an Aesthetic and Pedagogical Context for J. S. Bach's *Italian Concerto* BWV 971." In Geck (2003, 223–30).

———. 2004. "The Prélude to the Third English Suite BWV 808: An Allegro Concerto Movement in Ritornello Form." In Leahy and Tomita (2004, 93–101).

Butt, John. 1990. *Bach Interpretation: Articulation Marks in Primary Sources of J. S. Bach*. Cambridge: Cambridge University Press.

Carter, Stewart. 1991. "The String Tremolo in the 17th Century." *EM* 19:42–59.

Clark, Stephen L., ed. 1988. *C. P. E. Bach Studies*. Oxford: Oxford University Press.

———, ed. and trans. 1997. *The Letters of C. P. E. Bach*. Oxford: Clarendon Press.

Cole, Warwick. 2000. "Improvisation as a Stimulus to Composition in Bach's Partita II." *BACH* 31/1:96–112.

Collins, Dennis. 1996. "Spiegel-Kontrapunkt in Theorie und Praxis: Vorläufer für Contrapunctus 12 und 13 aus Bachs Kunst der Fuge." *BJ* 82:77–92.

Collins, Michael. 1966. "The Performance of Triplets in the Seventeenth and Eighteenth Centuries." *JAMS* 19:281–323.

Cone, Edward T. 1968. *Musical Form and Musical Performance*. New York: Norton.

———. 1974. "Bach's Unfinished Fugue in C Minor." In Marshall (1974, 149–55).

Couperin, François. 1717. *L'Art de toucher le clavecin*. Paris: Author. With German translation by Anna Linde and English translation by Mevanwy Roberts. Leipzig: Breitkopf und Härtel, 1933.

Dadelsen, Georg von. 1957. *Bemerkungen zur Handschrift Johann Sebastian Bachs, seiner Familie und seines Kreises*. Tübingen Bach-Studien, 1. Trossingen: Hohner.

———. 1958. *Beiträge zur Chronologie der Werke Johann Sebastian Bachs*. Tübinger Bach-Studien, 4–5. Trossingen: Hohner.

———, ed. 1975. *Joh. Seb. Bach: Suiten, Sonaten, Capriccios und Variationen*. Munich: Henle.

———, ed. 1988. *Johann Sebastian Bach: Klavierbüchlein für Anna Magdalena Bach 1725*. Documenta Musicologica, 2/25. Kassel: Bärenreiter. Facsimile of P 225, with commentary.

Dadelsen, Georg von, and Klaus Rönnau, eds. 1970. *Joh. Seb. Bach: Fantasien, Präludien und Fugen*. Munich: Henle.

Dahlhaus, Carl. 1967. *Musikästhetik*. Cologne: Musikverlag Hans Gerig. Translated by William W. Austin as *Esthetics of Music*, with new author's preface. Cambridge: Cambridge University Press, 1982.

Danckert, Werner. 1924. *Geschichte der Gigue*. Leipzig: Kistner and Siegel.

Dannreuther, Edward. 1893–95. *Musical Ornamentation*. London: Novello.

Dart, Thurston. 1970. "Bach's Early Keyboard Music: A Neglected Source (Brussels, B.R., Fétis 2960)." *Acta* 42:236–8. Reply in Dömling and Kohlhase (1971).

Daverio, John. 1992. "The 'Unraveling' of Schoenberg's Bach." In Benstock (1992).

David, Hans. 1945. *J. S. Bach's Musical Offering: History, Interpretation, and Analysis*. New York: G. Schirmer. Reprint, New York: Dover, 1972.

David, Johann Nepomuk. 1957. *Die zweistimmigen Inventionen von Johann Sebastian Bach*. Göttingen: Vandenhoeck und Ruprecht.

——. 1962. *Das Wohltemperierte Klavier: Versuch einer Synopsis*. Göttingen: Vandenhoeck und Ruprecht.

Dedel, Peter. 1975. "Dissemination and Dispute." In "Seminar Report" (see Wolff 1975), *CM* 19:50–4. On the *Art of Fugue*.

Dehnhard, Walter, ed. 1973. *Johann Sebastian Bach: Kleine Präludien und Fughetten*. Vienna: Wiener Urtext.

——, ed. 1977–83. *Johann Sebastian Bach: Das wohltemperierte Clavier*. 2 vols. Vienna: Wiener Urtext.

Deppert, Heinrich. 1987. "Anmerkungen zu Alfred Dürr, Ein Dokument aus dem Unterricht Bachs?" A response to Dürr (1986). *Musiktheorie* 2:107–8.

Derr, Ellwood. 1981. "The Two-Part Inventions: Bach's Composer's *Vademecum*." *MTS* 3:26–48.

Dirksen, Pieter, ed. 1992. *The Harpsichord and Its Repertoire: Proceedings of the International Harpsichord Symposium Utrecht 1990*. Utrecht: STIMU: Foundation for Historical Performance Practice.

——. 1998. "Zur Frage des Autors der A-Dur-Toccata BWV Anh. 178." *BJ* 84:121–35.

——. 2002. "Bachs 'Act Choralfughetten': Ein unbeachtetes Leipziger Sammelwerk?" In Leisinger (2002, 155–182).

——. 2003. "Überlegungen zu Bachs Suite f-moll BWV 823." In Geck (2003, 119–31).

Dömling, Wolfgang, and Thomas Kohlhase. 1976. "Kein Bach-Autograph: Die Handschrift Brüssel, Bibliothèque Royale, II. 4093 (Fétis 2960)." *Acta* 43:108–9.

Donington, Robert. 1973. *A Performer's Guide to Baroque Music*. New York: Scribner's.

——. 1977. "What *Is* Rhythmic Alteration?" *EM* 5:543–4.

——. 1982. *Baroque Music: Style and Performance: A Handbook*. New York: Norton.

Dorfmüller, Kurt. 1989. "Eine Themenverwandtschaft im Umkreis Bach-Benda." In Brusniak and Leuchtmann (1989, 71–7).

Douglass, Fenner, Owen Jander, and Barbara Owen, eds. 1986. *Charles Brenton Fisk, Organ Builder*. Vol. 1, *Essays in His Honor*. Easthampton, MA: The Westfield Center for Early Keyboard Studies.

Dreyfus, Laurence. 1987. *Bach's Continuo Group*. Cambridge, MA: Harvard University Press.

Dürr, Alfred. 1953. "Johann Gottlieb Goldberg und die Triosonate BWV 1037." *BJ* 40:51–80. Reprinted in Dürr (1988a).

——. 1978. "Tastenumfang und Chronologie in Bachs Klavierwerken." In Kohlhase and Scherliess (1978, 73–88). Reprinted in Dürr (1988a).

——. 1981. "Zur Form der Präludien in Bachs Englischen Suiten." In Ansehl, Heller, and Schulze (1981, 101–8). Reprinted in Dürr (1988a).

——. 1984. *Zur Frühgeschichte des Wohltemperierten Klaviers I von Johann Sebastian Bach*. Nachrichten der Akademie der Wissenschaften in Göttingen, I. Philologisch-Historische Klasse, Jahrgang 1984, Nr. 1. Göttingen: Vandenhoek und Ruprecht.

——. 1985. "The Historical Background of the Composition of Johann Sebastian Bach's *Clavier* Suite [*sic*]." *BACH* 16/1 (January):53–68.

——. 1986a. "Ein Dokument aus dem Unterricht Bachs." *Musiktheorie* 1:163–70.

——. 1986b. "Kein Meister fällt vom Himmel." *Musica* 40:309–12.

——. 1988a. *Im Mittelpunkt Bach: Ausgewählte Aufsätze und Vorträge*. Edited by the Board of the Johann-Sebastian-Bach-Institut, Göttingen. Kassel: Bärenreiter. Reprints of articles; references are to the original publications.

——. 1988b. "Das Präludium Es-Dur BWV 852 aus dem *Wohltemperierten Klavier*." In Bingmann, Hortschansky, and Kirsch (1988, 93–101).

——. 1998. *Johann Sebastian Bach: Das wohltemperierte Klavier*. Kassel: Bärenreiter (zweite Auflage, 2000).

——. 1999. *Die Kantaten von Johann Sebastian Bach*. 2 vols. Seventh printing (original: 1971). Kassel: Bärenreiter.

Edler, Arnfried. 1995. "Thematik und Figuration in der Tastenmusik des jungen Bach." In Heller and Schulze (1995, 87–110).

Edler, Arnfried, and Friedhelm Krummacher, eds. 1990. *Dietrich Buxtehude und die europäische Musik seiner Zeit: Bericht über das Lübecker Symposion 1987*. Kieler Schriften zur Musikwissenschaft, 35. Kassel: Bärenreiter.

Eichberg, Hartwig. 1975. "Unechtes unter Bachs Klavierwerke." *BJ*, 61:7–49.

Eisert, Christian. 1994. *Die Clavier-Toccaten BWV 910–916 von Johann Sebastian Bach: Quellenkritische Untersuchungen zu einem Problem des Frühwerks*. Mainz: Schott.

Emery, Walter. 1953. *Bach's Ornaments*. London: Novello.

Eppstein, Hans. 1964. "Zur Problematik von J. S. Bachs Sonate für Violine und Cembalo G-dur (BWV 1019)." *AMw* 21:217–42.

———. 1970. "Zur Vor- und Entstehungsgeschichte von J. S. Bachs Tripelkonzert a-moll (BWV 1044)." *Jahrbuch des Staatlichen Instituts für Musikforschung Preussischer Kulturbesitz* 3:44.

———. 1976. "Chronologieprobleme in Johann Sebastian Bachs Suiten für Soloinstrument." *BJ* 62:35–57.

———. 1986. "Johann Sebastian Bach und der galante Stil." In Birtel and Mahling (1986, 209–18).

Falck, Martin. 1913. *Wilhelm Friedemann Bach: Sein Leben und seine Werke*. Leipzig: Kahnt. 2d ed., 1919.

Fanna, Antonio, and Giovanni Morelli, eds. 1988. *Nuovi studi vivaldiani: edizione e cronologia critica delle opere*. Studi di Musica Veneta/Quaderni Vivaldiana, 4. 2 vols. Florence: Olschki.

Faulkner, Quentin. 1984. *J. S. Bach's Keyboard Technique: A Historical Introduction*. St. Louis: Concordia.

Fechner, Manfred. 1980. "Improvisationsskizzen und ausnotierte Diminutionen von Johann Georg Pisendel, dargestellt an in Dresden handschriftlich überlieferten Konzerten von Johann Friedrich Fasch und Johann Gottlieb Graun." In *Zu Fragen der Verzierungskunst in der Instrumentalmusik der ersten Hälfte des 18. Jahrhunderts*, 35–55. Studien zur Aufführungspraxis und Interpretation von Instrumentalmusik des 18. Jahrhunderts, 11. Blankenburg/Harz: n.p.

Federhofer, Hellmut. 1958. "Zur handschriftlichen Überlieferung der Musiktheorie in Österreich in der zweiten Hälfte des 17. Jahrhunderts." *Mf* 11:264–79.

Ferguson, Howard. 1975. *Keyboard Interpretation from the 14th to the 19th Century: An Introduction*. London: Oxford University Press.

Forchert, Arno. 1987. "Bach und die Tradition der Rhetorik." In Berke and Hanemann (1987, 1:169–78).

Forkel, Johann Nicolaus. 1802. *Ueber Johann Sebastian Bachs Leben, Kunst und Kunstwerke*. Leipzig: Hoffmeister und Kühnel. Facsimile, Frankfurt am Main: H. L. Grahl, 1950. Translation in NBR, 417–82. Edited by Walther Vetter. Kassel: Bärenreiter, 1968.

Franck, Wolf. 1949. "Musicology and Its Founder, Johann Nicolaus Forkel (1749-1818)." *MQ* 35:588–609.

Franklin, Don O., ed. 1989a. *Bach Studies*. Cambridge: Cambridge University Press.

———. 1989b. "Reconstructing the *Urpartitur* for WTC II: A Study of the 'London autograph' (BL Add. MS 35021)." In Franklin (1989a, 240–78).

———. 1991. "The Carnegie Manuscript and J. S. Bach." *BACH* 22/1 (Spring/Summer):5–15.

———. 1992. "The Fermata as Notational Convention in the Music of J. S. Bach." In *Convention in Eighteenth- and Nineteenth-Century Music: Essays in Honor of Leonard G. Ratner*, ed. Wye J. Allanbrook, Janet M. Levy, and William P. Mahrt, 345–81. Festschrift Series, 10. Stuyvesant, NY: Pendragon.

Franklin, Don, and Stephen Daw, eds. 1980. *Johann Sebastian Bach: Das Wohltemperierte Clavier II: Facsimile of the Autograph Manuscript in the British Library, Add. MS 35021*. London: The British Library.

Fritz, Barthold. 1757. *Anweisung, wie man Claviere, Clavecins, und Orgeln . . . gleich rein stimmen könne*. 2nd ed. Leipzig: Breitkopf. The first edition appeared the previous year.

Fuller, David. 1977. "Dotting, the 'French Style,' and Frederick Neumann's Counter-Reformation." *EM* 5:517–43.

———. 1985. "The 'Dotted Style' in Bach, Handel and Scarlatti." In Williams (1985a, 99–117).

———. 1990. "The Performer as Composer." In Brown and Sadie (1990, 117–46).

Fuller Maitland, J. A. 1925. *The "48": Bach's Wohltemperiertes Clavier*. 2 vols. London: Oxford University Press.

Gadamer, Hans-Georg. 1946. *Bach und Weimar*. Weimar: Hermann Böhlaus Nachfolger.

Geck, Martin, ed. 1969. *Bach-Interpretation*. Göttingen: Vandenhoeck und Ruprecht.

———, ed. 2003. *Bach's Musik für Tasteninstrumente: Bericht über das 4. Dortmunder Bach-Symposion 2002*. Dortmund: Klangfarben.

Gerber, Ernst Ludwig. 1790–2. *Historisch-biographisches Lexicon der Tonkünstler*. Leipzig: Breitkopf. Facs., ed. Othmar Wessely. Graz: Akademische Druck- und Verlagsanstalt, 1966–77.

Germann, Sheridan. 1985. "The Mietkes, the Margrave and Bach." In Williams (1985a, 119–48).

Glöckner, Andreas. 1981. "Neuerkenntnisse zu Johann Sebastian Bachs Aufführungskalender zu 1729 und 1735." *BJ* 67:43–75.

———. 1988. "Zur Echtheit und Datierung der Kantate BWV 150 'Nach dir, Herr, verlanget mich.'" *BJ* 74:195–203.

Glöckner, Andreas, et al., eds. 1988. *Bericht über die Wissenschaftliche Konferenz zum V. Internationalen Bachfest der DDR in Verbindung mit dem 60. Bachfest der Neuen Bachgesellschaft Leipzig, 25. bis 27. März 1985*. Leipzig: VEB Deutscher Verlag für Musik.

Godt, Irving. 1990. "Politics, Patriotism, and a Polonaise: A Possible Revision in Bach's *Suite in B Minor.*" *MQ* 74:610–22.

Graeser, Wolfgang. 1924. "Bachs 'Kunst der Fuge.'" *BJ* 21:1–104.

Groocock, Joseph. 2003. *Fugal Composition: A Study of Bach's "48."* Edited by Yo Tomita. Westport, CT.: Greenwood Press.

Gustafson, Bruce. 1979. *French Harpsichord Music of the 17th Century*. Studies in Musicology, 11. Ann Arbor, MI: UMI Research Press.

Haas, Robert. 1927. *Die estensischen Musikalien: Thematisches Verzeichnis*. Regensburg: Gustav Bosse.

Händel, Georg Friedrich. 1858–85. *Werke*. 94 vols. Edited by the Deutscher Händel-Gesellschaft. Leipzig: Breitkopf und Härtel.

Händel-Handbuch. 1978–. 5 vols. Kassel: Bärenreiter.

Hanks, Sarah Eliza. 1972. "The German Unaccompanied Keyboard Concerto in the Early Eighteenth Century, Including Works of Walther, Bach and Their Contemporaries." Ph.D. diss., University of Iowa.

Harris, Ellen T. 2001. *Handel as Orpheus: Voice and Desire in the Chamber Cantatas*. Harvard University Press.

Harrison, Daniel. 1990. "Rhetoric and Fugue: An Analytical Approach." *MTS* 12:1–42.

Heidlberger, Frank, Wolfgang Osthoff, and Reinhard Wiesend, eds. 1991. *Von Isaac bis Bach: Studien zur älteren deutschen Musikgeschichte: Festschrif Martin Just zum 60. Geburtstag*. Kassel: Bärenreiter.

Heinse, Wilhelm. 1903. *Hildegard von Hohenthal: Erster und zweiter Theil*. Sämmtliche Werke, 5. Edited by Carl Schüddekopf. Leipzig: Insel-Verlag.

Heller, Karl. 1989. "Norddeutsche Musikkultur als Traditionsraum des jungen Bach." *BJ* 75:7–19.

———. 1995. "Die Klavierfuge BWV 955: Zur Frage ihres Autors und ihrer verschiedenen Fassungen." In Heller and Schulze (1995, 130–40).

———. 2002. "Überlegungen zur Datierung der Reinken-Fugen Johann Sebastian Bachs." In Sandberger (2002, 231–44).

Heller, Karl, and Hans-Joachim Schulze, eds. 1995. *Das Frühwerk Johann Sebastian Bachs: Kolloquium veranstaltet vom Institut für Musikwissenschaft der Universität Rostock 11.–13. September 1990*. Cologne: Studio.

Helm, E. Eugene. 1989. *Thematic Catalogue of the Works of Carl Philipp Emanuel Bach*. New Haven, CT: Yale University Press.

Herz, Gerhard. 1984. *Bach-Quellen in Amerika/Bach Sources in America*. Bärenreiter: Kassel. German and English versions in parallel columns.

———. 1990. "Yoshitake Kobayashi's Article 'On the Chronology of the Last Phase of Bach's Work—Compositions and Performances: 1736 to 1750'—An Analysis with Translated Portions of the Original Text." *BACH* 21/1 (Spring):3–25.

Heussner, Horst, ed. 1964. *Festschrift Hans Engel zum siebzigsten Geburtstag*. Kassel: Bärenreiter.

Hill, John Walter. 1979. *The Life and Works of Francesco Maria Veracini*. Studies in Musicology, 3. Ann Arbor, MI: UMI Research Press.

Hill, Robert S. 1985. "*Echtheit angezweifelt*: Style and Authenticity in Two Suites Attributed to Bach." *EM* 13:248–55.

———. 1986. "Die Herkunft von Bachs 'Thema Legrenzianum.'" *BJ* 72:105–7.

———. 1987. "The Möller Manuscript and the Andreas Bach Book: Two Keyboard Anthologies from the Circle of the Young Johann Sebastian Bach." Ph.D. diss., Harvard University.

———. 1990a. "Stilanalyse und Überlieferungsproblematik: Das Variationssuiten-Repertoire J. A. Reinckens." In Edler and Krummacher (1990, 204–14).

———. 1990b. "Tablature versus Staff Notation: Or, Why Did the Young J. S. Bach Compose in Tablature?" In Walker (1990, 349–59).

———, ed. 1991. *Keyboard Music from the Andreas Bach Book and the Möller Manuscript*. Harvard Publications in Music, 16. Cambridge, MA: Department of Music, Harvard University (distributed by Harvard University Press). Foreword by Christoph Wolff.

———. 1995. "Johann Sebastian Bach's Toccata in G Major BWV 906/1: A Reception of Giuseppe Torelli's Ritornello Concerto Form." In Heller and Schulze (1995, 162–73).

———. 2002. Robert Hill, "'Streng' versus 'Frei': Ein Beitrag zur Analyse der frühen Tastenfugen von Johann Sebastian Bach." In Sandberger (2002, 176–80).

Hirschmann, Wolfgang. 1988. "Zur konzertanten Struktur der Ecksätze von Johann Sebastian Bachs Concerto BWV 971." *AMw* 45:148–62.

Hlawiczka, Karol. 1961. "Zur Polonaise g-moll (BWV Anh. 119) aus dem 2. Notenbüchlein für Anna Magdalena Bach." *BJ* 48:58–60.

Hofmann, Klaus. 1988. "Über Themenbildung und thematische Arbeit in einigen zweiteiligen Präludien des Wohltemperierten Klaviers II." In Wolff (1988b, 48–57).

———. 1988b. "'Fünf Präludien und fünf Fugen': Über ein unbeachtetes Sammelwerk Johann Sebastian Bachs." In Glöckner et al. (1988, 227–35).

———. 1991. "Zu Bachs zweiteiligen Klavierpräludien." In Szeskus (1991, 162–71).

———. 1992. "Notentextprobleme in Bachs Sechs Präludien für Anfänger auf dem Clavier (BWV 933–938)." In Beißwenger et al. (1992), 60–6.

———. 1993. "On the Instrumentation of the E-major Suite BWV 1006a by Johann Sebastian Bach." In Brainard and Robinson (1993, 143–54).

———. 1998. "Perfidia-Techniken und -Figuren bei Bach." In Steiger (1998, 281–99).

———. 2001. "Die Klangflächenpräludien des 'Wohltemperierten Klaviers' I: Überlegungen zur Frühgeschichte der Sammlung." In Staehelin (2001), 157–68.

Hogwood, Christopher. 1988. "A Supplement to C. P. E. Bach's *Versuch*: E. W. Wolf's *Anleitung* of 1785." In Clark (1988, 133–57).

———, ed. 2003. *The Keyboard in Baroque Europe: Keyboard Studies of the 17th and 18th Centuries*. Cambridge: Cambridge University Press.

Hogwood, Christopher, and Richard Luckett, eds. 1983. *Music in Eighteenth-Century England: Essays in Memory of Charles Cudworth*. Cambridge University Press.

Hoke, Hans Gunter, ed. 1979. *Johann Sebastian Bach: Die Kunst der Fuge, BWV 1080: Autograph; Originaldruck*. Faksimile-Reihe Bachscher Werke, 14. Mainz: Schott.

Hoppe, Günther, ed. 1998. *Beiträge zum Kolloquium "Kammermusik und Orgel im höfischen Umkreis: Das Pedalcembalo" am 19. September 1997 im Johanngeorgsbau des Schlosses Köthen*. Köthen: n.p. Includes his contribution: "Zu musikalisch-kulturellen Befindlichkeiten des anhaltköthenischen Hofes zwischen 1710 und 1730" (pp. 9–52).

Horn, Wolfgang. 1988. *Carl Philipp Emanuel Bach: Frühe Klaviersonaten*. Hamburg: Karl Dieter Wagner.

Jaccottet, Christiane. 1986. "L'influence de la musique française pour clavecin dans les *Suites Anglaises* de Johann Sebastian Bach et, plus spécialement, la première en La Majeur BWV 806." In Birtel and Mahling (1986, 195–99).

Johnson, Theodore O. 1986. *An Analytical Survey of the Fifteen Sinfonias (Three-Part Inventions) by J. S. Bach*. Lanham, MD: University Press of America.

Jones, Richard D. 1988. "The History and Text of Bach's Clavierübung I." Ph.D. diss., Oxford University.

———. 1991a. "Stages in the Development of Bach's *The Well-Tempered Clavier II*." *MT* 132:441–46.

———. 1991b. "Further Observations on the Development of *The Well-Tempered Clavier II*." *MT* 132:607–9.

———, ed. 2002. *J. S. Bach: The Art of Fugue BWV 1080*. London: Associated Board of the Royal Schools of Music.

Judd, Robert, ed. *Aspects of Keyboard Music: Essays in Honour of Susi Jeans on the Occasion of Her Seventy-Fifth Birthday*. Oxford: Positif Press, 1992.

Kaiser, Rainer, ed. 2001. *Bach und seine mitteldeutschen Zeitgenossen: Bericht über das Internationale Musikwissenschaftliche Kolloquium Erfurt und Arnstadt 13. bis 16. Januar 2000*. Schriften zur Mitteldeutschen Musikgeschichte, Band 4. Eisenach: Karl Dieter Wagner.

Karstädt, Georg. 1974. *Thematisch-systematisches Verzeichnis der musikalischen Werke von Dietrich Buxtehude: Buxtehude-Werke-Verzeichnis*. Wiesbaden: Breitkopf und Härtel.

Kast, Paul. 2003. *Die Bach-Sammlung: Katalog und Register nach Paul Kast:* Die Bach-Handschriften der Berliner Staatsbibliothek, *1958, vollständig erweitert und für die Mikrofiche-Edition ergänzt.* Edited by the Staatsbibliothek zu Berlin–Preußische Kulturbesitz. Munich: Saur.

Keller, Hermann. 1949. "Über Bachs Bearbeitungen aus dem 'Hortus musicus' von Reinken." In *Société Internationale de Musicologie: Quatrième Congrés Bâle . . . Compte rendu,* 161. Kassel: Bärenreiter.

————. 1950. *Die Klavierwerke Bachs.* Leipzig: C. F. Peters.

————. 1965. *Das Wohltemperierte Klavier.* Kassel: Bärenreiter. Translated by Leigh Gerdine. New York: Norton, 1976.

Kerman, Joseph. 2005. *The Art of Fugue: Bach Fugues for Keyboard 1715–1750.* Berkeley: University of California Press.

Kirkendale, Ursula. 1980. "The Source for Bach's *Musical Offering:* The *Institutio oratoria* of Quintilian." *JAMS* 33:88–141.

Kirkendale, Warren. 1979. "Ciceronians versus Aristotelians on the Ricercar as Exordium, From Bembo to Bach." *JAMS* 32:1–44.

Kirnberger, Johann Philipp. 1771–79. *Die Kunst des reinen Satzes in der Musik.* 4 pts. in 2 vols. Berlin and Königsberg: Christian Friedrich Voss in Commission (vol. 1), G. J. Decker and G. L. Hartung (vol. 2). Facsimile, Hildesheim, Germany: Olms, 1968. Translation by Jurgen Thym and David Beach of vol. 1 and of vol. 2, pt. 1, as *The Art of Strict Musical Composition.* New Haven, CT: Yale University Press, 1982.

————. 1773. *Die wahren Grundsätze zum Gebrauch der Harmonie.* Berlin: G. J. Decker and G. L. Hartung. Facsimile, Hildesheim, Germany: Olms, 1970.

Kittel, Johann Christian. 1808. *Der angehende praktische Organist.* Erfurt: Beyer und Maring.

Knowles, John, ed. 1996. *Critica musica: Essays in Honor of Paul Brainard.* Amsterdam: Gordon and Breach.

Kobayashi, Yoshitake. 1973. *Franz Hauser und seine Bach-Handschriftensammlung.* Göttingen: n.p.

————. 1978. "Neuerkenntnisse zu einigen Bach-Quellen an Hand schriftkundlicher Untersuchungen." *BJ* 64:43–60.

————. 1983. "Der Gehrener Kantor Johann Christoph Bach (1673–1727) und seine Sammelbände mit Musik für Tasteninstrumente." In Rehm (1983, 356–62).

————. 1988. "Zur Chronologie der Spätwerke Johann Sebastian Bachs: Kompositions- und Aufführungstätigkeit von 1736 bis 1750." *BJ* 74:7–72. Partial English translation in Herz (1990).

————. 1989. *Die Notenschrift Johann Sebastian Bachs: Dokumentation ihrer Entwicklung.* NBA, IX/2. Kassel: Bärenreiter.

————, 2001. "Bachs Eingriffe in wiederaufgeführte Werke: Aufführungspraktische Aspekte." In Staehelin (2001, 89–102).

Kohlhase, Thomas, and Volker Scherliess, eds. 1978. *Festschrift Georg von Dadelsen zum 60. Geburtstag.* Neuhausen-Stuttgart: Hänssler.

Kolneder, Walter. 1977. *Die Kunst der Fuge: Mythen des 20. Jahrhunderts.* 5 vols. Wiesbaden: Breitkopf und Härtel.

Koprowski, Richard. 1975. "Bach 'Fingerprints' in the Engraving of the Original Edition [of the *Art of Fugue*]." In "Seminar Report" (see Wolff 1975), *CM* 19:61–67.

Koster, John. 1999. "The Harpsichord Culture in Bach's Environs." In Schulenberg (1999, 57–77).

————. 2005. Review of Speerstra (2004) et al. *EM* 33:124–8.

Kretzschmar, Herrmann. 1910. "Das Notenbuch der Zeumerin." In *Jahrbuch der Musikbibliothek Peters für 1919,* 52–72. Leipzig: C. F. Peters.

Kross, Siegfried. 1969. *Das Instrumentalkonzert bei Georg Philipp Telemann.* Tutzing: Hans Schneider.

Krummacher, Friedhelm. 1991. "Bachs frühe Kantaten im Kontext der Tradition." In Szeskus (1991, 172–201).

Kunze, Stefan. 1969. "Gattungen der Fuge in Bach's Wohltemperiertem Klavier." In Geck (1969, 74–93).

Ladewig, James. 1991. "Bach and the *Prima prattica:* The Influence of Frescobaldi on a Fugue from the *Well-Tempered Clavier.*" *JM* 9:358–74.

Landowska, Wanda. 1924. *Music of the Past.* Translated from the French by William Aspenwall Bradley. New York: Knopf.

Landshoff, Ludwig. 1933. *Revisions-Bericht zur Urtextausgabe von Joh. Seb. Bach: Inventionen und Sinfonien.* Leipzig: C. F. Peters.

Leahy, Anne, and Yo Tomita, eds. 2004. *Bach Studies From Dublin.* Irish Musical Studies, vol. 8. Dublin: Four Courts.

Ledbetter, David. 1987. *Harpsichord and Lute Music in Seventeenth-Century France.* Bloomington: Indiana University Press.

———. 1990. Continuo Playing According to Handel: His Figured Bass Exercises. Oxford: Clarendon Press

———. 2002. *Bach's Well-tempered Clavier: The 48 Preludes and Fugues.* New Haven and London: Yale University Press.

Lee, Douglas A. 1988. "C. P. E. Bach and the Free Fantasia for Keyboard: Deutsche Staatsbibliothek Mus. ms. Nichelmann 1N." In Clark (1988, 177–84).

Lehman, Bradley. 2005. "Bach's Extraordinary Temperament: Our Rosetta Stone." *EM* 33:3–23 and 211–31.

LeHuray Peter. 1990. *Authenticity in Performance: Eighteenth-Century Case Studies.* Cambridge: Cambridge University Press.

Leisinger, Ulrich, ed. 1999. *Johann Sebastian Bach: Chromatische Fantasie und Fuge BWV 903 mit Frühfassung BWV 903a und der aus dem Umkreis Forkels überlieferten Fassung.* Vienna: Wiener Urtext, 1999.

———, ed. 2003. *Bach in Leipzig—Bach und Leipzig: Konferenzbericht Leipzig 2000.* Leipziger Beiträge zur Bach-Forschung, 5. Hildesheim: Olms.

———. 2003. "Idiomatischer Clavierstil in Johann Sebastian Bachs Konzertbearbeitungen für Tasteninstrumente." In Geck (2003, 73–86).

Leisinger, Ulrich, and Peter Wollny. 1993. "'Altes Zeug von mir': Carl Philipp Emanuel Bachs kompositorisches Schaffen vor 1740." *BJ* 79:127–204.

Lester, Joel. 1992. *Compositional Theory in the Eighteenth Century.* Cambridge, MA: Harvard University Press.

———. 2001. "Heightening Levels of Activity and J. S. Bach's Parallel-Section Constructions." *JAMS* 54:49–96.

Levin, Robert. 2000. Commentary to *Bach: The Well-Tempered Clavier, Book II. Robert Levin, harpsichord, clavichord, organ, and fortepiano.* Hänssler Edition Bachakademie, vol. 117. CD recording. Holzgerlingen: Hänssler.

Lindley, Mark. 1985. "Keyboard Technique and Articulation: Evidence for the Performing Practices of Bach, Handel and Scarlatti." In Williams (1985a, 207–43).

———. 1989a. "Early Fingering: Some Editing Problems and Some New Readings for J. S. Bach and John Bull." *EM* 17:60–9.

———. 1990. "Tuning and Intonation" and "Keyboard Fingerings and Articulation." In Brown and Sadie (1990, 169–85; 186–203).

Lockwood, Lewis, and Edward Roesner, eds. 1990. *Essays in Musicology: A Tribute to Alvin Johnson.* Philadelphia: American Musicological Society.

Löhlein, Georg Simon. 1765. *Clavier-Schule oder kurze und gründliche Anweisung zur Melodie und Harmonie.* Leipzig and Züllichau: Waisenhaus- und Fromannische Buchhandlung.

Loucks, Richard. 1992. "Was the *Well-Tempered Clavier* Performed on a Fretted Clavichord?" *Performance Practice Review* 5/1 (Spring):44–89.

Louwenaar, Karyl. 1982–3. "Which Comes First: Sarabande or Air? A Study of the Order of the Movements in Bach's Keyboard Partitas." *EKJ* 1:7–15.

———. 1983–4. "A Reconsideration of the Rhythmic Interpretation of the Gigue from Bach's Sixth Partita, BWV 830." *EKJ* 2:1–20.

McIntyre, Ray. 1965. "On the Interpretation of Bach's Gigues." *MQ* 51:478–92.

Marissen, Michael. 1988. "A Critical Reappraisal of J. S. Bach's A-Major Flute Sonata." *JM* 6:367–86.

———. 1994. "More Source-Critical Research on Bach's *Musical Offering.*" *BACH* 25/1 (Spring-Summer):11–27.

Marpurg, Friedrich Wilhelm. 1750. *Kunst des Clavierspielen.* Berlin: Henning. Revised edition, 1762. Facsimile of the revised edition. Hildesheim: Olms, 1969.

———. 1753–4. *Abhandlung von der Fuge.* 2 vols. Berlin: A. Haude and J. C. Spener. Facsimile, Hildesheim, Germany: Olms, 1970.

———. 1755. *Anleitung zum Clavierspielen.* Berlin: A. Haude and J. C. Spener. Facsimile of the second edition (Berlin, 1765), New York: Broude, 1969. Translation in Hays (1976).

———. 1756. *Principes du clavecin.* Berlin: A. Haude and J. C. Spener. Facsimile, Geneva: Minkoff Reprint, 1974. French language edition, with additions, of Marpurg 1755. Translation in Hays (1976).

Marshall, Robert L. 1972. *The Compositional Process of J. S. Bach: A Study of the Autograph Scores of the Vocal Works*. 2 vols. Princeton, NJ: Princeton University Press.

——, ed. 1974. *Studies in Baroque Music in Honor of Arthur Mendel*. Kassel: Bärenreiter.

——. 1976a. "Bach the Progressive: Observations on His Later Works." *MQ* 62:313–57. Reprinted in Marshall (1989, 23–58).

——, ed. 1976b. *Johann Sebastian Bach: Fantasia per il Cembalo, BWV 906/1*. Leipzig: Neue Bach-Gesellschaft. Facsimile edition with introduction. Translation as "The Autograph Fair Copies of the *Fantasia per il cembalo*, BWV 906" in Marshall (1989, 193–200).

——. 1983. "*Editore traditore*: Ein weiterer 'Fall Rust'?" In Rehm (1983, 183–91). Translated as "'Editore traditore': Suspicious Performance Indications in the Bach Sources" in Marshall (1989, 241–54).

——. 1986. "Organ or 'Klavier'? Instrumental Prescriptions in the Sources of Bach's Keyboard Works." In Stauffer and May (1986, 212–39). Reprinted as "Organ or 'Klavier'? Instrumental Prescriptions in the Sources of the Keyboard Works" in Marshall (1989, 271–93).

——. 1989. *The Music of Johann Sebastian Bach: The Sources, the Style, the Significance*. New York: Schirmer Books. Reprints of sixteen articles, those originally in German translated into English. References are to the original publications except where this volume contains new material.

——. 1990. "The Notebooks for Wilhelm Friedemann and Anna Magdalena Bach: Some Biographical Lessons." In Lockwood and Roesner (1990, 192–200).

——. 1996. "Bach's *tempo ordinario*: A Plaine and Easie Introduction to the System." In Knowles 1996, 249–78.

Mattheson, Johann. 1713. *Das Neu-Eröffnete Orchestre*. Hamburg: Author and Benjamin Schillers Witwe.

——. 1731. *Grosse General-Bass-Schule*. Hamburg: Johann Christoph Lissner. Facsimile, Hildesheim, Germany: Olms, 1968.

——. 1737. *Kern melodischer Wissenschaft . . . als ein Vorläuffer des Vollkommenen Capellmeisters*. Hamburg: Christian Herold.

——. 1739. *Der vollkommene Capellmeister*. Hamburg: Christian Herold. Facsimile ed. Margarethe Riemann. Kassel: Bärenreiter, 1954. New edition by Friederike Ramm. Kassel: Bärenreiter, 1999. Translated by Ernest C. Harriss as *Johann Mattheson's* Der vollkommene Capellmeister: *A Revised Translation with Critical Commentary*. Studies in Musicology, 21. Ann Arbor, MI: UMI Research Press, 1981.

Maul, Michael. 2004. "Johann Sebastian Bachs Besuche in der Reisdenzstadt Gera." *BJ* 90:101–19.

Melamed, Daniel R., ed. 1995. *Bach Studies 2*. Cambridge: Cambridge University Press.

——. 1999. "Constructing Johann Christoph Bach (1642–1703)." *ML* 80:345–65.

Milka, Anatoly P. 2003. "Zur Herkunft einiger Fugen in der Berliner Bach-Handschrift *P 296*." *BJ* 89:251–8.

Monelle, Raymond. 2000. *The Sense of Music: Semiotic Essays*. Princeton: Princeton University Press.

Morana, Frank. 1990. "The Presto in D Minor, BWV 970: Its Authenticity Reconsidered." *BACH* 21/3 (Winter):9–29.

——. 1993. "The 'Dobenecker' Toccata, BWV-Anh. II 85: An Early Bach Work?" *BACH* 24/2 (Fall-Winter):26–37.

Moroney, Davitt, ed. 1989. *Joh. Seb. Bach: Die Kunst der Fuge für Cembalo (Klavier) BWV 1080*. Munich: G. Henle.

——. 1992. "A New Completion for Bach's Unfinished Harpsichord Fugue in C Minor, BWV 906/2," in Judd (1992, 113–20).

Mozart, Leopold. 1756. *Versuch einer gründlichen Violinschule*. Augsburg: Verlag des Verfassers (Johann Jacob Lotter). Translation, from the first and third (1787) editions, by Edith Knocker as *A Treatise on the Fundamental Principles of Violin Playing*, 2d ed. Oxford: Oxford University Press, 1949.

Neumann, Frederick. 1965. "La note pointée et la soi-disant 'manière française.'" *Revue de musicologie* 51: 61–92. Translated by Raymond Harris and Edmund Shay as "The Dotted Note and the So-called French Style." *EM* 5 (1977):310–24.

——. 1974. "The Question of Rhythm in the Two Versions of Bach's French Overture, BWV 831." In Marshall (1974, 183–94).

——. 1977. "Facts and Fiction about Overdotting." *MQ* 63:155–85.

——. 1978. *Ornamentation in Baroque and Post-Baroque Music, With Special Emphasis on J. S. Bach*. Princeton, NJ: Princeton University Press.

——. 1979. "Once More: the 'French Overture Style.'" *EM* 7:39–115.

——. 1985. "Bach: Progressive or Conservative and the Authorship of the Goldberg Aria." *MQ* 71:281–94.

New Bach Reader, The: A Life of Johann Sebastian Bach in Letters and Documents. 1998. Edited by Hans T. David and Arthur Mendel. Revised and enlarged by Christoph Wolff. New York: Norton.

New Grove Dictionary of Music and Musicians, The. 1980. Edited by Stanley Sadie. 20 vols. London: Macmillan.

——. 2001. 2nd ed. Edited by Stanley Sadie. 29 vols. London: Macmillan. Citations without page number refer to the online version <www.grovemusic.com>.

Newman, William S. 1961. "Kirnberger's *Method for Tossing Off Sonatas.*" *MQ* 47:517–25.

——. 1965. "Emanuel Bach's Autobiography." *MQ* 51:363–72.

——, ed. 1967. *Carl Philipp Emanuel Bach's Autobiography—1773.* Hilversum, The Netherlands: Knuf. Facsimile edition from Burney (1773).

Niedt, Friedrich Erhardt. 1700–17. *Musicalische Handleitung.* 3 vols. Hamburg: Nicolaus Spieringk, 1700 (vol. 1); Benjamin Schiller, 1706 (vol. 2); Benjamin Schillers Erben, 1717 (vol. 3). Revised edition, ed. Johann Mattheson, Hamburg: Benjamin Schillers Witwe and Johann Christoph Kissner, 1721. Facsimile of the revised edition (Biblioteca Organologica, 32), Buren, The Netherlands: Knuf, 1976. Extracts from vol. 1 translated in Arnold (1931) and in *The Bach Reader* (1966); complete translation in Niedt (1989).

——. 1989. *The Musical Guide.* Translated by Pamela L. Poulin and Irmgard C. Taylor, with introduction and notes by Pamela L. Poulin. Oxford: Clarendon Press, 1989.

North, Nigel. 1995. Liner note for *"Aufs Lautenwerk": Music by J. S. Bach on the Lute-Harpsichord* (Kim Heindel, lautenwerk). Troy, N.Y.: Dorian (DIS-80126).

O'Donnell, John. 1979. "The French Style and the Overtures of Bach." *EM* 7:190–6, 336–45.

Oleskiewicz, Mary. 1999. "The Trio in Bach's *Musical Offering*: A Salute to Frederick's Tastes and Quantz's Flutes?" In Schulenberg (1999, 79–110).

——. 2000. "The Flutes of Quantz: Their Construction and Performing Practice." *Galpin Society Journal* 52:201–20.

——. 2004. Introduction to *Johann Joachim Quantz: Six Quartets for Flute, Violin, Viola, and Basso Continuo.* Ann Arbor, MI: Steglein Publishing.

Osthoff, Wolfgang, and Reinhard Wiesend, eds. 1987. *Bach und die italienische Musik.* Venice: Centro Tedesco di Studi Veneziani.

Osthoff, Wolfgang. 1991. "Imitatio, Allegorie, Symbol: Erwägungen zum Schlußsatz der Sonate BWV 963 und zu ähnlichen Soggetti von Johann Sebastian Bach." In Heidlberger et al., 1991, 273–85.

Patten, Nathan van. 1950. *A Memorial Library of Music at Stanford University.* Stanford, CA, n.p. Catalog of rare music books, scores, and manuscripts.

Petersen, Peter, ed. 1990. *Musikkulturgeschichte: Festschrift für Constantin Floros zum 60. Geburtstag.* Wiesbaden: Breitkopf und Härtel.

Pestelli, Giorgio. 1981. "Un'altra rielaborazione bachiana: La fuga della toccata BWV 914." *RIM* 16:40–4.

——. 1985. "Bach, Handel, D. Scarlatti and the Toccata of the Late Baroque." In Williams (1985a, 277–91).

Protz, Albert. 1957. "Zu Johann Sebastian Bachs 'Capriccio sopra la lontananza del suo fratello dilettissimo.'" *Mf* 10:407.

Quantz, Johann Joachim. 1752. *Versuch einer Anweisung die Flöte traversiere zu spielen.* Berlin: Johann Friedrich Voss. Facsimile of the third edition (Breslau: Johann Friedrich Korn der Ältere). Kassel: Bärenreiter, 1953. Translated by Edward J. Reilly as *An Essay on Playing the Flute.* Corrected reissue of the 2d ed. Boston: Northeastern University Press, 2001.

Radke, Hans. 1964. "War Johann Sebastian Bach Lautenspieler?" In Heussner (1964, 281–9).

Rameau, Jean-Philippe. 1722. *Traité de l'harmonie.* Paris: Jean-Baptiste-Christophe Ballard. Facsimile, New York: Broude, 1965. Translated by Philipp Gossett as *Treatise on Harmony.* New York: Dover, 1971.

Rampe, Siegbert. 1998. "Kompositionen für Saitenclaviere mit obligatem Pedal unter Johann Sebastian Bachs Clavier- und Orgelwerke." In Hoppe (1998, 143–85).

——, ed. 2002. *Bach: Das Wohltemperierte Klavier I: Tradition, Entstehung, Funktion, Analyse.* Munich: Katzbichler.

——. 2002a. "Sozialgeschichte und Funktion des Wohltemperierte Klaviers I." In Rampe (2002, 67–108).

———. 2002b. "'Monatlich neüe Stücke': Zu den musikalischen Voraussetzungen von Bachs Weimarer Konzertmeisteramt." *BJ* 88:61–104.

Rasch, Rudolf. 1986. "Does 'Well-Tempered' Mean 'Equal-Tempered'?" In Stauffer and May (1986, 293–310).

Rehm, Wolfgang, ed. 1983. *Bachiana et alia musicologica: Festschrift Alfred Dürr zum 65. Geburtstag am 3. März 1983.* Kassel: Bärenreiter.

Reidemeister, Peter, and Veronika Gutmann, eds. 1983. *Alte Musik: Praxis und Reflexion.* Winderthur, Germany: Amadeus.

Renwick, William. 1999. "*39. Praeludia et Fugen del Signor Johann Sebastian Bach?*: The Langloz Manuscript, SBB Mus. ms. Bach P 296." In Schulenberg (1999, 137–58).

Richter, Bernhard Friedrich. 1902. "Eine Abhandlung Joh. Kuhnaus." *Monatshefte für Musik-Geschichte* 34:147–54.

Riedel, Herbot Hugo. 1969. "Recognition and Re-Cognition: Bach and *The Well-Tempered Clavier I*." Ph.D. diss., University of California, Berkeley.

Riemann, Hugo, ed. 1912. *Musikgeschichte in Beispielen; eine Auswahl von 150 Tonsätzen.* Leipzig: E. A. Semmann. With commentary by Arnold Schering.

Rifkin, Joshua. 1985. "'. . . Wobey aber die Singstimmen hinlänglich besetzt seyn müssen . . .': Zum Credo der h-Moll-Messe in der Aufführung Carl Philipp Emanuel Bachs." *BJHM* 9:157–72.

———. 1995. "Some Questions of Performance in J. S. Bach's *Trauerode*." In Melamed (1995, 119–53).

———. N.d. Article to appear in *Bach Perspectives*, vol. 6.

Roberts, John H., ed. 1986. *Reinhard Keiser: La forza della virtù.* Handel Sources, 2. New York: Garland.

Rosen, Charles. 1972. *The Classical Style: Haydn, Mozart, Beethoven.* New York: Norton.

———. 1988. *Sonata Forms.* Rev. ed. New York: Norton.

———. 1990. "The Shock of the Old." *The New York Review of Books* 37/12 (July 19):46–52.

Ruhnke, Martin, ed. 1984. *Georg Philipp Telemann: Thematisch-Systematisches Verzeichnis seiner Werke. Instrumentalwerke.* Band 1. Kassel: Bärenreiter.

Ryom, Peter. 1966–7. "La comparaison entre les versions différentes d'un concerto d'Antonio Vivaldi transcrit par J. S. Bach." *Dansk Aarbog for Musik Forskning 1966–67*:91–111.

———. 1969. "A propos de l'inventaire des oeuvres de l'Antonio Vivaldi: Etude critique des catalogues et nouvelles découvertes." *Vivaldiana* 1:69–114.

———. 1979. *Verzeichnis der Werke Antonio Vivaldis. Kleine Ausgabe.* 2d ed. Leipzig: VEB Deutscher Verlag für Musik.

———. 1986. *Répertoire des Oeuvres d'Antonio Vivaldi: Les compositions instrumentales.* Copenhagen: Engstrøm & Sødring.

Sachs, Klaus-Jürgen. 1980. "Die 'Anleitung . . . , auff allerhand Arth einen Choral durchzuführen', als Paradigma der Lehre und der Satzkunst Johann Sebastian Bachs." *AMw* 37:135–54.

Sackmann, Dominik. 2003. "Konzerte des/für den Prinzen: Zu Funktion und Datierung von Bachs Konzertbearbeitung BWV 595/984." In Geck (2003, 133–43).

Sandberger, Wolfgang, ed. 2002. *Bach, Lübeck und die norddeutsche Musiktradition: Bericht über das Internationale Symposon der Musikhochschule Lübeck April 2000.* Kassel: Bärenreiter.

Scheibe, Johann Adolph. 1738–40. *Der critische Musicus herausgegeben von Johann Adolph Scheibe.* 2 vols. Hamburg: Thomas von Wierings Erben (vol. 1), Rudolph Beneke (vol. 2).

———. 1745. *Johann Adolph Scheibens, Königl. Dänis. Capellmeisters, Critischer Musicus. Neue, vermehrte und verbesserte Auflage.* Leipzig: Bernhard Christoph Breitkopf.

Scheide, William H. 1982. "'Nun ist das Heil und die Kraft' BWV 50: Doppelchörigkeit, Datierung und Bestimmung." *BJ* 68:81–102.

Schenker, Heinrich. 1925–30. *Das Meisterwerke in der Musik: Ein Jahrbuch.* 3 vols. Munich, Vienna, and Berlin: Drei Masken. Facsimile in one volume, Hildesheim, Germany: Olms, 1974.

———, ed. 1984. *J. S. Bach's Chromatic Fantasy and Fugue.* Trans. and ed., with a commentary, by Hedi Siegel. New York: Longman. Originally published Vienna: Universal, 1910.

Schering, Arnold. 1902–3. "Zur Bach-Forschung." *SIMG* 4:234–43.

———. 1903–4. "Zur Bach-Forschung II." *SIMG* 5:565–70.

Schleuning, Peter. 1969. "'Diese Fantasie ist einzig . . .': Das *Recitativ* in Bachs Chromatischer Fantasie und seine Bedeutung für die Ausbildung der Freien Fantasie." In Geck (1969, 57–73).

———. 1973. *Die Freie Fantasie: Ein Beitrag zur Erforschung der klassischen Klaviermusik.* Göppinger Akademische Beiträge, 76. Göppingen: Kümmerle.

————. 1992. "The Chromatic Fantasia of Johann Sebastian Bach and the Genesis of Musical 'Sturm und Drang.'" In Dirksen (1992, 217–29).

Schmieder, Wolfgang. 1990. *Thematisch-systematisches Verzeichnis der musikalischen Werke Johann Sebastian Bachs: Bach-Werke-Verzeichnis.* 2d ed. Wiesbaden: Breitkopf und Härtel. Originally published Leipzig: Breitkopf und Härtel, 1950.

Schneider, Michael. 2002. "Die 'Fried- und Freudenreiche Hinfarth' und die 'Franzose Art': Zur deutschen Rezeption des Tombeau im 17. Jahrhundert." In Sandberger (2002, 114–31).

Schott, Howard. 1998. "Parameters of Interpretation in the Music of Froberger." In *J. J. Froberger: Musicien européen.* [Paris:] Klincksieck. Pages 99–120.

Schreyer, Johannes. 1911–3. *Beiträge zur Bach-Kritik.* 2 vols. Leipzig: Merseburger.

Schröder, Karl-Ernst. 1995. "Zum Trio A-Dur BWV 1025." *BJ* 81:47–60.

Schulenberg, David. 1982. "Composition as Variation: Inquiries into the Compositional Procedures of the Bach Circle of Composers." *CM* 33:57–87.

————. 1984. *The Instrumental Music of Carl Philipp Emanuel Bach.* Studies in Musicology, 77. Ann Arbor, MI: UMI Research Press.

————. 1987. Review of Berg (1985). *JAMS* 40:105–12.

————. 1988. "Performing C. P. E. Bach: Some Open Questions." *EM* 16:542–51.

————. 1990. "Authenticity and Expression in the Harpsichord Works of J. S. Bach." *JM* 8: 449–76.

————. 1992. "Musical Expression and Musical Rhetoric in the Keyboard Works of J. S. Bach." In Benstock (1992).

————. 1995. "Composition and Improvisation in the School of J. S. Bach." In *Bach Perspectives*, vol. 1 (Lincoln: University of Nebraska Press, 1995), 1–42

————. 1995a. Review of Hill (1991). In *Bach Perspectives*, vol. 1 (Lincoln: University of Nebraska Press), 205–14.

————, ed. 1999. *Bach Perspectives*, vol. 4. Lincoln: University of Nebraska Press.

————. 1999a. "Versions of Bach: Performing Practices in the Keyboard Works." In Schulenberg (1999, 111–35).

————. 1999b. Review of NBA V/6.2 and VIII/2.1–2. *Notes* 55 (1998–9):755–60.

————. 1999c. "Tempo Relationships in the Prelude of Bach's Sixth English Suite: A Performance-Studies Approach," *Journal of Musicological Research* 18:139–60

————. 2003. "'Toward the Most Elegant Taste': Developments in Keyboard Accompaniment from J. S. to C. P. E. Bach." In Hogwood (2003, 157–68).

————. N.d. "The *Sonate auf Concertenart*: A Postmodern Invention?" In *Bach Perspectives,* vol. 7. University of Illinois Press, forthcoming. Preliminary version online at < http://www.wagner. edu/faculty/dschulenberg/sonata.html>.

Schulze, Hans-Joachim. 1966. "Wer intavolierte Johann Sebastian Bachs Lautenkompositionen?" *Mf* 19:32–9.

————. 1975. "Die Bach-Überlieferung: Plädoyer für ein notwendiges Buch." *AMw* 17:45–58.

————. 1976. "Melodiezitate und Mehrtextigkeit in der Bauernkantate und in den Goldbergvariationen." *BJ* 62:58–72.

————. 1978. "Das Stück in Goldpapier." *BJ* 64:19–42.

————. 1979a. "Cembaloimprovisation bei Johann Sebastian Bach: Versuch einer Übersicht." In *Zu Fragen der Improvisation in der Instrumentalmusik der ersten Hälfte des 18. Jahrhunderts,* 50–57. Studien zur Aufführungspraxis und Interpretation von Instrumentalmusik des 18. Jahrhunderts, 10. Blankenburg/Harz: n.p.

————. 1979b. "Ein 'Dresdner Menuett' im zweiten Klavierbüchlein der Anna Magdalena Bach. Nebst Hinweisen zur Überlieferung einiger Kammermusikwerke Bachs." *BJ* 65:45–64.

————, ed. 1979c. *Johann Sebastian Bach: Drei Lautenkompositionen in zeitgenössischer Tabulatur.* Leipzig: Zentralantiquariat der DDR.

————. 1983. "'Monsieur Schouster', ein vergessener Zeitgenosse Johann Sebastian Bachs." In Rehm (1983, 243–50).

————. 1984a. *Studien zur Bach-Überlieferung im 18. Jahrhundert.* Leipzig: Edition Peters.

————, ed. 1984b. *J. S. Bach: Fantasie und Fuge C-moll für Cembalo.* Facsimile of Dl Mus. 2405 T 52, Aut. 3 (autograph of BWV 906). Leipzig: Zentralantiquariat der DDR.

————. 1985. "Johann Christoph Bach (1671–1721), 'Organist und Schul Collega in Ohrdruf', Johann Sebastian Bachs erster Lehrer." *BJ* 71:55–81.

————. 1991. "Bach und Buxtehude: Eine wenig beachtete Quelle in der Carnegie Library zu Pittsburgh, PA." *BJ* 77:177–81.

Schwandt, Erich. 1990. "Questions concerning the Edition of the 'Goldberg Variations' in the *Neue Bach Ausgabe [sic]*." *Performance Practice Review* 3/1 (Spring):58–69.

Seidel, Elmar. 2002. "Wie rhythmisch ist Bachs Musik? Erwägungen über die Französische Suite in c-moll BWV 813." In Leisinger (2002, 219–33).

Selfridge-Field, Eleanor. 1990. *The Music of Benedetto and Alessandro Marcello: A Thematic Catalogue with Commentary on the Composers, Repertory, and Sources.* Oxford: Clarendon Press.

Sheldon, David A. 1975. "The Galant Style Revisited and Re-evaluated." *Acta* 4:240–70.

Siegele, Ulrich. 1960. "Die musiktheoretische Lehre einer Bachschen Gigue." *AMw* 17:152–67.

———. 1975. *Kompositionsweise und Bearbeitungstechnik in der Instrumentalmusik Johann Sebastian Bachs.* 2nd ed. Tübinger Beiträge zur Musikwissenschaft, 3. Neuhausen-Stuttgart: Hänssler.

———. 1983. "Bachs Stellung in der Leipziger Kulturpolitik seiner Zeit." *BJ* 69:7–50.

———. 1989. "The Four Conceptual Stages of the Fugue in C Minor, *WTC* I." In Franklin (1989a, 197–224).

Silbiger, Alexander, ed. 1987. *Bologna, Civico museo bibliografico musicale, MS DD/53; Florence, Biblioteca del Conservatorio de musica Luigi Cherubini, MS D 2534.* Seventeenth-Century Keyboard Music, 10. New York: Garland.

———. 1993. "Tracing the Contents of Froberger's Lost Autographs." *CM* 54: 5–23.

Snyder, Kerala J. 1987. *Dieterich Buxtehude: Organist in Lübeck.* New York: Schirmer Books.

Speerstra, Joel. 2004. *Bach and the Pedal Clavichord: An Organist's Guide.* Rochester: University of Rochester Press.

Spitta, Philipp. 1873–80. *Johann Sebastian Bach.* 3 vols. Leipzig: Breitkopf und Härtel. Translated by Clara Bell and J. A. Fuller Maitland. London: Novello, 1889. Reprint, New York: Dover, 1952.

Staehelin, Martin, ed. 2001. *"Die Zeit, die Tag und Jahre macht": Zur Chronologie des Schaffens von Johann Sebastian Bach: Bericht über das Internationale wissenschaftliche Colloquium aus Anlaß des 80. Geburtstages von Alfred Dürr Göttingen, 13.–15. März 1998.* Göttingen: Vandenhoeck & Ruprecht.

Stauffer, George. 1980. *The Organ Preludes of Johann Sebastian Bach.* Studies in Musicology, 27. Ann Arbor, MI: UMI Research Press.

———. 1983. "Johann Mattheson and J. S. Bach: The Hamburg Connection." In Buelow and Marx (1983, 353–68).

———. 1985. "Bach as Reviser of His Own Keyboard Works." *EM* 13:185–98.

———. 1989. "'This fantasia . . . never had its like': On the Enigma and Chronology of Bach's Chromatic Fantasia and Fugue in D Minor, BWV 903." In Franklin (1989a, 160–82).

———, ed. 1990. *The Forkel-Hoffmeister & Kühnel Correspondence: A Document of the Early 19th-Century Bach Revival.* New York: C. F. Peters.

———. 1993. "Boyvin, Grigny, D'Anglebert, and Bach's Assimilation of French Classical Organ Music." *EM* 21:83–96.

Stauffer, George, and Ernest May, eds. 1986. *J. S. Bach as Organist: His Instruments, Music, and Performance Practices.* Bloomington: Indiana University Press.

Steiger, Renate, ed. 1998. *Die Quellen Johann Sebastian Bachs: Bachs Musik im Gottesdienst.* Heidelberg: Manutius.

Stinson, Russell. 1989a. *The Bach Manuscripts of Johann Peter Kellner and His Circle: A Case Study in Reception History.* Durham, NC, and London: Duke University Press.

———. 1989b. "Toward a Chronology of Bach's Instrumental Music: Observations on Three Keyboard Works." *JM* 7:440–70.

———. 1990. "The 'critischer Musikus' as Keyboard Transcriber? Scheibe, Bach, and Vivaldi." *JMR* 9:255–71.

———, ed. 1992. *Keyboard Transcriptions from the Bach Circle.* Recent Researches in the Music of the Baroque Era, 69. Madison, WI: A-R Editions.

Swanton, Philip. 1985. "Der Generalbass in J. S. Bachs Kantaten mit obligater Orgel." *BJHM* 9:89–155.

Synofzik, Thomas. 2001. "Johann Gottlieb Preller und seine Abschriften Bachscher Clavierwerke: Kopistenpraxis als Schlüssel zur Aufführungspraxis." In Kaiser 2001, 45–64.

———. 2002. Synofzik, Thomas. "'Fili Ariadnæi': Entwicklungslinien zum Wohltemperierten Klavier." In Rampe (2002), 109–46.

Szeskus, Reinhard, ed. 1991. *Johann Sebastian Bachs historischer Ort.* Bach-Studien, 10. Wiesbaden and Leipzig: Breitkopf und Härtel.

Tagliavini, Luigi Ferdinando. 1986. "Bach's Organ Transcription of Vivaldi's 'Grosso Mogul' Concerto." In Stauffer and May (1986, 240–55).

Talbot, Michael. 1990. *Tomaso Albinoni: The Venetian Composer and His World*. Oxford: Clarendon Press.

———. 1995. "A Further Borrowing From Albinoni: The C-Major Fugue BWV 946." In Heller and Schulze (1995, 142–58).

Talle, Andrew. 2003. "Nürnberg, Darmstadt, Köthen: Neuerkenntnisse zur Bach-Überlieferung in der ersten Hälfte des 18. Jahrhnderts." *BJ* 89:143–72.

———. 2003a. "J. S. Bach's Keyboard Partitas and Their Early Audience." Ph.D. diss., Harvard University.

Tomita, Yo. 1993–5. *J. S. Bach's "Das wohltemperierte Klavier II": A Critical Commentary*. 2 vols. Leeds: Household Word.

Tovey, Donald Francis, ed. 1924. *Johann Sebastian Bach: Forty-Eight Preludes and Fugues*. 2 vols. (analytical commentary and musical text). London: Oxford University Press.

———. 1931. *A Companion to "The Art of Fugue."* London: Oxford University Press.

Vendrix, Philippe. 1989. "Zum Lamento aus J. S. Bachs Capriccio BWV 992 und seinen Vorläufern." *BJ* 75:197–201.

Viertel, Karl-Heinz. 1977. "Zur Herkunft der Polonaise BWV Anhang 130." *Muzikološki Zbornik* 13:36–43.

Walker, Paul. 1989. "Die Entstehung der Permutationsfuge." *BJ* 75:21–41.

———, ed. 1990. *Church, Stage, and Studio: Music and Its Contexts in Seventeenth-Century Germany*. Studies in Musicology, 107. Ann Arbor, MI: UMI Research Press.

———. 2000. *Theories of Fugue From the Age of Josquin to the Age of Bach*. Rochester: University of Rochester Press.

Walter, Horst. 1976. "Das Posthornsignal bei Haydn und anderen Komponisten des 18. Jahrhunderts." *Haydn-Studien* 4/1 (May):21–34.

Walther, Johann. 1708. *Praecepta der musicalischen Composition* [Ms.]. Edited by Peter Benary. Leipzig: VEB Breitkopf und Härtel, 1955.

———. 1732. *Musicalisches Lexicon oder Musicalische Bibliothec. . . .* Leipzig: Wolffgang Deer. Facsimile edited by Richard Schaal, Dokumenta Musicologica 1/3. Kassel: Bärenreiter, 1953.

Werbeck, Walter. 2003. "Bach und der Kontrapunkt: Neue Manuskript-Funde." *BJ* 89:67–95.

Wiemer, Wolfgang. 1977. *Die wiederhergestellte Ordnung in Johann Sebastian Bachs Kunst der Fuge*. Wiesbaden: Breitkopf und Härtel.

———. 1987. "Ein Bach-Doppelfund: Verschollene Gerber-Abschrift (BWV 914 und 996) und unbekannte Choralsammlung Christian Friedrich Penzels." *BJ* 73:29–73.

———. 1988. "Carl Philipp Emanuel Bachs Fantasie in c-Moll—ein Lamento auf den Tod des Vaters?" *BJ* 74:163–77.

Wilhelmi, Thomas. 1992. "Carl Philipp Emanuel Bachs 'Avertissement' über den Druck der Kunst der Fuge." *BJ* 78:101–5.

Williams, Peter. 1979. "Figurenlehre from Monteverdi to Wagner." *MT* 120:476–9

———. 1980–84. *The Organ Music of J. S. Bach*. 3 vols. Cambridge: Cambridge University Press.

———. 1981. "BWV 565: A Toccata in D Minor for Organ by J. S. Bach?" *EM* 9:330–37.

———. 1983a. "J. S. Bach's *Well-Tempered Clavier*: A New Approach." *EM* 11:46–52, 332–9.

———. 1983b. "The Snares and Delusions of Musical Rhetoric: Some Examples from Recent Writings on J. S. Bach." In Reidemeister and Gutmann (1983, 230–40).

———. 1984. "Bach's G Minor Sonata for Viola da Gamba and Harpsichord BWV 1029." *EM* 12:345–54.

———, ed. 1985a. *Bach, Handel, Scarlatti: Tercentenary Essays*. Cambridge: Cambridge University Press.

———. 1985b. "Encounters with the Chromatic Fourth; or, More on Figurenlehre, 1 [and 2]." *MT* 126:276–78, 339–43.

———. 1985c. "*Figurae* in the Keyboard Works of Scarlatti, Handel and Bach: An Introduction." In Williams (1985a, 327–46).

———. 1986a. "The Acquisitive Minds of Handel & Bach: Some Reflections on the Nature of 'Influences.'" In Douglass, Jander, and Owen (1986, 267–81).

———, ed. 1986b. *J. S. Bach: Kunst der Fuge*. London: Eulenburg.

———. 1986c. "The Snares and Delusions of Notation: Bach's Early Organ Works." In Stauffer and May (1986), 274–94.

———, ed. 1986d. *J. S. Bach: Musicalisches Opfer*. London: Eulenburg.

———. 1986–87. "Hints for Performance in J. S. Bach's *Clavierübung* Prints." *EKJ* 5:29–44.

———. 1989. "French Overture Conventions in the Hands of the Young Bach and Handel." In Franklin (1989a, 183–93).

———. 1993. "Two Case Studies in Performance Practice and the Details of Notation. 1: J. S. Bach and 2/4 Time." *EM* 21:613–22.

———. 1994. "Two Case Studies in Performance Practice and the Details of Notation. 2: J. S. Bach and Left-Hand–Right-Hand Distribution." *EM* 22:101–13.

———. 1997. *The Chromatic Fourth During Four Centuries of Music*. Oxford: Clarendon Press.

———. 1999. "Some Thoughts on Italian Elements in Certain Music of Johann Sebastian Bach." *Recercare* 11:185–200.

———. 2000. "Sui generis." *ML* 141:8–10.

———. 2001. *Bach: The Goldberg Variations*. Cambridge: Cambridge University Press.

———. 2003a. *The Organ Music of J. S. Bach*. Second edition of Williams (1980–4), vols. 1–2. Cambridge: Cambridge University Press.

———. 2003b. Review of Ledbetter (2002) et al. *MT* 144:64–6.

———. 2003c. "Is There an Anxiety of Influence Discernible in J. S. Bach's *Clavierübung I*." In Hogwood (2003), 140–56.

———. 2004. *The Life of Bach*. Cambridge: Cambridge University Press.

Wolf, Uwe. 2003. "Fassungsgeschichte und Überlieferung der Chromatischen Fantasie BWV 903/1." In Geck (2003, 145–58).

Wolff, Christoph. 1968. *Der stile antico in der Musik Johann Sebastian Bachs: Studien zu Bachs Spätwerk*. Wiesbaden: Franz Steiner.

———. 1971. "New Research on Bach's *Musical Offering*." *MQ*, 57:379–408. Also in Wolff (1991b, 239–58).

———. 1974. "Johann Sebastian Bach's 'Sterbechoral': Kritische Fragen zu einem Mythos." In Marshall (1974, 283–97). Translated as "The Deathbed Chorale: Exposing a Myth," in Wolff (1991b, 282–94).

———. 1975. "The Last Fugue: Unfinished?" Contribution to "Seminar Report: Bach's 'Art of Fugue': An Examination of the Sources." *CM* 19:71–77. Also as "Bach's Last Fugue: Unfinished?" in Wolff (1991b, 259–64).

———. 1976. "Bach's Handexemplar of the Goldberg Variations." *JAMS* 29:224–41. Also as "The Handexemplar of the Goldberg Variations," in Wolff (1991b, 162–77).

———. 1979. "Textkritische Bemerkungen zum Originaldruck der Bachschen Partiten." *BJ* 65: 65–74. Translated as "Text-Critical Comments on the Original Print of the Partitas," in Wolff (1991b, 214–22).

———. 1982. "Das Hamburger Buxtehude-Bild: Ein Beitrag zur musikalischen Ikonographie und zum Umkreis von Johann Adam Reinken." In A. Grassmann and W. Neugebauer, eds., *800 Jahre Musik in Lübeck*, 64–79. Lübeck: Der Senat der Hansestadt Lübeck—Amt für Kultur. Translated by Thomson Moore as "The Hamburg Group Portrait with Reinken and Buxtehude: An Essay in Musical Iconography." In *Boston Early Music Festival and Exhibition 8–14 June 1987* (program book), 102–12.

———. 1983b. Review of Franklin and Dow (1980). *BJ* 69:123–4.

———. 1983c. "Zur Chronologie und Kompositionsgeschichte von Bachs Kunst der Fuge." *BMw* 25:130–42. Translated as "The Compositional History of the Art of Fugue," in Wolff (1991b, 265–81).

———, ed. 1984. *Johann Sebastian Bach: Clavier-Übung Teil I–IV. Faksimile-Ausgabe nach Exemplaren der Musikbibliothek der Stadt Leipzig*. Leipzig: Peters. Four volumes plus commentary volume. Page references are to the latter, which is reprinted as "The Clavier-Übung Series" in Wolff (1991b, 189–213).

———. 1985a. "Bach's Leipzig Chamber Music." *EM* 13:65–75. Also in Wolff (1991b, 223–38).

———, ed. 1985c. *The Neumeister Collection of Chorale Preludes from the Bach Circle: Facsimile Edition of the Yale Manuscript LM 4708*. New Haven, CT: Yale University Press. "Introduction" reprinted as "The Neumeister Collection of Chorale Preludes from the Bach Circle," in Wolff (1991b, 107–27).

———, ed. 1985d. *Orgel, Orgelmusik und Orgelspiel: Festschrift Michael Schneider zum 75. Geburtstag*. Kassel: Bärenreiter.

———. 1986a. "Johann Adam Reinken und Johann Sebastian Bach: Zum Kontext des Bachschen

Frühwerkes." *BJ* 71:99–117. Translated as "Johann Adam Reinken and Johann Sebastian Bach: On the Context of Bach's Early Works" in Stauffer and May (1986, 57–80). Translation reprinted in Wolff (1991b, 56–71).

———. 1986b. "Johann Sebastian Bach's Third Part of the *Clavier-Übung*." In Douglass, Jander, and Owen (1986, 283–91).

———. 1987a. "Bach und das Fortepiano." In Osthoff and Wiesend (1987, 197–209).

———, ed. 1987b. *Johann Sebastian Bach: Die Kunst der Fuge.* 2 vols. Frankfurt: C. F. Peters.

———, ed. 1988b. *Johann Sebastian Bachs Spätwerk und dessen Umfeld: Perspektiven und Probleme. Bericht über das wissenschaftliche Symposon anlässlich des 61. Bachfestes der Neuen Bachgesellschaft Duisburg, 28–30. Mai 1986.* Kassel: Bärenreiter.

———. 1988c. "Vivaldi's Compositional Art and the Process of 'Musical Thinking.'" In Fanna and Morelli (1988, 1–17). Reprinted as "Vivaldi's Compositional Art, Bach, and the Process of 'Musical Thinking'" in Wolff (1991b, 72–83).

———. 1989. "From Berlin to Lodz: The Spitta Collection Resurfaces." *Music Library Association Notes* 46:311–27.

———. 1991a. "Apropos the Musical Offering: The Thema Regium and the Term *Ricercar*." In Wolff (1991b, 324–39). A revised translation of: (1) "Überlegungen zum 'Thema Regium,'" *BJ* 59 (1973):33–38, and (2) "Der Terminus 'Ricercar' in Bachs Musikalischem Opfer," *BJ* 53 (1967):70–81.

———. 1991b. *Johann Sebastian Bach: Essays on His Life and Music.* Cambridge, MA: Harvard University Press. Reprints of thirty-two articles, those originally in German translated into English. References are to the original publications except where this volume contains new material.

———. 1992. "The Identity of the 'Fratro Dilettissimo' in the Capriccio B-Flat Major [sic] and Other Problems of Bach's Early Harpsichord Works." In Dirksen (1992, 145–56).

———. 2000. *Johann Sebastian Bach: The Learned Musician.* New York: Norton.

———. 2001. "Johann Sebastian Bach." In NG2.

Wolffheim, Werner. 1912. "Die Möllersche Handschrift: Ein unbekanntes Gegenstück zum Andreas-Bach-Buche." *BJ* 9:42–60.

Wollny, Peter. 1993. "Studies in the Music of Wilhelm Friedemann Bach: Sources and Style." Ph.D. diss., Harvard University.

———. 1995. "Ein 'musikalischer Veteran Berlins': Der Schreiber Anonymus 300 und seine Bedeutung für die Berliner Bach-Überlieferung." *Jahrbuch des Staatlichen Instituts für Musikforschung* 38:80–113.

———. 2002. "Traditionen des phantastischen Stils in Johann Sebastian Bachs Toccaten BWV 910–916." In Sandberger (2002, 245–55).

———. 2002a. "Tennstedt, Leipzig, Naumburg, Halle: Neuerkenntnisse zur Bach-Überlieferung in Mitteldeutschland." *BJ* 88:29–60.

———. 2003. "'Allemande faite en passant le Rhin dans une barque en grand peril': Eine neue Quelle zum Leben und Schaffen von Johann Jakob Froberger (1616–1667)." *Jahrbuch des Staatlichen Instituts für Musikforschung Preussischer Kulturbesitz* 36:99–115.

Wotquenne, Alfred. 1905. *Catalogue thématique des oeuvres de Charles Philippe Emmanuel Bach (1714–1788).* Leipzig: Breitkopf und Härtel. Reprints, 1964, 1972, as *Thematisches Verzeichnis der Werke von Carl Philipp Emanuel Bach.*

Yearsley, David. 2002. *Bach and the Meanings of Counterpoint.* Cambridge: Cambridge University Press.

Zehnder, Jean-Claude. 1988. "Georg Böhm und Johann Sebastian Bach: Zur Chronologie der Bachschen Stilentwicklung." *BJ* 74:73–110.

———. 1991. "Giuseppe Torelli und Johann Sebastian Bach: Zu Bachs Weimarer Konzertform." *BJ* 77:33–95.

———. 1995. "Zu Bachs Stilentwicklung in der Mühlhauser und Weimarer Zeit." In Heller and Schulze (1995, 311–38).

Zietz, Hermann. 1969. *Quellenkritische Untersuchungen an den Bach-Handschriften P 801, P 802 und P 803.* Hamburg: Wagner.

Index

In addition to serving as an index, these pages provide a list of Bach's works mentioned in the text, as well as a *personalia* furnishing dates and brief descriptions of people mentioned. In general, musical sources (manuscripts and printed editions) and modern authors are not indexed, nor is matter in tables or in the lists of sources for individual works.

The principal discussion of a work or topic is in **boldface**; discussions accompanied by musical examples are in *italic*; principal discussions illustrated by examples are in ***boldface italic***. The Index of Works includes authentic as well as doubtful and spurious works that have been attributed to J. S. Bach ("JSB" below). Collections of pieces are listed first, then individual works.

Index of Works by J. S. Bach

General Index